SAGE was founded in 1965 by Sara Miller McCune to support the dissemination of usable knowledge by publishing innovative and high-quality research and teaching content. Today, we publish over 900 journals, including those of more than 400 learned societies, more than 800 new books per year, and a growing range of library products including archives, data, case studies, reports, and video. SAGE remains majority-owned by our founder, and after Sara's lifetime will become owned by a charitable trust that secures our continued independence.

Los Angeles | London | New Delhi | Singapore | Washington DC | Melbourne

Introduction to Urban Development and Planning

Introduction to Urban Development and Planning

B. K. Pattanaik

Professor, School of Extension and Development Studies, Indira Gandhi National Open University, New Delhi

SAGE | TEXTS

Los Angeles | London | New Delhi
Singapore | Washington DC | Melbourne

First published in 2020; second impression 2021

SAGE | TEXTS

SAGE Publications India Pvt Ltd
B1/I-1 Mohan Cooperative Industrial Area
Mathura Road, New Delhi 110 044, India
www.sagepub.in

SAGE Publications Inc
2455 Teller Road
Thousand Oaks, California 91320, USA

SAGE Publications Ltd
1 Oliver's Yard, 55 City Road
London EC1Y 1SP, United Kingdom

SAGE Publications Asia-Pacific Pte Ltd
18 Cross Street #10-10/11/12
China Square Central
Singapore 048423

Published by Vivek Mehra for SAGE Publications India Pvt Ltd. Typeset in 10/12 pt Cambria by AG Infographics, Delhi.

Library of Congress Cataloging-in-Publication Data

Names: Pattanaik, B. K. (Bikram K.) author.
Title: Introduction to urban development and planning / B. K. Pattanaik.
Description: Thousand Oaks : SAGE Publishing, 2020. | Includes index.
Identifiers: LCCN 2020014967 | ISBN 9789353883225 (paperback) | ISBN 9789353883232 (epub) | ISBN 9789353883249 (ebook)
Subjects: LCSH: City planning—Environmental aspects. | Cities and towns—Growth.
Classification: LCC HT241.P38 2020 | DDC 307.1/216—dc23 LC record available at https://lccn.loc.gov/2020014967

ISBN: 978-93-5388-322-5 (PB)

SAGE Team: Amit Kumar, Indrani Dutta, Shruti Gupta and Madhurima Thapa

Contents

Detailed Contents

List of Illustrations

Boxes

Exhibits

Figures

Tables

List of Abbreviations

ADB	Asian Development Bank
BCC	Behavioural change communication
BRT	Bid rent theory
CBD	Central business district
CBDM	Community-based disaster management
CBO	Community-based organization
CCTV	Closed-circuit television
CDP	City development plan
CFC	Central Finance Commission
CIP	City investment plan
CO2	Carbon dioxide
CSO	Civil society organization
CSR	Corporate social responsibility
DBMS	Database management system
DDA	Delhi Development Authority
DDC	District Development Committee
DDP	District development plan
DED	Decentralization to entrepreneurialism and to democratization
DFID	Department for International Development
DSS	Decision support system
FDI	Foreign direct investment
GDP	Gross domestic product
GER	Gross enrolment ratio
GHG	Greenhouse gas
GIS	Geographic information system
GNP	Gross national product
HDI	Human development index
HUDCO	Housing and Urban Development Corporation
ICT	Information and communication technology
IEC	Information, education and communication
ILO	International Labour Organization
IT	Information technology
JNNURM	Jawaharlal Nehru National Urban Renewal Mission

LSI	Local self-government institution
MDG	Millennium Development Goals
MML	Model Municipal Law
MoUD	Ministry of Urban Development
MSW	Municipal solid waste
NAC	Notified Area Committee
NCR	National Capital Region
NGO	Non-governmental organizations
O&M	Operation and maintenance
PPP	Public–private partnership
PRI	Panchayati Raj Institution
PT	Property Tax
PURA	Provision of Urban Amenities in Rural Areas
PVO	Private voluntary organization
RWA	Resident Welfare Association
SARC	Second Administrative Reforms Commission
SCP	Smart city proposal
SDG	Sustainable Development Goals
SFC	State Finance Commission
SGPC	Shiromani Gurudwara Prabandhak Committee
SPV	Special purpose vehicle
STD	Sexually transmitted disease
SWM	Solid waste management
TB	Tuberculosis
ULB	Urban local body
UN	United Nations
UNDP	United Nations Development Programme
WHO	World Health Organization
WTE	Waste to energy

Preface

More than half the world's population live in urban areas. Over the years, the number and percentage of population living in urban areas have been constantly rising. Globally, 55 per cent of the population lives in urban areas today. It is estimated that by 2045, the number of people living in cities will increase by 1.5 times to 6 billion. Besides, cities contribute to more than 80 per cent of global GDP. The World Bank has rightly commented, 'No country has grown to middle income without industrializing and urbanizing. None has grown to high income without vibrant cities. The rush to cities in developing countries seems chaotic, but it is necessary.' Urbanization is one of the preferred choices before the countries to achieve various goals of sustainable development. Cities are the hub of economic, social, cultural and political progresses. Cities are the torchbearers of economic growth and development of nation states. The status of urban development depicts the face, status and pace of modernization and globalization of nation states. On the contrary, it is true that cities across the developing regions face increasing poverty; lack of basic amenities and services such as water supply, electricity, sanitation, housing, education and healthcare; and worsening pollution and depletion of natural resources. Besides, crippling traffic congestion and declining safety and security are adding to the difficulties of the urban dwellers. With globalization, modernization and urbanization, the urban study has emerged as one of the contemporary areas of social science. It is also effectively found to be well integrated in the courses of urban planning being taught in technical courses such as architecture and civil engineering.

This book is based on my research and teaching experiences spanning over three decades. Over this period of time, I have also been involved in handling projects in various sectors of development—both in urban and rural areas. The content of this book will be useful not only to the students belonging to various disciplines of social sciences, such as geography, sociology, public administration and economics, but also to the architecture students and those who are pursuing degree and diploma programmes in urban planning and development. Besides, it would be useful to the planners, policymakers and administrators dealing with the urban development issues and challenges. The development practitioners, NGOs, research scholars and persons interested to know about the urban development can also refer to this book.

This book has been divided into 15 chapters. A brief of each chapter has been provided below.

Chapter 1: This chapter comprehensively covers various aspects which give a holistic idea about the urbanization and its issues and challenges. Some of the important aspects covered in this chapter are the concept and meaning, need and importance, causes, and trends of urbanization in developed and developing countries, along with important components of urbanization and urban development.

Chapter 2: This chapter deals with the urban planning and development theories and approaches. It covers various urban planning theories propounded by various exponents of urban development at different point of time. It also gives an account of different approaches to urban planning and development offered by classists, neoclassists and the modernists.

Chapter 3: This chapter gives an account of urban planning. Various aspects covered in this chapter are concept and meaning of urban planning, needs and importance of urban planning, types of urban planning, techniques of urban planning, and different issues and challenges related to urban planning. This is a core chapter of the book, as systematic and sustainable urban development is only possible through systematic urban planning.

Chapter 4: This chapter is on urban management. Systematic management of urban infrastructure and services is central to sustainable urban development. As there are various stakeholders of urban development and resources available at the disposal of the government are not adequate, there is a need for effective and efficient management of urban development services, projects and programmes in order to raise the quality of life of city dwellers. Various components covered in this chapter are concept and meaning of urban management, needs and importance of urban management, functions and process of urban management, aim and scope of urban management, urban activities and services management, systematic approach to urban development project management, deficiency in urban management and steps to be taken for the improvement of urban management.

Chapter 5: This chapter is on urban governance. Governance is a vital issue in development including urban development. This chapter deals in detail with the meaning of urban governance and its needs and benefits, attributes of urban governance, components and characteristics of good governance. It also covers the municipal governance and administration in India as well as citizen participation in governance. The lacunas of governance and the measures to strengthen governance have also been comprised in this chapter.

Chapter 6: This is an important chapter on urban development. This chapter deals with municipal finance. Finance is the lifeblood of development. The urban development programmes, projects and activities cannot kick-start without urban finance. This chapter deals in detail with the meaning of municipal finance and its importance in urban development. It broadly covers the following other important aspects of urban finance: fiscal decentralization, municipal revenue and expenditure, municipal financial management and municipal finance in India.

Chapter 7: This chapter deals with urban infrastructure, which is vital to urban development. It is required for the development of urban industrial and social sector activities. Moreover, it is required for enabling the urban dwellers to contribute effectively to the urban economic growth and development. At the outset, this chapter describes the meaning and importance of infrastructure to urban development. It gives an exhaustive analysis of various types of infrastructure required for urban areas. It also discusses how to measure urban infrastructure development. The deficiency and measures to strengthen urban infrastructure are also covered in this chapter.

Chapter 8: This chapter is on urban poverty, inequality and unemployment. This chapter is critically important to urban development. The urban development projects and programmes launched by the government broadly deal with these economic, social and human issues of development. The various aspects covered in these three crucial issues are: the concept and menacing, causes of poverty, inequality and unemployment, effects of urban poverty, inequality and unemployment, and measures to solve the problems of urban poverty, inequality and unemployment.

Chapter 9: This chapter gives an account of urban education and healthcare. It delineates the need and importance of urban education and healthcare for urban development. The other aspects covered are features of urban education and healthcare, determinants of the status of urban education and healthcare, the issues and challenges of urban education and healthcare, and various measures to be taken for the improvement of the status of urban education and healthcare. As education and healthcare are two important parameters of social development, this chapter on urban education and healthcare aims at urban social development through the improvement of the status of urban education and healthcare.

Chapter 10: This chapter deals with urban heritage. Urban heritage projects the historical backdrops and cultural strength of a city. A heritage city attracts tourists both from within and outside the nation states. Being a heritage city, it earns revenue for the economy through tourism and provides employment opportunity. The chapter covers the concept and meaning of urban heritage and the role and importance of urban heritage in urban development. Besides, it also covers different types of heritage assets and the issues and challenges pertaining to the maintenance of urban heritage. Last but not least, it also comprises the measures required for the maintenance of management of urban heritage. It is a small but important chapter from the standpoint of urban development.

Chapter 11: This chapter is on urban water bodies. Water bodies are significant from the environment and sustainable development points of view. The main components of this chapter are: meaning and types of urban water bodies, importance of water bodies to urban development, impact of urbanization on water bodies and measures to be taken for the revitalization of urban water bodies.

Chapter 12: This chapter deals with urban open space. The main contents covered in this chapter are: concept and meaning of water bodies, importance of water bodies to urban life, factors responsible for the deterioration of urban water bodies and the steps to be taken for the revitalization of urban water bodies. Urban open space has considerable significance in urban land space. It not only makes the life of the urban people healthy but also attracts tourists to the city.

Chapter 13: This chapter is on urban slums and informal settlements. This is a major issue in the developing countries. The growth of urban slums is a development paradox which none can deny. This chapter comprehensively covers the concept and meaning of slums and their informal settlements. It has delineated the factors responsible for the growth of slums in cities. Besides, the chapter also covers the issues and challenges of slums and measures to be taken for the improvement of the living conditions of slum dwellers.

Chapter 14: This is on urban safety and security. The three key components covered in this chapter are as follows: (a) urban crime and violence, (b) insecurity of tenure and forced eviction and (c) urban disaster. This is an important chapter, and in modern time, it influences the urban development a lot.

Chapter 15: This is an important chapter in contemporary urban development. This is on sustainable urbanization and smart cities. It describes the meaning and importance of sustainable urbanization, issues and challenges of sustainable urbanization and measures to promote sustainable urbanization. As far as smart city is concerned, it comprises the meaning of smart city, importance of smart city, dynamics and characteristics of smart city, issues and challenges of smart city and the measures to be taken to promote smart city in India. Smart city occupies an important place in the urban development scenario in the 21st century.

I highly appreciate the work of Sumit Kumar in helping me in computer-related work. I am also thankful to SAGE and two young editors Amit Kumar and Indrani Dutta of SAGE for giving valuable suggestions during the process of updating the manuscript. Last but not least, I underscore the invisible blessings of my late father which has always been a support in disguise to undertake any assignment and complete it with full dedication.

About the Author

B. K. Pattanaik is a Professor, currently Director, at the School of Extension and Development Studies in the Indira Gandhi National Open University (IGNOU), New Delhi. He is the editor of the *Political Economy Journal of India.* He is also on the editorial board of the *Journal of Economics and Development Studies,* American Research Institute for Policy Development, New York; *Asian Journal of Social Sciences & Humanities,* Oyama, Japan; and the *European Journal of Education Studies,* Bucharest, Romania. Professor Pattanaik holds a master's degree in economics, MA in human resource management and PhD in economics. He has more than 25 years of research and teaching experience to his credit in various national-level organizations, for example, the National Council of Educational Research and Training (NCERT), New Delhi; National Institute of Health & Family Welfare (NIHFW), New Delhi, and Centre for Research in Rural and Industrial Development (CRRID), an ICSSR Centre, Chandigarh. He has worked with and completed 26 projects sponsored by various international agencies such as the World Bank, the United States Agency for International Development (USAID), the Ford Foundation, the United Nations Children's Fund (UNICEF), the European Commission, the United Nations Fund for Population Activities (UNFPA; now United Nations Population Fund), the Bill & Melinda Gates Foundation, as well as projects sponsored by various government departments such as the Ministry of Panchayati Raj, Rural Development, Health and Family Welfare, Drinking Water and Sanitation, Agriculture and Farmer's Welfare, and Planning Commission of the Government of India. He has also completed projects and studies sponsored by various departments of the state governments of Punjab, Haryana and Himachal Pradesh in different areas of development, such as drinking water and sanitation, border areas, migrant labour, contract farming, studies on Scheduled Castes and Scheduled Tribes, health and family welfare, Panchayati Raj, education, rural development and decentralized planning, women and child welfare and preparation of district development plans.

So far, Professor Pattanaik has authored four books, co-authored four books and edited one book. He has more than 150 publications (research papers, articles, editorial column and book reviews) in various national and international journals. He has also been guiding PhD students in different areas of development studies, and seven candidates have already been awarded PhD degrees. He has been instrumental in designing the MA programme in development studies and the PG diploma programme in urban planning and development. He has visited countries such as the USA, China,

Spain and Finland, and attended international seminars, conferences and study tours. He has conducted an international conference on diaspora and development at IGNOU in which more than 100 participants from 25 different countries participated. Professor Pattanaik has been awarded the Distinguished Leadership Award in 1999 by the American Biographical Institute, USA, and the International Man of the Millennium by the International Biographical Centre, Cambridge, London. He has received Shelter Award 2019 from Shelter Council of India and Bharat Jyoti Puraskar 2017 by the Best Citizen Publishing House, New Delhi. He is also a member of the American Biographical Institute's Research Board of Advisors and of American Association of International Researchers (AAIR), USA.

1 Urbanization: An Overview

The world is undergoing the largest wave of urban growth in history. More than half of the world's population now lives in towns and cities, and by 2030 this number will swell to about 5 billion. Much of this urbanization will unfold in Africa and Asia, bringing huge social, economic and environmental transformations.

—UNFPA[1]

No country has grown to middle income without industrializing and urbanizing. None has grown to high income without vibrant cities. The rush to cities in developing countries seems chaotic, but it is necessary.

—World Bank (2009)

The city is one of the highest pinnacles of human creation.... Through agglomeration, cities have the power to innovate, generate wealth, enhance quality of life and accommodate more people within a smaller footprint at lower per capita resource use and emissions than any other settlement pattern.

—Robinson and Swilling (2012, p. iii)

With more than 80% of global GDP generated in cities, urbanization can contribute to sustainable growth if managed well by increasing productivity, allowing innovation and new ideas to emerge.

—World Bank[2]

Introduction

Urbanization is taking place rapidly in various countries of the world and most particularly in developing countries. Truly, urbanization is the order of the day and is one of the great paradigm shifts in the demographic situation in various countries of the world. Urbanization and urban development are the most common structural changes the countries of the world have been experiencing in recent years. In the World Urbanization Prospects 2014, the United Nations (UN) envisaged that Africa and Asia were urbanizing faster than other regions, and the urbanization is projected to become 56 and 64 per cent urban, respectively, by 2050. With 54 per cent of the world's population residing in urban areas in 2014, the UN also noted that globally more people were living in urban areas than in rural areas. In 2015, a report of the Global Taskforce of Local and Regional Governments envisaged that as the global population would grow from about 7 to more than 9 billion by 2050 in many countries, most of them would be absorbed by urban areas. Urban populations were projected to reach the 85 and 64 per cent levels in high-income in developing countries, respectively. In *World Urbanization Prospects: The 2018 Revision*, it has been noted that globally more people live in urban areas than in rural areas, with 55 per cent of the world's population residing in urban areas in 2018. In 1950, 30 per cent of the world's population was urban, and by 2050, 68 per cent of the world's population is projected to be urban. There is significant diversity in the urbanization levels reached by different geographic regions. The most urbanized geographic regions include Northern America (82% living in urban areas in 2018), Latin America and the Caribbean (81%), Europe (74%) and Oceania (68%). The level of urbanization in Asia is now approximating 50 per cent. By contrast, Africa remains mostly rural, with 43 per cent of its population living in urban areas (United Nations, 2019).

It is remarkable that abstract urbanization has been one of the most important demographic shifts worldwide during the past century and represents a substantial change from how most of the world's population has lived for the past several thousand years (Galea & Vlahov, 2005). Today, cities are playing a central role in creating national wealth and enhancing social and economic development. Cities are attracting direct foreign investment and boosting the economic growth rate of nation states. Cities also offer important stimulus for achieving sustainable economic growth. However, it has also been estimated that doubling the size of a city increases productivity by 3–8 per cent (Rosenthal & Strange, 2002). Therefore, urbanization can be termed as an opportunity as well as a challenge or concern for both developed and developing countries, especially for the latter. Randolph and Jain (2016) have also remarked that the truth is that cities are neither inherently good nor inherently bad. Their ability to generate economic, social and cultural opportunities depends on how well they are managed, which is why governments, the private sector and civil societies are paying increasing attention to promoting 'good urbanization'. Rather than viewing urbanization simply as a spatial consequence of economic growth, policymakers now realize that they must treat cities as key sites of policymaking in order to achieve the broader aims of sustainable development and inclusive growth (Randolph & Jain, 2016).

It is not a flight of fancy, but truly a rapid pace of urbanization is being observed in the low-income nations. It is noted that the most rapidly urbanizing cities are in less-wealthy nations, and the pace of growth varies among regions (Vlahov & Galea, 2002). The UN also supports the fact by envisaging that the global urban population is projected to grow by 2.5 billion urban dwellers between 2018 and 2050, with nearly 90 per cent of the increase concentrated in Asia and Africa (United Nations, 2019). The faulty process of urbanization taking place in the developing countries of Asia and Africa has put tremendous pressure on the government to meet the challenges of the growth of population in the urban areas. Stucki (2015), from the African cities' context, viewed that these cities are faced with poor urban planning, inefficient basic service delivery, poor infrastructure provision, inadequate transport services, unregulated traffic, increasing congestion and pollution, and inadequate technical, institutional and financial capacities. According to the United Nations (2019), the unplanned or inadequately managed urban expansion, in combination with unsustainable production and consumption patterns and a lack of capacity of public institutions to manage urbanization, can impair sustainability due to urban sprawl, pollution and environmental degradation, whereas well managed urbanization (among other factors) informed by an understanding of population trends over the long run can help to maximize the benefits of agglomeration while minimizing environmental degradation and other potential adverse impacts of a growing number of city dwellers, especially in low-income and lower-middle-income countries where the most rapid urbanization is expected between 2020 and 2050. Therefore, urbanization and its impact on the lives and livelihood of urban dwellers and on the economic growth and development of the nation states is hot development discourse. This chapter gives an overview of the urbanization.

LEARNING OBJECTIVES

After reading this chapter, you should be able to:

- Define urbanization and its characteristics
- Explain the need and importance of urban development
- Describe various dimensions of urban development
- Explain various dimensions and trends of urbanization
- Narrate various causes of urbanization
- Describe various issues and challenges of urbanization at a glance

Urbanization: Concept and Meaning

The word 'urbanization' has been derived from a Latin word *urbs*, a term used by the Romans to mean a city. The *Cambridge Dictionary* defines it as the process by which more and more people leave the countryside to live in cities. The *Macmillan Dictionary* defines it as the process by which towns and cities grow bigger, and more and more people go to live in them. Generally, urbanization means the rise of footprints in urban areas and the increase in the percentage of population living in urban areas of the nation states as compared to rural areas. In other words, urbanization refers to the movement of people from the countryside to the cities or urban areas. A few well-accepted definitions of urbanization are given below.

According to Henderson (2003), urbanization occurs as countries switch sectoral composition away from agriculture into industry and as technological advances in domestic agriculture release labour from agriculture to migrate to cities. He further says that urbanization, or the shift of population from rural to urban environments, is typically a transitory process, albeit one that is socially and culturally traumatic.

McGranahan and Satterthwaite (2014) have commented that urbanization is often used more loosely to refer to a broad-based rural-to-urban transition involving population, land use, economic activity and culture, or indeed any of these.

According to Chen et al. (2014), urbanization is not only about a simple increase in the number of urban residents, but also involves a series of changes from rural to urban styles in terms of industry structure, employment, living conditions and social public services.

Mishra (1998) had defined urbanization in the following way:

> Urbanization is not a product. It is a process by which a people, instead of living in predominantly dispersed agriculture villages, start living in towns and cities dominated by industrial and service

functionaries. It involves multiplication of urban places and/or an increase in size of cities. Growth of urban population is only one of dimensions of urbanization.

Kingsley Davis, one of the eminent demographers, has classified the process of urbanization into the following three stages. Stage I: This is the initial stage, characterized by traditional rural society with predominance in agriculture and dispersed pattern of settlements. Stage II: At this stage, the proportion of urban population gradually increases from 25 to 40 per cent, to 60 per cent and so on. This is otherwise called the stage of acceleration where the basic restructuring of economy and investments in social overhead capitals including transport and communication takes place. Stage III: This stage is also known as the terminal stage. Here urban population exceeds 70 per cent or more. At this stage, the level of urbanization remains more or less the same or constant.

UNICEF has rightly envisaged that an urban area can be defined in one or more of the following ways:

1. *Administrative criteria or political boundaries:* area within the jurisdiction of a municipality or town committee;
2. *Threshold population size:* where the minimum population for an urban settlement is typically in the range of 2,000, although this varies globally between 200 and 50,000;
3. *Economic function:* where a significant majority of the population is not primarily engaged in agriculture, or where there is surplus employment; and
4. *The presence of urban characteristics:* paved streets, electric lighting and sewerage.[3]

According to the Census of India, 2011, an urban area consists of:

1. All statutory towns with a Municipality, Corporation, Cantonment Board or Notified Town Area Committee and so on declared by the law of the State.
2. Census towns, which place and satisfy the following criteria:
   a. A minimum population of 5,000.
   b. At least 75 per cent of male working population engaged in non-agricultural pursuits.
   c. A population density of at least 400 persons per km^2.

From all these perspectives on urbanization, it can be said that urbanization is a process of migration of population from rural areas to the cities in order to pursue a different occupation and an improved way of life. Urbanization is a structural change of a nation state. In this phase, people move from the traditional agriculture sector towards the modern industrial and service sector, largely present in the cities, and from rural areas to urban areas. According to Drescher and Iaquinta (2002), urbanization occurs in five principal ways.

1. *Natural increase:* It is simply the excess of births over deaths in an area.
2. *International immigration to cities:* It involves the movement of individuals across national boundaries.
3. *Internal rural-to-urban migration:* Migration of rural population to urban areas in a country.
4. *Re-classification:* It occurs when a particular location reaches the administratively defined threshold to be redefined as urban.
5. *Metropolitanization:* It exerts its influence through a process of dominance whereby rural and peri-urban areas are either absorbed into the city itself or brought significantly within its sphere of daily activities.

Features of Urbanization

Some of the important features of urbanization are as follows:

1. *Sectoral influence:* One of the most universal features of urbanization is the migration of people from rural areas to urban areas. The influence of the agriculture sector is quite less in urban areas. Urban areas are largely found to be predominated by industry and businesses. Besides, service sector activities are also largely prevalent in urban areas. It is said that urbanization brings about industrialization and modernization. Malik and Ali (2015) argued that urbanization is a threat to agricultural land. With rapid economic growth due to urbanization, the economic structure shifts from agricultural to non-agriculture-based economy.
2. *Mobility:* The movement of the people from one occupation to the other and from one office to the other is usually characterized as mobility. The occupational options in urban areas are more than in rural areas. The other dimensions of mobility are the movement of people from one area to the other for houses, jobs and better urban services such as education and healthcare; a better city transport system; and e-mobility with information and communication technology (ICT) facilities. Therefore, mobility is one of the important features of urbanization.
3. *Social heterogeneity:* The urban society is a heterogeneous society where there is no occupational demarcation as that of the rural society. People across the nation state, belonging to different caste, class and ethnicity, present in urban areas are collectively called the urban community. Wilson (1986) was of the view that the large population size of the city not only maintains heterogeneity and unconventionality but also engenders them by bringing about the continual emergence of new or hybrid subcultures.
4. *Impersonal social relationship:* Impersonality in urban life is one of the convenient ways of urban living. Once a person migrates from a rural area to an urban area, his/her social acquaintance becomes limited. His/her large family network disappears and the friendship network takes its place. This friendship network is dynamic in nature as new friends add to this network and some old ones fade away with the change of occupation and place of living. Thus, relationship becomes impersonal and fragile.
5. *Materialism:* The urban society is more materialistic than the rural society. Man runs after money and becomes votary of luxury and comfort. Human beings residing in urban areas become materialistic and commercial. The attitude of fellow feeling and sacrificing fades away day by day with the increased stay period in urban areas. Urban people are exploring satisfaction in living through material and goods as well as from shopping malls which have become the significant platforms that are moulding people's behaviours and habits (Satt and others, 2017).
6. *Change in lifestyle:* As stated by Clark (2003), the concept of urbanization involves some urban lifestyle, which is a reflection of the pattern that is related to social, economic, behavioural, fashion culture, taste, identity, with all of this being a part of the aspirations of the people who live in it. The dress code and food habits and other cultural practices, which were influencing the lifestyle of the people in rural areas fade away in urban areas. Individuals aspire modernity and the modern way of living, and there are cross-cultural habits in urban areas.
7. *Man-made environment:* With the growth of population in urban areas, the flora and fauna diminish in urban areas. Cutting of trees for housing, official and commercial estates deeply affects the urban environment. Besides, with the rise in the number of vehicles and other

gadgets, the air of urban areas gets polluted. An artificial and man-made environment forcibly drives the natural environment from urban areas. In other words, houses and buildings take the places of grass and trees.

8. *Dynamism:* In the city, things are never fixed. A city is more agile and dynamic than a countryside. City life and activities are more hectic and pressing. All categories of people starting from the slum dweller and common man to rich millionaires, influential politicians, economists and artists reside in the city, and they all influence the lifestyle and living conditions of each individual. According to Kenji Doi, cities change with the passage of time, moving from growth to decay. To make an analogy with human life, cities pass from the period of childhood to adolescence (urbanization), young adulthood to middle age (suburbanization) and finally to old age (disurbanizaiton).[4]
9. *Individualism:* Another important feature of urbanization is individualism. People in urban areas are self-centred and more confined to their personal well-being rather than showing any concerns for others. In urban areas, there is the lack of social relationship, contacts and networking. A person in an urban area is identified through his/her house number and hardly by his/her name. The relationship is too personal and there is no concern for others. Ram Ahuja says that urbanism is a way of life, which is characterized by certain elements such as transiency (short-term relations), superficiality (impersonal and formal relations with limited number of people), anonymity (not knowing names and lacking intimacy) and individualism (people giving more importance to one's vested interests).[5]
10. *Modernity:* Modernity is a visible feature of urban cities. The lifestyle, dress code and food habits in urban areas are cosmopolitan in nature. There is less imprint of traditionalism, especially among the youth. Shopping complexes and marketing malls add sufficient values and flavour to modernity. Ibrahim (1972) noted that historically, urbanization and modernization had been directly linked in the evolution of Western Europe, North America, Soviet Russia and Japan.

Although there are many characteristics of urban areas, the aforementioned are some of the leading features of urban areas which are found in both developed and developing countries.

Need and Importance of Urban Development

Urbanization has become inevitable in the nation state which desires to promote growth, bring socioeconomic changes and raise human capital. According to Barofsk et al. (2016), the economic benefits of urbanization include agglomeration economies that raise workers' and businesses' productivity through enhanced resource sharing, quicker and better job matching, faster knowledge spillovers, infrastructure access, public goods and lower transaction costs. There is a need for urbanization, particularly in developing countries, in order to hasten their pace of development. The need and importance of urban development are as follows.

1. *Economic growth:* The increase in the national economic growth rate is one of the important contributions that urbanization has made. World Bank has remarked that with just 54 per cent of the world's population, cities account for more than 80 per cent of global gross domestic product (GDP). Urban growth may lead to a rise in the economic development of a country. It has also led to the expansion of business and economic activities in the

suburban areas. It can be considered as an indicator of the state of a country's economic condition. The economic condition has a direct effect on a country's economic development. Cities provide thick markets with large numbers of buyers and sellers of products, services, property and labour. Such market thickness in well-functioning cities has been shown to be a significant driver of economic growth in developed and developing economies (Moretti, 2013).

2. *Urbanization brings structural changes:* Industrialization leads to urbanization and vice versa. Urban areas enjoy the advantages of economies of scale. Inputs such as skilled labour and repair services are readily available in urban areas. It helps the producers to effectively utilize its resources and earn profit. According to the UN-Habitat, over the last two decades, cities and metropolitan areas have emerged as the world's economic platforms for production, innovation and trade. Urbanization can bring effective structural changes in both high-income and developing countries and more particularly in developing countries, where agriculture plays a predominant role. Cities can boost both industrial and service sector activities. The former can promote production activities, whereas the latter can promote consumption or service sector activities. Weber (1922) also contrasts 'consumption cities' and 'production cities': the former are cities that serve the needs of a political elite, whereas the latter address the needs of manufacturers and merchants.
3. *Urbanization brings modernization:* Customarily, urbanization means redistribution and shift of population from the countryside to towns and cities, whereas modernization more commonly implies attitudinal changes among the population towards greater acceptability of innovations, social change, rationality and the diffusion of the scientific outlook among most of the population in the society. Urbanization promotes a broader outlook among the people living in the cities. Modernization promotes cosmopolitanism and broadens the outlook of the people towards modern culture and the use of technology in the lifestyle. Modernization influences the dress code, food habits, dance, song and so on. With globalization, urbanization is boosting modernization at a faster pace in the cities. To Schnaiberg (1971), regardless of the exact conceptualization of 'urbanization' or 'modernization', we know that one affects another, so that a persistent co-variation is found, whether one looks at cross-sectional or longitudinal data.
4. *Urbanization increases employment opportunities:* Globally, urban centres are expanding due to their capacity to generate income, contribute to national wealth, attract investments and create jobs (WHO & UN-Habitat, 2010). A person working in both formal and informal sectors in an urban area gets a higher income than his/her countryside counterpart. Further, the quality of employment available in the cities is better than that in the countryside, which attracts the rural people to migrate to urban areas. The more the metropolitan area grows, the more employment it generates and the more it contributes to economic growth. It is remarked that since an urban market is thicker, it has more buyers and sellers than a non-urban market (Randolph & Jain, 2016). Enterprises can produce more, at cheaper prices, enabling them to grow faster, add employees and make productivity-enhancing investments (Hoover, 1975).
5. *Urbanization leads to the reduction of poverty:* Urbanization affects rural poverty. It generates new opportunities for rural workers in the urban informal sector, who shift from agriculture to more remunerative, non-farm activities in the city. This causes an influx of money into rural areas, mainly in the shape of remittances. Furthermore, the migration of agriculture workers into the city reduces the rural labour supply, thereby increasing rural wages.[6] It is also

remarkable that urbanization can help reduce poverty through its impact on economic growth, which is a prerequisite for poverty reduction (Demery & Squire, 1995). Therefore, cities have been described as 'real poverty fighters' (UN-Habitat, 2010). According to the UN-Habitat (2010), urbanization has helped millions escape poverty through higher levels of productivity, employment opportunities, improved quality of life via better education and health, large-scale public investment, and access to improved infrastructure and services.

6. *Urbanization enhances entrepreneurship and innovation:* Entrepreneurs and start-ups particularly benefit from ready access to a concentration of capital, business services and appropriately skilled labour, which are found readily available in urban areas. This, in turn, makes urban areas excellent breeding grounds for innovation and homes of the creative destruction that Schumpeter predicted would drive economic progress. Urban areas tend to be very good at supporting the entrepreneurial activity and innovation that can generate jobs and firm growth in more productive areas of economy (Gilles, 2013).
7. *Urbanization increases standard of living and quality of life:* The African Development Bank believes that planned urbanization can improve living conditions for the majority, help in the expansion of the middle-class and create conditions for economic transformation. Urban areas that provide better infrastructure and employment with higher wages than rural areas help the migrant rural population to access quality basic needs such as better housing, sanitation and safe drinking water, which boost the quality of life of common men. The rapid urban economic growth in India has helped to reduce poverty, increased standard of living by increasing job opportunities and declined dependency on agriculture (Mahey & Tripathi, 2016).
8. *Urbanization brings social change:* One of the important characteristics of urbanization is that it brings social change in nation states. Urban areas have good quality education and health institutions that promote education and health, which are important features of social development. Moreover, urban society being more heterogeneous, promotes development by negating social barriers imposed through caste, class, creed and gender. Women are socioeconomically more empowered in an urban society than in a rural society. They are vital actors of social change in an urban society. Muchadenyika and Williams (2016) are of the view that urbanization is an essential determinant of social change, and for social change to take place, the process of urbanization requires extensive management (through urban governance).

Dimensions of Urban Development

The 'urban' is in itself an opaque term (Boano & Marten, 2017). It amounts to more than its spatial and geographical parameters, and is characterized by what Edgar Pieterse, South African Research Chair in Urban Policy at the University of Cape Town, documents as the 'rich, complex and indeterminate dynamics of "cityness"' (Pieterse, 2013). With urbanization, transitions take place in various dimensions, such as societal, economic and environmental. All these dimensions of urbanization widely differ from those of rural areas. It has been rightly envisaged in the Habitat III in 2016 that:

> As the population, economic activities, social and cultural interactions, as well as environmental and humanitarian impacts, are increasingly concentrated in cities, this poses massive sustainability

challenges in terms of housing, infrastructure, basic services, food security, health, education, decent jobs, safety, and natural resources, among others.

The dimensions of urban development given by Safer (2004) are as follows: (a) urban society, (b) urban economy, (c) urban environment, (d) urban governance and (e) urban infrastructure. The urbanization is multidimensional.

With the effect of globalization, dimensions of urban development have changed, and more new dimensions have been added to the previously existing dimensions. Some of the important dimensions of urban development are as follows:

1. Urban society
2. Urban economy
3. Urban infrastructure
4. Urban governance
5. Urban environment
6. Urban planning
7. Urban management
8. Urban reforms

These are the eight dimensions for the achievement of inclusive and sustainable urban development (Figure 1.1).

Figure 1.1 Dimensions of Urban Development

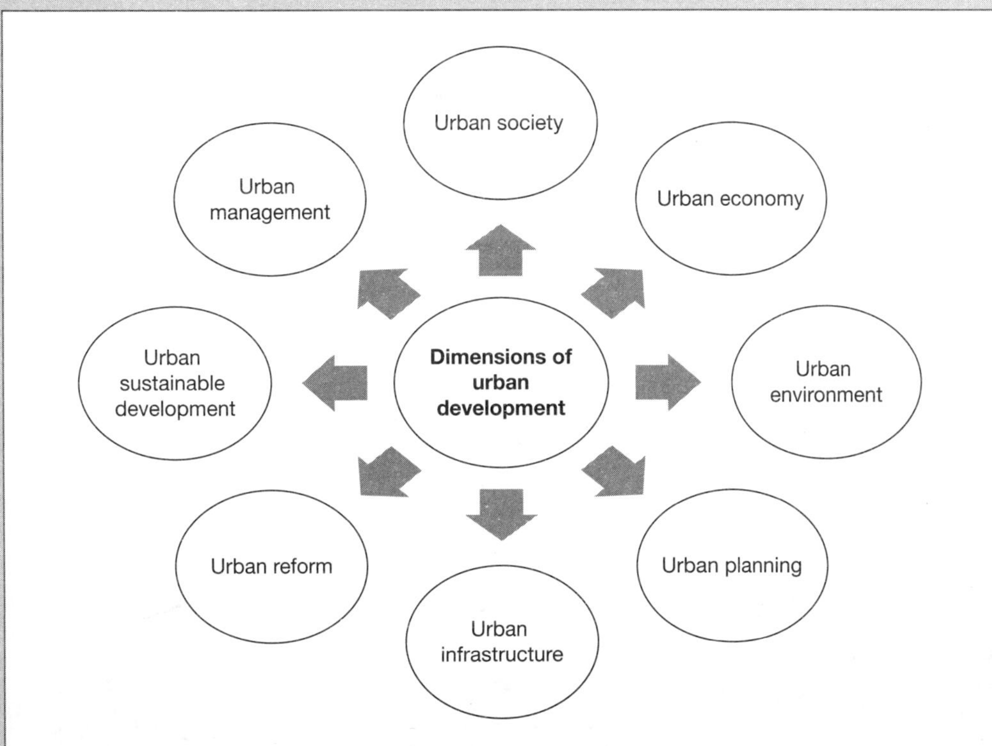

1. *Urban society:* An urban society is different from a rural one. The livelihood options available in an urban society are heterogeneous as compared to the rural society. The pattern of living in an urban society is also different from that of a rural society. Any discussion on urban society needs to cover the following aspects[7]:
   a. Social stratification and spatial segregation
   b. Urban poverty
   c. Informality
   d. Gender equality
   e. Social movements
   f. Cultural heritage
   g. Consumption habits and lifestyles

   Department for International Development (DFID) considers that cities are the major centres of struggle for social development—their concentration of large and diverse populations, and their attraction of migrants, provide the conditions for social innovation and changes in social relations that are vital to increasing social welfare for greater numbers. While, at the same time, they are the focal points of social struggles for an increased quality of life and social provision, and the centres of influence on changing values in wider societies. It has identified six areas for social transformation in cities, which are critical to urban development: (a) social inclusion, (b) urban livelihoods, (c) gender, (d) violence and human rights, (e) health, children and education and (f) culture and identity.[8]

   In the cities, opportunities available in the area of employment both in the formal and informal sectors, quality healthcare and education are higher than those in rural areas. This is one of the leading reasons for the migration of people from rural to urban areas. From the standpoint of social inclusiveness, urban society is more inclusive than rural society. There is hardly any cluster living on the basis of caste, religion and ethnicity. People belonging to different castes and communities reside in the same residential complex, be it single- or multi-storeyed. The other important feature of the urban society is that the individual identity is less revealed as there is less social interaction among the urban dwellers. It is often said that the identity of a person in an urban area is known from his/her house number rather than the name, designation, caste and other identity. Women in an urban society are comparatively more educated and empowered and have higher decision-making powers than those staying in rural areas. The consumption habit and lifestyle of an urbanite are different, and there is a greater degree of modernity. There is a lack of social cohesion, and the rate of crime is also higher in urban areas. The types and reasons of violence in urban areas are different from those in rural areas. The cluster living of the marginalized in the informal settlements has given rise to the issues of urban safety and security.
2. *Urban economy:* The urban economy, in general, and those of the metropolitan cities, in particular, are more exposed to globalization than the rural economies. In the urban economy, industrial and service sector activities contribute a large share to the national GDP. The contribution of an urban economy to the nation's economic growth is growing day by day and has virtually outstripped the contribution of a rural economy in most of the economies of the world. The urban economy gives a wide range of socioeconomic benefits, which are as follows:
   a. Reduction in poverty and social inequality;
   b. More economic and social opportunities in terms of better healthcare and education;

c. Division of labour and enhanced productivity;
d. Changing pattern of employment, livelihood and income;
e. Good quality infrastructure, such as road, market complexes, water supply and sanitation;
f. Effective e-governance and a better management of the urban economy with the help of technology;
g. Increased standard of living and quality of living;
h. Both public and private sectors play an important role in the generation of employment, income and productivity in an urban economy; and
i. Income and employment opportunities for women in the urban economy is higher than rural economy. In other words, in urban areas, the contribution of women to the economy is higher than those in rural areas.

It is remarkable that ongoing rapid urbanization has the potential to improve the well-being of societies. Although only around half of the world's people live in cities, they generate more than 80 per cent of GDP. Cities are also younger: home to relatively more young and working-age adults than rural areas, making them pivotal places to capture demographic dividends.[9] In developing countries, in urban economy, informal sector is an important actor of development and a large number of migrated populations from rural areas are engaged in informal sector activities. The labour market in the urban economy is dualistic in nature: one for informal sector employment and other for those who are skilled and semi-skilled and employed largely in the formal sector. According to Brown and McGranahan (2016), the urban informal economy includes a wide array of activities, from street vending to domestic service, from home-based enterprises to the informal employees of formal enterprises and from waste picking to urban agriculture. Urban finance is a key component of urban economy. It is one of the key requirements for provisioning of basic services and infrastructure facilities in urban areas. In the recent past, it has been seen that urban development programmes in developing countries are promoting interaction between rural and urban areas. An illustrious example is the concept used in India, that is, 'rur-urban' and 'rural–urban continuum'.

3. *Urban infrastructure:* Unban infrastructure is one of the important dynamics of urban development. It is said that the urban economic undertakings are dependent on infrastructures such as power, telecom, roads, water supply and transportation, sanitation and solid waste management (SWM).[10] People migrate from rural areas to urban areas with the hope that it will provide them better infrastructure facilities such as landscaping, housing, drinking water, electricity, sanitation, education and healthcare infrastructure. In terms of sectors, infrastructure can be classified broadly as follows (Kim, 2016): (a) transportation: surface (roads, parking, bridges), public transportation system (metro, buses), air (airports, navigation system) and sea (ports, canals), traffic interconnections; (b) environment: solid and liquid waste management, water supply, sanitation, land-use management; (c) social: educational institutions, such as schools and universities, health facilities, justice facilities, law enforcement agencies, cultural institutions, defence and security, money transfer institutions and social value systems; (d) energy: power generation plans, including hydro, geothermal, gas, solar, wind, biomass and nuclear, as well as distribution grids and networks; (e) telecommunications: fibre optics, towers, satellites, cables; (f) oil and gas: refineries and extraction facilities, storage; and (g) other: industries (mills, production

plants and so on), agriculture and mining. However, it varies across the different categories of cities. The landscaping and land development, urban transport system and the availability of technologies are also other infrastructural concerns. In India, the beautiful city of Chandigarh is famous for its infrastructure and land designing and utilization. The smart city concept coined by the Government of India (GoI) in recent years also aims at improving the urban infrastructure facilities. Urban infrastructure is the cornerstone of modern society and an inevitable necessity for economic growth and development. Starting from the construction of road to supply of energy and water, and the treatment of waste, to the provision of effective healthcare and education services, it is infrastructure that enables society to function effectively, grow and prosper.

4. *Urban environment:* Urban environment is a critical component of urban development. A healthy urban environment can be helpful to construct a healthy urban society. However, unplanned urbanization has adversely impacted the environment of the cities in most developing countries. The use of non-renewable sources of energy for various purposes, indiscriminate waste disposal and green house emission are severely affecting urban environment. It is causing a lot of health hazards in the cities in general and industrial cities in particular. Not only the cities but also the adjoining areas including the villages are found to be affected by the industrial pollution. The Sustainable Development Goals (SDGs) cannot be attained unless the environmental concerns in the cities are duly attended to. Ichimura (2003) has noted that urbanization does not have only local environmental impacts but also large so-called 'ecological footprints' beyond their immediate vicinity. He said that intensive and extensive exploitation of natural resources to support urban economy includes excessive extraction of energy resources (including fuelwood), quarrying and excavation of sand, gravel and building materials at large scales and over-extraction of water. These all contribute to the degradation of the natural support systems and irreversible loss of critical ecosystem functions, such as the hydrological cycle, carbon cycle and biological diversity, in addition to conflicts with rural uses of such limited resources. World Health Organization (WHO) has remarked that rapid, unplanned and unsustainable patterns of urban development are making developing cities focal points for many emerging environment and health hazards (WHO, 2002). Sustainable urbanization and smart city movement desire that the environmental issues need to be an integral part of the city design.
5. *Urban planning:* Urban planning and management are vital urban dynamics on which the fabric of urbanization stands. Urban planning deals with the complex management of change within the built and natural environment. Urban planning, as a form of collective decision-making, is related to spatial outcomes and is oriented keeping in mind the needs of individual, community and the nation states. Urban planning is defined as preparation of plans for partial or complete development of cities, with the current situation, as well as future scenarios in mind (Leksikon, 2016). This is to ensure that land use, transportation, buildings, landscapes, open places, infrastructure, economic investments, jobs and businesses are included in plans for development of communities (Rydningen & Rolfsen, 2016). The key stakeholders in the preparation of urban planning are urban local bodies (ULBs), development authorities; town and country planning organizations, urban parastatals and civil society organizations (CSOs) responsible for planning and implementing cities' path for development. It is not a flight of fancy, but delicately the

process of urban planning happens in a highly contested space where economic, political and historical factors play specific roles in shaping the future of a city and its adjoining region. In a nutshell, urban planning is primarily concerned with managing the spatial arrangements of cities and towns. This includes mentioning a few among many are the range of physical facilities and structures such as water and sewerage infrastructure, city road, hospitals, schools, offices, market complex, industry and housing. Besides, cultural, recreational, familial, civic, political and personal aspects of human life are accommodated within urban areas. It also looks into the effective use of urban open space such as parks, zoos, museums, playgrounds, open space for theatre and electioneering, and heritage during the planning process. This has to be contextualized in terms of the location, density, height and arrangements of structures. Successful urban planning has to integrate and balance the needs and challenges associated with 'everyday' and 'emergency' operations. Effective land use planning with the use of geographic information system (GIS) is being promoted in many cities of developed as well as developing countries for meeting the challenges of urbanization. Moreover, integration of environmental issues in the urban planning process will go a long way in the formation of a sustainable and resilient city.

6. *Urban management:* Urban management deals with the development of urban lifestyles. According to Mattingly (1995), the management of urban areas can be defined as the exercise of continuing responsibility for actions to achieve sustainable improvements in living conditions and productivity in urban areas. He was of the view that the highest priority actions comprising urban management will differ from time to time and from place to place, as particular conditions and contexts will determine them. The urban management has the responsibility to see that the tasks assigned to various agencies, authorities and bodies are performed effectively and efficiently so that the aims and objectives of urban development are achieved. Among many of the important aspects of urban management, some cropped up from time to time related to urban development: (a) safety and security services, (b) urban environment, (c) transport and traffic system, (d) drinking water services, (e) sanitation and waste management, (f) urban energy, (g) food security and public distribution and (h) education and healthcare services. Urban management can integrate and efficiently utilize scarce resources, vastly expanding the resource pool available for the needs of urban life (Mattingly, 1995). Sustainable urban management is an essential and vital component of urban development.
7. *Urban governance:* Urban governance is a major issue in urban development. Most of the democracies in the local self-government institutions (LSIs) are playing an important role in the process of urbanization and urban development. The governance issues such as transparency, accountability, rule of law, participatory and consensus-oriented governance are critical to urban governance particularly in developing countries. While commenting on urbanization in India, Ahluwalia (2014) has noted that the majority of cities in India have been facing huge challenges in all the fronts or in other words, for the government, the governance of urban areas is a big challenge. Avis (2016) has noted that effective urban governance depends on four key elements: (a) city–national interface; (b) municipal capacity; (c) role of private sector; and (d) political systems and institutions.

UNDP (2014) has emphasized two issues in urban governance.

a. Improved and inclusive urban governance, and greater resilience to climate-induced shocks should be part of broader governance reforms in countries, particularly local governance and development planning.
b. Improvements in public participation, transparency, accountability, responsiveness and equity are required for local governments in urban areas to respond more effectively to the challenges posed by climate change.

8. *Urban reforms:* Urbanization or urban development is a continuous process; therefore, countries in general and developing countries in particular have to introduce urban reform measures from time to time in order to accelerate the process of sustainable urban development. The reform process needs to analyse the past, present and future, and initiate projects and programmes for the development of cities and their peripheries. All the stakeholders such as the central and state government, ULBs, private and corporate sector and CSOs are to be effectively involved and engaged in the urban reform process. Urban reforms refer to both legislative and administrative reforms. The 74th Constitutional Amendment and empowerment of ULBs in India are an illustrious urban reform introduced in India since 1992. Besides, continuous amendments relating to ceiling regulation, land acquisition, urban e-governance are other reform measures several countries in the world are introducing for better and effective urbanization. Some of the urban reforms introduced by Jawaharlal Nehru National Urban Renewal Mission (JNNURM) are: (a) governance reforms—which includes the implementation of decentralization measures as envisaged in the 74th Amendment Act of the Constitution; transfer of activities under the 12th Schedule of the Amendment; Constitution of District Planning Committee and Metropolitan Planning Committee; administrative reforms; structural reforms and provision of basic services to the urban poor; (b) land and property reforms—reform of property tax (PT; arrangements for 90% coverage and 85% collection efficiency within the mission period of 7 years); earmarking at least 20–25 per cent of developed land in all housing projects for the Economically Weaker Section/Low Income Group; introduction of the computerized process of registration of land and property; repeal of Urban Land (Ceiling and Regulation) Act, 1976; introduction of property title certification system in ULBs, among others; (c) reforms for financial sustainability—levy of reasonable user charges by ULBs and states; internal earmarking of funds within local body budgets for basic services to urban poor; and (d) process-oriented/citizen responsive reforms—the adoption of modern accrual-based double entry system of accounting; introduction of system of e-governance; reform of rent control laws balancing the interests of landlords and tenants; rationalization of stamp duty (to no more than 5%); the enactment of Public Disclosure Law and the enactment of Community Participation Law to institutionalize citizen participation.[11]

   Urban reforms which also comprise urban policies and programmes aim at making cities more inclusive, sustainable and resilient. According to the United Nations World Urbanization Prospects—2014, urbanization is integrally connected to the three pillars of sustainable development: economic development, social development and environmental protection. The report has also recognized both the plight of the urban poor and the need for sustainable cities as matters of great urgency for the UN Development Agenda. The urban economy, society and environment have to cohesively work in order to achieve sustainable urban development. Any urban developmental actions taken in present have to take into considerations their impact on the quality of life and well-being of city dwellers in future. Besides, the urban development process has to take into consideration the needs of the marginalized and those who are in the informal settlements and integrate them effectively with the process of urban development. The urban reform process needs to emphasize the aspects which can make the city more resilient to deal with the future shocks.

Trends of Urbanization

Urbanization has almost become the order of the day and the trend of urbanization is on the rise. The world is experiencing a historical transition—human civilization will more and more coalesce into very large urban centres, and cities are the manifestation of the cultural, economic and social acceleration that we have experienced in the last century.[12] The UN has envisaged that the proportion of the world's population, which is urban, has been growing rapidly and a larger fraction of the total population lives within cities now than at any previous period in history (United Nations, 2007). Urbanization and growth of urban areas have been faster in developing countries after the globalization. The craze for cities has grown at a faster pace in developing countries than developed countries in recent years. The urban growth has three components: (a) natural increase of urban populations which results from an excess of births over deaths in urban areas; (b) migration to cities from rural areas or from abroad which contributes to urban growth whenever the number of in-migrants exceeds the number of out-migrants; and (c) reclassification which contributes to urban growth by enlarging the size of urban areas (United Nations, 2019). In World Urbanization Prospects: The 2018 Revision brought out by the UN[13] has noted the following trend in urbanization:

1. Striking differences in patterns of urbanization exist between the more developed regions and the less developed regions. While just under half of the population of the less developed regions currently lives in rural areas, the great majority in the more developed regions resides in urban areas. However, the urban population of the less developed regions has been growing considerably faster than that of the more developed regions and, as a result, its share of the world's urban population has been rising.
2. Globally, 55 per cent of the world's population is residing in urban areas in 2018. By 2050, 68 per cent of the world's population is projected to be urban.
3. Today in 2018, the most urbanized regions include Northern America with 82 per cent of its population living in urban areas; Latin America and the Caribbean with 81 per cent; Europe, 74 per cent and Oceania, 68 per cent. The level of urbanization in Asia is now approximating 50 per cent. In contrast, Africa remains mostly rural, with 43 per cent of its population living in urban areas.
4. Just three countries—India, China and Nigeria—together are expected to account for 35 per cent of the growth in the world's urban population between 2018 and 2050. India is projected to add 416 million urban dwellers, China 255 million and Nigeria 189 million.
5. Close to half of the world's urban dwellers reside in settlements with fewer than 500,000 inhabitants, while around one in eight live in 33 megacities with more than 10 million

inhabitants. By 2030, the world is projected to have 43 megacities, most of them in developing regions.

6. Tokyo is the world's largest city with an agglomeration of 37 million inhabitants, followed by Delhi with 29 million, Shanghai with 26 million and Mexico City and São Paulo, each with around 22 million inhabitants. Today, Cairo, Mumbai, Beijing and Dhaka all have close to 20 million inhabitants. The trend of urbanization in more developed and less developed regions is given in Table 1.1 and Figure 1.2.

Some of the features of urbanization as mentioned by WHO are as follows[14]:

1. More than half of the world's populations now lives in cities.
2. By 2030, 6 out of 10 people will be city dwellers, which will rise to 7 out of 10 people by 2050.
3. One in three urban dwellers lives in slums.
4. Urban air pollution kills around 1.2 million people each year around the world, mainly due to cardiovascular and respiratory diseases such as tuberculosis (TB), the incidence of which is much higher in big cities.
5. Urban environment tends to discourage physical activity and promote unhealthy food consumption.

Table 1.1 Trend of Urbanization in More-developed and Less-developed Regions, 1950–2050

	Population (Billion)					Average Annual Rate of Change (%)			
Development Group	**1950**	**1970**	**2011**	**2030**	**2050**	**1950–1970**	**1970–2011**	**2011–2030**	**2030–2050**
Total population									
World	2.53	3.70	6.97	8.32	9.31	1.89	1.55	0.93	0.56
More developed regions	0.81	1.01	1.24	1.30	1.31	1.08	0.51	0.23	0.06
Less developed regions	1.72	2.69	5.73	7.03	7.99	2.23	1.85	1.07	0.65
Urban population									
World	0.75	1.35	3.63	4.98	6.25	2.98	2.41	1.66	1.13
More developed regions	0.44	0.67	0.96	1.06	1.13	2.09	0.89	0.52	0.29
Less developed regions	0.30	0.68	2.67	3.92	5.12	4.04	3.33	2.02	1.34
Rural population									
World	1.79	2.34	3.34	3.34	3.05	1.36	0.87	−0.01	−0.44
More developed regions	0.37	0.34	0.28	0.23	0.18	−0.48	−0.48	−0.92	−1.14
Less developed regions	1.42	2.01	3.07	3.11	2.87	1.74	1.03	0.07	−0.40

Source: United Nations (2011, p. 4).

Figure 1.2 Urban and Rural Populations by Development Group, 1950–2050

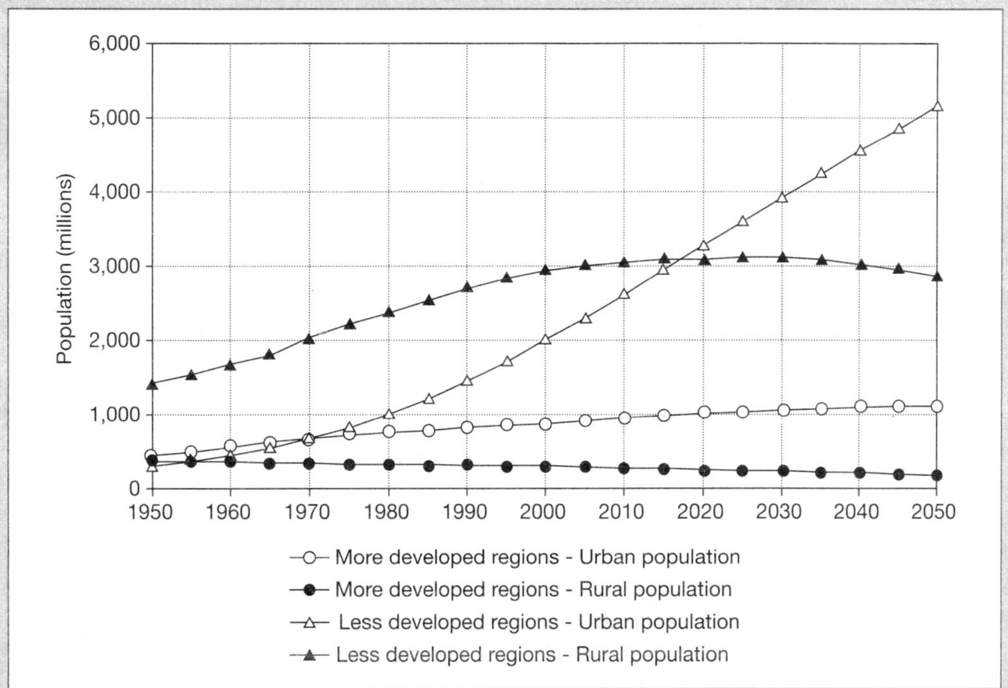

Source: United Nations (2011, p. 3).

Features of Urbanization in Developed Countries

Urbanization has taken place in developed countries much earlier than developing countries. In developed countries of North America and Europe, rapid urbanization took place during the period of industrialization in the 19th and early 20th centuries. Some of the important features of the trends of urbanization in developed countries are narrated further.

1. *Suburbanization:* One of the illustrious features of the urbanization process in developed countries of Europe and the USA is that there has been tremendous growth of suburbs. Suburbanization largely refers to the enhancement of city area and the area of residence to its periphery. Moreover, suburbanization also implies demarcation and separation of workplace and home; availability of better road infrastructure, transport facilities has supported the process of suburbanization in developed countries. Suburbanization has been caused due to migration of low- and lower-middle income group population who cannot afford to live in the centre of the city. Since 1945, the rate of suburban growth in the USA has been tremendous. Analysis of trends in the suburbanization of Whites, Blacks, Asians and Hispanics in the USA reveal that all groups are becoming more suburbanized,

though the gap between Whites and minorities remains large (Massey & Tannen, 2018). On the contrary, the suburbanization in big cities of China, which is a developing country, has placed many residents in locations that are far less accessible than their prior residences, requiring motorized travel (Cervero & Day, 2008).

2. *Urban renewal:* Urban renewal is one of the important trends of urban development activities in developed countries. Urban renewal generally means redevelopment, reconstruction and rehabilitation of the old areas of the cities that have fallen below the current standards of public acceptability. According to Egolum and Emoh (2017), urban renewal is most often undertaken to make life safe, more secure and comfortable to the urban dwellers to attract wealthier individuals to live in that area or to boost the economic base or activities in that area. To them, urban renewal, which may be also known as urban redevelopment is a veritable social gentrification technique. The old areas, which are central part of the cities, are found to be in dilapidated conditions with congested roads, old buildings, traffic problems, flooding and poor environmental conditions. Moreover, these areas are also facing the problems of social malaise and non-conforming uses.
3. *Megapolitan urban areas:* Megapolitan urban areas are one of the important trends observed in developed countries of Europe and the USA not in terms of growth of population but in terms of growth of their areas. Most of the cities are expanding physically. One of the merits of this physical expansion is the low density of population in urban areas of developed countries. According to Jean Gottmann, 'the megapolitan concept seems to have popularized the idea that the modern cities are better reviewed not in isolation, as centers of a restricted area only, but rather as parts of "city-systems," as participants in urban networks revolving in widening orbits'.[15] The megapolitan is more popular in the USA and also in European countries. The US megalopolis extends over 600 miles from Boston to Washington, DC. The Randstad megalopolis of the Netherlands comprises three major cities of Amsterdam, Rotterdam and The Hague.
4. *Gentrification:* It is the process of demolition of the entire city and construction of new city in its place. It is a process of urban renewal. For example, Greater London was totally renewed after the Great Fire of London in 1666; while Paris was razed to ground in the 1850s before it became 'the city of lights'. The gentrification process resulted into movement of middle-class population to the main city. In the USA, most of the main cities are now experiencing varying levels of gentrification in their central area neighbourhoods. However, Maurrasse and Bliss (2006) have remarked that gentrification is a daunting threat to many urban communities because of the unfortunate decrease in access to employment for low-income residents.

Features of Urbanization in Developing Countries

One of the most significant demographic phenomena of modern times and one that promises to loom even larger in the future is the rapid growth of cities in developing countries (Todaro, 1980). Urbanization in developing countries is moving at a faster pace than the developed nations. To Mountjoy (1978), the whole world is moving towards a more urban existence and whereas the process is more nearly completed in the small number of rich industrialized countries, it is only in recent years that marked urbanization has started to sweep across developing countries. Over the next 30 years, virtually all of the world's population growth is expected to be concentrated in urban areas in the developing world (Cohen, 2006). Some of the important features of urbanization in developing countries are as follows:

1. Urbanization takes place without much industrialization. This style of faulty urbanization has resulted in growth of informal sector in urban areas.
2. Urbanization in developing countries is largely due to migration of rural population to urban areas rather than natural growth of population in urban areas. Cohen (2006) has rightly remarked that because rates of natural increase are generally slightly lower in urban than in rural areas, the principal reasons for rising levels of urbanization are rural–urban migration, the geographic expansion of urban areas through annexations and the transformation and re-classification of rural villages into small urban settlements.
3. The density of population in urban areas is more in developing countries than in developed countries. In other words, there is faster addition of population to urban areas of developed countries than those of developing countries, leading to urban crisis. To Mountjoy (1978), all over the developing world, but especially in Latin America and Africa, there has begun a flight from the land: a tidal wave of country folk who now threaten to overwhelm the struggling cities and possibly even to bring about their social and economic disintegration.
4. The urban renewal in developed countries started much earlier than in developing countries. As compared to developed countries, developing countries lag behind in urban renewal mission.
5. Unplanned urbanization and the fast-paced migration of rural population to urban areas have led to the growth of slums in urban areas. In almost all developing countries, slums are being prevalent in the metropolitan cities.
6. One of the critical features of urbanization in developing countries is that the growth of population is at a faster pace in the metropolitan cities and class I cities than class II, class III and class IV cities. Henderson (2002) in his article 'Urbanization in Developing Countries' has also commented that the rapid urbanization in many developing countries over the past half century seems to have been accompanied by excessively high levels of concentration of the urban population in very large cities. In other words, the growth of smaller cities is slower than that of the metropolitan cities. This can be called imbalanced urbanization.
7. The suburbanization process is slower in developing countries than in developed countries. Except a few metropolitan cities, the suburbanization is slow in other cities.

Table 1.2 depicts that the projected rate of urbanization during 2030–2050 is the highest in Africa compared to other regions of the world.

Some of the features of the trends of urbanization in developing countries as given by UNESCO are as follows:

1. Globally, the number of cities with 10 million or more inhabitants is increasing rapidly, and most of these new 'megacities' are in the less developed regions. In 1960, only New York and Tokyo had more than 10 million people. By 1999, there were 17 cities of more than 10 million people around the world, 13 of these were in less developed regions.
2. Urbanization is projected to continue well into the next century. By 2030, it is expected that nearly 5 billion (61%) of the world's 8.1 billion people will live in cities. The less

Table 1.2 Percentage Urban by Major Area, Selected Period, 1950–2050

	Percentage Urban					Rate of Urbanization (%)			
Major Area	**1950**	**1970**	**2011**	**2030**	**2050**	**1950–1970**	**1970–2011**	**2011–2030**	**2030–2050**
Africa	14.4	23.5	39.6	47.7	57.7	2.47	1.27	0.98	0.96
Asia	17.5	23.7	45.0	55.5	64.4	1.52	1.57	1.10	0.74
Europe	51.3	62.8	72.9	77.4	82.2	1.02	0.36	0.31	0.30
Latin America and the Caribbean	41.4	57.1	79.1	83.4	86.6	1.61	0.80	0.28	0.19
Northern America	63.9	73.8	82.2	85.8	88.6	0.72	0.26	0.22	0.16
Oceania	62.4	71.2	70.7	71.4	73.0	0.66	-0.02	0.05	0.12

Source: United Nations (2011, p. 11).

developed regions will be urbanized at a rate of more than 57 per cent. Latin America and the Caribbean will actually have a greater percentage of inhabitants living in cities than Europe.[16]

Trends of Urbanization in India

Urbanization is taking place at a faster pace in India since the beginning of the 20th century. According to Bhagat (2011), the declining trend in the urban population growth rate observed during the 1980s and 1990s was reversed at the national level, and the level of urbanization increased rapidly during 2001–2011. He also further remarked that for the first time since Independence, the absolute increase in the urban population was higher than that in the rural population. The impact of globalization and modernization has triggered off the pace of urbanization in India putting population pressure in the metropolitan cities of India. However, the urbanization taking place without much industrialization is one of the main issues of the trend of urbanization in India. A few important trends of urbanization are discussed further (given in Table 1.3).

1. The urban population growth is largely due to the natural growth of population in urban areas. Kundu (2006) has calculated that urban population expansion is due to the natural growth of population (accounted 59.4% in 1991–2001); the emergence of new cities (accounted 6.2% in 1991–2001); rural-to-urban migration (accounted 21% in 1991–2001) and re-classification of rural areas as urban (accounted 13% in 1991–2001).
2. The contribution of the urban sector to the national GDP shows a rising trend (Table 1.4). It is envisaged in the draft of the 11th Five-Year Plan that in 1950–1951, the contribution of the urban sector to India's GDP was only 29 per cent, which increased to 47 per cent in 1980–1981 and presently it is contributing 62–63 per cent and is likely to be 75 per cent by 2021.[17]
3. The urbanization is largely taking place in the metropolitan cities. In other words, the growth of population in the metropolitan cities of India is higher than that in class I,

Table 1.3 Urbanization and Urban Population from 1901 to 2011

Various Census	Number of Urban Agglomeration/Towns	Total Population	Urban Population	Urban Population in %
1901	1,827	238,396,327	25,851,873	10.84
1911	1,825	252,093,390	25,941,633	10.29
1921	1,949	251,321,213	28,086,167	11.18
1931	2,072	278,977,238	33,455,989	11.99
1941	2,250	318,660,580	44,153,297	13.86
1951	2,843	361,088,090	62,443,709	17.29
1961	2,363	439,234,771	78,936,603	17.97
1971	2,590	598,159,652	109,113,977	19.91
1981	3,378	683,329,097	159,462,547	23.33
1991	3,768	844,324,222	217,177,625	25.72
2001	5,161	1,027,015,247	285,354,954	27.78
2011	7,935	1,210,193,422	377,105,760	31.16

Note: Compiled on the basis of various census reports.

Table 1.4 Urban GDP as Percentage of Total NDP, India

Year	% Share to Total NDP
1970–1971	37.65
1980–1981	41.09
1993–1994	45.73
1999–2000	51.70
2004–2005	52.02

Source: Tripathi (2013).

class II, class III and other smaller cities. The rise in population in the metropolitan cities has further given rise to sundry problems in these cities (see Table 1.5 and Figure 1.3).

4. There has been steady growth of urban agglomerations and town over the decades in India. This shows that there is a genuine emphasis on urbanization in the country. The pace of urbanization is on the rise. It is remarked that the new town accounts for almost 30 per cent of the urban growth in the last decade, and this unexpected increase in the number of census towns in the last census (Census 2011) has thrust them into the spotlight (Deshmukh, 2015).
5. The urbanization in the states such as Goa, Delhi, Tamil Nadu, Maharashtra, Gujarat and Kerala is higher compared to Odisha, Assam, Bihar and Himachal Pradesh. Urbanization

Table 1.5 Percentage of Urban Population in Size Class of Cities and Towns, India, 1951–2011

Year	Million Cities (1,000,000 and Above)	Cities (100,000 to 1,000,000)	Large Towns (50,000–100,000)	Medium Towns (20,000–50,000)	Small Towns (Less than 20,000)
1951	19.07	25.75	9.96	15.72	29.69
1961	23.34	28.08	11.23	16.94	20.41
1971	26.02	31.22	10.92	16.01	15.83
1981	26.93	33.49	11.63	14.33	13.62
1991	33.18	32.01	10.95	13.19	10.66
2001	37.80	30.78	9.73	12.29	9.36
2011	42.62	23.09	9.33	12.73	11.75

Note: Compiled on the basis of various census reports.

Figure 1.3 Percentage of Urban Population in Size Class of Cities and Towns, India, 2011

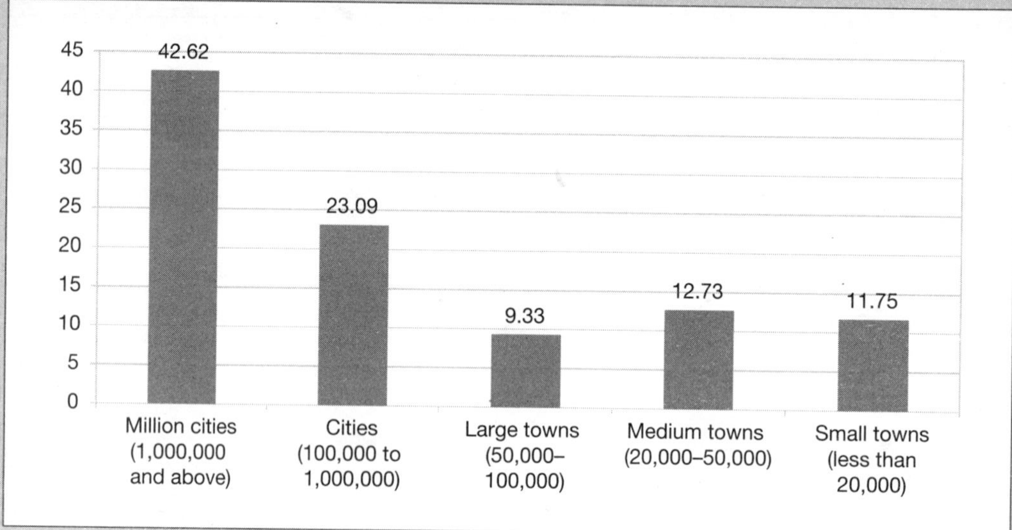

across the states of India is given in Table 1.6. The former categories of states show a higher rate of urbanization than the national average and the latter are below the national average. It is rightly remarked that at the state level, the pattern of urbanization is very diverse, but economically advanced states more or less show higher levels of urbanization (Deshmukh, 2015).

Table 1.6 Urbanization across States of India, 2011

Level of Urbanization	States
50% & above (3)	Delhi, Goa, Mizoram
40–50% (4)	Tamil Nadu, Kerala, Maharashtra, Gujarat
30–40% (7)	Karnataka, Punjab, Haryana, Andhra Pradesh, Manipur, West Bengal, Uttarakhand
20–30% (11)	Nagaland, Madhya Pradesh, Jammu & Kashmir, Tripura, Sikkim, Rajasthan, Jharkhand, Chhattisgarh, Arunachal Pradesh, Uttar Pradesh, Meghalaya
Below 20% (4)	Odisha, Assam, Bihar, Himachal Pradesh
31.2%	All India

Source: Deshmukh (2015).

6. Urbanization has led to the growth of informal settlements and slums in the cities of India and most particularly in the metropolitan cities. The World Bank Report has highlighted that messy urbanization is reflected in almost 65.5 million Indians who, according to the country's 2011 Census, live in urban slums (Peter & Mark, 2016).
7. One of the trends of the urbanization of the Indian metropolitan cities is that it is expanding to the territories of the cities of the other states. For example, the National Capital Region (NCR) of Delhi such as Gurugram, Faridabad and Noida is entering into the cities' territory of Haryana and Uttar Pradesh. The World Bank Report has noted that for major cities such as Delhi, Mumbai, Hyderabad and Kolkata, population growth has been fastest on their peripheries in areas beyond their official administrative boundaries (Peter & Mark, 2016).

Causes of Urbanization

Urbanization is taking place on a massive scale both in developed and developing countries of the world. The urbanization in both developed and developing countries happened because of some of the common reasons, such as industrialization, modernization, commercialization, social benefits, employment opportunities, change in lifestyle and rural-to-urban transformation. A few important causes of urbanization are elaborated further.

1. *Structural change:* Almost all economies of the world and most particularly the developing economies of Asia and Africa are going for structural changes in order to attain higher economic growth rate and development. The industrial sector and the service sector, particularly the latter, are expanding at a faster speed in urban areas leading to migration of people from the rural to urban areas. It is remarked that small towns are defined as 'first-tier markets and service providers for rural enterprises and development' and originate as villages that due to agglomeration economies develop over time as urban centres by virtue of their functions and services.[18]
2. *Declining importance of agriculture sector:* Agriculture provides employment to a gigantic percentage of rural population in developing countries. Over the period, the contribution of

the agriculture sector to the economic growth rate is declining in many developing countries. Moreover, the wage rate in the agricultural sector is low and seasonal in nature. Further, with the increase in the level of education in rural areas, rural youth are not interested to work in the agriculture sector. Many of them are migrating to urban areas and cities in search of jobs and also for pursuing higher education. This has added to the pace of urbanization particularly in developing countries. On the contrary, it is remarked that urbanization also presents challenges to farmers, and negative externalities associated with urbanization increase the cost of farming and threaten the viability of the agricultural economy (Wu et al., 2011).

3. *Industrialization:* One of the important reasons for urbanization in the European countries is industrialization. Also, in developing countries, industrialization is a vital factor for the growth of urban areas. Industrialization provides both direct and indirect employment to a lot of people who migrate from rural areas to work in the industrial sector in urban areas. A few examples of industrial urban areas are Ludhiana (Punjab), Rourkela (Odisha) and Kanpur (Uttar Pradesh). According to Jonathan Rees, between 1880 and 1929, industrialization and urbanization expanded in the USA faster than ever before. Industrialization means manufacturing in factory settings using machines plus a labour force with unique, divided tasks to increase production, stimulated urbanization, leading to the growth of cities in both population and physical size.[19]
4. *Modernization:* One of the reasons for the proliferation of urbanization is modernization. Availability of modern education, health and entertainment facilities in the cities led to the migration of people from rural to urban areas. Modernization and development in general, and modernization and urban development in particular, go hand in hand. The availability of better infrastructure facilities such as transport, electricity, water works and telecommunication makes living in city attractive to common men, leading to urbanization in greater scale. According to Fox et al. (2019), modernization believed to set in motion a set of additional normatively positive developments that may improve urbanization.
5. *Migration:* Migration is an important cause of urbanization. Migration of population from the rural to urban areas due to various social and economic reasons led to the growth of population in urban areas. At the initial stage, it is the growth of population due to migration and in later stages, it also leads to natural increase in population in urban areas. The urban pull and rural push factors are responsible for migration of population from rural to urban areas. Migration is a very important aspect of urbanization in Africa and other Third-World countries.[20]
6. *Social and cultural change:* Social and cultural changes are also important factors for urbanization in developing countries. It is remarked that urbanization changes the nature of the cause of both economic and social implications, and the role of the internal relationships, families of redefining the concepts of individual and social responsibility (Gilbert, 1989). With the advent of modernization, there is a rapid change in the social status of the population in rural areas. The rising literacy and level of education among the countryside population have pushed many of them to urban areas either for jobs or for higher education. Better healthcare facilities and healthcare institutions are also available in urban areas. Moreover, the cities have become the hub of cultural and entertainment activities. Many of the cultural and religious places, for example, in India, Haridwar (Uttarakhand) and Amritsar (Punjab) have been urbanized because of their religious importance. Besides the cultural heritage being a reason, Agra (Uttar Pradesh) and many

cities in Rajasthan such as Udaipur and Jaisalmer have also been urbanized because of cultural tourism and cultural activism.

7. *Infrastructure development and communication:* Rapid infrastructural and communication facilities have enabled people in general, and educated and unemployed people in particular, to migrate from rural to urban areas. Both in developed and developing countries, infrastructural development is one of the important reasons of urbanization. The unprecedented infrastructure development in China has created huge opportunities for urban land development and economic activity. Both intra- and intercity infrastructure developments, including streets within cities, and intercity express highways and railways connecting cities, have positive impacts on urban expansion.[21] The World Bank has remarked that infrastructure is the vehicle for transforming low- and middle-income countries into emerging or developing nations.
8. *Agglomeration:* Urbanization is characterized by agglomeration of production and consumption, which stimulates overall economic growth (Iimi, 2005, pp. 88–109). Agglomeration of production and consumption is one of the vital causes of urbanization. Urban areas and the cities are the hub of economic activities and a place for high production of non-agricultural goods and their consumption. To Iimi (2005), agglomeration of production in urban areas means concentration of consumption. This is because the labour force as centralized in urban areas has an element of production, which generates large demand, forming a huge consumer market.
9. *Emphasis on economic growth and smart city:* The contribution of urban areas to the economic growth rate of the nation states is higher than that of rural areas. Therefore, government of many developing countries, which are urbanizing at a faster pace, are laying stress on urban development leading to urbanization and movement of people from rural to urban areas for various urban development activities per se urban infrastructure development. Moreover, the smart city project of the Government of India is one of the measures to promote urbanization and city development in India.

Urban Issues and Challenges

The faulty urbanization in developing countries in particular has posed a number of issues and challenges. Both the urban dwellers and the government are facing a Herculean task to overcome these issues and challenges. UN-Habitat envisaged in the World Cities Report of 2016 that the current urbanization is unsustainable in many respects, puts many people at risk, creates unnecessary costs, negatively affects the environment and is intrinsically unfair. McGranahan and Satterthwaite (2014) have very nicely noted that 'there is an emerging consensus that urbanization is critically important to international development, but considerable confusion over what urbanization actually is; whether it is accelerating or slowing; whether it should be encouraged or discouraged; and, more generally, what the responses should be'. In the context of India, the World Bank has expressed that meeting the needs of India's soaring urban populations is and will continue to be a strategic policy matter. Critical issues that need to be addressed are as follows:

1. Poor local governance;
2. Weak finances;

3. Inappropriate planning that leads to high costs of housing and office space; in some Indian cities, these costs are among the highest in the world;
4. Critical infrastructure shortages and major service deficiencies that include erratic water and power supply, and woefully inadequate transportation systems; and
5. Rapidly deteriorating environment.[22]

Some of the important issues and challenges of urban development are as follows.

1. *Urban poverty:* The percentage of people living below the poverty line, of course, is lower in urban areas than that in rural areas; yet, it is a challenge before the government to overcome it. In almost all the countries, and particularly in developing countries, the urban poor lack access to healthy housing, sanitation, safe drinking water facilities, nutrition and healthcare facilities, and also educational facilities. According to the Asian Development Bank (ADB), unlike rural poverty, urban poverty is complex and multidimensional—extending beyond the deficiency of income or consumption, where its many dimensions relate to the vulnerability of the poor on account of their inadequate access to land and housing, physical infrastructure and services, economic and livelihood sources, health and education facilities, social security networks, and voice and empowerment.[23] According to the International Labour Organization (ILO), in absolute terms, Asia represents the largest concentrations of urban poverty in the world. In the developing world, African cities have the highest percentage of poverty, with 41 per cent of the urban population living below the poverty line.[24]
2. *Urban inequality:* Inequality between the poor living in unorganized colonies and in the slums and the rich living in the cities is a glaring feature of urbanization both in developed and developing countries. The social and economic inequalities in terms of access to education and healthcare, income and employment, and overall quality of life are high among the rich and poor in urban areas. According to Ricky Burdett, all cities display some level of inequality. Some are more pronounced than others, depending on their national and regional contexts, and the level of economic development and informalization. What we are observing today, especially in cities of the developing world, is that social inequality is becoming increasingly spatialized.[25]
3. *Urban unemployment:* Urban unemployment is a vital issue and has posed a formidable challenge for the government. Unemployment and underemployment are the critical features of cities. Mostly, the migrants from rural to urban areas are found to be working in the informal sector under poor working conditions. Besides, because of the rising youth population and their education level, most of them are found to be underemployed in urban areas. According to ILO, most urban unemployment in developing countries takes the form of underemployment in which people are obliged to undertake any available economic activity, however poorly paid and unproductive, because there are no social safety nets and no alternatives in the form of unemployment insurance or job training for the formal sector work. In Ghana, for example, one survey put the unemployment rate at 1.6 per cent of the workforce, but the rate of underemployment was nearly 25 per cent.[26]
4. *Urban law and order, and crime:* With the growing population in urban areas and more particularly in the metropolitan cities, the law and order problem has become a critical issue. It has posed surmountable challenges before the government. The laxity in law and order has resulted in the rise of crime in urban areas. The cases of chain snatching,

molestation, eve-teasing and so on are rising day by day. The security of women is a challenge as with the proliferation of the services sector in urban areas, women employment is on the rise. UN-Habitat in its report has envisaged that the rapid pace of urbanization is associated with increased crime rates in some of the world's regions as it places increased pressures on the ability of authorities to meet public security and safety demands.[27]

5. *Urban transport:* Urban transport is one of the pressing issues in both developed and developing countries. The growing number of vehicles in urban areas has caused traffic problems, particularly during the pick hours, causing a lot of inconvenience to the commuters. It has resulted in increased road congestion, increased noise pollution, parking problems and rise in the accident rates. Customarily, it is seen that in most of the urban areas and particularly in the metropolitan cities, the growth rate of traffic is greater than that of the road space. Some of the issues identified for sustainable urban transportation in cities in developing countries are as follows: (a) road infrastructure, (b) rail-based public transport, (c) road-based public transport, (d) support for non-motorized travel modes, (e) technological solutions, (f) awareness raising campaigns, (g) pricing mechanisms, (h) vehicle access restrictions and (i) control of land uses (Pojani & Stead, 2015).
6. *Urban waste management:* Urban waste management is a challenging issue in most of the urban areas, more particularly in the megacities. Several categories of waste generated in urban areas, such as household wastes, medical wastes, industrial wastes; waste generated in the marketplaces and even the erratic throwing of wastes by the individual in the streets and the vacant places are major challenges before the municipal government. SWM is a major concern for many cities of developing countries where people are not sensitized to various waste disposal and management practices. As urbanization is occurring on a rapid scale around the world, the importance of an efficient and effective SWM system is more critical than ever before. It is rightly remarked that in developed countries, the problems usually centre on the difficulties and high cost of disposing of the large volume of waste generated by households and businesses. In developing countries, the main problems are related to collection and disposal, with one-third to half of all solid waste generated in the Third-World countries remaining uncollected (Hoornweg & Bhada-Tata, 2012).
7. *Urban education and healthcare:* Social development is a key concern in urban areas. With growing urban population, provisioning of education and healthcare to these people and particularly those who are residing in the unorganized areas and in the slums is a Herculean task. It is remarked that even though the health needs of the urban poor are high, they have virtually no access to healthcare. The World Report has envisaged that '...1 million Indian babies are born in slums every year with little or no medical assistance.'[28] The lack of sanitation and urban air pollution has increased the occurrences of respiratory problems in urban areas. As far as urban education is concerned, it is vexed with the lack of fund and infrastructure, high dropout rates, excessive teacher attrition, low enrolment rates and low standardized test scores, particularly in the school run in the urban informal settlements. There is a great need to look after the healthcare and education of the girl children and children belonging to the marginalized sections of the society in urban areas.
8. *Urban infrastructure:* One of the gigantic problems of the urbanization is the infrastructural development. The growing population in urban areas has caused infrastructural deficiencies. The demand for public infrastructure such as road, sewerage system, telephone connectivity, water supply, housing, schools and colleges, and hospitals is rising and governments of

many developing countries have failed to provide these facilities to the growing urban population. ADB has envisaged that there exists an enormous gap between demand for infrastructure services and capacity to finance urban development. In 2004, conservative estimates suggested that about $250 million per year in infrastructure investments would be needed to support urban growth over the next 25 years.[29]

9. *Urban governance:* The urban governance is a key issue in the urbanization process of developing countries. The maintenance of law and order, active administration and responsive ULBs are the areas of concern. The coordination between the ULBs, urban administration and the legislatures of urban areas are many a time lacking which further hampers urban development. The decentralized urban governance with accountability is the need for the better development of urban areas. According to UN-Habitat, governance is the enabling environment that requires adequate legal frameworks, efficient political, managerial and administrative processes to enable the local government response to the needs of citizens. It also emphasized that effective urban governance is characterized as democratic and inclusive; long-term and integrated; multi-scale and multilevel; territorial; proficient and conscious of the digital age.[30]
10. *Urban management:* Urban management refers to the political and administrative structures of cities and the major challenges that they face to provide both social and physical infrastructure services.[31] These include managing urban economic resources, particularly land and the assets of the built environment, creating employment and attracting investment in order to improve the quality and quantity of goods and services available (Clarke, 1991). The management of urban infrastructure, finance and services is critical to urban development. The effective and efficient management of urban infrastructure and finance will stimulate urban development and raise the quality of life of city dwellers. The management of roads, sanitation, drinking water, garbage, electricity, information technology (IT) and so on is sine qua non for a smart city. The urban management largely covers areas, such as urban population management, finance management, waste management, land management, slum management, management of urban environment and urban development projects and programmes management.
11. *Urban slums:* Slums, small or big, are largely present in almost all the cities of developed and developing countries. However, unplanned urbanization in developing countries have ensured the existence of slums in the cities of these countries. According to UN-Habitat, the slums are home to approximately 828 million people, one-third of the world's urban population. As far as India is concerned, according to 2011 Census, nearly 17 per cent of urban population lives in slums. Some of the important features of slums are dilapidated and temporary houses, lack of sanitation and safe drinking water supply, poor environmental conditions, and there is lack of primary healthcare and primary education facilities in most of the unorganized slums in developing countries. UN-Habitat defines a slum as an area lacking at least in one of the following: (a) access to safe water, (b) access to sanitation, (c) safe and secure tenure or (d) durable housing structures.[32] The quality of life of the people living in slums is very poor and they are subject to many health hazards, such as plague, cholera and dengue, and also man-made and natural hazards.
12. *Urban informal sector:* The informal economy is the hallmark of urban economies of developing countries of South Asia and Africa. The faulty urbanization and migration of

rural people to urban areas have strengthened the roots of the informal sector in the urban economy. Hart, who coined this term informal sector during his field study in Ghana, found that a large number of new entrants to urban areas, who are unable to get employment in the formal organized sector are engaged in self employment activities. The income of the workers employed in the informal sector is very low, there is no legal binding, they work for longer hours without any job security and there is also lack of social and health security in this sector. In India, 9 out of 10 people work in the informal sector. The percentage of women engaged in the informal sector workforce in urban areas is higher than the men. Moreover, the child labour activities are also seen in the urban informal sector. Alison Brown has mentioned that despite its importance—in some cities the informal economy accommodates up to 80 per cent of urban workers—social protections rarely include informal workers, regulations affecting workers are complex and conflicting, and evictions are commonplace.[33] Timelsina (2011) has noted that the urban authority and informal activities are confronted with the problems of licensing, taxation, encroachment of public places and pavements, and on increasing social problems.

13. *Urban environment:* One of the greatest issues in the metropolitan cities of developing countries is the environmental pollution and its effect on human health. Increase in the number of vehicles and the dust generated in the construction process has made the air of urban areas poisonous to inhale. Besides, sound pollution due to the increase in the number of vehicles is also a problem in many cities. WHO and United Nations Environment Programme (UNEP) have mentioned that rapid, unplanned and unsustainable patterns of urban development are making developing cities focal points for many emerging environment and health hazards. As urban populations grow, the quality of the urban environment will play an increasingly important role in public health with respect to issues ranging from solid waste disposal, provision of safe water and sanitation, and injury prevention to the interface between urban poverty, environment and health.[34]
14. *Urban finance:* With scanty resources at their disposal, many countries and more particularly developing countries are facing daunting challenges to meet the expenses of urban development and more particularly the exigencies of urban infrastructure and urban services. The ULBs are excessively dependent on the grant-in-aid from the government and their own sources of funds are very low. Moreover, many ULBs have poor financial capabilities to raise municipal bonds in the market. The public–private partnership (PPP) in urban financing is not encouraging in many developing countries. The ULBs are lacking capabilities in financial management. In the Indian context, UNESCAP has envisaged in a document that municipal dependence on external sources and inability to mobilize requisite funds confirm that municipal governments suffer from vertical and horizontal imbalances. On the whole, municipal-owned sources constitute barely around half of the municipal finance, and the other part of the revenue from the vertical transfers is at best ad hoc and not linked to actual requirement of funds at the ULB level.[35]
15. *Urbanization and climate change:* The climate change and unplanned urbanization have led to urban flooding in many of the cities during the rainy season. Excessive growth of urban population and dumping of urban wastes in the open spaces and water bodies have led to closing of water bodies, which fail to soak the water. Moreover, constructions of houses and concrete roads in the cities have restricted the capacity of the soil to soak excess water.

The urban flood-based disaster is frequently occurring in many cities of India. It is an annual disaster in cities such as Mumbai and Chennai. The urban flooding has led to many problems. To name a few among many are traffic jams, damage to public and private property, vector-borne and waterborne diseases and disruption of power supply and telecommunication. The urbanization in the hilly areas has affected the climate change in those areas. The cloudbursts and frequent floods in the hilly areas are due to climate change being affected through urbanization. UN-Habitat has noted that the effects of urbanization and climate change are converging in dangerous ways. Hundreds of millions of people in urban areas across the world will be affected by rising sea levels, increased precipitation, inland floods, more frequent and stronger cyclones and storms, and periods of more extreme heat and cold.[36]

Summing Up

The world is urbanizing very fast. Not only developed countries but also developing countries of the world are emphasizing urbanization in order to boost their economic growth and ensure better quality of living to their citizens. Now, more than half of the world population is living in urban areas and the percentage is on the rise. Edward Glaeser noted that 'Cities are the best path we know out of poverty. They are the best transformers of civilizations. But, there are also demons that come with density.'[37] Cities are positive and potent force for addressing sustainable economic growth, development and prosperity of the nation states. They are also driving force of innovation, consumption and investment in both developed and developing countries. Increased productivity and employment opportunities due to urbanization have strengthened the weight of urban areas as a potent instrument to reduce poverty. Gradually, cities have become important to national and global economies. Indeed, the prosperity of nations and regions is increasingly dependent on the economic performance of cities. According to UN-Habitat, urbanization has helped millions escape poverty through higher levels of productivity, employment opportunities, improved quality of life via better education and health, large-scale public investment and access to improved infrastructure and services. Moreover, unplanned urbanization in most of the developing countries has brought many problems in urban areas, such as urban poverty, disparities and inequality, unemployment, deficiency of urban infrastructure, urban safety and security, growth of slums and informal activities. Systematic, sustainable and smart urbanization is the need of the hour, which on the one hand, raises contribution of urban areas to the GDP and on the other hand, provides a sustainable quality of living to city dwellers. At a UN session, India said that unplanned urbanization and migration pose serious development challenges in terms of delivery of services and living conditions, and therefore called for a comprehensive approach to deal with the issues of sustainable cities and human mobility.[38]

Keywords

Urbanization, Materialism, Urban Governance, Urban Management, Urban Society, Urban Environment, Urban Renewal, Urban Reform, Gentrification

REVIEW QUESTIONS

1. Define urbanization and discuss its various characteristics.
2. What is urbanization? Explain various causes of urbanization.
3. Describe the trends of urbanization in developed and developing countries.
4. Explain the various factors responsible for the growth of urbanization in developing countries.
5. Describe in detail four important dimensions of urban development.
6. Discuss the important issues and challenges of urbanization.
7. Write short notes on the following:
   a. Urban reform
   b. Urban economy
   c. Trends of urbanization in developing countries
   d. Define urbanization from Indian perspectives
   e. Gentrification
   f. Megapolitan
   g. Urban society
   h. Urban governance

Notes

1. https://www.unfpa.org/urbanization (accessed on 20 June 2018).
2. http://www.worldbank.org/en/topic/urbandevelopment/overview (accessed on 26 June 2018).
3. https://www.unicef.org/sowc2012/pdfs/SOWC-2012-DEFINITIONS.pdf (accessed on 21 June 2018).
4. https://www.iatss.or.jp/common/pdf/en/publication/commemorative-publication/iatss40_theory_01.pdf (accessed on 11 October 2019).
5. http://www.sociologydiscussion.com/urbanism/urbanism-as-a-way-of-life-concept-and-characteristics/2619 (accessed on 11 October 2019).
6. https://richmondvale.org/en/blog/effects-of-urbanization-on-poverty (accessed on 13 March 2019).
7. http://www.ombudsman.gov.ph/UNDP4/wp-content/uploads/2012/12/Chap-03.-Urban-Society-30Nov06-UPF.pdf (accessed on 22 June 2018).
8. https://www.ucl.ac.uk/dpu-projects/drivers_urb_change/urb_society/index.htm (accessed on 14 March 2019).
9. http://hdr.undp.org/en/content/rapid-urbanisation-opportunities-and-challenges-improve-well-being-societies (accessed on 12 March 2019).
10. http://psrcentre.org/images/extraimages/49.%201312606.pdf (accessed on 22 June 2018).
11. http://www.skoch.in/images/stories/knowledge_repository/urban/Implementing%20Urban%20Reforms.pdf (accessed on 26 June 2018).
12. http://braungardt.trialectics.com/projects/geography/world-urbanization-trends/ (accessed on 25 June 2018).
13. https://esa.un.org/unpd/wup/publications/Files/WUP2018-KeyFacts.pdf (accessed on26 June 2018).
14. https://www.who.int/bulletin/volumes/88/4/10-010410/en/ (accessed on 16 June 2020).
15. https://placesjournal.org/article/megapolitan-america/ (accessed on 27 June 2018).
16. http://www.unesco.org/education/tlsf/mods/theme_c/popups/mod13t01s009.html (accessed on 2 July 2018).

17. https://economictimes.indiatimes.com/news/economy/infrastructure/urban-ministry-seeks-rs-2-6-lakh-crore-in-11th-plan/articleshow/2568886.cms?from=mdr (accessed on 17 June 2020).
18. https://www.researchgate.net/publication/325420959_Structural_Changes_and_Implications_for_Urbanization (accessed on 10 July 2018).
19. http://americanhistory.oxfordre.com/view/10.1093/acrefore/9780199329175.001.0001/acrefore-9780199329175-e-327 (accessed on 10 July 2018).
20. https://repository.up.ac.za/bitstream/handle/2263/24073/02chapter3.pdf?sequence<hig>=</hig>3 (accessed on 11 July 2018).
21. https://www.researchgate.net/publication/318162817_Infrastructure_Development_and_Urbanization_in_China (accessed on 23 July 2018).
22. http://www.worldbank.org/en/news/feature/2011/07/04/indias-urban-challenges (accessed on 16 August 2018).
23. https://www.adb.org/publications/urban-poverty-asia (accessed on 14 August 2018).
24. http://www.ilo.org/global/about-the-ilo/newsroom/news/WCMS_008055/lang—en/index.htm (accessed on 14 August 2018).
25. http://www.oecd.org/social/inequality-urban-growth.htm (accessed on 14 August 2018).
26. http://www.ilo.org/global/about-the-ilo/newsroom/news/WCMS_008055/lang—en/index.htm (accessed on 14 August 2018).
27. https://www.thelancet.com/action/showPdf?pii<hig>=</hig>S0140-6736%2811%2960215-8 (accessed on 15 March 2019).
28. https://www.thelancet.com/journals/lancet/article/PIIS0140-6736(11)61083-0/fulltext (accessed on 24 November 2019).
29. https://www.adb.org/themes/urban-development/issues (accessed on 14 August 2018).
30. https://unhabitat.org/governance/ (accessed on 17 August 2018).
31. http://archive.unu.edu/unupress/unupbooks/uu26ue/uu26ue10.htm (accessed on 15 October 2019).
32. https://unhabitat.org/the-urban-informal-economy-alison-brown/ (accessed on 15 March 2019).
33. http://www.who.int/sustainable-development/cities/health-risks/slums/en/ (accessed on 20 August 2018).
34. http://www.who.int/heli/risks/urban/urbanenv/en/ (accessed on 21 August 2018).
35. https://www.unescap.org/sites/default/files/4.Financing%20urban%20infrastructure_Mahesh%20Purohit.pdf (accessed on 21 August 2018).
36. https://unhabitat.org/urban-themes/climate-change/ (accessed on 25 June 2019).
37. https://www.brookings.edu/blog/africa-in-focus/2016/09/07/can-rapid-urbanization-in-africa-reduce-poverty-causes-opportunities-and-policy-recommendations/ (accessed on 13 March 2019).
38. https://www.indiatoday.in/india/story/unplanned-urbanisation-migration-pose-serious-development-challenges-india-to-un-1209540-2018-04-11 (accessed on 15 October 2019).

References

Ahluwalia, I. J. (2014). *Transforming our cities: Postcards of change.* Noida: HarperCollins publisher. http://www.ijsrd.com/articles/IJSRDV6I80362.pdf (accessed on 14 April 2020).

Avis, W. R. (2016). *Urban governance* (Topic Guide). Birmingham: GSDRC, University of Birmingham. https://gsdrc.org/wp-content/uploads/2016/11/UrbanGov_GSDRC.pdf (accessed on 14 March 2019).

Barofsk, J., Siba, E., & Grabinskey, J. (2016). *Can rapid urbanization in Africa reduce poverty? Causes, opportunities, and policy recommendations.* https://www.brookings.edu/blog/africa-in-focus/2016/09/07/can-rapid-urbanization-in-africa-reduce-poverty-causes-opportunities-and-policy-recommendations/ (accessed on 13 March 2019).

Bhagat, R. B. (2011). Emerging pattern of urbanization in India. *Economic & Political Weekly, 46*(54), 10–12.

Boano, C., & Marten, R. (2017). *Think urban and learn from the city: Exploring urban dimension of humanitarianism*. UCLP. http://pubs.iied.org/pdfs/G04286.pdf (accessed on 21 June 2018).

Brown, D., & McGranahan, G. (2016). The urban informal economy, local inclusion and achieving a global green transformation. *Habitat International, 53*, 97–105.

Cervero, R., & Day, J. (2008). Suburbanization and transit-oriented development in China. *Transport Policy, 15*(5), 315–323.

Chen, M., Zhang, H., Liu, W., & Zhang, W. (2014). The global pattern of urbanization and economic growth: Evidence from the last three decades. *PLoS One, 9*(8). http://journals.plos.org/plosone/article?id=10.1371/journal.pone.0103799 (accessed on 21 June 2018).

Clark, D. (2003). *Urban world/global city* (2nd ed.). New York, NY: Routledge.

Clarke, G. (1991). Urban management in developing countries. A critical role. *Cities, 8*(2), 93–107.

Cohen, B. (2006). Urbanization in developing countries: Current trends, future projections, and key challenges for sustainability. *Technology in Society, 28*(1–2), 63–80.

Demery, L., & Squire, L. (1995). *Poverty in Africa: An emerging picture*. Washington: World Bank.

Deshmukh, M. S. (2015). Emerging trends of urbanization in India. *EPRA International Journal of Economic & Business Review, 3*(12), 146–153.

Drescher, A. W., & Iaquinta, D. L. (2002). *Urbanization: Linking development across the changing landscape*. http://www.fao.org/fileadmin/templates/FCIT/PDF/sofa.pdf (accessed on 22 April 2019).

Egolum, C. C., & Emoh, F. I. (2017). The issues and challenges of urban renewal in a developing economy. *International Journal of Development and Economic Sustainability, 5*(1), 32–44.

Fox, A., Feng, W., & Asal, V. (2019). What is driving global obesity trends? Globalization or 'modernization'? *Globalization and Health, 15*(32), 2–16. https://globalizationandhealth.biomedcentral.com/track/pdf/10.1186/s12992-019-0457-y (accessed on 14 October 2019).

Galea, S., & Vlahov, D. (2005). Urban health: Evidence, challenges, and directions. *Annual Review of Public Health, 26*, 341–365.

Gilbert, O. L. (1989). *The ecology of urban habitat*. London: Chapman and Hall.

Gilles, D. (2013). *Growing through cities in developing countries*. Philadelphia: Wharton School, University of Pennsylvania. https://assets.publishing.service.gov.uk/media/57a089efe5274a27b200032b/What_are_the_features_of_urbanisation_and_cities_that_promote_productivity_employment_and_salaries.pdf (accessed on 13 March 2019).

Henderson, J. V. (2003). *Urbanization, economic geography and growth*. Providence: Brown University. https://pdfs.semanticscholar.org/b86f/f2d4af0f3b7de5389208cc29d16d96ce7942.pdf (accessed on 21 June 2018).

Henderson, V. (2002). Urbanization in developing countries. *The World Bank Research Observer, 17*(1), 89–112.

Hoornweg, D., & Bhada-Tata, P. (2012). What a waste: A global review of solid waste management (Urban Development Series, Knowledge Papers, No. 15). Washington: World Bank.

Hoover, Edgard M. (1975). *An introduction to regional economics* (2nd ed.). https://www.theigc.org/wp-content/uploads/2016/06/Randolph-Jain-2016-Policy-paper.pdf (accessed on 13 March 2019).

Ibrahim, S. E. M. (1972). The relationship between urbanization and modernization in Yugoslavia. *International Review of Modern Sociology, 2*(2), 143–160.

Ichimura, M. (2003). *Urbanization, urban environment and land use: Challenges and opportunities*. Asia-Pacific Forum for Environment and Development Expert Meeting. http://citeseerx.ist.psu.edu/viewdoc/download?doi=10.1.1.523.396&rep=rep1&type=pdf (accessed on 25 June 2018).

Iimi, A. (2005). Urbanization and development infrastructure in the East Asian Region (no. 10). Tokyo: JBICI.

Kim, J. (2016). *Handbook on urban infrastructure finance*. Montréal: NewCities Foundation. https://www.unido.org/sites/default/files/files/2018-02/BRIDGE%20for%20Cities_Issue%20Paper_3.pdf (accessed on 13 March 2019).

Kundu, A. (2006). Urbanization and urban governance: Search for a perspective beyond neoliberalism. In A. Shaw (Eds.), *Indian Cities in Transition* (29–58). Hyderabad: Orient Longman.

Leksikon, S. N. (2016). *Definition of urban planning.* https://www.ntnu.edu/documents/139799/1273574286/TPD4505.Trine.Kirkhaug.pdf/b5be429a-a89f-459f-993f-4489d9f0f7f4 (accessed on 24 June 2019).

Mahey, K., & Tripathi, S. (2016). Urbanization and economic growth in Punjab (India): An empirical analysis (MPRA Paper No. 71325). https://mpra.ub.uni-muenchen.de/71325/1/MPRA_paper_71325.pdf (accessed on 13 March 2019).

Malik, R., & Ali, M. (2015). The impact of urbanization on agriculture sector: A case study of Peshawar, Pakistan. *Journal of Resources Development and Management, 8*, 79–85.

Massey, D. S., & Tannen, J. (2018). Suburbanization and segregation in the United States: 1970–2010. *Journal of Ethnic and Racial Studies, 41*(9), 1594–1611.

Mattingly, M. (1995). Urban management in less developed countries (Working Paper No. 72). https://www.ucl.ac.uk/bartlett/development/sites/bartlett/files/migrated-files/WP72_0.pdf (accessed on 14 March 2019).

Maurrasse, D. J., & Bliss, J. B. (2006). Comprehensive approaches to urban development: Gentrification, community, and business in Harlem, New York. *Northwestern Journal of Law & Social Policy, 1*(1). https://scholarlycommons.law.northwestern.edu/cgi/viewcontent.cgi?article=1008&context=njlsp (accessed on 28 June 2018).

McGranahan, G., & Satterthwaite, D. (2014). Urbanization concepts and trends (IIED Working Paper). London: Human Settlement Group. http://pubs.iied.org/pdfs/10709IIED.pdf (accessed on 21 June 2018).

Mishra, R. P. (1998). *Urbanisation in India challenges and opportunities.* Shillong: ICSSR North Eastern Regional Centre.

Moretti, Enrico M. (2013). Cities and growth (Evidence Paper No. 11). London: International Growth Centre. https://assets.publishing.service.gov.uk/media/57a089efe5274a27b200032b/What_are_the_features_of_urbanisation_and_cities_that_promote_productivity_employment_and_salaries.pdf (accessed on 13 March 2019).

Mountjoy, A. B. (1978). *Urbanization in the Third World.* https://link.springer.com/chapter/10.1007/978-1-349-16030-3_10 (accessed on 13 October 2019).

Muchadenyika, D., & Williams, J. J. (2016). Social change: Urban governance and urbanization in Zimbabwe. *Urban Forum, 26*(3), 253–274.

Peter, E., & Mark, R. (2016). *Leveraging urbanization in South Asia: Margining spatial transition for prosperity and livability.* http://www.worldbank.org/en/country/india/brief/leveraging-urbanization-india (accessed on 22 April 2019).

Pieterse, E. (2013). *Rogue urbanism: Emergent African cities.* Cape Town: Jacana Media and ACC.

Pojani, D., & Stead, D. (2015). Sustainable urban transport in the developing world: Beyond megacities. *Sustainability, 7*(6), 7784–7805.

Randolph, G., & Jain, D. (2016). Promoting job-rich urbanization in Zambia (ZIPAR 'More and Better Jobs' Policy Paper No. 2). https://www.theigc.org/wp-content/uploads/2016/06/Randolph-Jain-2016-Policy-paper.pdf (accessed on 13 March 2019).

Robinson, B., & Swilling, M. (2012). *Urban patterns for a Green economy: Optimizing infrastructure.* Nairobi: United Nations Human Settlements Programme (UN-Habitat).

Rosenthal, S. S., & Strange, W. C. (2002). Evidence on the nature and sources of agglomeration economies. Prepared for the *Handbook of urban and regional economics* (Vol. 4). https://assets.publishing.service.gov.uk/media/57a089efe5274a27b200032b/What_are_the_features_of_urbanisation_and_cities_that_promote_productivity_employment_and_salaries.pdf (accessed on 13 March 2019).

Rydningen, U., & Rolfsen, C. N. (2016). *Making education on sustainable community planning tangible.* https://www.ntnu.edu/documents/139799/1273574286/TPD4505.Trine.Kirkhaug.pdf/b5be429a-a89f-459f-993f-4489d9f0f7f4 (accessed on 24 June 2019).

Saat, M. K., Shaari, S., & Fauzi, T. A. (2017). *Materialism and consumerism through urban social lifestyle in the context of shopping malls: Malaysian perspective.* https://www.researchgate.net/publication/322293296_Materialism_and_Consumerism_Through_Urban_Social_Lifestyle_In_The_Context_of_Shopping_Malls_Malaysian_Perspective (accessed on 14 April 2020).

Safier, M. (2004). *Inter-dimensional analysis of urban development, a guide to the organization of cases and their linkages*. http://pubs.iied.org/pdfs/G04286.pdf (accessed on 21 June 2018).

Schnaiberg, A. (1971). The modernizing impact of urbanization: A causal analysis. *Economic Development and Cultural Change*, *20*(1), 80–104.

Stucki, M. (2015). Policies for sustainable accessibility and mobility in urban areas of Africa (Working Paper No. 106). SSATP. https://www.ssatp.org/sites/ssatp/files/publications/SSATPWP106-Urban%20 Mobility_IO.pdf (accessed on 11 October 2019).

Timelsina, K. P. (2011). An urban informal economy: Livelihood opportunity to poor or challenges for urban governance. *Global Journal of Human Social Science*, *2*(2), 25–31.

Todaro, M. P. (1980). Urbanization in developing nations: Trends, prospects, and policies. *Journal of Geography*, *79*, 164–174.

Tripathi, S. (2013). *An overview of India's urbanization, urban economic growth and urban equity* (MPRA Working Paper No. 45537). https://mpra.ub.uni-muenchen.de/45537/ (accessed on 19 March 2020).

UN-Habitat. (2010). *State of the World Cities 2010–11, bridging the urban divide*. Nairobi: UNHSP.UNDP. (2014). The impact of decentralization and urban governance on building inclusive and resilient cities (Asia-Pacific Urbanization and Climate Change Issue Brief Series No. 2). http://www.undp.org/content/dam/rbap/docs/Research%20&%20Publications/poverty/RBAP-PR-2014-Urbanization-Climate-Change-Issue-Brief-02.pdf (accessed on 25 June 2018).

United Nations. (2007). *State of World Population 2007: Unleashing the potential of urban growth*. New York: United Nations.

United Nations. (2011). *World urbanization prospects: The 2011 revision*. New York: Population Division, Department of Economic and Social Affairs, United Nations.

United Nations. (2019). *World urbanization prospects: The 2018 revision*. New York, NY: Department of Economic and Social Affairs Population Division, United Nations.

Vlahov, D., & Galea, S. (2002). Urbanization, urbanicity, and health. *Journal of Urban Health*, *79*(4 Suppl 1), S1–S12.

Weber, M. (1922). *Wirtschaft und Gesellschaft*. Tubingen: Mohr Possible. http://citeseerx.ist.psu.edu/viewdoc/download?doi=10.1.1.498.7780&rep=rep1&type=pdf (accessed on 23 June 2019).

WHO. (2002). *The World Health Report 2002—Reducing risks, promoting healthy life*. Geneva: World Health Organization.

Wilson, T. C. (1986). Community population size and social heterogeneity: An empirical test. *American Journal of Sociology*, *91*(5), 1154–1169.

World Bank. (2009). *World Development Report 2009: Reshaping economic geography*. Washington: World Bank.

Wu, J., Fisher, M., & Pascual, U. (2011). Urbanization and the viability of local agricultural economies. *Land Economics*, *87*(1), 109–125.

2 Theories and Approaches of Urban Development and Planning

Urban theory is in itself is a highly heterogeneous field of knowledge that has developed from various academic disciplines within the social sciences (especially urban geography and urban sociology) and humanities as well as urbanism and planning. Within all such disciplines urban theories are outcomes of systematic reflection that sharpen our understanding of cities and more specific urban issues.[1]

Neoliberalisation of urban development in the past decade has led to significant changes in social demands and subsequent political transformation, culminating in an important paradigm shift over the recent years.

—Sik (2016)

Introduction

Globally, more than half of the population lives in urban areas today (~4 billion). By 2045, the number of people living in cities will increase by 1.5 times to 6 billion, adding 2 billion more urban residents. With more than 80 per cent of global GDP generated in cities, urbanization can contribute to sustainable growth if managed well by increasing productivity, allowing innovation and new ideas to emerge.[2] Over the centuries, cities have become focal points for economic activities and engines of economic growth in both developed and developing countries. They are centres of excellence for education, healthcare, culture, technological innovation, entrepreneurship, social services, government administration and communications with the world. They create opportunities for jobs, employment and livelihood.[3] Urbanization gives rich dividends if it is planned. However, unplanned urbanization, particularly in developing countries, has resulted in several problems such as unemployment and underemployment, informalization of the urban economy and rise in urban poverty. Besides, the slums of the cities have also become breeding grounds of crime and criminal activities. There is a breakdown of security and urban law-and-order problem. For the growing urban population, urban infrastructure such as housing, sanitation, drinking water and road are falling short. Therefore, there is a need that the rapid rate of urbanization needs to be effectively managed to ensure that the potential economic and social development arising from urbanization is fully optimized. It will help to reduce poverty, improve the quality of life and protect the environment. Proper planning of cities and its neighbourhood is sine qua non for sustainable urban development.

Being a pertinent issue in the world today, urban studies are an emerging area of teaching and research in the contemporary world. In this perspective, knowledge about various urban development theories and approaches would be helpful to strategically deal with the urban issues and challenges.

LEARNING OBJECTIVES

After reading this chapter, you should be able to:

- ❐ Explain various theories of urban development
- ❐ Describe different approaches to urban development

I
URBAN DEVELOPMENT AND PLANNING THEORIES

Theory provides justifications for decisions, offers guidance on possibilities, and facilitates ethical behavior. Theory attempts to extract rules to describe, explain, and predict the world.

—Grant (2006)

The planning profession needs theory to inform practice.

—Friedmann (1979)

Theory is a foundational part of knowledge as it describes how a particular field has been evolved and established over a period of time. The history of the process and pattern of growing urbanization can be better understood by consulting various existing theories of urbanization. Urban growth theories explain the internal demographic, spatial and economic growth of cities. According to Scott and Stopper (2014), all cities consist of dense agglomerations of people and economic activities, even though there are strong ambiguities about where and how a lower size limit should be drawn. They, therefore, were of the view that urban theory is hence faced with the task of how to take in hand a complex array of similarities and differences. By asking further questions, it is also further argued that as urban growth involves various actors with different patterns of behaviour, scientific understanding must be based on elaborated complexity theory and a multidisciplinary framework: Can we group all cities together as a common class of phenomena? Or, must we divide them into several different and incommensurable classes and, in the extreme case, into as many classes as there are individual cities? Urban growth theories explain the internal demographic, spatial and economic growth of cities. These three features of a city's growth are interlinked.[4] Theoretical analysis can provide a guideline for selecting modelling methods currently available in complexity modelling and in remote sensing and GIS environments.[5] The exponents of urban development theories have tried to put forth theoretical perspectives and models for better planning of cities.

Some of the important theories of urban development are described further.

Concentric Zone Theory

This theory was propounded by E. W. Burgess and is based on his extensive work conducted in and around the Chicago city during 1920–1925. This model states that the growth of a city starts from its central region and gradually expands outwards from the central region in a series of rings. The five important rings or zones formulated by this model are as follows.

Zone I—Central business district (CBD): This is the central area of a city. It is exclusively predominated by business and commerce activities. In other words, this is mainly a non-residential area. The people from other zones and residential areas commute to this place for commercial activities. Road transport is the main means of communication from the peripheries to the central zone.

Zone II—Zone of transition: This is the old area of the city having dilapidated houses, factories and abandoned buildings. In the modern days, it is popularly called old city. This zone is characterized with dilapidated houses and poor infrastructure facilities. The industrial activities are basically observed in this area. People and most particularly the higher and middle-income group give least preference to live in this area. According to Ratcliff, what characterizes this transitional commercial fringe are 'pawn shops, food stores, pool halls, beer gardens, strip joints, automotive supply shops, shoe repairers, cheap photographers and cheap restaurants'.

Zone III—Zone of workers' homes: This zone is predominantly a working-class zone. Here people are found to be living in old houses. They are mainly factory workers, shopkeepers, daily wagers and so on. This zone is characterized by lack of amenities such as proper road connectivity, sewerage and drinking water system for better living.

Zone IV—Residential zone: This zone is a new area having new and spacious houses. Residents of this zone are businessmen of small- and medium-sized enterprises, professional people, clerks and largely middle-class people. This area is not far off from the business zone. The government official residences for the clerks are also found in this area.

Zone V—Commuters' zone: This zone is a bit far away from the city and largely predominated with high-class people who can afford to commute to the business zone by using their own transport. This is largely a suburb area. This zone is well connected to the main city, and many real estate people are interested in the construction of residences in this zone.

The basic proposition of this model is that there is a direct relationship with the household's economic status and place of residence. The economically lower class people reside near the city, whereas those who are well up live at a distance away from the city. According to Ernest Burgess, this changing pattern of households brings about the process of 'invasion' and 'succession' in which the outward growth of CBD involves the invasion of the neighbouring residents, making them move outwards, resulting in city expansion.[6] The concentric zone model is given in Figure 2.1.

Some of the criticisms labelled against the centric zone theory are as follows:

1. It gives a static view of urbanization where activities of each zone are more or less stratified; however, it has not been true for recent years.
2. The condition is that the land is not the same everywhere and its price varies. In most of the cities in the developing countries, it is found that high-class people reside in the transition zone where the rental values and price of land are very high.
3. There is decentralization of activities, each zone has various activities and there is less compartmentalization in recent cities.

Figure 2.1 Concentric Zone Model

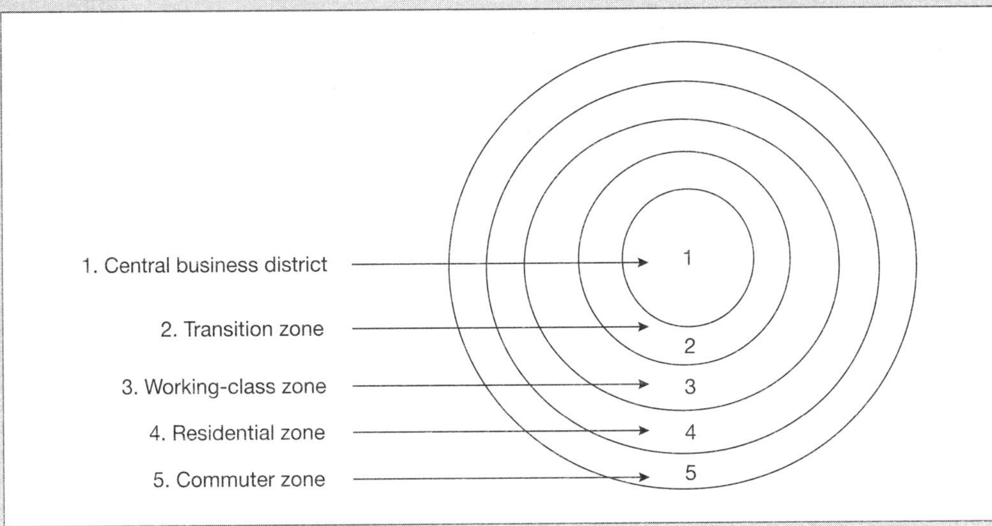

4. With urban regeneration and renewal, more costly houses are found to be constructed in the workers' zone and even middle-class residential areas.
5. The urban land and city development are found to be influenced by the LSI and Smart Cities Mission.

Sector Theory

The sector theory is attributed to the work of Hoyt in 1939. It is a modified version of the centric zone theory given by E. W. Burgess. This theory was developed by Homer Hoyt during the 1930s and was the result of an analysis of more than 200,000 neighbourhood blocks in approximately 70 American cities.[7] The characteristic feature of the sector theory of urbanization is that the development of city is not based on the zone formed of several 'rings', rather it is based on the zone in the form of 'sectors'. The sector model considers that the activities in each sector would remain the same throughout the sector because of its functioning and purpose. Besides that, the land use pattern would also remain the same throughout the sectors. The sector model (Figure 2.2) has categorized the land use pattern into the following types.

1. *CBD:* It is the hub of all business and commercial activities. It is at the heart of the city.
2. *Factories and industries:* This sector is largely confined to factory and industrial activities. Customarily, this sector is found adjacent to the railway line.
3. *Working-class residential:* In this sector, mostly working-class people reside who work in various offices. This sector is found to be lacking in amenities. The inhabitants of this sector largely work in factories. They live near the industries to avoid the cost of transportation. Pollution makes the environmental condition of this sector poor. There are low-cost houses in this sector.

4. *Middle-class residential:* In this sector, people belonging to the middle-class reside. This sector has the largest residential areas. The environmental condition is also very poor in this sector.
5. *High-class residential:* This sector is placed at the edge of the city. This area is more neat and clean with less pollution. The quality of houses is good. It is less congested with less traffic problem. There is less noise and pollution in this area as it is far away from the industrial areas. The houses are very costly and mostly get constructed by the rich section of the population.

Figure 2.2 Sector Model

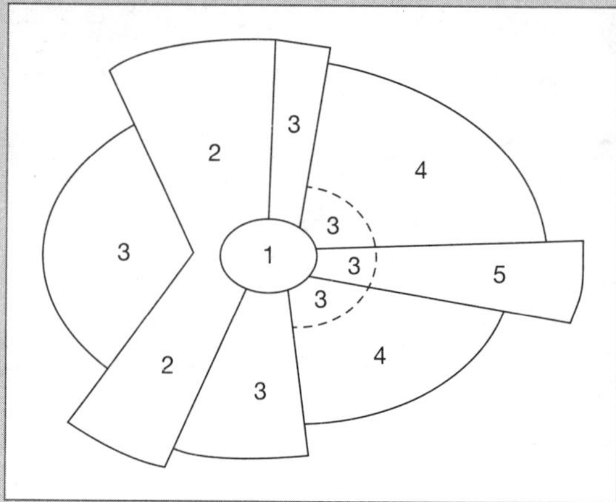

Source: Ghosh (2008, p. 108).
Note: 1 = CBD; 2 = Wholesale and light manufacturing; 3 = Low-class residential; 4 = Middle-class residential; 5 = High-class residential.

Both the centric zone and sector theories have more or less the same approach to urbanization; however, the latter theory differs from the former one on the ground that it considers 'sector' as a unit of urbanization as against the 'ring' approach devised by the centric-zone theory. The sector model is given in Figure 2.2.

Some of the criticisms of this theory are as follows:

1. In recent cities, there is decentralization of activities and each zone has various activities. Therefore, less compartmentalization in activities is seen in recent times.
2. With urban regeneration and renewal, more costly houses are found to be constructed in workers' zone and even middle-class residential areas.
3. The urban land and city development are found to be influenced by the LSI and Smart Cities Mission.

Multiple Nuclei Theory

Multiple nuclei theory was developed by Harris and Ullman in 1945. It is an expansion of the Hoyt sector theory. The proponents of this theory viewed that CBD is not the only centre of an urban area or city activities. They asserted that urbanization and cities can be evolved with more than one business district which they name 'nuclei'. The 'nuclei' are the multiple smaller growth centres that develop around the metropolitan areas. These nuclei can be ports, universities, airports, neighbourhoods, and business and government centres. They are connected with CBD through the transport system. The main aim of this model was to move away from the concentric zones and search for the complex nature of large urban areas. The nodes of the multiple nuclei theory are as follows.

1. *CBD:* It is the primary nucleus around which all other nuclei revolve. It is the main hub of business and commercial activities in a city. The new nuclei developed after this primary nuclei competes with the CBD in the following manner:
2. *Light manufacturing:* These are consumer-oriented business areas around CBD and are found near residential areas. The wholesale business such as clothes, furniture, electrical and electronic items and grocery shops are found in this zone.
3. *Low-class locality:* This locality is observed next to the manufacturing and industrial corridors. Workers working in the manufacturing and other industries reside here. The housing quality is low and hence houses are less costly. Being in proximity to the industrial areas, people living in this type of locality are exposed to pollution and environmental hazards.
4. *Middle-class locality:* This area is situated away from the industrial locality. It is subjected to less pollution and the living condition of the people here is better than that in the low-class locality. The people who reside here commute to CBD through transport. This middle-class sector is the largest sector in the cities.
5. *High class:* This is a high-class zone being occupied by the higher income group of population. This sector is clean and has less traffic than other sectors. It is less polluted, and the real estate developers prefer to develop their residential complexes here.
6. *Heavy manufacturing:* This is basically an industrial zone where heavy industries are found. These industries produce materials such as chemicals, steel and heavy machines.
7. *Outlying business district:* This zone is developed on the pattern of CBD and competes with CBD for residents. This zone is comprised of business malls, airports, universities, community business centres and so on.
8. *Residential suburbs:* These suburbs are customarily single-family houses on a small plot of land on the outskirts of the city. This zone is well connected to CBD through the road transport system.
9. *Industrial suburbs:* This zone is created by the workers working in the heavy industry sector. As industries create pollution, this zone is created for the industrial workers at the outskirts of the city.

Figure 2.3 Multiple Nuclei Model

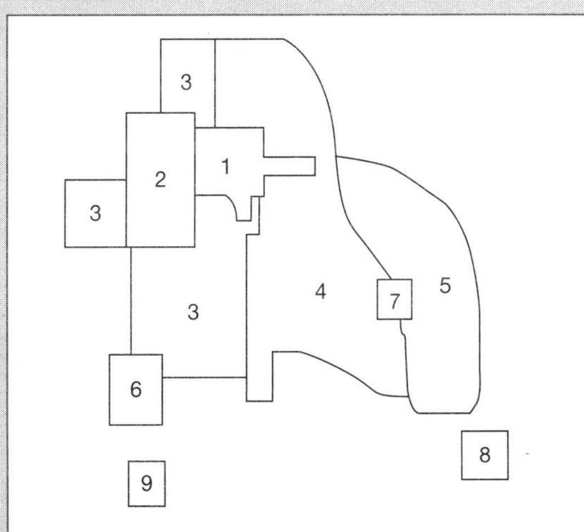

Source: Ghosh (2008, p. 108).
Note: 1 = CBD; 2 = Wholesale light manufacturing; 3 = Low-class residential; 4 = Medium-class residential; 5 = High-class residential; 6 = Heavy manufacturing; 7 = Outlying business district; 8 = Residential suburb; 9 = Industrial suburb.

The crux of the multiple nuclei theory is that every city has a scope of expansion. The city might start with a single CBD, but over the period of time, more activities are added and thus it gets modified. The multiple nuclei model is given in Figure 2.3.

Some of the limitations of this theory are as follows:

1. The cities, particularly old cities, are mostly congested and therefore further expansion through nuclei will make the living conditions in the city worse.
2. This concept may not be applicable to oriental cities having cultural, economic, social and political backdrops.
3. It is not a simple model of urbanization and rather gives a critical outlook.

Bid Rent Theory

Bid rent theory (BRT) is a geographical economic theory. This theory was initially developed by Von Thunen in the year 1826. It was later further developed by William Alonso in the year 1960. It is commented that one of the seminal work on land use economics is William Alonso's bid rent theory (Andrew, 2014). BRT states that the prices and demand for the land by the landowners and real estate developers depend on the distance of land from CBD. Shorter is the distance of land from CBD, higher will be the price and more will be the demand for land and vice versa. Thus, the theory states that land prices and demand for land change, depending on the distance of land from CBD.

Figure 2.4 BRT Model

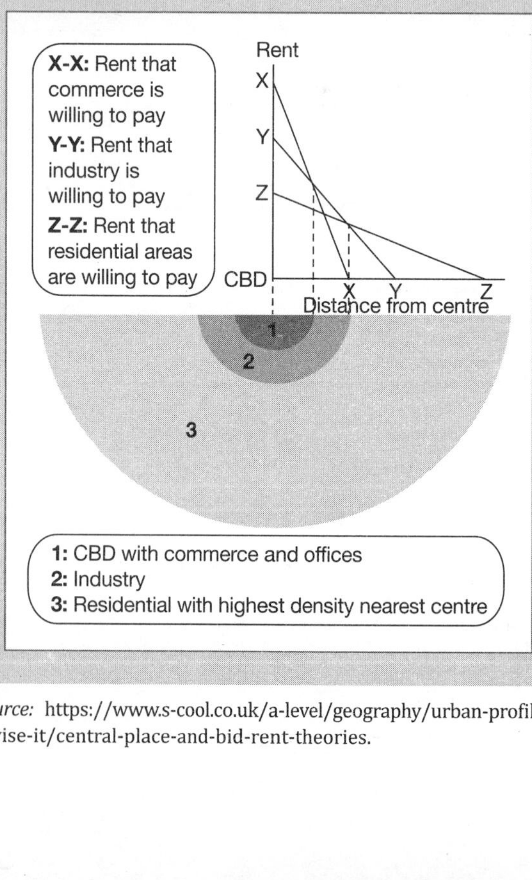

Source: https://www.s-cool.co.uk/a-level/geography/urban-profiles/revise-it/central-place-and-bid-rent-theories.

According to BRT, the central place of a city or urban areas will be CBD. The next ring of land after CBD will be occupied by industry. Thus, the industrial sector comes after CBD, which pays slightly less prices for land than CBD. The third sector is the residential sector which is away from CBD, in which a large number of people reside. Here, the size of land is larger, which is mostly situated in the outskirts or in the periphery. The price of land and rent of the houses in this area are low as compared to CBD (Figure 2.4).

The three important assumptions of BRT are as follows: (a) the inner city or CBD is wealthier than the periphery; (b) people pay more rent in CBD area as compared to those who stay in the periphery residential areas; and (c) the land area as per the BRT is less as compared to the periphery. Some of the criticisms of BRT are as follows: (a) it is not always true that there is rigid compartmentalization of zones on the basis of land; (b) in the developing countries, the business and commercial activities are not only confined to CBD but they also, on parallel several sectors, compete with CBD for business and commercial activities and (c) the land price and demand depend on the locality and the categories of population, quality of land access to transport facilities and other amenities and many other criteria.

New Urban Area Development Theories

The new urban area development theories are largely known for urban area planning theories. Some of the important theories of new urban area development theories are discussed further.

Garden City Theory

Garden city theory was developed and propounded by the British social activist Ebenezer Howard. The basic aim of this theory is the systematic construction of new urban areas which offer healthy life and livelihood to city dwellers. Howard in his books *Tomorrow: a Peaceful Path towards Real Reform* and *Garden Cities of Tomorrow* was of the view that the nation should try to build ideal cities having all amenities of both rural and urban areas. These types of cities he termed as 'garden cities'. Howard established a company called the Garden City Co. Limited and raised fund and purchased a piece of land 56 km away from London for the establishment of garden city. The first garden city was Letchworth Garden City. The second garden city, Welwyn Garden City, was constructed 36 km north-west of London.

Some of the features of garden city are as follows:

1. Both rural and urban areas are combined in a garden city.
2. The size of a garden city should be such that it should offer enough to sustain a rich social life.
3. It should be surrounded by a permanent belt of agricultural land. The residents of the city work in agriculture and produce fresh grain and vegetables.
4. The total area of a garden city needs to be 6,000 acres (1 acre = 0.405 ha), with coverage of 1,000 acre at the centre and 5,000 acres of agricultural land around it.
5. The total residents of the city need to be 32,000 out of which 30,000 people live in the city and 2,000 people are scattered around the country.
6. A garden city needs to have a park of about 145 acres at the centre of the city.
7. The outer region of the city may be used for the construction of factories, warehouses and marketplaces.
8. One of the important features of a garden-city theory is that a chain of garden cities built around the central city is to be called 'urban agglomerations free of slums and smokes'.

The garden-city theory received attention worldwide and the European nations tried to emulate the pattern of garden city in order to ensure a good living condition to the urbanites.

Satellite City Theory

The concept of 'satellite city' was popularized during the mid-1990s and the 20th century. It will not be mistaken to say that the concept of satellite city was taken from the concept of garden city. The satellite cities are built around the central city. Looking from the top of the central city, the cities developed around the main city are seen like satellites. The *Oxford Dictionary of Architecture* defines satellite towns as follows:

> Towns that are self-contained and limited in size, built in the vicinity of a large town or city to house and employ those who would otherwise create a demand for expansion of the existing settlement, but dependent on the parent-city for population and major services.[8]

Some of the features of satellite city are as follows:

1. The satellite cities are smaller in size as compared to that of central city.
2. The satellite cities are huge and are controlled by the central city in terms of administration, economy, culture and life.
3. The main purpose of building satellite cities is to disperse population density in the central city.
4. The satellite cities provide employment opportunities and an improved quality of life to the people residing there.

The origin of the satellite cities was triggered in London. Gradually, it attracted attention of other countries of Europe and Asia also. Many cities of Japan and China have built satellite cities, and satellite cities are gradually found to be popular in the developing countries of Asia.

Theory of Urban Agglomeration Economies

It derives its essence from the writings of illustrious German economist Alfred Weber. Alfred Weber's illustrious book *Industrial Location Theory* veritably envisages about the theory of urban agglomeration. He has argued for strengthening the role of economic agglomeration for urban development. He defined agglomerate economy as a benefit or as an economy which gained from production or sale because of the production being carried out at the same place according to a certain scale (Shao, 2015). According to this theory, agglomeration improves efficiency and reduces cost through economies of scale and scope. Under urban agglomeration, varieties of industries march towards cities and agglomerate in urban areas. This is called 'urban agglomeration economy'. Beside industries, the urban agglomeration also attracts flow of population, information, technologies, commodities and services to urban areas. As a result, the city expands in size and form. However, when the scale of development reaches a certain degree, it gradually starts declining. The robust diseconomies of agglomeration constantly impair the role of agglomeration economy (Shao, 2015). The increase in the number of industries and population severely affects the environment of urban areas. This dissuades people to stay in urban areas and they gradually start moving towards the urban suburbs.

The examples of theory of urban agglomeration economies are seen in developing countries. In India, Ludhiana (Punjab) and Kanpur (Uttar Pradesh) are two prominent examples among many.

Urban–Rural Integration Theory

This theory was propounded by the British social activist Ebenezer Howard. In his book *Tomorrow: A Peaceful Path towards Real Reform,* he advocated to 'replace the old social structure of urban–rural division with the new social structure of urban–rural integration'. He also noted that 'city and country have their own advantages and corresponding disadvantages although urban–rural integration can avoid the disadvantages on both.' He further opined that 'the city and country must get married and the happy combination ignites new hope, new life and new civilization.' Some of the characteristic features of urban–rural integration theory are as follows:

1. At the outset, a city must occupy the agricultural land of the country as little as possible.
2. The optimum size of the city population should not be larger than 32,000.
3. The urban dweller who purchases urban land needs to set up or join a stock company.

The examples of urban and rural integration are seen in many developing countries and, in fact, developing countries are promoting urban–rural integration in order to offer better quality of living to the people residing in countryside. In India, the urban–rural continuum of Kerala and rur-urban project of Gujarat are illustrious examples.

II
APPROACHES TO URBAN DEVELOPMENT

The theoretical frameworks describing the phenomena of urbanization are tied to larger issues of social change and economic development, and that these are rooted in different philosophical and ideological assumptions.[9]

Cities are complex and socio-technical in nature. Many cities have their own illustrious past, scintillating present and glorious future. Theoretical and practical efforts to create better cities have a long history. As urban planning is more practical in nature, many a time, theoretical approaches are being argued along with urban planning theories. The classical, neoclassical, the developmentalists and modernization theorists have put forward many approaches towards growth and development of urban areas in both developed and developing countries. The theoretical approaches to urban development can be categorized as follows:

1. Classical approach
2. Developmentalist approach
3. Modernist approach
4. Sustainable urban development approach
5. Smart city approach

The Classical Approach

Adam Smith's Perspectives on Urbanization and Development

Adam Smith, a great classical economist, in his illustrious book *The Wealth of Nations* has pointed out that the growth of city is in a natural order which helps the individual to acquire 'finer things of life'. According to Smith, after fulfilling two basic rights, such as the right of survival and the right to a level of living beyond subsistence, man can search for and discover the 'finer things of life'. This can be possible through accumulation of capital, enhancing productivity of labour through the application of technology and raising the productivity of physical material goods. Smith (1827) has noted that:

> According to natural course of things, the greater part of the capital of every growing society is, first, directed to agriculture, afterwards to manufactures and last of all to foreign commerce...cultivated before any considerable towns could be established and some sort of coarse industry of the manufacturing kind must have been carried on in those towns, before they could well think of employing themselves in foreign commerce.

In the order of development stated by Smith, at the outset, the first and foremost emphasis is laid on agriculture, followed by manufacturing, industry and finally trade and commerce. The latter two lead to the growth of city and urban areas. Smith pointed out that this natural order of development has been followed in all of the modern states of Europe. This classical thought of an illustrious classical economist indicates that Smith has emphasized the growth of city and urban areas in the natural process of development of a country, visible in the pattern of development of cities in the European countries.

Karl Marx's Perspectives on Modern Cities

Karl Marx in his popular political theory of public and private has highlighted about the modern capitalist cities and the contemporary urban life and urban social movements in the capitalist societies. In Marx's views, the modern cities and industrial capitalism were the materialistic bases of public action. Marx has distinguished between private and public life. Marx's concept of private life in capitalist society is the privatized self or personality. While, on the other hand, public life is a social space in which human beings are both social and political. Marx established the public realm as an arena in which actors take hold of and create anew their social bonds and the meanings of their actions through new stories, accounts and images of collective life. To Marx, the great modern cities are the social spaces in which public life in capitalist society emerges. He was of the view that modern civilization is in true sense an urban civilization. The modern cities systematically educate, civilize and socialize human beings and their capabilities. Here, human beings are the public actors. In modern cities, these public actors unite and fight for socialism. In other words, to Marx, public life in the modern cities is a means to achieve the ends of socialism. In real sense, Marx identified society itself in terms of the modern city.

> The city was to be praised for at least one thing, the escape it offers from what he called 'the idiocy of village life'. He no doubt had in mind the primitive meaning of the word 'idiot', which is not a mentally deficient person, nor yet an uncouth and ignorant person, but a private person, one 'who does not hold public office': a person who is not a participant in society as Marx understood it. For Marx, the working out of the historical process, and therefore the essential life of man, could take place only in cities where the classes confront each other, where men in the mass demonstrate the nature and destiny of mankind. (Trilling, 1972)

Some of the features of Marxian city and urban development are as follows:

1. The modern cities in the capitalist society were the social, spatial and historical setting for the creation of public life.
2. Cities enhance the beauty of social and public life where human beings participate in association with others.

3. Some of the characteristics of modern cities are industrialization, mechanization and concentration of population, division of labour and cosmopolitanism which abolishes local narrowness.
4. Modern society, whether capitalist or socialists, would be an urban society.
5. The modern cities provide opportunity to the labour in a capitalist society. They also provide opportunities for public action, sociability and political association.

Engels' Perspectives on Cities and City Life

Engels' perspectives on urbanization and urban problems are based on his observations on the industrial cities of England. Engels' illustrious book *The Condition of the Working Class in England in 1844* is one of the masterpiece works on urban sociopolitics. It is remarked that the entire tradition of the 20th-century urban planning, capitalist and socialist alike owes an enormous debt to Engels.[10] According to Engels, life in the city is too mechanical. People regard each other only as useful objects. The rich capitalists and industrialists exploit the poor workers. There is large-scale concentration of power in the hands of the industrialists and capitalists. The strong treads the weaker under foot. Some of the features of Engels' perspectives on urbanization and urban development are as follows:

1. The modern cities are the hub of manufacturing, mechanization and concentration. The cities are the breeding grounds of industries.
2. It is the place where capital, manufacturing, population and capable human powers are concentrated.
3. Cities are the birthplaces of working class and labour movement.
4. Modern cities give a paradox of wealth, poverty, luxury and degradation.
5. The environmental pollution makes urban life unfit for human and civilized activities.
6. Urbanization sharpens the division of labour between the town and the countryside.
7. Insecurity, poverty, uncertainty, complexity and exclusion are inherent to urban culture.

Engels was of the opinion that the working class in cities is largely from rural areas. They are strangers to each other. They lead miserable lives and work in deplorable working conditions in the private sector. They are victims of exclusion under the privatization. However, urban life gives them an opportunity to unite and fight for their common interest. Thus, cities are the fighting grounds of productive power of industrialists and capitalists on the one hand, and the power of the common people on the other. 'The Great Towns', Engles wrote:

> have transformed the disease of the social body, which appears in chronic form in the country, into an acute one, and so made manifest its real nature and means for curing it. Without the great cities and their forcing influence upon the popular intelligence, the working class would be far less advanced than it is. (Engels, 1892)

Developmentalist Approach

The developmental economists have emphasized urban development for enabling the developing countries to achieve higher economic growth rate and socioeconomic development. Some of the developmental theories are the 'big push' theory of Rosenstein-Rodan; two-sector model of Arthur

Lewis, Ragnar Nurkse's theory of balanced growth and W. W. Rostow's stages of economic growth. The big push theory advocates that in the countries where economic growth and development are in a nascent stage, then a certain type of big investment and big economic push is required in order to drag these economies from the spectre of economic backwardness and underdevelopment. In his view, investment on industry is required to take these economies forward towards the boon of economic prosperity and progress. The investments on industry itself connote the growth of urbanization and focus on industrialization. In other words, the growth of cities requires big investments in various sectors of development.

The two-sector model of Arthur Lewis is comprised of traditional agriculture sector and modern industrial sector, and predicts that the development of the underdeveloped countries can be possible only when the surplus labour existing in the agriculture sector is successfully transmitted and gainfully employed in the modern industrial sector. The development of the industrial sector will lead to the growth of industrial cities. He believes that the underdeveloped countries have a lot of potential to achieve economic growth and development. This they could achieve through industrialization and transfer of labour from the agriculture to the modern industrial sector. In India, Rourkela, Bokaro, Tatanagar and so on are illustrious examples of urbanization through industrialization.

The balanced growth theory propounded by Ragnar Nurkse asserts that the underdeveloped economies are unable to develop because of three reasons, that is, vicious circle of poverty, low capital formation and small size of market. Nurkse advocated large-scale investment in industrial sector for the development of the underdeveloped countries. Through balanced growth, Nurkse perceived that a large-scale increase in supply sweeping across a large number of industrial sector would, at the same time, be met by a large-scale increase in demand created by the same expansion (Cypher & Dietz, 2006). According to Nurkse (1953), in development programmes, 'all sectors of the economy should grow simultaneously, so as to keep a proper balance between industry and agriculture and between production of more consumption and production for exports...the logic of this proposition is an unassailable as its simplicity.'

W. W. Rostow in his classic book *The Stages of Economic Growth: A Non-Communist Manifesto*, published in 1960, noted that countries would pass through five stages of development process before they achieve the hallmark of high economic growth. The five stages are: (a) the traditional society; (b) the pre-conditions of take-off; (c) the take-off; (d) the drive to maturity; and (e) age of high mass consumption. According to Rostow (1960), 'the stages are not merely descriptions. They are not merely a way of generalizing certain factual observations about the sequence of development of modern societies. They have an inner logic and continuity; they have an analytical bone-structure rooted in a dynamic theory of production.' The last three stages such as the take-off stage, the drive to maturity and age of high mass consumption are possible and can be achieved through high investment, innovation, industrialization and modernization. At this stage, the process of development of urbanization starts and matures further. It has happened in most of the developed countries and of the West, and the giant Asian nations such as Japan, Singapore, South Korea and Taiwan have also experienced various stages of economic growth and development and urbanization. Thus, according to Rostow's stages of economic growth, the urbanization takes place in an economy when it attains certain stages of economic growth and development. Thus, from the analysis of stages of the economic growth of Rostow, it is amply clear that drive to maturity can happen when there is fast-paced urbanization and industrialization which would lead to consumerism and progress.

From all these discussions of developmentalists, it is amply clear that the industrialization and urbanization are the only answers to the development of the underdeveloped countries. Doucette and Park (2018) have rightly remarked that it is difficult to examine East Asian urbanization without taking the legacy of developmentalism into account. They have also further viewed that under big push industrialization efforts across East Asia, urban processes took place very rapidly in strategically selected areas of political and economic importance.

Modernist Approach

The modernization theory was originated in America and Europe during 1945–1960. It remained as the most vital paradigms of development during 1950–1970. The modernization theory was propounded by Max Weber, Emile Durkheim, Talcott Parsons, David McClelland and Daniel Lerner to name a few among others. The main proposition of modernization theory is that the underdeveloped economies can also become developed economies through the adoption of the modernization approach. The primary intension of the modernization theorists is to provide a formula for bringing modernity to the Third-World countries of Asia, Africa and Latin America in order to break the jinx of 'underdevelopment'. The modernization theory advocates that the modernization process experienced by USA and several Western European countries has provided a model which could be applied to other countries to enable them to develop through modernization (Kreutzamann, 1998). The modernist school of thought believed that the underdevelopment problem of Third-World countries was not due to the colonialism but because of internal shortcomings of prevalence of traditionalism inherent to the underdeveloped societies. Therefore, at the heart of the modernization theory is the idea that economic growth can be stimulated in any country by following a US/European Model (Green, 2008). In their opinion, modernization and urbanization go hand in hand.

Max Weber, one of the prolific propounders of the modernization theory of development, has viewed that the growth of capitalism and modernization of economic system depends on how to overcome traditionalism. To them, traditionalism tends to put restriction on the development of the underdeveloped economies. Another strong protagonist of the modernization theory is Talcott Parsons. Talcott Parsons noted that the developing societies are guided by the 'traditional' values, which is the greatest obstacle to development. He advocated that modernity is the only solution for the development of the underdeveloped countries which are mostly traditional in nature. The developed countries have undergone a high degree of modernization in terms of democratization, industrialization, urbanization and technological revolution compared to their counterpart underdeveloped countries which are still characterized by dominance of agriculture, less industrialization and technological backwardness. Therefore, modernization is essential for the development of the underdeveloped countries. Lerner, another prolific propounder of modernization, considers that in modern society people are more advanced, educated and media suave. They are mostly urbanized. Lerner has categorized individuals into two types, that is, 'traditional' and 'transitional or modern'. He was of the opinion that the modern individuals are better informed, happier and relatively younger as compared to traditional individuals. Inkeles and Smith (1974) have given a few features of traditional and modern man (Table 2.1).

In view of modernization theorists, urbanization is sometimes treated synonymous to modernization. The modernist approach believes that modernization which directly means

Table 2.1 Traditional Man and Modern Man

Traditional	Modern
Not receptive to new ideas	Open to new experience
Rooted in tradition	Oriented towards change
Only interested in things that benefit them quickly	Interested in outside world
Denial of different opinions	Acknowledges different opinions
Uninterested in new information	Eager to seek out new information
Oriented towards the past	Punctual; oriented towards the present
Concerned with short-term	Values planning
Distrustful of people beyond the family	Calculability; trust in people to meet obligations
Suspicious of technology	Values technical skills
High value placed on religion and the sacred	High value placed on formal education and science
Traditional patron–client relations prevail	Respect for the dignity of others; belief that rewards should be distributed according to rules
Particularistic	Universalistic
Fatalistic	Optimistic

Source: Inkeles and Smith (1974).

industrialization and urbanization are the only solution to the development of the developing countries. The modernization has enabled the developed countries of the West to achieve higher development as compared to the developing countries which are mostly traditional and rural in nature.

Sustainable Urban Development Approach

Cities around the world today are facing surmountable challenges of intense degradation, pollution, overpopulation and so on. Sustainable development refers to the environmental, economic and sociological processes in the city and its physical structure.[11] Therefore, in the 21st century, urban sustainability has become a prominent element in the day-to-day debate on urban policy (Yigitcanlar & Teriman, 2015). According to Stephen (1996), sustainable urban development seeks to create cities and towns that improve the long-term health of the planet's human and ecological systems. It means to achieve this objective, the following actions can be taken: protecting and restoring natural ecosystems in urban areas, creating community environments that nurture human potential, using land and resources wisely and facilitating human lifestyles that contribute to global sustainability.

The key elements of sustainable development are environment, society and economy. The unbridled growth of population in urban areas, more particularly in the developing countries, has created a ramshackle urban environment. The excessive growth of vehicles and heat-generating gadgets have not only polluted the urban environment but also posited climate change on urban areas. Moreover, poor waste management is also detrimental to urban environment. The sustainable urban development calls for protection of urban environment. The urban economy contributes nearly 60 per cent of national GDP of many countries. However, urbanization process has failed to manage the infrastructure to be available for the growing urban population causing harm to urban society, economy and environment. Some of the important concepts associated with the sustainable city are as follows.

1. *Green city:* Green city is one of the important forms of sustainable city which intends to use green energy and enhance footprints of green belts in the city in order to check pollution and improve the quality of life of city dwellers. Six types of investments are required for creating green cities for ensuring the long-term survival of the urban environment: (a) low-carbon transport systems; (b) a green industrial sector; (c) energy-efficient buildings; (d) greening of the city itself; (e) green, resilient infrastructure; and (f) intelligent systems (Lindfield & Steinberg, 2012).
2. *Garden city:* The garden city movement of urban planning was launched by Sir Ebenezer Howard in 1898 in the United Kingdom. The main intention behind the garden cities was that the city is to be planned and must have self-contained communities surrounded by 'green belts', containing proportionate areas of residences, industry and agriculture. The garden city would be self-sufficient and when it reached full population, another garden city would be developed nearby. Howard envisaged a cluster of several garden cities as satellites of a central city of 50,000 people, linked by road and rail.[12]
3. *Low-carbon city:* Low-carbon city is another type of sustainable city approach which aims at reducing the anthropogenic carbon footprint by minimizing the utilization of non-renewable sources of fossil fuel energy. The leading cause of climate change is the anthropological expansion of greenhouse gases (GHGs), including carbon dioxide (CO_2), nitrous oxide and methane in the atmosphere. About 70 per cent of global CO_2 emission is associated with urban areas because they cluster socioeconomic activities that generate climate change-related emissions (Rimi & Aliyu, 2019).
4. *Eco-city:* The other name of green city is eco-city. The city which adheres to the ecological norms and maintains the ecological health of the city without causing any harm to the environment is called eco-city. White (2002) defines an eco-city as 'a city that provides an acceptable standard of living for its human occupants without depleting the ecosystems and biochemical cycles on which it depends'. Another definition of the eco-city has identified it as:

> an ecologically healthy city. Such a city is the result of a healthy human ecological process leading to sustainable development within the carrying capacity of local ecosystems through changes in production modes, consumption behavior, and decision instruments that are based on ecological economics and systems engineering. (Wang & Ye, 2004)

The World Commission on Environment and Development announced the following principles as the essential features of a sustainable city:

1. Increasing enough economic and social opportunities for the urban population;
2. Reducing the share of energy in urban growth;
3. Optimal use of water;

4. Land and other resources required for such urban growth;
5. Minimizing the waste produced and maximizing the recycling of waste;
6. Creating enough power and performance management systems to achieve economic, social and environmental objectives;
7. Directing the technology used in the city towards SDGs; and
8. Strengthening different areas of the city in order to prevent or respond to threats and achieve economic, social and environmental objectives as a result of which natural or human factors arise, and also enhancing the flexibility in the face of unexpected disruptions in the city.

It is also commented that the sustainable city is a city where improvements in social justice, diversity and high quality of life may be realized (Azizi, 2001).

The sustainable urban development approach needs to take into consideration the following aspects:

1. Control of urban population to an optimum level which is tolerant to their well-being putting not much pressure on urban environment;
2. Effective management of urban economy which ensures basic needs and amenities to all urban dwellers;
3. Controlling urban pollution by regulating vehicles and effective traffic and crime control;
4. Urban waste management and ensuring education and proper healthcare to all urban dwellers;
5. Control of urban poverty and inequality;
6. Ensuring sustainable energy to urban population;
7. Judicious urban land use planning taking into consideration urban housing, open space, water bodies and heritage;
8. Effective urban slum management;
9. Effective use of technology for urban e-governance and sustainable development;
10. Capacity building and empowerment of ULBs on sustainable urban development;
11. Promoting urban biodiversity and checking urban pollution; and
12. Focus on resilient city by developing appropriate strategies for urban disaster management.

Smart City Approach

Another important approach of the 21st century for city development is smart city approach. The smart city is a versatile concept and is difficult to define precisely. The alternative names used for smart city are hi-tech city, resilience city, knowledge city, sustainable city, green city, eco-city and so on. However, as the urbanization is going on at a faster pace in developing countries, the smart city is of immense importance for providing good quality of life to city dwellers. According to the Government of India (2015), smart cities are those which provide core infrastructure and give decent quality of life to its citizens, a clean and sustainable environment and application of 'smart' solutions. While mapping smart city, the European Union (2014) defined it as follows: 'a smart city is a city seeking to address public issues via ICT-based solutions on the basis of a multi-stakeholder, municipally based partnership.' William D. Eggers and John Skowron have noted that the goal of smart city is to enable better decision-making through the use of data for all stakeholders—

Box 2.1 Some of the Important Elements of Smart City

- *Smart citizens:* It should be a knowledgeable society, where people are educated and empowered to carry out their business and activities smartly.
- *Smart mobility:* The public transport system should be very smart and responsive to the needs of various types of users. There needs to be multiple user-friendly means of transport such as metro rail, buses, paid taxis and autorickshaws. This may vary from one city to another. There should be e-traffic system for the management of traffic.
- *Smart governance:* Smart government is alternatively used as e-governance. It should promote the use of ICT in public services such as e-payment, e-redressal of grievances and the motto is to bring public transparency.
- *Smart economy:* The smart city needs to encourage and provide support to the government for entrepreneurship and creativity through financial assistance and transactions. The smart city economy needs to contribute sustainably to green growth.
- *Smart environment:* A smart city should provide active and adaptive response to environmental concerns. The city needs to be free from pollution and should promote green environment.
- *Smart local self-government:* The smart cities need to have educated, trained and e-equipped LSIs. They need to carry out their duties responsibly and work for the well-being of marginalized dwelling in the slums and informal settlements.
- *Smart quality of life:* Residents of a smart city must have access to healthy housing, sanitation, safe drinking water, smart energy and e-health and effective health services.

government, business and residents. The focus of any smart city should be its people, providing benefits such as:

1. A better quality of life for residents and visitors.
2. Economic competitiveness to attract industry and talent.
3. An environmentally conscious focus on sustainability.

These three goals—quality of life, economic competitiveness and sustainability—can provide the foundation for a smart city initiative.[13] The aim of the smart city is to effectively involve all the stakeholders such as government, private sector, non-governmental organizations (NGOs), CSO and people at large in city building in order to ensure a sustainable environment and good quality of life to city dwellers. It also aims at the use of technology and other smart infrastructure facilities to make city not only beautiful but resilient to the future shocks and also be responsive to the needs of the urban dwellers. Some of the basic elements of smart cities are given in the Box 2.1.

The Smart Cities Mission is an innovative and new initiative by the GoI to drive economic growth and improve the quality of life of people by enabling local development and harnessing technology as a means to create smart outcomes for citizens. The objective is to promote cities that provide core infrastructure and give a decent quality of life to its citizens, a clean and sustainable environment and application of 'smart' solutions.

The core infrastructures required for the smart city are:

1. Adequate water supply;
2. Assured electricity supply;

3. Sanitation, including SWM;
4. Efficient urban mobility and public transport;
5. Affordable housing, especially for the poor;
6. Robust IT connectivity and digitalization;
7. Good governance, especially e-governance and citizen participation;
8. Sustainable environment;
9. Safety and security of citizens, particularly women, children and the elderly; and
10. Health and education.[14]

Summing Up

The urban development theories and approaches are equally important to urban planning and development studies. In this chapter, some of the important theories of urban development and approaches to urban development have been discussed. These are critical backdrops which will provide inputs to the urban planners and policymakers to take appropriate steps for sustainable urban development. However, no single urban theory or approach is a one-time solution to city development. It will vary from city to city depending on spatial, socioeconomic, cultural and political conditions of the nation states. As Leitner and Sheppard (2015) write: '...no single theory suffices to account for the variegated nature of urbanization and cities across the world, without asserting the necessity of different distinct theories for different contexts.' And 'Our position, then, is that there can be no single urban theory of ubiquitous remit.' However, theories and approaches are guiding spirit and try to provide basic understanding on urban development process and lead to further innovations in the approaches to urban development.

Keywords

Garden City, Satellite City, Smart City, Smart Governance, Smart Economy, CBD, Green City

REVIEW QUESTIONS

1. Critically explain the concentric theory and sector theory of urban planning.
2. Describe the multiple nuclei theory and BRT of urban planning.
3. Explain any two new urban area development theories.
4. Explain the classical and neoclassical approach to urbanization and urban development.
5. Describe the developmentalist approach to urbanization and development.
6. Explain the sustainable and smart city approach to urbanization and urban development.
7. Write short notes on the following:
   a. Modernization approach to urban development
   b. Satellite city theory
   c. Urban–rural integration theory
   d. Garden city theory

Notes

1. https://aho.no/en/news/urban-theory-and-history (accessed on 21 August 2018).
2. https://www.worldbank.org/en/topic/urbandevelopment (accessed on 18 March 2019).
3. https://www.adb.org/themes/urban-development/issues (accessed on 18 March 2019).
4. http://www.csun.edu/~sg61795/310/3a.html (accessed on 4 April 2019).
5. https://pdfs.semanticscholar.org/f544/aa99b3c610258373c44e0fc24d52acedb310.pdf (accessed on 15 October 2019).
6. https://www.worldatlas.com/articles/what-is-the-concentric-zone-model.html (accessed on 21 April 2018).
7. https://core.ac.uk/download/pdf/35469545.pdf (accessed on 21 April 2018).
8. https://www.encyclopedia.com/education/dictionaries-thesauruses-pictures-and-press-releases/satellite-town (accessed on 24 November 2019).
9. https://architexturez.net/doc/az-cf-166806 (accessed on 27 August 2018).
10. http://faculty.wwu.edu/zaferan/472%20engles%20article.pdf (accessed on 28 April 2018).
11. https://www.id-press.eu/seejad/article/view/265 (accessed on 15 October 2019).
12. https://www.geni.com/projects/The-Garden-City-Movement/15255 (accessed on 16 October 2019).
13. https://www2.deloitte.com/insights/us/en/focus/smart-city/overview.html (accessed on 4 April 2019).
14. india.gov.in/spotlight/smart-cities-mission-step-towards-smart-india (accessed on 4 April 2019).

References

Azizi, M. M. (2001). Sustainable urban development: Analytical approach from a global perspective. *Scientific-Research Journal of School of Architecture and Urban Planning,* 11, 33. Also see https://www.iaiest.com/data-cms/articles/20191108095817amIAJSE1510020.pdf (accessed on 16 June 2020).

Cypher, J. M., & Dietz, J. L. (2006). *The process of economic development.* New York, NY: Rutledge.

Doucette, J., & Park, B. G. (2018). Introduction: Interrogating urban development in East Asia. *Studies in Critical Social Sciences, 130.* https://brill.com/view/book/edcoll/9789004383609/BP000001.xml?lang=en (accessed on 9 March 2019).

Engels, F. (1892). *Condition of the working class in England in 1844.* London: Swan Sonnenschein.

European Union. (2014). *Mapping smart cities in the EU.* Brussels: European Union Policy Department, European Parliament. https://www.europarl.europa.eu/RegData/etudes/etudes/join/2014/507480/IPOL-ITRE_ET(2014)507480_EN.pdf (accessed on 14 April 2020).

Friedman, A. (1979). *The good society*. Cambridge: MIT Press.

Ghosh, S. (2008). *Introduction to settlement geography.* Kolkata: Orient BlackSwan.

Government of India. (2015). *Smart cities mission statement and guidelines.* New Delhi: Ministry of Urban Development of India, Government of India.

Grant, J. (2006). *Planning the good community new urbanism in theory and practice.* London: Routledge.

Green, Phil. (2008). Are development theories of the 1950s,1960s and 1970s still relevant today? Discuss with reference to modernization theory. https://philmgreen.files.wordpress.com/2010/08/modernisation-theory-today.pdf (accessed on 16 June 2020).

Inkeles, A., & Smith, D. H. (1974). *Becoming modern—Individual change in six developing countries.* Cambridge: Harvard University Press.

Kreutzamann, H. (1998). From modernization theory towards the 'clash of civilization: Directions and paradigms shifts in Huntington, S (eds.) Analysis and prognosis of global development, *GeoJournal, 46,* 255–265.

Leitner, H., & Sheppard, E. (2015). Provincializing critical urban theory: Extending the ecosystem of possibilities. *International Journal of Urban and Regional Research.* http://eprints.lse.ac.uk/65351/1/Current%20debates_author.pdf (accessed on 16 October 2019).

Lindfield, M., & Steinberg, F. (Eds.). (2012). Introduction. In M. Lindfield & F. Steinberg (Eds.), *Green city* (pp. 1–2). Manila: Asian Development Bank.

Nurkse, R. (1953). *Problems in capital formation in underdeveloped countries.* Oxford: Oxford University Press.

Rimi, A. S., & Aliyu, B. Y. (2019). *Low carbon city: Strategies and case studies.* https://link.springer.com/referenceworkentry/10.1007%2F978-3-319-71061-7_24-2 (accessed on 20 March 2019).

Rostow, W. W. (1960). *The stages of economic growth: A non-communistic manifesto.* Cambridge: Cambridge University Press.

Scott, A. J., & Stopper, M. (2014). The nature of cities: The scope and limits of urban theory. *International Journal of Urban and Regional Research.* https://luskin.ucla.edu/sites/default/files/ScottStorperpubliblished.pdf (accessed on 24 June 2019).

Shao, Z. (2015). Relevant theories on new urban area development. In Z. Shao (Ed.), *The new urban area development* (pp. 23–30). Berlin: Springer.

Sik, I. C. (2016). Community-based approaches to urban development in Singapore and Seoul. In I. C. Sik & B. Kriznik B (Eds.), *Community based urban development* (pp. 89–146). Berlin: Springer.

Smith, A. (1827). *An inquiry into the nature and causes of the wealth of nations.* Edinburgh: University Press of Thomas Nelson and Peter Brown.

Stephen, W. (1996). Sustainable urban development: A literature review and analysis. Oakland: Institute of Urban and Regional Development, University of California.

Trilling, L. (1972). *Sincerity and authenticity.* Cambridge: Harvard University Press.

Wang, R., & Ye. Y. (2004). Eco-city development in [the People's Republic of] China. *Ambio, 33*(6), 341–342.

White, R. R. (2002). *Building the ecological city.* Cambridge: Woodhead Publishing Ltd.

Yigitcanlar, T., & Teriman, S. (2015). Rethinking sustainable urban development: Towards an integrated planning and development process. *International Journal of Environmental Science and Technology, 12*(1), 341–352.

3 Urban Planning

Urban planning is designed to regulate the use of land and other physical resources in the public interest and can make a tremendous difference in the quality of life and wellbeing of people living in cities.[1]

Urban planning is an important source of development and a tool for reducing inequality.

—UN-Habitat[2]

The urban world is changing rapidly. Whether in the west or in countries in transition, the changes taking place in our cities are of revolutionary proportions. It thus becomes vitally important to look at how cities develop and how they are planned.

—Duhl and Sanchez (1999)

Introduction

Urbanization is going on at a faster pace in both developed and developing countries. More than 70 per cent of the population in the developed countries is now living in urban areas. On the other hand, in the developing countries, the process of urbanization is going on at a faster pace. Urbanization has the ability to transform the socioeconomic, human, cultural and political development fabric of a nation. An urban area has the potential to enhance the economic growth of the nation states. It is found that the contribution of urban areas to economic growth is higher as compared to rural areas. It is pertinent to note the view of Scott and Storper (2014) that most of us have little hesitation in dealing with everyday propositions to the effect, say, that cities are now growing rapidly at locations all over the globe or that urbanization is moving ahead more forcefully than at any other time in human history. Urbanization is good but unplanned urbanization is a cause for concern as it puts tremendous pressure on urban planning and development. Unplanned urbanization in developing countries created a host of problems including urban unemployment, poverty, inequality and growth of urban slum and rise of urban informal sector and environmental issues. Sofi et al. (2017) from their study in Srinagar (Jammu & Kashmir) have noted that unplanned urbanization has led to human and environment problems such as overpopulation, haphazard housing service, health burdens, urban poverty, crime, child labour, erratic education system, mismanagement of waste, air, water, sound and soil pollutions, carbon emission, environmental hazards, traffic jam, unemployment, improper drainage system, inadequate entertainment facilities, drug abuse, vulnerable ecosystem, medley lifestyle and culture. Urban planning emphasizes the planned use of physical, human and financial resources earmarked for the development of urban areas for making city dwelling pleasant and comfortable. According to Thooyavan (2011), urban planning by its nature is concerned with shaping the future of urban settlements and allocation of land for residential, commercial, institutional and industrial development. He further noted that planning and development means the physical and economic growth which meets effectively the social needs of the human society. According to Ahmadi and Toghyani (2011), urban planning has an important role to form the framework of urban sustainable development and the goal of sustainable urban development process is to achieve the status of 'sustainability' in urban communities. Therefore, for the developing countries, urban planning has a key role to play in offering better quality of life to the people living in the cities.

LEARNING OBJECTIVES

After reading this chapter on urban planning, you should be able to:

- Define urban planning and the need for urban planning
- Explain different types of urban planning
- Techniques of urban planning
- System approach to urban planning
- Issues and challenges relating to urban planning

Urban Planning: Concept and Meaning

'Planning' can be defined as a process that enables a nation state to set goals, formulate vision and mission, objectives and development of strategies. It also emphasized prudent sector-wise allocation of resources in order to accomplish the developmental goals and objectives within a particular time period. For Cole (1993), planning is an activity which involves decisions about ends as well as means and about conduct as well as result. Invancevich et al. (1994) perceived planning as embracing all the activities that lead to the determination of objectives and the appropriate courses of action that lead to their achievements. The United Nations (1975) has rightly said that 'a plan is a programme of action for achieving definite objectives or goals. In this sense, a plan is a policy statement and planning means policy making.' The urban development planning may be defined as formulating, implementing, regulating and controlling economic activity by a nation state according to set priorities with a view to achieving well-defined objectives of urban development within a given time period. With scanty resources at disposal to be spent for the development of urban areas without proper planning, effective development of urban areas could not be possible.

Urban planning is the planning for city development. It includes land use planning, planning for urban infrastructure, planning for allocation of resources, budgeting for various city development activities, participation in city development and all other need-based activities necessary for the development of urban areas and cities and to raise the quality of life of city dwellers. Let us give a few definitions of urban planning gathered from various sources.

Urban planning is a technical and political process concerned with the development and use of land, protection and use of the environment, public welfare and the design of the urban environment, including air, water and the infrastructure passing in and out of urban areas, such as transportation, communications and distribution networks.[3]

Urban planning is the process that seeks to control the development of cities through local regulations and direct interventions to fulfil a number of objectives, such as mobility, quality of life and sustainability.[4]

Urban planning is a large-scale concept concerned with planning and development at all levels such as architectural, infrastructural, ecological, economical and even political.[5]

Another comprehensive definition of urban planning is given as follows: urban planning is a term that encapsulates both science and art, which has strong relevance to several disciplines and brings them under a single umbrella. It encompasses almost all aspects of a city, whether it be physical, social or cultural. In response to urbanization, these aspects vary from the construction of children's playgrounds to highway or railroad infrastructures; from the construction of residential, industrial or commercial sites to governmental plants and buildings.[6]

Urban planning is defined as preparation of plans for partial or complete development of cities, with the current situation, as well as future scenarios in mind (Store Norske Leksikon, 2016). This is to ensure that land use, transportation, buildings, landscapes, open places, infrastructure, economic investments, jobs and businesses are included in plans for development of communities (Rydningen & Rolfsen, 2016).

To Alnsour (2014), the improved urban planning includes institutional change, improvement of the performance of human resources, a reassessment of the funding allocated to municipalities from the public budget, institutionalization of the relationship between citizens and municipalities, increasing the participation of people in the decision-making process, the development of PPP, the establishment of a centre for environmental research and reassessment of the current laws for urban planning.

Need and Importance of Urban Planning

The need for urban planning has arisen due to the following reasons:

1. At the outset, as urban areas are contributing a gigantic share of the GDP of a nation state, formulation of an appropriate and effective planning is necessary for faster urban development so that contribution of urban area to the national GDP is increased. It is remarked that the central goal of urban and economic development planning is to produce policies and programmes to promote economic growth and enhance the quality of life in the community in which people live and work (Nahavandi, 2013). Pro-growth urban planning has resulted in the systematic development of cities in China and enhancing their contribution to local economic growth rate. Zhu while studying about the urban planning and pro-growth strategies in China has rightly envisaged that pro-growth urban planning intends to be in favour of progressive new interests,

responsive to market changes and conducive to local growth in the context of rapid urbanization and economic transition.[7]

2. Urban planning is essential for the effective planning of land use in urban areas. According to a definition widely cited in the 1960s and 1970s, urban planning is 'the art and the science of ordering the use of land and the character and siting of buildings and communication routes so as to secure the maximum practicable degree of economy, convenience and beauty' (Keeble, 1969). The appropriate distribution of scanty land of cities for various purposes such as commercial complexes, residential complexes, recreation purposes and purposes of social services such as education, health and road are critical to city development and essential for ensuring a good quality of life to the urban people. The garden city, radiant city, city beautiful and so on are illustrious examples of visionary urban planning. Good spatial planning can minimize the urban land use footprints and increase the efficiency of service provision.
3. Urban planning will lead to better sectoral management of resources and activities. The sectoral need assessment during the process of urban planning can check the wastage of resources and appropriate allocation of resources to various sectors as per the need. The urban planning strategies would lead to coordination among various sectors and actors of development engaged in the development process of the cities. The concept of rur-urban and rural–urban continuum desires the proper coordination between the LSIs working in the rural and urban areas. One of the objectives of urban planning is the optimum and judicious allocation of resources and proper coordination among various sectors and actors of development.
4. Urban planning is needed for better urban management. The planning strategy must clearly delineate the management of various urban services, such as water supply, sanitation, health, education and waste management. The management of urban growth necessitates adequate supply of land and appropriate plans for its use and deployment of infrastructure. Urban management systems, therefore, need to include the ability to plan and adopt various available models that optimize transportation and the built environment, resources including energy and water, and other natural resources. For example, PPP in sustainable infrastructure development should be explored during the strategic planning phase in the key service development areas such as water supply, sewage treatment, SWM and public transport.
5. One of the important exigencies of urban planning is to improve urban governance. The decentralized local governance by entrusting more and more functions, functionaries and funds to the LSIs would enhance service delivery system at the grassroots level. Good governance encourages participatory development with involvement of people at the grassroots level. The introduction of decentralized, community-based and participatory approaches and processes for the design, development and implementation of urban programmes and projects increases the prospects for democracy, accountability and transparency, and promotes the development of local involvement and enablement.[8]
6. Urban planning is required for raising the standard of living of city dwellers and to offer them good quality of life. The planning process will identify the needs of the cities and slum development is one of the important activities for ensuring better living conditions to the slum dwellers in the cities. The decentralized planning process must initiate discussion with all the stakeholders, that is, resident associations, investors and the people at large and ask them how to improve their living and working conditions. The suggestions and feedback

given by them can be incorporated in the grassroots planning process. In a nutshell, the planning process must deal with the various dimensions which influence the quality of life such as physical, environmental, social, psychological, economic and political.

Types of Urban Planning

Different types of urban planning being used in the planning for urban and city development are as follows:

1. Urban strategic planning
2. Master plan
3. City development plan
4. Urban land use planning
5. Planning for city region
6. Participatory urban planning
7. Decentralized urban planning

Urban Strategic Planning

Also known as long-term planning, urban strategic planning helps the planners and the urban administrators to know the direction and movement of development of the cities and urban areas for a longer period. The cosmetic short-term planning is not the right approach to develop cities and city region holistically. The inclusive and strategic approach to planning puts primary emphasis on the dynamic character of the planning process, engagement of stakeholders and the importance of the development of action plans and securing financial outlays for the implementation of selected priority projects (Ludeking & Belpaire, 2007). The three issues which the strategic planning tries to answer are as follows.

1. *Where we are—The strategic situation:* This is done by doing (a) situation analysis and need assessment; (b) doing exercises on planning framework; (c) assessment of the capacities for investment and development; and (d) contemplating consolidated urban diagnosis.
2. *Where do we want to go? The strategic direction:* This pertains to (a) setting the vision of city and urban area development; (b) preparation of a mission for city and urban area development; and (c) setting the strategic priorities and direction of city developmental actions.
3. *How do we go? The strategic action:* This comprises (a) the action and tasks required; (b) implementation strategies; (c) financial allocation; (d) setting of time frame; (e) monitoring and evaluation; and (f) impact assessment.

In the UN-Habitat Conference Towards Defining the New Urban Agenda, seven orientation points have been envisaged[9]: (a) Orientation 1: consolidating the role of local authorities as the main contracting authority; (b) Orientation 2: making strategic urban planning part of a political and contextualized vision of the city; (c) Orientation 3: involving the territory's stakeholders by the use of democratic local urban governance; (d) Orientation 4: promoting an integrated approach; (e) Orientation 5: regulating land use for an urban development that is inclusive; (f) Orientation 6: development of information services of the city and territories; and (g) Orientation 7: building the capacities of local actions as pillars of strategic territorial planning. The differences between strategic and conventional planning are given in Exhibit 3.1.

Exhibit 3.1 Strategic Planning versus Conventional Planning

Strategic Planning	Conventional Planning
• Process and action-oriented	• Product oriented (the plan)
• Starts with consensus on issues	• Starts with power to enforce rules
• Proactive	• Reactive
• Focused and selective	• Comprehensive
• Places high value on intuition and judgement	• Places high value on quantitative analysis
• Addresses organizational values	• Values not considered
• Strengths and weaknesses are addressed	• Strengths and weaknesses not considered
• Interactive with shareholders	• Interaction limited to date
• Political awareness and involvement	• Administrative orientation
• Takes account of implementation capability	• Implementation capability is assumed
• Oriented to allocation of organizational resources	• Planning, resource mobilization, allocation separated
• Contingency planning included	• Excludes contingency planning
• Commitment to vision developed through interaction	• Vision (if included) is an idealized end-state
• Managers and implementers are the planners	• Planning specialists do planning as a staff function
• Implementation by empowerment	• Implementation by directive

Source: Retrieved from http://www.rrojasdatabank.info/ump/ump26p28-69.pdf (accessed on 25 June 2020).
Note: The table above distinguishes between the extreme forms of these planning approaches. In practice, many of the aspects are not completely mutually exclusive. For example, although process oriented, some 'products' may be included in strategic planning, and similarly, despite its product orientation, conventional planning may incorporate processes and actions.

Master Plan

The Third Five-Year Plan of India has defined the term 'master plan' as a statutory instrument for controlling, directing and promoting sound and rational development and redevelopment of an urban area with a view to achieving maximum economic, social and aesthetic benefits. Master plan is a tool and an exercise which aims to promote growth and regulates future development of the cities and urban areas for a perspective time span of 20–25 years. It is multidimensional and comprehensive in nature. The master plan exercise takes into consideration various multidimensional aspects such as social, demographic, spatial, financial, infrastructural, economic and environmental while preparing the long-term plan for the development of a city. The master plan document gives an account of the vision and mission of the city development plan (CDP). The master plan calls for systematic exercises, which take into consideration the existing situation and is also based on the future need assessment of the development of city. Besides, master plan also takes note of regional dimensions, which have a bearing on the development of different areas of the city. The JNNURM has envisaged that it is an instrument to work out land and infrastructure requirements for various urban and rural uses, and allocate land for various uses to result in harmonious and sustainable distribution of activities so that towns/cities are provided with a form and structure within which they can perform all their economic and social functions efficiently and effectively.[10]

Some of the salient features of the master plan are as follows:

1. It is a multi-stage and multidimensional exercise.
2. It is a long-term plan of 20–25 years.
3. It is a statutory instrument and is prepared with the help of professional planners and policymakers.
4. It takes regional aspects into consideration.
5. It is more comprehensive and integrated in nature.

It is pertinent to mention here that the master plan for Delhi was first prepared in the year 1962; the second master plan was prepared in the year 2001, and the third master plan of Delhi is due in the year 2021. However, ironically, all these master plans are silent on investments required and sources of funding. I. J. Ahluwalia in her paper 'Planning for Urban Development in India' has envisaged that the principal flaw of the master planning approach in India has been that it has not allowed the market forces to play a role in determining the scale and location of economic activity. Being restricted to physical planning of a city and its immediate periphery, master plans have not been able to pay attention to the challenges of metropolitan and regional planning.[11]

City Development Plan

CDP was emphasized in the JNNURM. The main aim of CDP is to create economically productive, efficient, equitable and responsive city. A CDP is both a perspective and a vision document for the future development of a city. Developing a vision for the city is central to the preparation of a CDP which in fact is a statement where the city wishes to go, within a given time frame, and is often expressed in terms of clear expectations (Meshram, 2006). It defines the potential of a city and reflects its unique attributes in terms of comparative and competitive advantages, values and preferences of a city's residents (Meshram, 2006). Some of the important features of CDP are: (a) physical resources, which are concerned with the availability of land, adequacy of land availability taking into consideration legal and statutory provisions and allocation of land for various uses and purposes, and gaps and finances required for land acquisition; (b) infrastructure development in which the development of economic, social and cultural infrastructure in terms of quantity and quality, and identification of gap between supply and demand of infrastructure for various services is taken care of; (c) city investment plan (CIP) which is an estimation of level of investment required for the implantation of CDP; (d) financial strategy, which includes financial help from the government, CSO and the people as a whole; and (e) institutional coordination, which is required between the central and state governments and with the ULBs and parastatal bodies. It also aims at coordination between the line departments. CDP does an in-depth analysis and review of the existing situation which covers the demographic, economic, financial, infrastructure, physical, environmental and institutional aspects before and during the plan preparation. The detailed aspects also cover urban governance, urban economy, slum development, urban heritage, open space, conservation and so on. Although there are no watertight differences between the master plan and CDP, it can be said that master plan is a generic plan related to urban development or development of an urban area, while CDP is specific to a city. Smart Cities Mission

Exhibit 3.2 Master Plan versus City Development Plan

MASTER PLAN	CITY DEVELOPMENT PLAN
• Comprehensive integration of all aspects	• More focused towards financing and project implementation
• Long-term perspective year of 20 years or more	• Perspective of five years
• Takes into account regional linkages	• Emphasizes city and internal growth
• Aims to promote growth, regulate present and future development of towns and cities, allocates land to various uses of land	• Main focus is to improve financial conditions of local bodies, ensure investment of funds to fulfil deficiencies in urban infrastructure
• Contributes to planned development both conceptually and operationally	• Contributes to development more operationally rather than being conceptual

Source: Retrieved from https://planningtank.com/planning-techniques/city-development-plan-cdp-comparison-master-plan (accessed on 25 June 2020).

in India is an illustrious example of CDP. The differences between master plan and city development plan are given in Exhibit 3.2.

Urban Land-use Planning

Land is an essential and important prerequisite for city development. Selection of appropriate land and location is sine qua non for sustainable and smart city development. After the selection of land, the next step is the land-use planning which is crucial for sustainable city development. According to Metternicht (2017), land-use planning is the systematic assessment of land and water potential, alternatives for land use and economic and social conditions, in order to select and adopt the best land use options. Its purpose is to select and put into practice those land uses that will best meet the needs of the people while safeguarding resources for the future. Further, another definition of land-use planning says that it is a public policy exercise that designates and regulates the use of land in order to improve a community's physical, economic and social efficiency and well-being. Land-use planning is based on the broad-based assessment of the current land uses, associated problems and the opportunity for better and effective use of land for city development. For this, several techniques such as zoning, land evaluation and land suitability analysis are used. Once the assessment of land is over, a scoping study taking into consideration the public opinion and social impacts needs to be carried out by using participatory planning tool. The basic objective of land-use planning is to ensure the efficient and effective use of land, which promotes smart city development and ensures better quality of life to city dwellers.

Some of the essential aspects needed to be taken into consideration during the land use planning are as follows:

1. The land-use planning approach needs to be flexible and adoptive.
2. It should be well structured and should be based on the demand, capacities, rules, institutional structures and ecosystem of the place.

3. It should be based on clear-cut objectives, vision, mission and strategies.
4. It should follow integrated and participatory approach and must encourage the multi-sectoral and multi-stakeholders' engagement.
5. It should take into consideration sociopolitical, economic and legal contexts.
6. It should plan for vertical integration of national, provincial and local plans.
7. It should take into consideration various resources such as physical, financial and material available at various levels for city development.
8. Land-use planning is a process and is largely implementation oriented.
9. It should take into consideration the trade-off between the agriculture, ecosystem, water and biodiversity.

The urban land-use planning takes into consideration the following pattern of land use in an urban area such as land for residential use, commercial use, industrial use, use for open space for park and recreation, garbage disposal sites, use for public social and economic development activities such as opening of schools, hospitals and other public sector offices such as banks, insurances and IT. It is rightly remarked that land use does not consider production only but also land functions such as protected areas, land recreation, road building, waste disposal sides and use of restricted areas such as buffer zones for exhaust gases, areas for regenerating groundwater and buffer zones for traffic noise pollution.[12]

Planning for City Region

Cities, particularly the bigger ones, or the metropolitan cities, largely comprise the main city and the peripheral areas, which are largely known as the city regions. The people in the city many a time prefer to dwell in the city region for several reasons such as availability of cheap rented accommodation, comparatively cheaper land price and lower housing price and better environment. Through transport system, such as buses and metro rails and other means, people of the city region frequently interact with the main city. It is often said that the cities are somehow or other dependent on their surrounding regions for their existence and growth. To Weber et al. (2016), the term 'city region' reflects associations of multiple municipalities and scales of government in which responsibility for urban development is distributed, both formally and informally. According to Vermeijden (2001), 'The "city region" [denotes] a spatial hierarchy of satellite towns surrounding a central core city, on which the satellite settlements would depend for both employment and services.' According to Scott et al. (2001), city regions are becoming increasingly central to modern life and all the more so because globalization has reactivated their significance as bases of all forms of productive acidity, no matter whether in manufacturing or services, in high-technology or low-technology sectors. According to them, there are now more than 300 city regions around the world with population greater than 1 million. The popularization and widespread use of the city region concept for policymaking has important implications for the design and implementation of development strategies (Rodriguez-Pose, 2008). It is argued that 'city regionalization' would improve service delivery for a range of functions relating to the promotion and management of sustainable economic change.[13] To Scott and Storper (2003), city regions are locomotives of the national economies within which they are situated, in that they are the sites of dense masses of interrelated economic activities that also typically have high levels of productivity by reason of their jointly generated agglomeration economies and their innovative potentials.

In a document titled 'A Framework for City-Region' published by the Office of the Deputy Prime Minister (London) in 2006, a few important functions of city regions have been mentioned, which are as follows:

1. City regions are the enlarged boundaries from core urban areas.
2. City regions have greater economic and cultural resonance than current administration regions and local authority districts.
3. The geography of city regions is fuzzy and varies depending on different functions.
4. City regions governance is decentralized on a comprehensive basis as part of a wider local government reform.[14]

City region is being termed as *urban agglomeration,* where the urban activities expand to its nearby areas. To Fang and Yu (2017), urban agglomeration is a highly developed spatial form of integrated cities. It occurs when the relationships among cities shift from mainly competition to both competition and cooperation. Cities are highly integrated within an urban agglomeration, which renders the agglomeration one of the most important carriers for global economic development. Other forms of city regions are the *peri-urban* areas. These areas are adjacent to the city and the feature of these areas is not homogeneous. The residents of the peri-urban areas belong to the high- and middle-income groups, and the other sections are industrial workers and migrant labourers who reside in cheap accommodations. The peri-urban areas in many cases demonstrate the features of both rural and urban areas and there is a constant change of land use, land market and land prices in these areas because of various reasons such as migration of people to the city and infrastructure development. The second category of city region is the *satellite town.* These towns are situated at a distance from the city and are well connected with the city with proper infrastructure and the people in the satellite towns commute to the main city through various means of transport. The third category is the *suburbs.* These are the areas very close to the city. The suburbs are integral part of the rural–urban fringe and are largely dominated by the migrant population from various parts of the provinces of the nation states. The fourth category of city region which is used in Delhi of India is the NCR. The cities adjoining the main city of Delhi such as Gurugram, Faridabad, Noida and Ghaziabad are collectively called the NCR of Delhi. The former two cities belong to Haryana, while the latter two belong to Uttar Pradesh. Both the state and the national government make necessary efforts to improve the infrastructure and other facilities in these areas to provide good quality of life to the people. The fifth category of the city region is the polycentric urban region. The *polycentric urban region* develops around urban areas when the economic activity of urban areas is found to be clustering in several centres of activity around it. Koolsterman and Mustered (2001) have remarked that polycentrism, basically denoting the existence of multiple centres in one area, seems to have become one of the defining characteristics of the urban landscape in advanced economies.

Participatory Urban Planning

The participatory approach is nowadays being considered as one of the effective methods of planning. It is rightly remarked that an inclusive city is defined as 'a place where everyone, regardless of wealth, gender, age, race, ethnicity or religion, is enabled to participate productively and positively in the opportunities cities have to offer' (UN-Habitat, 2002). The participation customarily means two types of participation: (a) stakeholders' participation and (b) citizens' participation in urban planning. There are several types of stakeholders, whose participation is considered vital to urban development, such as plan formulation, implementation, monitoring and evaluation. The stakeholders in urban planning are the government, the parastatals, the private and corporate sector and the LSIs. On the other hand, in case of citizen participation, the citizens are largely being consulted either directly or through their representatives during various stages of urban planning and development. Research has shown that planners and politicians think of participation as more important to ensure democratic processes and hearing of all parties in the society (Falleth & Hansen, 2011). In a broad sense, public participation can be defined as 'taking part in the processes of formulation, passage and implementation of public policies with actions aimed at influencing decisions made by public representatives' (Parry et al., 1992).

The participation of stakeholders is vital to the development of the smart city. PPP is one of the illustrious examples of stakeholder participation in urban development. The stakeholders' participation is sought by the government for a few important purposes such as (a) providing information to the stakeholders about CDP and strategies, and their possible role; (b) collecting input from the stakeholders; (c) negotiation with the stakeholders; and (d) supporting stakeholders' initiatives in city development. The stakeholders' participation can take various forms such as contribution in cash and kind; vision and mission formulation; development of CDP, infrastructure development and other developmental projects implementation; adoption of the city and creation of awareness.

On the other hand, community participation in urban development is one of the arduous tasks. However, successful community participation in urban planning is fundamental to sustainable urbanization. Many community participation methods can be used for encouraging community participation in urban planning, such as conducting consultative meetings, public meetings, community forums, focus group discussions and social surveys. The community participation can be resorted to various purposes of urban planning such as assessment of needs, collection of data, development of plans, formulation of strategies, implementation of plan, monitoring and evaluation of the plan. A framework of role of participation by activity as envisaged in one of the UN documents is given in Table 3.1.

Decentralized Urban Planning

Most of the countries in the world, both developed and developing, are promoting democratic decentralization in order to enable the grassroots level institution and effective participation of the people in the development planning process both in urban and rural areas. The simplest meaning of decentralization is the devolution of functions, functionaries and funds to the lower level democratic institution closer to the people. These institutions in India are Panchayati Raj Institutions (PRIs) in rural areas and LSIs in urban areas. The Local Government Declaration to the World Summit on Sustainable Development held in 2002 maintains that 'we live in an increasingly inter connected, interdependent world. The local government cannot afford to be insular and inward looking.' The democratic decentralization is premised on the assumption that local governments will be more responsible to the needs of the citizens and take their preferences into account in determining the services to be provided, the level of resources required

Table 3.1 Role of Participants by Activity

Planning Activities	Participants		
	Beneficiaries/ Citizen	**Planners/ Professionals**	**Public Officials/ Decision-makers**
Situation analysis (sector performance)	+	++	+
Identifying problems and their causes	++	++	+
Assessing community values	++	+	0
Determining goals and objectives	++	+	++
Needs assessment	++	+	0
Data collection	+	++	0
Design criteria and standards	+	++	+
Developing alternative plans	++	++	+
Choosing an alternative	++	+	++
Detailed plan preparation	0	++	+
Plan modification and approval	++	+	++
Project development	+	++	+
Prioritization	++	0	+
Implementation	+	++	++
Monitoring	0	++	+
Reviewing of plan	++	+	++

Source: So (1979).
Notes: ++ = Major role; + = Facilitating or supportive role; 0 = Marginal role.

and the optimal means of ensuring effective delivery (Robinson, 2007). Haque (1977) argued that the decentralization is a way of increasing the effectiveness of development programmes by making them more relevant and responsive to local needs and conditions, allowing greater flexibility in their implementation, thus making the state more participatory, more acceptable and more effective and efficient.

As per Table 3.2, in many countries, the LSIs are involved in the urban planning process. In India, the LSIs, that is, the Nagar Panchayats, Municipal Councils and the Municipal Corporations are engaged in the decentralized planning process. These institutions actively participate in the process of formulation of the district development plan (DDP). The DDP is an integration of rural area plan and urban area plan. Rural area plans are being prepared by various PRIs: (a) the village panchayat development plan is prepared by the village panchayats; (b) the block development plan is prepared by the block panchayat (intermediate panchayat), which congregates all the village panchayat development plans of the block; and (c) finally the DDP (rural) is prepared by the Zilla Parishad (district panchayat), which congregates plans of all village and block panchayats. On the other hand, urban area plans are prepared by the ULBs: (a) each ward in the Nagar Panchayats,

Table 3.2 Comparative Responsibilities of Local Governments in Selected Countries in the Region

Country	Planning	Basic Education	Basic Social Welfare	Basic Health Services	Water Supply	Electricity Supply	Public Transport	Business Development Support
Australia	Yes	No	No	No	Yes	No	Yes	Yes
China	Yes	Yes	Yes	Yes	Yes	Yes	No	Yes
India	Yes	Yes	No	Yes	Yes	No	Yes	Yes
Indonesia	Yes	Yes	Yes	Yes	Yes	No	Yes	Yes
Japan	Yes	Yes	Yes	Yes	Yes	No	Yes	Yes
Malaysia	Yes	No	No	No	Yes	No	Yes	Yes
New Zealand	Yes	No	No	No	Yes	No	Yes	Yes
Pakistan	Yes	Yes	Yes	Yes	Yes	No	Yes	Yes
The Philippines	Yes	No	Yes	Yes	Yes	No	No	Yes
Republic of Korea	Yes	Yes	Yes	Yes	Yes	No	Yes	Yes
Thailand	Yes	Yes	Yes	No	Yes	No	Yes	Yes
Vietnam	Yes	Yes	Yes	Yes	Yes	No	Yes	Yes

Source: UCLG (2008).

Municipal Council and Municipal Corporation prepares their development plan; (b) in the second stage, all these wards plans are congregated at each ULBs and are called the Nagar Panchayat Development Plan, the Municipal Council Development Plan and the Municipal Corporation Development Plan; (c) finally, all these plans of the ULBs are comprehended in the DDP along with the plans prepared by the PRIs. Finally, the DDP is approved by the District Development Committee (DDC) of each district.

Various steps for preparation of the DDP are as follows.

Step I: Each municipal ward needs to prepare its own municipal ward plan through filed survey and focus group discussions with the elected representatives of the municipal ward, opinion leaders and CSOs. Each municipal ward needs to prepare its own municipal ward and plan, and get it approved in the Ward Sabha. The ward plan is then sent to the ULBs be it Nagar Panchayat or Municipal Council or Municipal Corporation.

Step II: The line department functionaries of the ULBs conduct need assessment of their respective ULBs in the city. The holistic ULB plan is prepared by merging it with the municipal ward plan. This becomes the plan of either the Nagar Panchayat Plan or the Municipal Council Plan or the Municipal Corporation Plan. These are the draft plans of the respective ULBs.

Step III: These draft plans prepared by various ULBs are presented before the Nagar Panchayat Committee, the Municipal Council Committee and the Municipal Corporation Committee, respectively. The comments and suggestions of these committees are incorporated and the final plan is prepared. This becomes the Nagar Panchayat Development Plan, the Municipal Council Development Plan and the Municipal Corporation Development Plan.

Step IV: Finally, these development plans prepared by various ULBs existing within a district are merged and it becomes the district urban development plan.

Step V: Just like this, the rural development plans are also prepared by various PRIs. The district urban development plan and district rural development plan are merged together. This finally becomes the DDP.

Step VI: The DDP is placed before the DDC, which constitutes the representatives of both PRIs and ULBs for approval. The comments and suggestions of the DDC are incorporated and the final DDP after approval of the DDC is sent to the state government for approval and necessary action. The district plan strategy is given in Figure 3.1.

During the process of formulation of their own plan by various ULBs, these institutions need to collect data from various line departments such as education, health, public works, water and sanitation and so on, relating to existing situation and their needs. The gaps are identified and the physical target along with the activities and task mapping and financial allocation is prepared department wise. The district authorities in most of the cases in the preparation of decentralized development plan take the help of research organizations and the creditable NGOs and universities for the preparation of the DDP.

Some of the merits of decentralization planning are as follows: (a) it accommodates people's felt needs; (b) it is democratic in nature; (c) it bridges the gap between people and bureaucracy, and, as a result, government and the people come closer; and (d) it helps in the mobilization of local resources. Sighting the example of Kerala's decentralized planning, Jafar (2014) noted that it has been widely acknowledged that democratic governance is best promoted through the widest participation of the people in local democracy and decentralized planning. Though with

Figure 3.1 District Decentralized Plan Strategy

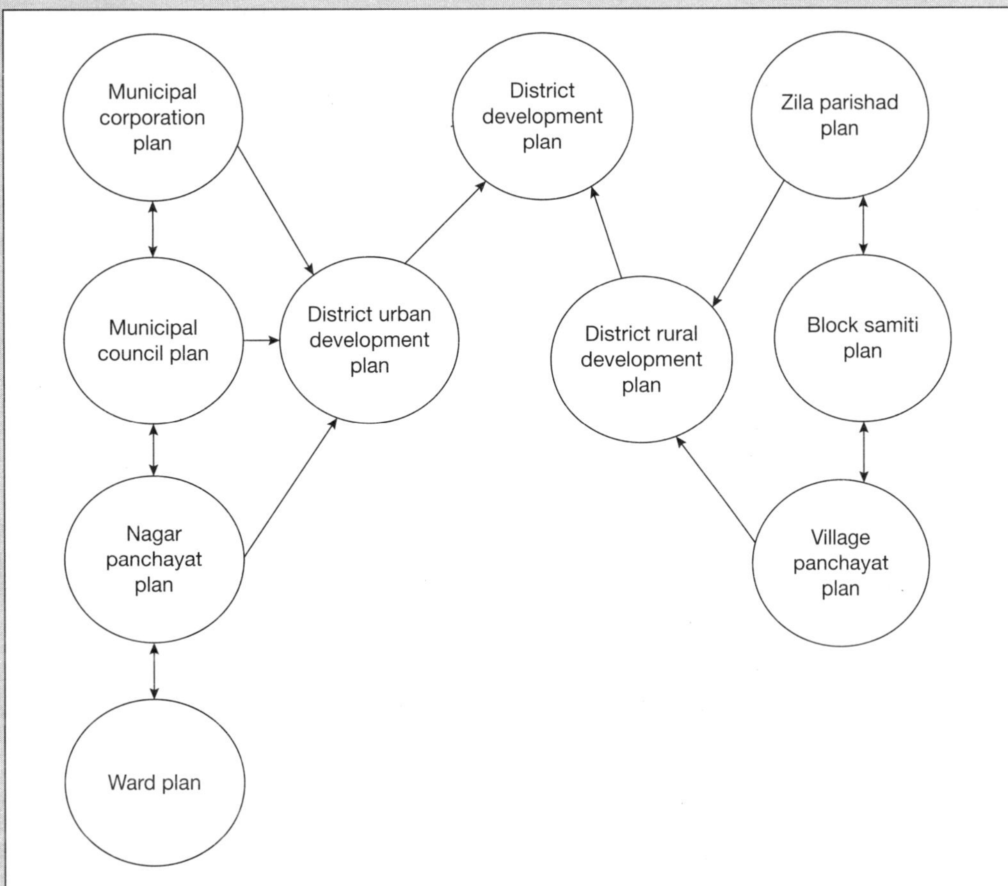

its own unique local context, Kerala's achievements in micro-level planning and democratic participation can be treated as a useful example to understand, plan and engage with local development process.

Techniques and Methods of Urban Planning

There are various techniques and methods of urban planning and a few important of them are narrated further.

1. *Survey research technique:* Survey is one of the popular and old methods of planning process. The organization involved in the urban planning process conducts urban need

assessment surveys and on the basis of these surveys prepares a documented plan to be implemented by the urban development authority. Conducting a survey involves various processes. At the outset, a survey project proposal is prepared. The project proposal comprises the following aspects: (a) objectives of the survey; (b) methods and tools of data collection; (c) data analysis; and (d) preparation of survey report. On the basis of survey report, the urban development authority prepares a detailed action plan and strategies for the implementation of action plan and puts it before the urban administration for approval. After approval, the plan is implemented.

2. *Demographic and socioeconomic analysis:* It is one of the important methods of urban planning. Population is fundamental to any planning process including urban planning. Schmitt (1952) had noted that population analysis is important to city planning because design standards are usually expressed in terms of population. He was of the opinion that almost everything the planner does is measured in relation to population—its size, distribution and composition. For example, the National Park Service suggested that one acre of play area should be allotted for a population of 1,500–2,500 beyond school age, and for each child enrolled in various schools the minimum recommended space is as follows: (a) elementary schools, 75 square feats; (b) junior high schools, 100 square feats; and (c) senior high schools, 200 square feats (mentioned in Menhinick, 1948).[15]

   The demographic data for analysis may comprise the variables such as population, family size, birth rate, death rate, fertility rate, age, sex, race, caste and class compositions. While the economic analysis could cover the variables such as family income, poverty, labour force participation, employment and so on, the social analysis may comprise the health status such as immunization rate, infant and maternal mortality rate, morbidity rate, education and literacy rate, gross enrolment ratio and level of education. For example, the beautiful city of Chandigarh was planned for a population of 5 lakh; now, the population in the city has increased more than three times causing a lot of challenges for the urban planners and policymakers of the city's government.

3. *Forecasting technique:* The forecasting methods are nowadays being used in the urban planning process. Customarily, forecasting means predicting the future or estimating for the future. The forecasting covers both qualitative and quantitative dimensions of estimation for future city development. It is remarked that the term 'forecasting' is often used for both quantitative predictions of future developments and for qualitative explorations of possible futures (Armstrong, 1985; Makridakis et al., 1998; Pourahmadi, 2001).
   a. *Qualitative methods of forecasting:* The qualitative method of forecasting is based on personal judgement. This method is used when there is little or non-availability of data on the historical facts in order to access the future predictability. Further, it is also used when the forecast is of long-time horizon. The two popular methods of qualitative approaches to forecasting are the Delphi method and scenario building method.
      i. *Delphi method:* This method was developed in 1950 by RAND Corporation, a US-based think tank. The Delphi method is based on the anonymous exchange of opinion through the structured questionnaire of the participants. It is said that the anonymous exchange of opinions is the most important characteristic of a Delphi approach, as in a group setting opinions can be influenced by many things, including the dominant positions of some participants, personal characteristics and 'alleged expertise' (Ike & Voogd, 2004). The procedure commonly adopted in the Delphi method is as follows: at the outset, the participants are selected and a set of

questionnaire is sent to them asking them to give their opinion which are essentially kept anonymous; then all the answers are tabulated with the help of computer; the results derived through analysis are sent to each participants interviewed with the request to review their earlier opinion and this process continues till a consensus or near-to-consensus solution is arrived at. The main aim of this method is to forecast the consensus solution to future possibilities.

ii. *Scenario building method:* Customarily, a 'scenario' is a description of the possible future, a course of events, which enables a system to move from its present situation to a future situation. The scenario approach to forecasting was propounded by Wiener and Kahn (1967) in their book published in 2000. The main aim of the scenario is to provoke thinking among the planners and the policymakers, who would prepare the necessary action plan for the fulfilment of the scenario.

b. *Quantitative method of forecasting:* The quantitative methods use numerical data for forecasting of the future. The basic objective of this method is to use the past available data and various statistical techniques and econometric models for the forecasting of the future. The two popular methods used in the forecasting are the time series methods and casual forecasting methods. The time series methods used in the forecasting are moving average, exponential smoothing and least square trend analysis. The casual forecasting methods are multiple regression analysis, econometric models and simulation models.

4. *Cost–benefit analysis:* The city planners and policymakers can formulate alternative plans and projects for the development of a city which will provide much benefit to the city development with minimum cost. The cost–benefit analysis is one of the ways to do so. According to Lichfied (2007), city planning proposals are made for the purpose of increasing the community's welfare in the evolution of cities. Ideally, the particular proposals made would be those likely to yield the largest attainable combination of net benefits, as compared with the costs of attaining them. A formula of cost–benefit analysis is given as follows:

$$BCR = \frac{\sum_{t=1}^{t=n} \frac{Bt}{(1+r_2)^t}}{\sum_{t=1}^{t=n} \frac{Ct}{(1+r_2)^t}}$$

5. *Decision analysis:* Modern planning theories encourage approaches that consider all stakeholders with a variety of discourse values to avoid political and manipulative decisions and therefore in the last decade, application of quantitative approaches such as multi-criteria decision-making techniques in urban planning procedures has increased (Afshari et al., 2016). The decision analysis is a systematic technique which helps to choose the better alternatives among the available alternatives. Its main aim is to overcome the limitations associated with the individual and group methods of decision-making. The decision-making technique of urban planning involves a multi-stage process, that is, clearly defining the objectives, selection of criteria to measure objectives, specifying alternatives, assessing weightage to the criteria and applying mathematical algorithm for ranking alternatives. The decision-making analysis technique is used in

various areas of urban planning such as urban land use planning, SWM and water management. Lotfi et al. (2009) have proved that multi-criteria decision analysis can provide an appropriate framework for solution of the complicated issues of urban spatial planning when it is integrated to GIS, such as urban land compatibility for urban development.

6. *GIS:* GIS is one the computerized systems, which integrates the data from various sources and helps the urban planners to make decisions effectively for urban planning. It serves as a database as well as a toolbox for urban planning and development. GIS is defined as a system for capturing, storing, checking, integrating, manipulating, analysing and displaying of data, which are spatially referenced to the earth. The GIS is being increasingly used in both developed and developing countries in the land use planning process of urban areas. The advantages of GIS are as follows: the data are maintained in both hardware and software form in the computer; large number of data can be stored and maintained and are used in the future for the decision-making purpose and both geographic and non-geographic information are also maintained in the computer. To UN-Habitat, with the increase in user-friendliness and functions of GIS software, and the marked decrease in the prices and increase in performance of GIS hardware, GIS is now an affordable, operational and effective spatial planning support system.[16] The hardware and software functions of a GIS include: (a) acquisition and verification, (b) compilation, (c) storage, (d) updating and changing, (e) management and exchange, (f) manipulation, (g) retrieval and presentation, and (h) analysis and combination.[17]

   The many benefits in using GIS in urban planning include the following (Royal Town Planning Institute 1992):

   a. *Improved mapping:* Better access to maps, improved map currency, more effective thematic mapping and reduced storage cost.
   b. Greater efficiency in retrieval of information.
   c. Faster and more extensive access to the types of geographical information important to planning and the ability to explore a wider range of 'what if' scenarios.
   d. Improved analysis.
   e. Better communication to the public and staff.
   f. Improved quality of services, for example, speedier access to information for planning application processing.

GIS is one of the formalized computer-based information systems capable of integrating data from various sources to provide the information necessary for effective decision-making in urban planning (Han & Kim, 1989). Other information systems for urban planning include database management system (DBMS), decision support system (DSS) and expert system.[18] DBMS is a technology solution mainly used for optimizing, managing the storage and retrieving data from databases. It is useful for providing a centralized view of data which can be accessed by multiple users, from multiple locations, in a controlled manner. A DSS is a computerized system that gathers and analyses data, synthesizing it to produce comprehensive information reports. It helps in informed decision-making, timely problem-solving and improved efficiency in planning and programme management. An expert system belongs to a field of artificial intelligence, and it is a computer program or software, which can do the same task of a human expert. It can give reliable advice in a specific area of expertise (its domain) and get new conclusions about difficult activities to examine.[19] The district planning process through GIS is given in Figure 3.2.

Figure 3.2 Planning Process through GIS

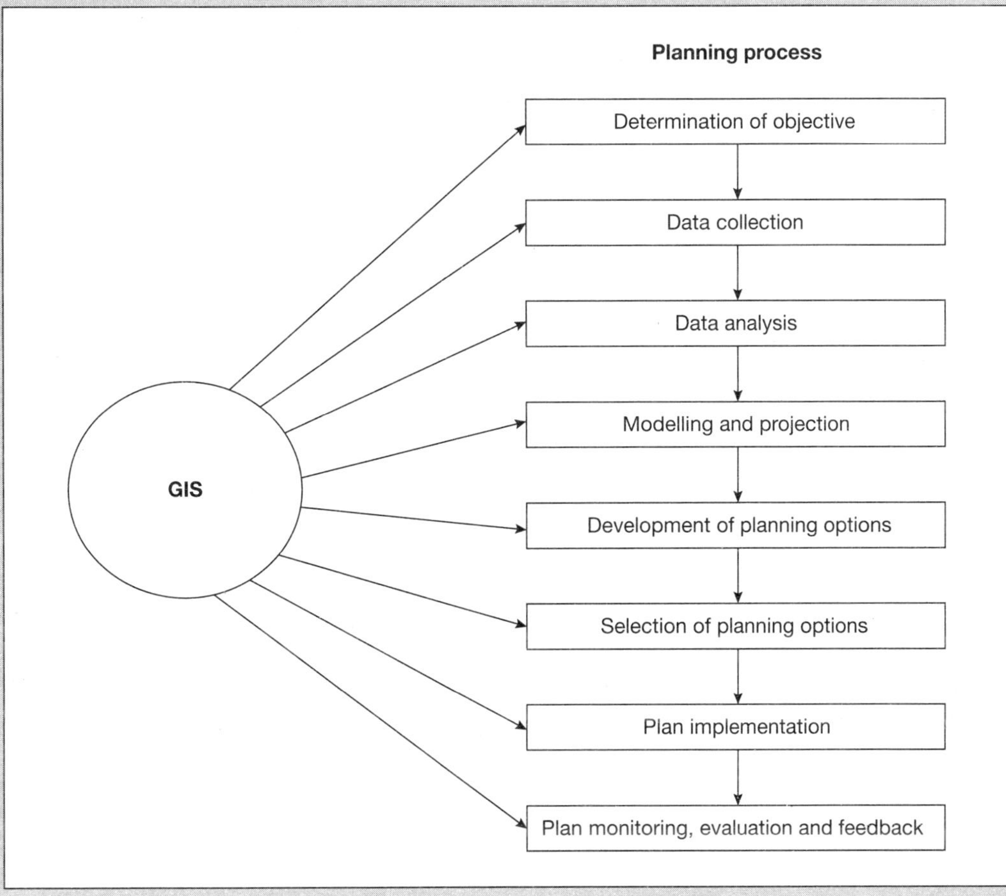

Systems Approach to Urban Planning Process

The urban planning process needs to adopt a system approach for the development of the smart cities and sustainable cities. Cooper et al. (1971) have envisaged that the systems approaches possess an ability of dealing with large numbers of interacting variables and relations. The various steps in the system approach to urban planning are as follows.

1. *Define and prioritize objectives:* At the outset, the urban planner has to formulate objectives of the urban development plan and priorities them according to their necessity and urgency. Formulation of *SMART* objective will enable the planners to complete the urban development plan and project effectively within the stipulated time frame.

   S—Simple. The statement must be very simple to understand which can also be implementable.

   M—Measurable. The stated objectives can be measured in quantitative or qualitative terms.

A—Attainable. The objectives must be attainable within the stipulated time period.

R—Realistic. The objectives should be realistic which can be put into operation without much difficulty.

T—Time-bound. The formulated objectives should be such that it can be achieved within the set time period of the development projects or programmes.

After the formulation of objectives, the planner has to prioritize them keeping in mind their exigencies and funds available for their implementation.

2. *Develop appropriate strategies consistent with objectives:* The second important task before the urban development planner is to formulate appropriate strategies consistent to the objectives. The strategies may vary in terms of their objectives. In this phase, the planner has to take into consideration the available resources and also to formulate various tasks and activities for the accomplishments of those tasks.
3. *Identify and quantify inputs:* Identification and quantification of inputs such as manpower, finance and physical inputs are critical to development planning and its implementation including the urban development planning. Proper layout of government funding, community funding, funding by the voluntary organizations and corporate sector and international agencies has to be plotted and quantified. For example, in case of land use planning, the identification and quantification will include to quantify the cost of developing new land, how much money the government is going to invest in acquiring new lands, how much will be borrowed and recovered, then how much land is to be acquired or used in order to develop the roads and other public assets such as parks, schools and hospitals; and finally how many government employees and consultants will have to be used to implement the strategy.
4. *Identify and quantify outputs:* The quantification of output is very vital to urban planning. The quantification may mean how much hectare of land is acquired, how many kilometres of road is prepared, number of public institutions established and so on. Without quantification of output, the plan document will be weak and may invite criticism from various corners.
5. *Implement the project for urban development:* The plan document must systematically delineate the implementation process with the timeline and Gantt chart. It will help the urban authorities to implement the urban plan objectives with the time frame as suggested.
6. *Monitor the process of implementation and outputs:* Monitoring the progress and keeping eye on the output is very vital to the success of the project. For example, monthly and quarterly monitoring of the progress on various front and taking appropriate measures in case of delay in the deliverables is an essential requirement of the plan documents.
7. *Evaluate output and outcome:* The planning process must clearly reveal the evaluation strategies. The assessment of the impact of the project on the end users or the beneficiaries is important. The plan document must provide the variables and indicators to be affected due to the project implementation and the expansion of urbanization.
8. *Identify the gaps if any and initiate measures to overcome them:* The last but not the least step of systems approach to urban planning is the gap identification and measures for the eradication of gaps. The plan process involves a lot of stakeholders and actors, and it also has to take into consideration a host of variables and indicators. The lapses and gap may occur inadvertently or due to laxity in effective implementation. Therefore, the planners have to design accordingly for the probable gaps which might occur during various stages leading to poor outcome. The mechanisms of gap eradication and corrective measures have to be formulated.

Challenges of Urban Planning

Some of the important challenges of the urban planning are narrated as follows.

1. *Urban complexities:* Urban development is a more complex affair as compared to rural areas. The economic, social and infrastructural requirements of urban areas are more and diverse as compared to rural areas. Moreover, in urban areas, people from all sections of the society in respect of religion, caste and class reside there. It is remarked that the planners, operating in the complex environment comprised of many interconnected elements, are constrained by lack of certainty as to the future consequences of planning actions (Myers, 2001). Thus, the planning process in urban areas is more complex one and has to be meticulously formulated taking into various development variables into considerations.
2. *Change is more uncertain:* Urban areas are being concurrently affected and influenced by the globalization and development happening in urban areas around the world. According to the Organisation for Economic Co-operation and Development (OECD), the contemporary cities continuously undergo rapid, profound and unpredictable changes (OECD, 1994). Often traditional planning techniques developed 'in a lineal and incremental world do not have the flexibility needed to address multi-faceted and rapidly paced change' (Ratcliffe, 2002, p. 9).
3. *Inaccuracy in urban projections:* Projections many a time give misleading outcome, which creates suspicion in the minds of the general public and intelligentsia on the intention of the planners. Forecasters have been often criticized for failing to present the assumptions on which forecasts have been developed, and for stating the results of forecasts without presenting alternatives arising from the changes of the input variables (Wachs, 2001). Planners have also been blamed for using projections as if they described the most probable future and as if this future was desired (Isserman, 1985).
4. *Urban planning many a time exclusively focuses on spatial planning:* In many countries, particularly developing countries, urban planning largely focuses on the spatial dimensions of urban development. However, the other dimensions such as social and cultural, and urban paradox dimensions such as urban crime, law and order, and so on, also need attention in the urban planning. It is remarked that for many years urban planning has been mainly focused on shaping the physical form of cities and the provision of necessary services (Krawczyk & Ratcliffe, 2005). Myers and Kitsuse (2000) argue that a strong focus on spatial analysis has often led to the neglect of the future aspect.
5. *Lack of integrated and holistic approach:* The urban system is very vast and the urban development activities spread across various sectors and engage various actors in the development and management process. The single and little sector plan focus will not fulfil the holistic development needs of the cities. It is rightly remarked that consideration of different urban elements separately often leads to neglecting important connections and interdependencies between them which results in ineffective policies and decisions (Ratcliffe, 2002). Plans developed in one sector rarely relate to the wider spatial impacts of activities and policies, and usually apply only a single sectoral perspective (Koresawa & Konvitz, 2001).
6. *Lack of effective participation and collaboration between stakeholders:* Decisions about the future involve gaining agreement among a great number of stakeholders, many of whom vary in their valuations of key factors and hold different, often emotionally based views (Myers, 2001). The urban development process needs to involve several stakeholders in the

process of urban development. Besides the government, LSIs, corporate sectors, non-governmental organizations (NGOs), CSOs and so on are a few important actors which are nowadays playing an important role in urban development. The planning process in many nation states hardly records and envisages the role of various actors involved in the process of urban development and their contribution in various forms. There is a need to build 'convergence of values and meanings that go beyond the specialized knowledge of a few experts in order to investigate the diversity of experience, attitudes and values' of different groups and communities (Puglisi, 2000).

7. *Lack of clear vision and mission of urban development:* As the urban development is a more complex one in terms of its dimensions and spread, any plan document prepared for the development of urban areas and the cities must have clear-cut vision and mission. All the activities and actions have to be undertaken based on the vision and mission. However, many authors have pointed out the lack of visionary approach towards the future (Brooks, 1988; Isserman, 1985; Myers & Kitsuse, 2000; Ratcliffe, 2002). Isserman (1985) argued that too often planning 'has lost sight of the future' and it lacks a vision that would lead the present to the future.

Suggestions for Better Urban Planning

Some of the suggestions for the improvement in the urban planning are as follows:

1. One of the important steps to be taken for the balanced development of the cities is the identification of key issues and problems of urban areas on the short-term and long-term basis based on the characteristic of the present situation. The issues and challenges vary from one city to another. Further, the issues of the metropolitan cities are different from those of smaller cities such as municipalities and Nagar Panchayats. This involves collecting a whole range of factual and statistical information as well as knowledge on community perceptions, memories, values, wishes, fears and so on.
2. Exploration of the past and present plan, decisions, policies and factors that have led to the development of the present situation. These should be considered at the local, regional and national levels. It is appropriate that the decentralized planning process at all levels such as Nagar Panchayats, municipalities and Municipal Corporations are prepared and need-based revisions be made from time to time based on the need assessment survey at each level.
3. Need-based and appropriate planning technique must be used in the urban planning process. It must vary from one city to another. The planning technique for the city region will vary from those of CDP. According to A. W. Drescher, for developing countries, a more appropriate and dynamic planning tool is structural planning. This provides a broad framework for local decision-making, thereby encouraging public participation. This method is more indicative than a master plan, in that it requires not only projections of the future demands and needs of a community, such as housing, infrastructure, employment, transport and local markets but also environmental aspects like waste management.[20]
4. It is must recognize the main actors and stakeholders in urban planning. In the neoliberalized world, corporate sectors have been emerged as important stakeholders of

Table 3.3 Log Frame of Development Planning: Deficiency Analysis and Need Assessment

Components	Desired Level	Existing Level	Gap	Needs
Pukka houses	Ensuring pukka houses to all	Number of households having pukka houses at present	Desired level—existing level	1. Number of pukka houses to be constructed 2. Number of beneficiaries to be covered 3. Total amount of money required
Piped drinking water	Ensuring piped drinking water to all	Number of households having piped drinking water at present	Desired level—existing level	1. Number of houses to get piped water connection 2. Number of community water point to be installed 3. Total amount of money required
Sanitary toilets	Ensuring sanitary latrine to all households	Number of households at present having toilets	Desired level—existing level	1. Number of houses to get sanitary toilet 2. Number of community toilets to be constructed 3. Total amount of money required
Solid and liquid waste management	Ensuring sewerage system and safe garbage disposal to all households	Number of households at present having sewerage facility	Desired level—existing level	1. Number of households to get sewerage facility 2. Number of dustbins to be provided at the ward and cluster level 3. Amount of money required
LPG connection	Ensuring LPG connection to all households	Number of households at present having LPG connections	Desired level—existing level	1. Number of households to get LPG connection 2. Amount of money required
Ward-level street light	Ensuring street light in all roads at the municipality and municipal ward level	Number of streets at present having street light facility	Desired level—existing level	1. Number of streets to get street light 2. Amount of money required
Ward-level street roads	Ensuring street roads at the municipality and municipal ward level	Number of streets at present having street road	Desired level—existing level	1. Number of streets to get street road 2. Amount of money required
Ward-level health clinic	Ensuring health clinics at the municipality and municipal ward level	Number of municipal wards at present having health or mohalla clinic	Desired level—existing level	1. Number of municipal wards to get mohalla clinic 2. Amount of money required

(Table 3.3 Continued)

(Table 3.3 Continued)

Components	Desired Level	Existing Level	Gap	Needs
Ward-level pre-primary and primary schools	Ensuring pre-primary and primary education to all children	Number of Anganwadi centres established as per population and number of primary schools opened	Desired level—existing level	1. Number of Anganwadi centres and primary schools required 2. Amount of money required
Skill and vocational education, development training linked to economic activities	Ensuring skill education to youth and women at the municipality level	Number of youth and women at municipality level need skill training	Desired level—existing level	1. Number of youth and women need skill and vocational training 2. Number of skill and vocational training centres need to be established 3. Amount of money required
Providing self-employment	Ensuring self-employment to the working-age group population, who are unemployed or seeking employment	Number of working group population provided with institutional financial support to start self-employment activities.	Desired level—existing level	1. Number of unemployed and people seeking employment requiring institutional financial support to start self-employment activities 2. Amount of bank loan required to provide self-employment to the unemployed seeking self-employment opportunities
Maintenance of heritage, water bodies and open space	Ensuring financial and manpower support for the maintenance to the heritages, water bodies and open spaces existing at the municipality and municipal ward level	Number of heritages, water bodies and open spaces existing at the municipality and municipal wards levels are properly maintained	Desired level—existing level	1. Number of heritages, water bodies and open spaces require maintenance and upgradation facility 2. Amount of money required for the purpose

urban development not only in developed countries but also in the developing countries. The PPP model needs to be implemented for city development. The corporate sector has to be encouraged to participate in the adoption of cities. At the same time, the role of LSIs and CSOs such as Resident Welfare Association (RWA) is recognized. They should be effectively participated and engaged in the plan formulation and implementation process. To Krause (2014), the benefits of participation in planning processes are as follows:

a. It makes the decision-making processes more transparent.
b. It raises mutual understanding between citizens and administration.
c. It considers ideas, concerns and everyday knowledge.
d. It improves the knowledge basis.
e. It has a positive influence on planning processes as it increases acceptability.

5. Improved information system and technology can be used for information gathering and city development. The GIS is one of such examples. The citizen service centre is needed to be established for collection of fee and user charges and taxes and grievance redressals. More use of technology in urban planning and plan implementation process is sine qua non for smart city projects. All these service delivery mechanisms are to be a part of the broader city plan development. Ana Virtudes and Joao Sa have noted that with the use of ICT, urban planning authorities are more likely to be aware of the city features in their multiple aspects, being able to define and monitor the public policies, suitable to each situation, reinforcing the democracy and transparency of local governance.[21]
6. There should be integrated district planning for the development of the municipal and village areas of the city. For this, there should be effective coordination between the village panchayats and the municipalities for the effective development of the villages existing within the city areas. The Manual for Integrated District Planning by the Planning Commission, Government of India, has envisaged that participative district planning is multidimensional, and therefore calls for following a clearly organized sequence of steps to arrive at a meaningful plan. The participative district planning design process, led by local governments, needs to take numerous factors into account, the foremost being the duality that exists between the constitutional and legal aspects of the framework that governs rural and urban local governments. The next most important feature consists of the several levels within the local government structure; the three levels of panchayats in rural areas and the wards that exist and Area Sabhas that are envisaged under each municipality. Then comes the multiplicity of development sectors to be addressed (health, education, nutrition, sanitation, livelihoods and so on), a variety of funding sources (central, state, centrally sponsored, local and so on), an intertwined group of departmental and programmatic machinery and a broad spectrum of stakeholders, each seeking fulfilment of their own expectations (which may sometimes conflict with each other) from a district plan.[22]
7. The plan document and the detailed project report of the city development must include the vision and mission. The sectoral development and action plan can be an integrated aspect of city development. The aspect to deal with urban paradoxes such as poverty, underemployment, inequality, crime, law and order situation, slums and so on is to be the focal point along with the urban infrastructure development. The Global Platform for Sustainable Cities has rightly envisaged that planning for the short-term, medium-term and

long-term, with an integrated, multi-sectoral approach is essential when intervening in the urban system. Doing so is efficient and can ensure the co-creation of plans and result in cross-sectoral co-benefits.[23]

8. *Formulation of a multidisciplinary team for architecting plan document:* The Ministry of Urban Development (MoUD) at the central and state levels should formulate a multidisciplinary team for the formulation and documentation of an urban plan. The team should consist of engineers, architects, town planners, economists, geographers, demographers, sociologists, statisticians, management expert, legal experts, cost accountant and so on. The Urban Regional Development Plans Formulation and Implementation Guidelines 2014, MoUD, has rightly noted that planning for development is an envisioning process which requires a sound assessment of the ground realities and providing options for sustainable development within the bounds of the demographic, physical, socioeconomic, jurisdiction and financial aspects.[24]

Urban planning is one of the key components of urban development studies. One of the economists of World Bank has rightly remarked that the well-planned cities allow the socioeconomic benefits of urbanization to be fully harnessed and can create vibrant, liveable, urban spaces. However, it will be a long-term process and will require a strong commitment from government, citizens and the private sector.[25]

Summing Up

Urban planning is one of the vital branches of the tree of urban development. The effective urban development and smart cities can only be thought of if there is strong and systematic urban planning. Systematic planning leads to effective utilization of resources allotted for the development of urban areas and the cities. There are various types of urban planning and also different techniques used for urban planning. The urban planner has to judiciously choose as per the need of the development of urban areas. However, urban planning is a continuous process and the nation states need to adopt appropriate urban planning techniques at different points of time and for the exigencies of the development of various categories of cities. It is also commented that an important challenge for urban planning is of capacity both at the local government level to envision and prepare a CDP, a master plan and a financial plan, and at the level of the state government to provide legislative and administrative support and an enabling environment for facilitating the process of planning at local and regional level.[26] There are limitations in the process of urban planning; however, those limitations could be overcome by taking appropriate policy measures.

Keywords

Rural–Urban Continuum, Strategic Planning, Master Plan, Sustainable Urban Development Planning, Urban Land Use Planning, Urban Agglomeration, Satellite Town, Suburbs, NCR, Cost–Benefit Analysis, Decision Analysis, GIS

REVIEW QUESTIONS

1. What is urban planning? Why is there a need for urban planning? Explain.
2. Explain four different types of urban planning.
3. Urban land use planning is essential for systematic development of urban areas. Illustrate.
4. Explain three different techniques of urban planning.
5. What is GIS? Describe the need and benefits of GIS in city planning.
6. Planning for city region is vital to smart city development. Illustrate.
7. Describe in detail system approach to urban planning.
8. What are the limitations of urban planning? Explain how these limitations can be overcome.
9. Write short notes on the following:
   a. Urban land use planning
   b. Planning for city region
   c. GIS
   d. Satellite town
   e. NCR
   f. Qualitative method of forecasting
   g. Cost–benefit analysis
   h. Decision analysis
   i. Master plan for city development
   j. System approach to urban planning

Notes

1. http://unpei.org/sites/default/files/e_library_documents/Guide%20for%20the%20creation%20of%20Municipal%20Territorial%20Development%20Plans%20with%20an%20ecosystems%20approach.pdf (accessed on 9 September 2018).
2. https://unhabitat.org/urban-planning-important-for-development-and-inequality-reduction-dr-clos-tells-minurvi/ (accessed on 10 August 2018).
3. https://www.quora.com/What-is-the-definition-of-urban-planning (accessed on 19 March 2019).
4. http://kwhs.wharton.upenn.edu/term/urban-planning/ (accessed on 19 March 2019).
5. http://www.eltis.org/participate/forum/urban-planning-definition-problems-and-solutions (accessed on 19 March 2019).
6. http://www.ilkercolak.com.tr/main-characteristics-of-urban-planning-and-its-effects-on-fundamental-rights-and-freedoms-%E2%80%93with-special-reference-to-turkish-law/ (accessed on 19 March 2019).
7. http://siteresources.worldbank.org/INTURBANDEVELOPMENT/Resources/336387-1269364687916/6892589-1269394475210/zhu.pdf (accessed on 11 September 2018).
8. http://www.rrojasdatabank.info/ump/ump26p28-69.pdf (accessed on 12 September 2018).
9. https://www.pfvt.fr/fr/docman/doc-download/125 (accessed on 24 November 2019).
10. http://www.itpi.org.in/pdfs/07_01.pdf (accessed on 17 September 2018).
11. http://icrier.org/Urbanisation/pdf/Ahluwalia_Planning_for_Urban_%20Development.pdf (accessed on 22 March 2019).

12. https://www.mpl.ird.fr/crea/taller-colombia/FAO/AGLL/pdfdocs/gtz-lup.pdf (accessed on 18 September 2018).
13. http://webarchive.nationalarchives.gov.uk/20070507024923/http://www.communities.gov.uk/pub/588/AFrameworkforCityRegionsResearchReportPDF814Kb_id1163588.pdf (accessed on 19 September 2018).
14. http://webarchive.nationalarchives.gov.uk/20070507024923/http://www.communities.gov.uk/pub/588/AFrameworkforCityRegionsResearchReportPDF814Kb_id1163588.pdf (accessed on 19 March 2020).
15. https://www.jstor.org/stable/2571595?seq=1#metadata_info_tab_contents (accessed on 24 September 2018).
16. http://mirror.unhabitat.org/downloads/docs/gis.pdf (accessed on 8 October 2018).
17. http://shodhganga.inflibnet.ac.in/bitstream/10603/108205/12/12_chapter%204.pdf (accessed on 10 October 2018).
18. https://www.geos.ed.ac.uk/~gisteac/gis_book_abridged/files/ch62.pdf (accessed on 30 October 2019).
19. https://www.intechopen.com/books/enhanced-expert-systems/introductory-chapter-enhanced-expert-system-a-long-life-solution (accessed on 5 November 2019).
20. https://www.ruaf.org/sites/default/files/Discussionpaper%203%20Tools%20for%20integrating%20UPA%20in%20urban%20land%20use%20planning_1.pdf (accessed on 31 October 2019).
21. https://iopscience.iop.org/article/10.1088/1757-899X/245/5/052086/pdf (accessed on 31 October 2019).
22. http://planningcommission.nic.in/reports/genrep/mlp_idpe.pdf (accessed on 31 October 2016).
23. https://www.thegef.org/sites/default/files/events/GPSC%20COP24%20Session%20Concept%20Draft_10.12.18_link%202.pdf (accessed on 31 October 2019).
24. http://www.naredco.in/notification/pdfs/Volume-I%20Main%20URDPFI%20Guidelines%202014a.pdf (accessed on 31 October 2019).
25. https://www.worldbank.org/en/news/press-release/2017/12/20/urban-planning-can-improve-quality-of-life-and-opportunities-in-phnom-penh (accessed on 10 October 2018).
26. http://icrier.org/Urbanisation/pdf/Ahluwalia_Planning_for_Urban_%20Development.pdf (accessed on 22 March 2019).

References

Afshari, A. R., Vatanparast, M., & Cockale, D. (2016). Application of multi-criteria decision making to urban planning—A review. *Journal of Engineering Management and Competitiveness, 6*(1), 46–53.

Ahmadi, F., & Toghyani, S. (2011). The role of urban planning in achieving sustainable urban development. *International Journal of Sustainable Development, 20*(11), 23–26.

Alnsour, J. (2014). The effectiveness of urban management in Jordanian municipalities. *The Sustainable City*, 1, 271–282. https://www.witpress.com/Secure/elibrary/papers/SC14/SC14023FU1.pdf (accessed on 23 April 2019).

Armstrong, J. S. (1985). *Long range forecasting: From crystal ball to computer*. New York: Wiley.

Brooks, M. (1988). Four critical junctures in the history of the urban planning profession: An exercise in hindsight. *APA Journal, 54*(2), 241–248.

Cole, G. A. (1993). *Management: Theory and practice* (2nd ed.). London: DP Publications.

Cooper, W., Eastman, C., Johnson, N., & Kortanek, K. (1971). Systems approaches to urban planning: Mixed, conditional, adaptive and other alternatives. *Policy Science, 2*(4), 397–405.

Duhl, L. J., & Sanches, A. K. (1999). *Healthy cities and the city planning process: A background document on links between health and urban planning*. Copenhagen: WHO Regional Office of Europe. http://www.euro.who.int/__data/assets/pdf_file/0009/101610/E67843.pdf (accessed on 15 April 2019).

Falleth, E. I., & Hansen, G. S. (2011). Participation in planning: A study of urban development in Norway. *European Journal of Spatial Development*. https://snl.no/byplanlegging (accessed on 19 March 2019).

Fang, C., & Yu, D. (2017). Urban agglomeration: An evolving concept of an emerging phenomenon. *Landscape and Urban Planning, 162*, 126–136.

Han, S. Y., & Kim, T. J. (1989). Can expert systems help with planning? *Journal of the American Planning Association, 55*(3), 296–308.

Haque, S. (1977). Local governance in developing nations: Re-examining the question of accountability'. *Regional Development Dialogue, 18*(2), 4–23.

Ike, P., & Voogd, H. (2004). Forecasting in planning. In H. Voogd & G. Linden (Eds.), *Environmental and infrastructure planning* (157–180). Groningen: Geo Press.

Ivancevich, J. M., Lorenzi, P., Skinner, S. J., & Crosby, P. B. (1994). *Management quality and competitiveness.* Illinois: lrwin.

Isserman, A. (1985). Dare to plan: An essay on the role of the future in planning practice and education. *Town Planning Review, 56*(4), 483–491.

Jafar, K. (2014). *A note on Decentralised Planning Initiative: Possible lessons from the Kerala experience.* Hyderabad: Council for Social Development. https://mpra.ub.uni-muenchen.de/65710/9/MPRA_paper_65710.pdf (accessed on 20 October 2019).

Keeble, L. (1969). *Principles and practice of town and country planning.* London: Estates Gazette.

Koolsterman, R. C., & Mustered, S. (2001). The polycentric urban region: Towards a research agenda. *Urban Studies, 38*(4), 623–633.

Koresawa, A., & Konvitz, J. (2001). *Towards a new role for spatial planning.* Paris: OECD.

Krause, J. (2014). Partizipation und Beteiligung bei kommunalen Verkehrsprojekten. In J. Gies & M. Hertel (Eds.), *Beteiligungsprozesse – unterschätztes Potenzial in der Verkehrsplanung* (pp. 33–48). Dokumentation der Fachtagung "kommunal mobil" am 26/27 September 2013 in DessauRoßlau, Berlin, Germany: Deutsches Institut für Urbanistik gGmbh. file:///C:/Users/ignou/Downloads/citizen-and-stakeholder-involvement-a-precondition-for-sustainable-urban-mobility.pdf (accessed on 31 October 2019).

Krawczyk, E., & Ratliffe, J. (2005). *Imagine ahead, plan backwards: Perspective methodology in urban and regional planning.* Dublin: Dublin Institute of Technology. https://arrow.dit.ie/cgi/viewcontent.cgi?referer=https://www.google.co.in/&httpsredir=1&article=1003&context=futuresacart (accessed on 10 September 2018).

Lichfied, N. (2007). Cost benefit analysis of city planning. *Journal of American Institute of Planners*, 273–279. https://www.tandfonline.com/doi/abs/10.1080/01944366008978426 (accessed on 14 April 2020).

Lotfi, S., Habibi, K., & Koohsari, M. J. (2009). An analysis of urban land development using multi-criteria decision model and GIS (A case study of Babolsar city). *American Journal of Environmental Sciences, 5*(1), 87–93.

Ludeking, G., & Belpaire, E. (2007). Preface. In An introduction to urban strategic planning (Vol. 1), *Inclusive and sustainable urban planning: A guide for municipalities.* Nairobi: UN-Habitat.

Makridakis, S., Wheelwright, S. C., & Hyndman, R. J. (1998). *Forecasting: Methods and applications* (3rd ed.). New York; London: Wiley.

Metternicht, G. (2017). *Global land outlook working paper: Land use planning.* United Nations Convention to Combat Desertification. https://www.oecd-ilibrary.org/sites/208beaaa-en/index.html?itemId=/content/component/208beaaa-en (accessed on 14 April 2020).

Menhinick, H. K. (Ed.). 1948. *Local planning administration* (2nd ed.). Chicago: International City Managers' Association.

Meshram, D. S. (2006). Interface between city development plans and master plans. *ITPI Journal, 3*(2), 1–9. http://www.itpi.org.in/pdfs/07_01.pdf (accessed on 17 October 2019).

Myers, D. (2001). Symposium: Putting the future in planning. *Journal of the American Planning Association, 67*(4), 365–367.

Myers, D., & Kitsuse, A. (2000). Constructing the future in planning: A survey of theories and tools. *Journal of Planning Education and Research, 19*(3), 221–231.

Nahavandi, A. (2013). *Urban planners, economic development planners and economic growth.* Austin, TX: The University of Texas at Austin. https://repositories.lib.utexas.edu/bitstream/handle/2152/24320/NAHAVANDI-MASTERSREPORT–2013.pdf?sequence=1&isAllowed=y (accessed on 11 September 2018).

OECD. (1994). *Cities for the 21st century*. Paris: OECD.

Parry, G., Moyser, G., & Day, N. (1992). *Political participation and democracy in Britain*. Cambridge: Cambridge University Press.

Pourahmadi, M. (2001). *Foundations of time series analysis and prediction theory*. New York; London: Wiley.

Puglisi, M. (2000). *Futures studies and the challenges of participatory urban planning: The use of interactive scenarios in Barletta*. Paper presented at the seminar 'The Quest for the Futures', Turku School of Economics and Business Administration, Turku, Finland, 13–15 June.

Ratcliffe, J. (2002). *Imagineering cities: creating future 'prospectives' for present planning*. Conference paper presented at Turkish Real Estate Seminar III, Istanbul, 2–4 May.

Robinson, M. (2007). Introduction: Decentralizing service delivery? Evidence and Policy Implications. *IDS Bulletin*, *38*(1), 1–7.

Rodriguez-Pose, A. (2008). The rise of the 'city region' concept and its development policy implications. *European Planning Studies*, *16*(8), 1025–1046.

Royal Town Planning Institute. (1992). *Geographic information systems: A planner's introductory guide prepared by the Institute's GIS Panel*. London: The Royal Town Planning Institute.

Rydningen, U., & Rolfsen, C. N. (2016). *Making education on sustainable community planning tangible*. http://www.witpress.com/elibrary/wittransactions-on-ecology-and-theenvironment/204/35706 (accessed on 19 March 2019).

Scott, A. J., & Storper, M. (2003). Regions, globalization, development. *Regional Studies*, *37*(6–7), 579–593.

Scott, A. J., & Storper, M. (2014). The nature of cities: The scope and limits of urban theory. *International Journal of Urban and Regional Research*. https://luskin.ucla.edu/sites/default/files/ScottStorperpubliblished.pdf (accessed on 17 October 2019).

Scott, A. J., Agnew, J., Soja, E. W., & Storper, M. (2001). Global city regions. In A. J. Scott (Ed.), *Global city regions: Trends, theory, policy* (pp. 11–30). Oxford: Oxford University Press.

So, Frank S. (1979). *The practice of local government planning*. Washington, DC: International City Management Association. unescap.org/sites/default/files/pub_2308.pdf (accessed on 19 March 2020).

Sofi, M. A., Dar, A. A., & Banoo, F. (2017). Impacts of unplanned urbanization on the socio-economic conditions and environment. *International Journal of Multidisciplinary Education and Research*, *2*(4), 48–50.

Store Norske Leksikon. (2016). *Urban planning*. https://snl.no/byplanlegging (accessed on 19 March 2019).

Thooyavan, K. R. (2011). Urban planning and real estate development. *Institute of Town Planners, India Journal*, *8*(1), 90–94.

UCLG. (2008). *Denaturalization and local democracy in the world: First global report*. Barcelona: UCLG. http://www.fukuoka.unhabitat.org/programmes/ccci/pdf/2_The_Impact_of_Decentralization_and_Urban_Governance_on_Building_Inclusive_and_Resilient_Cities.pdf (accessed on 19 March 2020).

UN-Habitat. (2002). *Tools to support participatory urban decision making*. Nairobi: UN-Habitat.

Vermeijden, B. (2001). Dutch urban renewal, transformation of the policy discourse 1960–2000. *Journal of Housing and the Built Environment*, *16*(2), 203–232.

Wachs, M. (2001). Forecasting versus envisioning: A new window on the future. *APA Journal*, *67*(4), 367–372.

Weber, R., Tammi, I., Anderson, A., & Wang, S. (2016). A spatial analysis of city-regions: Urban form and service accessibility (Working Paper No. 2). Stockholm: Nordregio.

Wiener, A., & Kahn, H. (1967). *The year 2000*. New York: Macmillan.

4 Urban Management

In the field of urban development in the Third World, the last two decades have witnessed the ascendency of urban management programmes as probably the most significant force in shaping the direction of development interventions in human settlements.

—Corubolo (1998)

Urban management enables optimal functioning of city administration, which is oriented towards improving economic and social conditions in the city.

—Mumtaz and Wegelin (2001)

Introduction

Urban management is a vital component of urban development. It believes in effective and efficient management of urban resources such as financial, physical and human for the development of cities. Besides, it also aims at effective management of urban development activities and services; projects and programmes in order to ensure better lifestyle to city dwellers. It is a holistic aspect which comprises the management of municipal affairs or the affair of the LSIs as well as the management of the activities and the involvement of all stakeholders in the development of urban affairs. It is remarked that urban management can husband and efficiently utilize scarce resources, vastly expanding resource pool available for the needs of urban life (Mattingly, 1995). The urban management programme of UNDP, the United Nations Centre for Human Settlements and World Bank together aim at the objectives of improving access to land, the provision of infrastructure and municipal finance as well as reducing poverty and protecting urban environment (Urban Management Program, 1991). Therefore, urban management is an important component of urban development studies.

LEARNING OBJECTIVES

After reading this chapter, you should be able to:

- ❒ Explain the meaning and scope of urban management
- ❒ Narrate the functions and process of urban management

- Describe various components of urban management
- Discuss the system approach to urban management
- Describe the deficiencies of urban management and suggestions for improving the urban management

Urban Management: Concept and Meaning

Urbanization is taking place at a faster pace in both developed and developing countries. As estimated by the World Bank, today, over 4 billion people around the world, that is, more than half of the population in the globe, live in cities. If this trend continues, it is expected that the urban population will double than the current size and nearly 7 out of 10 people in the world will live in cities. The unplanned urbanization has led to sundry problems in the developing countries. Those problems are urban population growth, the rise of million-plus cities, increasing urban poverty level, urban unemployment, urban inequality, inadequate basic services, environmental degradation and so on. The management of urban services is becoming a growing concern. Urban management deals with the development of cities and an effective management of urban services. The urban management process comprises a set of instruments, activities, tasks and functions which aim at effective management of urban services such as healthcare, sanitation, drinking water, energy and waste management to enhance the quality of life of city dwellers.

Etymologically, urban management develops, promotes and strengthens innovative urban management practices and provides inputs to the urban managers for the effective and efficient management of urban development projects, programmes, activities and services. It tries to deal with the broad spectrum of aspects of a city in terms of economic, environmental, social, cultural and infrastructural. A few definitions of urban management are given further.

As viewed by Van Dijk (2006, p. 56), 'urban management is an effort to coordinate and integrate public as well as private actions to tackle the major issues the inhabitants of the cities are facing, to make a more competitive, equitable and sustainable city.'

Rakodi (1991) believes that:

> Urban management aims to ensure that the components of the system are managed so that they make possible the daily functioning of a city which will both facilitate and encourage economic activity of all kinds and enable residents to meet their basic needs for shelter, access to utilities and services, and income generating opportunities.

Davidson and Nientied (1991) have tried to understand urban management through its active role in the urban process; for them, 'the essence of urban management is taking an active role in developing, managing and coordinating resources to achieve a town's urban development objectives.'

As viewed by Ilaria Bramezza (1996), 'urban management can be defined as the co-ordinated development and execution of comprehensive strategies with the participation and involvement of all relevant urban actors, in order to identify, create and exploit potentials for the sustainable development of the city.'

Kenneth Davey (1993) believes that:

> Urban management is concerned with the policies, plans, programs and practices that seek to insure that population growth is matched by access to basic infrastructure, shelter and employment. While such access will depend as much, if not more, on private initiatives and enterprise, these are critically affected by public sector policies and functions that only government can perform.

Clarke (1991) states that urban management includes managing of urban economic resources, particularly land and assets of the built environment, creating employment and attracting investment in order to improve the quality and quantity of goods and services available.

Need and Importance of Urban Management

There is a need for urban management, particularly in the developing countries; otherwise, in the faster changing world, the developing countries cannot hasten their pace of growth and development. It is remarked that there is a strong rationale for improved urban management to encourage efficiency and equity in the use of technical, human and financial resources in both public and private sectors (Clarke, 1991). The role and importance of urban management are narrated further.

1. *Enhance the contribution of urban areas to economic growth rate:* In most of the countries of the world, the contribution of urban areas to the economic growth rate is higher as compared to rural areas. The UN believes that urbanization brings both opportunities and challenges. Cities are the agents of economic, social, cultural, technologic and political changes and advancement. If properly managed and planned for, urbanization could be an engine of economic growth and industrialization (UN-Habitat, 2011). Application of urban management principles and approaches would be not only to hasten the pace of urbanization but also enhance its contribution to the economic growth rate. A well-developed city or a metropolitan area plays an important role and becomes the hope of development centre and economic engine for economic growth.
2. *Make the urbanization process sustainable:* The goal of sustainable city development can be better accomplished through effective urban management. It is pertinent to mention here that the urban management, like economic management, emphasizes on the management of scarce resources in ways that are sustainable, equitable and efficient. Traditional economic factors of production such as land, labour and capital are effectively and efficiently utilized within the framework of urban economies in order to build sustainable urban economies. It is envisaged that improving management to deal with immediate problems and addressing long-term issues of sustainability must go together.[1]
3. *Better utilization of resources:* The urban development management system is required for the effective utilization of scarce resources allotted for urban development. For the effective utilization of urban finance, the urban management system is sine qua non. With effective management of city affairs, a city could improve its social, cultural and economic climate and be enabled to offer more livelihood options to city dwellers and migrants from rural areas. Moreover, it can also support small- and medium-scale entrepreneurship and other activities of a commercial nature. All this will lead to better and effective utilization of city resources in the generation of livelihood opportunities for city dwellers.

4. *Promote effective PPP and community participation in the process of urban development:* Integrated urban management system calls for management of urban development projects and programmes through the effective participation of all stakeholders and beneficiaries of urban development. This can be possible only through the establishment of an urban management system. PPP in the supply, management and maintenance of public services is becoming a popular urban management instrument, especially because of the problems derived from budget restrictions, decreasing revenues and cuts in public sector expenditures and the search for the efficiency that private sector seems to offer.[2] Shabbir Cheema (1993) and Zenker et al. (2013) state that the main purpose of urban management is to create a city that is competitive, equitable and sustainable through a real partnership between the public and private sectors. Moreover, community participation in the management of urban services is also becoming popular under the participatory development model. The elected representatives of LSIs will play an important role in the management of urban services in their respective ULBs. It is said that the local governments are now expected to take the main responsibility for urban management (Mattingly, 1995).
5. *Enhances the capabilities of city administration:* The assumption was that urban management enables optimal functioning of city administration, which is oriented towards improving economic and social conditions in the city (Mumtaz & Wegelin, 2001). The benefit of an effective urban management system is that it enhances the capabilities of the urban administrators and the elected representatives of ULBs to discharge their duties and responsibilities efficiently and effectively. Farvacque and McAuslan (1992) argue that the fundamental purpose of urban management development is to provide a policy and administrative framework in order to provide smooth implementation of the services.
6. *Urban risk and security management:* Urban management would be helpful to effectively deal with urban risk and disasters in urban areas. Cities, particularly with disaster-prone locations, have to have a strong urban management system. Moreover, better urban management is also sine qua non for the safety and security of a city's population. The issue of security in urban areas is subject to the constant changes which take place in cities and municipalities, and is an important consideration for those deciding where to live and work (EBP, 2018). Systematic risk management plays an essential role in achieving a high level of security in cities and communities and thus ensuring good quality of life (EBP, 2018).
7. *Better management of urban infrastructure and services:* Creation and maintenance of urban infrastructure and services is one of the key issues and challenges of the LSIs. Urban management provides input to the urban administrators and elected representatives of the municipalities how to effectively manage the city infrastructure. McGill (1998) suggests that urban management is the capacity of a city's government to plan for, provide and maintain its infrastructure and services.

Functions and Processes of Urban Management

The urban development management process applies general development management principles and processes in order to effectively accomplish various tasks of urban development. The managers of the urban development projects and programmes have to apply the principle of POSDCCBR—P for planning; O for organizing; S for staffing; D for directing; C for coordinating, C for controlling; B for budgeting mechanism and R for reporting—in development processes to effectively and efficiently achieve urban development goals and objectives. According to G. R. Terry,

Figure 4.1 Development Management: Functions and Processes

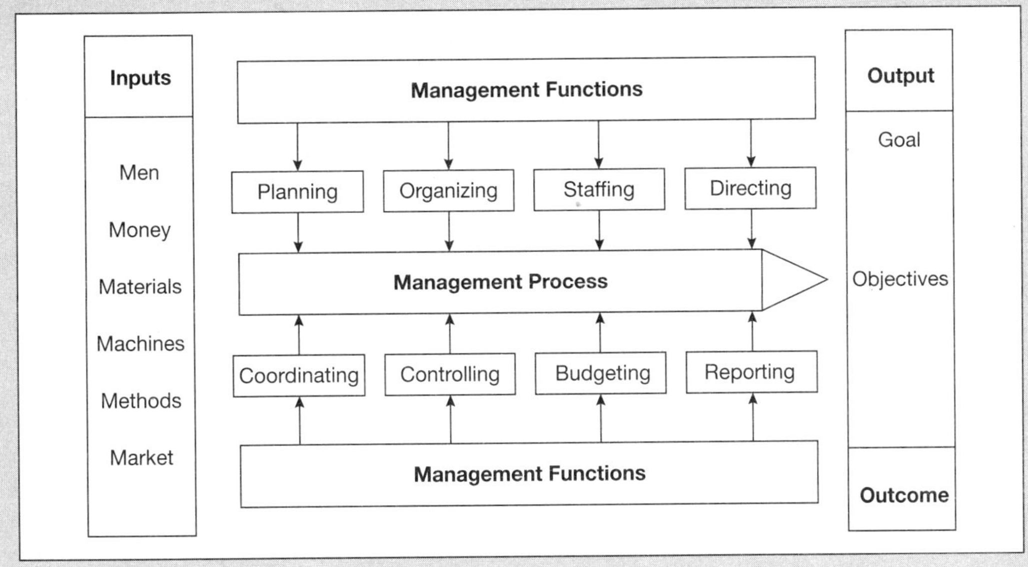

'management is a distinct process consisting of planning, organizing, activating and controlling to determine and accomplish the objectives by the use of people and resources.' The development management functions and processes are given in Figure 4.1.

The urban development management processes apply general management principles in order to accomplish various tasks of urban development. Inputs such as men, material, machines are applied with proper methodology in the market in order to achieve the goal, objectives, outputs and outcomes of the implemented urban development projects. The details of the urban management processes and principles are narrated further.

- *Planning:* Planning is the starting point of the process of urban management. At the outset, the urban development manager has to meticulously prepare a CDP. Whether it is a strategic plan or a master plan, at the outset, it has to be prepared following various steps of system approaches to planning. All the required steps, that is, need assessment, goals and objectives formulation, output, financing and activity mapping, implementation strategy, monitoring and evaluation strategy must be clearly documented in the plan DPR.
- *Organizing:* The urban development managers have to organize properly before undertaking any urban development task. He/she has to see that before initiating any action, everything is in proper order. The development managers during the process of organizing various tasks have to conform to the following important questions to himself/herself: who will do what? What will be done when? How it will be done by whom? And try to get an answer to them. It is customarily observed that most of the development plans have failed due to poor organization, blame game and shifting and transfer of responsibility from one person to another. It can be said that half of the work is done when you organize properly.
- *Staffing:* Manpower recruitment or staffing is a crucial function of development management. Recruitment is a vital component of development management function. It is one of

the important determinants of success and failure of a development project or programme. Putting the right man in the right job is a Herculean task before the development manager. Experienced, qualified and hardworking people are an asset to an organization. Hiring of efficient people would make the accomplishment of development task easier.

- *Directing:* Directing is an important process of urban management. The manager who is the leader in the front has to properly direct the team member by effectively orienting them about the vision, mission and objectives of the urban development programmes and projects. Leading the team in the right and proper direction is vital to the achievement of set development targets and goals. A directionless development manager might be ended in non-linear achievement, while the manager with the right direction, on the other hand, may be able to achieve curve linear output. Division of work, placing the right man in the right job, fixing the task, who will do what, how and when and building their capacities is one of the vital components of directing.
- *Coordinating:* One of the important functions of urban development manager is to coordinate various activities relating to urban development projects and programmes. By coordinating, it means harmonizing working relationships and unifying individual endeavours for the accomplishments of development goals. Poor coordination will lead to confusion, controversy and distractions which may not be helpful to achieve set goals and objectives.
- *Controlling:* Controlling means tapping the progress and taking corrective measures from time to time. According to Reeves and Woodward (1970), 'controlling refers to the task of ensuring that activities are producing the desired results. Control, in this case, is limited to monitoring the outcome of activities, reviewing feedback information about this outcome and if necessary, taking corrective actions.' The development managers need to have complete command over the project and all of its activities and resources engaged in it.
- *Budgeting:* It is the vital component of development management. DPR includes budgeting. The planning of development activities, projects and programmes is meaningless without budgeting or allocation of resources to various planned tasks and activities. According to Waldron, Vasanthakumar and Arulraj, budgeting means making financial plans, maintaining accounting and management control of revenue and keeping cost in line with objectives.
- *Reporting:* To prepare a report is another essential function of urban development management. The project report gives an overview of the progress made by the project and programme, and its output and impact on the targeted beneficiaries. The report may be monthly, six-monthly or annual. The type of report includes appraisal report, monitoring, report, evaluation report, impact assessment report and so on as required by the management.

Aims of Urban Management

The aims of urban development management are as follows:

1. To promote faster and effective urban development through best alternative ways and in a cost-effective manner.
2. To improve the efficiency and capabilities of the urban development managers engaged in the formulation and implementation of various urban development projects and programmes.
3. To make the city and urban areas beautiful and liveable. To see that the urban dwellers enjoy a good quality of life.

4. To prepare a good urban development plan for the city and effectively implement it.
5. To create sustainable urban infrastructure and their management system.
6. To promote inclusive and sustainable urban development. In other words, it aims at constructing a sustainable and resilient city.
7. To adopt a participatory approach in development projects and programmes (formulation, implementation, monitoring and evaluation) instead of a one-sided top-down approach. In other words, it follows the bottom-up approach undertaken in the spirit of partnership and inclusiveness, and the motto is participatory development management.
8. To create institutions and build capabilities of the LSIs and the parastatal bodies.
9. To develop alternative models of urban and city development to be more efficient, effective and productive, and check wastage of resources.
10. To develop an eco-city, heritage city, smart city and so on by applying the need-based approach of city development.
11. To effectively engage the private and corporate actors in the city development. The motto is PPP for urban development.
12. To promote community participation in the city development process.

Scope of Urban Management

As urban development is taking place at a faster pace in the developing countries, effective urban management will help them to properly develop the cities and ensure good quality of life to city dwellers. The scope of urban management is discussed further.

1. *Urban management as a process:* Urban management will fasten the urban development process. Effective urban management will help the urban development management to systematically use scanty allocated resources and manpower in the process of urban development. Cartwright (1989) was of the view that urban management should lay less emphasis on defining specific targets and more emphasis on creating a better and stronger process of social decision-making.
2. *Effective management of urban services:* Urban management will be helpful to make systematic management of urban services such as urban infrastructure, traffic management, education and healthcare services and other urban amenities. The endeavour needs to be to provide cost-effective services to city dwellers. The urban services can be broadly categorized as follows:
    a. *Public utility services:* Water supply, electricity, gas pipeline, sewerage, sanitation and telephone.
    b. *Social services:* Education, health, housing, social welfare and old-age home.
    c. *Transport and traffic:* Urban transport services, traffic management, street light and city road.
    d. *Security, and law and order:* Maintenance of security, and law and order through effective surveillance system.
    e. *Other services:* Parks, recreation, open space, market, cemeteries, disaster management services and urban forestry.
3. *Management of urban development projects and programmes:* Urban development management veritably teaches how to effectively manage various projects and programmes

launched in various sectors by the Department of Urban Development. It will help the manager to effectively manage various physical, financial and human resources involved in the implementation of urban development projects and programmes.

4. *Inter-sectoral coordination:* Urban management promotes inter-sectoral coordination that would help the urban government to deliver urban services such as health, education, sanitation and drinking water effectively and efficiently through mutual cooperation. For example, several departments such as education, labour and employment, micro, small and medium enterprises are involved in the process of skill development. It is commented that inter-sectoral collaboration is important for policy implementation; however, effective collaboration may be difficult to achieve because of poor internal drive to collaborate, disagreements on framing the problem, institutional constraints and poor leadership (Li et al., 2015).
5. *Use of technology in urban management:* Urban management makes the use of IT services and technology for the speedy and effective management of urban services. The use of GIS in the process of urban land management is one of the illustrious examples. The sustainable smart cities use ICT for improving the quality of life of city dwellers. The UN-Habitat has envisaged that the emergence of cloud-based services, more powerful mobile devices, sensors, big data and analytics present a huge opportunity for cities to enter a new phase of technological development and enable new ways to deliver services to citizens.[3]
6. *Decentralization:* Urban management can promote a decentralized system in the management of urban affairs. The urban management will strengthen the role of ULBs in the management of urban basic services in coordination with the government grassroots functionaries of the urban development department at various levels. It is rightly remarked that the urban management approach stresses strengthening local government through supporting decentralization with the objective of moving decision-making on resource allocation closer to beneficiaries, and stressing their participation (Jenkins, 2000).
7. *Stakeholder participation:* One of the objectives of urban management is to promote stakeholder participation in the management of urban development programmes, projects and activities. The urban management scope can go beyond the management of urban affairs by the urban development administration and functionaries, and could include other community actors in the process of urban development. It will effectively engage other stakeholders such as the RWA, Youth Clubs, *mahila mandals* and other active citizenries in the delivery and management of urban affairs particularly the urban services. It is rightly remarked that good stakeholder engagement and coordination can enable agencies to leverage opportunities for greater scale to benefit from and support local response mechanisms, to do no harm and to contribute to the resilience and long-term development of a city.[4]
8. *PPP:* Urban management may include the private sector in the implementation of urban development programmes and projects and the development of sustainable smart cities. The PPP could be promoted in the areas of technical support and resource sharing. PPPs in urban development can be best defined as a true partnership of public officials and private developers who 'have development ambitions that they could not complete alone' (Sagalyn, 2007). In this form of public (municipalities) and private sector (private companies such as construction and property development firms, private banks and investment companies) cooperation, the aim usually is to accomplish a public task or a project by funding and/or

operating on the basis of a partnership in which the financial risks of the public sector are to be reduced (Tasan-kok & Zaleczna, 2010). The adoption of a city through PPP by the private sector is one of such examples of partnership. In India, Tatanagar is a good example to show the role of the private sector in a city's development.

9. *Urban development policies:* The scope of urban management includes the formulation and implementation of urban development policies. In the Indian context, as the urban development is a state subject, the centre can, at the most, 'issue directives, provide advisory services, set up model legislation and fund programmes which the states can follow at will' (Shaw, 1996). However, Ramachandran (1989) points out: despite the fact that states have been empowered to make urban policy, they have rarely done so. As decentralization is in vogue in many countries of the world, the urban local self-government can also formulate policy for the development of the ULBs. A comprehensive urban development policy could include policies relating to various sectors such as health, education, sanitation, waste management, drinking water, housing, traffic and crime management and management of urban slums. The urban development managers provide policy input to the legislatures and the government.
10. *Interdisciplinary approach:* It applies interdisciplinary approach and takes the help of architect, engineers and social scientists from various disciplines such as geography, economics, sociology, public administration and management for the effective management of urban affairs. It is rightly remarked that because of its elusive nature, urban management was claimed by a number of disciplines (architecture, sociology, urban sociology, urbanism, political science and so on), each of which understood and defined the concept differently (Stren, 1993).
11. *Institutional arrangement and capacity building:* The urban management process builds institutions for the management of urban services. The establishment of urban parastatal bodies and other institutions by the government has strengthened the management of urban infrastructure and services. Many institutions are being found to be involved in the research, education and training programme concerning to urban development. Last but not the least, the urban management also takes into consideration the capacity building of the urban development functionaries and elected representatives of the ULBs at various levels for the effective delivery and management of urban services. A paper prepared for the UN-Habitat conference with the help of several experts have noted as follows:

    > Capacity building is the backbone of the New Urban Agenda. Without strong institutions that are capable to plan, manage and implement development policies and can rely on well-trained staff who are capable to respond adequately to the challenges of urbanization and the demands of cities and its citizens, it is nearly impossible to assure that cities will become a sustainable place to live and work in dignity and peace.[5]

Components of Urban Management

Urban management is a very broad and complex wing of urban development. It overlaps with urban planning on the one hand and urban governance on the other. However, it broadly covers many areas such as urban land use and infrastructure management, transport and traffic management, urban services management, management of urban safety and security. Some of the important components of urban management are discussed further.

Urban Land Management

Acquisition and utilization of land for various purposes in a city is a critical function of urban management. Every city requires land for its growth and development. City placement and development do not take place in air. Land is a reality and unavoidable requirement for the city. It is remarked that land problems are inherently complex both in theory and in practice, particularly because of the interdependencies of land use, the specificity of location advantages, transfer costs, social taboos and inhibitions, and many other market imperfections, not the least the opportunities land transactions provide for corruption (Dunkerley, 1983). Selection and acquisition of land of site for development of cities, urban corridors and fringe are vital functions of urban development and is rest with the people and organizations dealing with urban land management. According to the World Bank, as urban growth continues, some 600,000 hectares of rural land must be transformed into urban use during the last two decades of the century, or enough space to accommodate 20 new cities the size of Mumbai.[6]

Land management requires covering some of the pertinent aspects, which are as follows:

1. Information about the vulnerable land, common land and abandoned land;
2. Identifying available lands and their ownership;
3. Effective and sustainable land management requires protecting watershed, vegetation, topography, drainage courses and so on. The water-logging in various cities (e.g., the recent disaster in Kashmir [India] in 2014) is an illustrious example of the construction of houses on the watercourses. In the same vein, frequent urban disasters occur during the rainy season in the metropolitan cities such as Delhi, Mumbai and Chennai;
4. Land development through mechanisms of land pooling, land banking and so on;
5. Locating the land in close proximity to socioeconomic opportunities;
6. Acquiring land for ensuring services to city dwellers such as road, park, recreation, water, sanitation, power and SWM; and
7. Formulation of suitable land policy for the development of a city.

The merits of land use management are as follows:

1. To guarantee ownership and security of land tenure;
2. To develop and monitor land markets;
3. To protect and manage state lands;
4. To reduce land disputes and facilitate land reforms;
5. To improve urban planning and infrastructure development;
6. To support environmental and heritage management;
7. To use land inclusively and sustainably for a city's development;
8. To protect water bodies and wetlands; and
9. To effectively utilize the open land space of the city.

Urban Infrastructure Management

Urban infrastructure development and management is a key function of the urban development department, its functionaries and the elected representatives of the LSIs. Infrastructure maybe defined as 'the network of services in a society which are essential for its cohesion and for the efficient functioning of the economy' (Penguin and Macquarie Dictionary of Economics and

Finance, 1988). The infrastructure includes road, public transport, waterworks, drainage, sewerage, public utilities, housing, public park and so on. The management of the urban infrastructure, in particular, is in shambles in most of the developing countries. The fight between the provincial government and the local self-government; the lack of participation of private sector and poor community participation in the urban infrastructure management are a few among many issues in urban infrastructure management. In its 'World Development Report 1994: Infrastructure for Development', the World Bank had laid down principles for reform in the provision and operation of infrastructure, which are as follows:

1. Manage infrastructure like a business, not like a bureaucracy;
2. Introduce competition directly if feasible, indirectly if not; and
3. Give users and other stakeholders a strong voice and real responsibility.[7]

Some of the essential aspects which have to be taken into consideration for the effective management of urban infrastructure are as follows:

1. Improving participation of the local self-government in the management of urban infrastructure. This calls for dynamic local government leadership;
2. Healthy climate and cooperation with the corporate, private and business sectors in the management of urban infrastructure with their physical and financial support;
3. Partnership with the NGOs and community-based organizations (CBOs) for the management of urban infrastructure at the local and at the municipal ward level;
4. Empowering people to take care of infrastructure management. In other words, enhancing the involvement of RWAs in the management of urban infrastructure at the local level;
5. Mobilization of private resources for the management of infrastructure;
6. Employing a GIS system for urban infrastructure management;
7. Improving urban governance for the efficient management of urban infrastructure;
8. Capacity building of LSIs for the management of infrastructure at the local level;
9. An integrated approach to infrastructure management;
10. Applying system approach to urban infrastructure by involving the stakeholders and the beneficiaries at the infrastructure planning, implementation and maintenance level; and
11. Creation of smart and sustainable infrastructure.

The UN document has envisaged that the smart infrastructure project needs to be:

1. *People-centred and inclusive:* It should be chosen and designed with a deep understanding of people's lifestyles, cultures, behaviour and needs.
2. *Resilient and sustainable:* It should be resilient to external shocks and ensure sustainability.
3. *Interoperable and flexible:* It should be designed in order to be flexible with regard to future modification and enhancements.
4. *Risk mitigating and safe:* It should be accompanied by appropriate risk management and risk mitigation strategies (United Nations, 2016).

Urban Basic Services Management

The third essential component of urban management is the management of urban basic services such as food security to the poor, housing, safe drinking water supply, household sanitation, safe and sustainable energy, basic education and basic healthcare services, urban road and telecommunication. Customarily, the urbanization process aims at the transformation from the rural characteristics of people towards a modern one in order to raise the quality of life of city dwellers. Basic Needs & Response Analysis Framework Report has envisaged that the concept of basic needs refer to the essential goods, utilities, services or resources required on a regular or seasonal basis by households for ensuring survival and minimum living standards, without resorting to negative coping mechanisms or compromising their health, dignity and essential livelihood assets. However, in most of the developing countries, the lifestyle of people residing in the cities has not been changed satisfactorily. It is felt that the positive role of urbanization has often been overshadowed by the deterioration in the physical environment and quality of life in urban areas caused by a widening gap between demand and supply of essential services and infrastructure.[8]

The management of urban basic services essentially could include the following:

1. Provisioning and management of public distribution system which would provide essential food and nutritional care services to the urban poor with particular emphasis on those who are in the informal settlements and in urban slums.
2. Management of urban housing facilities, especially for the poor and providing healthy housing to the poor having proper accommodation with facilities of kitchen, bathing and toilet. Besides, every household needs to have the required furniture for eking a minimum living style. Besides, making strong legal provision in the real estate sectors in order to ensure timely housing to the home buyers.
3. Provisioning and management of safe drinking water facilities for all. The safe drinking water facility needs to include access to drinking water from safe sources such as dip borewells, tube well and tap water. The safe drinking water management will have to take into consideration the following aspects: (a) sources of supply of drinking water to the city; (b) water preservation and purification; (c) water supply system, that is, supply through tankers, piped water and so on; (d) water pricing; and (e) water conflict. On the other hand, the sanitation and waste management may include: (a) source of waste generation such as household waste, hospital waste, industrial and business waste; market and shopping complex waste, pedestrian waste, waste generated in the religious places and during festivals; waste generated in the institutions and open spaces such as parks and schools; (b) collection and segregation of waste; (c) processing of waste for energy and other useful things; (d) community participation in waste collection and segregation; and (e) fee and charges for waste management particularly for waste collection.

Management of Urban Energy

Cities currently account for about two-thirds of the world's annual energy consumption and about 70 per cent of GHG emissions (International Energy Agency, 2008). It is not a flight of fancy, but truly the cities which occupy less than 3 per cent of land surface and have houses 50 per cent of the world's population exert high demand of energy. A gigantic percentage of this energy demand comes from fossil fuel which is more scarce and getting depleted day by day. The increased urbanization therefore, in the long run, requires management of energy in order to meet energy deficiency and also to protect the environment. Smart cities and sustainable urban

Box 4.1 **Goal 7: Ensure Access to Affordable, Reliable, Sustainable and Modern Energy for All**

7.1. By 2030, ensure universal access to affordable, reliable and modern energy services.
7.2. By 2030, increase substantially the share of renewable energy in the global energy mix.
7.3. By 2030, double the global rate of improvement in energy efficiency.
7.4. By 2030, enhance international cooperation to facilitate access to clean energy research and technology, including renewable energy, energy efficiency and advanced and cleaner fossil-fuel technology and promote investment in energy infrastructure and clean energy technology.
7.5. By 2030, expand infrastructure and upgrade technology for supplying modern and sustainable energy services for all.

Source: https://sustainabledevelopment.un.org/post2015/transformingourworld (accessed on 22 March 2019).

development necessitate sustainable, and safe and clean energy. This urges the use of more and more renewable sources of energy in order to control urban pollution. The four major sectors in urban areas using energy are domestic, transport, industry, and services and commercial. Use of solar energy, wind energy, smokeless *chulas* (traditional cooking stove), LPG gas, biogas and so on is being promoted in different cities as sources of clean, cheap and sustainable energy. The management of energy needs to take into consideration the following: (a) sources of energy; (b) energy generation; (c) energy distribution; (d) energy pricing; (e) energy consumption; and (f) energy conflict. Bose and Anandalingam (1996) have noted that the sustainability objectives of energy management include the following: (a) meeting the minimum useful energy demand of each end user in different sectors, (b) maximizing the capacity utilization of power stations and the stock of modal fleet, (c) minimizing expenditure on energy within the budget limits, (d) minimizing emissions of different pollutants with respect to the 1990 loading; and (e) minimizing overutilization of energy resources.

The UN has envisaged how to ensure access to affordable, reliable, sustainable and modern energy for all. It is given in Box 4.1.

Urban Education Management

Ensuring primary and elementary education for all and with particular emphasis on those who are staying in the urban slums and other makeshift and informal settlements of the cities. This is to be done with the help of various actors and stakeholders engaged in the educational development of the cities such as LSIs, private and corporate sector, NGOs, CBOs and voluntary organizations. Special attention has to be given for the education of the disadvantaged sections, such as girl child education, education of the socioeconomically backwards and differently-abled children. In the World Conference on Education for All in Jomtien, Thailand, 1990, it was stated that:

> Every person—child, youth and all—shall be able to benefit from educational opportunities designed to meet their basic learning needs. These needs comprise both essential learning tools (such as literacy, oral expression, numeracy, and problem solving) and the basic learning content (such as knowledge, skills, values and attitudes) required by human beings to be able to survive, to develop their full capacities, to live and work in dignity, to participate fully in development, to improve the quality of their lives, to make informed decisions and to continue learning.

The management of primary and elementary education in urban areas needs to take into consideration the following aspects: (a) conduction of education survey and need assessment; (b) opening of primary and elementary education institutions such as preschools, that is, *anganwadis*, *balwadis* and crèches; primary schools and elementary schools; (c) management of educational institutions run by public sectors, private sectors, NGOs and voluntary sectors; (d) overseeing enrolment, dropout and retention rate; (e) monitoring of mid-day meal and other support programmes; (f) educational pricing; (g) community participation in education at the grassroots level; and (h) monitoring of both quality and quantity of education such as gross enrolment rate, teacher–pupil ratio, quality of the teacher, training of the teacher, pass-out and dropout rate, curriculum, availability of other facilities such as the library, playground, boundary wall, support to students with disabilities and gender ratio. Other aspects of urban education include the opening of vocational schools and offering vocational education through them with special organizational and instructional approach. Teachers are the key component of urban education for imparting quality education; there is a need to decrease class size and increase the number of teachers with advanced degrees. This will require increase in per capita spending on education of the children. Smith in his article 'Urban Education: Model That Works' has suggested that a school's success depends on the following: more teacher feedback; data-driven instruction; students spending more time in school; small group tutoring; and culture and expectations. He also further emphasized on developing a culture of education that values students and does not treat them as widgets; establishing goals with accompanying curricula and measuring students' progress; relying on data-driven instruction and investing in teachers and rewarding them with pay for performance.[9] The cities are also known for provisioning higher education institutions, particularly technical education. The sustainable city, therefore, needs to emphasize on offering quality education with good hi-tech infrastructure facilities and teachers with advanced degrees. Development of human capital through education, training and capacity building with the help of primary, secondary, tertiary educational institutions, technical and vocational education institutions, teacher training institutions, educational research and innovations need to be the primary thrust of the urban education management.

Urban Healthcare Management

One of the vital basic services critical to human need is provisioning and management of minimum healthcare services in urban areas critical to human survival. Kumar et al. (2018) in their article on 'Urban Health: Needs Urgent Attention' have noted that there is a strong need to set up primary healthcare system in urban areas and systematically deal with urban health challenges in terms of vector-borne diseases, rising incidence of non-communicable diseases, air pollution and acute respiratory infections, road traffic accidents, trauma and injuries. They have suggested that the initiatives to address these challenges do not remain confined to health sector alone but also need to be supported by sectors other than health such as social welfare, women and child development, road transport and highways, school education, drinking water and sanitation. We really need to address the wider and social determinants of health to effectively improve the urban health scenario.

According to the WHO, it is the 'minimum collection of essential health services that all the population need to have guaranteed access to. The essential services are those services which if not provided, will result in the most negative impact on the health status of the overall population'. The management of primary healthcare services includes: (a) effective management of the delivery of primary healthcare services such as immunization, treatment of common illness, communicable and non-communicable diseases and timely referral healthcare services to the urban poor and marginalized; (b) provisioning of primary healthcare infrastructure, manpower and essential medicine at the primary healthcare centres and below-level healthcare delivery centres; (c) promotion of inter-sectoral coordination and community participation at the grassroots level for the effective delivery of healthcare services; (d) encouraging the involvement of NGOs, CBOs and voluntary organizations at the grassroots level; (e) capacity building of the grassroots level of health functionaries and health-related functionaries from time to time; (f) effective linkage of healthcare services with the sanitation, safe drinking water and nutritional care services; (g) strengthening the school healthcare programme; and (h) effective engagement of local self-government in the healthcare system.

Moreover, urban areas are also known for their secondary and tertiary healthcare system. In urban areas, both public and private sector play an important role in delivering specialized healthcare services to the people. However, the improper management of the healthcare services delivery with regard to affordability, accessibility and availability still holds the key. It is not a flight of fancy, but truly healthcare institutions in urban areas of the developing countries like India not only provide the healthcare services to the urban population but also emergency and referral care services to the rural population which has migrated at a large scale from rural areas to urban areas. Therefore, the capacity of urban healthcare institutions and capabilities of the urban healthcare personnel need to be improved. Moreover, these institutions need to be provided with modern healthcare technology and infrastructure to cater to the healthcare needs effectively and efficiently.

Urban Transport and Traffic Management

Urban transport is a critical problem in the cities, particularly in metropolitan cities. After the liberalization and globalization, and with the increase in the number of vehicles, the urban transport problem has become a pain for the urban government. There are several categories of transport system consisting of personal, private and public transport system such as two-wheelers/bike and scooters, personal cars, private cars, three-wheelers/autorickshaws, e-rickshaws and hand rickshaws, metro rail, trams, and public and private buses. Besides, there are pedestrians and bicyclists who are also the creators as well as victims of traffic problems. With the increase in the number of vehicles due to burgeoning population in urban areas, the traffic problem has become a common problem in the cities. The management of the transport system and traffic is a critical issue and challenge for the urban government and municipalities.

Traffic congestion is caused by inefficient road operation, a growing number of vehicle and users, and inadequate traffic sensing infrastructure and traffic controlling personnel. Moreover, people in many cities also lack sense of traffic ethics and many are habitual violators. Traffic management is the organization, arrangement, guidance and control of both stationary and moving traffic, including pedestrians, bicyclists and all types of vehicles. Its aim is to provide for safe, orderly and efficient movement of persons and goods, and to protect and, where possible, enhance the quality of the local environment on and adjacent to traffic facilities.[10] The number of vehicles is also to be controlled within the city and more number of ring roads need to be constructed for diversion of traffic from the busy city roads. Besides, the construction of metro rail will also reduce the load on surface transport for daily commuters.

Urban Safety and Security Management

Crime and violence are fundamental threats to human security and safety from crime and violence—including the resulting fear and insecurity—is increasingly being acknowledged internationally as a public good, as well as a basic human right (UN-Habitat, 2007). In recent decades, urban areas both in developed and developing countries have become increasingly larger and more densely populated. Poor urban planning and faulty urbanization have promoted armed conflicts in the cities. A recent study has shown that 60 per cent of urban dwellers in developing and transitional countries have been victims of crime (UN-Habitat, 2007). Some of the factors which are responsible for the rise in the crime in the cities are poverty, inequality, inflow of rural population to urban areas, poor safety and security arrangement and lack of security policy and prevention mechanism. The types of crimes seen in urban areas are murder, snatching, molestation, burglary, robbery, eve-teasing, homicide and so on. Acts of terrorism and radicalization of young people are increasingly witnessed in urban areas. Many of those who commit terrorist acts are being radicalized in their local urban communities. Besides, the concentration of populations in urban areas also makes cities attractive targets for terrorist attacks. It is not a flight of fancy, but delicately urban crime and violence still bring dramatic and unacceptable direct and indirect costs to communities and individuals residing in the cities. Many studies have shown that street harassment and violence against females are prevalent in almost all cities of the world.

There is a need for controlling urban crime and providing safety and security to city dwellers. Smart and sustainable cities must be secured and made safe for its dwellers. Urban safety and security mean identification and remediation of threats and vulnerability. It means prevention of urban crime and atrocities. Not only the government but also all the stakeholders, LSIs, RWAs and citizens as a whole have to work in tandem to control and prevent urban crime. Sensitization of the migrant population on safety and security issues is critical to controlling urban crime. Some of the suggestions given are as follows: (a) installation of more surveillance cameras to monitor daily activities; (b) deployment of more armed security guards (with guns, tear gas, pepper spray and clubs); and (c) establishment of more checkpoints to scan and examine people and baggage.[11]

Urban Waste Management

The rapid growth of population and the proliferation of industrial and service sector activities in urban areas give rise to waste generation in urban areas. Moreover, the growing urban area population has also created a lot of household wastes. Therefore, waste management has become an imminent problem in rapidly growing urban centres, particularly in developing countries. The unsustainable production and consumption patterns result in waste that can harm health and the environment. Waste management largely includes the following activities: (a) generation of waste; (b) collection of waste; (c) segregation of waste; (d) processing and treatment of waste; and (e) use of waste in landfilling (solid waste). At the outset, the endeavour needs to be not to generate adequate amount of waste. Generated waste are of the following types, such as household wastes, industrial wastes, waste produced in business and marketplaces, medical wastes, waste produced by hotels and waste generated during ceremonies and festivals and in religious places. Second, a systematic attempt has to be made for the segregation of waste such as degradable and non-degradable waste and process these two types of waste accordingly. It is remarked that composting is an environment-friendly and simple solution for organic waste that is often successful at the household level. Another option is biogas production, which can be used to produce electricity or can be used as fuel for vehicles.[12] The segregation of waste at the source is a recommended means to avoid cost in waste segregation. Finally, the segregated waste has to be treated for generation of wealth such as manures, recycling and materials. In other words, from waste to wealth should be the approach. Moreover, solid waste can be used in the refilling of pits and other sites that require to be refilled.

Urban Environment Management

Preservation and protection of the urban environmental condition are essential for the healthy living of city dwellers. Pollution-related diseases in urban areas are on the rise because of the increased number of vehicles, dust generated due to construction, burning of wastes and so on. Lack of proper waste disposal system is responsible for urban water pollution, air pollution and land pollution causing a lot of health hazards and hazardous epidemics. The degree of pollution is more acute in industrial cities. Moreover, it is also noticed that GHG emissions taking place in various countries of the world are associated with activities largely taking place in cities. Integrating GHG emissions reduction strategies in urban planning and management can reduce the impact that cities have on the global environment while improving the quality of life for urban residents.[13] World Bank has highlighted that global emissions originating from intensive energy use in urban areas and from fossil fuel consumption contribute to climate change. In turn, climate change exacerbates the frequency and intensity of natural disasters, many of which affect cities with increasingly high human and economic costs.[14]

Cities which are clean and green are more attractive. Therefore, integrating the environmental issues and challenges in urban planning and management will not only contribute to global environmental goals and sustainable development but also can generate substantial economic and social co-benefits. The Brown Agenda, which aims at improving the urban environment in various countries would enable the nation states to improve their environmental management system. All the actors of development and especially ULBs have to be proactive in launching various activities for greening the urban environment. However, the role of the private sector, NGOs, CSOs and urban dwellers will go a long way in the direction of urban environmental management and development. According to UNEP, the urban environment can be defined as the intersection and overlay of the natural environment, the built environment and the socioeconomic environment. Effective urban environmental management requires (a) management of all three spheres (natural, built, socioeconomic), (b) an understanding of their interdependencies and linkages, (c) a balance of the demands and needs of all stakeholders; and (d) a commitment to sustainable development.[15]

Four key steps recommended for urban environment management are as follows:

1. Identifying priority urban environmental issues and involving the stakeholders.
2. Formulating urban environmental action plans.
3. Capacity building and institutionalizing environmental management strategies and routines.
4. Formulating and implementing environmental action plans (UNCHS, 1995).

Urban Road Infrastructure Management

Construction and maintenance of urban road and surface communication are vital to urban development. Roads are vital public assets. A systematic process of maintaining, upgrading and operating this asset is also vital for traffic management and standard of living of city dwellers.

The agencies engaged for the transport infrastructure must maintain, operate, improve, replace and preserve this asset. Both the intra and intercity road connectivity are vital to raising the contribution of urban areas to economic growth and development. Roads will raise the level of education and be indirectly helpful to reduce the mortality rate. Moreover, greater attention has to be given to the road connectivity between city and villages in order to enable the countryside population to have access to employment opportunities, healthcare and education facilities, which are available in greater scale in urban areas. The smart and sustainable city requires a sustainable road transport system. An ecosystem road according to weather and climate of the cities is required for sustainable road development.

Information Technology Infrastructure Management

Like the surface or road transport system, the management of IT infrastructure is in equal vein important for urban development. For more than two decades, information technology or ICT has been playing a vital role in enhancing the economic growth and development of the nation states. It is largely playing an important role in urban areas in promoting accessibility, transparency and accountability in the delivery of urban services. The smart cities are also being called electronic cities or information cities. Harrison et al. (2010) argue that a city is smart when it manages to connect the physical infrastructure, the IT infrastructure, the social infrastructure and the business infrastructure to leverage the collective intelligence of the city. When considering the implementation of a smart ICT plan for a city, the key step for any policymaker is to foster the development of a rich environment of broadband networks that support digital applications, ensuring that these networks are available throughout the city and to all citizens (Komninos et al., 2013). It was found that municipalities used a number of software applications to carry out different work processes that were grouped into five categories; planning and scheduling, designing, financing and accounting, managing and monitoring processes (Zeb et al., 2012). Computers are used in municipalities for issuance of birth and death certificates, maintenance of land record, payment of electricity and water bills and so on under a single-window system called e-governance. Therefore, management of information technology infrastructure is vital to municipal administration and local governance. Moreover, the GIS is also a vital information technology infrastructure used in the urban planning process.

Management of Urban Open Space, Water Bodies and Heritage

Urban green spaces play a key role in maintaining sustainable development and the liveability of an area (Levent & Nijkamp, 2004). The quality and viability of cities depend largely on the design, management and maintenance of urban green areas and open spaces. At the same time, good quality green space plays a vital role in enhancing the quality of urban life. Such space helps to make an area more attractive to live in by providing opportunities for people to relax, exercise, play sports and meet with friends (Office of the Deputy Prime Minister, National Audit Office, 2006). It is the duty and responsibility of the ULBs to create, upgrade and maintain the open spaces in its municipal areas. It will not only enhance the lifestyle of city dwellers but also can generate revenue for the local bodies.

Like the open spaces, the water bodies in urban areas are found to be vanishing or in decay because of city expansion and globalization. The water bodies are essential for the environmental health of the city. These are critical for strengthening biodiversity. Biodiversity is a key element that underpins the ecosystem functions and process that provide humans with vital goods and services (Schwarz et al., 2017). The Curitiba Declaration on Cities and Biodiversity (2007)[16] affirmed the importance to integrate biodiversity in urban planning and development, with a view on improving the lives of urban residents.

Management of urban heritage is another important dimension of urban management. Heritage is the asset of a city which not only glorifies its name but also attracts tourists and earns revenue to the municipalities. Management of urban heritage is one of the important functions of the urban municipality. It includes allocation of revenue for the maintenance of heritage sites, strengthening infrastructure in heritage sites and making it one of the vital aspects of city planning and development. According to the UN-Habitat (2015), urban heritage represents a social, cultural and economic asset and resource reflecting the dynamic historical layering of values that have been developed, interpreted and transmitted by successive generations and accumulation of traditions and experiences recognized as such in their diversity. It urged for urban heritage or urban conservation related to urban planning processes aimed at preserving cultural values, assets and resources through conserving the integrity and authenticity of urban heritage while safeguarding intangible cultural assets through a participatory approach.

System Approach to Management of Urban Development Projects and Programmes

Urban management is a complete technical exercise in order to accomplish any urban development activity *per se* the creation of an urban infrastructure. The manager of urban development projects needs to apply a system approach in order to effectively manage urban development project undertaken in cities. In this connection, two definitions of urban management are worth quoting. Mattingly (1994) has opined that urban management is 'taking sustained responsibility for actions to achieve particular objectives with regard to a particular object...this responsibility is to determine what needs to be done, to arrange that it be done, and then make certain that it is done for the city's development'. Giles Clarke (1991) considers urban management as a tool for encouraging efficiency and equity in the use of technical, human and financial resources in both public and private sectors. Therefore, in Clarke's view, the city is an engine of growth, and urban management is a tool with which economic power can be fully developed. While Chakrabarty (1998) defines the concept similarly. In his words, 'with urban management concept we are getting things done, i.e. achieve objectives and solve urban problems using efficiently the physical, financial, human and other resources within the control of an urban sector entity.'

Application of system approach helps the urban manager to effectively utilize its resources for the faster growth and development of urban areas and effective delivery of urban services. Various steps in the system approach to urban management are as follows: urban development needs identification; planning and formulation of task and activities; planning of strategies to accomplish those tasks and activities; resourcing; developing; operating and maintaining. The various steps of system approach to project management cycle are diagrammatically given in Figure 4.2.

1. *Identifying:* At the outset, the need for urban development projects in various sectors of urban development, such as housing, sanitation, safe drinking water, road, energy, health and education in cities has to be identified by conducting a need-assessment survey.

Figure 4.2 Urban Development Project Management Cycle

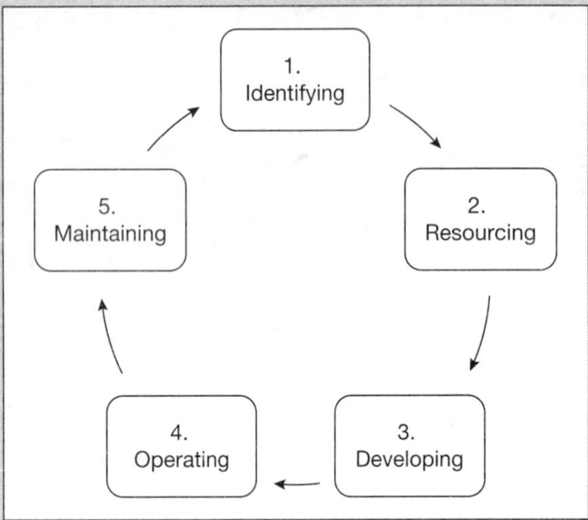

The project team engaged in the formulation of questionnaire and strategies for need assessment should consist of engineers, architects and social scientists. The participatory urban need assessment with the effective involvement of all stakeholders and beneficiaries such as the private sector, NGOs, private voluntary organizations (PVOs), CBOs, LSIs and the residents at large is a suggested methodology. The participatory urban need assessment would create a feeling of ownership among the stakeholders and beneficiaries, and will entice them to contribute in terms of money, manpower and materials in the long run for the maintenance of urban development projects after the withdrawal of project interventions. A Gantt chart is a graphical depiction of a project schedule and it helps in scheduling, managing and monitoring project activities, tasks and resources. A detailed project management report may be prepared at this stage.

2. *Resourcing:* Resource is one of the vital requirements of the project and resource mobilization is one of the important activities of urban development project management. Mobilization of resources from various sources to perform the development activities and tasks is a key concern of the project manager. Besides, other resources which are to be taken into consideration in this phase are human resources; material resources; institutional resources and information resources. Human resources are manpower requirements; material resource is the material required to accomplish the task particularly important in urban infrastructure management project; institutional resources are sometimes the LSIs and municipalities lack adequate expertise and manpower to accomplish the project tasks and activities and therefore they can seek the help of other institutions—private and NGOs. Thus, identification of institutional resources, particularly the local institutional resources, is important for the project management team to complete the project in time without compromising quality. Finally, information resources are also vital aspects of urban development management projects and programmes. The project team in order to maintain transparency ethics has to disseminate the progress of the project from time to time. It is remarked that information is essential to the actions of management, so much so that the communication of it is universally singled out for attention if management is to be improved (Mattingly, 1995).
3. *Developing:* After all these steps are over, the project management team starts real action. Here developing means creating. As a process of management, it creates institutions and assets, and capital goods for the government, private and community sectors, such as schools, hospitals, roads, waterworks, garbage disposal sites, parks and public offices and

other infrastructure which are necessary to provide services. Most of the corruption takes place at this stage of the project management cycle. The project management team has to be honest enough to carry out their duties and responsibilities in a fair and transparent manner. Development of weak capital goods and public assets is a wastage of national resources and ineffective use of taxpayers' money. E-tendering nowadays is being used for assigning tender to the competent organization. Good quality capital assets require less maintenance cost.

4. *Operating:* After the construction, the infrastructure and other assets created by the project management team in the cities are put into use or become operational. Operations are the day-to-day activities of urban management which deliver services to the public. In this process, governments collect refuse, manage street lights and treat wastes and so on. Moreover, it also puts to use the city roads, bridges and flyovers and other assets created and developed by the management system of the concerned municipalities. Operating requires the ability to command resources of staff, money, equipment and materials in adequate amounts and of appropriate qualities in order to perform various tasks.
5. *Maintaining:* The maintenance of public assets created by the urban government is an issue which has dragged considerable attention nowadays. Proper maintenance conserves facilities and saves a considerable amount of expenditure of the government in reconstruction. Maintenance is important for sustaining improvements in urban conditions. Maintenance of services facilities such as roads, sewerage systems, urban housing, waterworks and flyovers is absolutely essential if the benefits they bring are to be sustained. Nowadays, the external donors are ensuring the maintenance guarantee from the nation states before financing any project. The community maintenance of public works project is in practice in a few places. Complaints of ineffective maintenance of the public assets are being frequently reported in the developing countries.

Deficiencies of Urban Management

In the developing countries in particular, there are a lot of deficiencies in urban management. Because of this, the urban development process is slow and has not adequately fulfilled the aspiration of city dwellers. Studies issued by international organizations such as World Bank, UNDP and United Nations Centre for Human Settlements have argued that urban management effectiveness consists of a set of elements including financial viability, efficiency in the use of resources and technical competence.[17] Some of the deficiencies of urban management are as follows.

1. *Poor urban governance:* Poor governance is one of the vital deficiencies of urban management. Lack of accountability, poor leadership quality and transparency in the city management system are weak areas of urban management in most of the developing countries. There is large-scale corruption in the implementation of various urban development projects and programmes. This has also delayed the city development mission. Poor decentralized governance and weak transfer of funds, functionaries and functions to the LSIs is also a responsible factor for poor urban management.
2. *Poor urban planning:* Urban planning is the starting point of urban management. Unsatisfactory urban planning would lead to poor urban management. As the urban

planning and urban management are in the hands of a different set of people, therefore poor planning may lead to poor management. Shanghai Manual has rightly envisaged that urban management systems should include the ability to plan and model whole systems that optimize transportation and the built environment, resources including energy and water, and natural systems.[18]

3. *Weak participatory management system:* The development of urban areas could be effectively planned and managed through a well set-up participatory management system. All the actors and stakeholders have to be effectively involved in the process of urban development management. However, because of the predominance of the bureaucratic system over other stakeholders, the process of urban management has become a one-sided public affair and other stakeholders are seen to be sidelined. Weak participatory management system leads to a slow pace and unorganized urban development in most of the cities, particularly in the developing countries.
4. *Weak urban development administration:* Development administration has a key role to play in the planning, implementation and management of development projects and programmes. However, in most of the developing countries, development administration is weak; rather it is only administration. There is utter lack of participatory development administration. The role of efficient, effective and participatory urban development administration cannot be ignored in urban management.
5. *Poor financial management:* City development requires finance. Not only mobilization of resources but also its effective management is sine qua non for faster urban development. Weak financial management system is a responsible factor for poor urban management. It is rightly noted that researching and assessing potential financing mechanisms and tools should be part of the integrated management strategy.[19]
6. *Inadequate information system:* The GIS is weak in most of the cities. This has resulted in poor urban planning, especially urban land management. It is an integrated management information and decision support system that can assist city authorities in managing growth and changes within a city based upon key performance indicators related to areas such as traffic, environment and finance.[20]
7. *Inadequate law pertaining to urban management:* The laws pertaining to urban management in various countries are not only inadequate but also vary from one province to the other. Hollis and Fulton (2002) argue that urban management literature tends to focus on describing policy instruments rather than evaluating their influences. There is also poor implementation of law because of lack of clarity.
8. *Limited institutional capabilities:* In the developing countries in particular, there is less number of institutions pertaining to urban management. Further, the number of institutions varies from one province to the other. This is a major handicap for which the city administration fails to build up the capabilities of urban managers.

Measures to Strengthen Urban Management

Urban management is an important wing of urban development. It has to be strengthened in order to enable the nation state to achieve sustainable urban development. Michael Mattingly (1994) pointed out, without a more conceptually rich and diverse approach to urban management and support from the research community around the world, the concept has little potential for survival within the rapidly changing international marketplace of development ideas. Some of the steps needed to be taken for the improvement of urban management are as follows:

1. Improvement in the urban governance system and decentralization of development decision-making. Empowering the ULBs to take up city management. The managerial capabilities of the political and administrative heads of the ULBs need to be improved through capacity building. Moreover, effective transfer of functions, functionaries and funds to the ULBs will enable them to effectively participate in city development management process.
2. The municipal act and law need to emphasize on the urban management system. The inter and intrastate coordination among the ULBs in the management of municipal affairs would enable them to better manage municipal affairs by learning from each other. Moreover, they have also to coordinate with the local bodies in rural areas (PRIs in India) for better management of emerging municipalities which are transforming from rural to urban areas. It is rightly remarked that the laws pertaining to urban management are inadequate in many respects and focus on the key nature of the power relationship between the state and its citizens (Alnsour, 2011).
3. The urban planning process must be strengthened and participatory planning will be helpful to promote participatory urban management. It is envisaged that when communities, CSOs and other local actors are recognized as genuine interlocutors, participation is enhanced and urban planning and management can benefit from democratic decision-making. Participatory management can help reduce potential conflict and build local people's feeling of ownership in the government's plan.[21]
4. The institutional capabilities of the bodies dealing with urban management need to be enhanced. Institutional change, improving the performance of human resources and enhancing technical competences would be an important step in improving the effectiveness of urban management. The need for capacity building and actual performance should also be addressed.[22] Moreover, the managerial capabilities of urban parastatal bodies also need to be improved. The interstate study tours and replication of best practices on urban management by the municipalities from the best municipal management practices case studies of other municipalities will also be helpful to promote better management of urban development issues and challenges.
5. Strengthen the urban information system for the effectiveness of urban management. The GIS and other ICT instruments need to be improved and used by the city manager for the effective management of urban affairs including provisioning of urban services. It is envisaged that urban information systems are powerful means for governments in meeting long-term strategic planning and management challenges. For example, the information from a geographic information database helps in planning, zoning, transportation, utilities, flood management, urbanization and its impact on the environment and the use of demographics in making a public policy. It provides a heightened awareness of the interdependency among environmental, social and economic health and the impact of decisions made by neighbouring jurisdictions, state and federal agencies and private business.[23]
6. Appropriate urban project appraisal, monitoring and evaluation tools need to be developed and used for the effective management of urban development projects and programmes. In this respect, each urban development authority and institutions need to

have multidisciplinary team consisting of engineers, architects, planners and social scientists. Moreover, if required, the urban administration can take the help of NGOs and research organizations having experience in conducting studies and training programmes on urban development issues for the monitoring and evaluation of urban development programmes and projects.

7. Ensure that citizens are effectively involved throughout a city's development management process. This often requires balancing the need for action with the need for citizen engagement in various areas: information, consultation, involvement, collaboration, empowerment, or all of these. Moreover, the Municipal Ward Sabhas which are grassroots institutions to promote citizen participation needs to be strengthened. Alnsour (2014) by taking the mayors' response in Jordanian municipalities stated that there are several communication instruments which are used to expedite communication between a municipality and its citizens, which are as follows:
   - Commissioning local citizens to become members of their local municipal council.
   - Reliance on experienced counsellors' opinions to recognize the needs of citizens.
   - Facilitating the ability of citizens to make complaints.
   - Public meetings to discuss local topics of interest.

Summing Up

Improving urban management is a crucial precondition for developing smart and sustainable cities. The urban management deficits are critically prevalent in the management of various cities. It has its historical roots. However, an array of contemporary problems relating to urban management needs to be overcome if improvements are to be realized. Effective urban management requires sustained effort over the long period of time. However, institutionalizing such arrangements is the key to success. It is envisaged that the urban management, broadly defined, is about government's responsibility for the planning, development and day-to-day operations of a city. Moreover, effective urban management requires the involvement of private sector and community organizations.[24]

Keywords

Urban Management, Risk and Security Management, Organizing, Staffing, Directing, Coordinating, Stakeholder Participation, Decentralization, Interdisciplinary Approach, Urban Land Management, Management of Urban Energy, System Approach to Urban Management

REVIEW QUESTIONS

1. What is urban management? Describe the need for and importance of urban management to urban development.
2. Briefly explain the aim and scope of urban management.

3. Describe the functions and process of urban management.
4. Define urban management. Explain four important components of urban management.
5. Discuss in detail the system approach to urban management.
6. What are various deficiencies of urban management? Explain the steps to be taken to overcome them.
7. Write short notes on the following:
   a. PPP and urban management
   b. Management of urban energy
   c. Management of urban basic services
   d. Functions of urban management
   e. System approach to urban management
   f. Urban education and healthcare management

Notes

1. https://www.ucl.ac.uk/dpu-projects/drivers_urb_change/official_docs/Tow_Sust_Urb_EU_Guidelines.pdf (accessed on 24 October 2019).
2. http://www.claudioacioly.com/downloads/articles/Acioly%202003_Meaning%20of%20Urban%20Management.pdf (accessed on 20 October 2018).
3. https://www.ericsson.com/assets/local/news/2014/9/the-role-of-ict-in-the-new-urban-agenda.pdf (accessed on 29 October 2019).
4. https://www.rescue.org/sites/default/files/document/1853/weburbanstakeholderengagementand-coordinationweb.pdf (accessed on 29 October 2019).
5. http://capacitybuildingunhabitat.org/wp-content/uploads/Trainings%20and%20publications/2019_09_30/Capacity%20Building%20in%20New%20Urban%20Agenda_PositionPaper%20v2.pdf (accessed on 29 October 2019).
6. http://citeseerx.ist.psu.edu/viewdoc/download?doi<hig>=</hig>10.1.1.456.7016&rep<hig>=</hig>rep1&type<hig>=</hig>pdf (accessed on 19 October 2018).
7. https://crawford.anu.edu.au/rmap/devnet/devnet/db-45.pdf (accessed on 20 October 2018).
8. http://shodhganga.inflibnet.ac.in/bitstream/10603/51778/9/09_chapter%202.pdf (accessed on 20 October 2018).
9. https://www.philadelphiafed.org/community-development/publications/cascade/81/08_urban-education-models-that-work (accessed on 22 March 2019).
10. https://trid.trb.org/view/362282 (accessed on 21 October 2018).
11. https://www.un.org/ruleoflaw/files/urbansafetyandsecurity.pdf (accessed on 21 October 2018).
12. https://www.sida.se/contentassets/22c694f1c252402ea44353d05e731b1a/urban-solid-waste-management_1067.pdf (accessed on 21 October 2018).
13. http://www.citiesalliance.org/sites/citiesalliance.org/files/publications/integrating_the_environment.pdf (accessed on 24 October 2018).
14. https://www.preventionweb.net/files/2595_288170PAPER0Ur1ent010infrastructure.pdf (accessed on 21 October 2018)
15. http://www.unep.or.jp/ietc/Focus/eco.pdf (accessed on 24 October 2018).
16. file:///C:/Users/Administrator/Downloads/2010vermonden_thesis_-_key_factors_for_biodiversity_of_urban_water_systems.pdf (accessed on 30 June 2019).

17. https://www.witpress.com/Secure/elibrary/papers/SC14/SC14023FU1.pdf (accessed on 28 October 2018).
18. http://www.un.org/esa/dsd/susdevtopics/sdt_pdfs/shanghaimanual/Chapter%202%20-%20Delivering%20effective%20urban%20management.pdf (accessed on 28 October 2018).
19. http://www.un.org/esa/dsd/susdevtopics/sdt_pdfs/shanghaimanual/Chapter%202%20-%20Delivering%20effective%20urban%20management.pdf (accessed on 28 October 2018).
20. http://www.un.org/esa/dsd/susdevtopics/sdt_pdfs/shanghaimanual/Chapter%202%20-%20Delivering%20effective%20urban%20management.pdf (accessed on 28 October 2018).
21. https://unhabitat.org/un-habitat-for-the-sustainable-development-goals/11–3-sustainable-urbanization/ (accessed on 4 November 2018).
22. https://www.witpress.com/Secure/elibrary/papers/SC14/SC14023FU1.pdf (accessed on 28 October 2018).
23. http://www.reading.ac.uk/PeBBu/scope_definition/themes/12_information_systems.htm (accessed on 28 October 2018).
24. http://www.urbanlandmark.org.za/downloads/sourcebook_mod05.pdf (accessed on 28 October 2018).

References

Alnsour, J. (2011). Illegal housing in Jordan. *Jordan Journal of Social Sciences, 4*(3), 339–354.

Alnsour, J. (2014). The effectiveness of urban management in Jordanian municipalities. *The Sustainable City IX, 1*, 271–282.

Bose, R. K., & Anandalingam, G. (1996). Sustainable urban energy—Environment management with multiple objectives. *Energy, 21*(4), 305–318.

Bramezza, I. (1996). *The competitiveness of the European city and the role of urban management in improving the city's performance.* Rotterdam: EUR.

Cartwright, T. J. (1989). Urban management as a process, not an output: Reflections of an international workshop. *Review of Urban and Regional Development Studies, 1*(2), 107–111.

Chakrabarty, B. K. (1998). Urban management and optimizing urban development models. *Habitat, 22*(4), 503–522.

Clarke, G. (1991). Urban management in developing countries: A critical role. *Cities, 8*(2), 93–107.

Corubolo, E. (1998). Urban management and social justice (Working Paper No. 92). Endsleigh Gardens, London: Development Planning Unit, University College London.

Davey, K. (1993). *Elements of urban management.* Washington, DC: The World Bank.

Davidson, F., & Nientied, P. (1991). Introduction. *Cities, 8*(2), 82–86.

Dunkerley, H. (1983). *Urban land policy: Issues and opportunities.* New York: Oxford University Press.

EBP. (2018). *Urban security (safety and security).* https://www.ebp.ch/en/topics/safety-and-security/urban-security-safety-and-security (accessed on 4 September 2019).

Farvacque, C., & McAuslan, P. (1992). *Reforming urban land policies and institutions in developing countries.* Washington: World Bank.

Harrison, C., Eckman, B., Hamilton, R., Hartswick, P., Kalagnanam, J., Paraszczak, J., & Williams, P. (2010). Foundations for smarter cities. *IBM Journal of Research and Development, 54*(4). http://ijsrcseit.com/paper/CSEIT183187.pdf (accessed on 24 April 2019).

Hollis, L. E. & Fulton, W. (2002). *Open space protection: Conservation meets growth management.* Washington: Brookings Institution, Center on Urban and Metropolitan Policy.

International Energy Agency. (2008). Energy use in cities. *World Energy Outlook 2008.* Paris: Organization for Economic Co-operation and Development; International Energy Agency.

Jenkins, P. (2000). Urban management, urban poverty and urban governance: Planning and land management in Maputo. *Environment & Urbanization, 12*(1), 137–152.

Komninos, N., Pallot, M., & Schaffers, H. (2013). Special issue on smart cities and the future Internet in Europe. *Journal of the Knowledge Economy, 4*(2), 119–134.

Kumar, S., Kumar, S., & Gupta, B. (2018). Urban health: Needs urgent attention. *Indian Journal of Public Health, 62*(3), 214–217.

Levent, T. B., & Nijkamp, P. (2004). Urban green space policies: Performance and success conditions in European cities, in *Preliminary Vision: 44th European Congress of the European Regional Science Association, Regions and Fiscal Federalism*. Portugal. https://reader.elsevier.com/reader/sd/pii/S2226585618300815?token=376D15907205594834AFE0D06D58367A8540CAAF9532E4337AB9A98F9D3F806E38DA7DB35402C675AD93C1C63AED7A3C (accessed on 29 June 2019).

Li,.B., Huikuri, S., Zhang, Y., & Chen, W. (2015). Motivating intersectoral collaboration with the Hygienic City Campaign in Jingchang, China. *Environment & Urbanization, 27*(1), 285–302.

Macquarie Library. (1988). The Penguin Macquarie Dictionary of Economics & Finance (Penguin Australia Reference Book). Australia: Penguin Books Australia Ltd.

Mattingly, M. (1994). Meaning of urban management. *Cities, 11*(3), 201–205.

Mattingly, M. (1995). Urban management in less developed countries (Working Paper No. 72). https://www.ucl.ac.uk/bartlett/development/sites/bartlett/files/migrated-files/WP72_0.pdf (accessed on 4 September 2019).

McGill, R. (1998). Urban management in developing countries. *Cities, 15*(6), 463–471.

Mumtaz, B., & Wegelin, E. (2001). *Guiding cities*. Washington: World Bank.

Office of the Deputy Prime Minister, National Audit Office. (2006). *Enhancing urban green space*. London: The Stationery Office. https://reader.elsevier.com/reader/sd/pii/S2226585618300815?token=376D15907205594834AFE0D06D58367A8540CAAF9532E4337AB9A98F9D3F806E38DA7DB35402C675AD93C1C63AED7A3C (accessed on 29 June 2019).

Rakodi, C. (Ed.). (1991). *The urban challenge in Africa*. Tokyo: United Nations University Press.

Ramachandran, R. (1989). *Urbanization and urban systems in India*. New Delhi: Oxford.

Reeves, T. K., & Woodward, J. (1970). The Study of Managerial Control. In J. Woodward (Ed.), *Industrial organization: Behavior and control*. London: Oxford University Press. http://faculty.baruch.cuny.edu/tkdas/publications/flamholtz-das-tsui_aos85_control_35-50.pdf (accessed on 15 April 2020).

Sagalyn, L. B. (2007). Public/private development: Lessons from history, research and practice. *Journal of the American Planning Association, 73*(1), 7–22.

Schwarz, N., Moretti, M., Bugalho, M. N., Davies, Z. G., Haase, D., Hack, J., & Knapp, S. (2017). Understanding biodiversity—Ecosystem service relationships in urban areas: A comprehensive literature review. *Ecosystem Services, 27*, 161–171.

Shabbir Cheema, G. (1993). The challenge of urban management: Some issues. In G. Shabbir Cheema (Ed.), *Urban management: Policies and innovations in developing countries* (pp. 1–16). Westport: Greenwood Praeger Press.

Shaw, A. (1996). Urban policy in post-independent India: An appraisal. *Economic & Political Weekly, 31*(4), 224–228.

Stren, R. E. (1993). Urban management in development assistance: An elusive concept. *Cities, 10*(2), 125–139.

Tasan-kok, T., & Zakeczna, M. (2010). *Public–Private partnerships in urban development projects. Polish practices and EU regulations*. https://www.ey.com/Publication/vwLUAssets/Public-private_partnership.pdf/$FILE/ATTDGMR2.pdf (accessed on 29 October 2019).

UN-Habitat. (2007). *Enhancing urban safety and security: Global report on human settlements 2007*. London: UN-Habitat.

UN-Habitat. (2011). *The economic role of cities*. Nairobi: UN-Habitat.

UN-Habitat. (2015). *Habitat III issue papers—4: Urban culture and heritage*. New York: UN-Habitat.

UNCHS. (1995). *Sustainable city news*. Nairobi: UN-Habitat.

United Nations. (2016). *Smart cities and infrastructure* (E/CN.16/2016/2). Commission on Science and Technology for Development, Nineteenth Session, Geneva, 9–13 May. https://unctad.org/meetings/en/SessionalDocuments/ecn162016d2_en.pdf (accessed on 23 April 2019).

Urban Management Program. (1991). *Revised prospectus: Capacity building for urban management in the 1990s.* Nairobi: World Bank. https://www.ucl.ac.uk/bartlett/development/sites/bartlett/files/migrated-files/WP72_0.pdf (accessed on 4 September 2019).

Van Dijk, M. P. (2006). *Managing cities in developing countries: The theory and practice of urban management.* Cheltenham: Edward Elgar Publishing.

Zeb, J., Froese, T., & Vanier, D. (2012). Survey of information technology use for municipal infrastructure management. *Journal of Information Technology in Management, 17*, 179–193.

Zenker, S, Eggers, F., & Farsky, M. (2013). Putting a price tag on cities: Insights into the competitive environment of places. *Cities, 30*(1), 133–139.

5 Urban Governance

A lot of the writing on the concept of urban governance has focused on empirical case studies that have led to the exploration of outcomes of different institutional arrangements for the characteristics of cities.

—Mello and Baiocchi (2006)

Effective urban governance is characterized as democratic and inclusive; long-term and integrated; multi-scale and multilevel; territorial; proficient and conscious of the digital age.

—UN-Habitat[1]

UN-Habitat recognizes that good urban governance is characterized by the interdependent principles of sustainability, equity, efficiency, transparency and accountability, security, civic engagement and citizenship.[2]

Urban governance is the software that enables the urban hardware to function.

—UN-Habitat[3]

Introduction

Governance is the most frequently used term in the nation state of the developing countries. The aim of governance is to provide an efficient, effective, accountable and transparent legislative, executive and judiciary system which would put an end to red-tapism and corruption, and enable the nation states to hasten their pace of economic growth and development, and give better quality of life to their people. It will also enable nation states to effectively utilize their scanty resources for the attainment of higher economic growth and development. Governance plays an effective role in the management of various affairs of the nation states and is an indispensable instrument for facilitating faster development. Governance is sine qua non not only for the effective functioning of government institutions but also for private, NGOs and other CSOs implementing various public funding projects and programmes in partnership with the government and dealing with the public affairs. According to Acemoglu et al. (2003), good governance is not only critical to development but also it is the most important factor in determining whether a country has the capacity to use resources judiciously and effectively to promote economic growth and development. Governance and adherence to its principles have become inevitable for improving the performance of various actors and sectors of development. It is equally important for the development of both urban and rural areas and enhancing their contribution to economic growth and development.

The urbanization process is going on at a faster pace in the developing countries. In order to enable these nation states to have effective urban development, effective urban governance is a vital necessity. Customarily, urban governance is a form of modern state intervention which aims to improve the functioning of the functionaries of the government and LSIs at various levels and enable them to provide developmental services to the people with honesty, accountability and responsiveness. The UN-Habitat claims that, as a concept, it makes cities inclusive, meaning that they show 'unity in diversity' (Obeng-Odoom, 2012). To the votaries and advocators of urban governance, the end of urban governance is to make city development inclusive and sustainable in partnership with various stakeholders of the urban society. Although there is no watertight difference between urban governance and urban management, urban governance is different from the urban management in much respect. Now it is popularly suggested that there should be a shift from urban management to urban governance for better management of urban affairs and effective implementation of urban development projects and programmes. Urban governance is a means to effectively manage urban affairs or to perform urban management. In other words, effective urban governance is a means to effective and efficient urban management. Urban governance involves a number of structures, skills, principles, processes and tools in order to be effective and enable sustainable urban development. The differences between urban governance and urban management has been rightly summarized as management implies a unilateral approach to administration and planning, whereas governance entails multilateral, plural and diverse ways of administering cities, drawing on stakeholders at local, national, regional and international levels (Kearns & Paddison, 2000). This chapter deals with urban governance.

LEARNING OBJECTIVES

After reading this chapter, you should be able to:

- Define urban governance
- Explain the need for urban governance
- Describe the characteristics of good urban governance
- Distinguish between centralized and decentralized urban governance
- Discuss different deficiencies of urban governance
- Explain various measures to make urban governance effective

Urban Governance: Concept and Meaning

The UN Human Settlements Programme defines urban governance as follows:

> the sum of the many ways individuals and institutions, public and private, plan and manage the common affairs of the city. It is a continuing process through which conflicting or diverse interests may be accommodated and cooperative action can be taken. It includes formal institutions as well as informal arrangements and the social capital of citizens. (UN-Habitat, 2002)

According to Hendriks (2013), urban governance refers to more or less institutionalized working arrangements that shape productive and corrective capacities in dealing with urban steering issues involving multiple governmental and non-governmental actors.

The defining feature of urban governance is that the management of cities is not the sole preserve of government or the private sector but is the preserve of a wide variety of actors that interact with one another to govern cities (Maloutas & Malouta, 2004).

Urban governance refers to partnership in urban development between urban local governments and other stakeholders, such as business leaders and landowners (Obeng-Odoom, 2012).

Urban governance substantially transcends the boundaries of governments, making use of a cluster of ideas, ranging from decentralization to entrepreneurialism and to democratization (Blakeley, 2005; Gilbert, 2006; Mello & Baiocchi, 2006).

Urban governance is identified as a scientific pursuit to explore the depth and completeness of how to improve cities by addressing four fundamental research questions scientifically, or four H's: (a) How do cities work? (b) How should cities work? (c) How are plans and decisions made? and (d) how should plans and decisions be made?[4]

Customarily urban governance means how to plan, finance and manage urban affairs with the help, coordination and participation of various stakeholders of urban development such as government functionaries, elected representatives of ULBs, CSOs and RWAs. It involves continuous dialogue, negotiation and contestation with various stakeholders over the allocation of financial, physical and material resources. It helps to establish synergy between the urban administration and LSIs for the effective implementation of urban development programmes, projects and activities formulated by the national and provincial government. Some of the important aims of urban governance are as follows:

1. To apply governance principles in the urban administration and local governance to bring transparency and accountability in delivery of urban development services;
2. To establish coordination between all stakeholders for the effective implementation and management of urban development services;
3. To bring accountability, transparency and responsiveness in urban administration and LSIs;
4. To increase efficiency and effectiveness in urban administration and LSIs at all levels; and
5. To strengthen a decentralized democratic system by effectively empowering the LSIs.

Need and Importance of Urban Governance

There is an emerging consensus that good governance is the sine qua non for sustainable human and settlements development (UN-Habitat, 2002). As the urbanization is taking place at a faster pace, urban governance is of utmost importance for the effective management of urban affairs. According to Slack and Cote, urban governance:

1. Plays a critical role in shaping the physical and social character of urban regions;
2. Influences the quantity and quality of local services and efficiency of delivery;
3. Determines the sharing of costs and distribution of resources among different groups; and
4. Affects residents' ability to access local government and engage in decision-making, influencing local government accountability and responsiveness to citizens' demands.[5]

The need for and benefits of urban governance are as follows:

1. At the outset, the urban governance is needed for the effective utilization of urban resources in order to enhance contribution of urban areas to economic growth and development. It will enable the elected representatives of LSIs to effectively utilize the allotted resources for the development of their municipal area. It will make the elected representative sensitive and accountable to the development needs of city dwellers.
2. Decentralized urban governance will take the governance system closer to the people. Decentralized governance aims at effective devolution of functions, functionaries and funds to the lower level of governance institutions. It will lessen the corruption and red-tapism and will make the elected representative as well as municipal administration accountable and responsive towards the needs of the people. ADB has rightly remarked that many governments have decentralized responsibilities to local governments. This gives local governments a more strategic role in planning and decision-making in urban development.[6] A report on Commission on Global Governance has envisaged that:

   > Local governance is the sum of the many ways in which individuals and institutions, public and private, manage their common affairs. It is a continuing process through which conflicting or diverse interests may be accommodated and cooperative action may be taken. It includes formal institutions and regimes empowered to enforce compliance, as well as informal arrangements that people and institutions either have agreed to or perceive to be in their interest.[7]

3. Urban governance is needed for effective coordination among various stakeholders of urban development. It aims at effective engagement of all stakeholders such as NGOs, private and corporate sectors and CSOs in the process of urban development. The key stakeholders in the urban context include municipal elected officials and non-officials, council and committees, employees and their trade unions, parastatals, government departments, ratepayers' associations, resident welfare groups, chamber of commerce, business associations, NGOs, CBOs, neighbourhood committees, self-help groups, professional organizations, the media and the like. Thus, effectiveness of municipal governance depends on how the interactions between various stakeholders are managed to produce the desired goals of providing civic infrastructure and services to the citizens in a transparent and accountable manner.[8] ADB has urged that cities need to partner with private sector, other cities and organizations to exchange information, build capacities, expand resources and enhance revenues, and implement improvements in urban management.[9]
4. Urban governance is needed for better coordination between the urban administration and LSIs. Better coordination between the urban administration and the elected representatives of the ULBs is needed for faster implementation of urban development policies, projects, programmes and activities at the grassroots level. Moreover, good urban governance will make the municipal administrators accountable to the people. It will also bring transparency in urban administration.
5. Urban governance believes in pluralistic characteristics of the urban society. It aims at holistic development of urban areas by taking into consideration the effective development of the marginalized sections of the society. The people staying in slums and informal settlements in urban areas would be benefitted through the adherence of good urban

governance principles. According to UN-Habitat, strong and capable local governments are the key levers to ensure inclusive and sustainable urban development, accountable and transparent city management and a dynamic multi-stakeholder engagement.[10]

6. Urban governance will lead to better development of the city regions. Every city is expanding in its size and in terms of its population also. Better management of the city region is critical to urban development. It, with the help of good urban governance, can be developed effectively and would provide better lifestyle to the people living in the city regions.
7. One of the goals of good urban governance is to promote peoples' participation in the process of urban development. The city dwellers need not to be considered as passive beneficiaries but active contributors to city development. The active and genuine public involvement is essential in order to (a) develop and deliver programmes effectively and efficiently, (b) build public confidence and trust in decision-making, (c) generate greater understanding of issues, concerns, priorities and solutions at the grassroots level and (d) build broader support for programmes and initiatives, and make the development programme the peoples' programme.

Arms of Urban Governance

The four important arms of urban governance are (a) urban administration, (b) the urban legislatives, (c) constitutional amendments and acts, and (d) other stakeholders: private/corporate sector, bilateral and multilateral organizations, NGOs and CVOs. The effective coordination among different arms of urban governance is sine qua non for urban good governance (Figure 5.1).

1. *Urban administration:* The urban administration is the executive wing of the urban governance. The urban administrations in most of the democracies have been decentralized. Decentralized urban administration starts from the urban development ministry in the centre: having secretaries, directors and other officials and supporting staff; urban development ministry in the states: having secretaries, directors and the official and other staff and the municipal administration system at district and below level levels: chairman/executive officer and other functionaries of the various LSIs at various levels. Good urban governance expects that the functionaries of the urban administration have to discharge their duties and responsibilities in a transparent manner without corruption and with greater degree of accountability and responsiveness. They are also required to follow the rule of law while discharging their duties and responsibilities. Moreover, for the effective delivery of urban services, urban parastatal bodies have been created. The Housing and Urban Development Corporation (HUDCO) is one of the illustrious examples of urban parastatal bodies in India. The administrative system in these bodies has to also follow the principles of good governance while implementing their vision and missions, and also in discharging their duties and responsibilities. The Right to Information and Citizen Charter are instruments aimed at improving the urban governance in India. Making the availability of documents and information about the tasks of urban development agencies, as well as the names and contacts of the functionaries, their duties and responsibilities, period of completing the assignments in the citizen information board and portal are important steps towards improving the accountability of urban administration towards citizens. Pandey

Figure 5.1 Arms of Urban Governance

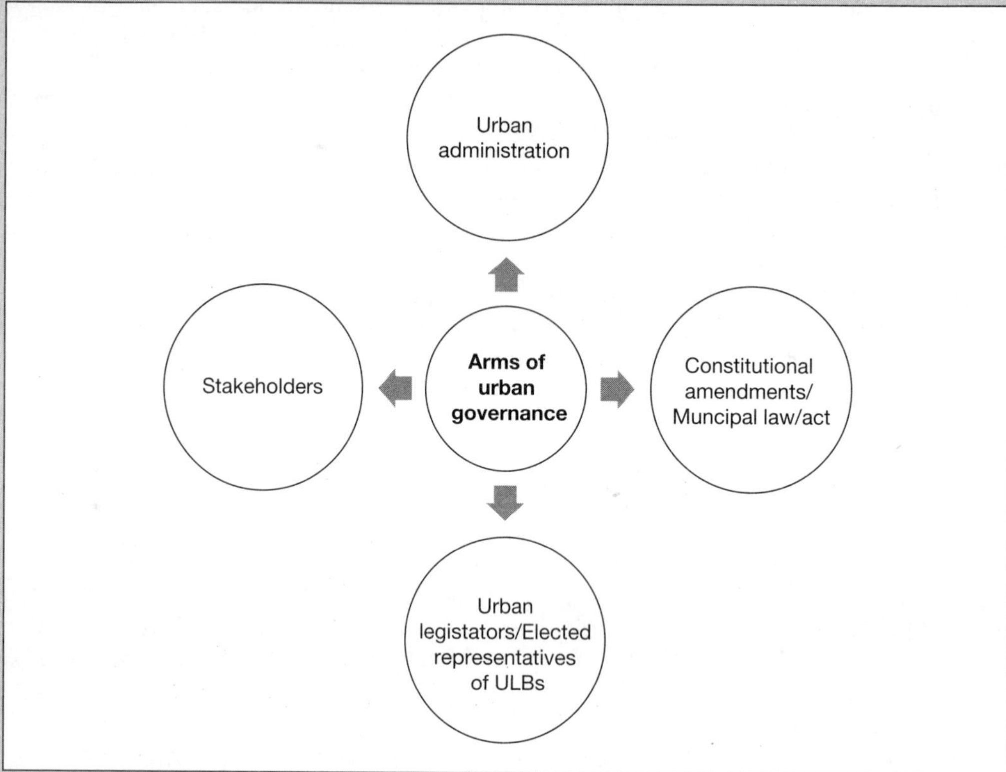

(2012) was of the view that the administration of urban development assumes special connotation with the objective to achieve decentralization, equitable and affordable access to infrastructure and services, poverty alleviation and capacity building of stakeholders at different levels of governance.

2. *Urban legislative system:* The decentralized urban legislative functions start at the centre from the MoUD having the minister of urban development; at the state level, Minister of Urban Development and at the sub-governments level there are chairman/presidents of various ULBs, the designation may vary from one nation state to another. Moreover, the parliamentarian, State Legislative Assembly members and the elected representatives of the ULBs also look after urban development activities at the grassroots level in the cities. In a few European countries, the municipalities are found to have assigned portfolios to councillors to look after specific services such as education, sanitation and health. The ministers, parliamentarians, legislatures at the centre and state level oversee the implementation of urban development policies and programmes in urban areas of their constituencies. In the same vein, the elected representatives of the ULBs also are accountable to their constitutionally assigned duties and responsibilities. They are involved in the

effective implementation of the urban development programmes in their area. Therefore, the good governance principle desires that they need to be responsive to the development of their local areas under the municipalities. The Ward Sabha is considered as local assembly to which the elected representatives are accountable to present their report cards before the people of wards. The Indian democracy considers ULBs as the third-tier democratic institution after the Parliament and State Legislative Assemblies. The Second Administrative Reforms Commission (SARC) in its report on 'Ethics in Governance' had observed: 'If the legislators are beholden to the executive, the legislature can no longer retain its independence and loses the ability to control the Council of Ministers and the army of officials and public servants.' It has suggested that an effective mechanism like empowered legislative committees is therefore needed to enhance the legislators' role to give them an opportunity of exercising positive power for public good.

3. *Constitutional amendments, laws and acts:* The third arm of urban governance is the urban development-related constitutional amendments, laws and acts. Municipal laws in India are very old. Therefore, after the 74th Constitutional Amendment, the GoI developed a Model Municipal Law (MML) in 2003 to guide states to enact municipal legislations (Box 5.1). The basic objectives of MML are to implement the provisions of the 74th Constitutional Amendment and urban sector reform agenda. A model Municipal Law (2003) of the Ministry of Urban Development and Poverty Alleviation, GoI, includes the following:
   a. The Constitution and the government;
   b. Municipal revenue;
   c. Urban environmental infrastructure and services;
   d. Urban environmental management, community health and public safety;
   e. Regulatory jurisdiction; and
   f. Powers, procedures, offences and penalties.[11]

   The 74th Constitutional Amendment of the GoI which is related to empowerment of urban LSIs is an illustrious example of urban governance. It has not only delineated about the structure of ULBs but also assigned them with 18 duties and responsibilities to be carried out for the development of the city. Each state government has formulated their Municipal Act and are also making necessary amendments from time to time to fulfil urban reform agendas and for improving functioning of the ULBs. The good urban governance desires that the elements of Municipal Law and Act have to be religiously implemented for the effective development of the cities. However, these laws and acts are needed to be flexible and made people-centred. Well-formulated Municipal Acts and their effective implementation is sine qua non for good municipal governance. It remarked that the Municipal Act is a comprehensive guiding legal document for the local government officials and the elected representatives, and by-laws are framed to further clarify the administrative procedures (Aijaz, 2006).

4. *Stakeholders:* It is rightly noted that maximizing the potential of urban areas requires institutionalizing mechanisms of coordination, planning and accountability among diverse stakeholders in a way that recognizes the complexity of urban challenges (Applied Knowledge Service, 2016). The stakeholders of the municipal governance are the bilateral and multilateral agencies, the private and corporate sector, NGOs and CVOs. These stakeholders are actively participating in the municipal affairs in order to improve the governance and the service delivery system of municipal government. For example, the World Bank, ADB, European Commission are giving funds to developing countries for the improvement of urban governance system and capacity building of the functionaries and elected representatives of

Box 5.1 Model Municipal Law

The GoI prepared MML in 2003 to address the problems of differences and deficiencies of state municipal acts. The salient features of MML are as follows:

1. A unified law for three levels of ULBs;
2. Executive power of a ULB to be exercised by the 'Empowered Standing Committee';
3. A municipal fund with separate accounts for various services;
4. Indirect election of mayor/chairperson for a five-year term;
5. Constitution of wards and Wards Committee;
6. State-level Municipal Audit Committee to review the staff status;
7. Classification of functions into: (a) core municipal functions (including water supply, drainage, sewerage, SWM, roads and so on); (b) functions assigned by government; and (c) other functions;
8. State government may dissolve an elected body if it shows default in performance or abuse of powers, after giving due notice and review by a committee constituted by the state government. Election has to take place within six months;
9. A State Municipal Accounting Manual with improved system of accounting including double-entry system;
10. State government can appoint a professional chartered accountant as auditor of a ULB;
11. Each ULB to prepare an annual balance sheet of the assets and liabilities;
12. Appointment of a Municipal Accounts Committee similar to the Public Accounts Committee;
13. ULB to prepare an inventory of properties of the municipality each year;
14. State government to frame a Debt Limitation Policy laying down the general principles of borrowings commensurate with ULBs financial capacity;
15. Empower ULBs to generate internal revenues, particularly through PT Assessment System on area or capital value basis;
16. Participation of private sector in construction, financing and delivery of services including billing and collection;
17. Provision of a State Municipal Regulatory Commission to determine user charges and standard of services, to suggest avenues of private sector participation and ensure fair deal to citizens;
18. Provide for the representation of ULBs in District/Metropolitan Planning Committees (MPCs) and provision for the implementation of development plans by ULBs; and
19. ULBs to prepare annual environment and subsidy reports.

Source: CRRID (2006).

the ULBs. Smart Cities Mission in India has involved the private and corporate sectors in the development of smart cities under the aegis of PPP. The last but not the least, role of NGOs, CVOs like RWAs and urban residents as a whole cannot be overemphasized in urban governance system. The effective participation of these institutions in the governance system of the local self-government is helpful to improve the urban governance in the developing countries. This is called participatory urban governance. It is remarked that the purpose of municipal governance and strategic urban planning in a country is to create effective, responsive, democratic, transparent, accountable local governance framework organized according to a rational structure that promotes responsiveness and accountability; to provide responsive policy guidance and assistance to sub-national entities; to strengthen the legal, fiscal, economic and service delivery functions of municipalities and to foster greater citizen participation in the governance of local bodies (Chandrakala, 2017).

Attributes of Good Governance

For the effective urban governance, it is pertinent to discuss various attributes of good governance. UN Economic and Social Commission for Asia and the Pacific has envisaged eight characteristics of good governance, namely participatory, consensus-oriented, accountable, transparent, effective and efficient, equitable and inclusive, and follows the rule of law. Similarly, a 'White Paper on European Governance 2001' of the European Commission has mentioned five good governance principles: openness, participation, accountability, effectiveness and coherence. Customarily, good governance requires a legal framework that is enforced impartially by an independent judiciary. Its decisions and enforcement are transparent or carried out in a manner that follows established rules of law. Some of the common important characteristics of good governance (Figure 5.2) are described further.

1. *Accountability:* One of the important characteristics of good governance is accountability. All the functionaries working in various sectors and also in the organizations of various sectors have to be accountable to their duties and responsibilities. They cannot shy away from their responsibilities. There should not be a tendency to shift the accountability from one person to the other. Shifting of responsibility from one person to another for failure and fighting for taking credit for success are adversaries to accountability. Development projects and programmes have failed largely to improve the quality of life of the city population because of poor accountability on the part of organizations responsible for the implementation of these projects and programmes.

Figure 5.2 Characteristics of Good Governance

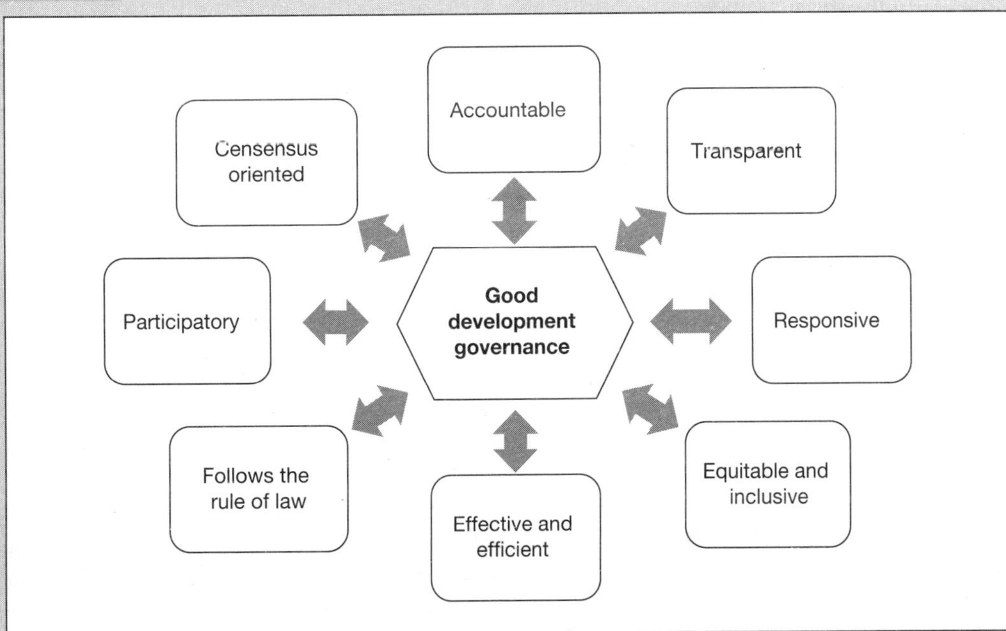

2. *Transparency:* The actors of governance such as government, semi-government organizations, private sector and NGOs and CSOs must be well-intentioned and open to public scrutiny. This is a vital ingredient in preventing corruption. Transparency presupposes that rules and regulations, and procedures must be simple, clear and understandable with fewer amounts of contradictions. Honesty is an important ingredient of transparency.
3. *Responsiveness:* The dictionary meaning of the word 'responsiveness' is quick to react in the way that is needed, suitable or right for a particular situation. Delay in reply is an indication of an attempt to conceal a fact or showing callousness towards a genuine problem. Therefore, institutions and processes try to respond to the queries of stakeholders and beneficiaries of development within a reasonable time. Punctuality is an essential characteristic of responsiveness.
4. *Equitable and inclusive:* The governance needs to follow the principle of equity and inclusiveness. People irrespective of caste, sex, gender and ethnicity must be treated equally. No one should feel having excluded and discriminated. Moreover, to be equitable means assigning preferential benefits to the unequal or have-nots over haves.
5. *Effectiveness and efficiency:* Effectiveness and efficiency are the two important pillars of governance. Efficiency is a productivity metric which means how fast one can do things. While effectiveness is a quality metric meaning how good a person is in doing things. In management terminology, efficiency means doing the things in the right manner, while effectiveness is doing the right things. Both these concepts are two important sides of the coin of good governance and one is meaningless without the other.
6. *Rule of law:* Good governance must apply the rule of law in the development process. According to Sachiko and Durwood (2005; pp. 15–21), the term 'rule of law' is used to mean independent, efficient and accessible judicial and legal systems, with a government that applies fair and equitable laws equally, consistently, coherently and prospectively to all of its people. The key elements of the rule of law are fair, impartial and accessible justice system used for the common good of the people.
7. *Participatory:* Good governance emphasizes on participatory decision-making. Participatory process believes that decisions are not imposed rather followed and accepted through popular participation. According to Haque and Zaffarullah (2006), one of the critical elements of development governance is empowerment of the people, particularly the poor and those marginalized at the grassroots, by expanding their capabilities and enlarging the domain of their participation in and influence over the process of development.
8. *Consensus oriented:* 'Consensus oriented' conventionally means that decision should not be imposed rather be derived. All the stakeholders have to be involved in the decision-making process. It believes in democratic processes rather than in the authoritarian nature of decision-making. UNESCAP (2009) envisages that good governance requires mediation of the different interests in society to reach a broad consensus in society on what is in the best interest of the whole community and how this can be achieved.

Components of Good Governance

Some of the important components of good governance required for the urban governance are explained further.

Decentralized Governance

Most of the countries of the world are now emphasizing upon the decentralized system of governance in the process of rural and urban development. It is aimed at taking effectively governance process closer to the people and makes the development process people-centred. Bardhan and Mokherjee (2000) opined that decentralization, by shifting central rights from the central bureaucrats to a local government, typically tends to expand service deliveries as authority goes to those more responsive to user needs. While betting for the decentralized governance, UN (2000) envisaged that 'men and women have the right to live their lives and raise their children in dignity, free from hunger and from fear of violence, oppression from injustice. Democratic and participatory governance based on the will of the people best assure these rights.' Three important forms of decentralization are devolution, delegation and de-concentration. The devolution aimed at both the authority and functions is transferred from the higher level of government to the lower level of governments. While on the other hand in delegation, the power and sometimes the authority are not transferred, and if transferred, they can be taken away by the power transferring authority. In the case of de-concentration, only the functions and responsibilities are transferred from the higher to the lower government, but not the authority.

The decentralization emphasizes the three main types of decentralization such as political decentralization, administrative decentralization and financial decentralization. The political decentralization aims at transfer of functions and power from the higher level of political institutions and political representatives to the lower level of political institution and representatives and in particular to the LSIs and their representatives. The administrative decentralization aims at transfer of administrative functionaries from the higher level of government to the lower level government while financial decentralization means transfer of funds from a higher level of the government to a lower level of government. According to the World Bank (Decentralization Thematic Group), political decentralization aims to give citizens or their elected representatives more power in public decision-making. In case of the administrative functions performed by the central government are transferred to geographically and administratively distinct administrative units (Pattanaik, 2016). According to the World Bank (Decentralization Thematic Group), administrative decentralization seeks to redistribute authority, responsibility and financial resources for providing public services among different levels of government. It also emphasizes upon the transfer to functionaries from the central and provincial government to the LSIs. The financial decentralization aims at transfer of financial responsibilities from the central and provincial government to the sub-national governments. This means the sub-national governments be endowed with devolution of funds and are empowered to collect local revenue through tax and fees for making the LSIs self-sustaining. It is remarked that in most countries decentralization involves providing for (a) local elections; (b) a division of spending responsibilities or competencies among types of governments; (c) sub-national (e.g., municipal) own taxing authority; (d) rules and regulations relating to local borrowing and debt management; and (e) a special status for capital cities (Slack & Chattopadhyay, 2009).

Participatory Governance

Participatory local governance is one of the important instruments of sustainable development. The participatory governance calls for a political 'space' which only decentralization can provide. In the participatory development governance process, people govern themselves and through their representatives for their own development. In the process of participatory governance, the government and other development agencies only play a catalyst role. According to the World Bank (1996), participatory development is a process by which people, especially disadvantaged people, influence decisions that affect them. Participatory development is an empowering process in which people in partnership with government and other development agencies identify problems and needs, mobilize resources and assume responsibility themselves to plan, manage, control and assess the development projects and programmes which are meant for them. According to ADB (1996), 'participatory development is a process through which stakeholders can influence and share control over development initiatives and over the decisions that affects themselves.' According to Fischer (2012), participatory governance seeks to deepen citizen participation in the governmental process by examining the assumptions and practices of the traditional view that generally hinders the realization of a genuine participatory democracy. Speer (2012) has also remarked that participatory governance mechanisms have been widely promoted in developing countries and they are claimed to bring about several public policy benefits, including increased accountability, higher government responsiveness and better public services. In the Indian context, in the participatory governance, the shared decision-making in the formulation and implementation of urban development activities are entrusted with the Ward Sabhas of the municipalities. The aim of participatory governance is to make the development process need-based and people-centred. It makes peoples' representative accountable to the people of their area as they are one of the stakeholders in the decision-making process.

E-governance

E-governance is commonly defined as the application of electronic means in the interaction between government and citizens, and government and business as well as in internal government operations to simplify and improve the democratic and business aspects of governance (Backus, 2001). According to Heeks (2001), e-governance is the use of ICTs to support good governance. The World Summit on the Information Society which emphasizes on Internet governance (i-governance) intends the 'development and application by governments, the private sector and civil society in their respective roles, of shared principles, norms, rules, decision-making in procedures and programmes that shape the evolution and use of the internet'. The World Summit on the Information Society's declaration principles expressed:

> a common desire and commitment to build a people-centered, inclusive and development-oriented information society, where everyone can create, access, utilize and share information and knowledge, enabling individuals, communities and peoples to achieve their full potential in promoting their sustainable development and improving their quality of life.

Some of the advantages of e-governance are as follows: (a) cost-saving; (b) time-saving; (c) transparent; (d) citizen-centric; and (e) easy accessibility. The urban e-governance centres are providing a lot of services to people at a commonplace. The various angles of urban e-governance are described in Figure 5.3.

Figure 5.3 Angles of Urban E-governance

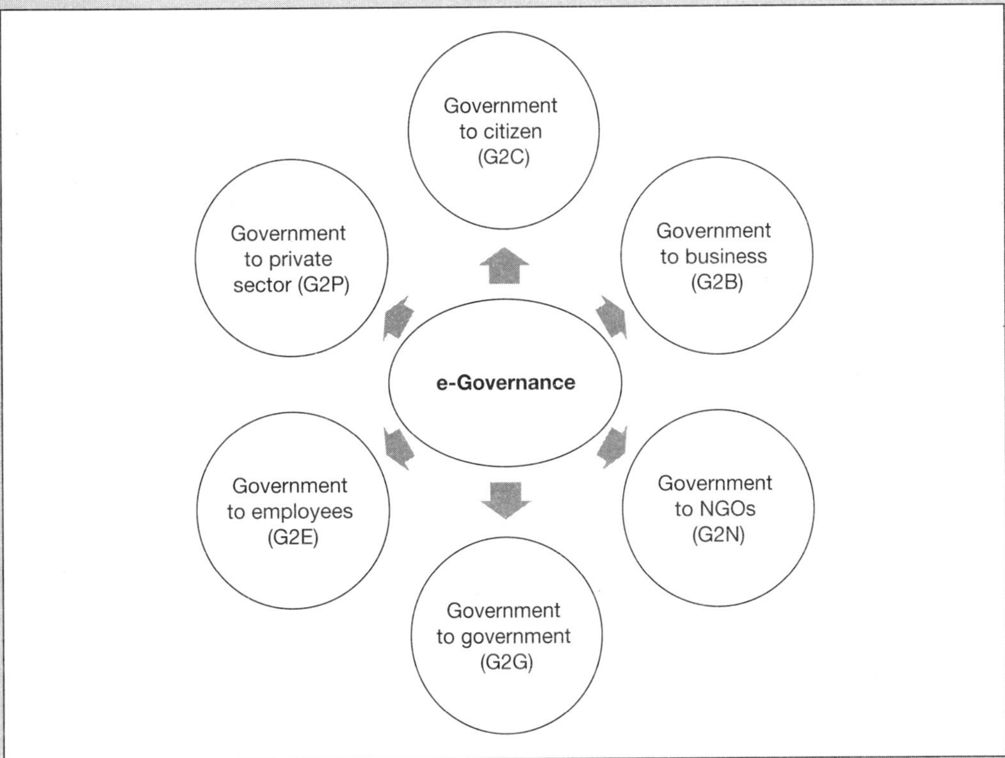

Box 5.2 Sampark Centres, Chandigarh City

The following services are provided in Sampark Centres:

1. Payment of taxes
2. Payment of water and sewerage bills
3. Payment of electricity bills
4. Payment of stickers/postal challan
5. Issue of bus pass
6. Issue of senior citizen cards
7. Issue of birth and death certificates
8. Space booking
9. Tenant registration
10. Domestic servant registration
11. Passport applications
12. Telephone bill payments

Municipal Governance in India

The municipal system in India has a glorious past. The evidence of urban life was found in India since Indus Valley Civilization (2300–1750 BC). In the Indus Valley Civilization, the organized urban life with wide roads, drainage and sewerage system, marketplaces, office places, were found. During the Mauryan period, urban governance was evidenced. The chief executive officers were appointed in urban areas to perform functions related to the city administration. The Greek Ambassador, Megasthenes, who visited the court of Chandragupta Maurya in 303 BC described the City Council which governed Pataliputra comprising six committees with 30 members. Later on, during the Gupta period (320–540 AD), the cities were found to be governed by a council with the provision of an elected administrative officer. However, during the Mughal period, the municipal system was not given adequate importance.

During the British period, the municipal governance in India gained importance. Madras Municipal Corporation was established in 1667. Later on, in 1726, Calcutta Municipal Corporation and Bombay Municipal Corporation were established. In 1850, improvement in Towns Act was made which established a system of councillor and entrusted them with administrative authority. Some of the important resolutions which took place during the British period are narrated further.

1. *Lord Mayo's Resolution 1870:* This resolution triggered off the municipal movement in India. The important features of the resolution are: (a) it provided for decentralization of administration from the centre to the provinces; (b) municipalities were established in every town of importance; and (c) however, these municipal bodies lack autonomy and were completely under the control of the district magistrate.
2. *Lord Ripon's Resolution 1882:* The features of Lord Ripon's Resolution are as follows: (a) at the outset, it advocated for the establishment of a network of LSIs; (b) reduction of the official element of not more than a third of the total membership; (c) measures of financial decentralization; and (d) adoption of election as a means of constituting local bodies.
3. *Government of India Act, 1919:* Government of India Act, 1919, had recommended the following steps for strengthening LSIs: (a) responsibility for local government transferred from the hands of the district officers to a department controlled by a popular minister; (b) franchise for election to local bodies substantially widened; and (c) in some provinces, the municipal bodies were given the power to raise or lower rates of taxes within the statutory limits.

Development of Local-self Governance after India's Independence

After independence and with the formulation of Indian Constitution, the GoI made a sincere attempt to empower LSIs both in rural and urban areas. The Constitutional Provision (1950) put urban local government within the legislative competence of the states. Following ULBs were being created:

1. *Municipal corporation:* Municipal corporations are created largely for the big cities having a population of more than 0.3 million. In the state, these bodies are being created by passing an Act in the state assemblies. While for the union territories, they can be established by the Acts of Indian parliament.
2. *Municipal council:* The municipalities are being created for the administration of smaller cities and towns. It is created for the cities having a population between 50,000 and 0.1 million.

In different states, municipal councils are being created by the Acts of the respective State Legislative Assemblies. While for the union territories, they can be established by the Acts of Indian Parliament.

3. *Notified Area Committee:* A Notified Area Committee (NAC) is established to take care of the administration of an area which is growing fast as a town and is yet to fulfil the condition to create a municipality. Many small cities in various states were being created as NAC but gradually developed into a municipality. It is created after a state government gazette notification and is regulated by the State Municipal Act.
4. *Cantonment board:* These boards are being created for the municipal administration for civilian population dwelling in the cantonment areas. The cantonment board is created and administered by the union government. The provisions enumerated in the Cantonments Act, 2006, a central government act, are applicable for the regulation of the cantonment board. It is to be noted that a cantonment board functions under the administrative control of union defence ministry.
5. *Port trust:* The port trusts are created in the port areas such as Kolkata, Chennai, Mumbai and Paradeep. The main objective behind the creation of a port trust is to manage and protect the ports. A port trust is set up by an act of parliament. Its members include both elected and nominated. The chairman of the port trust is an official. Its civic functions are almost similar to those of a municipality.

Local-self Governance after 73rd and 74th Constitutional Amendment

The 73rd and 74th Constitutional Amendments of 1992 are a watershed in the history of empowerment of LSIs in India. The 73rd Constitutional Amendment deals with the PRIs for rural areas, while the 74th Constitutional Amendment is related to the ULBs for urban areas. Features of the 74th Constitutional Amendment are narrated as follows:

1. Constitution of a uniform typology of ULBs such as Municipal Corporations, Municipal Councils and Nagar Panchayats (the types of ULBs are given in Table 5.1).
2. Constitution and composition of Wards Committees.
3. Periodic election of the ULBs in every five years.
4. Reservation of seats for women, SCs,/STs and OBCs.
5. Establishment of State Election Commission for conduction of election of the LSIs.
6. Establishment of State Finance Commission (SFC) for the powers, authority and responsibilities of municipalities.
7. Constitution of SFCs to look after the financial matter of the LSIs.
8. Formation of the District Planning Committee for the formulation of development plan for the rural and urban areas with the help of LSIs.
9. Assignment of duties and responsibilities to the ULBs under the 12th Schedule of the Constitution. As per the Powers, Authority and Responsibilities of Municipalities (Article 243 - W):

   Subject to the provisions of this Constitution, the Legislature of a State may, by law, endow

   (a) the Municipalities with such powers and authority as may be necessary to enable them to function as institutions of self-government and such law may contain provisions for the devolution of powers and responsibilities upon Municipalities, subject to such conditions as may be specified therein, with respect to:

(i) the preparation of plans for economic development and social justice;

(ii) the performance of functions and the implementation of schemes as may be entrusted to them including those in relation to the matters listed in the Twelfth Schedule;

(b) the Committees with such powers and authority as may be necessary to enable them to carry out the responsibilities conferred upon them including those in relation to the matters listed in the Twelfth Schedule.

As per the Twelfth Schedule, the duties and responsibilities assigned to the ULBs are as follows:

1. Urban planning, including town planning;
2. Regulation of land use and construction of buildings;
3. Planning for economic and social development;
4. Roads and bridges;
5. Water supply for domestic, industrial and commercial purposes;
6. Public health, sanitation, conservancy and SWM;
7. Fire services;
8. Urban forestry, protection of the environment and promotion of ecological aspects;
9. Safeguarding the interests of the weaker sections of society, including the differemtly-abled;
10. Slum improvement and upgradation;
11. Urban poverty alleviation;
12. Provision of urban amenities and facilities, such as parks, gardens and playgrounds;
13. Promotion of cultural, educational and aesthetic aspects;
14. Burials and burial grounds; cremations, cremation grounds and electric crematoriums;
15. Cattle pounds; prevention of cruelty to animals;
16. Vital statistics, including registration of births and deaths;
17. Public amenities, including street lighting, parking lots, bus stops and public conveniences; and
18. Regulation of slaughterhouses and tanneries.

Table 5.1 Types of Urban Local Bodies after the 74th Constitutional Amendment

Types	Name of the Elected Member	Political Head	Administrative Head	Area
Municipal corporation	Councillor directly elected by the people and MPs and MLAs as ex-officio members	Mayor	Municipal commissioner	Larger urban areas. More than 3 lakh population
Municipal council	Councillor directly elected by the people and MPs and MLAs as ex-officio members	President	Executive officer	Smaller urban areas. Population of 50,000 to 1 lakh
Nagar Panchayat	Councillor or ward members	Chairman	Executive officer	Transitional areas from rural to urban

The ULBs are being governed by the municipal administration. The municipal administration is customarily governed by the Municipal Act of various states. Usually, there are two wings: (a) Deliberative Wing and (b) Executive Wing. The Deliberative Wing comprises the following: (a) president, (b) vice-president, (c) councillor and (d) subcommittees. On the other hand, the Executive Wing comprises the following: (a) chairman or executive officer, (b) secretary and (c) other functionaries of the municipal administration.

Deliberative Wing

The deliberate wing of the LSI consists of the following:

1. *President:* President is the head of the Deliberative Wing and is elected by the elected members of the Municipal Council or Committee. He performs both deliberative and executive functions of the council and oversees the executive and financial administration of the council. The election of the president or chairman of the Municipal Corporation and Council varies from state to state. Some states have direct election, while the others have indirect election among the elected members of the council.
2. *Vice-president:* Vice-president is elected among the elected members of the council. He performs all those duties assigned to him/her by the president with the approval of the council. The position and the election process vary from state to state.
3. *Subcommittees:* The subcommittees are the statutory bodies constituted with the approval of the state government. The subcommittees of several types such as finance subcommittee, public works subcommittee, sanitation and water supply subcommittee. The subcommittees also vary from state to state depending on their State Municipal Act.

Executive Wing

The Executive Wing is the administrative wing of the council and is headed by the executive officer. It implements the plans and policies approved by the Deliberative Wing. The executive officer is being assisted by the secretary and other official staff of the council. There are various departments within the council to look after different activities such as general branch, accounts branch, public health branch, waterworks branch, taxation branch and municipal engineering branch. It varies from state to state.

The SARC of India has looked into the metropolitan governance and has specifically recommended a suitable institutional framework covering the following:

1. A Metropolitan Police Authority in all cities with a population above 1 million to oversee community policing, improve police–citizen interface, suggest ways to improve the quality of policing, approve annual police plans and review the working of such plans.
2. A Unified Metropolitan Transport Authority in all megacities should exist to coordinate the planning and implementation of urban transport solutions with overriding priority to public transport.
3. For metropolitan corporations, with a population exceeding 5 million, MPCs may be constituted with the chief minister as the chairperson, whereas other MPCs may have a routine structure of governance.

Box 5.3 Democratic Decentralization in Finland

Finland, a sovereign parliamentary republic, has a democratic administration and governance consisting central–state; intermediate–regional and municipal–local government. The local government enjoys full autonomy and complete freedom to run its affairs without any interventions from either the nation or the provincial government. The Finish Constitution has clearly envisaged that:

> The provincial government has no right to interfere in municipal affairs or to give command to a municipality. The municipalities are not under the administration of the provincial government. If municipality has not performed its task defined in the law or state subsidies, the Provincial Government may command the municipality to complete such a task.

Some of the key features of the autonomy of municipalities are as follows:

1. Municipalities are self-governing units where the highest decision-making authority is vested in local councils elected by the residents.
2. Municipalities provide adequate and quality basic services relating to social welfare, healthcare, education, management of schools, vocational training, libraries, culture, environment and infrastructure such as urban streets, water supply, sewerage, electricity and waste management.
3. The fiscal domain of municipalities is very strong. The budget of municipalities and the joint local authorities exceeds €27 billion.

Source: CRRID (2006).

4. All cities with a population exceeding 5 million should have a Metropolitan Environment Authority to carry out environmental management within the city limits.
5. Due cognizance should be given to primacy of ULBs in a metropolitan region and development authorities should be transferred to ULB or profit made by the development authorities should be shared with ULBs.[12] The constitutional provision of autonomy given to municipality in Finland is given in Box 5.3.

Citizen Participation in Municipal Governance

Citizen participation in local governance is essential in order to make the development programme more democratic and people-centred. The participation process will create an ownership feeling among the people. Platt (1996) has noted three types of participation of local communities and individuals. These are as follows.

1. *Physical participation:* Being present, using one's skills and efforts.
2. *Mental participation:* Conceptualizing the activity, decision-making, organization and management.
3. *Emotional participation:* Assuming responsibility, power and authority.

Zanna (2015) has remarked that citizen participation in local government affairs will bring about development programmes in direct contact with the people and encourage them to become innovative and take initiative. He also suggested that the well-established democratic structure of local government should enhance citizenship participation, local officials should be engaged in building an innovative spirit to improve the delivery of services and the government should also design a people-oriented development programmes at all levels. The basic philosophy of participation is to give locals a meaningful role in local government decisions that affect them.

In India, the municipal governance is a state subject. In compliance with the 74th Constitutional Amendment of India, many states have provided the institution of Wards Committees. The states have adapted the recommendations of the 74th Constitutional Amendment according to their convenience. It is observed that many states have made the provision of the Wards Committees in their State Municipal Act. The constitution and composition of Wards Committees, in general, are as follows:

1. Wards Committees are constituted in municipalities having a population of 0.3 million or more. In some states, they are constituted even if the population is less than 0.3 million. In such cases, certain conditionality like the minimum annual income of the municipality is imposed.
2. Each Wards Committee shall consist of 5–10 wards.
3. The Wards Committee shall consist of the members elected from the wards for which the Wards Committee is constituted.
4. The chairperson of the Wards Committee shall be elected by the members from among themselves. There would be a secretary to assist the Wards Committee in its functioning. The secretary is an official of the municipality to be identified by the commissioner.

The powers and functions of the Wards Committee, in general, are as follows:

1. Maintenance of sanitation, SWM and drainage/sewerage.
2. Maintenance of water work and water supply.
3. Maintenance of roads and street lighting.
4. Maintenance of markets, parks and playgrounds.
5. Maintenance of school buildings, dispensaries and maternity and child welfare centres.
6. Review of revenue collections.
7. Preparation of draft annual budget of its jurisdictions and forwarding the same to the council for consideration and incorporation in municipal budget.
8. Approval of capital and maintenance works to certain limits in some states.

The Ward committees in several states of India are actively participating in the implementation of various urban development programmes in their locality. As representatives of the people, they are raising peoples' concern before the government officials engaged in the implementation of various programmes and projects. They are engaging people to contribute in cash and kind towards development of their own locality. It is argued that an effective participation or empowered people can make governance more accountable, more transparent and more legitimate (JICA, 1995).

WHO has rightly glorified the role of citizen participation in the following words (Nakajimo, 1982):

> People are the true measure of the success of policies and programmes. At the same time, people are the determinants of success. Experience teaches us that, whether in the most sophisticated cities or in the most remote villages, when people act with determination and understanding in pursuit of goals they deem essential, they achieve success. Previously insoluble problems are solved and resources are mobilized. Miracles happen.

Merits of Citizen Participation in Local Governance

Some of the merits of citizen participation in local governance are as follows.

1. *Improve citizen participation in public service:* This is essential for the effective delivery of government welfare scheme launched for the benefit of common men. Citizen participation will make programme and projects need-based and people-centred.
2. *It will make public service demand-driven:* The supply-driven model of government services has been failed to fulfil the needs and aspirations of the common men. Involvement of people will make them responsible and also engage them to contribute towards the programmes.
3. *It will strengthen the decentralization process:* One of the aims of decentralization is to promote peoples' participation. The goal of decentralization will be realized only when there is peoples' participation in the government action and activities.
4. *Improve the implementation and monitoring process:* These two processes are vital in the launching of any programmes and projects. Citizens' involvement in the implementation and monitoring process will reduce the cost and also enable the implementing agencies to effectively find out the gaps.
5. *Enhance the knowledge and skill of local people:* Peoples' involvement is an effective way to enhance on-hand knowledge and skill of local people. It will indirectly reduce the cost of capacity building. It will also better promote networking between the government functionaries and the people.
6. *It will lead to better convergence:* Citizen participation is a better way to promote convergence of the actions of various stakeholders of development including government. A citizen can better coordinate with the private, NGOs and other parallel bodies functioning at the grassroots for the local area development.
7. *It will strengthen grassroots democracy:* Citizen participation is a vital means to promote the end of good democracy. Citizen participation will not only promote their role in the implementation of development programmes but also lead to strengthen grassroots democracy and their participation in the election process to the various democratic institutions such as parliament, Legislative Assemblies and LSIs and grassroots-level parallel bodies.

Barriers to Citizen Participation in Local Governance

Some of the important barriers to citizen participation in local governance are as follows:

1. *Lack of community-level organization and community membership:* The community participation will be strengthened only when there are strong community-level organizations such as youth clubs, self-help groups, cooperative societies and farmers' associations. These institutions are found to be either not present or even if present are not effectively involving themselves in the urban development affairs. Any urban development project or programme which does not get adequate community support at the grassroots level cannot be effective enough to attain its desired goals and objectives.
2. *Weak community interaction and social networking:* Social networking is essential for effective citizen participation in local area development. The wards where there is weak

social networking among different communities, effective citizen participation in local area development may not be possible. In the era of the e-networking era, people have greater access to mobile phone and Internet services in municipalities. The urban development functionaries and the stakeholders of urban development have to take advantage of this networking system.

3. *Weakness of the capabilities of statutory bodies:* The statutory bodies within the LSIs are either not formulated or, if formulated, are weak to carry out their duties and responsibilities. For example, if the Ward Sabha, which is a statutory body of the ULBs, is weak then it cannot promote effective community participation for the local area development. Moreover, weak capacity building of these bodies is also one of the vital factors for their ineffective functioning.
4. *Lack of community members' skills and knowledge:* The members of various community-level organizations lack skills and knowledge about their roles and functions. This does not help them in facilitating effective community participation in municipal affairs.
5. *Lack of incentives and promotions to citizen participation:* The national and provincial governments do not take the necessary initiative and also do not incentivize citizen participation in the functioning of the LSIs. In India, except Kerala, no other states have incentivized citizen participation in the local area development.
6. *Lack of political and bureaucratic will:* There is lack of political and bureaucratic will to involve the citizen in development affairs. The fear of being exposed and altruistic motive to indulge in corruption also are responsible factors which dissuade them to involve public in local development programmes and projects.
7. *Lack of awareness about values of people's participation:* There is lack of public awareness about the power of citizen participation and its effect on local area development. There is also lack of awareness about various case studies on benefits of public participation in local affairs.
8. *Administrative centralization:* Too much centralization and mindset of bureaucratic authoritarianism are deterrent to democratic decentralization. The weak devolution of functions, functionaries and funds to the LSIs in many states of India are illustrious examples of authoritarianism. It is pertinent to mention here that the DDC which is supposed to be chaired by the political head of the zilla parishad in many places is being chaired by the administrative head of the district. As the representatives of the ULBs are closer to the people, they can more effectively promote citizen participation than other administrative heads.
9. *Lack of social capital:* The strong social-level institutions such as *mahila mandals* (women groups), youth organizations, religious and cultural associations and RWAs are needed for effective citizen participation. It is found to be lacking in many municipalities and localities which prevent citizen participation in local area development.

Characteristics of Good Urban Governance

Urban areas nowadays contribute significantly towards the economic growth of the developed as well as developing countries. Good governance of the municipalities would enable them to enhance their contribution to GDP. Some characteristics of good urban governance given in Figure 5.4 are narrated further.

1. *Urban governance as democratization:* The urban governance needs to follow the principle of democratization. There should be free and fair periodic elections to the ULBs. Effective

representation of the disadvantaged sections of the society such as women, and people belonging to different castes, communities and ethnic group will strengthen the local area democracy. The lower level democratic institutions such as Ward Sabhas have to be strengthened in order to promote peoples' voice in their own local area development. This, in other words, emphasizes on inclusive representation in the ULBs. The 'deep democracy' approach focuses on the potential benefits of (a) more inclusive representation at the local level (for instance, through quotas); (b) proximity between voters and elected representatives; and (c) increased possibilities of participation—thus suggesting that the local could be the locus of regeneration of democracy.[13]

Brillantes (1997) remarked that:

> Local governments indeed play a central role in any democratizing polity. For one, being in the frontline, they are regarded by many citizens as THE government. If local governments fail and are not responsive to the basic needs of the people, then government to these people is failure, regardless of the grandiose plans and visions of the national government.

2. *Urban governance as decentralization:* One of the important principles of the good urban development governance is decentralization of urban governance. The functions, funds and functionaries must be transferred to the ULBs those are closer to the people. The decentralization emphasizes on entrusting authority to the lower level of LSIs. One of the major promises of decentralization is that it brings popular participation and accountability to local governance and, therefore, makes the local government more responsive to citizens' desires and more effective in delivering services (Clarke & Gaile, 1998; Harvey, 1989).
3. *Urban governance as pluralistic:* The good urban governance has to emphasize upon the pluralistic culture of urban areas. The urban paradox is very much revealed in most of the cities of the developing countries. The countryside people migrate to urban areas for better employment opportunities. These are people belonging to various castes, communities and ethnic groups. In recent years also, women of various age groups flung to urban areas for jobs. An urban area is an agglomeration of different cultures. The pluralism believes that the religion and culture of various people groups have to be respected. Besides, various actors of development such as the corporate sector, private sector, business groups and NGOs are also found to be present in urban areas and are performing various activities in different areas of urban development. Urban pluralism believes that the ethos, attitudes, cultures of various actors have to be taken into consideration while formulating plans for urban development.
4. *Urban governance as entrepreneurialism:* In recent years, governments in both developed and developing countries have encouraged entrepreneurialism in the growth and development of modern cities. The government is encouraging PPP in city development. In India, Tata Steel City is an illustrious example where the Tata Company has developed Tatanagar, an industrial city which provides good quality of life to city dwellers. It has been remarked that 'the new urban entrepreneurialism typically rests...on a public–private partnership focusing on investment and economic development with the speculative construction of place rather than amelioration of conditions within a particular territory as its immediate (though by no means exclusive) political and economic goal.'[14] According to Harvey (1989), urban governance has become increasingly preoccupied with the exploration of new ways in which to foster and encourage local development and employment growth and such an entrepreneurial stance contrasts with the managerial practices of earlier

decades which primarily focused on the local provision of services, facilities and benefits to urban populations.[15] Good urban governance needs to encourage entrepreneurialism. It will reduce the burden on the government. The private entrepreneurs need to be encouraged to invest in various areas of urban development such as education, health, sanitation, drinking water and communication. The entrepreneurialism needs to be the engine of urban development.

5. *Urban governance as localization:* Localization is described as 'the process of defining, implementing and monitoring strategies at the local level for achieving global, national, and sub-national sustainable development goals and targets'.[16] The good urban governance needs to be closer to the people and work to resolve local issues working in close coordination with the local-level institutions and with the participation of local people. In the decentralized model of development, LSIs are primarily expected to work with the local people, assess their developmental needs and help them to resolve through various issues of urban development with the cooperation of different actors of development such as government, corporate sector, private sector and NGOs. Further, close coordination between national and local governments and also between other stakeholders desires a clear division of roles and responsibilities. It needs to address gaps in terms of capacity, information and resources.
6. *Urban governance as institutionalization:* The good urban governance principle desires that the decentralized institutions formulated for carrying out urban development activities are properly institutionalized. It also means that these decentralized institutions must be entrusted with functions, functionaries and funds so that they carry out their roles and responsibilities with full freedom. For example, in the decentralized model of local governance in India, the institutions working at the various levels for the development of urban areas are the Municipal Corporation, Municipal Council and Nagar Panchayats. At the grassroots level, these institutions are supported by the grassroots-level statutory bodies such as the municipal wards and Ward Sabhas. These institutions are to be strengthened and effectively institutionalized and empowered. Besides, the other related institutions such as the Finance Commission (FC) at the central and state level, State Election Commission and so on and parastatal bodies have to be empowered to discharge their duties and responsibilities effectively. In India, the Kerala government has taken several steps for the effective institutionalization of the LSIs. The path-breaking decision that paved the way to strengthen LSIs in Kerala was to earmark one-third of the development fund to the local governments as untied funds (1996) and to transfer institutions and officials relating to the 28 subjects, to the three-tier panchayats and ULBs (1995).[17]
7. *Urban governance as participatory:* Peoples' participation in urban governance is an instrument to guide local development and governance. There are various ways of involving citizens in the governance process, including providing information; enabling citizens to take part in decision-making, implementation or evaluation and sharing benefits.[18] Michels and Graaf (2010) in their study in two municipalities of the Netherlands revealed that citizen participation has a wide range of positive outcomes, including increasing citizens' feelings of responsibility, encouraging people to listen to diverse opinions and enhancing the legitimacy of decision-making. Citizen participation has been characterized as necessary to ensure a good relationship with the public, better service quality and better decision-making which in turn requires a shift in policy, budget and commitment (Office of the Deputy Prime Minister, 2002). Moreover, citizen participation is thought to promote accountability, legitimacy, transparency

and empowerment (Bohman, 2005; Schillemans, 2008). The participatory mechanism is considered as one of the effective mechanisms for urban governance.

8. *Urban governance as collective wisdom:* It is largely felt that good governance suffers from democratic deficits. It requires collective actions and group leadership to solve common problems existing at the local level both in rural and urban areas. Collective wisdom is an essential need for good governance. Collective wisdom is otherwise known as 'collective intelligence' and 'inclusive decision-making'. Landemore (2012) was of the view that people flock together because they know they can achieve more as a group than they could on their own, and they make decisions collectively because they believe that the expected quality of such decisions will be, on average, smarter than the expected quality of those that only one of them would make on their behalf. It is remarked that from the governance perspective, which transcends the public and private sectors as well as the civil society, the focus should be on networks rather than hierarchical relations, reinforced by diversified resources and actors and their knowledge and experience (Dool et al., 2015). UN-Habitat (2001) in the Asian context has also recognized that:

> Governance of human settlements in Asia today involves multiple actors and stakeholders, interdependent resources and actions, shared purposes and blurred boundaries between the public and the private, formal and informal, and state and civil society sectors. The active involvement of these varied actors in governance indicates a greater need for coordination, negotiation and building consensus.

Figure 5.4 Features of Urban Good Governance

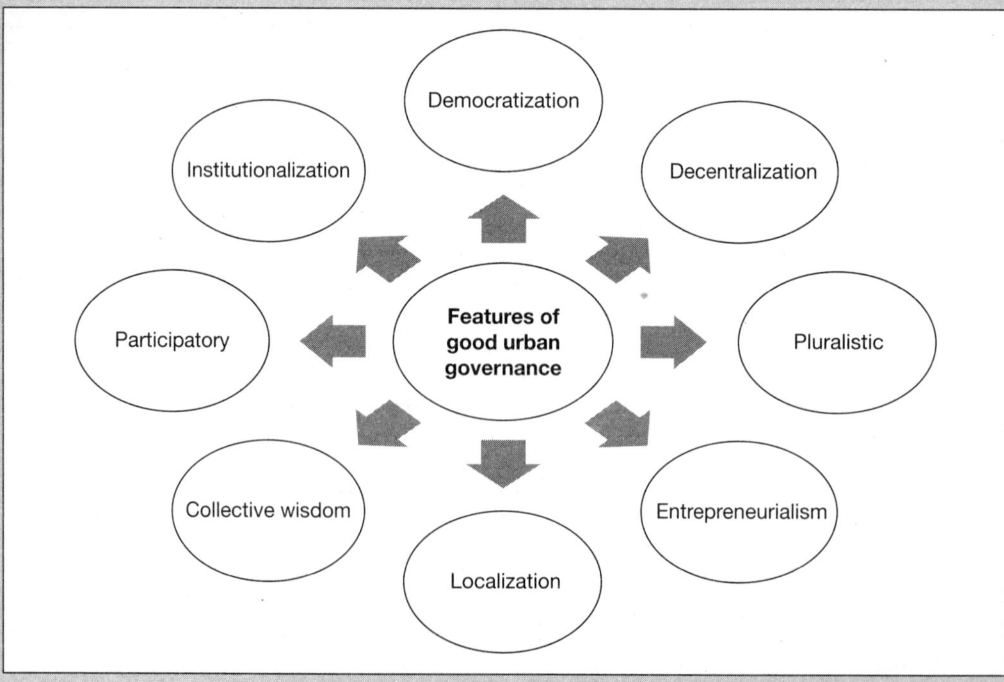

Lacunas in Urban Governance

The local self-governments in many developing countries are not effectively and efficiently functioning due to poor urban governance. Some of the impediments in effective urban governance are discussed further.

1. *Ineffective urban reform:* The urban reform process which includes urban governance is very slow and ineffective. Lack of political and bureaucratic willpower is also responsible for the ineffective formulation of urban reform measures leading to poor urban governance. The urban reforms as enshrined in the 74th Constitutional Amendment are not uniformly implemented across different states of the Indian union. For example, many states in India are slow in the implementation of the democratic decentralized governance process as mandated in the 74th Constitutional Amendment dealing with the ULBs.
2. *Weak decentralization:* The decentralization process in many countries is very poor and the process also varies from one province to the other in the same country. The higher-order legislative and bureaucratic representatives and functionaries, respectively, are reluctant to transfer power to the sub-national bodies. This has created hurdle in the path of smooth urban governance and transfer of functions, functionaries and funds to the ULBs. One of the studies on urban governance has noted that the city governments face challenges such as poor fiscal decentralization, dominance of the state government in taking decisions and unavailability of property records for efficient PT collection. The city governments also lack the capacity to budget and utilize money. Any fiscal decision needs the approval of the Directorate of Municipal Administration equivalent to the state government. Thus, the city governments cannot take decisions and depend on the state.[19]
3. *Lack of citizen participation:* There is poor peoples' participation in the process of urban governance. The grassroots-level government functionaries and the elected representatives of the municipalities do not take adequate interest to woo people to participate in municipal affairs. People are also not aware of the benefit of citizen participation in municipal governance. It is remarked that people lack knowledge on the legal and institutional aspects of citizen participation in urban local government.[20]
4. *Lack of capacity building:* Many of the elected representatives of the LSIs at the grassroots level lack knowledge about the municipal act and also their duties and responsibilities. Because of lack of knowledge, they are unable to discharge their duties and responsibilities effectively and efficiently. Moreover, the functionaries of the LSIs are also not well aware about how to promote community participation in municipal governance. This leads to delay in the implementation of various urban development projects and programmes.
5. *Poor e-governance:* The e-governance at the grassroots level in the municipalities, especially at the ward level, is very poor. This resulted in lack of transparency in the distribution of development benefits to the people. Besides, proper maintenance of records in computer hardware and software, poor collection of fee and taxes at the local level is because of poor e-governance system. To Sangita and Dash (2005), the issues such as inadequate skilled manpower, lack of proper attitudinal orientation on the part of officials and people, inadequate e-infrastructure, instances of people misusing the technology, lack of proper awareness on the part of the general public, lack of adequate funding and so on, which hinder the progress of electronic governance in India.

6. *Deficiency of social capital*: There is a deficiency of social capital at the grassroots level. The social networking among different groups of population belonging to different caste, class and ethnic groups is still prevailing at the grassroots level in various transformational ULBs. The social-level institutions such as *mahila mandals*, self-help groups, youth clubs and other associations can play an important role in social networking among different groups of population in urban municipalities. As Maloney et al. (2000) put it, 'the governance of an area is affected by social capital, but is itself an influence on social capital.' If governments are able to affect the development of social capital, it may be possible to break out of 'un-civic' vicious circles and actively promote the 'virtuous' combination of civic engagement and good governance.

Measures to Strengthen Urban Governance

Some of the measures to strengthen urban governance are as follows:

1. *Formulation of urban reforms for urban governance:* The urban reform needs to be a continuous process and nation states have to initiate urban reform process from time to time keeping in mind the globalization. The developing countries have to continuously look at the case studies of good urban governance and urban reforms available in various countries of the world. The urban land reform and reform in urban governance need to be given priorities. To Vaidya (2009), the second generation of urban reforms should further focus on regulation, innovative financing and PPP, and climate change initiatives.
2. *Strengthening the process of decentralization:* One of the attributes of urban governance is the decentralization, that is, transfer of power from central and provincial governments to the LSIs. However, it is seen that the decentralization process in most of the developing countries is very poor. The LSIs are not effectively empowered to carry out their duties and responsibilities with full freedom. Effective decentralization is the answer to good governance. It is rightly remarked that decentralization is promoted as a means of strengthening the state for developing countries suffering from low organizational capacity, poor public service provision and sectarian violence (Brancati, 2004).
3. *Capacity building at all levels:* Effective urban governance calls for capacity building of the elected representatives and functionaries of various ULBs at various levels. Capacity building of elected representatives of the LSIs and their functionaries are essential to empower them to effectively follow various principles of good governance. Moreover, the integrated capacity building programme of the elected representatives and functionaries of the various development departments and functionaries of other stakeholders functioning at the grassroots level will promote participatory governance. Aijaz (2010) has identified that the capacity building of municipal functionaries as an approach to strengthen municipal work practices and thereby improve the performance of municipalities in India.
4. *Institutionalizing urban governance institutions:* The institutions involved in the urban governance process such as State Election Commission, SFC, District Planning Committees and the Ward Sabhas have to be established and empowered. Institutional functioning is vital to urban governance and development. Moreover, the effective institutionalizations of the parastatal bodies are also equally important to urban governance. Vaidya (2009) said

that the institutional arrangement for municipal governance and urban service delivery mainly comprises the Constitutional provisions, state municipal laws, the role of SFC and Central Finance Commission (CFC) and the status of ULBs and parastatals.

5. *Institutionalization of e-governance:* The e-governance is the need of the hour in the digital world. It will strengthen the efficacy of urban governance. It will make the urban governance more transparent and accountable. Direct digital transfer of benefits to the beneficiaries of various development programmes in India is one of the illustrious examples of e-governance. For example, the government of Madhya Pradesh has implemented e-governance in the local body through their portal.[21] By using this central portal, a citizen of MP can get many e-governance services. While Gujarat has no central portal for the implementation of all ULBs, various municipal corporations had implemented their own portal for providing e-governance to the citizens of respective corporation. For example, the Rajkot Municipal Corporation has its own portal.[22]
6. *Enhancement of peoples' participation in urban governance:* The good governance necessitates that peoples' participation may be vigorously promoted in urban governance. Peoples' participation in urban governance will make urban development cost-effective and transparent, and more accountable. Moreover, peoples' participation is a milestone of participatory governance. H. Ramachandran has remarked that all political power in democracy stems from people. Central, therefore, to governance is the empowerment of people by increasing their control over governance.[23]
7. *PPP in urban governance:* The example of PPP in urban governance is being reported in many countries. With the globalization, private sectors are becoming important stakeholders in urban governance both in developed and developing countries. The effective division duties and responsibilities between the private and public sector with regard to various areas of urban governance are required; however, it is lacking and needs to be promoted. PPPs are the preferred vehicles for the planning, financing and implementation of contemporary urban development (Goldstein & Mele, 2016).
8. *Social capital formation:* Social capital is considered as the best way to promote participatory urban governance for urban development. Strengthening social institutions at the grassroots level is critical to the effective implementation of urban development projects and programmes. According to the Second Administrative Reforms Commission (2008), GoI, there are several ways in which social capital can improve government performance. First, it can broaden government accountability; government must be responsive to citizens at large rather than to narrow sectarian interests. Second, it can facilitate the agreement where political preferences are polarized. Third, it induces innovation in policymaking.

Summing Up

The urbanization is going on at a rapid pace in both developed and developing countries. With growing urbanization, the role of urban governance in the process of urbanization has become vital. Urban governance stresses on the effective and smooth management of urban affairs; effective and efficient implementation of urban development projects and programmes, and establishment of urban governance-related institutions and their capacity building for carrying out urban affairs effectively and efficiently. The smart governance or good governance aims at establishment of smart cities, which is empowered to raise the quality of life of urban dwellers. It emphasizes on e-governance and participatory governance in order to deal with urban issues such as poverty, unemployment, pollution and crime more effectively and efficiently. The United Nations (2002) conference held in Nairobi envisaged that 'good urban governance' principles have become a global standard in urban policies. This concept is advocated as a strategy for improving the quality of life in urban settlements both in developed and developing countries where sustainable growth and inclusive urban policies are threatened from rapid urbanization. According to UN-Habitat's Human Settlements Programme, these indicators are subsidiarity, sustainability, equity, efficiency, transparency, accountability, civic engagement, citizenship and security. According to the Human Development Report 1993, where decentralization has taken place, it has often been quite successful, encouraging local participation, increasing accountability of local officials, reducing costs and increasing efficiency.[24]

Keywords

Governance, Accountability, Collective Wisdom, Institutionalization, Decentralization, E-governance, Participatory Governance, Social Capital, ULBs, Urban Reforms, Localization, Ward Committee

REVIEW QUESTIONS

1. Define urban governance. Explain the merits of urban governance.
2. Describe the importance of urban governance in urban development.
3. Explain the attributes of good governance.
4. Discuss in detail various features of good urban governance.
5. Explain the features of the 74th Constitutional Amendment in India. Critically discuss its role in urban governance.
6. Describe the weaknesses of urban governance. Suggest the measures to be taken in order to strengthen urban governance.
7. Define citizen participation. Discuss the role of citizen participation in urban governance.
8. What are the merits of citizen participation in urban governance? Suggests steps to be taken for the promotion of citizen participation in governance.

Notes

1. https://unhabitat.org/governance/ (accessed on 28 October 2018).
2. https://unhabitat.org/wp-content/uploads/2014/03/Hub-Urban-Governance.pdf (accessed on 1 November 2019).
3. https://unhabitat.org/governance/ (accessed on 12 April 2019).
4. http://www.ntpu.edu.tw/ipug/files/IPUG-AnIntroductiontoUrbanGovernance.docx (accessed on 24 November 2019).
5. https://gsdrc.org/topic-guides/urban-governance/concepts-and-debates/what-is-urban-governance/ (accessed on 15 April 2019).

6. https://www.adb.org/themes/urban-development/issues (accessed on 30 October 2018).
7. https://www.adb.org/themes/urban-development/issues (accessed on 30 October 2018).
8. https://unhabitat.org/governance/ (accessed on 12 April 2019).
9. https://cgg.gov.in/core/uploads//2017/07/Municipal_Accountability_Transparency.pdf (accessed on 2 November 2019).
10. See Constitutional Provisions Relating to Village Panchayats and Municipalities in India (1999: 13–14; 18–19).
11. https://www.indiawaterportal.org/articles/model-muncipal-law-ministry-urban-development-and-poverty-alleviation-2003 (accessed on 16 April 2019).
12. https://journals.openedition.org/samaj/3188 (accessed on 13 April 2019).
13. https://journals.sagepub.com/doi/10.1177/097542531200300110 (accessed on 13 April 2019).
14. https://journals.sagepub.com/doi/10.1177/097542531200300110 (accessed on 13 April 2019).
15. https://www.uclg.org/sites/default/files/towards_the_localization_of_the_sdgs.pdf (accessed on 22 November 2018).
16. https://cgg.gov.in/core/uploads//2017/07/Municipal_Accountability_Transparency.pdf (accessed on 24 November 2019).
17. https://epress.lib.uts.edu.au/journals/index.php/cjlg/article/view/5451/5907 (accessed on 22 November 2018).
18. https://epress.lib.uts.edu.au/journals/index.php/cjlg/article/view/5451/5907 (accessed on 22 November 2018).
19. http://iopscience.iop.org/article/10.1088/1757–899X/245/8/082017/pdf (accessed on 26 November 2018).
20. https://praja.org/praja_docs/praja_downloads/Regional%20Consultation%20Phase%201-%20Key%20Findings.pdf (accessed on 2 November 2019).
21. http://www.mpenagarpalika.gov.in (accessed on 24 March 2020).
22. rmc.gov.in (accessed on 24 March 2020); http://www.ijsrp.org/research-paper-0217/ijsrp-p6216.pdf (accessed on 28 April 2019).
23. http://planningcommission.gov.in/reports/genrep/bkpap2020/15_bg2020.pdf (accessed on 28 April 2019).
24. http://planningcommission.gov.in/reports/genrep/bkpap2020/15_bg2020.pdf (accessed on 28 April 2019).

References

Acemoglu, D., Johnson, S., Rohinson, J., & Thaicharoen, Y. (2003). Institutional causes, macro-economic symptoms: Volatility, crises and growth. *Journal of Monetary Economics, 50*(1), 49–123.

ADB. (1996). *Framework for mainstreaming participatory development process into bank operation.* Manila: Asian Development Bank.

Aijaz, R. (2006). Challenges of urban local governments in India (Asia Research Centre Working Paper No. 19). London: London School of Economics and Political Science. http://www.lse.ac.uk/asiaResearchCentre/_files/ARCWP19-Aijaz.pdf (accessed on 16 April 2019).

Aijaz, R. (2010). Capacity building of municipal functionaries for good governance in Uttarakhand, India. *Habitat International, 34*(4), 386–391.

Applied Knowledge Service. (2016). *Urban governance.* Birmingham: GSDRC International Development Department, College of Social Science, University of Birmingham. http://gsdrc.org/wp-content/uploads/2016/11/UrbanGov_GSDRC.pdf (accessed on 29 April 2019).

Backus, M. (2001). E-governance and developing countries (*Research Report*, 3). Hague: IICD.

Bardhan, P., & Moorkherjee, D. (2006). *Decentralization and local governance in developing countries.* Cambridge: MIT Press.

Blakeley, G. (2005). Local governance and local democracy: The Barcelona model. *Local Government Studies, 31*(2), 149–165.

Bohman, J. (2005). From demos to demoi: Democracy across borders. *Ratio Juris, 18*(3), 293–314.

Brancati, D. (2004). Can federalism stabilize Iraq? *The Washington Quarterly, 27*(2, Spring), 7–21.

Brillantes, Alex Jr. (1997). Local governments in a democratizing polity: Trends and prospects. In Felipe Miranda (Ed.), *Democratization: Philippine perspectives* (p. 97). Quezon City: University of Philippines Press.

Chandrakala, M. (2017). Administrative system of municipal corporations in India. *Asian Review of Social Sciences, 6*(2), 40–44.

Clarke, S. E., & Gaile, G. L. (1998). *The work of cities.* Minneapolis: University of Minnesota Press.

CRRID. (2006). *Manual for capacity building of local self-government institutions in Punjab.* Chandigarh: Centre for Research in Rural and Industrial Development.

Dool, L. van den, Hendriks, F., Gianoli, A., & Schaap, A. (2015). *The quest for good urban governance: Theoretical reflections and international practices.* Wiesbaden: Springer.

Gilbert, A. (2006). Good urban governance: Evidence from a model city? *Bulletin of Latin American Research, 25*, 392–419.

Goldstein, B. T., & Mele, C. (2016). Governance within public–private partnerships and the politics of urban development. *Journal of Space and Polity, 2*(2), 194–211.

Haque, A. S., & Zafarulla, H. (2006). Introduction: Challenges of governing development. In A. S. Haque, & H. Zafarulla (Eds.), *International development governance* (pp. 1–12). London: Taylor and Francis.

Harvey, D. (1989). *From managerialism to entrepreneurialism: The transformation in urban governance in late capitalism.* https://www.tandfonline.com/doi/abs/10.1080/04353684.1989.11879583 (accessed on 22 November 2018).

Heeks, R. (2001). *Building e-governance for development: A framework for national and donor action* (I-Government Working Paper Series, No.12). Manchester, UK: Institute for Development Policy & Management, University of Manchester.

Hendriks, F. (2013). Understanding good urban governance: Essentials, shifts, and values. *Urban Affairs Review, 50*(4), 553–576.

JICA. (1995). 'Participatory development and good governance report of the aid study committee'. Study Reports. https://www.anzam.org/wp-content/uploads/pdf-manager/864_ANZAM2010-203.PDF (accessed on 16/11/2018).

Kearns, A., & Paddison, R. (2000). New challenges for urban governance. *Urban Studies, 37*(5–6), 845–850.

Landemore, H. E. (2012). Why the many are smarter than the few and why it matters. *Journal of Public Deliberation, 8*(1), 1–14.

Maloney, W., Smith, G., & Stoker, G. (2000). Social capital and urban governance. *Political Studies, 48*(4), 802–820.

Maloutas, T., & Malouta, M. P. (2004). The glass menagerie of urban governance and social cohesion: Concepts and stakes/concepts as stakes. *International Journal of Urban and Regional Research*, 28, 449–465.

Mello, M., & Baiocchi, G. (2006). Deliberative democracy and local governance: Towards a new agenda. *International Journal of Urban and Regional Research, 30*(3), 587–600.

Michels, A., & Graaf, L. D. (2010). Examining citizen participation: Local participatory policy-making and democracy. *Local Government Studies, 36*(4), 477–491.

Nakajimo, H. (1982). *Editorial: A grand alliance.* New York: World Health Organization.

Obeng-Odoom, F. (2012). On the origin, meaning, and evaluation of urban governance. *Norwegian Journal of Geography, 66*(4), 204–212.

Office of the Deputy Prime Minister (ODPM). (2002). *Public participation in local government: A survey of local authorities.* London: Demelza Birch, Local and Regional Government Research Unit, Office of the Deputy Prime Minister. https://epress.lib.uts.edu.au/journals/index.php/cjlg/article/view/5451/5907 (accessed on 22 November 2018).

Pandey, K. K. (2012). *Administration of urban development and urban service delivery.* Theme paper for the 56th Members' Annual Conference 2012, Indian Institute of Public Administration, New Delhi. http://www.iipa.org.in/upload/theme%20paper%20members%20conference.pdf (accessed on 28 April 2019).

Pattanaik, B. K. (2016). *Introduction of development studies*. New Delhi: SAGE.

Platt, I. (1996, August). *Review of participatory monitoring and evaluation*. Report prepared for Concern Worldwide. Dublin: Concern Worldwide.

Sangita, S. N., & Dash, B. C. (2005). Electronic governance and service delivery in India: Theory and practice (Working Paper No. 165). Bengaluru: Institute for Social and Economic Change. http://www.isec.ac.in/WP%20-%20165.pdf (accessed on 2 November 2019).

Sachiko, M., & Durwood, Z. (2005). *Rule of law, good governance, and sustainable development*. Paper presented at Seventh International Conference on Environmental Compliance and Enforcement. https://core.ac.uk/download/pdf/82226798.pdf (accessed on 15 April 2020).

Schillemans, T. (2008). Accountability in the shadow of hierarchy: The horizontal accountability of agencies. *Public Organization Review*, *8*(2), 175–194.

Second Administrative Reforms Commission. (2008). *Social capital: A shared destiny*. Ninth Report. New Delhi: Government of India. https://darpg.gov.in/sites/default/files/Social_Capital9.pdf (accessed on 28 April 2019).

Slack, E., & Chattopadhyay, R. (Eds.) (2009). *Finance and governance of capital cities in federal system*. Montreal and Kinston: McGill-Queen's University Press.

Speer, J. (2012). Participatory governance reform: A good strategy for increasing government responsiveness and improving public services? *World Development*, *40*(12), 2379–2398.

UNESCAP. (2009). *What is good governance?* Bangkok: United Nations Economic and Social Commission for Asia and the Pacific.

UN-Habitat. (2001). *Cities in a globalizing world, global report on human settlements*. Nairobi: UN-Habitat; London: Earthscan.

UN-Habitat. (2002). *Global campaign on urban governance*. Concept Paper (2nd revised edition). Nairobi: UN-Habitat.

Vaidya, C. (2009). *Urban issues, reforms and way forward in India*. New Delhi: Department of Economic Affairs, Ministry of Finance, Government of India. https://dea.gov.in/sites/default/files/Urbanissues_reforms.pdf (accessed on 28 April 2019).

World Bank. (1996). *The World Bank participatory source book*. Washington, DC: The World Bank.

6 Municipal Finance

There is a consensus that cities' resources should be in line with their responsibilities—for example, larger cities need to spend more and therefore need to mobilize more local revenues—fiscal theory recognizes that local governments have a limited tax base.

—Bird (2009)

Local governments throughout the world are under increasing financial pressure to do more with less.

—Kopanyi and Morrell (2014)

Municipal finance is about the revenue and expenditure decisions of municipal governments.

—UN-Habitat (2009)

Finance is the lifeblood of urban development. To meet the rising demands of urbanization, municipalities need adequate revenue tools to pay for services and infrastructure (UN-Habitat, 2009). It is not a flight of fancy, but truly development measures cannot be undertaken, and development projects, programmes and activities cannot be effectively and properly implemented unless and until adequate and sustainable finances are assured. In the democratic decentralized system, most of the local area city development projects and programmes are being implemented through LSIs; therefore, sustainable finance to LSIs is sine qua non for sustainable development of urban areas through ULBs at various levels. The municipal finance is pertinent for the infrastructure development and provisioning of essential services to city dwellers. Shortage of finance and mis-utilization of financial resources are reported as main municipal financial concerns in most municipalities of the developing countries. Thus, finance is the kingpin of municipal development. Way back, Claw (1896) said that in connection with city affairs, the topic most needing scholarly investigation is finance; budget, classification of city functions, taxation, local monopolies, debt and sinking funds are subjects which are required a knowledge of their history and theory for adequate treatment. The Zero Draft for the Addis Ababa Accord, released in March, recognizes that '...in more and more countries, responsibilities for revenues, expenditures and investments in sustainable development are being devolved to the sub-national level and municipalities, which often lack adequate technical capacity, financing and support.'[1] Urban finance in the true sense means municipal finance. It is rightly remarked that municipalities cannot deliver services to the community without sufficient municipal finances, and have to raise income from taxes, levies, rates and service charges paid by ratepayers (Mazibuko & Fourie, 2013). Considering significance of municipal finance, it can be emphatically said that any discussion on the subject of urban development will not be complete if it does not give adequate coverage to urban finance. Even urban planning will be futile without assured municipal finance. This chapter deals with municipal finance.

LEARNING OBJECTIVES

After reading this chapter, you should be able to:

- ❐ Explain the meaning of municipal finance
- ❐ Narrate the need and importance of municipal finance in urban development
- ❐ Describe fiscal decentralization and municipal finance
- ❐ Explain the various sources of municipal revenue and types of municipal expenditure
- ❐ Describe urban financial management and its exigencies
- ❐ Discuss the issues and challenges of municipal revenue before the municipal administration
- ❐ Suggests measures to be taken to strengthen municipal finance

Municipal Finance: Concept and Meaning

In simple term, 'municipal finance' means revenue and expenditure of the ULBs or municipal government. The 74th Constitutional Amendment of GoI has been broadly categorized as LSIs in India as the Nagar Panchayats, Municipal Councils and the Municipal Corporations. They have been recognized as the third-tier democratic institutions in Indian democracy. Several studies on urban finance have noted that the financial empowerment of these LSIs is one of the critical areas of concerns. In general parlance, municipal finance means income and expenditure system of the LSIs. According to UN-Habitat, municipal finance covers the sources of revenue that are used by municipal governments—taxes (property, income, sales, excise and taxes), user fees and intergovernmental transfers. It also addresses issues around expenditures at the local level and the accountability for expenditure and revenue decisions including the municipal budgeting process and financial management (UN-Habitat, 2009). The coin of municipal finance has two sides. One side of municipal revenue of the LSIs largely comprises revenue transfers from the central and state government and their power to raise revenue through other sources such as tax, fee, loans and bonds. The other side deals with the expenditure incurred by the LSIs for provisioning urban infrastructure and other essential services to city dwellers.

Municipal Finance: Need and Importance

Finance is the backbone and the lifeblood of central, state as well as local governments. It is a fuel for the administrative machinery to undertake urban development programmes, projects and activities. The sound fiscal policy is of crucial importance to the government, whether central, state or local. Kautilya (1956), the great Indian philosopher, remarked 'all undertakings depend upon finance; hence foremost attention should be paid to the treasury.' Hicks (1966) said that 'If local bodies are to play any significant part in economic or social development, they must clearly have access to adequate finances.' The Economic Survey 1991–1992 has rightly stated: 'The financial sector is the centre of economic activity; its health affects the entire economy, municipal governments are directly linked with the availability and utilization of financial resources.'

According to the World Bank, if local governments and private organizations are to carry out decentralized functions effectively, they must have an adequate level of revenues—either raised locally or transferred from the central government—as well as the authority to make decisions about expenditures.[2] For faster and effective urban development at the grassroots level in urban areas, ULBs need finance. A few important reasons for the need and importance of municipal finance are as follows:

1. Regular flow of finance will enable the development administration to implement urban development projects and programmes smoothly. Finance is the key to the implementation of any development projects and programmes. The importance of finance is so great in administration that Lloyd George once remarked that 'government is finance' (Sharma 1978). It will help to build urban infrastructure and provide urban utility services.
2. Many of the experts have remarked that too much dependence of the ULBs on the central and state government funding will not make them self-sustainable. For self-sustaining LSIs, the ULBs need financial empowerment. Timely, effective and adequate devolution of finance is also very important from the standpoint of economic empowerment of municipal bodies. In another words, for sustainable urban development, sustainable finance is essential. The UNDP has rightly said that governments at the sub-national level need to be able to access and mobilize diverse sources of finance to make long-term investments in sustainable urban development.[3]
3. In recent years, particularly in India, the ULBs are being constitutionally assigned 18 duties and responsibilities. For exercising their duties and responsibilities, these local bodies require finance. The proper financial management and financial administration is required for the efficient management of urban finance. Financial administration is the art and science of planning, organizing, implementing, monitoring and evaluating the financial resources to ensure their best use for the achievement of the objectives, goals and targets of municipal development projects and programmes. While financial management deals with financial accounting, budgeting, auditing and reporting of municipal finance.
4. The urban finance includes the empowerment of ULBs for the collection of taxes and fees from the citizen in order to provide quality services to the people. Article 243W and 243X of the Constitution of India impose a duty upon the state legislature to endow the municipalities with such powers and functions in the form of taxation, fee and so on to enable them to perform their functions. The availability of finance through tax and fee will empower the ULBs with untied money to spend on need-based infrastructure development and provisioning of utility services at the grassroots level.
5. Urban finance is required for improving urban governance. It will make functionaries and the elected representatives of the LSIs accountable to the people. It would enable them to serve the people of their local area in a transparent manner and through social auditing in coordination with the functionaries of ULBs. IMF (2001) has envisaged that fiscal decentralization—the assignment of expenditure and revenue mobilization functions to

sub-national levels of government—is associated with various indicators of governance, such as corruption, rule of law and government effectiveness.

6. Urban finance will enhance the contribution of urban areas to the economic growth of the nation states. Investment in the infrastructure such as road, electricity, sewerage system, drinking water and sanitation will raise the quality of life of the urban people. It is pertinent to mention here that in most of the countries of the world, the contribution of urban areas to the GDP is much higher than the contribution of the rural areas. It will enable them generate employment in the local areas. Municipal finance even affects poverty reduction through its impact on the ability of municipal governments to undertake effective pro-poor programmes in the areas of social, economic, health, education and community development.
7. To USAID (2006), municipal finance affects the quality of the natural environment through its impact on municipal services such as water supply, sewage treatment, SWM and public transportation. Through effective SWM, the ULBs can control pollution. The financial investment in smart transport will also be helpful to control environmental pollution.
8. Urban finance and financial investment in slum upgradation would make the city life sustainable and inclusive. Moreover, investment in the education, healthcare, welfare of women, children, disabled and other marginalized urban dwellers will not only make city inclusive but can improve country's achievement in the world ranking of SDGs.
9. Finance is critical to make the city smart by investing in smart infrastructure development. It will enable the urban administration to make effective planning for a sustainable and smart city. Moreover, for the renewal of old cities, finance is very vital. To Deloitte (2017), government financial officers can play a key role in enabling city reinvestment and modernization using fiscal policy, PPPs and performance-based revenue models.
10. Finance is critical to disaster management that is largely happening in cites of various countries. The super earthquake in the city of Surat (Gujarat), and the flood-related disasters in Chennai (Tamil Nadu) and Mumbai (Maharashtra) are a few examples among many where the finance is vital to the reconstruction of damage done due to disasters. To World Bank (2018), for many cities around the world, strengthening urban resilience is a multibillion-dollar agenda that requires strong partnerships and new sources of capital.
11. Decentralization in general and intergovernmental decentralization of financial resources in particular, will be helpful in nation-building and in the eradication of regional and inter-regional disparities. In some countries, decentralization has been a strategy to promote national cohesion and to defuse tensions if society is fragmented by ethnicity, religion, language, endowment of natural resources or other conditions (Muwonge & Ebel, 2014).

Fiscal Decentralization

Fiscal decentralization is an important area of municipal finance. The discussion on urban finance basically starts from fiscal decentralization. In other words, fiscal decentralization is one of the vital starting points of discussion on municipal finance. Effective fiscal decentralization and devolution of funds from the central and provincial government to the sub-national governments will enable them to effectively undertake developmental activities at the grassroots level in urban areas. Fiscal decentralization aims at shifting of financial responsibilities such as revenue and expenditure from the central and state government to local governments. It is one of the important dimensions of economic empowerment of the ULBs. To Coady (2017), fiscal decentralization is a transfer of responsibility for fiscal policies from the national level to the region, sub-region or local levels. It could increase accountability of sub-national governments to their citizens and also encourage competition between sub-national governments.

To begin with, decentralization is the devolution or reassignment of specific powers 'with all of the administrative, political, and economic attributes that these [powers] entail' from central government to sub-national governments which are autonomous within their own geographic and functional spheres of authority (Faguet, 2014). The decentralization aims at devolution of functions, functionaries and funds to the sub-national government with full autonomy. As far as financial devolution is concerned, it means the devolution of funds from the central and state government to the sub-national governments. According to Kenneth Davey, fiscal decentralization comprises the financial aspects of devolution to regional and local government and it covers two interrelated issues: (a) first is the division of spending and (b) the amount of discretion to be given to regional and local governments to determine their expenditures and revenues.[4] According to the Overseas Development Institute (ODI), fiscal decentralization means the manner in which control and responsibility for the handling of funds is shifted from central government to sub-national government.[5]

According to the World Bank,[6] the fiscal decentralization can take many forms, including:

1. Self-financing or cost recovery through user charges;
2. Co-financing or co-production arrangements through which the users participate in providing services and infrastructure through monetary or labour contributions;
3. Expansion of local revenues through property or sales taxes, or indirect charges;
4. Intergovernmental transfers that shift general revenues from taxes collected by the central government to local governments for general or specific uses; and
5. Authorization of municipal borrowing and the mobilization of either national or local government resources through loan guarantees.

Need and Importance of Fiscal Decentralization

Decentralization in general, and fiscal decentralization in particular, is critical to the financial and economic empowerment of the local bodies. It is one of the vital principles of devolution. Customarily, fiscal decentralization means the devolution of finance from the higher level of government to the local government with full autonomy. This calls for fiscal sector reform and willingness on the part of the legislative and bureaucratic system to religiously adhere to the decentralization principles and practices. Shah (2004) has rightly envisaged that the elements of a comprehensive package of fiscal system reforms would include: (a) clarifying roles of various levels of government in public service delivery; (b) reassigning taxing responsibilities to ensure local revenue autonomy, accountability and efficiency without endangering an internal common market; (c) designing fiscal transfers to ensure regional fiscal equity and to create an enabling environment for innovative and competitive service delivery; (d) facilitating responsible credit market access to sub-national governments; (e) designing institutional arrangements for intergovernmental fiscal relations to better coordinate policies; and (f) aligning operational capacity with the authorizing environment through the 'accountability for results' framework of public management.

Some of the factors which are critical to the need and importance of fiscal decentralization are discussed further.

1. *Fiscal federalism:* The fiscal decentralization to the LSIs, which is recognized as the third-tier democratic intuitions aims at promoting fiscal federalism. It is remarked that fiscal decentralization is a mechanism of fiscal federalism and can be considered as a necessary condition of the latter because there is no point in a vertical financial structure of the public sector without a certain level of decentralization (Yushkov, 2015).
2. *Effective provisioning of public goods to the local people:* If financial autonomy is given to the sub-national government which is closer to the people, they can spend it more effectively as per the needs and aspirations of the people. It will make development programmes demand driven and people-centric. According to Musgrave, the federal government should be responsible for macroeconomic stabilization and income redistribution, whereas sub-national (regional and local) authorities, which are closer to citizens and possess more information on their preferences, should ensure the efficiency of public goods provision within their jurisdictions (Musgrave, 1959).
3. *Participatory governance:* Decentralized democratic system intends to promote decentralized governance in the democratic institutions that are closer to the people. It places greater accountability on the functionaries and elected representatives of the local government and responsiveness on the citizen. The fiscal federalism and devolution of finance to the LSIs will bring transparency in the administration as people will be involved in the planning, implementation and monitoring of the development projects and programmes. According to Joshi (2010), collective accountability mechanisms are better suited to use by the poor and vulnerable, and are more likely to result in improved public good benefits as opposed to the private benefits that can be the outcomes of individual action and in particular collective accountability is more likely to result in reduced corruption and increased empowerment of people as citizens.
4. *Participatory budgeting:* One of the aims of fiscal decentralization is to promote participatory budgeting. Under participatory budgeting, people are actively involved along with local government and other stakeholders to decide the allocation of funds to their locality and modality of expenditure and public contribution. It is remarked that under participatory budgeting, citizens are empowered to deliberate part of the resource allocation in their communities while the role of politicians is reduced to executing the resulting budget. Some of the acclaimed results of participatory budgeting experiences are as follows: (a) better accountability; (b) lower levels of corruption; (c) improvement of public service delivery; (d) reversion of priorities/pro-poor policies; (e) more social justice/redistribution in allocating resources; and (f) efficiency gains and more rational administration.[7] It is also commented that participatory budgeting aims to improve accountability and responsiveness by opening up the 'black box' of budgetary design and implementation to the whole of society. This allows narrowing down the information asymmetries between policymakers and citizens, and encourages further checks by the latter on the former's activities—particularly relevant in a context characterized by widespread clientelistic and corrupt practices as is the case in Brazil.[8]
5. *Fiscal empowerment of local government:* Fiscal decentralization means fiscal empowerment of the local government, that is, their power to raise resources at the local level, spend funds for the development of people and prepare the road map of expenditure to be incurred by

the local government. Fiscal decentralization with fiscal autonomy to raise revenue and incur expenditure will make the devolution process effective and efficient taking into considerations the aspirations of the people. Bahl considers fiscal decentralization as 'the empowerment of people by the [fiscal] empowerment of their local governments'.[9]

6. *Urban development governance:* Fiscal decentralization is called for improving the urban development governance at the grassroots level. It helps to promote sustainable and inclusive development at the grassroots level. In the fiscal decentralization, funds are effectively used for the following reasons: (a) utilization fund is demand-driven rather than supply-driven as there is high degree of local involvement; (b) it makes financial operation transparent and accountable; (c) it is free from red-tapism and government interventions; (d) it is inclusive as it is carefully targeted towards improving the quality of life of the poor; and (f) finally, it promotes sustainable development by allocating judiciously towards the fulfilment of basic needs of the marginalized sections of the society. C. R. Hankla considers decentralization's impact on three policy outcomes: (a) the targeting and efficient provision of public goods; (b) inequality and regionalism; and (c) macroeconomic stability.[10]

Criteria for Fiscal Decentralization

Local government financial management is very vital for the effective utilization of finances available to the ULBs from various sources. Moreover, the transfers of funds from the central and state government to the local bodies are to be based on certain rationale and criteria so that equity in the distribution of financial resources to various local bodies is adhered to. Some of the criteria to be followed during the process of the devolution of funds to the local bodies are discussed further.

1. *Clarity:* While allocating grants to the ULBs, the grant objectives must be clearly spelt out so that the grants are being used for the allocated purpose only. Lack of clarity will lead to deviation which can defeat the purpose of devolution.
2. *Autonomy:* The local bodies must have complete autonomy and given full flexibility to set out their priorities for which the grants are to be used. The sub-national government should be given the freedom to use the allotted financial resources based on the needs of the local areas.
3. *Responsiveness:* The grant given for the various urban development programmes to different ULBs should be flexible to meet the responsiveness of the localities. In other words, grants allotted need to have the flexibility to accommodate unforeseen changes in the fiscal situations of the cities. An example of responsiveness is the action to meet the disaster response.
4. *Equity (fairness):* One of the notable quotes on equity is that 'from each according to one's ability and to each according to one's needs'. The size, need of resources and development attainments vary from one municipality to the other. Therefore, it would be better if the allocated funds vary and are directly linked to the fiscal need factors.
5. *Predictability:* The grant mechanism needs to ensure predictability of the total size of the financial allocation to be made available to the local bodies annually or for the period of five years. This will help the local bodies to plan their developmental activities accordingly.
6. *Simplicity:* The formula for the transfer of funds to the various local bodies needs to be very simple and understandable so that it will not create any confusion and doubt in the minds of the local bodies. Both the central and provincial governments have to devise their own

formula based on various criteria such as socioeconomic conditions, demography and geography of the allocation of resources to the ULBs. Grant allocation should be based on objective factors over which individual units can have little control.

7. *Absorptive capacity:* It is recommended that the resources needed to be transferred based on the capability of the ULB to utilize them within the given financial years or earmarked stipulated time period. This indicates performance-based allocation.
8. *Incentive:* The financial allocation could be based on such a design which would provide incentives for sound fiscal management. The ULBs generating adequate self-finance through taxes and fees may be given incentive for their endeavour. It will encourage others and also make the ULBs self-sustaining and competitive.
9. *Inclusiveness:* Removal of urban poverty needs to be the first priority in the allocation of fiscal resources to the ULBs. Besides, special grants should be made available for the inclusive development purpose such as upgradation of the living standard of the slum dwellers, development of the village areas of the cities and other disadvantage sections of city dwellers. This will make the urban development process inclusive.
10. *Sustainability:* The focus of the 21st century is to make the city sustainable and smart. The allocation of finance on these two vital critera has become popular in recent years in the developing countries, particularly in India. The sustainable criteria emphasize the sustainability of the development work of the municipal areas after the withdrawal or closing of the project or programme. Its main aim is to develop alternative sources of funding through corporate and community participation.
11. *Accountability for results:* The allocation of finance needs to be based on the accountability of the ULBs to produce developmental outputs and service delivery at various fronts of city development. Allocation of funds without accountability can sometimes lead to underutilization and less effective utilization of finance allocated to the ULBs. It is remarked that output-based transfers respect local autonomy and budgetary flexibility while providing incentives and accountability mechanisms to improve service delivery.[11]

Municipal Revenue and Expenditure

The revenues and expenditures of municipalities determine their ability to deliver services. Weaknesses in revenue and expenditure management could constrain the ability of a municipality to contribute to poverty reduction and economic development.[12] The municipal revenue basically refers to the various sources of income of the ULBs, while municipal expenditure gives an account of the spending of the earned income on various developmental activities and services. The revenue and expenditure status of the municipalities also influences the governance aspects of the municipalities.

Municipal Revenue

Nowadays how to finance cities by municipalities has become a big challenge, as access to favourable and sustainable revenue sources leads municipalities to play a more active role in an urban environment and properly meet the needs of citizens (Hajilou et al., 2018). Most of the municipalities in the developing countries lack adequate financial resources to carry out the developmental activities in their municipal areas. Lack of finance is a critical challenge before the urban managers, most particularly in the cities of the developing countries. The financial problems of these cities arise due to the lack of sustainable sources of finance from the central as well as provincial governments, scanty own sources of taxable and non-taxable revenue and their inability to raise revenue through municipal bonds. Because of poor sources of revenue, most of the municipalities heavily depend on fiscal transfer from the central and state governments. It is largely felt that generation of adequate sources of revenue and to receive finance through devolution from the central and state governments are revenue challenges before the ULBs.

The sources of revenue for local governments vary across countries but generally include taxes, user fees and charges, and intergovernmental transfers. Other revenues may include investment income, property sales, and licenses and permits (Freire & Garzon, 2014). However, experiences of different countries indicate that the most important financial sources of municipalities are supplied by taxes, tolls and state supports in the form of current budgets of local governments and local establishments and equipment and finally, borrowings and loans (Ayatollahi, 2008).

The common sources of revenue for the municipalities are discussed further.

1. *Intergovernmental transfer:* The central and state government transfers a percentage of their taxable income to the sub-national governments. It varies from country to country. In India, the fiscal transfer is based on the recommendations of the CFC and SFC constituted in every five year.
2. *Tax:* Some of the important sources of taxable income of the municipal bodies are PT, house tax, sales tax, motor vehicle tax, individual income tax, corporate tax, toll tax, show tax and so on. In India, municipalities do not collect income tax; however, in the European countries, for example, Finland, municipalities collect individual income tax.
3. *Fee and charges:* These include education fee, hospital fee, entertainment fee, advertisement fee, parking fee, construction and development fee, *tehbazari* fee, slaughterhouse fee, dead animal fee, sale of land, garden and roadside trees, dangerous and offensive trade licenses and so on. The municipalities also charge the users for using various utilities such as the use of facilities of the common service centres, electricity, water, sewerage, cable connection, solar energy, gas connection, slaughterhouse fee and market fee.
4. *Municipal bond:* A revenue bond is a municipal bond supported by the revenue from a specific project, such as a toll bridge, highway or local stadium. Revenue bonds are municipal bonds that finance income-producing projects and are secured by a specified revenue source.[13] In India, municipal bonds are fixed-income instruments or debt securities which are issued by Municipal Corporations, government and semi-government institutions to raise funds.[14] The

Exhibit 6.1 Pune Municipal Bond

Like any other bond, municipal bonds are debt instruments—a promise to repay a fixed principal amount with interest periodically, which can be paid at fixed intervals or at the end of the tenure, with the principal. For instance, the coupon rate for Pune municipal bonds was 7.5 per cent semi-annual. In the case of Pune municipal bonds, the money collected will be used to provide uninterrupted municipal water supply in the city.

Source: https://www.livemint.com/Money/nVebfz5LBzbz4LDVp7lKxJ/Municipal-bonds-of-Indian-cities.html (accessed on 5 December 2018).

Municipal Bond was first issued in 1997 by the Bangalore Municipal Corporation to raise revenue from the market. An example of Pune Municipal Bond is given in Exhibit 6.1.

5. *Borrowings/Loans:* Loan borrowed by the ULBs from the central and state governments and from other banking and non-banking financial institutions for meeting capital expenditures.
6. *Development assistance:* There are two types of development assistance such as domestic assistance (i.e., disaster relief) by the state governments, private and corporate sector and other individual donors and international development assistance from various agencies, for example, World Bank, the UNDP, ADB and so on for meeting the unforeseen situations arising in the city to build up city infrastructure.
7. *Municipal development fund:* Municipal development funds (MDFs) are financial intermediaries that provide credit to local governments and to other institutions investing in local infrastructure. Around the world, more than 60 countries have established financial intermediaries of this kind. In larger, federal nations such as Brazil and India, individual states often have established their own MDFs.[15] MDF is created above the individual local government level primarily with a purpose to invest in infrastructure development at the municipality level. The MDF is being managed by different institutions or government agencies and is being called Municipal Development Intermediaries. These are being found in Western European countries and also in Japan. The MDFs lend money to local governments for long-term investment at preferential rates which cover interest and administration costs.

The sources of local revenue of selected countries are given in Tables 6.1 and 6.2. Examples of sources of revenue of municipalities of Finland and Spain are given in Exhibit 6.2. Truly, the local government's revenue sources in most of the countries in the world are dependent on the transfer from central and state governments. Their own sources of revenue through tax, fee and other charges are very low to carry out infrastructure and other utility service activities. One of the findings shows that the total revenue of the municipal sector accounts for about 0.75 per cent of GDP

Exhibit 6.2 **Examples of Source of Revenue for Finland and Spain**

Sources of revenue of municipalities of Finland (2003) are as follows:

- Taxes: 47 per cent
- State grants: 17 per cent
- Sales of goods and services: 27 per cent
- Borrowings: 6 per cent
- Other revenues: 3 per cent

Types of taxes paid by the people in municipal area of Spain are as follows:

- House tax
- Garbage tax
- Vehicle tax
- Enterprise tax
- Energy tax
- Water tax

Source: CRRID (2006).

Table 6.1 Local Government Revenue Sources of a Few Countries

Country	Sources of Local Government Revenue
Australia	Grants and general or special purpose payments of federal and state governments comprise 23% of local government revenues. Other sources include tax on immovable property, fees and fines, net operating surplus of trading enterprises and interest.
India	Tax revenue—properties, octroi, professions and vehicles; non-tax revenue—licenses and services charges, grants-in-aid and state/central government loans and borrowing.
Kenya	Fees and charges, water and sewerage fees, local property, taxes and business permits.
Pakistan	Tax and octroi (comprising 60% of local governments revenues) and non-tax sources. Property-related taxes (such as local rates or leases on all land assessable to either rent, land revenue or use).
Sri Lanka	Rate, taxes, duties, fees, fines, penalties and other charges as well as money from sales, leases or other transaction, revenues derived from properties and grants from other government spheres.
Ghana	Taxes, user fees and charges.

Source: http://www.clgf.org.uk/default/assets/File/Publications/reports/2006%20Municipal%20Finance%20 Paper.pdf (accessed on 10 April 2019).

Table 6.2 Structure of Local Revenues, Selected Countries, 2006 (%)

	Local Taxes					
Country	Property Tax	Income and Business Tax	Total Local Taxes (Including Shared Taxes	Grants	Other Revenues (Including Fees and Sales of Assets	Total
Australia	39	0	39	14	47	100
Canada	38	0	20	70	10	100
Finland	2	44	47	29	24	100
Sweden	–	58	59	22	19	100
Spain	16	10	52	36	12	100
Brazil	4	–	13	63	24	100
Kenya	16	0	21	33	46	100
Thailand	8	–	55	31	14	100
Mumbai (India)	19	–	65	4	31	100

Source: http://documents.worldbank.org/curated/en/403951468180872451/pdf/888780PUB0Box300EPI1983 00June182014.pdf (accessed on 11 April 2019).

in India. In contrast, the ratio is 4.5 per cent for Poland, 5 per cent for Brazil and 6 per cent for South Africa.[16] Therefore, it can be rightly commented that they are not local self-governments in the true sense but the local self-government dependent on the central and state governments having less fiscal empowerment and autonomy to carry out developmental activities of their own with untied sources of revenue. According to the UN-Habitat (2009), dependence on intergovernmental transfers by local governments is widespread but the extent of that dependence varies in different countries. For example, government transfers are still the most significant revenue source for local governments in many countries, but they have been decreasing in many North American and European jurisdictions. Therefore, the UN-Habitat (2009) had envisaged that the challenge for local governments is to keep cities economically viable by delivering a high level of services and, at the same time, keeping taxes sufficiently low so as not to discourage individuals and businesses from locating in their jurisdiction. Freire and Garzon (2014) have envisaged two key principles of local revenue management: (a) the services that municipalities provide should be clearly linked to the revenue sources needed to finance them; and (b) services should be financed by their beneficiaries—'the general benefit principle'—directly or indirectly. Moreover, the discussion on municipal revenue and expenditure also needs to emphasize a few important aspects such as revenue planning, revenue forecasting, revenue mobilization strategies and revenue collection efficiency. The local government sources of revenue and revenue structure of a few countries are given in Table 6.1 and Table 6.2, respectively.

Municipal Expenditures

Public expenditures are a powerful tool to guarantee access to essential goods and services for all strata of society; however, in many cases, distortion and misallocation of public monies—more often than the lack of resources—prevent this from happening (Goncalves, 2013). Local governments make expenditures on a variety of services including transportation, policing, fire protection, water and sewers, garbage collection and disposal, housing, health, recreation and culture, education and social expenditures (UN-Habitat, 2009). As compared to the revenue earned by the municipalities, the expenditure incurred by them on various developmental activities is very high. In the developing countries, the municipal expenditure to the total GDP of the nation is low as compared to the developing countries (Table 6.3). In the similar vein, per person spending by the municipalities in the developing nation states is lower than those of developed countries (Table 6.4). This clearly shows that in the developing countries the capabilities of the municipalities to spend on infrastructure development and services in the municipal areas is very low. Lack of capability to spend affects the quality of life of city dwellers. Some of the important areas of municipal expenditure are:

1. General supervision, collection of revenue and so on;
2. Health and sanitation;
3. Sewerage and SWM;
4. Education and libraries;
5. Conservancy scavenging and street cleaning;
6. Road;
7. Energy and public lighting;
8. Water supply;
9. Garden and open space;
10. Creation and maintenance of water bodies;
11. Heritage and sites;
12. Administrative expenses and salaries; and
13. Other infrastructure development.

Table 6.3 Municipal Expenditure as Percentage of GDP in Various Countries

Country	Local Government Expenditure as % of GDP	Local Government Expenditure as % of Total Government Expenditure
Australia	2.4	6.7
Denmark	32.9	62.0
Finland	19.7	39.3
Italy	15.4	32.0
Russia	6.3	19.8
China	13.7	74.6
South Africa	5.1	16.9
Kenya	0.06	1.3

Source: UN-Habitat (2009).

Table 6.4 Local Government per Person Spending in Selected Countries (2003)

Country	Local Government per Person Expenditure ($)
UK	2,797.97
Canada	1,984.86
India	799.18
South Africa	692.64
Australia	480.43
New Zealand	588.74
Kenya	8.69
Ghana	12.22

Source: http://www.clgf.org.uk/default/assets/File/Publications/reports/2006%20Municipal%20Finance%20Paper.pdf (accessed on 10 April 2019).

Municipal infrastructure is essential to the economic, social and environmental development of cities. Cities not only have to provide roads, transit, water, sewers and other 'hard' services, they also have to provide 'soft' services that enhance the quality of life in their communities such as parks, libraries, social housing and recreational facilities (UN-Habitat, 2009). Without adequate revenue in hand, the municipalities in most of the developing countries of the world are constrained to spend on creation and maintenance of infrastructure and provisioning of basic and essential services to the satisfaction of city dwellers. The municipal expenditure in India constitutes just more than 1 per cent of the GDP. In the European countries, it is more than 5 per cent of the

GDP (Table 6.3). The imbalance between expenditures and revenues at the local level makes it critically important that cities spend the resources they have as efficiently and effectively as possible (Bird, 2001). This is because of inability of the municipalities to earn income through taxes and fees, and insufficient devolution of fund from the central and state government to the sub-national government. This has enticed the municipalities to look forward to the participation of the private sector in development of cities. Therefore, the government in the developing countries are nowadays encouraging PPP for making a city smart and development of new smart cities. A principal advantage of PPPs is that they relieve municipalities of the financial responsibility for upfront capital costs (Tassonyi, 1997) and allow them to build facilities without incurring municipal debt. There are many factors which influence the expenditure quantum as well as pattern of the municipalities. A few of them among many are density of population, access to basic needs by city dwellers, the number of informal settlements and slum dwellers, poverty rate, institutional arrangements, household income and so on.

Some of the features of municipal financing, that is, municipal revenue and expenditure are as follows:

1. The pattern of municipal revenue and expenditure varies from country to country and within same country from one province to another. In India, the raising of municipal revenue through taxes and fee are determined by the Municipal Acts of respective states.
2. The main types of municipal expenditure are infrastructure development and their maintenance and provisioning of basic and essential services to city dwellers.
3. Generally, the municipality's ability to raise revenue is less as compared to their willingness to spend on municipal development activities and services.
4. It is not a flight of fancy, but truly with constraint of financial resources, the municipalities have to learn how to perform more with less revenue at hand.
5. The devolution of fund from the central and state government to the sub-national government is not only slow but also small.
6. Last, but not the least, there is general lack of willingness among the legislature and executive at higher levels for the fiscal empowerment of the sub-national governments or LSIs.

Municipal Financial Management

With low revenue at their disposal, it is essential that the municipalities have to effectively paltry finance at their disposal. Financial management is a crucial element of municipal management. If required, they have to take the help of financial consultant in order to perform this job. Financial management systems are fundamental elements of transparency, accountability, and efficient and effective service delivery in every municipality in the world (Mantzaris, 2014). It enables the local government to plan, mobilize and use financial resources in an efficient and effective manner, as well as fulfil its obligation to be accountable to its citizens (Venkateswaran, 2014). Fiscal decentralization, coupled with a growing demand for accountability and transparency at the local level, has resulted in greater public participation in the municipal budgetary process and more rigorous financial management techniques by local governments in many countries (UN-Habitat, 2009). Financial accountability is about promoting and reporting publicly on performance and it requires transparent rules-based expenditure and financial management systems that ensure that resources are allocated in accordance with citizens' preferences (Yilmaz & Beris, 2008). Mazibuko and Fourie (2013) were of the view that municipal financial management takes into account interconnected management aspects such as enhancing the developmental mandate of local government, planning and budgeting, a transparent and participatory trajectory, continuous capital investment, setting aside money for that capital investment, maintenance of and repairs to existing infrastructure, generating revenue, debt collection, managing cash and expenditure within the applicable limits. It is also further suggested that reforming financial management in the municipalities need to involve a whole bundle of regulatory, institutional and mental changes on both the revenue and the expenditure management side of the municipal finance (OECD, 2001).

Need and Importance of Urban Financial Management

1. Financial management is one of the most important aspects of municipal finance. It helps the municipalities to cost and effectively implement various development projects and programmes in the municipal areas. Some of the reasons of need for and importance of urban financial management are as follows: The concepts and technique of financial management help local governments in utilizing their limited financial resources in an efficient and transparent manner. They also help them to function accountably. Budgeting, accounting and financial reporting are the pillars of good financial management. Well-developed financial management systems are the foundation of good governance, which is the very opposite of corruption, graft, fraud, poor management of resources, nepotism, incompetency and general negligence of the basic principles of management and leadership (Mantzaris, 2014).
2. Modern IT has enabled the municipalities to effectively deal with the financial management system. Introduction of computerized financial management systems and the use of ICT instruments have accelerated the information flows, and data security and improved the process of financial management of municipalities in developed countries. Mitullah et al. (2005) did a survey of 175 local authorities in Kenya on the effectiveness of information systems. The research found that the information system was instrumental in enhancing the proper management of revenue sources in the local authorities.
3. The municipal financing management system will enable the municipalities to better plan development activities in their municipal area. It will be helpful in the formulation of financial policy for the municipal system. They can do better mapping and forecasting of municipal resources and formulate future and long-term strategies. The revenue and expenditure management, particularly the sound financial management capacity of a municipality, determines the ability of a municipal system to contribute to poverty reduction and economic development (Mazibuko & Fourie, 2013).
4. The concepts and tools of financial management are important for the local government managers. They can better their performance in adopting at the outset simple but fundamental tools and techniques, and gain proficiency in their practice. It will save time and raise the accuracy of the municipal financing system. To Gidisu (2012), the introduction of an automation system has impacted reducing the cost of tax administration and increasing the effectiveness of revenue collection. Thus, any weaknesses in financial management are likely to be reflected in the emergence of other long-term governance challenges in the municipality which may lead communities to complain of a lack of adequate delivery of services (Mazibuko & Fourie, 2013).

5. Last, but not the least, municipal financial management improves service delivery system of municipalities. The financial management helps the municipal manager to take prudent decision on what to spend, where to spend, on what activities to spend and so on. It is said that the financial management challenges, in particular, have an effect on service delivery to urban and rural populations regarding water, electricity, sanitation and housing, and refuse collection (Mazibuko & Fourie, 2013).

Components of Financial Management

The four essential components of financial management are: budgeting, accounting, auditing and financial reporting (Figure 6.1). All these are discussed further.

Figure 6.1 Components of Financial Management

Budgeting

Budget and budgeting are starting point of any financial activities. Budgeting has always been important as a means of controlling expenditures and identifying revenues (UN-Habitat, 2009). The budget is a very important document because, if properly prepared, it will eliminate unnecessary expenditures, increase efficiency in the methods of collecting revenues and preserve the credit rating of the municipality (Tassonyi, 1997). The municipal budget serves two primary purposes. At the outset, it sets out a programme of expenditures of the municipality during the coming year to forecast the revenues that will be used to finance those expenditures. It provides a method to control expenditure so that municipal expenditures do not exceed municipal revenues (Wrenshall, 1937). According to Venkateswaran (2014), a budget is the annual financial plan of a local government, which defines its operational and development priorities for the ensuing financial year and describes how the plans will be financed.

Harry Kitchen (2002) has set out the purposes of municipal budgeting by noting that municipal budgets should be designed to achieve the following objectives:

1. To provide for the management of financial control;
2. To provide information essential for useful and efficient management decisions; and
3. To improve programme and financial planning.

There are two types of budget: operating and capital. Operating budget deals with recurrent and short-term expenditure such as salaries, phone bills, fuel and stationery. On the other hand, capital budget takes into account the expenditure on assets with a lifespan of more than a year or expenditure on existing assets that improves the lifespan of the asset or improves the productivity of the existing assets on a long-term basis.

A system approach is followed in the budgeting process. At the outset, each head of the departments, independent units, agencies, prepares their respective departmental budgets, both operating and capital, for the upcoming financial year and sends it to the finance officer or the budget committee. The chief finance officer, who works under the supervision of the mayor and budget committee, looks after the day-to-day affair of budget preparation. The mayor presents the budget before the council which is approved by the council before putting into operation.

A good municipal budget needs to provide transparency, accountability, feasibility, predictability and prioritization of resources. Besides, budgeting exercise must be objective oriented. It needs to review the data and demand justifications and check the sufficiency in availability of funds before making budgetary allocations. A well-prepared budget is a tool which can enhance decision-making; become an effective financial plan and policy document. Moreover, it can be an operational guide for municipal financial management. William Feather has rightly commented that 'a budget tells us what we cannot afford, but it does not keep us from buying it.'[17]

Accounting

The municipal accounting system provides complete, up-to-date and exact information concerning revenues, expenditures, assets and liabilities of the municipality. Within a local government, accounting records provide information on billing taxpayers and receiving tax payments, paying employees, and paying vendors and contractors for goods, work and services.[18] Accounting systems also inform management and external stakeholders about the financial resources, the efficiency of the organization's financial management and its financial position during and at the end of the financial year (Lee & Johnson, 1998). Improper accounting system puts a question mark not only on the functioning of the municipality but also on its integrity.

Two types of accounting system are generally used by the municipalities. These are narrated further.

1. *Double-entry accounting system:* This system is followed in order to make the accounting process simple and transparent. It is a continuous process and is carried out by the organization on a daily basis. The vouchers are prepared every day for all financial transactions and these are meticulously entered into the account book. The information in the accounts book is compiled in the form of the following: monthly report (trial balance and receipts and payments account), and annual report (financial statements).

   The key process of the double-entry system involves the following:
   a. Identification of transactions on a daily basis.
   b. Preparation of voucher (after passing) on a daily basis.
   c. Recording transaction in a book of prime entry on a daily basis.
   d. Preparation of trial balance on a daily basis.
   e. Posting to general ledger on a daily basis.
   f. Preparation of financial statements at the end of the year.

Merits of the double-entry accounting system are as follows: (a) it is easier to detect errors and frauds under this system; and (b) it helps in more accurate calculation of income and loss.

2. *Accrual system of accounting:* Under the accrual system of accounting, income and expenditures are identified when these are incurred. However, income that is earned but yet to be received is shown as 'receivable assets'. The expenses that are incurred but yet to be paid are shown as 'payable liabilities'.

A few merits of the accrual system of accounting are as follows: (a) it records the actual income during a period, thereby helping the authority in taking financial decisions; and (b) here expenses are matched with the income earned in the same period; thus, it helps the authority to understand the true performance of the organization.

Some of the principles of a good accounting system of a municipality are as follows:

1. At the outset, it is important for municipalities to make sure that the basic accounting functions such as preparing ledgers, posting transactions on a daily basis, tallying cash balances at the close of a business day are religiously taking place.
2. The double-entry accounting system is the appropriate system to be followed by the municipalities at the initial years before they move to accrual-based accounting or any other financial management system.
3. Timely completion of the annual financial statement is a must. If statements are delayed, their informational value is eroded.
4. If the annual audit is done by independent external auditors, it enhances the credibility of financial statements. In order to enhance transparency and accountability, the municipality should also publish the audit report.
5. The computerization of accounting procedures improves efficiency of the municipalities. It makes the accounting system more transparent.
6. It is important to strengthen the technical and managerial skills and capacities of the staff who manage the accounting systems. The capacity building of the accounting staff from time to time will enable them to do their task effectively and efficiently.
7. Accounting forms the backbone of the financial record system of any organization. It should be seen as the organization's financial information system, providing valuable information regarding operational and financial efficiencies and conveying the financial performance of the organization to citizens and stakeholders.[19]

Auditing

Auditing is a systematic process of objectively obtaining and evaluating evidence regarding assertions about economic actions and events (Venkateswaran, 2014). Auditing is an important aspect of financial management of any organization. An audit is an 'examination of records, facilities, systems, and other evidences to discover or verify desired information' (Mikesell 2011). The audit seeks to discover deviations from accepted rules and practices, and bring out instances of any illegal or irregular transactions or decisions and it also aims at holding management accountable and preventing repetition of inappropriate actions in the future (Venkateswaran, 2014). The financial auditing is taking stock of the financial records. It is the critical evaluation of the expenditure made during a financial year and assessing their accuracy and to see whether these are being incurred as per the financial guidelines or not.

The auditing is done with the following purposes in mind: (a) whether the financial resources are utilized and managed properly in compliance with the laws and regulations; (b) whether money spent is achieving their objectives and desired outcomes; and (c) whether services are provided economically, effectively and efficiently.

Various types of audit are done at the municipality level. Those are as follows.

1. *Financial audit:* It is an independent evaluation done with a purpose of observing and certifying the fairness, accuracy and reliability of the financial data. It focuses on whether financial statements prepared by the Municipality reflect its financial position or not.
2. *Compliance audit:* It is done with a purpose to find out whether the municipality has complied with the rules and procedures regarding the spending of money.
3. *Management audit:* Management audit is a holistic audit. It is a future-oriented, independent and systematic evaluation of the activities of the organization. It is prepared with the objective of helping the municipality to attain its objectives. A management audit is otherwise called a 'performance audit'. To Venkateswaran (2014), it evaluates the organization's performance against its stated plans and analyses the reasons for any variance in performance, with the aim of drawing lessons for the future.
4. *Social audit:* From the point of view of municipalities, social audit is now used for bringing more transparency to the audit system and making the authorities accountable to the people. In the social audit, people through the community-level institution, such as Ward Sabha, participate in auditing all the aspects of the municipalities, that is, activities performed, financial allocation made and objectives fulfilled. According to the Ministry of Housing & Urban Poverty Alleviation, Government of India (2011), the major objectives of the social audit are as follows: (a) to assess the physical and financial gaps between the needs and resources; (b) to create awareness among beneficiaries and providers; (c) to increase efficacy and effectiveness, and ensure transparency; (d) to scrutinize various policy decisions; (e) to popularize good governance; and (f) to sensitize citizens to demand accountability. The system approach to be followed in the conduction of a social audit is as follows: (a) defining boundaries of social audit; (b) stakeholder identification and consultation; (c) identification of key issues and data collection; and (d) social audit findings and verifications.

Financial Reporting

It is important on the part of the municipality to disseminate its financial aspects to the general public. It will make municipal affairs transparent and also give an opportunity to other stakeholders to assess the performance of the municipality. Financial reporting provides a consolidated set of information to a wide range of stakeholders such as government and private agencies, employees, citizens and suppliers that require information about an entity. Financial reports are means of communicating to the users of financial information material that they use to make choices among alternative uses of scarce resources future (Venkateswaran, 2014).

It is envisaged that financial reporting involves the disclosure of financial information to the various stakeholders about the financial performance and financial position of the organization over a specified period of time. These stakeholders include investors, creditors, public, debt providers, governments and government agencies. The typical components of financial reporting are as follows.

1. Financial statements which include balance sheet, profit and loss account, cash flow statement and statement of changes in stockholder's equity;
2. The notes to financial statements;
3. Quarterly and annual reports (in case of listed companies);
4. Prospectus (in case of companies going for initial public offerings); and
5. Management discussion and analysis (in case of public companies).[20]

The three prominent objectives of financial reporting as identified by Schaeffer (2000) are as follows:

1. Financial reporting should assist in fulfilling the government's duty to be publicly accountable and should enable users to assess that accountability;
2. Financial reporting should assist users in evaluating the operating results of the government entity for the year (and year over year); and
3. Financial reporting should assist users in assessing the level of services provided by the local municipality and its ability to meet these obligations as they are due.

Every municipality needs to prepare and publish its financial report for wider consumption. Some of the useful characteristics of good financial reporting are: (a) it needs to be relevant; (b) it is a faithful representation; (c) it should be consistent and comparable; (d) it is understandable; and (e) the information should be accurate so that it should not misguide the interpreters.

Municipal Finance in India

Backdrops of Local Government Finance

Municipal finance system in India is marred with limited autonomy. They are largely tied with the rope of the Municipal Act being formulated by the state government from time to time. Customarily, the municipalities do not have the power to fix adequate tax rates to determine the tax exemption policy, fee collection autonomy and to raise fund through capital markets. Their taxing and spending powers have existed under the provisions of state laws. The state laws vary from one state to another. But generally state laws often deny municipalities their power either to impose a particular tax or fee and other charges. The state laws largely do not make adequate provision for the protection of municipal fiscal domain nor do these lay down a policy governing transfers.

There is a dire need for the financial empowerment of the LSIs as they carry out most of the developmental activities at the grassroots level. The Reserve Bank of India (1962) in its bulletin has rightly stressed the importance of local government finances as follows:

> With the increasing industrialization and urbanization under the impetus of development and planning, the local authorities from a growing part of the expanding public sector, with powers to raise and spend considerable amounts of public funds for development purpose. Local authorities form an important segment of public sector in India. The contribution of the local bodies to income in general and capital formation is of considerable significance, in view of their large number and the area and population they cover.

The four important milestones with which the financial empowerment of the local bodies is concerned are as follows:

1. *Government of India Act, 1919:* The Government of India Act, 1919, which came into force in 1921 envisaged a local list of taxes which comprises the following taxes:
    a. Toll
    b. Tax on land and land values
    c. Tax on buildings
    d. Tax on vehicles and boats
    e. Tax on menials and domestic servants
    f. Tax on animals
    g. Octroi
    h. Terminal tax
    i. Tax on trade, professions and callings
    j. Tax on private markets
    k. Tax imposed in return for services rendered, such as (a) water rate, (b) lighting rate, (c) drainage rate, (d) fees for use of markets and (e) other public conveniences[21]
2. *The Local Finance Enquiry Committee 1951:* The Local Finance Enquiry Committee 1951 recommended a list of 13 taxes to be exclusively utilized by or for local government. The 13 taxes recommended by the Committee were as follows:
    a. Terminal tax on goods or passengers carried by railway, sea or air
    b. Tax on lands and buildings
    c. Tax on mineral rights
    d. Tax on the entry of goods into a local area for consumption, use or sale therein
    e. Tax on consumption or sale of electricity
    f. Tax on advertisements other than advertisements published in the newspapers
    g. Tax on good and passengers carried by road or on inland waterways
    h. Tax on vehicles
    i. Tax on animals and boats
    j. Tolls
    k. Tax on professions, trades, callings and employment
    l. Capitation tax
    m. Tax on entertainments[22]
3. *The Taxation Enquiry Commission (1953–1954):* The Taxation Enquiry Commission (1953–1954) had also addressed the issue of specific taxes be devolved to the local government. It had recommended a list of 10 taxes to be reserved for the local government, adding, however, that 'the recommendations should not be construed as precluding transfer of other taxes to any local body, wherever appropriate, if the state governments consider such a source desirable.' The recommended taxes were:
    a) Tax on lands and buildings
    b) Octroi
    c) Tax on vehicles other than those mechanically propelled
    d) Tax on animals and boats
    e) Tax on professions, trades, callings and employment
    f) Theatre tax

g) Tax on advertisements other than those published in newspapers
h) Duty on transfer of property
i) Toll
j) Tax on foods and passengers carried by road or inland waterways[23]

4. *The Constitutional Amendment 1992:* The 73rd and 74th Constitutional Amendment of 1992 are path-breaking from the standpoint of empowerment of the LSIs. The 1992 Amendment made important changes with regard to the transfer of funds to ULBs. The provisions of financial transfer are outlined in Articles 243 I and Y of the Constitution which state that the state governments are required to constitute, once every five years, an FC whose mandates include making recommendations on: (a) taxes, levies and duties that should be assigned to municipalities; (b) taxes, duties and levies that should be shared between the states and municipalities; (c) grants-in-aid; and (d) any other measure that would augment the finances of municipalities. While Article 280(3)(a) envisages that the CFC is required to make recommendations on the 'measures needed to augment the Consolidated Fund of a state to supplement the resources of the municipalities on the basis of the recommendations made by the finance commission of the States'. The purpose underlying these constitutional provisions is to establish a uniform system for assessing the financial requirements of municipalities and making appropriate recommendations on both the grants and shared revenues by the central and state government with the ULBs.

Revenue Sources of Local Bodies in India

Indian cities accommodate 377 million of population which is 31 per cent of India's current population. The urban areas contribute 63 per cent of the GDP. Therefore, the urban areas in India like those of any other countries have utmost significance from the standpoint of the economic growth and development of the nation states. With the increasing recognition of the contribution of urbanization to economic growth, the strengthening of the fiscal position of ULBs through finance reforms has become a key component in the GoI's development agenda. However, the sources as well as quantum of revenue of the ULBs arc less. Most assessments have pointed out to the unsatisfactory state of municipal finances, highlighting: (a) the inadequacy of internally generated revenues for meeting revenue expenditures, (b) the discretionary and *ad hoc* nature of the transfers and grants-in-aid and (c) high level of expenditure on establishment (wages and salaries) vis-à-vis expenditure on operations and maintenance of services (Asian Development Bank, 2013).

The municipal revenue constitutes a minimal share of India's GDP. The Eleventh and Twelfth FCs data show that the ratio was around 0.7 per cent which according to the Thirteenth FC has gone up to 0.94 per cent in 2007–2008. The Thirteenth FC data reflect that the municipal tax to GDP ratio is a meagre 0.5 per cent as compared to central tax to GDP ratio at 12 per cent and states' tax to GDP ratio at 5.6 per cent for 2007–2008, while PT to GDP ratio is only 0.25 per cent. While stipulating the modalities, the Fourteenth FC envisages that a detailed procedure for the disbursal of the performance grant to ULBs would have to be designed, subject to certain eligibility criteria. Under the Fourteenth FC, an amount of ₹871.43 billion are to be devolved towards the ULBs over a time period of five years, from 2015–2020. Total 80 per cent of this amount forms the basic grant and 20 per cent of the amount is the performance grant. These funds are only to be devolved for basic services and O&M purposes by ULBs.[24]

The various sources of revenue of the ULBs in India are as follows:

1. *Tax revenue:* ULBs levy a few taxes in their areas such as octroi, PT, professional tax, entertainment tax, advertisement tax, animal tax, market tax, water tax, pilgrim tax and toll tax. It varies from state to state. It is pertinent to mention here that octroi tax has been abolished by the state with the implementation of GST.
2. *Non-tax revenue:* The non-tax revenue earned by the ULBs in the states generally consists of fees, fines, rent and income from the remunerative activities. Besides, fees are also collected from park, exhibition grounds, marriage places, parking of vehicles, public markets and so on. The user charges need to be based on benefit principle to the consumers. Bandyopadhyay (2014) was of the view that the user charges are useful to the extent that they help in bringing about 'efficiency' in revenue collection for the municipalities, help in 'rationing' of services and most importantly help the municipalities with more funds to work with.
3. *Assigned (shared) revenue/transfers:* The ULBs get grant as per the recommendations of the CFC and SFC. Shared taxes are revenues based on tax assignment rules. Entertainment tax, motor vehicles tax, stamp duty/surcharge are some of the common shared revenue sources which are not uniform across states. On an average, nearly half of the total revenues of the municipal bodies come from transfers.
4. *Grants-in-aid:* Grants-in-aid largely comprise the following: (a) grants made available through planned transfers from the upper tier of government under various projects, programmes and schemes, and (b) grants made available to compensate for the loss of income and some specific transfers.
5. *Loans/Borrowings:* Loan borrowed from the central and state governments and from other banking and non-banking financial institutions for meeting capital expenditures. The state governments permit urban local governments to borrow under their respective municipal laws, which lay down the framework for borrowing: the projects for which the borrowing is allowed, the volume of borrowing and the security to be pledged, the procedure for applying to the state for the permission to borrow and the manner in which accounts must be kept. Most states have issued guidelines for local borrowing such as that borrowing should be for less than 30 years, that the interest rate should not exceed the interest rate on government securities and that there should be sufficient provisioning for debt servicing. By and large, most borrowing by municipal corporations has been from public institutions such as HUDCO or Life Insurance Corporation for housing and water supply schemes.[25]

Table 6.5 Share of Tax Revenue in India (%)

Categories	Share of the Tax Revenue (%) in 2008
Centre	50.0
States	48.1
Municipalities	1.7
Panchayats	0.2
Total	100

Source: Indian Public Finance Statistics, Government of India, and Thirteenth Finance Commission.

Table 6.6 Revenue Sources of Municipal Corporations in India 1998–2002

Revenue Head/Category	Sources of Revenue
Tax revenue	Property tax, octroi, advertisement tax, tax on animals, vacant land tax and taxes on carriages and carts.
Non-tax revenue	User charges, municipal fees, sale & hire charges, lease amounts.
Other receipts	Sundry receipts, law charges costs recovered, lapsed deposits, fees, fines and forfeitures, rent on tools and plants, miscellaneous sales and so on.
Assigned (shared) revenue	Entertainment tax, surcharge on stamp duty, profession tax, motor vehicles tax.
Grants-in-aid	1. Plan grants made available through planned transfers from upper tier of government under various projects, programmes and schemes.
	2. Non-plan grants made available to compensate against the loss of income and some specific transfers.
Loans	Loans borrowed by the local authorities for capital works and so on (HUDCO).
	LIC, state and central governments, banks and municipal bonds.

Source: https://m.rbi.org.in/scripts/bs_viewcontent.aspx?Id=1161 (accessed on 5 December 2018).

6. *Bonds:* Municipal bonds are issued by the municipalities in order to meet expenditure on infrastructure project. A few municipalities such as Pune Municipal Corporation and Bangalore Municipal Corporation have issued municipal bonds in the capital markets. Pune Municipal Corporation raised ₹2 billion in June 2017 through municipal bonds.[26]
7. *Other receipts:* The other receipts comprise sundry receipts, law charge costs recovered, lapsed deposits, fees, fines and forfeitures, rent on tools and plants, miscellaneous sales and so on.

The various sources of revenue of the Municipal Corporations in India are given in Table 6.6.

Mechanism to Improve Municipal Revenue

Mobilization of adequate revenue will enable the ULBs to carry out development activities smoothly in the cities. Some of the steps the ULBs can take for the mobilization of adequate revenue to make LSIs self-sustaining are discussed further.

1. *PT collection and innovations:* PT is one of the important sources of revenue of the ULBs. In most of the cities, property records are not updated and PT is not properly assessed. ULBs can increase revenue by improving PT inventories, record management, public awareness and participation and effective tax collection. It is remarked that assessment of properties is one of the biggest challenges for the ULBs which are plagued with issues such as unscientific methods, lack of transparency and issues with incomplete records of properties (Bandyopadhyay, 2014). Some of the innovative actions to be taken for effective mobilization of property tax are given in Exhibit 6.3.
2. *Effective tax governance and administration:* The tax governance and administration calls for addressing the issue of under assessment, tax theft by retaining exemption from the PT. These

Exhibit 6.3 Innovative Actions to Mobilize Property Tax

- PT should be levied on built properties as well as vacant land.
  - PT under area-based system/capital value method
  - Vacant land tax @0.5 per cent of ready reckoner capital value
- Timely and periodic valuation
- Autonomy to fix rates to ULBs
- Complete listing using GIS mapping to have accurate register of taxpayers/base
- Service components like water/sewerage tax to be separated
- Setting up of PT Board
- Organize collection camps/collection through vendors/banks and so on
- Insurance cover on timely payment (as done by Mumbai)
- Attachment of bank account of defaulters (as done by Delhi)

Source: http://www.iipa.org.in/upload/Theme%20Paper%20Members%20Conference.pdf (accessed on 28 February 2018).

issues have to be properly addressed. However, online submission of tax will get rid of many deficiencies and can check tax evasion and corruption. Good tax administration requires strong technical capacity of the administrative agency and a well-designed tax structure.

3. *Energizing the tax system:* A study on municipal finance conducted by ADB in 2013 has envisaged that municipal finance system in India has limited autonomy in fixing tax rates, determining the tax exemption policy, accessing capital markets or restructuring personnel policies. Formulation of municipal revenue policy by the state governments will go a long way to improve the municipal finance. The state governments need to have willpower to assign more power to the ULBs to raise revenue through taxes.
4. *Explore generation of revenue in the capital market:* The ULBs must explore the alternative sources of raising the municipal revenue in the capital market by selling municipal bond. All the upcoming smart cities can go for municipal bonds for raising revenue for their infrastructural projects. In the view of Bagchi (2001), the accessing of capital market funds for financing capital investments in urban basic services by the city governments is not beyond their capacity. However, it would need certain financial, structural, institutional, administrative changes and restructuring of city governance.
5. *Willpower to raise non-tax revenue:* The state governments need to assign the municipalities to raise their non-tax revenue sources. One of the important components of non-tax revenue is user charge. It is remarked that user charges are useful to the extent that they help in bringing about 'efficiency' in revenue collection for the municipalities, helps in 'rationing' of services and most importantly help the municipalities with more funds to work with (Bandyopadhyay, 2014).
6. *Timely transfer of revenue from the central and state governments:* Transfers consist of shared taxes between the Municipality and the state government and grants from the central government and CFC. As it is a major source of revenue for the local bodies, the transfer needs to be transparent and timely so that local bodies are able to perform their developmental duties and responsibilities. It is remarked that performance-based transfer systems are intended to promote and create incentives for governance and institutional development reforms, including financial management, transparency and citizen involvement and participation (Muwonge & Ebel, 2014).

There is a necessity to raise the base of the taxable and non-taxable sources of revenue of the municipalities. It will enable them to become self-sustainable and spend on need-based development acidities. Bandyopadhyay (2014) from his study has suggested that the ULBs in India are confronted with lack of proper decentralization of functions and finances, inadequate revenue generation, expenditure shortfalls leading to poor service delivery. Another challenge is the variation in revenue among the municipalities. Mathur, Debdulal and Nilesh (2009) finds that there are large intercity variations with Mumbai Municipal Corporation having per capita revenue of ₹1,334 while the Municipal Corporations of Patna and Dhanbad, respectively, had only ₹25 and ₹40. It is remarked that various ways of augmenting the resources of municipal bodies in the country, including essential reforms in the PT system and adequate exploitation of user charges and fees for various services delivered as well as ways of strengthening and improving central and state transfers to urban local governments, need to be explored.

Expenditures of Urban Local Bodies in India

LSIs or ULBs directly influence the welfare of the people by providing civic, social and economic infrastructure services and facilities in both urban and rural areas.[27] The LSIs in urban areas perform a range of developmental activities as assigned to them under the constitution. The developmental activities at the grassroots level in the cities are largely performed by the municipal government. In order to perform these activities, these local bodies make expenditures. The expenditures incurred by the ULBs can be categorized under two broad heads: (a) revenue expenditures and (b) capital expenditures. The revenue expenditures broadly comprise (a) establishment expenditures; (b) administrative expenditures; (c) operation and maintenance expenditures; and (d) interest payments on loans while the capital expenditures comprise (a) expenditure on capital formation and (b) principal repayment. Various categories of expenditures made by the ULBs in India are given in Table 6.7.

Table 6.7 Categorization of Municipal Expenditures in India

Expenditure Category	Expenditure Items
Establishment expenditure	Staff salaries, allowances, wages, pensions and retirement benefits and so on.
Administrative expenditure	Rents, rates and taxes, office maintenance, communications and books.
	Periodicals, printing and stationary, travel expenditure, law charges and so on.
Operations and maintenance	Power and fuel, bulk purchases, stores, hire charges, repairs and expenditure, maintenance and interest payments made on loans.
Capital expenditure	Buildings, water supply and sewerage, energy/lighting, solid waste management, roads, bridges, culverts, causeways, health and sanitation, parks and recreation spaces, furniture and fittings, tools and plant, equipment and principal repayments of loans.
Other expenditure	Miscellaneous expenses not accounted for in the above.

Source: https://m.rbi.org.in/scripts/bs_viewcontent.aspx?Id=1161 (accessed on 5 December 2018).

Table 6.8 Urban Local Bodies Spending Levels in India

Type of Urban Local Bodies	Share of Urban Population (%)	Share of Municipal Expenditures (%) 2007–2008
Municipal Corporations	41.2	71.9
Municipal Councils	38.8	22.5
Nagar Panchayats	11.5	5.0
NAC	0.9	0.5
Non-Municipal Census Towns	7.5	–
Total	100.0	100.0

Source: https://m.rbi.org.in/scripts/bs_viewcontent.aspx?Id=1161 (accessed on 5 December 2018).

A report of the Reserve Bank of India envisages that a gigantic share of total expenditure done by the ULBs in India is done by the Municipal Corporations (Table 6.8).

Steps to Augment Municipal Finance

The municipal revenue and expenditure in India are a minute percentage of the GDP. According to the statistics, the municipal revenue constitutes only 0.96 per cent of GDP while expenditure is just 1.01 per cent (given in Table 6.9). Therefore, it can be rightly said that the municipal finance is of minor importance or is given less importance in the financial system of the various levels of government. In other words, the decentralization of finance and financial empowerment of local bodies is very poor in the decentralization process of India.

Some of the measures suggested by Rao and Bird (2010) for strengthening municipal financing in India are as follows: (a) development charges should be used more effectively; (b) more should also be done to utilize public lands more effectively; (c) to a considerable extent, capital expenditure requirements will have to be financed through borrowing so further development of the municipal bond market is important; and (d) PPPs should be used more and more effectively.

Some of the suggested measures for making judicious expenditures of the limited available municipal revenue are narrated further.

1. *Performance budgeting:* The performance-based budgeting will rationalize the municipal expenditure. Through this technique, the municipal administration can link financial outlay with the physical targets and achievements. This will check unnecessary expenditure by doing effective cost and benefit analysis. Performance budgeting is basically a process where there has to be a positive linkage between the funds allocated and measurable results. There has to be a shift in focus from the emphasis being on funds allocated for programmatic activities to more specifically result that can be achieved.[28]
2. *Efficient accounting and internal audit system:* A proper system of accounting and auditing with control over finances will ensure proper expenditure and check unnecessary expenditure and also corruption. It pinpoints the maladies in financial management. The

Table 6.9 The Finances of Municipalities, All States

Finances	2002–2003		2007–2008		
	Amount ₹ Crore	Per Capita ₹	Amount ₹ Crore	Per Capita ₹	CAGR (%)
Revenue income					
Own tax revenue	8,838.13	311	15,277.72	492	11.57
Own non-tax revenue	4,441.84	156	8,243.66	265	13.16
Total own revenue	13,279.97	466	23,521.38	757	12.11
Assignment and devolution	3,657.06	128	9,171.11	295	20.19
Grants-in-aid	2,259.76	79	5,676.25	183	20.23
Others	1,137.52	40	2,818.32	91	19.90
Transfers from the central government	308.86	11	2,372.97	76	50.35
FC transfers	276.53	10	869.02	28	25.74
Total revenue income	20,919.69	733	44,429.05	1430	16.26
Expenditure					
Revenue expenditure	15,691.46	550	28,431.45	915	12.62
Capital expenditure	5,938.28	208	18,594.08	598	25.64
Total expenditure	21,629.74	758	47,025.53	1,513	16.80
GDP (India)	2,261,415	21,415	4,320,892	37,969	13.83
Own tax as % of GDP	0.39		0.35		
Own revenue as a % of GDP	0.59		0.54		
Municipal expenditure as % of GDP	0.96		1.09		

Source: Asian Development Bank (2013).
Note: GDP at factor cost (current prices).

audit *paras* and objections should be carefully attended to. Moreover, the audit should be timely and strict. Ozuomba Chidinma et al. (2016) were of the opinion that internal audit serves a major management control tool to provide an assurance to management that the financial information furnished to management to aid decision-making is reliable, accurate and based on reliable records and where otherwise to draw the attention of management to deficiencies in the organization or system of internal control and to highlight areas of management practices requiring corrective actions. Mustafa Baltaci and Serdar Yilmaz of World Bank Institute noted that an internal control and audit framework aims at improving financial and administrative management capacity by limiting fiscal behaviours that result in waste, misallocation and corruption.[29]

3. *Effective utilization of existing resources:* The meagre financial resources of the ULBs have to be utilized in an economic and effective manner. In this regard, it is necessary that there should be clear priorities. Wastage of money needs to be checked.

4. *Financial governance:* The public finance system is strengthened in line with the principles of good financial governance. Some of the principles of good financial governance are transparency, efficiency and accountability. Good financial governance enhances public confidence in local government and helps to ensure that a council is in a position to make decisions that are properly responsive to the interests of its community.[30]
5. *Follow participatory expenditure process:* Effective peoples' participation in the process of income and expenditure of the local bodies will not only curtail the cost of the project but also expenditure through public contribution. The community contribution in welfare project would reduce public expenditure. Participation in sub-national planning and budgeting is a key tool in making local constituents understand and appreciate local development initiatives. One innovation could be citizens 'deciding who to tax and how much, and how to spend these revenues'.[31] The functionaries and the elected representatives of the LSIs should jointly operate the account and draw the amount with joint signature for spending for various development works at their respective local institutions. The participatory decision-making process for expenditure needs to be followed by involving committees or Ward Sabhas at the grassroots level. This is known as true participatory expenditure process.
6. *Equity in distribution of finance:* It is observed that the flow of finance largely goes to the Municipal Corporation, Municipal Council and Nagar Panchayats in India on the basis of a set formula designed by the CFC and SFCs. However, there are intra-local differences within these local bodies. The equity consideration in the allocation of financial resources will bring the weaker and laggard ULBs at par with their stronger/forward counterparts. The Third SFC Report of Uttarakhand has envisaged that 'Equity, as distinguished from equality in its absolute sense, emphasizes equality in outcomes. Instead of treating everyone identically, equity considerations accept the possibility of giving special consideration to the weaker units in order to bring about some degree of equality and narrowing of differences.'[32]
7. *Private and corporate expenditure and financing:* The government needs to encourage the participation of private, business and corporate sectors in spending on infrastructure development and utility services in the ULBs. Besides, state municipal acts also can encourage private and corporation participation in municipal development in terms of sharing financial expenses burden. The private sector is found to be making investments in transport, education, health and housing in many countries in urban areas.
8. *Community financing:* The ULBs must encourage community financing of various developmental activities such as sewerage system, water connection and solar energy through Ward Sabhas. For the sustainability of the utility services, community financing must be encouraged. The UNDP has emphasized on crowd funding to support the central and state financial transfers. It has noted that crowd funding initiatives can be especially effective for small projects that are popular with citizens, such as public parks, bike lanes or a museum/cultural institution. Governments at the sub-national level can use such platforms in a variety of ways to, for example, secure 'last mile' financing (raise those last few dollars to make a project reality), create momentum to secure larger donations/contributions from other sources or to raise matching funds to fulfil grant requirements.[33]
9. *Corporate social responsibility and expenditure on urban development:* Under the corporate social responsibility (CSR), corporate sectors are found to be spending on education, health, nutrition, housing and so on in the development of slum areas of many cities. The corporate sector under the CSR needs to be encouraged by the ULBs for provisioning of utility services in the urban slums and informal settlements.

10. *Inter-municipal cooperation in municipal expenditure:* The adjoining municipalities can share their expenditure with regard to expenditure on infrastructure and utility services. The municipalities that want to jointly finance and provide some public services on a collective basis can create or join a community. These supra-municipal structures coexist with the municipal structures but have different responsibilities, depending on member municipalities' 'choices regarding the competences to transfer to their community'.[34] It will be helpful to reduce cost and even become cost-effective.

Summing Up

The decentralization process is taking place in various countries of the world, both developed and developing countries. It has met with various degrees of progress and its success varies from country to country and within the country from one province to another. However, customarily, it is seen that the devolution of functions and funds, and more particularly funds from the higher level of government to the lower level has not taken place in many of the countries. One of the common reasons for this is lack of political and bureaucratic willpower to adhere to the ethics and constitutional mandates of decentralization. It has been rightly remarked that among the most important pending issues are the needs to: (a) clarify the distribution of responsibilities among the levels of government and (b) strengthen the resource base of local governments (Farvacque-Vitkovic, 2014). It is therefore felt that the ULBs have to be effectively economically empowered and be allocated with adequate financial resources to carry out various development activities in the cities. They are needed to be empowered to raise tax and collect fees from their municipal areas and also get due share of the grants-in-aid from the central and provincial governments. It is remarked that the financial aspects of intergovernmental relations that strongly influence the nature, scope and depth of decentralization (Muwonge & Ebel, 2014). Rao and Bird (2010) were of the view that good policies, good local governance systems and sound arrangements to finance public services are critical elements in sustainable urban development. Moreover, effective and efficient urban financial management system will go a long way to improve the financial health of the local bodies. It has been rightly noted in the UN-Habitat Global Report 2005 that local authorities have had to: (a) enhance their economic competitiveness; (b) meet the demands for public services; (c) expand and diversify the local tax base; and (d) generate funding for capital investments. Thus, municipal finance is one of the most important areas of urban development system. It has further mentioned that in advanced economies, the combination of strong local tax bases, structured central/local fiscal relations and well-targeted transfers give local governments the means to drive their own economic, social and physical development, partner with private sector entities on development initiatives and work with NGOs on social programmes.[35] For the sustainable development of the city and in order to make cities smart, urban finance is the key requirement without which the quality of life of the people residing in the urban areas cannot be adequately improved.

Keywords

Fiscal Decentralization, Fiscal Federalism, Participatory Governance, Participatory Budgeting, Accounting, Auditing, Predictability, Municipal Bond, Financial Management, Double-entry Bookkeeping, Accrual System of Auditing, Management Audit, Compliance Audit, Social Audit

REVIEW QUESTIONS

1. What is municipal finance? Describe the need and importance of municipal finance.
2. What is fiscal decentralization? Why is it important for municipal governance?
3. Why is there a need for fiscal decentralization? Describe various criteria for good fiscal decentralization.
4. Describe four important sources of municipal revenue and expenditure.
5. What is municipal financial management? Discuss various components of municipal financial management.
6. Describe various sources of municipal revenue and expenditure in India.
7. Explain various sources of municipal revenue in India? What are the lacunas and what steps are to be taken to improve the municipal revenue in India?
8. Write short notes on the following:
   a. Fiscal federalism
   b. Fiscal devolution of municipal finance
   c. Participatory budgeting
   d. Social auditing
   e. Municipal bond
   f. Double-entry bookkeeping
   g. Accounting

Notes

1. https://delog.org/web/wp-content/uploads/2015/01/Background-Paper-of-LRGs-on-FfD3.pdf (accessed on 28 November 2018).
2. http://www1.worldbank.org/publicsector/decentralization/fiscal.htm (accessed on 29 November 2018).
3. https://www.undp.org/content/undp/en/home/blog/2018/Meeting-the-urban-finance-challenge.html (accessed on 12 April 2019).
4. http://unpan1.un.org/intradoc/groups/public/documents/UNTC/UNPAN017650.pdf (accessed on 29 November 2018).
5. https://www.odi.org/sites/odi.org.uk/files/resource-documents/11063.pdf (accessed on 29 November 2018).
6. https://www.odi.org/sites/odi.org.uk/files/resource-documents/11063.pdf (accessed on 29 November 2018).
7. https://pdfs.semanticscholar.org/0273/e2123f96b465b0e4e4a68fb046e679202f83.pdf (accessed on 29 November 2018).
8. http://policydialogue.org/files/publications/Effects_of_Participatory_Budgeting.pdf (accessed on 5 December 2018).
9. https://www.jstor.org/stable/24440097?seq<hig>=</hig>1#metadata_info_tab_contents (accessed on 29 November 2018).
10. https://www.jstor.org/stable/pdf/40272230.pdf (accessed on 29 November 2018).
11. https://openknowledge.worldbank.org/handle/10986/18725 (accessed on 4 December 2018).
12. http://www.treasury.gov.za/publications/igfr/2008/lg/Chapter%203%20-%20Revenue%20and%20expenditure%20trends.pdf (accessed on6 December 2018).
13. https://www.investopedia.com/terms/r/revenuebond.asp#ixzz5YmSCVeRa (accessed on 5 December 2018).

14. https://www.financialexpress.com/market/municipal-bonds-what-they-are-who-can-buy-them/1238448/ (accessed on 5 December 2018).
15. http://siteresources.worldbank.org/INTMF/Resources/339747–1251914038224/77p.pdf (accessed on 5 December 2018).
16. https://m.rbi.org.in/scripts/bs_viewcontent.aspx?Id<hig>=</hig>1161 (accessed on 5 December 2018).
17. https://c.ymcdn.com/sites/mocities.site-ym.com/resource/resmgr/Budgeting_&_Financial_Contro.pdf (accessed on 7 December 2018).
18. http://documents.worldbank.org/curated/en/403951468180872451/pdf/888780PUB0Box300EPI198300June182014.pdf (accessed on 10 December 2018).
19. http://documents.worldbank.org/curated/en/403951468180872451/pdf/888780PUB0Box300EPI198300June182014.pdf (accessed on 10 December 2018).
20. https://www.edupristine.com/blog/financial-reporting (accessed on 10 December 2018).
21. http://shodhganga.inflibnet.ac.in/bitstream/10603/40555/10/12_chapter3.pdf (accessed on 11 December 2018).
22. http://shodhganga.inflibnet.ac.in/bitstream/10603/40555/10/12_chapter3.pdf (accessed on 11 December 2018).
23. http://shodhganga.inflibnet.ac.in/bitstream/10603/40555/10/12_chapter3.pdf (accessed on 11 December 2018).
24. https://amrut.gov.in/writereaddata/Toolkit-for-pg.pdf (accessed on 12 November 2018).
25. https://munkschool.utoronto.ca/imfg/uploads/77/rao_bird_urban_governance_and_finance_in_india.pdf (accessed on 11 December 2018).
26. https://www.hindustantimes.com/cities/pmc-to-raise-another-rs-200-crore-through-municipal-bonds/story-YGqErww3e6EjKTLQDHtQ0O.html (accessed on 7 June 2020).
27. https://www.researchgate.net/publication/23777672_Municipal_Finance_in_IndiaAn_Assessment (accessed on 12 December 2018).
28. https://link.springer.com/chapter/10.1007/978–3-030–02077–4_7 (accessed on 30 April 2019).
29. http://documents.worldbank.org/curated/en/458411468178144890/pdf/358640WBI0Inte1tLocalLevel01PUBLIC1.pdf (accessed on 30 April 2019).
30. https://www.lga.sa.gov.au/webdata/resources/files/23%20-%20Financial%20Governance%202015.pdf (accessed on 30 April 2019).
31. https://publicadministration.un.org/publications/content/PDFs/E-Library%20Archives/2005%20Participatory%20Planning%20and%20Budgeting%20at%20the%20Sub-national%20Level.pdf (accessed on 30 April 2019).
32. http://uk.gov.in/files/3rd%20stte%20finance%20report/chapters/8.pdf (accessed on 1 April 2019).
33. https://www.undp.org/content/undp/en/home/blog/2018/Meeting-the-urban-finance-challenge.html (accessed on 14 May 2019).
34. https://halshs.archives-ouvertes.fr/halshs-00730555/document (accessed on 1 May 2019).
35. http://i2ud.org/documents/Municipal_Finance_to_distribute_11.14.05.pdf (accessed on 3 November 2019).

References

Asian Development Bank. (2013). India: India municipal finance study (Technical Assistance Consultant's Report Project Number: TA 7334). https://nipfp.org.in/media/medialibrary/2013/08/IMFR_FINAL_REPORT.pdf (accessed on 10 April 2019).

Ayatollahi, A. (2008). *The financing of French municipalities.* Tehran: Department of Finance and Administration, Municipal Finance Conference Abstracts. Publications of Tehran Municipality. file:///C:/Users/new%20world/Downloads/388-Article%20Text–657–1–10–20171225%20(1).pdf (accessed on 5 December 2018).

Bagchi, S. (2001). Financing capital investments in urban infrastructure: Constraints in accessing capital market by urban local bodies. *Economic & Political Weekly, 36*(4), 385–387.

Bandyopadhyay, S. (2014). *Municipal finance in India: Some critical issues* (International Center for Public Policy, Working Paper) 14–21 May. Georgia: Andrew Yong School of Policy Studies, Georgia State University.

Bird, R. M. (2001). Setting the stage: Municipal and intergovernmental finance. In M. Freire & R. Stren (Eds.), *The challenge of urban government: Policies and practices* (pp. 113–128). Washington: World Bank Institute.

Bird, R. M. (2009). Tax assignment revisited. In J. Head & R. Krever (Eds.), *Tax reform in the 21st century* (pp. 441–470). New York: Wolters Kluwer.

Claw, F. R. (1896). Suggestions for the study of municipal finance. *The Quarterly Journal of Economics, 10*(4), 455–466.

Coady, D. (2017). *Fiscal decentralization: Objectives, principles and challenges.* Washington: Division Chief, Expenditure Policy Division Fiscal Affair Department, IMF. https://www.who.int/health_financing/events/D3S1-Coady-Fiscal-Decentralization-Objectives-Principles-and-Challenges.pdf (accessed on 12 April 2019).

Deloitte. (2017). *Funding and financing smart cities.* New York: Deloitte Center for Government Insights. https://www2.deloitte.com/content/dam/Deloitte/us/Documents/public-sector/us-ps-funding-and-financing-smart-cities.pdf (accessed on 28 April 2019).

Faguet, J. P. (2014). Decentralization and governance. *World Development, 53,* 2–13.

Farvacque-Vitkovic, C. (2014). Introduction. In C. Farvacque-Vitkovic & M. Kopanyi (Eds.), *Municipal finance: A handbook for local governments.* Washington: World Bank.

Freire, M. E., & Garzon, H. (2014). Managing local revenues. In C. Farvacque-Vitkovic & M. Kopanyi (Eds.), *Municipal finance: A handbook for local governments* (pp. 147–214). Washington: World Bank.

Gidisu, T. E. (2012). Automation system procedure of the Ghana Revenue Authority on the effectiveness of revenue collection: A case study of customs division (Unpublished MBA Thesis). Kumasi: Kwame Nkrumah University of Science and Technology. file:///C:/Users/new%20world/Downloads/Mccluskey-263-263.pdf (accessed on 29 April 2019).

Goncalves, S. (2013). The effects of participatory budgeting on municipal expenditure ad infant mortality in Brazil. *World Development, 20,* 1–17.

Hajilou, M., Mirehei, M., & Var, M. P. (2018). Studying sustainable revenue sources of municipalities (Case: Shabestar, East Azerbaijan Province). *Urban Economics and Management, 5,* no.4(20), 1–23.

Hicks, U. K. (1966). *Development from below: Local government and finance in Developing countries of the Commonwealth.* Oxford: Clarendon Press.

IMF. (2001). Fiscal decentralization and governance: A cross-country analysis (Working Paper No. 01/71). https://www.imf.org/en/Publications/WP/Issues/2016/12/30/Fiscal-Decentralization-and-Governance-A-Cross-Country-Analysis-4105 (accessed on 12 December 2018).

Joshi, A. (2010). Background paper on service delivery. In R. McGee & J. Gaventa (Eds.), *Review of impact and effectiveness of transparency and accountability initiatives.* Brighton: Institute of Development Studies, also see http://www.chance2sustain.eu/fileadmin/Website/Dokumente/Dokumente/Publications/D6.1_-_Framework_-_Participatory_Governance.pdf (accessed on 29 November 2018).

Kautilya. (1956). *Arthashastra.* Mysore: Raghuveer Printing Press.

Kitchen, Harry. (2002). Management issues affecting expenditure controls. In *Issues in municipal financing: Spending, revenues, governance, and administration* (Chapter 10). Toronto: Canadian Tax Foundation. https://www.ctf.ca/ctfweb/Documents/PDF/2002ctj/2002ctj1_tassonyi.pdf (accessed on 7 December 2018).

Kopanyi, M., & Morrell, L. (2014). Managing local expenditure. In C. F. Farvacque-Vitkovic & M. Kopanyi (Eds.), *Municipal finances: A handbook for local governments* (pp. 215–274). Washington: World Bank.

Lee, Robert E., & Johnson, R. D. (1998). *Public budgeting systems.* Gaithersburg: Aspen Publishers.

Mantzaris, E. (2014). Municipal financial management to fight corruption and enhance development: A holistic approach. *African Journal of Public Affairs, 7*(2), 80–92.

Mathur, O. P., Debdulal, T., & Nilesh, R. (2009). *Urban property tax potential in India.* New Delhi: National Institute of Public Finance and Policy.

Mazibuko, G., & Fourie, D. (2013). Municipal finance: Relevance for clean audit outcomes. *Administratio Publica, 21*(4), 130–152.

Mikesell, J. (2011): *Fiscal administration*. Boston, MA: Wardsworth.

Ministry of Housing & Urban Poverty Alleviation, Government of India. (2011). *Social audit methodology and operational manual for BSUP & IHSDP projects*. New Delhi: Ministry of Housing & Urban Poverty Alleviation, Government of India. http://mohua.gov.in/upload/uploadfiles/files/13Social%20Audit%20 Toolkits%20(Methodology_OperationalGuidelines_SocialAudit).pdf (accessed on 12 April 2019).

Mitullah, W. V., Odhiambo, M., & Akivaga, K. S. (2005). *Management of resources by local authorities: The case of local authority transfer fund*. Nairobi: Claripress. file:///C:/Users/new%20world/Downloads/ Mccluskey-263-263.pdf (accessed on 29 April 2019).

Musgrave, R. (1959). *The theory of public finance*. New York: McGraw-Hill.

Muwonge, A., & Ebel, R. D. (2014). Integrating finance in a decentralized world. In C. Farvacque-Vitkovic & M. Kopanyi (Eds.), *Municipal finance: A handbook for local governments* (pp. 1–11). Washington: World Bank.

OECD. (2001). *Management of municipal finance for environmental infrastructure in the new independent states*. OECD EAP Task Force. Prepared by the EAP TF Secretariat Final, 12 April. http://www.oecd. org/environment/outreach/2008522.pdf (accessed on 3 November 2019).

Ozuomba Chidinma, N., Nwadialor Eugene, O., & Ifureze, S. M. (2016). Effective internal audit as a tool for improving institutional governance and accountability in the public sector. *Advances in Applied Science Research, 7*(4), 1–10.

Rao, M. G., & Bird, R. M. (2010). Urban governance in India (Rotman School of Management Working Paper No. 1568858). https://papers.ssrn.com/sol3/papers.cfm?abstract_id=1568858 (accessed on 13 December 2018).

Reserve Bank of India. (1962). Chapter on local government finances. *Reserve Bank Bulletin*. http://shodhganga. inflibnet.ac.in/bitstream/10603/40555/10/12_chapter3.pdf (accessed on 11 December 2018).

Schaeffer, M. (2000). Municipal budgeting (Urban and Local Government Background Series No. 4). Washington: World Bank.

Shah, A. (2004). Fiscal decentralization in developing and transition economies: Progress, problems and the promises (Policy Research Working Paper No. 3282). Washington: World Bank. https://openknowledge. worldbank.org/handle/10986/14114 (accessed on 12 December 2018).

Sharma, M. P. (1978). *Public administration: Theory and practice*. Allahabad: Kitab Mahal.

Tassonyi, A. (1997). Financing municipal infrastructure in Canada's city-regions. In P. A. R. Hobson & F. St-Hilaire (Eds.), *Urban governance and finance: A question of who does what* (pp. 171–204). Montreal: Institute for Research on Public Policy.

UN-Habitat. (2009). *Guide to municipal finance*. Nairobi: United Nations Human Settlements Programme.

USAID. (2006). *Making cities work assessment and implementation toolkit*. Washington: Municipal Finance, USAID. https://urban-links.org/wp-content/uploads/2017/05/municipal-finance-assessment.pdf (accessed on 27 April 2019).

Venkateswaran, R. K. (2014). Municipal financial management. In C. F. Farvacque-Vitkovic & M. Kopanyi (Eds.), *Municipal finances: A handbook for local governments* (pp. 93–146). Washington: World Bank.

World Bank. (2018). *City resilience programme*. https://www.worldbank.org/en/topic/disasterriskmanagement/ brief/city-resilience-program (accessed on 28 April 2019).

Wrenshall, C. M. (1937). *Municipal administration and accounting*. Toronto: Pitman.

Yilmaz, S., & Beris, Y. (2008). Good governance and the emergence of a new accountability agenda. In G. Péteri (Ed.), *Finding the money: Public accountability and service efficiency through fiscal transparency*. Budapest: Local Government and Public Service Reform Initiative.

Yushkov, A. (2015). Fiscal decentralization and general economic growth: Theory, empirics and the Russian experience. *Russian Journal of Economics, 1*(4), 404–418.

7 Urban Infrastructure and Waste Management

The adequacies of infrastructure—which can contribute to diversifying production, expanding trade, and coping with population growth, reducing poverty, or improving environmental conditions—helps determine a country's success.

—World Bank (2004)

The link between infrastructure and development is not a once for all affair. It is a continuous process and progress in development has to be preceded, accompanied and followed by progress in infrastructure, if we are to fulfill our declared objectives of a self-accelerating process of economic development.

—V. K. R. V. Rao[1]

Managing solid waste well and affordably is one of the key challenges of the 21st century, and one of the key responsibilities of a city government. It may not be the biggest vote-winner, but it has the capacity to become a full-scale crisis, and a definite vote-loser, if things go wrong.

—UN-Habitat (2010a)

Introduction

The urban areas are known for their infrastructure facilities which distinguish them from the rural areas. These facilities enable investment which allows the urban areas to contribute efficiently and effectively towards economic growth and development of a nation state. One of the dictionary meanings of infrastructure is the basic facilities and installations that help a government or community run, including roads, schools, phone lines, sewage treatment plants and power generation. It is the term for the basic physical systems of a business or nation—transportation, communication, sewage, water and electric systems are all examples of infrastructure.[2] Infrastructure promotes the multidimensional development of the urban areas. Quality infrastructure facilities promote sustainable development. It improves the face value of the city and attracts investment from within and also from foreign countries. It also helps to improve the quality of life of the people. Smart cities necessitate smart infrastructure. The World Development Report 1994 asserts that a strong association exists between the availability of certain basic infrastructure and economic development measured in terms of GDP.

On the other hand, urban SWM is is an important concern for urban municipalities and pain for the city managers. If the wastes are not properly managed, then it will lead to unhealthy environment which can cost human life and adversely affect the sustainable development goal of the nation states. According to the World Bank (1999), urban areas in Asia generate about 760,000 tonnes of municipal solid waste (MSW), or approximately 2.7 million cubic metres, per day. In 2025, this figure will increase to 1.8 million tonnes of waste per day, or 5.2 million cubic metres of waste. Management of solid wastes is one of the important components of urban development issues and challenges.

This chapter deals with urban infrastructure and SWM.

LEARNING OBJECTIVES

After reading this chapter, you should be able to:

- ❒ Define infrastructure
- ❒ Explain the importance of infrastructure in urban development
- ❒ Describe various types of urban infrastructure
- ❒ Narrate the issues and challenges associated with urban infrastructure
- ❒ Suggest measures to upgrade infrastructure of a nation
- ❒ Explain the meaning and importance of SWM
- ❒ Describe various types of solid wastes and different strategies of SWM
- ❒ Narrate various issues and challenges of SWM

I
URBAN INFRASTRUCTURE

Urban Infrastructure: Concept and Meaning

Infrastructures are the physical facilities such as road, sanitation, drinking water, housing, transport, telecommunication and electricity, which are required for boosting economic growth and enhancing the quality of life of the people. Donald (1974) defined infrastructure as the physical structure and facilities that are developed or acquired by public agencies to enhance governmental function and provide water, power, waste disposal, transportation or similar services to facilitate the achievement of common social and economic objectives. Mody (1997) was of the view that infrastructure can be defined as activities that provide society with the services necessary to conduct daily life and to engage in productive activities. In the opinion of Srinivasu and Rao (2013), infrastructure is the stock of basic facilities and capital equipment needed for the functioning of a country or area; the term to refer collectively to the roads, bridges, rail lines, and similar public works that are required for an industrial economy, or a proportion of it, to function. According to UN-Habitat (2011), broadly, infrastructure refers to all basic inputs and requirements for the proper functioning of the economy. The economic infrastructure essentially are transport, energy, ICT technology, water, sanitation and irrigation, and the social infrastructure, on the other hand, encompasses services such as health, education and recreation (UN-Habitat, 2011).

The importance of infrastructure for economic growth has been widely acknowledged by the international agencies. DFID (2002) has identified various channels through which investment in infrastructure can contribute to sustainable growth. These are: (a) reducing transaction costs and facilitating trade flows within and across borders; (b) enabling economic actors—individuals, firms and governments—to respond to new types of demand in different places; (c) lowering the costs of inputs for entrepreneurs for making existing business more profitable; (d) creating employment; (e) enhancing human capital; and (f) improving environmental conditions. It remarked that infrastructure services—including power, transportation, telecommunications, provision of water and sanitation, and safe disposal of wastes—are central to economic production and urban growth.[3]

Richard R. Mudge and Kenneth I. Rubin while asking the question 'Why is infrastructure?' viewed that infrastructure generates additional investment or economic activity through a multiplier effect on private firms or other public agencies. This process occurs in several ways:

1. By making better use of underutilized resources that previously were very costly or difficult to obtain.
2. By enabling more efficient trade-offs among factors of production.
3. By reducing costs and thus increasing economic efficiencies.
4. By expanding markets as improved efficiency results in more effective competition with other countries or regions.[4]

Need and Importance of Urban Infrastructure

Urban infrastructure is vital to urban development because of the following reasons:

1. *Stimulates economic growth:* The investment in building quality infrastructure in cities is a growth-boosting investment. The good-quality infrastructure such as road, sewerage system, waste management system, housing, telecommunication and traffic system will save a lot of time and generate motivation among the stakeholders to contribute towards economic growth and development. Cities having superior and good-quality infrastructure are found to be attracting more private investments and foreign direct investments (FDIs) and contributing more to the national growth in the developing countries. The World Bank has rightly remarked that infrastructure development lies at the nexus of economic growth, productive investment, job creation and poverty reduction.[5]
2. *Attracts private investment:* Quality infrastructure in cities attracts investors from within the country as well as from foreign countries. In India, it is observed that most of the FDIs are made in the cities such as New Delhi, Mumbai, Bangalore, Hyderabad and Chennai which have good-quality infrastructure as compared to other cities. As per an OECD (2014) document, infrastructure has a strong impact on a country's investment attractiveness. The extensiveness of the road network, the efficacy of the port system and the length of container wait times, for instance, have clear implications for the timely and cost-effective delivery of goods. Policymakers and planners have used infrastructure systems to attract private investments for housing and economic development.[6]

3. *Stimulates urban land development:* Infrastructure plays an important role in urban land development. The need for various urban infrastructures such as good road, housing complex, marketing complex and recreation centre enables effective utilization of urban land by the government. Good-quality infrastructure also raises land prices of the urban areas. It is commonly agreed that infrastructure plays an important role in stimulating urban land development and private economic activity (Démurger, 2001). Further, availability of urban infrastructure also enhances the land prices in the cities having better and quality infrastructure. Serra et al. (2004) viewed that urban land supply is determined by topography and physical conditions, patterns of land ownership, availability of infrastructure—roads, water, electricity—and government regulations.
4. *Regional balance:* The infrastructure, in general, and road infrastructure, in particular, connect one region with the other through cities. In other words, infrastructure in cities acts as a go-between. Wisely targeted infrastructure investment is not a silver bullet. But it can rebalance the economy and connect cities and regions to internal and external markets for employment, goods and services.[7] The infrastructure is one of the important yardsticks for the measurement of regional development.
5. *Promotes trade and commerce:* The infrastructure provides both forward and backward linkages for development, which means that businesses prefer to be near to their suppliers and customers; this allows for reductions in cost, greater oversight of the supply chain and improved productivity.[8] A nation cannot flourish its trade and commerce without good infrastructure network. The commercial cities such as Kolkata and Mumbai in India are known for their infrastructural provisioning. E-commerce depends on the availability of telecommunication infrastructure. To Munim and Schramm (2018), it is vital for developing countries to continuously improve the quality of port infrastructure as it contributes to better logistics performance, leading to higher seaborne trade, yielding higher economic growth.
6. *Promotes inclusive and sustainable development:* According to ADB, the role of infrastructure is to promote inclusive sustainable development, and it recognizes the importance of developing regional and international infrastructure to achieve this objective.[9] Infrastructure not only glorifies cities but also links cities with the semi-urban and rural areas and thus promotes inclusive development. It enables the disadvantaged to have access to cities for employment and raise their quality of life. Sustainable development can be possible only with quality infrastructure. SDG has an element of sustainable infrastructure within its ambit. The UN has envisaged that investments in infrastructure—transport, irrigation, energy and ICT—are crucial to achieving sustainable development and empowering communities in many countries.[10]
7. *Promotes industrialization:* Industrialization requires good-quality infrastructure for the transport of raw materials. Besides, the industrial cities both in government and private industries ensure good quality infrastructure facilities to the city dwellers. Thinking of industrialization without the provision of infrastructure is impossible. The good infrastructural facilities available in various cities of the European countries are because of industrialization which started in the 17th century. Infrastructural development and industrialization go hand in hand. It is being remarked that a functioning and resilient infrastructure is the foundation of every successful community. To meet future challenges, our industries and infrastructure must be upgraded.[11]

8. *Promotes service sector activities:* Infrastructure development gives stimulation to the service sector. The availability of services such as banking, insurance, education, health and information technology depends on the availability of good-quality infrastructure for these services. The investors both inside and outside the countries are attracted to invest in service sector activities in the cities having good infrastructure facilities. ADB has envisaged that services are a vital source of output, growth and jobs in the region, but suffer from very low productivity levels. It advocated that the complementary investments in physical infrastructure will also speed up service sector development.[12]
9. *Promotes social and human development:* Providing social infrastructure such as health institutions and educational institutions will promote social and human development. It is not a flight of fancy, but delicately all quality educational and health institutions are available in urban areas. The level of education is high and the health status in terms of infant and maternal mortality rate is lower in urban areas as compared to rural areas. Literacy rate and infant mortality rate are the two vital components of human development index (HDI). Therefore, it has long been recognized that growth in productivity and incomes, and improvements in health and education outcomes require investment in infrastructure.[13] It is remarked that successful human socioeconomic development seems to require the simultaneous co-evolution of social structures and infrastructural networks and services (Holston, 2008; Jacobs, 1970).
10. *Raises quality of life:* Last but not least, availability of quality infrastructure such as healthy houses, sanitation, safe drinking water and energy for cooking and lighting are essential requirements of life. In urban areas, the availability of these basic infrastructure facilities will raise the quality of life of city dwellers. Nwagbara (2003) opined that quality of life in cities depends on the degree of people's accessibility to adequate healthcare, housing, educational facilities, power supply and other infrastructure. It can be argued that improved quality of life is strongly infrastructure based.[14]

Types of Urban Infrastructure

Infrastructure is fundamental to development and its importance is more ascertaining in urban areas and cities. Eleventh Five-Year Plan document of GoI had rightly envisaged that Indian cities will be the locus and engine of economic growth over the next two decades, and the realization of an ambitious goal of 9–10 per cent growth in GDP depends fundamentally on making Indian cities much more liveable, inclusive, bankable and competitive.[15]

1. *Housing:* Housing is a basic need and a healthy house with required rooms, separate kitchen and bathrooms and toilet, and proper ventilation will raise the quality of life of the people living in urban areas. However, ensuring healthy house to the urban slum population is a challenge before the government and local bodies. It has been rightly remarked that adequate housing is necessary for social welfare as it provides protection from weather, a place to bring up families and a place to work. While policy debates have more or less accepted that urbanization is an irreversible phenomenon with more positive than negative externalities, the biggest challenge associated with urbanization is that it has not kept pace with the housing needs of those living in cities and those migrating to the cities.[16] UN-Habitat (2010b) has noted that more than 30 per cent of the world's urban population is either living in poor housing conditions in slums or is homeless.

2. *Road:* Roads are the arteries through which the economy pulses. By linking producers to markets, workers to jobs, students to schools and the sick to hospitals, roads are vital to any development agenda.[17] A road within the city and connecting road to the city will not only make urban life comfortable and save the precious time of the urban dweller, but it will also enhance the trade and commerce activities of the cities. Bombay–Delhi corridor is intended to enhance commercial activities between Delhi, the capital city of India, and Mumbai, the business city of India. The inner city road in many smaller cities is not in a good condition of the developing countries.
3. *Intracity transport:* The World Bank has envisaged that the pressures on urban transport systems are increasing in most developing countries as part of the process of growth. Because demand for transport is essentially a derived demand, urban transport must be viewed strategically as an integral component of the city economy and hence of its development strategy.[18] Ensuring pollution-free transport facilities to the city dwellers is an essential requirement of the smart cities. The transport-related pollution and increasing number of vehicles are cause for concern for the health of city dwellers. The air qualities of most of the metropolitan cities are in highly dangerous stage. Reducing the number of diesel vehicles within the cities is called for. Besides this, traffic jam and sound pollution are other associated problems with more vehicular transport. The metro rail and monorail facilities in many cities have reduced the transport-related concerns to some extent in the populated cities. The World Bank has expressed its concern that deteriorating transport conditions associated with urban sprawl and increased motorization are damaging the economy of large cities.
4. *Intercity communication:* The cities and urban areas within the state and in the adjoining states of the nation need to be connected with rail, air and bus services. Connecting the cities by air will not only save the time of the passengers but also raise the commercial activities in the cities. Good communication facilities to heritage and religious cities will enhance the state revenue and employment opportunities in these cities. The prominent examples in India are Agra and Haridwar. It is remarked that transport differs from other problems faced by developing societies because it is getting worse rather than better with economic development.[19] Maintenance of intercity roads is a big challenge before the governments of the developing countries.
5. *Information technology:* In the globalized era, the world has become a single village through modern information technology. The information communication facilities such as broadband Internet connectivity and mobile phones in the cities are vital for its development. More emphasis needs to be given to the smaller cities in the economically backward states and situated in the hilly and inaccessible areas of the nation states. The concept of smart cities and the 'Fourth Industrial Revolution' are the buzz words that have dominated urban thinking and discussion in recent years. Developments in artificial intelligence, robotics, the Internet of Things, autonomous vehicles, virtual reality, 3D printing, nanotechnology, biotechnology, materials science, energy storage and quantum computing are promising a new era of contemporary urban development.[20]
6. *Sewerage and drainage system:* Drainage and sewerage system in urban areas is an important priority because of rapid urbanization, industrialization and population growth in the cities and urban areas. Besides, there has been an increase in urban slum population through migration of rural population to urban areas mostly in the developing countries. It is frequently reported that the urban living conditions become precarious during floods and heavy rains. The main reason is the lack of proper drainage system. Generally in the

developing countries, the many urban slums lack proper sewerage facilities which affect the health and quality of living to a great extent. Jonathan Parkinson has remarked that in poorly drained areas, urban run-off mixes with sewage from overflowing latrines and sewers, causing pollution and a wide range of problems associated with the increased risk of waterborne diseases.[21]

7. *Solid waste and garbage disposal:* SWM is a stupendous problem in the metropolitan cities of both developed and developing countries. Shortage of landfill sites has further aggravated the situation in many countries. The generation of solid wastes from various sources in the cities has grown manifold because of unplanned urbanization. The World Bank has envisaged that around the world, waste generation rates are rising. In 2016, the worlds' cities generated 2.01 billion tonnes of solid waste, amounting to a footprint of 0.74 kilograms per person per day. With rapid population growth and urbanization, annual waste generation is expected to increase by 70 per cent from 2016 levels to 3.40 billion tonnes in 2050. It urged that managing waste properly is essential for building sustainable and liveable cities, but it remains a challenge for many developing countries and cities.[22] The infrastructure required for the purpose largely includes identification of landfill sites, garbage disposal tanks, dustbins, garbage transport vehicles, treatment plants and so on.
8. *Water supply:* Piped and safe drinking water supply to the city population and building up infrastructure for safe drinking water are important responsibilities of the government. Supply of safe drinking water is also one of the necessary conditions for a smart and sustainable city. With half of the world's population staying in the cities, the demand for key services such as safe drinking water and sanitation is likely to emerge as a major challenge in coming days (Cohen, 2006). Van der Bruggen et al. (2010) have explained the water supply problems in urbanized regions of the developing countries as the interaction of three interrelated factors, namely (a) high population growth, (b) lower than required investments in water supply infrastructure and (c) availability of water sources. The government and urban local bodies have to formulate an appropriate strategy to overcome the difficulties in the supply of safe drinking water to the city dwellers.
9. *Energy infrastructure:* Building urban energy infrastructures such as power grids, gas pipelines, petroleum and diesel pumps and solar systems is essential for the sustainable development of the modern cities. A smart and sustainable city depends on smart energy. Smart energy infrastructure needs to provide a pollution-free smart environment to the city dwellers. It has been noted that today, municipalities around the globe are striving to improve the livelihood of their inhabitants by producing and integrating renewable energy, aiming to reduce their carbon footprint, transitioning to distributed electrical power systems, promoting and developing sustainable transportation and so on.[23] Energy self-sufficiency through renewable sources is an alternative to promote a closed energy cycle in urban areas to the extent that it should replace technologies, which require fossil resources.[24] In his survey, Garsous (2012) found that, *ceteris paribus* (with other conditions remaining the same), studies focusing on the energy sector are more likely to find a robust positive impact than any other infrastructure sector. In other words, investing in the energy sector may be the safest bet to achieve a high social rate of return.
10. *Sociocultural infrastructure:* Social and cultural development plays an important role in urban development as well. There should be emphasis on cultural and recreational infrastructure in the cities in order to attract tourists from within and outside the country. The cities need to have parks, stadiums, museums, sanctuaries, cinemas, theatres, art

galleries, aquariums and so on. It is remarked that the development of new 'hard' cultural infrastructure has long been part of the urban regeneration toolkit (Hoffman et al., 2003). It can be used at a number of spatial scales, for example, as part of an urban regeneration scheme or as a major investment intended to enhance the overall image of a city.[25]

The cities need to have social infrastructure like quality educational infrastructure such as schools, colleges and universities and health infrastructure such as hospitals and dispensaries. Julie Brown and Austin Barber were of the view that the social infrastructure framework is designed to integrate policies and programmes for housing, education, social services, health, leisure and emergency services and to plan public service provision jointly. They also opined that providing services and facilities that meet the needs of residents, promoting social interactions and enhancing the quality of life are vital for building sustainable communities.[26]

11. *Law and order infrastructure:* Law and order is a vital issue in cites of the developing countries of Asia and Africa. The citizens must feel safe and be protected from the criminal elements. An adequate number of police booths and night patrolling police must be deployed in the cities. A safe city is a smart and sustainable city. Adequate city lighting facilities and CCTV cameras are other law and order exigencies for the safe city. PwC has envisaged that safe city solutions incorporate a wide array of technology-driven sub-systems. The detection system may be driven electronically using high-definition closed-circuit television (CCTV) cameras, infrared radars, lasers, handheld devices or simply an incident reported by a vigilant citizen through a mobile or social media.[27] The aim of the law and order infrastructure is to prevent occurrences of crimes and violence occurring in the streets, colonies, organizations and other places of the cities.
12. *Traffic infrastructure:* Unplanned urbanization and globalization has enhanced the number of vehicles—two wheelers, three wheelers and four wheelers—in the cities. Most of the cities in the developing countries lack adequate traffic infrastructure. In many of these countries manual traffic management is still going on. Inadequate traffic infrastructure and management have resulted in accidents in the cities. According to a traffic management streamlining think tank, the traffic management technologies have been divided into five groups which are: (a) short-term traffic management techniques which include regulatory techniques, demand management techniques, bus priority techniques and others; (b) passive traffic management systems which include fixed-time traffic signals, signal hardware, passive passenger information systems, violation detectors; (c) incremental infrastructure which includes road improvements, flyovers, pedestrian subways, parking lots and others; (d) active traffic management systems which include detector-based traffic signals, variable message signs for parking/incident/violation detection, traffic sensors; and (e) expert traffic management systems.[28] The cities, in general, and metropolitan cities, in particular, need to have adequate traffic management equipment and trained personnel for traffic operation in order to control traffic jam and accidents.
13. *Old-age homes:* Taking care of the elderly population is an emerging issue in both high-income and developing countries. The demographic changes have revealed a rising percentage of old-age population in the demographic pyramid of the nation states. Small family size and migration of children away from the parents are serious demographic concerns in the cities. The municipalities of the developing countries like those of the developed countries are needed to construct and manage old-age homes with the help of private and corporate sectors and NGOs. In the cities, customarily, there is a growth of

individualism, and the generational gap and clashes between young and old generations distress the old. It is true that many of the problems which the elderly face in urban areas do not exist in the villages. Therefore, a good number of the elderly of urban areas prefer to stay in old-age homes. Construction of old-age homes is a social responsibility of the welfare state.

14. *Market complexes and shopping malls:* With liberalization and globalization, the market economy is proliferating in most developing countries of the world. The modernization and inter- and intra-country trade and business are growing in cities. Therefore, the government and the urban municipalities in the developing countries, in particular, have to build market and shopping complexes in order to enhance its own sources of revenue. Most of the FDIs in recent years are invested in the retail business. Shopping malls act like public magnets. They attract people who spend their leisure times and also purchase their necessary and other items at a common place called 'shopping mall'. They also attract tourists and it is observed that the tourists largely visit popular shopping malls in the cities. Market complexes and shopping malls are infrastructures worth creating by the city municipalities.

Measurement of City Infrastructure Development

Identification of variables for the measurement of infrastructure development in the city is important for developing competitiveness among the cities with regard to the development of their infrastructure. UNDP in the calculation of city development index has used following variables in infrastructure development of a city: (a) water connection, (b) sewerage, (c) electricity, (d) waste disposal and (e) waste treatment.[29] Some of the variables that need to be taken into consideration for the assessment of infrastructure competitive index of the cities are as follows:

1. Quality of city road
2. Electricity connectivity and supply
3. Cooking gas connection
4. Sewerage system
5. Piped drinking water
6. Waste disposal
7. Waste treatment
8. Automatic traffic management system
9. Transport system
10. Telephone and Internet connectivity
11. Infrastructure for safety and security (number of police posts per thousand populations).
12. Dispensaries and hospitals
13. Schools, colleges and higher education institutions
14. Market complexes and shopping malls
15. Use of open space, that is, parks, gardens, footpaths and so on
16. Infrastructure facilities in the city slums

It is pertinent to mention here that in the Infrastructure Raking Global Competitive Index, Asian giants, Singapore and Japan, occupy first and fifth places, respectively, keeping the USA behind (Table 7.1). The municipal service level gaps in India are given in Table 7.2.

Table 7.1 Infrastructure Ranking, Global Competitive Report, 2018

Countries	Score	Rank
Singapore	95.7	1
Japan	91.5	5
United States	89.5	9
China	78.1	29
India	68.7	63

Source: http://reports.weforum.org/global-competitiveness-report-2018/competitiveness-rankings/#series=GCI4.A.02 (accessed on 12 January 2019).

Table 7.2 Service Level Gaps in India

Service Indicators	National Benchmark	India Status
Water Supply		
Per capita supply of water	135 lpcd	69 lpcd
Extent of metering of water connections	100%	13%
Extent of non revenue water (NRW)	20%	32%
Cost recovery in water supply services	100%	39%
Sewerage		
Coverage of toilets	100%	70%
Collection efficiency of the sewage network	100%	10%
Solid Waste Management		
Household level coverage	100%	35%
Extent of scientific disposal of municipal solid waste	100%	10%
Stormwater Drainage		
Coverage of stormwater drainage network	100%	46%

Source: https://www.teriin.org/projects/apn/pdf/day2/Financing_of_Infrastructure_Development_TERIGoa.pdf (accessed on 1 May 2019).

Issues and Challenges of Urban Infrastructure

Some of the issues and challenges of urban infrastructure are as follows:

1. *Rapid urbanization:* The most important challenge before urban infrastructure and urban development is rapid urbanization. The rapid unplanned urbanization in the developing countries with the migration of rural population to urban areas is a formidable challenge of urbanization. The municipality's budget on infrastructure building and their maintenance is escalating year by year. This has inflicted issue of shortage and poor maintenance of

infrastructure in urban areas. It has been reported that an excessive increase in urban population leads to aggravation of living infrastructure in urban areas.[30] John Scott was of the opinion that we need to recognize this rapid urbanization; often, unplanned urbanization brings risks of profound social instability, risks to critical infrastructure, potential water crises and the potential for devastating spread of diseases. These risks can only be further exacerbated as this unprecedented transition from rural to urban areas continues.[31]

2. *Upgradation of urban infrastructure:* The urban infrastructure in most of the old cities is in bad shape. The upgradation of civil infrastructures such as roads, sewerage system, drinking water projects and SWM are sin qua non for ensuring a good standard of living to the city population. Effective implementation of urban renewal mission is a challenge. One of the objectives of the smart city mission is to modernize cities by providing core infrastructure and give a decent quality of life to its citizens, a clean and sustainable environment and application of 'smart' solutions.[32]
3. *Financing urban infrastructure:* One of the major challenges of developing countries is financing the urban infrastructure. Having scanty resources, these countries have to invest in the infrastructure development of both urban and rural areas. The maintenance of urban infrastructure is poor because of lack of finance. According to Mathur, financing urban infrastructure centres around four questions: (a) How much is invested in urban infrastructure? (b) Who invests? (c) What are the key sources and financing instruments? (d) Are the investment levels adequate or proportionate to the demand?[33] It can be rightly said that in urban areas of the developing countries, the financing for the creation of infrastructure compared to rapid pace of urbanization is falling short of demand.
4. *Operation and maintenance of urban infrastructure:* The operation and maintenance (O&M) of the urban infrastructure is a vital challenge. On one hand, existing infrastructure is falling short in front of the huge demand for urban infrastructure, while on the other hand, these infrastructures are falling into disrepair before completing their design life. O&M has been identified by the urban planners and policymakers as the key to enhancing the sustainability of existing infrastructure and assets. Proper operation of services refers to the activities involved in the delivery of a service; it depends on both users and providers using the facilities and equipment with care in order to ensure the long life of services of the infrastructure and to reduce maintenance needs. Maintenance refers to the activities that ensure that infrastructure remains in a serviceable condition; it covers preventative maintenance, corrective maintenance and crisis maintenance (Davies & Brikke, 1995). Most of the developing countries find it difficult to maintain the created infrastructure in its urban areas.
5. *Lack of skilled manpower:* Most of the developing countries lack skilled manpower for infrastructure, planning, development, operation and maintenance. The hiring of a foreign expert is a costly affair for the developing countries. The metro rail transport in India is being developed with the help of Japan's technical support. While analysing the skilled manpower requirement in the urban real estate sector, it was felt that with rapid urbanization, skilled manpower for the real estate sector is very much in demand but supply is an issue. Experts believe that reducing the massive demand–supply gap of skilled professionals is fundamental for the industry to be able to deliver projects of the highest quality, on time and cost.[34]
6. *Regional imbalance:* The intra-state and inter-state imbalance in urban infrastructure is a cause of concern in the developing countries. It is generally observed that the capital cities have good infrastructural facilities as compared to other middle-sized and smaller cities.

For the sustainable city development, all cities within a nation state have to be developed so that they can contribute towards the nation's economic growth and development. The challenge is proper planning and allocation of resources for city infrastructure development. Ghosh and Dey from their study have concluded that: first, regional disparity has been rising in the recent period, and plan outlay has not played any major role in this regard; second, regional imbalance in physical infrastructure has been found to be responsible for rising income disparity across the states.[35]

7. *Research and development:* The research and development activity in the infrastructure sector is poor in the developing countries. This is the sole factor responsible for the development of poor-quality infrastructure in the developing countries. Research and development in urban infrastructure is a weak area of urban development. It is remarked that urban infrastructure shapes our cities socially, environmentally and politically. Infrastructure can divide communities and bring communities together; it can address one environmental concern and create a new one; it can be bought, sold and co-owned. Urban infrastructure decisions may also affect different parts of the city to different degrees, which can result in varying patterns of socio-spatial disadvantage and inequity.[36] However, research related to urban infrastructure on cost-effectiveness, social impact needs assessment, environmental impact and designing is critically lacking. The study of infrastructure has been described by Star (1999) as 'mundane to the point of boring, involving things such as plugs, standards and bureaucratic forms'.[37]
8. *Creating fiscal and financially self-sustaining ULBs:* ULBs play an important role in the formulation, operation and maintenance of urban infrastructure project. The devolution of finance to ULBs will make the urban infrastructure project more self-sustaining. The NITI Aayog has rightly remarked that the provisioning of adequate infrastructure requires huge finances. A look at the urban local finances in India indicates that most of the ULBs are lacking in mobilization of resources and financial autonomy. Further, the existing pattern of municipal finances has not been able to meet the required expenditure on infrastructure development in urban areas.[38]
9. *Presence of multiple authorities having overlapping jurisdictions:* The infrastructure development is a critical area cross-cutting multiple jurisdictions such as central, state, municipal and village panchayats. Sometimes forest and other departments such as education and health are also being involved. Getting clearances from various departments and agencies is a herculean task which results in delay in the starting and completion of infrastructure projects. FICCI has rightly envisaged that urban infrastructure, more than any other sector, faces the drag of multiple authorities having jurisdiction over different aspects of the same infrastructure facility. For example, in a large urban infrastructure project, it is usual to require approval for the implementation of the relevant project, depending on the city, of the municipality, the urban town and country planning department, a development authority, state government public works department, state government irrigation department, city police, city fire department and the state government.[39]
10. *Urban land-use planning*: Last, but not least, are the issues and challenges related to urban infrastructure development in the urban land-use planning. Land acquisition for the development of urban infrastructure is an arduous task. It faces a lot of resistance from the public. Moreover, systematic land-use planning is also an issue for the effective development of sustainable urban infrastructure. It has been suggested that at the city level, local governments must be encouraged to carry out an integrated land-use planning to comprehensively address adverse impacts of urbanization, including environmental

problems. Zoning techniques, which may be applied to implement the master plan and to guide urban development to spatially appropriate areas, include designation of sensitive land resources and areas, establishment of buffer zones, management of hazard-prone lands, protection of cultural resources, conservation of open spaces and urban green, management of prime agricultural land, and guiding and discouraging of an excessive urban sprawl.[40]

Measures to Promote Urban Infrastructure Development

It is not a flight of fancy, but delicately investment in infrastructure will help urban areas to effectively contribute to economic growth and development of the nation states. In the developing countries, generation, operation and maintenance of infrastructure in urban areas is poor and not satisfactory. For sustainable and smart cities, sustainable infrastructure is sine qua non. The following measures are needed to improve the infrastructure development in urban areas.

1. *Planned urbanization and migration:* The unbridled migration of rural population to urban areas needs to be checked. One of the objectives of planned urbanization is to check unwanted migration of rural population to urban areas. If the urban amenities are being provided to the countryside population, then it would dissuade them to migrate to urban areas. The planned urbanization process desires an optimum population for a city to attain the goal of a sustainable city. Moreover, the Kerala model of rural–urban continuum will also be helpful to check rural to urban migration. It is rightly remarked that the capacity of cities and towns to absorb population growth and enable such good living (as measured by wealth and quality of life) depends, among other factors, on the quality of its urbanization process.[41]
2. *Infrastructure financing:* Urban infrastructure financing is a major problem for the creation, operation and maintenance of urban infrastructure. Various sources of infrastructural financing in India are local government capital budget allocation, bank and institutional loans, grants from state and central governments, long-term municipal funds/bonds, leveraging municipal assets and private equity, and pooled bonds issued by urban infrastructural funds. The other sources of municipal infrastructural funding that need to be explored and used for infrastructure development in the cities are public–private partnership, funds from bilateral and multilateral agencies and user charges and community financing.
3. *Skill upgradation:* There is need for skill upgradation in urban infrastructure sector of the functionaries belonging to public, private and ULBs. The public works department and private sectors engaged in the infrastructure development in the cities need to be oriented on modern technologies used in infrastructure development. The UN has also emphasized for conducting skills gap analyses in workforces, including in public sector entities, with regard to the skills required for the design, development and management of infrastructure.[42]
4. *Financial empowerment of ULBs:* The financial empowerment of urban local self-government institutions is critical to urban infrastructure development. More and more funds need to be devolved from the central and state governments for the development and management of urban infrastructure by the municipalities in their areas. Moreover, the local self-government must be empowered to raise funds through taxes and other sources. Pethe and Lalvani (2006) suggested that there is a need to create virtual

entities—self-help groups among ULBs—that could expand the domain of ULBs eligible to access the credit market for infrastructure building.

5. *PPP:* The government alone cannot develop and manage sustainable infrastructure in the cities. Therefore, the role of the private sector through PPP has to be promoted to develop and manage infrastructure in the cities. To Pongsiri (2011), PPPs are arrangements between government and private sector entities for the purpose of providing public infrastructure, community facilities and related services. It is being suggested that PPPs undertake urban construction projects to facilitate joint development and renewal of problematic urban zones.[43]
6. *Community participation:* Community participation in infrastructure development, operation and maintenance are vital for effective management of infrastructure projects. The people in various municipalities in India are participating in the planning and management of infrastructure project, particularly, drinking water, electricity, school and heath institutions projects, solid waste disposal and management and so on through Ward Sabhas, a statutory body of the local self-government institutions. More and more community participation in various infrastructural development projects is required. The community participation in infrastructure development can take place in different ways: (a) providing consultancy, (b) giving land for infrastructure development, (c) cost-sharing, (d) creating community fund for management of infrastructure and (e) giving user charges. Alfredo Stein from his study in various social projects in Nicaragua has noted that through participatory micro-planning exercises, the communities and families involved have identified, prioritized, negotiated and coordinated their projects with local governments, and the loans with a commercial bank. Likewise, project committees and community working groups have been established to participate directly in the building, administration, supervision and maintenance of the infrastructure works.[44]
7. *Research and development:* The research and development activities in infrastructure have to be strengthened, particularly in developing countries. A holistic multidisciplinary research is required for effective planning, development and management of various infrastructural projects. It has been rightly remarked by Wendy Steele and Crystal Legacy that urban infrastructure, despite its pervasiveness and criticality, is an under-explored area of critical urban research, policy and practice.[45]
8. *Proper infrastructure planning and management:* Planning and management of infrastructures is important for their sustainability. Yvo de Boer has remarked, 'Infrastructure, if intelligently designed, planned and delivered, is probably one of the best hopes we have of achieving a sustainable future against the impacts of climate change'.[46] A multidisciplinary team with town planners, engineers, social scientists, management experts as its members is being suggested for the planning and management of infrastructure. The participatory infrastructure planning and management will involve the community in effective operation and maintenance of infrastructure.

The UN document has envisaged that the smart infrastructure project needs to be:

a) *People-centred and inclusive:* It should be chosen and designed with a deep understanding of people's lifestyles, cultures, behaviour and needs.
b) *Resilient and sustainable:* It should be resilient to external shocks and ensure sustainability.
c) *Interoperable and flexible:* It should be designed in order to be flexible with regard to future modification and enhancements.

d) *Risk mitigating and safe:* It should be accompanied by appropriate risk management and risk mitigation strategies.

In the World Development Report 1994: Infrastructure for Development, the World Bank had laid down principles for reform in the provision and operation of infrastructure. These are as follows:

a) Manage infrastructure like a business, not like a bureaucracy.
b) Introduce competition—directly, if feasible and indirectly, if not.
c) Give users and other stakeholders a strong voice and real responsibility.[47]

II
URBAN SOLID WASTE MANAGEMENT

Waste management is a problem in rapidly growing urban centres in developing countries. The unsustainable production and consumption patterns result in waste that can harm health and the environment.

—Sida[48]

The overall goal of urban solid waste management is to collect, treat and dispose of solid wastes generated by all urban population groups in an environmentally and socially satisfactory manner using the most economical means available.

—World Bank[49]

Waste is generated by human activities. Urban waste is generated by human activities performed in urban areas. Urban waste management is a crucial component of urban development. According to UN-Habitat (2010), a working definition of MSW is 'wastes generated by households, and wastes of a similar nature generated by commercial and industrial premises, by institutions such as schools, hospitals, care homes and prisons, and from public spaces such as streets, markets, slaughter houses, public toilets, bus stops, parks, and gardens'. Generation of waste is a fact and has to happen in the cities, however, wastes have to be managed properly so that they do not negatively affect the health and quality of life of the city dwellers. Managing waste efficiently and sustainably is a unique challenge before the urban municipalities. The smart and sustainable city relies on the effective management of urban waste in order to provide a sustainable and healthy living environment to the urban population. It is estimated that urban areas in India generate more than 100,000 million tonnes of waste per day: (a) a large metropolis like Mumbai generates about 7,000 million tonnes of waste per day, (b) Bangalore generates about 5,000 million tonnes and (c) other large cities such as Pune and Ahmedabad generate waste in the range of 1,600–3,500 million tonnes per day.[50] China produces around 300 million tonnes of waste a year, majority of which comes from cities.[51] Waste management is a crucial issue before the municipal administration. It is well commented that there is a need for a complete rethinking of 'waste'—to analyse if waste is indeed waste. A rethinking that calls for:

WASTE to become WEALTH
REFUSE to become RESOURCE
TRASH to become CASH[52]

Need for Urban Waste Management

Why management of urban waste is important? It is a pertinent question posed before various sectors, actors, stakeholders and general city dwellers at large. According to UN-Habitat (2013), cities are in fact the protagonists, responsible for 70 per cent of global greenhouse gas emissions, 60 per cent of global energy consumption and 70 per cent of global waste. Urban waste management can be defined as the management related to prevention and minimization of generation of waste, its storage, collection, transport or transfer, disposal and processing of solid waste materials in a way that best addresses the range of issues associated with public health, environment, engineering, economics and aesthetic consideration of city dwellers. Sustainable waste management would make cities smart and enhance the quality of life of the city dwellers. According to some research reports, every year, 62 million tonnes of waste is generated out of which only 28 per cent of waste is recycled and 72 per cent is left on the roads and the landfill areas for several years, which is fraught with hazardous consequences.[53] Therefore, there is need for urban waste management for ensuing waste-related free diseases to the city dweller and improvement of city environmental sanitation conditions. A few reasons for the management of urban waste are discussed as follows:

1. Waste problem is directly or indirectly related to social, economic and political development issues. These issues, on the other hand, would have a profound impact on health, public order and security and have other related problems. Therefore, the implementation of management of waste should be in an integrated way with other development issues.[54]
2. Smart waste management is a key factor for a smart city. It will create a feel-good factor among the city dwellers as well as visitors to the cities. It will make the city smart, beautiful and green. Borghi et al. (2014) were of the view that smart waste management is a key issue for translating integrated strategic approaches for smart cities into the wider idiom of a circular economy, transcending the urban dimension.
3. Waste management is required in order to improve the health and well-being of the city dwellers. It is generally studied that a city where the wastes are well managed there is less prevalence of waste-related diseases such as plague and dengue. The existing evidence on the linkage between poor SWM and adverse health outcomes calls for action by all stakeholders in understanding, prioritizing and addressing the issue of solid waste in our midst to ensure that our environment and health are preserved (Ziaraba et al., 2016).
4. It helps in the reduction of environmental pollution. The waste and the small produce out of it spoil the environmental health of the city. It not only affects the human being but also other creatures. Chadar and Chadar (2017) have opined that solid waste is harmful for the environment whether it exists in solid, liquid or gaseous form. Solid waste pollution is caused mainly through urbanization and through industrial waste. It causes various diseases in humans such as bacillary dysentery, diarrhoea and amoebic dysentery, plague, salmonellosis, trichinosis, endemic typhus, cholera, jaundice, hepatitis and gastroenteric diseases. The management of waste, which includes safe disposal and treatment of waste, protects the environment from man-made pollution.
5. Waste management is necessary for creating renewable sources of energy. It helps to generate electricity and thus reduces the load on non-renewable sources of energy. Electricity is produced by burning MSW as a fuel. MSW power plants, also called waste to energy (WTE) plants, are designed to dispose of MSW and to produce electricity as a by-product of the incinerator operation. Japan is the highest producer of WTE in the world.

6. The treatment of biodegradable wastes to convert them into compost is used for raising agricultural productivity in many places. A review shows that MSW compost is being increasingly used in agriculture not only as a soil conditioner but also as a fertilizer.[55]
7. Waste management has provided employment to unskilled, semi-skilled and skilled workforce in the cities. It has provided livelihood and generated income for the sanitation workers, rag pickers, waste collectors (*kabadiwala*). It has been noted that in Ahmedabad, collaboration between the municipality and local workers' unions led to waste pickers' monthly earnings increasing from ₹1,500 ($21) to ₹6,000 ($84), a significant increase in household incomes.[56]

Types of Wastes

There may be different types of wastes, which are narrated as follows:

1. *Domestic waste:* Generated by households in the city;
2. *Commercial wastes:* Waste generated in the marketplaces and business shops such as malls of the city;
3. *Institutional wastes:* Wastes generated from various categories of institutions situated in the city such as health institutions, educational institutions, hotels and offices;
4. *Waste in open space*: The waste in various open spaces of the cities such as parks, water bodies, playgrounds and recreation clubs;
5. *Wastes generated in religious and cultural places:* Wastes generated in the religious institutions and also during cultural festivals, marriages, birthday parties in the banquets, palaces, farmhouses;
6. *Industrial/Factory wastes:* Waste generated by the industrial houses and businesses;
7. *Construction wastes:* Waste generated during the construction of houses, roads, buildings, flyovers and so on in the cities causes industrial pollution;
8. *E-wastes:* The e-wastes nowadays constitute major problems. The wastes of computers, televisions, music systems and other information, education and communication (IEC) materials and their accessories are cause for concerns for waste management;
9. *Liquid wastes:* Water used for different industries, tanneries, distilleries, thermal power plants;
10. *Plastic wastes:* Plastic bags, bottles, bucket and so on; and
11. *Metal wastes:* Unused metal sheets, metal scraps and so on.

These wastes can be further categorized as biodegradable wastes (wet wastes) and non-biodegradable wastes (dry wastes) (Agarwal et al., 2015).

Wet waste (biodegradable) includes the following:

1. Kitchen waste including food waste of all kinds, cooked and uncooked, including eggshells and bones;
2. Flower and fruit waste including juice peels and house-plant waste;
3. Garden sweeping or yard waste consisting of green/dry leaves;
4. Sanitary wastes;
5. Green waste from vegetable and fruit vendors/shops;
6. Waste from food and tea stalls/shops; and
7. Paper and paper products.

Table 7.3 Types of Municipal Solid Waste

Types	Materials
Organic	Food scraps, yard (leaves, grass, brush) waste, wood, process residues
Paper	Paper scraps, cardboard, newspapers, magazines, bags, boxes, wrapping paper, telephone books, shredded paper, paper beverage cups Though organic, unless contaminated by food residue, it is not classified so.
Plastic	Bottles, packaging, containers, bags, lids, cups
Glass	Bottles, broken glassware, light bulbs, coloured glass
Metal	Cans, foil, tins, appliances, (white goods) railings, vehicles
e-Waste	Batteries, electric and electronic equipment, wires, CFLs, LEDs
other	Textiles, leather, rubber, multi-laminates, ash, other inert materials

Source: Hoornweg and Bhada-Tata (2012).

Dry waste (non-biodegradable) includes:

1. Plastic and all kinds of poly bags and waste plastic products;
2. Cardboard, cartons and containers;
3. Containers of all kinds;
4. Packaging of all kinds;
5. Glass of all kinds;
6. Metals of all kinds;
7. Rags, rubber;
8. House sweeping (dust);
9. Ashes;
10. Foils, wrappings, pouches, sachets and tetra packs (rinsed);
11. Discarded electronic items from offices, colonies, namely cassettes, computer diskettes, printer cartridges and electronic parts; and
12. Discarded clothing, furniture and equipment.

The types of MSW as given by Hoornweg and Bhada-Tata (2012) are given in Table 7.3.

Urban SWM

Waste, in general, and MSW, in particular, are a global issue and municipal challenge. If not properly dealt with, it would create a lot of public health and environmental problems. Therefore, there is a need for effective waste management for the promotion of human, societal and environmental health of the cities. It is one of the basic duties of the municipalities to provide effective SWM services to the city dwellers. As waste management is one of the essential utility services, therefore, it is also regarded as a basic human right. Solid or MSW management refers to the planning, financing and implementation of programmes for solid waste collection, transportation, treatment and final disposal in an environmentally and socially acceptable manner

(United Nations, 1997). The scope of SWM includes all administrative, financial, legal, planning and engineering functions involved in the whole spectrum of solutions to problems of solid wastes thrust upon the community by its inhabitants (Tchobanaglous, et al., 1997). To MoUD (2014), GoI, SWM is essentially a municipal function and it is mandatory for all municipal authorities to provide this service efficiently to keep the cities and towns clean, process the waste and dispose of the residual MSW in an environmentally acceptable manner. It is pertinent to discuss various strategies of urban SWM.

Integrated Urban SWM Strategy

The waste management strategy may include hierarchically following aspects, that is, waste prevention, waste minimization, waste collection, waste storing, waste segregation, waste reuse, waste recycling, energy recovery, waste transportation and finally waste disposal. Let us discuss them one by one.

1. *Waste prevention:* It is well said that prevention is better than cure. It is wise on the part of the individuals and all other institutions and agencies generating waste to formulate strategies so that the waste is either prevented from being generated or is generated with a low quantity. It will reduce the cost of waste management. According to the European Union (2012), waste prevention can be achieved by reducing the quantity of material used in the creation of products and increasing the efficiency with which products, once created, are used. Preventing waste by limiting unnecessary consumption and by designing and consuming products that generate less waste are forms of strict avoidance of waste.
2. *Waste minimization:* Waste or source reduction initiatives (including prevention, minimization and reuse) seek to reduce the quantity of waste at generation points. It involves looking at the entire process, that is, manufacturing, processing, packaging, storage, recycling and disposal to identify opportunities to manage waste and minimize them. To MoUD (2014), GoI, the most preferred option for waste management is to prevent the generation of waste at various stages including product design stage, production, packaging, and use and reuse stages of a product.
3. *Waste collection:* A daily waste collection service provided for the collection of wastes from the sources of its generation. At the household level hand rickshaws, small motored vehicles which can easily travel within the narrow lanes are found to be used in the collection of waste from various sources. The municipalities and the residential welfare associations in many cities are also found to have engaged the sanitation workers for the collection of wastes from the doorsteps of the households. Management Resources for Good Governance (2005) has envisaged two methods of waste collection: (a) door-to-door waste collection services and subsequent disposal at dumpsites by MSW management personnel, and (b) Outsourced waste collection and subsequent disposal at dumpsites by a private company.
4. *Waste storing:* Storing is being carried out at household level, as municipal bins of different sizes and colours are being used by municipalities for the storing of waste at the immediate sites closer to the residential colonies, marketplaces and so on. Moreover, informal recycling trade middlemen such as *kabadiwala,* rag pickers and wholesale dealers are also found to be working and providing first-hand help in storing of waste. However, throwing of waste in the street is a disastrous way of dealing with waste management. The UNEP

document has envisaged that there are two main types of storage: on-site and off-site. On-site storage is within the premises of the waste generator, while off-site storage removes the wastes from the premises on which they were generated. Both types of storage are dealing with the treatment or disposal of the wastes. Storage of hazardous wastes must be done in a way which minimizes accidental release. Among the most important provisions to ensure these are:

a) Appropriate physical design of the storage area, and of any containers;
b) Correct labelling of the waste containers;
c) Clear signage for the storage area;
d) Emergency capability and contingency plans;
e) Hazard communication plans;
f) Appropriate duration of storage; and
g) Employee training.[57]

5. *Waste segregation:* Most of the waste is generated in households, marketplaces, cities, towns, institutions and industrial zones. However, very few households segregate waste at the household level. There is also minimal waste segregation at source within industries, marketplaces, institutions and so on in most towns/cities. The segregation of degradable and non-degradable wastes is essential before reuse and recycling. Preferably, sorting could be carried out at household level, at the municipal bin, central sorting facility, waste processing site or the landfill site.
6. *Wastes reuse:* Reusing items by repairing, selling or donating these to charity and community groups reduces the quantity of waste. Reuse is preferable to recycling because these items do not need to be reprocessed. The reuse of wastes can have important social and cultural benefits.
7. *Wastes recycling:* One of the important advantages of recycling is to reduce the amount of deposited waste and use the rest for productive purposes and generation of energy out of it. Recycling diverts waste from landfills, saves energy and water and creates less air pollution. Besides, the organic wastes can be recycled and turned into organic fertilizer, vermiculture and larvae for fish food.
8. *Recovery (for energy):* Much of the household wastes generated from food and beverage are biodegradable and can be composted rather than sent to a landfill. In the composting process, bacteria helps convert complex organic matter into CO_2, water, plant nutrients and humus. Another recovery process is combustion. In this process, wastes are reused as fuel for energy production.
9. *Transportation:* The transportation of waste is the movement of waste from different site sources to the waste disposal spot through vehicles such as trains, tankers, trucks, barges or other vehicles. The transportation of chemical and other hazardous waste is to be done in a safe manner.
10. *Disposal:* Solid waste disposal in developing countries is carried out by filling up landfill sites. Incineration or combustion is another type of disposal method in which MSWs are burned at high temperatures so as to convert them into energy. However, in many smaller cities of developing countries open dumping causes a lot of health problems to the urban dwellers. Joseph (2002) considered open dumps as a 'primitive stage of landfill development' yet remains the most common method of waste disposal in low-income communities owing to their limited budget, lack of facilities and low technical know-how. However, open dumps present serious environmental and public health danger due to release of leachate into

Figure 7.1 Waste Management Hierarchy

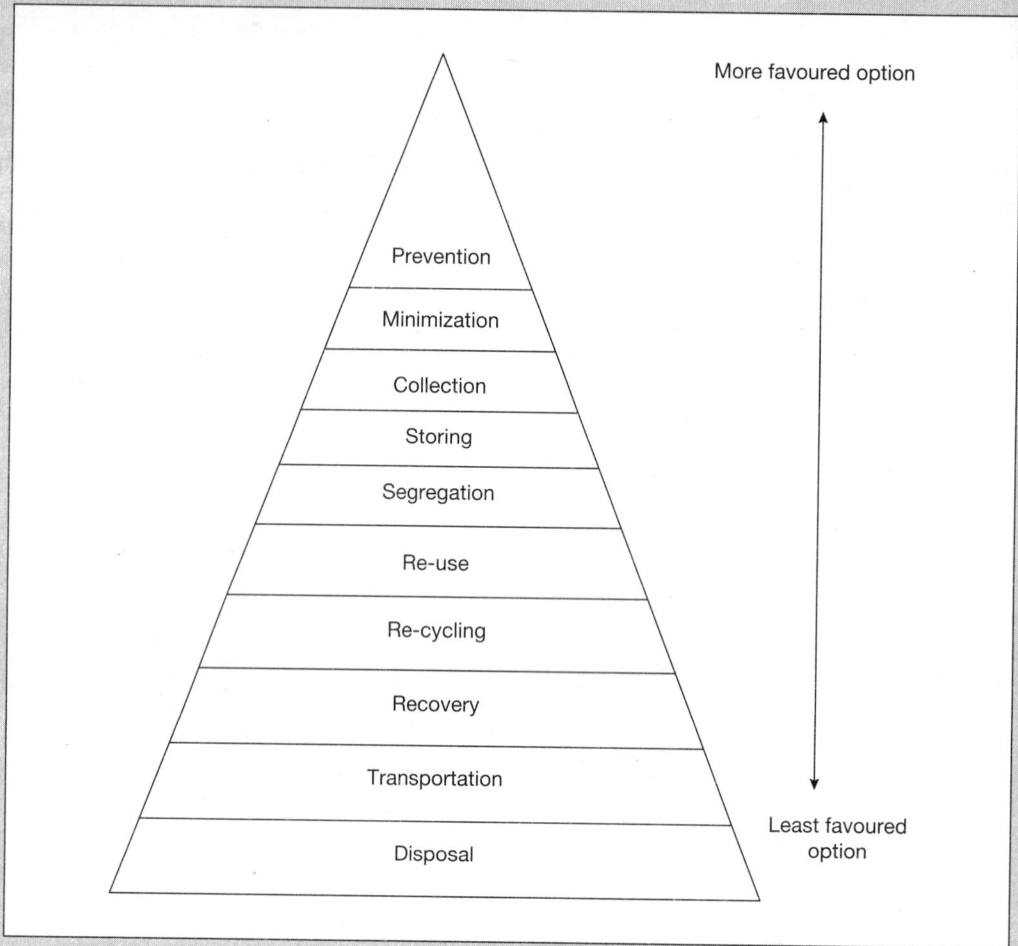

surface and groundwater, insect and rodent infestation is also common (Joseph, 2002). Therefore, UNEP emphasized on sanitary landfill. A sanitary landfill is an engineered method of waste disposal together with environmental protection measures (UNEP, 2005).

WHO believes that the improved collection, management and disposal of urban waste is one important strategy that can yield multiple improvements in both climate and health.[58]

The SWM strategy of a bilateral organization like Swedish International Development Cooperation Agency (Sida) and a multilateral organization, that is, the World Bank are worth citing here. Strategic areas for action as suggested by Sida are as follows:

1. Institutional development, including clear division of responsibilities, structural reforms, by-laws and regulations, planning, training and general management capacities.
2. Physical planning, environmental impact assessments.

3. Complementary interventions in environmental sanitation, for example, drainage, for maximum impact.
4. Promotion of primary waste collection, sorting and recycling through micro-enterprises.
5. Safety and health of scavengers and other waste workers.
6. Hazardous waste management, chemicals policy.
7. Appropriate technologies for landfills, biogas production and collection systems.[59]

The World Bank has given an investment strategy for the management of solid waste projects by the nation states. The World Bank's SWM projects and investments include the following:

1. *Infrastructure:* The World Bank provides capital investments to build or upgrade waste sorting and treatment facilities, close dumps, construct or refurbish landfills and provide bins, dumpsters, trucks and transfer stations.
2. *Legal structures and institutions:* Projects advise on sound policy measures and coordinated institutions for the municipal waste management sector.
3. *Financial sustainability:* Through the design of taxes and fee structures, and long-term planning, projects help governments improve waste cost containment and recovery.
4. *Citizen engagement:* Behaviour change and public participation is key to a functional waste system. The World Bank supports designing incentives and awareness systems to motivate waste reduction, source separation and reuse.
5. *Social inclusion:* Resource recovery in most developing countries relies heavily on informal workers, who collect, sort and recycle 15–20 per cent of generated waste. Projects address waste pickers' livelihood through strategies such as integration into the formal system as well as the provision of safe working conditions, social safety nets, child labour restrictions and education.
6. *Climate change and the environment:* Projects promote environmentally sound waste disposal. They support greenhouse gas mitigation through food loss and waste reduction, organic waste diversion and the adoption of disposal technologies that capture biogas and landfill gas. Waste projects also support resilience by reducing waste disposal in waterways and safeguarding infrastructure against flooding.
7. *Health and safety:* The World Bank's work in municipal waste management improves public health and livelihoods by reducing open burning, mitigating pests and vector-borne diseases, and preventing crime and violence.
8. *Knowledge creation:* The World Bank helps governments plan and explore locally appropriate solutions through technical expertise, and data and analytics.[60]

Issues and Challenges Associated with Integrated Waste Management

Some of the important issues and challenges associated with the integrated SWM are narrated as follows.

1. *Infrastructure development:* At the outset, up-to-date waste management infrastructure has to be provided to the urban municipalities in order to enable them to efficiently and effectively carry out the SWM activities. The capital investments in waste sorting and treatment facilities, close dumps, constructing or refurbishing landfills are required.

Moreover, the municipalities have to be provided bins, dumpsters, trucks and transfer stations.

2. *Institutional, legal and policy initiatives:* Formulation of appropriate legal structure for dealing with waste management. Moreover, formulation of sound policy measures and its religious implementation at the municipality level will go a long way in the effective management of urban wastes. Some of the legal frameworks related to waste management in India are: (a) 74th Constitutional Amendment Act, 1992; (b) Hazardous Wastes (Management and Handling) Rules, 1989; (c) Environment (Protection) Act, 1986; (d) National Environment Tribunal Act, 1995; (e) National Environment Appellate Authority Act, 1997; (f) Water (Prevention and Control of Pollution) Act, 1974; and (g) Water (Prevention & Control of Pollution) Cess Act, 1977. Some of the policy initiatives taken by the Government in India are: (a) National Urban Sanitation Policy, 2008; (b) National Environment Policy, 2006; (c) Policy Statement for the Abatement of Pollution, 1992; and (d) National Conservation Strategy and Policy Statement on Environment and Development, 1992.[61]

   In Canada, provincial governments are responsible for setting up regulations that govern environmentally sound and safe disposal of waste materials within their jurisdiction (Environment Canada, 2013). However, municipalities or local governments are free to adopt waste management approaches that suit their constituencies. Private sector participation is common in most provinces because residents consider them more cost-effective and efficient (Statistic Canada, 2005).

3. *Financial sustainability:* Providing good SWM services while also ensuring financial sustainability of the system continues to be a major challenge in cities of developing countries. Some suggestions for the financial sustainability of the SWM system are: (a) improved fee collection efficiency by linking the fees of solid waste collection to water supply; (b) increasing the value chain by sales of organic waste recycling products; (c) diversifying revenue streams and financing mechanisms (polluter pays, cross-subsidy and business principles); and (d) cost reduction and improved cost-effectiveness (Lohri et al., 2014).

4. *Citizen engagement:* Citizen participation in SWM is vital for the effective management of wastes. People and the residential association have to actively participate in various stages of waste management. Their cooperation in the minimization of urban waste, prevention of urban waste, segregation of waste at the household level would certainly reduce the burden on the municipal authorities. Moreover, public- and people-led residential associations need to pay for waste collection at the household level. It is found that participation by local communities might involve separating waste at household level, handing over separated waste to the waste collector and composting of organic waste in backyards (Rigasa et al., 2017). Most importantly, participation by local communities in waste management has adequately converted household waste from burden to resources through separation at source (Sujauddin et al., 2008).

5. *PPP:* Government alone cannot perform effectively this huge task of waste management, particularly in the metro cities. Therefore, there is need for cooperation of private sector in SWM. In order to overcome the technical and financial deficiencies associated with the current system, state and local governments in India are increasingly resorting to the use of private contractors for collection, transportation and disposal and private capital to supplement the mechanization/improvisation process.[62] Under the PPP model, various

Table 7.4 Waste Management Services in Various PPP Projects in India

Services on PPP	PPP Projects in India
Door to door collection	Bangalore, Ahmadabad, Nagpur, Jaipur, North Dumdum, Gandhinagar, Delhi
Street sweeping	Surat, Hyderabad
Storage and transportation	Surat, Ahmadabad, Mumbai, Delhi
Integrated treatment and disposal	Delhi, Bangalore, Coimbatore, Kolkata, Chennai, Ahmadabad
Integrated primary collection, street sweeping, storage and transportation	Chennai
Integrated MSWM (complete value chain)	Gawhati, Hyderabad

Source: http://swachhbharaturban.gov.in/writereaddata/Tookit-Public.pdf (accessed on 30 March 2019).

integrated waste management services are being provided in different cities of India (Table 7.4).

6. *Capacity building:* The capacity building of the municipal functionaries in how to effectively manage urban waste is critical to SWM. The manpower engaged in waste collection, segregation, recycling and so on needs to be trained on new methods of SWM from time to time. The national level health and health-related training institutions and NGOs need to take the responsibility of capacity building on the SWM system. The target groups for capacity building are elected representatives and functionaries of municipal bodies, waste generators, elected representatives of residential welfare associations, filed staffs, NGOs/CVOs, sanitary inspectors, middle and senior officers. The curriculum of the training and orientation programme will vary from one target group to the other. Some of the topics to be covered are: SWM—technical, institutional, financial and legal aspects; waste management strategies—collection, segregation, storage, transportation and so on; safety and security, PPP, community participation and behavioural change communication (BCC).
7. *BCC and advocacy:* The most important aspect relating to SWM is to change the behaviour and attitude of the people towards sanitation. For this, awareness camps for CBOs such as youth clubs, *mahila mandals*, functionaries of the Ward Sabhas and people at large are essential. Moreover, the awareness camps need to be organized in various educational institutions of the cities. Creating BCC and advocacy for sanitation and SWM is very vital and a cost-effective way to deal with the SWM problem in the cities. This includes: (a) adoption of the 4R concept—reduce, reuse, recycle and recover the waste; (b) storage and segregation at source; (c) imbibing the civic responsibility of keeping the premises clean; and (d) willingness to accept the civic responsibilities of citizens.[63] Various methods such as print media, electronic media, posters, hoardings, use of public transport, debates, rallies and advertisements by celebrities may be used for BCC in SWM.
8. *Waste management projects and programmes:* The governments both central and provincial need to formulate innovative projects and programmes on SWM. The Swachh Bharat Mission of the GoI is an illustrious example of SWM. The construction and maintenance of

Box 7.1 Swachh Bharat Mission (Urban) 2014–2019

In keeping with the vision of the NUSP and GoI's priority to make India clean, litter-free and ODF, the Swachh Bharat Mission (SBM) (with separate components for rural and urban) was launched in October 2014. Estimated at a cost of approximately INR 62 lakh crore (INR 62 billion), the SBM urban has the following objective:

- Eliminate open defecation;
- Eradicate manual scavenging;
- 100 per cent collection and scientific processing/disposal of municipal solid waste;
- Bring about a behavioural change in people regarding healthy sanitation practices;
- Generate awareness among citizens about sanitation and its linkages with public health;
- Strengthen ULB to design, execute and operate systems; and
- Create an enabling environment for private sector participation in capital and operation expenditure.

The Mission has been launched and received priority and attention at all levels, including national, state and cities and towns. This has provided the much-needed priority to sanitation and hygiene, and has given a great push forward to achieving clean, healthy cities as envisaged by the NUSP.

Source: https://www.wsp.org/sites/wsp/files/publications/Community%20Slum%20Sanitation%20in%20India.pdf (accessed on 24 June 2019).

public toilets, garbage disposal tanks and innovative ways of waste to wealth programmes would be helpful for the better management of urban wastes. The JNNURM programme launched by the GoI has also laid emphasis on waste management. The objectives of the Swatch Bharat Mission by GoI in urban areas of India are given in Box 7.1.

9. *Research, innovations and use of technology in waste management:* Research and innovation of SWM will go a long way to strengthen the system of SWM. The technical institutions such as IITs and NITs must be given fund for conducting innovative projects and research programmes on SWM. Besides, social science research institutions and the universities must undertake studies on social impact assessment of various SWM programmes and projects. The technologies to treat MSW and further reduce emissions include landfilling with biogas recovery, composting of selected waste fractions, anaerobic digestion and thermal processes including incineration, gasification and pyrolysis (Potdar et al., 2016). The applications of these technologies depend on local, regional and national drivers for both waste management and GHG reduction (Lino & Ismail, 2013).
10. *Social inclusion:* In most of the developing countries, the informal sanitary workers play a key role in the SWM system. The municipalities rely heavily on informal workers, who collect, sort and recycle the generated waste. They are not treated well either by the government or by the public, are socially excluded and are found living in the slums and informal settlements. Their integration into the formal system, as well as the provision of safe working conditions, social safety nets, child labour restrictions and education are critical to SWM system.
11. *Banning of single-use plastics:* There is enormous use of plastic bags and more particularly single-use plastic bags in urban areas. The convenience in the use of plastic bags costs a lot to environmental health. It also does a lot of harm to the health of human being, animals, birds and marine life. Moreover, in the megacities, it is also one of the reasons for disaster

Table 7.5 SWM Matrix

Dimensions and level of Decision Making	Household	Neighbourhood	City	Nation
Social	*	*	*	
Technology	*	*	*	
Economic	*	*	*	*
Political		*	*	*
Administrative		*	*	*

Source: http://www.gdrc.org/uem/waste/swm-matrix.html (accessed on 22 April 2019).
Note: *Focal Area of Action

during the rainy seasons as the plastic bags choke the gutters. Ritch et al. (2009) viewed that plastic bags can choke waterways and exacerbate natural disasters. In 1988, poor drainage resulting from plastic bag litter clogging drains contributed to devastating floods in Bangladesh, causing several deaths as two-thirds of the country were submerged. According to UNEP (2018), plastics in the environment pose significant hazards to wildlife both on land and in the ocean. High concentrations of plastic materials, particularly plastic bags, have been found blocking the breathing passages and stomachs of hundreds of different species. According to Clapp and Swanston (2009), in developing countries, with inadequate solid waste management regulations, plastic bag litter can aggravate pandemics. By blocking sewage systems and providing breeding grounds for mosquitoes and other pests, plastic bags can raise the risk of transmission of vector-borne diseases such as malaria. Besides, plastic bags are also injurious to the ecosystem as they are not easy to recycle.

12. *Health and social security provisioning:* The health and security of the sanitation workers is very important. For those who deal with the sanitation of the hazardous waste, it is further vital. They need to be provided with health insurance and life insurance facilities by the employer, be it municipality or the private sector dealing with urban sanitation. The social security measures like pension to the family is also needed to be ensured to the sanitation workers particularly engaged in handling hazardous wastes.
13. *Decision-making:* UNEP considers that decision-making at various levels is vital to the effective and efficient management of solid wastes. It has developed a matrix of decision-making called SWM matrix which has delineated focal areas for action at various levels. It is given in Table 7.5. Effective decision-making at various levels would holistically be helpful to deal with waste management.

These are some of the issues and challenges and also measures to be taken for effective management of solid waste in the urban areas.

Sanitation Policy

The country should formulate an urban sanitation policy in order to set the priorities of sanitation and waste management. It should clearly delineate its vision, mission and objectives to achieve the goal of sanitation and development. The National Urban Sanitation Policy of GoI formulated in the year 2008 runs as follows:

1. *Vision:* The vision for urban sanitation in India is—all Indian cities and towns become totally sanitized, healthy and liveable and ensure and sustain good public health and environmental outcomes for all their citizens with a special focus on hygienic and affordable sanitation facilities for the urban poor and women.
2. *Key sanitation policy issues:* In order to achieve the above vision, following key policy issues must be addressed.
   a) *Poor awareness:* Sanitation has been accorded low priority and there is poor awareness about its inherent linkages with public health.
   b) *Social and occupational aspects of sanitation:* Despite the appropriate legal framework, progress towards the elimination of manual scavenging has shown limited success; little or no attention has been paid towards the occupational hazard faced by sanitation workers daily.
   c) *Fragmented institutional roles and responsibilities:* There are considerable gaps and overlaps in institutional roles and responsibilities at the national, state and city levels.
   d) *Lack of an integrated city-wide approach:* Sanitation investments are currently planned in a piece-meal manner and do not take into account the full cycle of safe confinement, treatment and safe disposal.
   e) *Limited technology choices:* Technologies have been focused on limited options that have not been cost-effective, and sustainability of investments has been in question.
   f) *Reaching the unserved and poor:* Urban poor communities as well as other residents of informal settlements have been constrained by lack of tenure, space or economic constraints, in obtaining affordable access to safe sanitation. In this context, the issues of whether services to the poor should be individualized and whether community services should be provided in non-notified slums should be addressed. However, provision of individual toilets should be prioritized. In relation to 'pay and use' toilets, the issue of subsidies inadvertently reaching the non-poor should be addressed by identifying different categories of urban poor.
   g) *Lack of demand responsiveness:* Sanitation has been provided by public agencies in a supply-driven manner, with little regard for demands and preferences of households as customers of sanitation services.
3. *Policy goals:* The overall goal of this policy is to transform urban India into community-driven, totally sanitized, healthy and liveable cities and towns. The specific goals are as follows.
   a) *Awareness generation and behaviour change:* This includes generating awareness about sanitation and its linkages with public and environmental health among communities and institutions, and promoting mechanisms to bring about and sustain behavioural changes aimed at adoption of healthy sanitation practices.
   b) *Achieving open defecation free cities:* All urban dwellers will have access to and use safe and hygienic sanitation facilities and arrangements so that no one defecates in the open. In order to achieve this goal, the following activities shall be undertaken:
      i. Promoting access to households with safe sanitation facilities (including proper disposal arrangements).

ii. Promoting community-planned and managed toilets, wherever necessary, for groups of households who have constraints of space, tenure or economic constraints in gaining access to individual facilities.
iii. Adequate availability and 100 per cent upkeep and management of public sanitation facilities in all urban areas to rid them of open defecation and environmental hazards.

c) *Integrated city-wide sanitation—reorienting institutions and mainstreaming sanitation*: This includes the following:
i. Mainstream thinking, planning and implementing measures related to sanitation in all sectors and departmental domains as a cross-cutting issue, especially in all urban management endeavours.
ii. Strengthening national, state, city and local institutions (public, private and community) to accord priority to sanitation provision, including planning, implementation and O&M management.
iii. Extending access to proper sanitation facilities for poor communities and other unserved settlements.

d) *Sanitary and safe disposal:* All the human excreta and liquid wastes from all sanitation facilities including toilets must be disposed of safely. In order to achieve this goal, the following activities shall be undertaken:
1. Promoting proper functioning of network-based sewerage systems and ensuring connections of households to them wherever possible.
2. Promoting recycle and reuse of treated wastewater for non-potable applications wherever possible will be encouraged.
3. Promoting proper disposal and treatment of sludge from on-site installations (septic tanks, pit latrines and so on).
4. Ensuring that all the human wastes collected are safely confined and disposed of after treatment so as not to cause any hazard to public health or the environment.

e) *Proper O&P of all sanitary installations:* This includes promoting proper usage, regular upkeep and maintenance of household, community and public sanitation facilities and strengthening ULBs to provide or cause to provide, sustainable sanitation services delivery.

f) *Implementation of support strategy:* GoI recognizes that sanitation is a state subject and on-ground implementation and sustenance of public health and environmental outcomes require strong city-level institutions and stakeholders. Although there are some common elements across urban areas of India, there are a number of factors, constraints and opportunities that are peculiar to specific situation of states and cities with respect to sanitation, climate, physiographic factors, economic, social and political parameters, and institutional variables and so on. Therefore, each state and city needs to formulate its own sanitation strategy and their respective city sanitation plan in overall conformity to the national policy.[64]

Summing Up

By 2050, it is estimated that 70 per cent of global population will live in the cities. The pace of urbanization will be faster in the developing countries of Asia and Africa. With rapid and unplanned urbanization, urban infrastructure would become one of the most pressing challenges in the developing countries in the coming years. Infrastructure plays on important role in the growth and development of the nation. Adequate quantity and good-quality infrastructures would enhance the contribution of cities to the growth rate of the nation states. In both developed and developing countries, cities are striving to provide a raft of critical infrastructure; more effective transportation systems, reliable and low-carbon energy, safe and secure water networks, waste management and efficient and scalable social infrastructure all will play central roles in the smooth transition to urbanization. The smart cities vision as envisioned by the developing countries would be possible only through smart, secure and safe infrastructure. Smart infrastructure aims at sustainable infrastructures which are cost-effective, consumer friendly and long lasting. The World Development Report, 1994, published by the World Bank under the title 'Infrastructure for Development' rightly mentions that 'the adequacy of infrastructure helps determine one country's success and another's failure—in diversifying production, expanding trade, coping with population growth, reducing poverty, or improving environmental conditions.' Second, SWM is going to be a key challenge for the cities in times to come. The developing countries, in particular, have to create appropriate infrastructure and formulate strategies and implement them effectively in order to make the cities smart and sustainable. The UN-Habitat has rightly said that in a rapidly urbanizing global society, SWM will be a key challenge facing all the world's cities.[65]

Keywords

Smart Infrastructure, Public—Private Partnership, Infrastructure Financing, Infrastructure Bond, Infrastructure Fund, Energy Infrastructure, Law and Order Infrastructure

REVIEW QUESTIONS

1. Define infrastructure? Discuss importance of infrastructure for urban development.
2. Explain four main urban infrastructures? Describe how to improve those infrastructure facilities in urban areas.
3. What are the major issues and challenges in infrastructure development in the developing countries?
4. What measures nation states have to take to improve the infrastructure provisioning in the urban areas?
5. Discuss the role of PPP in infrastructure development in the developing countries.
6. What is SWM? Explain strategies of SWM.
7. Explain various types of solid waste. Describe a few important measures of SWM.
8. Define MSW. Discuss why management of solid waste is important in urban development.
9. Explain five important issues and challenges of SWM.

10. Write short notes on:
    a. Smart infrastructure
    b. Infrastructure bond
    c. PPP in infrastructure development
    d. Smart energy
    e. Waste management infrastructure
    f. SWM pyramid

Notes

1. https://shodhganga.inflibnet.ac.in/bitstream/10603/8497/12/12_chapter%202.pdf (accessed on 14 April 2016).
2. https://www.yourdictionary.com/infrastructure (accessed on 7 January 2019).
3. https://www.investopedia.com/terms/i/infrastructure.asp (accessed on 24 November 2019).
4. https://www.lincolninst.edu/sites/default/files/pubfiles/infrastructure-urban-development-chinese-cities_0.pdf (accessed on 8 January 2019).
5. https://www.nap.edu/read/1096/chapter/18 (accessed on 8 January 2019).
6. https://www.worldbank.org/en/topic/financialsector/brief/infrastructure-finance (accessed on 8 January 2019).
7. https://www.lincolninst.edu/sites/default/files/pubfiles/infrastructure-urban-development-chinese-cities_0.pdf (accessed on 8 January 2019).
8. http://www.wsp-pb.com/PageFilesn/81292/WSPPB%20ACE%20-%20Cities%20and%20Infrastructure%20-%20White%20paper%20-%20DPS.pdf (accessed on 7 January 2019).
9. http://www.wsp-pb.com/PageFilesn/81292/WSPPB%20ACE%20-%20Cities%20and%20Infrastructure%20-%20White%20paper%20-%20DPS.pdf (accessed on 7 January 2019).
10. https://www.adb.org/sites/default/files/publication/218316/adbi-wp626.pdf (accessed on 8 January 2019).
11. https://www.un.org/sustainabledevelopment/infrastructure-industrialization/ (accessed on 8 January 2019).
12. https://www.globalgoals.org/9-industry-innovation-and-infrastructure (accessed on 8 January 2019).
13. https://www.adb.org/publications/developing-service-sector-engine-growth-asia (accessed on 8 January 2019).
14. https://www.un.org/sustainabledevelopment/infrastructure-industrialization/ (accessed on 8 January 2019).
15. https://www.researchgate.net/publication/265999112_Urban_Infrastructure_and_Quality_of_life_A_Case_Study_of_Warri_Metropolis (accessed on 8 January 2019).
16. http://planningcommission.gov.in/plans/planrel/fiveyr/11th/11_v3/11v3_ch11.pdf (accessed on 9 January 2019).
17. http://www.gdn.int/sites/default/files/3_3_Pritika%20Hingorani_Paper_T3%20%28Revised%29.pdf (accessed on 9 January 2019).
18. http://blogs.worldbank.org/developmenttalk/how-roads-support-development (accessed on 9 January 2019).
19. http://siteresources.worldbank.org/INTURBANTRANSPORT/Resources/chapter2.pdf (accessed on 9 January 2019).

20. https://www.sutp.org/files/contents/documents/resources/A_Sourcebook/SB1_Institutional-and-Policy-Orientation/GIZ_SUTP_SB1a_The-Role-of%20Transport-in-Urban-Development-Policy_EN.pdf (accessed on 9 January 2019).
21. https://www.ifhp.org/role-technology-urban-development (accessed on 9 January 2019).
22. https://www.ircwash.org/sites/default/files/Parkinson-2002-Urban.pdf (accessed on 9 January 2019).
23. http://www.worldbank.org/en/topic/urbandevelopment/brief/solid-waste-management (accessed on 9 January 2019).
24. https://www.ryerson.ca/content/dam/cue/pdfs/White%20Paper%20-%20Urban%20and%20Energy%20Planning.pdf (accessed on 9 January 2019).
25. https://www.witpress.com/Secure/ejournals/papers/SDP120307f.pdf (accessed on 9 January 2019).
26. https://www.tandfonline.com/doi/pdf/10.1080/00291950701553848 (accessed on 10 January 2019).
27. https://www.researchgate.net/publication/232723026_Social_infrastructure_and_sustainable_urban_communities (accessed on 10 January 2019).
28. https://www.pwc.com/gx/en/psrc/assets/pwc-psrc-safe-cities-the-india-story.pdf (accessed on 10 January 2019).
29. https://tifac.org.in/index.php/8-publication/188-traffic-management-streamlining-technologies (accessed on 10 January 2019).
30. http://www.un.org/ga/Istanbul+5/116.pdf (accessed on 13 January 2019).
31. https://www.jica.go.jp/jica-ri/IFIC_and_JBICI-Studies/jica-ri/english/publication/archives/jbic/report/review/pdf/report10_3.pdf (accessed on 10 January 2019).
32. https://www.zurich.com/en/knowledge/articles/2015/01/the-risks-of-rapid-urbanization-in-developing-countries (accessed on 10 January 2019).
33. https://www.indianeconomy.net/splclassroom/major-urban-infrastructure-development-programmes-in-india/ (accessed on 10 January 2019).
34. http://ris.org.in/pdf/aiib/19April2018/Urban%20Development%20Background%20Note.pdf (accessed on 10 January 2019).
35. https://housing.com/news/indian-realty-sector-taking-skill-gap-problem-seriously/ (accessed on 10 January 2019).
36. https://www.jstor.org/stable/pdf/4407415.pdf (accessed on 10 January 2019).
37. https://www.tandfonline.com/doi/pdf/10.1080/08111146.2017.1283751?needAccess=true (accessed on 11 January 2019).
38. https://www.tandfonline.com/doi/full/10.1080/08111146.2017.1283751 (accessed on 10 January 2019).
39. https://niti.gov.in/content/financially-empowering-municipalities-way-forward (accessed on 10 January 2019).
40. http://ficci.in/spdocument/20122/Urban_infra.pdf (accessed on 10 January 2019).
41. https://www.kas.de/c/document_library/get_file?uuid=0a33e97c-fdaf-56ac-0043-36765fea265a&groupId=252038 (accessed on 11 January 2019).
42. http://capacitybuildingunhabitat.org/wp-content/uploads/workshops/2017-fundamentals-of-urbanization/Principles%20of%20Planned%20Urbanization_20-07-2016.pdf (accessed on 19 May 2019).
43. https://unctad.org/meetings/en/SessionalDocuments/ecn162016d2_en.pdf (accessed on 11 January 2019).
44. https://sustainabledevelopment.un.org/content/documents/2288desaworkingpaper148.pdf (accessed on 11 January 2019).
45. http://www.microfinancegateway.org/sites/default/files/mfg-en-case-study-participation-and-sustainability-in-social-projects-the-experience-of-the-local-development-program-prodel-in-nicaragua-jun-2000.pdf (accessed on 11 January 2019).
46. https://www.tandfonline.com/doi/pdf/10.1080/08111146.2017.1283751?needAccess=true (accessed on 11 January 2019).

47. See https://home.kpmg/content/dam/kpmg/pdf/2012/05/Cities-Infrastructure-a-report-on-sustainability.pdf (accessed on 11 January 2019).
48. https://www.sida.se/contentassets/22c694f1c252402ea44353d05e731b1a/urban-solid-waste-management_1067.pdf (accessed on 26 March 2019).
49. http://web.worldbank.org/WBSITE/EXTERNAL/TOPICS/EXTURBANDEVELOPMENT/EXTUSWM/0,,menuPK:463847~pagePK:149018~piPK:149093~theSitePK:463841,00.html (accessed on 26 March 2019).
50. https://smartnet.niua.org/content/078f931c-d842-43b2-8e34-80a362a6377a (accessed on 26 March 2019).
51. https://www.thenatureofcities.com/2015/02/01/ways-forward-from-chinas-urban-waste-problem/ (accessed on 26 March 2019).
52. http://www.gdrc.org/uem/waste/waste-intro.html (accessed on 26 March 2019).
53. https://www.indiacelebrating.com/environmental-issues/waste-management-meaning-types-methods-importance-benefits-and-solutions/ (accessed on 26 March 2019).
54. https://iopscience.iop.org/article/10.1088/1757-899X/309/1/012017/pdf (accessed on 26 March 2019).
55. https://www.researchgate.net/publication/231181421_A_Review_of_the_Use_of_Composted_Municipal_Solid_Waste_in_Agriculture (accessed on 26 March 2019).
56. https://newclimateeconomy.report/workingpapers/wp-content/uploads/sites/5/2018/09/CUT18_Leeds_Waste_Final-1.pdf (accessed on 26 March 2019).
57. www.unep.fr/shared/.../3182/.../Management%20practices/5.1%20intro%20final.doc (accessed on 20 May 2019).
58. https://www.who.int/sustainable-development/cities/strategies/urban-waste/en/ (accessed on 29 March 2019).
59. https://www.sida.se/contentassets/22c694f1c252402ea44353d05e731b1a/urban-solid-waste-management_1067.pdf (accessed on 21 October 2018).
60. http://www.worldbank.org/en/topic/urbandevelopment/brief/solid-waste-management (accessed on 9 January 2019).
61. http://home.iitk.ac.in/~anubha/H16.pdf (accessed on 30 March 2019).
62. https://assets.publishing.service.gov.uk/government/uploads/system/uploads/attachment_data/file/186990/ReportPPPMunicipalSolidWasteManagement270812.pdf (accessed on 30 March 2019).
63. http://ud-hp.in/pdf/Community_Mobilisation_Strategy_for_SWM.pdf (accessed on 30 March 2019).
64. http://www.indiaenvironmentportal.org.in/files/nusb.pdf (accessed on 24 June 2019).
65. https://unhabitat.org/books/solid-waste-management-in-the-worlds-cities-water-and-sanitation-in-the-worlds-cities-2010-2/ (accessed on 31 March 2019).

References

Agarwal, R., Chaudhary, M. & Singh, J. (2015). Waste management initiatives in India for human wellbeing. *European Scientific Journal* (special issue), 105–127.

Borghi, A. D., Gallo, M., Strazza, C., Magrassi, F., & Castanga, M. (2014). Waste management in smart cities: The application of circular economy in Genoa (Italy). *Impresa Progetto Electronic Journal of Management, 4*. http://www.liguriacircular.it/wp-content/uploads/2015/09/CEinGenoa.pdf (accessed on 19 May 2019).

Chadar, S. N., & Chadar, K. (2017). Solid waste pollution: A hazard to environment. *Recent Advances in Petrochemical Sciences, 2*(3), 1–3.

Clapp, J., & Swanston, L. (2009). Doing away with plastic shopping bags: International patterns of norm emergence and policy implementation. *Environmental Politics, 18*(3). https://wedocs.unep.org/

bitstream/handle/20.500.11822/25496/singleUsePlastic_sustainability.pdf (accessed on 16 April 2020).

Cohen, B. (2006). Urbanization in developing countries: Current trends, future projections, and key challenges for sustainability. *Technology in Society, 28*(1–2), 63–80.

Davies, J., & Brikke, F. (1995). *Making your water supply work* (IRC Occasional Paper Series OP29). IRC International Water and Sanitation Centre. https://dspace.lboro.ac.uk/dspace-jspui/bitstream/2134/3862/1/ASCE%20%2322261-UP.pdf (accessed on 10 January 2019).

Demurger, S. (2001). Infrastructure development and economic growth: An explanation for regional disparities in China? *Journal of Comparative Economics, 29*(1): 95–117.

DFID. (2002). *Making the connections: Infrastructure for poverty reduction.* Department of International Development.

Donald, C. S. (1974). *Professional education in public works/environmental engineering administration* (95th ed.). Chicago: American public works and association.

Environment Canada. (2013). *Managing and reducing wastes.* Government of Canada. https://umanitoba.ca/institutes/natural_resources/pdf/theses/Oyegunle,%20Ahmed.MNRM%202016.pdf (accessed on 22 May 2019).

European Union. (2012). Preparing a waste prevention programme (Guidance document). BioIntelligence Service S.A.S., in association with Copenhagen Resource Institute, Copenhagen Regional Environmental Center. http://ec.europa.eu/environment/waste/prevention/pdf/Waste%20prevention%20guidelines.pdf (accessed on 20 May 2019).

Garsous, G. (2012). *How productive is infrastructure? A quantitative survey.* ECARES Working Paper. Université Libre De Bruxelles. Also see https://www.ifc.org/wps/wcm/connect/054be8804db753a6843aa4ab7d7326c0/INR+Note+1+-+The+Impact+of+Infrastructure+on+Growth.pdf?MOD=AJPERES (accessed on 12 January 2019).

Hoffman, L., Fainstein, S., & Judd, D. (Eds.). (2003). *Cities and visitors: Regulating people, markets and city space.* Blackwell. https://www.tandfonline.com/doi/pdf/10.1080/00291950701553848 (accessed on 10 January 2019).

Holston, J. (2008). *Insurgent citizenship.* Princeton University Press.

Hoornweg, D., & Bhada-Tata, P. (2012). *What a waste: A global review of solid waste management.* The World Bank.

Jacobs, J. (1970). *The economy of cities.* Jonathan Cape Ltd.

Joseph, K. (2002). *Solid waste dump sites to sustainable landfills.* Centre for Environmental Studies, Anna University. https://umanitoba.ca/institutes/natural_resources/pdf/theses/Oyegunle,%20Ahmed.MNRM%202016.pdf (accessed on 22 May 2019).

Lino, F. A. M., Ismail K. A. R. (2013). Alternative treatments for the municipal solid waste and domestic sewage in Campinas, Brazil. *Resource Conservation, Recycling, 81*, 24–30. Also see https://reader.elsevier.com/reader/sd/pii/S1878029616301670?token=AA55FDA3B2F85A04DE831F1D494692F1AC6880FDC5763F50D31B8A85569DA6ADAE2CC277035BF19523382D378665CE0F (accessed on 30 March 2019).

Lohri, C. R., Camenzind, E. J., & Zurbrugg, C. (2014). Financial sustainability in municipal solid waste management—costs and revenues in Bahir Dar, Ethiopia. *Waste Management, 34*(2), 542–552.

Management Resources for Good Governance. (2005). Solid waste management strategy guiding principles and strategic options. Management Resources for Good Governance, Sri Jayawardenapura Kotte Municipal Council UN-Habitat Basic Urban Services Initiative International Water & Sanitation Centre (IRC). http://www.fukuoka.unhabitat.org/programmes/scp/sri_lanka/pdf/CCA_2-2_Summary_Kotte_SWM_strategy.pdf (accessed on 20 May 2019).

Mody, A. (Ed.). (1997). *Infrastructure strategies in East Asia: The untold story.* The World Bank.

MoUD. (2014). *Municipal solid waste disposal manual.* Central Public Health & Environmental Engineering Organization (CPHEEO), Ministry of Urban Development, Government of India.

Munim, Z. H., & Schramm, H. J. (2018). The impacts of port infrastructure and logistics performance on economic growth: The mediating role of seaborne trade. *Journal of Shipping and Trade, 3*(1), 2–19.

Nwagbara, A. C. (2003). *Population/family life education, women and gender issues in Nigeria.* TAIT Publications.

OECD. (2014). *Creating an environment for investment and sustainable development. Development Co-operation Report 2014, Mobilising Resources for Sustainable Development.* https://www.oecd-ilibrary.org/docserver/dcr-2014-16-en.pdf?expires=1557991374&id=id&accname=guest&checksum=4F5C457158777E3BF890A8DB7868D983 (accessed on 16 May 2019).

Pethe, A., & Lalvani, M. (2006, February 18). Towards economic empowerment of urban local bodies in Maharashtra. *Economic & Political Weekly, 41*(7), 635–641.

Pongsiri, N. (2011). Public private partnerships and urban infrastructure development in south east Asia. *International Public Management Review, 12*(1), 48–60.

Potdar, A., Singh, A., Unnikrishnan, S., Naik, N., Naik, N. I., & Patil, V. (2016). Innovation in solid waste management through clean development mechanism in developing countries. *Procedia Environmental Sciences, 35*, 193–200. Also see https://reader.elsevier.com/reader/sd/pii/S1878029616301670?token=AA55FDA3B2F85A04DE831F1D494692F1AC6880FDC5763F50D31B8A85569DA6ADAE2CC277035BF19523382D378665CE0F (accessed on 30 March 2019).

Rigasa, Y. A., Badamasi, A. G., Galadimawa, N., & Abubakar, G. U. (2017). Community based solid waste management strategy: A case study of Kaduna metropolis. *WIT Transactions on Ecology and the Environment, 210*, 761–772.

Ritch, E., Brennan, C., & MacLeod, C. (2009). Plastic bag politics: Modifying consumer behavior for sustainable development. *International Journal of Consumer Studies, 33*(2), 168–174.

Serra, M. V., Dowall, D. E., Motta, D., & Donovan, M. (2004). *Urban land markets and urban land development: An examination of three Brazilian cities: Brasília, Curitiba and Recife* (Working Paper 2004–03). Institute of Urban and Regional Development University of California at Berkeley. https://www.econstor.eu/obitstream/10419/39268/1/513250654.pdf (accessed on 16 May 2019).

Srinivasu, B., & Rao, P. S. (2013). Infrastructure development and economic growth: Prospects and perspective. *Journal of Business Management & Social Sciences Research (JBM & SSR), 2*(1): 81–91.

Star, S. L. (1999). The ethnography of infrastructure. *American Behavioral Scientist, 43*(3), 377–391. https://www.imtfi.uci.edu/files/articles/Star.pdf (accessed on 15 April 2020).

Statistics Canada. (2005). Human activities and the environment. Catalogue No. 16–201-XiE. https://umanitoba.ca/institutes/natural_resources/pdf/theses/Oyegunle,%20Ahmed.MNRM%202016.pdf (accessed on 22 May 2019).

Sujauddin, M., Huda, S. M. S., & Hoque, A. R. (2008). Household solid waste characteristics and management in Chittagong, Bangladesh. *Waste Management*, 28(9), 1688–1695.

Tchobanaglous, G., Theisen, H., & Eliassen, R. (1997). *Solid wastes: Engineering principles and management issues.* McGraw-Hill Publications.

UNEP. (2005). *Training Module: Closing of an open dumpsite and shifting from open dumping to controlled dumping and to sanitary landfilling.* Nairobi: United Nations Environment Programme.

UNEP. (2018). *Single-use plastics: A roadmap for sustainability.* https://wedocs.unep.org/bitstream/handle/20.500.11822/25496/singleUsePlastic_sustainability.pdf (accessed on 16 April 2020).

UN-Habitat. (2010a). *Solid waste management in the world's cities: Water and sanitation in the world's cities. UN-Habitat.* https://unhabitat.org/solid-waste-management-in-the-worlds-cities-water-and-sanitation-in-the-worlds-cities-2010-2 (accessed on 15 April 2020).

UN-Habitat. (2010b). State of world's cities 2010/11. Press release. United Nations Human Settlement Programme, UN-Habitat.

UN-Habitat. (2011). Infrastructure for economic development and poverty reduction in Africa. The global urban economic dialogue series. United Nations Human Settlement Programme.

UN-Habitat. (2013). Planning and design for sustainable urban mobility: Global report on human settlements. https://iopscience.iop.org/article/10.1088/1757-899X/245/6/062002/pdf (accessed on 18 April 2019).

United Nations. (1997). *Studies in methods.* Department for Economics and Social Information and Policy Analysis. https://www.ncbi.nlm.nih.gov/pmc/articles/PMC5184495/ (accessed on 19 May 2019).

Van der Bruggen, B., Borghgraef, K., & Vinckier, C. (2010). Causes of water supply problems in urbanized regions in developing countries. *Water Resource Management, 24*(9), 1885–1902.

World Bank. (1999). What a waste: Solid waste management in Asia. http://documents.worldbank.org/curated/en/694561468770664233/What-a-waste-solid-waste-management-in-Asia (accessed on 15 April 2020).

World Bank. (2004). Infrastructure for development. In *World Development Indicators.* Oxford University Press.

Zairaba, A. K., Haregu T. N., & Mberu, B. (2016). A review and framework for understanding the potential impact of poor solid waste management on health in developing countries. *Archives of Public Health, 74*(55). https://www.ncbi.nlm.nih.gov/pmc/articles/PMC5184495/ (accessed on 19 May 2019).

8 Urban Poverty, Inequality and Unemployment

Many analysts believe that the locus of poverty and under-nutrition is gradually shifting from rural to urban areas.

—Haddad, Ruel, and Garrett (1999)

Urban inequality reminds us that cities are, in part, unequal because they manage to attract both skilled and unskilled people, which are in many ways a reflection of urban strength.

—Glaeser, Resseger, and Tobio (2009)

Youth unemployment is a problem that affects most countries. In developing countries, youth face not only the challenge of obtaining productive employment, but also obtaining safe and acceptable work.

—Broussard and Tekleselassie (2012)

Introduction

Poverty, income inequalities and unemployment are paramount problems in the urban areas of the developing countries. The urban paradox where the ultra rich with all luxurious amenities and the poorest of the poor living in the slums and squatters struggling for two square meal a day co-exist revealing one of the bizarre features of urban society and economy in many developing countries. In other words, a small percentage of high-salaried officials and businessmen along with the people working in the informal sector lacking job and social security are co-existing in many cities of both developed and developing countries. To be more precise, poverty in the urban areas is pervasive among the impoverished sections of the population largely staying in the unorganized slums, make-shift arrangements and engaged in informal sector activities. According to the International Institute for Environment and Development, around a billion urban dwellers live in informal settlements, most of which are affected by:

1. Poor quality, overcrowded housing;
2. Risk of forceful eviction;
3. Lack of safe and readily available water supplies;

4. Poor provision for sanitation, drainage and solid waste collection;
5. Lack of access to healthcare, emergency services and police;
6. Lack of access to government schools; and
7. High risk of disasters and with risk levels increasing because of climate change.[1]

However, urban areas provide hopes to the impoverished to eke out a sustainable livelihood. DFID (2001) has rightly envisaged,

> [F]or poor people, cities present tremendous opportunities for social and economic development. They represent key centers where poor people can and do demand their right to a share of the opportunities that urban development presents, and where they can actively participate in processes of socioeconomic and political change.

Unlike poverty, income inequality is more pervasive in urban areas. According to Kuznets (1955),

> a) the average per capita income of the rural population is usually lower than that of the urban;
> b) inequality in the percentage shares within the distribution for the rural population is somewhat narrower than in that for the urban population—even based on annual income; and this difference would probably be wider for distributions by secular income levels.

Any study or education on urbanization and urban development cannot be holistic if it does not cover these three vital issues and challenges of development.

LEARNING OBJECTIVES

After reading this chapter, you should be able to:

- ❒ Define poverty, inequality and unemployment
- ❒ Analyse various characteristics of poverty, inequality and unemployment
- ❒ Explain the causes of poverty, inequality and unemployment
- ❒ Describe effects of poverty, inequality and unemployment
- ❒ Suggest measures to reduce poverty, inequality and unemployment

I
URBAN POVERTY

Unlike rural poverty, urban poverty is complex and multidimensional—extending beyond the deficiency of income or consumption, where its many dimensions relate to the vulnerability of the poor on account of their inadequate access to land and housing, physical infrastructure and services, economic and livelihood sources, health and education facilities, social security networks, and voice and empowerment.

—ADB (2014)

Deprivation is a multi-dimensional concept. In the sphere of economics, deprivation manifests itself as poverty; in politics, as marginalisation; in social relations, as discrimination; in culture, as rootlessness; in ecology, as vulnerability. The different forms of deprivation reinforce one another. Often the same household, the same region, the same country is the victim of all these forms of deprivation. We must attack deprivation in all its forms. None of the other dimensions of deprivation, however, can be tackled unless we address the problem of poverty and unemployment.

—United Nations (1993)

Poverty deserves only to be in the museums, where small children can see it in the future and be shocked how we allowed such an inhuman condition to exist for so many people for so long.

—Yunus (2006)

Those who are poor and hungry will often destroy their immediate environment in order to survive: They will cut down forests; their livestock will overgraze grasslands; they will overuse marginal land; and in growing numbers they will crowd into congested cities.

—WCED (1987)

Poverty whether exists in rural or urban areas is a curse on humanity. The UN considers that urban poverty is one of the major issues of the 21st century (United Nations, 2002). Although the percentage of population living in poverty in the urban areas is lower as compared to the rural areas, it is a cause for concern for the government of both developed and developing countries. It is not a flight of fancy, but delicately 'poverty' is a most frequently used term and is a cause for concern for the government of developing countries, in particular. Ali (2000) was of the view that the most demanding of the urban challenges, unquestionably, is the challenge posed by urban poverty. It can be said emphatically that 'poverty' is the simplest term being frequently used by both illiterate and wise, however, is the most difficult term to define comprehensively and measure precisely. It is one of the most relative concepts and realized by the person who suffers from it. It is rightly remarked that poverty is a multidimensional phenomenon and less amenable to simple solutions (Haughton & Khandkar, 2009). The National Human Development Report, 2001, of the GoI envisaged that 'poverty is a state of deprivation'. In absolute terms, it reflects the inability of an individual to satisfy certain basic minimum needs for a sustained, healthy and a reasonably productive living (Planning Commission of India, 2002). According to Streeten (1979), 'poverty' is a state of affairs of not being able to meet 'basic needs' which refer to physical (food, healthcare, education, shelter and so on) and non-physical (participation, identity and so on) requirements of a meaningful life. The definition of poverty is nicely synthesized by the World Bank (2000) as 'poverty is pronounced deprivation in well-being'. Thus, from all these definitions of poverty, it can be said that poverty is an economic situation when an individual or his/her household is unable to afford or lack access to basic minimum livelihood needs, that is, (a) healthy house with a separate kitchen and bathroom, (b) a square meal a day with minimum required calorie, (c) necessary clothing for his or her family, (d) access to sanitation (household toilet) and safe drinking water, (e) access to safe energy for cooking and lighting, (f) provide basic education to their children; and (g) access and to affordable critical medical care for their family members. The urban poverty in the African countries and in the South Asian countries is higher as compared to the urban poverty in the European countries. The percentage of population living below national poverty line of a few selected countries is given in Table 8.1 while the urban poverty head-count ratio in India for the past few years is given in Table 8.2.

Table 8.1 Percentage of Urban Population below National Poverty Line in Selected Countries

Countries	Year	%
Argentina	2017	4.7
Bangladesh	2016	21.3
Colombia	2017	24.1
Ethiopia	2015	25.7
India	2011	13.7
Kenya	2015	33.7
Pakistan	2015	18.2
Sri Lanka	2016	2.1

Source: http://wdi.worldbank.org/table/1.1 (accessed on 18 December 2018).

Table 8.2 Urban Poverty Head Count Ratio (% of Population) in India

Year	%
1995	31.8
2006	25.7
2011	20.9
2013	13.7

Source: https://www.indexmundi.com/facts/india/poverty-headcount-ratio (accessed on 24 November 2019).

Urban Poverty: Meaning and Characteristics

Urban poverty is a concern for the governments of the developing countries. According to Ravallion (2007), the urban sector's share of the poor is rising over time. Among those living on no more than $1 a day, the proportion found in urban areas rose from 19 per cent to 24 per cent between 1993 and 2002; over the same period, the urban share of the population as a whole rose from 38 per cent to 42 per cent. (Ravallion, 2007).

McDonald and McMillen (2008) viewed that urban poverty is usually defined in two ways: as an absolute standard based on a minimum amount of income needed to sustain a healthy and minimally comfortable life, and as a relative standard that is set based on the average standard of living in a nation. While Moser (1998) defined it as asset vulnerability, that is, as the limited ways in which the urban poor can manage their 'asset portfolio', which includes labour, human capital, housing, household relations and social capital (Moser, 1998). Urban poverty is more complex than rural poverty. As much of urban poverty is a transition from rural poverty, therefore, the addition of rural poverty to urban poverty makes the feature of urban poverty more complicated. According to Mitlin (2003), 'it is likely that the urban chronically poor live in diverse economic and political situations, facing different livelihood opportunities and different physical conditions. Furthermore, chronic poverty may be caused by the process of transition from rural to urban rather than the specific conditions in any particular urban settlement.' Satterthwaite (2001) argued that urban poverty tends to exhibit eight major aspects. These are as follows.

1. *Inadequate income* which gives rise to inadequate consumption of necessities including food, safe and sufficient water and often problems of indebtedness with debt repayments significantly reducing income available for necessities.
2. *Inadequate, unstable or risky asset base,* both material and non-material, including educational attainment and housing for individuals or communities.
3. *Inadequate shelter*, which is typically of poor quality, overcrowded and insecure.
4. *Inadequate provision of 'public' infrastructure* comprising piped water, sanitation, drainage, roads, footpaths and so on, which increase health burden and often work burden.
5. *Inadequate provision of basic services* such as daycare centres, schools, vocational training centres, healthcare facilities, emergency services units, public transport, communications and law enforcement.
6. *Limited or no safety net* to ensure that basic consumption can be maintained when income falls as well as to ensure access to shelter and healthcare when these can no longer be paid for.
7. *Inadequate protection of poorer groups' rights through the operation of the law* including laws and regulations regarding civil and political rights, occupational health and safety, pollution control, environmental health, protection from violence and other crimes, and protection from discrimination and exploitation.
8. *Poorer groups' voicelessness and powerlessness* within political systems and bureaucratic structures, leading to little or no possibility of receiving entitlements, organizing, making demands and getting a fair response.

Following are some of the characteristics of urban poverty:

1. Urban poverty is high in many developing countries of South Asia, Africa, Latin America and the Caribbean. While in the urban areas of developed nations of North America and in European countries the percentage of people living in poverty is very less as compared to the developing countries.
2. In the urban areas of the developing countries, poverty is more pervasive among the population who are working in the informal sector. To Chaudhuri (2015), significantly, a large number of urban poor work in the informal sector as they have less skill, less education and less capital.
3. Poverty is generally high among the unskilled population in urban areas as compared to skilled population. It is also high among those who are engaged in petty self-employment activities. To Unni (2009), the self-employed workers face specific problems of access to credit, markets and space and also incur various 'hidden costs'. Therefore, the self-employed among the urban workers in the 15–64 years group have shown higher poverty rates than the salaried.

4. The poverty in the urban areas of the developing countries is higher among the population migrated from rural to urban areas. It is rightly said that urban poverty is fuelled by rural poverty. Singh (2009) had observed that poverty incidence was found less among migrants as compared to non-migrants, but it was higher among rural to urban migrants.
5. The poverty in the urban areas is found to be concentrated in the population residing in the slums and make-shift houses as compared to those who are residing in the organized colonies and sectors. In other words, slums are the breeding ground of urban poverty. To D'Souza (1979), the poor and the slum dwellers happen to be more or less the same people in the urban setting. However, with the slum upgradation taking place, the degree of poverty varies from organized to unorganized slums.
6. Urban poverty is characterized by multiple deprivations, that is, deprivation of quality healthcare and education, lack of sanitation and healthy housing, poor quality of employment and deprivation of nutrition.
7. Urban poverty-stricken people are largely marginalized. The urban poor tend to live in disadvantaged neighbourhoods, where average income is low, employment is informal and public services are limited. Residence on the outskirts of the city, where links to work opportunities are restricted, is also a characteristic of urban poverty (Grant, 2010).
8. The urban poverty rate in many of the developing countries is declining with the improvement in the socioeconomic indicators in these countries. For example, the poverty head count ratio in India in the urban India has declined from 31.8 per cent in 1995 to 13.7 per cent in 2013.
9. The urban poverty is reflected in various ways through child labour, child marriage, infant mortality and morbidity, and lack of education and malnutrition in the developing countries.

Dimensions of Urban Poverty

ADB has rightly envisaged that unlike rural poverty, urban poverty is complex and multidimensional—extending beyond the deficiency of income or consumption, where its many dimensions relate to the vulnerability of the poor on account of their inadequate access to land and housing, physical infrastructure and services, economic and livelihood sources, health and education facilities, social security networks, and voice and empowerment.[2] Some important dimensions of urban poverty given by Baker and Schuler (2004) are: (a) commoditization (reliance on the cash economy); (b) overcrowded living conditions (slums and unsafe houses); (c) environmental hazard (stemming from the density) and hazardous location of settlements, and exposure to multiple pollutants; (d) social fragmentation (lack of community and inter-household mechanisms for social security, relative to those in rural areas); and (e) crime and violence. Urban poverty is being caused and have been effected by many factors and in this context, it is pertinent to discuss various dimensions of urban poverty.

1. *Income and employment dimension of poverty:* In the urban areas, there is a wide income inequality between various sections of urban population. The people employed in the formal sector get considerable higher income than those who are engaged in the informal

and unorganized sector. The high percentages of people living in poverty are usually found among those who are working in the informal sector having lower income as compared to their counterparts working in the formal sector. It is remarked that although people in poverty are more likely to work informally, their pay rates and total income from informal work are lower than for other population groups, meaning that the informal economy reinforces their marginalized position (William, 2014). Besides, it also varies according to types of employment; the casual and contractual workers and self-employed people in petty business activities in urban areas are more vulnerable to poverty as compared to the regular employed. In urban areas, it is observed that skilled workers are prone to less poverty as compared to the unskilled workers.

2. *Basic-needs dimension of poverty:* Lack of access to basic minimum needs such as healthy shelter, minimum clothing, safe drinking water, sanitation, electricity, primary healthcare services and elementary education has been a determinant of poverty in recent years. UNDP's Multidimensional Poverty Index includes these basic needs variable in the calculation of the index. The access to basic needs also determines the standard of living of the households. The basic-needs poverty line developed by Samoa include food and non-food basic needs and the non-food basic needs include expenditure for housing/shelter, essential transport and communications, school fees and other education-related costs, medical expenses and clothing (UNDP, 2010).
3. *Nutrition dimension of poverty:* Malnutrition is defined as the risk of being malnourished and having access to food which lacks required micronutrients. Nutrition determines the standard of health on which the productivity capacity of an individual depends. Malnourished children are prone to forgetfulness and lack mental ability to read and memorize. The malnourished children are not only a burden on their family but also on the society and the nation. It is found that the urban-poor group of children is disproportionately affected by malnutrition as it cumulates indices of thinness—that are worse than in their urban-rich or rural counterparts (Ejike, 2016). Malnourishment among the adults affects the productivity of a nation and thus influences economic growth rate and development. Poverty and malnutrition go hand in hand and constitute a vicious circle. The Rio Group has envisaged that 'adequate nutrition is one of the most basic human needs and it is therefore a central element in the construction of absolute poverty lines'.[3]
4. *Gender and ethnicity dimension of poverty:* The percentage of people living in poverty varies across gender and various ethnic groups, particularly in the developing countries both in rural and urban areas. Worldwide poverty is higher among women-headed households. Further, the percentage of women living in poverty is higher than men. Women account for a growing percentage of the world's poor. And a publication of the UNDP states, '70% of the world's poor are women'.[4] In India, percentage of the Scheduled Castes living BPL is higher as compared to the general caste population in the urban areas. Besides, poverty also varies across the various Scheduled Caste groups of population. According to a World Bank sponsored study in India, on the head count index, the poverty ratio among the Scheduled Tribes, Scheduled Castes and other groups of population in 2004–2005 are 43.8, 37.9 and 22.7, respectively.[5]
5. *Human poverty dimension:* Human dimension of poverty was emphasized by the UNDP in 1997. Lifting the family out of the vicious circle of poverty depends on the capability of a person. Therefore, human poverty is one of the important dimensions of poverty. The National

Human Development Report, 2001, brought out by the National Planning Commission in 2002 had developed human poverty index (HPI) which measures the state of deprivation in the society. HPI considered three types of deprivation with multiple indicators: (a) health deprivation—this deprivation includes life expectancy below 40, proportion of population without access to basic medical services, proportion of deliveries not receiving medical attention and proportion of children not immunized; (b) education deprivation—it includes illiteracy rate and children in the school-going age group not enrolled in schools; (c) economic deprivation—it comprises proportion of population living BPL, proportion of population without access to sanitation, proportion of population living in *kutcha* houses, proportion of population without access to safe drinking water and proportion of population without electricity. Human poverty dimension is more relevant for the developing countries where the deprivation of basic needs is very high in percentage as compared to developed countries.

The World Bank Group (2000) provided a powerful description of poverty which reflects various dimensions of poverty in the following words:

> Poverty is hunger. Poverty is lack of shelter. Poverty is being sick and not being able to see a doctor. Poverty is not being able to go to school and knowing how to read. Poverty is not having a job, is fear for the future, living one day at a time. Poverty is losing a child to illness brought about by unclean water. Poverty is powerlessness, lack of representation and freedom.

The Multidimensional Poverty Index developed by UNDP has three dimensions and ten indicators given in Figure 8.1.

Figure 8.1 **Multidimensional Poverty Indicators**

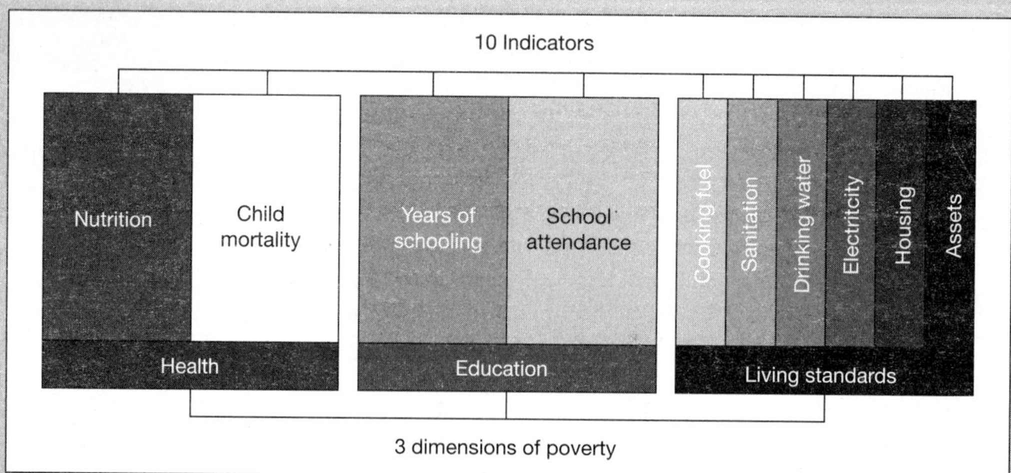

Source: http://www.indiaenvironmentportal.org.in/files/file/global_MPI_Report-2018.pdf (accessed on 19 December 2018).

Causes of Urban Poverty

It is vital to identify the cause of urban poverty in the developing countries so that appropriate steps could be taken for the removal of urban poverty. According to the Urban Management Programme of the UN Centre for Human Settlements (Habitat), urban poverty encompasses three main issues: lack of adequate employment, lack of appropriate urban services and insufficient social integration.[6] Some of the important causes of urban poverty are discussed as follows:

1. *Urban poverty a spillover of rural poverty:* The migration of impoverished rural population to urban areas for employment is one of the vital causes of urban poverty. It is rightly remarked that there have been many important studies which referred to the 'spillover' effect of rural poverty while commenting on urban poverty (Mitra, 1992). Dandekar and Rath (1971) observed,

   > ...The character of urban poverty is the consequence of the continuous migration of the rural poor into the urban areas in search of a livelihood, their failure to find adequate means to support themselves there and the resulting growth of pavement and slum life in the cities.

   This indicates that rural to urban migration of rural poverty-stricken households is the main cause of urban poverty.
2. *Lack of employment opportunities:* The poverty in urban areas is generally found in the population having less access to wage and self-employment. Moreover, people engaged in casual labour and petty self-employment also suffer from poverty. A study on unemployment and urban poverty in China has found that with more and more rural migrants moving to the towns and cities, laid-off workers are struggling to find alternative employment in the non-state sector. Consequently, a significant proportion of the households with laid-off workers has been trapped in poverty (Yao, 2004).
3. *Informal sector and low wage rate:* It is observed that people engaged in the informal sector in the urban areas and getting lower wage rate suffer from poverty. The standard of living and the cost of living in the urban areas is higher as compared to the rural areas. Therefore, those who are getting wage rate lower than the subsistence wage rate suffer from poverty. It is rightly remarked that low wage rates and income levels of the informal sector suppress workers' standard of living to a bare minimum level, forcing people to live in squatter communities and creating much misery in many developing countries (Fukuchi, 1998).
4. *Large family size:* The impoverished and upper-income group of population residing in the urban slums and other unorganized colonies are generally found to have large family size. The large family size with lower income dampens the per capita income and pushes the family to vicious circle of poverty in urban areas. Musgrove (1980) from his study in Latin America concluded that poverty is quite markedly associated with large household size and with low overall employment rates, both of which reflect large numbers of children per adult member. Low wages and high dependency together, of course, virtually guarantee that a family will be poor; but dependency alone can explain much of poverty.
5. *Low level of education and lack of skill education:* These are two important variables of poverty. People with low level of education and lack of technical skill are engaged in menial

work and get lower wage rate. They are prone to poverty at different point of time. The World Bank has categorically remarked that 'low skill perpetuates poverty and inequality. Skills development can reduce unemployment, raise incomes and improve standard of living. Helping young people develop skills makes economic sense'.[7]

6. *Social exclusion and labour market discrimination:* Many people succumb to poverty because of social exclusion and labour market discrimination in the urban labour market. The discrimination on the basis of skill, sex and ethnicity is sometimes responsible for poverty in urban areas of the developing countries. DFID (2005) has noted that socially excluded people are often denied the opportunities available to others to increase their income and escape from poverty by their own efforts. So, even though the economy may grow and general income levels may rise, excluded people are likely to be left behind, and make up an increasing proportion of those who remain in poverty.
7. *Lack of economic empowerment of women:* Women constitute around 50 per cent of urban population. Their workforce participation in the urban areas of the developing countries is lower as compared to the men. Lack of women economic empowerment affects per capita family income. If the quality of employment is low, there is a likelihood that the family will suffer from poverty. It is rightly remarked that women are more likely to be poor than men and at risk of hunger because of the systematic discrimination they face in education, healthcare, employment and control of assets (World Bank, 2012).
8. *Internal migration:* The excessive unplanned migration of rural population to the urban areas is also one of the vital causes of poverty in the developing countries. It can be said that urban poverty is the migration of rural poverty from rural to urban areas. Generally, the jobless and poverty-stricken people from the rural areas move to urban areas with a hope to get better employment and job opportunity in the developing countries.
9. *Urbanization without adequate industrialization and modernization:* In the developing countries, urbanization takes place with less industrialization and modernization. Therefore, the quality of employment opportunity available in the urban areas is poor, which gives rise to poverty in the cities of the developing countries.
10. *Poor implementation of urban poverty eradication programmes:* Because of poor governance the poverty eradication programmes in the developing countries are not being effectively implemented. Poor implementation of urban poverty eradication programmes is also responsible for poverty.

Consequences of Urban Poverty

The urban poverty can produce following consequences:

1. *Standard of living:* Poverty has a serious impact on the standard of living. The poverty-stricken households have poor living conditions. They cannot afford quality basic needs such as healthy houses, safe drinking water, toilets and cooking gas connections. Besides, their paltry income does not permit them to provide quality education and healthcare to their children. Poverty has an inverse relationship with standard of living.
2. *Economic inequality:* Economic inequality is a cause and effect of poverty. Poverty increases the income gap between the rich and poor. Poverty and inequality are inextricably linked to

one another. In urban areas, it is found that the rich businessmen and officials live in the posh colonies and the poor live in the filthy environment near the railway satiations, in slums or near the sewerage line.

3. *Environmental degradation:* Poverty can have an adverse impact on environment. Poverty-stricken households are more likely to defecate in open places and use unsafe cooking methods which can cause pollution. Jack M. Hollander had remarked that the poor in an effort to survive overuse resources and pollute their environment and thus the real enemy of the environment is poverty.[8]
4. *Malnutrition:* Malnutrition in the developing countries is customarily a product of poverty. Poverty and malnutrition are positively correlated. Higher is the intensity of poverty more is the number of people to be affected by malnutrition. Where there is poverty, there is malnutrition. Mydlikova (2013) from his study in Ethiopia has concluded that malnutrition is a manifestation of extreme poverty.
5. *Child labour:* Child labour is largely found in households reeling under acute poverty. Owing to poverty and indebtedness, children are compelled to do child labour activities for earning for the family rather than going to school for education. Traeger (2011) was of the view that poor families are typically larger because they use children as a source of generating income via child labour.
6. *Prostitution:* Poverty also produces a bizarre effect on prostitution. The poverty-stricken separated divorced women-headed households during extreme poverty may be compelled to engage women in flesh trade. The principal cause of prostitution is poverty and parents often feel obligated to sell their children to pimps because their low salary does not allow them to meet the needs of their family.[9]
7. *Feminization of poverty:* Poverty is rampant among households either headed by women or where women are not engaged in income earning activities. Thus, poverty is feminized and the gender-related effect of poverty is widely seen in the urban slum areas of India. UNIFEM describes it as 'the burden of poverty borne by women, especially in developing countries'.
8. *Criminal and unsocial activities:* The poverty in the urban slums may lead to anti-social and criminal activities in the cities. Most of the metropolitan cities are found to be facing a lot of criminal activities against women mostly committed by the youths belonging to the upper-income and poverty-stricken strata of urban society. According to Ghani (2017), key factors that persuade criminal behaviours of potential offenders include: unemployment, poverty, bad governance and weaknesses in law enforcement or crime-control agencies.

Measures to Tackle Urban Poverty

Whilst many development agencies have focused their work on rural areas, there have been many projects and programmes that have sought to address poverty in urban areas (UNCHS, 1996). Within a range of programmes seeking to reduce poverty in low-income urban settlements, two particular approaches can be identified. The first emphasizes the need for income generation, and the second concentrates on neighbourhood improvements in housing, basic services and/or infrastructure.[10] As poverty is a multidimensional problem in urban areas, therefore, no single approach is likely to be adequate for the eradication of poverty from the urban areas.

Some of the measures for eradication of urban poverty are as follows.

1. *Controlling rural to urban migration:* At the outset, in the metropolitan cities of the developing countries, specific measures need to be taken to check rural to urban migration of people in order to control relative urban poverty. Although in developed countries the migration to urban areas from the rural is medium of mitigation of rural poverty. However, in the developing countries, the addition of impoverished rural population can generally be termed as an addition to urban poverty. This should be restricted as far as possible.
2. *Formalization of informal sector:* Poverty is seen to be bred in the urban informal sector where there is low wage rate and lack of employment and social security. Therefore, formalization of the urban economy is the need of the hour. Attia (2009) from a study in Egypt has concluded that formalizing the informal economy may lead to economic growth and accordingly reducing and even eradicating poverty in Egypt taking into account the fact that most or nearly all the poor are in the informal sector.
3. *Control of urban slum:* Growth of slums in the urban areas needs to be checked and slum upgradation programmes in the existing slums need to be implemented by the government. Moreover, the role of NGOs, private and corporate sector will go a long way in the eradication of poverty from the urban slums. UN-Habitat (2007) has suggested that slum policies should be integrated with broader, people-focused urban poverty reduction policies that deal with the varied aspects of poverty, including employment and incomes, shelter, food, health, education and access to basic urban infrastructure and services.
4. *Capacity building and skill upgradation:* Capacity building and skill upgradation programmes for the urban poor will go a long way to enable them get higher income and raise their standard of living. Skill development contributes to social and economic integration. Providing training in vocational skills plays an important role in equipping young people and adults with the skills required for work and social integration and poverty reduction (IIEP, 2006).
5. *Economic empowerment of women:* Economic empowerment of women belonging to families living BPL in urban areas will enable those families to improve their standard of living. Women empowerment is one of the effective solutions for lifting the families from below to above poverty line.
6. *Launching of self and wage employment programmes:* The governments of the developing countries need to launch self and wage employment programmes for the urban poor. This will enable them to have access to basic needs.
7. *Strengthening industrial and service sectors:* The governments of the developing countries need to strengthen the industrial and service sectors in the urban areas. It will enhance employment opportunity for both male and female workforce in the urban areas.
8. *Access to land:* Like rural areas, in urban areas also land distribution, particularly, the land for housing purpose, may be done by the government. Regularization of slums is one of the measures in that direction.

Urban poverty is a cause for concern for the developing countries. It is sustaining because of persistent migration of rural population to urban areas. It can be remarked that cities are the best place to foster poverty and destitution. As cities flourish, so do the city slums, 'welcoming' and 'accommodating' more rural migrants and aggravating urban poverty. This otherwise can be termed as 'urbanization of poverty'. Thus, poverty is likely to increase, alongside the rise in urban populations. Controlling urban population and urban poverty is a major challenge before the nation states which are urbanizing at a faster pace.

II
URBAN INEQUALITY

Any city however small, is in fact divided into two, one the city of the poor, the other of the rich.

—Plato[11]

During the 18th and 19th centuries, political economists wrote about inequality as a central issue of their time, important as a mechanism of development and for its links with poverty and social harmony.

—Jolly (2005)

The world is not only divided by differentiated access to opportunities, consumption, public spaces and services, education, technology and employment, but more and more by access to income. More than two thirds of the world's population lives in cities that are more unequal today than 20 years ago.

—UN-Habitat (2014)

Widening inequalities can create social divisions in society and it's much more stark in cities because you have the wealthy living right next door too often to the urban poor in small spaces.

—Judy Baker[12]

Urbanization features strongly in the classic analysis of inequality and development.

—Kuznets (1955)

The concept of 'urban inequality' is now a routine topic of urban debate (Stephenes, 2012). Although not poverty, urban inequality is one of the pertinent urban issues and challenges haunting the mind of the urban planners and policymakers. It is remarked that inequality within the USA has been rising since the 1970s; inequality in almost every metropolitan area has risen since 1980. In many cases, the increase in inequality has been considerable.[13] Urban inequality since the advent of urbanization has dragged the attention of the urban planners and policymakers. Hamnett (2010) has remarked that the nature and extent of urban social divisions and inequalities is of major importance for social scientists, politicians and policymakers, not least because they have a bearing on social and economic conditions in cities where the majority of the world's population now live. This section deals with urban inequality. An example of urbanization process in Latin America is given Box 8.1.

Box 8.1 Latin America Is the Most Urbanized Region on the Planet

- 75% of Latin American cities are marked by a high level of inequality. Eight out of the 20 most unequal countries in the world are in Latin America, and the rest are in Africa.
- Across the region, two-thirds of GDP comes from urban areas, but 111 million urban residents in Latin American live in underserved neighborhoods.
- 80% of natural disasters occur in cities, and 75% of greenhouse gas emissions come from urban areas.

Source: https://www.avina.net/wp-content/uploads/2019/07/03_SustainableCities.pdf (accessed on 7 October 2019).

Urban Inequality: Meaning and Characteristics

Inequality is a major concern for human well-being. Inequality is typically viewed as different people having different degrees of something, often considered in terms of income or consumption but equally applicable to other dimensions of living standards that show a continuous pattern of variation, like the level of education or the degree of malnutrition (McKay, 2002). Income inequality is an extreme concentration of wealth or income in the hands of a small percentage of a population. It has been described as the gap between the richest and the rest.[14] American Community Survey on household income in 2016 has shown that relatively wealthy cities including Boston, New York and San Francisco, as well as cities struggling with high poverty such as Buffalo, Miami, New Orleans and Providence, also registered high rates of income disparity.[15] It is well said that in the urban areas the rich and wealthy man's dogs are better nourished than the children of the families living on the footpaths and urban slum areas. The income inequality is one of the prominent factors which boost social inequality in terms of education and health status. Urban inequality customarily means difference in income among the individuals and among the urban households. The income and wage earning inequality in urban areas is observed in the following: (a) the income and earnings of the individuals working in the urban formal sector are different and always higher than those who are working in the informal sector; (b) in the formal sector, there is income and earnings difference among those who are working in the regular positions and those who are in contractual positions; (c) in the private and non-governmental sectors, income and earnings difference is observed between the skilled and unskilled workers; and (d) there is gender disparity in income and wage rate across all the sectors. The growth of informal sector and casualization of work in urban areas have led to income and earnings disparities.

One of the UNDP write-ups envisages that income inequality measures the distribution of income across households or individuals in an economy. This is usually measured using the Gini index of inequality which varies between 0 and 100, with 0 reflecting complete equality and 100 indicating absolute inequality.[16]

The Gini coefficient is calculated with the help of Lorenz Curve which provides graphical representation of a nation's income distribution. The Gini coefficient is equal to the area between the line of equality and the Lorenz Curve divided by the total.

The formula used is:

$$\text{Gini Coefficient} = \frac{A}{A+B}$$

If the income is distributed completely equally, then the Lorenz Curve and the line of equality are merged and the Gini coefficient is zero. Larger the difference between the line of equality and Lorenz Curve, higher is the inequality. In other words, higher the value of Gini coefficient, larger is the inequality.

There is a growing body of evidence that income inequality (at least) within and between countries has been increasing over the last two decades. ODI Inequality Briefings has noted that there are several reasons why development agencies should be concerned with inequality, including: (a) inequality matters for poverty; (b) inequality matters for growth; (c) inequality matters in its own right; (d) inequality is often a significant factor behind crime, social unrest or

Graph 8.1 Inequality Measure

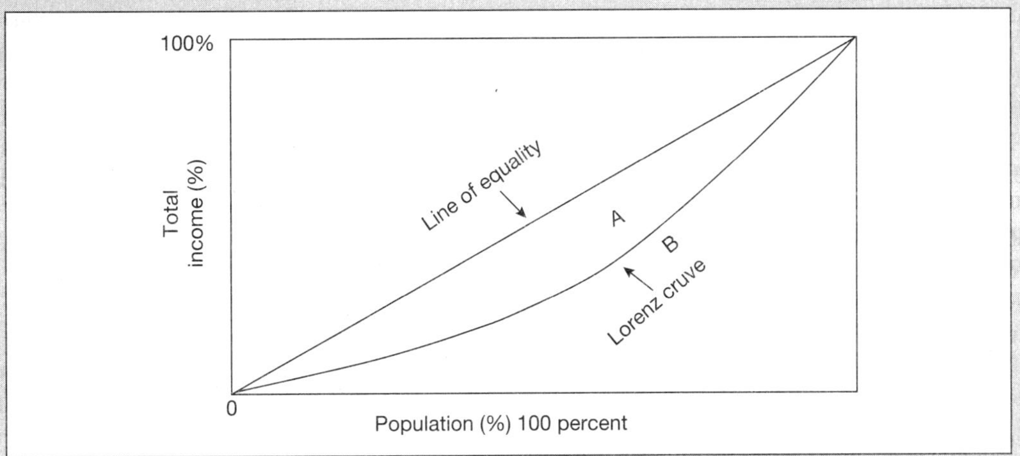

violent conflict; and (e) inequality is likely to be critically important for the attainment of the Millennium Development Goals (MDG).[17]

Unplanned urbanization in the developing countries has enhanced inequality in the cities and more particularly in the metropolitan cities of these nations. One of the studies has found that urbanization contributed about 300 per cent of the increase in inequality at the national level in the Philippines, more than 50 per cent in Indonesia, slightly less than 15 per cent in India (Zhuang & Kanubur, 2013). It is said that rapid urbanization and rising inequality are two main characteristics of China's development over the past more than three decades. According to official statistics, China's income Gini index increased from 0.3 in 1978 to around 0.5 in 2014 and a recent survey estimated that the national wealth Gini index could be as high as 0.73.[18]

Characteristics of Urban Inequality

Some of the characteristics of urban inequality are as follows:

1. The urban inequality varies from one city to that of the other and from the cities in the developed countries of Europe and America to that of the cities of Asia, Africa, Latin America and Caribbean countries.
2. The degree of income inequality is different from other inequalities such as social and political depending on the social and political development of the nation states. Income inequality in many cases influences social and political inequality. Bayarjargal (1996) from his study found that social inequality is positively and significantly associated with income inequality in a highly democratic society implying that income inequality enlarges as social freedom worsens. The similar relationship is found for political inequality. In other words, in a country with a high level of social inequality, higher political inequality expands income disparity.

3. The income inequality in the urban areas varies from one residential zone to the other residential zone. The income inequality between the central zone and periphery zone are also characteristic features of many developing countries.
4. The urban inequality varies according to the size of the city. Larger the city size higher is the inequality.[19] The inequalities in the metropolitan cities are different from those of the municipal councils and Nagar Panchayats in India.
5. The inequality varies according to the categories of city, that is, industrial city, religious city, heritage city and so on.
6. Income inequality in urban areas varies on the skill, education and migration status of the population.
7. Income inequality in the urban areas is glaring between the populations living in the slums from those who are living posh areas.
8. The inequalities are pervasive among those who are working in the formal sector to those who are working in the informal sector.
9. Gender disparities in the urban labour market have also led to urban inequality. Kim's (1987) study on 'Urban Unemployment and Labor Force Participation in Korea' clearly indicates that 'sexual dualism' is pervasive in the urban labour market in Korea. Market discrimination against women is quite evident.

Causes of Urban Inequality

Some of the causes of urban inequality are as follows:

1. *Differences in income and wage rate:* This is one of the outstanding causes of income inequality in the developing countries. There are staggering differences in income between the organized and unorganized sector employees. Moreover, those who are engaged in the casual labour activities also earn less compared to the regular employees, this creates income inequality. Litwin (2015) from his study concluded that increases to the minimum wage can cause a decrease to income inequality until the minimum wage exceeds a maximum effectiveness value, at which point the effect starts to reverse itself.
2. *Casualization of employment and jobs:* The casualization of employment in the formal and informal sector is also a leading cause of income inequalities in the urban areas of the developing countries. The casualization of work is more prominent in informal sector than the formal sector. Under the casualization of employment, the wage rate and terms and conditions of employment depend on the whim of the employer. The casual or contractual workers not only get lower income but also work for more hours. There is no job and social security.
3. *Poor implementation of wage laws:* In the developing countries the minimum wage acts are not religiously implemented in various sectors of development. Moreover, there is no rigorous punishment for those who are violating the wage laws. McCulloch (1977) was of the view that minimum wage legislation is frequently advocated in the belief that it creates a more nearly equal distribution of income.
4. *Unequal access to property and land:* In the urban areas, the property and particularly the landed property are unequally distributed. The business class, high-paid officials and local people whose lands come within the urban areas have high income as compared to the

houseless migrants to the cities. Unequal access to property is leading cause of income inequality in urban areas.

5. *Corruption and poor governance:* Poor governance and corruption is also an important cause of income inequality. People in the urban areas, even those employed as lower-level clerical assistants positioned in lucrative departments, are found to have amassed lot of income through illegal means. To Gupta and Abed (2002), corruption can affect income inequality and poverty through various channels, including overall growth, biased tax systems and poor targeting of social programmes as well as through its impact on asset ownership, human capital formation, education inequalities and uncertainty in factor accumulation.
6. *Globalization:* Globalization is also one of the leading causes of income inequalities. It has helped the skilled manpower to earn more as compared to the unskilled workforce. Income differences between the technical workforce and the non-technical workforce are glaring. To Bukhari and Munir (2016), the impact of globalization is not evenly distributed among all segments of the society, especially the effect of globalization on employment and income. It is widely accepted that increase in globalization is associated with rising income inequality in the world. UNDP (2005) found that combined incomes of 500 richest individuals in the world are greater than 2.5 billion poor people.

   With globalization, the inequality in wealth, income and consumption in India is on rise in the urban areas as compared to rural. The glaring income difference between those who are working in formal and informal sectors is one of the leading reasons for income inequalities. The Gini-coefficient of rural and urban areas of India is given in Table 8.3.

Table 8.3 Gini Coefficient of Rural and Urban Areas of India

Year	Total	Rural	Urban
Wealth			
1991	0.65	0.62	0.73
2002	0.66	0.63	0.71
2012	0.74	0.67	0.77
Consumption			
1993–94	0.33	0.29	0.34
2004–05	0.36	0.30	0.38
2011–12	0.37	0.31	0.39
Income			
2004–05	0.54	0.51	0.48
2011–12	0.54	0.53	0.50

Source: As retrieved from Income Inequality and Polarization in India: The Role of Caste by Anjana Thampi and Ishan Anand, Paper prepared for the IARIW-ICIER Conference on New Delhi, India, on Experiences and Challenges in Measuring Income, Inequality, and Poverty in South Asia. November 23–25, 2017. http://www.iariw.org/India/thampi.pdf (accessed on 27 September 2019).

Consequences of Inequality

Unequal outcomes, particularly income inequality, it is argued, play a key role in determining variations in human well-being. This is made evident by the strong association between income inequality and inequalities in health, education and nutrition (WHO, 2008). Moreover, when the privileged exercise sufficient political control and influence, and when this kind of influence affects job availability or access to resources, then income inequality compromises the economic, political and social lives of the less privileged and limits the opportunities they have to secure their well-being (Birdsall, 2005).

Some of the consequences of income inequalities are discussed as follows.

1. *Social tension and crime:* One of the leading effects of income inequalities in the urban area is the growing incidence of crime and social unrest in the cities. The unemployed youths and those who are getting lower income are found to indulge in anti-social activities such as crime, molestation and chain snatching. Extreme inequality may damage trust and social cohesion and thus is also associated with conflicts, which discourage investment.[20]
2. *Inclusive growth:* Inclusive growth presupposes that each and every person has to contribute towards the economic growth and development of the nation. However, lower income and income disparities de-motivate many to religiously contribute towards economic growth and development of the nation states. Higher inequality lowers growth by depriving the ability of upper-income households to stay healthy and accumulate physical and human capital, thereby lowering labour productivity.[21]
3. *Social development:* The income inequality also produces adverse impact on the access to quality healthcare and education among the lower-income groups. Customarily, the mortality and morbidity are higher among the lower-income groups in urban areas as compared to those having higher income.
4. *Human development:* Per capita income is one of the important parameters of the HDI. One of the reasons for which most of the developing countries are lagging in HDI as compared to the developed countries is income inequality.
5. *Hamper poverty reduction:* Income inequality affects the pace at which growth enables poverty reduction (Ravallion, 2004). The countries having a high level of income inequality cannot have distributive justice and will have lower tickle down effect to reduce poverty.

Measures to Tackle Income Inequalities

Some of the measures to be taken to tackle urban income inequality are as follows:

1. *Higher economic growth rate:* It is generally felt that in the developing countries higher economic growth rate will reduce income inequality if the tickle-down effect of the economic growth benefits the poor.
2. *Education and skill development:* The educational empowerment in general and skill education in particular will empower the upper-income group to raise their income and standard of living. Education is a powerful instrument to fight with poverty and inequality.
3. *Effective implementation of rule of law:* The effective implementation of the law that equal wage for equal work needs to be religiously implemented. This can reduce the income gap between the rich and poor.

4. *Reduction of the size of informal sector:* The developing countries, in particular, have to formalize their economy and particularly their urban economy. It will enable the urban economy to reduce the income gap in urban areas.
5. *Labour market reform:* There is an urgent need for labour market reform in the developing countries. It should focus on reduction of discrimination in terms of sex, class and ethnicity in the labour market. This will reduce income gap in the urban areas.
6. *Good governance:* Restriction on corruption and good urban governance is one of the measures which the developing countries have to seriously think about. All the developed countries, particularly the Scandinavian countries, have reduced poverty and inequalities and raised their positions in HDI through better governance.
7. *Infrastructure development:* Infrastructure development in the smaller cities and municipalities will open up employment opportunities in these cities. Moreover, the rural population migrating to the bigger metropolitan cities will move to smaller cities in their own states for jobs. Infrastructure will also directly provide employment opportunity to the people with various educational levels and more particularly the less skilled people.

Income inequality is a major concern in the cities of developed as well as developing countries. It makes the cities unequal and unsustainable. Income inequality creates both spatial and social divides within the city. The aim of harmonious and just city cannot be accomplished if there is greater degree of income inequality. The UN-Habitat has rightly remarked that today the world is more unequal than it was 20 years ago: 75 per cent of the world's cities have higher levels of income inequalities than two decades ago.[22]

III
UNEMPLOYMENT

The unemployment is the cankerworm that eats deep into the development of the economy and thus has a lot of negative consequences such as youth restiveness, juvenile delinquency, and high incidence of armed robbery among others.

—Odonwodo and Abdullahi (2009)

A country's prosperity depends on how many people are in work (employed) and how productive they are which in turn rests on the skills they have and how effectively those skills are used.

—ILO (2011)

Unemployment in a very low income society may well mean economic waste; it certainly constitutes a threat to political stability.

—Malenbaum (2011)

The growing mass of urban unemployed and underemployed is regarded by many as a great social evil and prime source of human tragedy.[23] Unemployment in urban areas is more pressing and growing with the migration of rural population to urban areas. It is said that unemployment exists in its open variety—with people lined up at employment exchanges, particularly in urban industrial area (Malenbaum, 2011). Frank (1968) opined that one of the characteristics of the low-income economies of the world is a rapidly growing urban population and urban workforce combined with a much slower increase in employment opportunities in the larger scale urban establishments. Unemployment is a serious problem in the urban areas of the developing countries and it has been troubling the planners and policymakers since long. Zenou (1999) has remarked that urban unemployment is one of the growing problems of our society due to its implications in terms of poverty, ghettos and segregation. The massive youth's unemployment in any country is an indication of far more complex problems (Okarfor, 2011). Citing the example of Nigeria, Ajufo (2012) said consequence of youth unemployment is exemplifier by increasing militancy, violent crimes, kidnapping, restiveness and political instability. In recent years, in the countries like India, it has become a parameter of winning or losing political elections. The fact is that the urban unemployment and underemployment are more open than the rural disguised employment. The persistence of urban unemployment has given rise to the growth of urban informal sector. As far as India is concerned, recent statistics have shown that the unemployment rates in urban areas are higher than those in rural areas. In rural areas, the unemployment rate is 5.3 per cent, whereas in urban areas, it is 7.8 per cent according to the usual status. The overall unemployment rate is 6.1 per cent in India according to the usual status.[24]

Unemployment: Meaning and Types

Unemployment customarily means a person is willing to do work but not getting work. It generally means involuntary unemployment. However, a person with requisite skill and dexterity but prefers not to do any work and not seeking for any job may not be treated as unemployed. In the developing countries defining unemployment in strict sense is very difficult. According to the *Encyclopedia Americana* (Americana Corporation, 1995), unemployment literally applies to all persons without work and actively looking for work. Englama (2001) points out that the unemployment rate in an economy is the number of people unemployed expressed as a percentage of the total labour force. The total labour force is defined as the number of people employed plus the number of people unemployed within the age bracket of 18–60 years. Unemployment is one of the most complex terms to be precisely defined. Pigou (1933) has viewed that any man is said to be unemployed when he is both not employed and also desires to be employed, while the notion of desiring to be employed must be interpreted in relation to established facts as regards: (a) hour of work per day, (b) rates of wage and (c) a man's state of health.

The labour survey undertaken by ILO envisaged that to be unemployed an individual must (a) be aged 16–65 years, (b) have been out of work for four weeks, (c) be able to start work in the next two weeks so he/she must be readily available for work and (d) be available for work for one hour per week, so part-time unemployment is included in the measurement, though these workers are unlikely to claim unemployment benefits.[25] The National Human Development Report, 2001, brought out by the Planning Commission of India in the year 2001, has used the following method in the calculation of workforce participation:

> Persons in the labour force participation rates is the portion of persons in the age group 15 years and above who are either working (i.e employed) on the usual principal and subsidiary status or seeking or available for work. A person (15 years and above) considered working or employed, if the

person was engaged for a relatively longer time during the preceding year in any one or more work related activities. The activity in which a person spends relatively longer time in the preceding 365 days from the date of survey is considered as the principal status of the person. A person categorized as a non-worker (i.e unemployed or out of labour force), who pursued some economic activity in subsidiary capacity is called a subsidiary status employed. The principal status workers and subsidiary status workers together constitute all workers as per the usual status classification. (Planning Commission of India, 2002)

A few types of employment observed in the cities are: (a) public sector employment both regular, contractual employees and daily wagers; (b) private sector employment in industrial and services sector with large, medium, small and individual enterprises; (c) self-employed in petty income earning activities such as petty business, vendors, street sellers, hawkers, cobblers, rickshaw pullers, auto and taxi drivers, motor and cycle mechanics and housemaids; and (d) contractors, builders engaging workers in urban infrastructure buildings and housing and real estate.

The urban unemployment can be categorized as follows.

1. *Frictional unemployment:* Frictional unemployment occurs when young people search for jobs that best suit their skills and preferences. Frictional unemployment represents the unusual amount of unemployment resulting from young people who have left jobs that did not work out and are searching for new jobs, or young people who are either entering or re-entering the labour force to search for jobs.
2. *Structural unemployment:* Structural unemployment is one of the determinant of urban youth being unemployed. It usually results from shifts in the pattern of demand for goods and services or changes in technology in the economy that affect the profitability of hiring young workers in specific industries. Structural unemployment often requires that young workers who lose their jobs learn new skills or move to another location to find satisfactory new jobs. This occurs largely due to the changes in the structure of the economy and functioning of the industries within an economy.
3. *Technological unemployment:* Technological unemployment is manifested in some urban centres. This type of unemployment arises due to the advancement of science and technology, resulting in the invention of labour-saving machines and other devices to accelerate production. Technological development necessitates new skills in many industries, leaving those workers who have outdated skills without a job.
4. *Cyclical unemployment:* Cyclical unemployment is evident among young people in most of the urban centres. Cyclical unemployment results from recurring depressions and cyclical fluctuations in business activities and government projects. It is also attributable directly to a cyclical decline in real gross national product (GNP). Cyclical unemployment is the amount of unemployment resulting from declines in real GNP during periods of construction or recession when the economy fails to operate at its potential level. The increase in urban youth unemployment observed here is due to political instability, uneven distribution of services and economic growth.
5. *Underemployment:* It is one kind of unemployment where the employed people consider that they are not effectively employed as per their educational qualification and skill. For example, an engineering graduate working as a clerk. This is a stupendous problem in most of the developing countries. It is a characteristic feature of the informal sector within the urban sector (Figure 8.2).

Figure 8.2 Diagrammatic Presentation of Underemployment

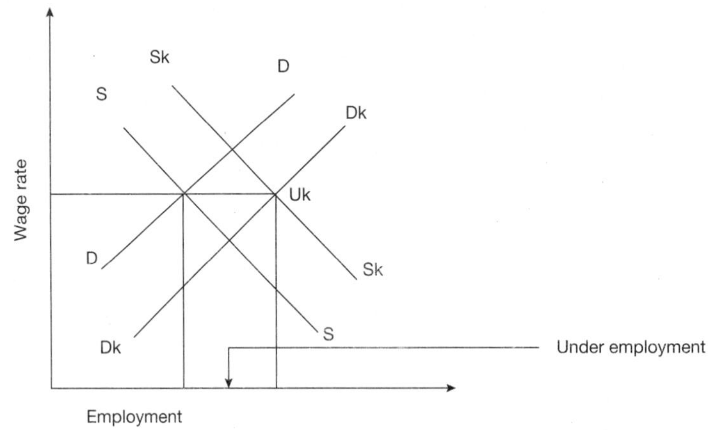

The unemployment rate in urban areas is generally higher as compared to the rural areas. The migration of people from rural to urban areas for the job and non-availability of adequate job in urban economy is one of the reasons for urban unemployment. The unemployment figures given in Table 8.4, for selected countries, reveals that unemployment rate is higher in urban areas as compared to the rural areas at least in many developing countries.

As far as unemployment rate among the youth in urban India is concerned, Table 8.5 reveals that the unemployment rate is higher among the youth who are qualified graduates and above. If these youth remain unemployed for a longer period in urban areas, particularly males, there is every chance that they will indulge in anti-social activities. The higher the youth unemployment in urban areas, higher will be the security risk.

Table 8.4 Unemployment (%) in Urban Areas of Selected Countries

Country	Unemployment (%) Urban	Unemployment (%) Rural
South Africa (2013)	51.2	61.70
Tanzania (2013)	35.8	14.80
Ethiopia (2005)	19.7	1.15
Nepal (2013)	34.6	21.60
Malawi (2007)	20.1	6.40
Zambia (2012)	23.2	14.70
India (2004)	12.5	5.10

Source: https://assets.publishing.service.gov.uk/media/5b97f2b640f0b6786cf0f4ca/012_Unemployment_and_underemployment_data__K4D_template_.pdf (accessed on 28 September 2019).

Table 8.5 Youth Unemployment Rate (15–29) Urban Areas of India

Categories	Male	Female
Not literate	2.5	1.6
Literate & upto primary level	4.8	4.3
Middle school	5.1	5.8
Secondary	5.5	15.1
Higher secondary	12.0	14.6
Diploma/certificate	12.5	17.3
Graduation & above	16.3	23.4
All India	8.1	13.1

Source: https://www.niti.gov.in/sites/default/files/2019-01/article-skill.pdf (accessed on 29 September 2019).

Causes of Urban Unemployment

The most common cause of unemployment is that the demand for labour in the urban labour market, both public and private, is lower than the supply of labour, thus forcing many urbanites to remain unemployed. As far as private employment of labourers is concerned, many labourers stand in the labour chowk (street) and few of them are picked up by the contractors as per their requirement and others remain unemployed for the day and this process continues. On an average, a labourer in city gets job for 15–20 days and the rest of the days he remains unemployed. As far as youth public sector unemployment in urban areas is concerned, there is stiff competition for public sector jobs, where the posts are in hundreds and the applicants in lakhs, for which a lot of youth are forced to remain unemployed after continuous endeavours. A few of them get the job and others remain unemployed. Zenou (1999) identifies three causes of urban unemployment: (a) Since workers are tempted to shirk, and since it is costly to monitor workers, firms set a self-enforcing contract by paying their workers an efficiency wage that induces them not to shirk and to remain employed. This (efficiency) wage is greater than the market clearing wage and thus, since all firms behave in the same way in equilibrium, there will be a durable level of (involuntary) unemployment in the city.; (b) urban search frictions—it has been observed that workers, who are the furthest away from jobs, have poor information and thus their probability of finding a job is low and (c) spatial mismatch—there is a 'spatial mismatch' between worker's residence and their workplace yielding urban unemployment that persists because of housing discrimination.

Some of the important causes of urban unemployment are described as follows.

1. *High population growth and rural to urban migration:* High population growth due to migration of rural population from rural to urban areas in the developing countries has led to higher unemployment in the urban areas particularly in the metropolitan cities. According to Simelane (1995), the location of more service points supplying a variety of services to the urban areas attracts rural dwellers to the urban areas, thereby contributing to rural-urban migration and leading to urban unemployment. Todaro (1992) points out

that the high rate of urban unemployment is a result of continuous transfer of economic activities and youths from rural to urban areas.

2. *Lack of investment and capital formation:* The developing countries are largely the capital poor countries. Because of lack of investment in the industrial and service sector activities in the urban areas, the people who migrate from rural to urban areas with the hope of getting a job remain unemployed. Eite and Ashipala (2010) from their study have found that there is a negative relationship between unemployment and investment. An increase in investment causes unemployment to decrease. The coefficient of investment is statistically significant for all the variations of the estimated unemployment function. Investment must be promoted in order to generate jobs for majority of the unemployed people.
3. *Aspirations of youth and informal employment:* Youth who have either migrated from the rural areas to the urban areas or live in the urban areas have lots of aspirations from the urban areas. However, these aspirations are not fulfilled for all and many remain unemployed and underemployed. Urban youth unemployment, according to Onah (2001, in Ezeani & Otaki, 2003), stands for the conglomerate of youths with diverse background, willing and able to work in urban areas. Given the lack of employment opportunities in the formal sector, young people are compelled to engage in casual work and other unorthodox livelihood sources, often of a criminal nature (Gibb & George, 1990).
4. *Supply and demand mismatch:* The supply and demand mismatch of the labour market is a potent factor for urban unemployment. According to Adebayo (1999), unemployment arises whenever the supply of labour exceeds the demand for it at the prevailing wage rate. Goldstein and Hollister (1994) argued that the high population growth rate has resulted in rapid growth of the labour force which is far outstripping the supply of jobs.
5. *Faulty government policy:* Sometimes faulty government policy which creates economic inequality is also one of the responsible factors which lead to urban unemployment. The implementation of hiked pay commission in every 10 years by the GoI leads to decadal unemployment in the public sector because of inability of state government to create jobs for more people. This picture continues in a multiplier way. The policy of the government in enhancing pay and allowances through the Pay Commission and enhancement of dearness allowances from time to time puts financial burden on the central government. These measures put pressure on public exchequers for the payment of enhanced salary, allowances and social security benefits. It is not a flight of fancy but delicately these measures curtail the scope of public sector job creation.
6. *Lack of investment by the private and corporate sector:* In the developing countries the private and corporate sectors are not creating adequate job opportunities. However, the economic ups and downs also create frictional unemployment in these sectors.
7. *Poor emphasis on skill development:* One of the factors responsible for the rising unemployment in urban areas is less emphasis on industry-linked skill development. The World Bank believes that skill development can reduce unemployment, raise incomes and improve standard of living. Helping young people develop skills makes economic sense.
8. *Impact of globalization:* Globalization has impacted the employment scenario of various countries of the world. The fictional unemployment in urban areas of the developing countries is due to global economic slowdown in various developed countries of the world. Mary Hall was of the view that unemployment is the result of a recession whereby as economic growth slows, companies generate less revenue and lay off workers to cut costs. A

domino effect ensues, where increased unemployment leads to a drop in consumer spending, slowing growth even further, which forces businesses to lay off more workers.[26]

Effects of Urban Unemployment

Youth urban unemployment has implications on the economy of any nation. Some of the implications of the urban unemployment are discussed as follows.

1. *Criminal activities:* One of the ugly impacts of faulty urbanization is that it can promote criminal activities in the urban areas of the developing countries. According to Chigunta (2002), the unemployed youths survive by engaging in various activities such as petty trading, casual work, borrowing, stealing, pickpocketing, prostitution, touting and other illegal activities. Bennel (2000) argued that urban society is becoming increasingly criminalized, especially with the proliferation of youth gangs.
2. *Growth of informal sector:* The growth of population in the urban areas, particularly of the rural unskilled and illiterate population, would lead to growth of urban informal sector. This sector provides low wage rate and does not have concrete social and job security policy. This sector is also promoter of urban poverty and inequality.
3. *Rise in urban poverty and inequality:* The unemployment is a responsible factor for rising poverty and inequality in the urban areas. The urban workforce who are unemployed and underemployed mostly belong to the lower-income group and are susceptible to poverty and inequality. It is remarked that long-term unemployed workers are much more likely to be poor. The relationship between growing long-term unemployment and poverty runs both ways, where poverty can reinforce joblessness just like joblessness can increase poverty.[27]
4. *Hamper social and human development:* The rise in urban unemployment will lead to social human development problem. The unemployed workforce cannot afford the cost of quality education and healthcare services which would ultimately affect their social and human development status.
5. *Growth of urban slum:* One of the bizarre effects of urban unemployment is the growth of slums in the urban areas. It is seen that urban slums are the breeding ground of urban unemployed and underemployed people. The lower wage rate and uncertainty in employment condition force the people in shaky informal sector to reside in slums or create a slum colony along with its fellow informal sector workers, leading to growth of slums in the city.
6. *Rising of non-working population:* The urban unemployment will lead to growth of non-working population. This will enhance urban dependency ratio. This may not only lead to fall in per capita income of urban families but could also promote urban unrest such as crime, conflict and riot. Rising non-working population in developing countries is a cause of concern.
7. *Urban paradox:* Last, but not least, effect of urban unemployment is the urban paradox. The urban paradox such as poverty, inequality, crime, pollution, prostitution and breakage of law and order in urban areas is the cause and effect of urban unemployment. The inability to find decent work, particularly in the urban areas, enhances a sense of vulnerability among the youth. This can lead to social ills such as crime, violence and conflicts. It will also enhance the number of informal settlements in the cities.

Measures to Control Urban Unemployment

The opportunity costs and losses arising from unemployed and underemployed young people have, and will continue to exert, tremendous impacts on society if these problems are not addressed quickly and sufficiently.[28] Therefore, it is pertinent on the part of the government to control the problem of unemployment in its urban areas. Some of the suggested measures are as follows.

1. *Reduce rural to urban migration:* At the outset, governments in the developing countries should try to create employment opportunities in the rural areas through the modernization of agriculture and opening of small- and medium-scale industries in rural areas. This will check rural to urban migration. Kerala is a unique example of rural–urban continuum. The Provision of Urban Amenities in Rural Areas (PURA) would also check rural to urban migration and be helpful to control urban unemployment problem.
2. *Strengthen urban service sector:* The government needs to try to develop service sector activities both in public and private sectors. It is seen in urban areas that schools, hospitals, banks, IT and insurance sector both in public and private sector have created a lot of employment opportunities.
3. *Development of more categories of cities:* The government should identify and develop more prospective cities and smart small towns having employment and growth potential. The government needs to develop activities in the heritage and religious cities. It will create self-employment opportunities for the illiterate and semi-literate people in those areas. As a result, employment pressure will reduce in the metropolitan and larger cities. Moreover, infrastructure development and industrial and service sector activities need to be promoted in the smaller cities, which would create employment opportunities.
4. *PPP in city development:* PPP needs to be promoted in city development. Moreover, more private actors need to be involved in the creation of jobs for the skilled and semi-skilled youths in the urban areas. The corporate sector needs to be encouraged by the government for the adoption of city and develop it into an industrial, business or heritage smart city. Tata Nagar is an illustrious example. *Desisting from populist wage enhancement and age of retirement measures:* The governments of the developing countries must desit from vote bank politics of hiking pay and enhancing retirement age at least in public sector which largely exist in urban areas. This would further elongate the income disparities between the organized and unorganized sector and pauperise urban poor further. In many countries, high pay scale and high retirement age of employees have tightened the hand of the government to create employment in the public sector.
5. *Creation of more employment:* The governments of the developing countries need to launch more wage employment programmes in the urban areas. Creation of employment in the public and corporate sectors through investment in infrastructure will reduce the rate of unemployment in the developing countries. The programmes like urban employment guarantee schemes would go a long way to deal with problem of unemployment in urban areas.
6. *Reduce the size of informal economy in urban areas:* There is a need to reduce the size of informal sector, particularly in the urban areas of the developing countries. This sector is responsible for the underemployment and vulnerable employment in urban areas. Payment of minimum wage rate, social and health security to the employees will remove the fear of unemployment from the minds of the people working in informal sector of the urban economy.

7. *Educational reform and skill education:* The governments of the developing countries need to enhance the skill and vocational education facilities in urban areas. It will not only enhance opportunities in the urban areas but also raise the standard of living of urban workforce by enhancing their income. The educational reform in the developing countries should be formulated with a background of industry-linked education system and sector-specific job-based education.
8. *FDI:* The governments of the developing countries and states need to attract FDIs with the condition of generation of employment. Moreover, some rules and regulations are required to be made for the investment of remittances in creation of employment opportunities in rural and urban areas.
9. *Urban capital formation:* Last but not least, urban capital formation in both public and private sectors and in the industrial and service sectors will go a long way to create employment opportunities in the urban areas. The urban poor needs to be encouraged to save and contribute a mite to the urban capital formation.

Employment creation is central to urban development which contributes substantially to economic growth of the nation states. The World Bank in its 2013 World Development Report noted that jobs are the cornerstone of economic and social development. Indeed, development happens through jobs. People work their way out of poverty and hardship through better livelihoods. Economies grow as people get better at what they do, as they move from farms to firms, and as more productive jobs are created and less productive ones disappear. Societies flourish as jobs bring together people from different ethnic and social backgrounds and nurture a sense of opportunity. Jobs are thus transformational—they can transform what we earn, what we do and even who we are.[29] Unemployment in general and urban unemployment in particular give rise to several social evils in the urban society such as crime, chain snatching, violence, conflicts and youth unrest. The government has to formulate an appropriate policy that creates jobs in the urban market. The attraction of FDIs, good governance and incentive to corporate sector will go a long way to deal with urban unemployment problem.

Summing Up

Urban poverty, inequalities and unemployment are the key challenges for urban development. Sustainable urban development cannot be possible unless and until these three key issues and challenges persists in urban areas. These are interrelated and have strong cause and effect relationship. The cause, effect and measures to tackle poverty, inequalities and unemployment in urban areas are invariably same with little variations. However, if these problems persist for longer period in urban areas, then it will lead to social unrest and conflict. Many African countries are experiencing the effect of urban poverty and unemployment on social unrest and conflict. The nation states have to take measures to tackle urban poverty, inequality and unemployment. Faulty urbanization without industrialization and systematic development of service sector activities are seen to be the causes of these three problems. However, unbridled urban population growth through rural to urban migration is one of the major causes of urban poverty and unemployment. Strategic balanced rural and urban development will go a long way to tackle these three problems in the developing countries. Ann Bernstein has remarked that developing countries must create cities of hope for the poor. However, many middle-income countries have seen wasteful congestion, the creation of slums, worsening air quality, floods, inadequate sanitation and joblessness. Overcoming these problems requires effective city management, and the integration of the urban agenda into national plans to promote job-rich growth, to provide safety and security, public goods and quality education.[30]

Keywords

Poverty Index, Human Poverty, Multidimensional Poverty, Income Inequality, Disguised Unemployment, Underemployment, Frictional Unemployment, Urban Paradox, Cyclical Unemployment, Technological Unemployment

REVIEW QUESTIONS

1. Define poverty. Discuss causes and effects of urban poverty.
2. Explain various dimensions of poverty.
3. Suggest measures to eradicate urban poverty from the developing countries.
4. What is income inequality? Describe factors which cause urban inequality.
5. Explain in detail the cause and effect of urban inequality.
6. How income inequality is measured? Suggests measures to overcome income inequality.
7. What are the different types of unemployment that exist in urban areas? Suggests measures to control unemployment in urban areas.
8. Explain the cause and effect of unemployment.
9. Write short notes on:
    a. Underemployment
    b. Frictional unemployment
    c. Multidimensional poverty
    d. Income inequality
    e. Gini coefficient
    f. Measurement of poverty
    g. Measurement of inequality
    h. Urban paradox

Notes

1. https://www.iied.org/introduction-urban-poverty (accessed on 3 October 2019).
2. https://www.adb.org/publications/urban-poverty-asia (accessed on 19 December 2018).
3. https://www.justice.gov.za/commissions/FeesHET/hearings/set5/set05-d1-DrPaliLehohla-MeasuringPovertyReport.pdf (accessed on 5 April 2016).
4. http://www.cpahq.org/cpahq/cpadocs/Feminization_of_Poverty.pdf (accessed on 24 November 2019).
5. http://siteresources.worldbank.org/EXTINDPEOPLE/Resources/407801-1271860301656/Chapter_6_India.pdf (accessed on 24 November 2019).

6. http://encyclopedia.uia.org/en/problem/136978 (accessed on 25 March 2019).
7. https://www.worldbank.org/en/topic/skillsdevelopment (accessed on 28 May 2019).
8. https://www.ucpress.edu/book/9780520243286/the-real-environmental-crisis (accessed on 25 March 2019).
9. https://www.humanium.org/en/child-prostitution/ (accessed on 25 August 2017).
10. https://www.jstor.org/stable/4029376?seq=1#metadata_info_tab_contents (accessed on 25 March 2019).
11. https://www.azquotes.com/quote/667432 (accessed on 25 March 2019).
12. https://www.nst.com.my/business/2017/10/287033/urban-inequality-growing-risk-asia-world-bank (accessed on 25 March 2019).
13. https://www.hks.harvard.edu/sites/default/files/centers/taubman/files/urban_inequality_final.pdf (accessed on 21 December 2018).
14. https://www.investopedia.com/terms/i/income-inequality.asp (accessed on 7 October 2019).
15. https://www.brookings.edu/research/city-and-metropolitan-income-inequality-data-reveal-ups-and-downs-through-2016/ (accessed on 7 October 2019).
16. http://documents.worldbank.org/curated/pt/361761468761690314/140540323_20041118130703/additional/multi-page.pdf (accessed on 25 March 2019).
17. https://www.odi.org/sites/odi.org.uk/files/odi-assets/publications-opinion-files/3876.pdf (accessed on 25 March 2019).
18. https://www.ncbi.nlm.nih.gov/pmc/articles/PMC4951071/ (accessed on 25 March 2019).
19. https://www.weforum.org/agenda/2014/07/cities-urbanization-rich-poor-inequality/ (accessed on 25 March 2019).
20. https://counterview.org/2015/06/19/benefits-dont-trickle-down-increase-in-income-share-of-top-20-by-1-leads-to-decline-in-gdp-by-0-08-in-next-five-years/ (accessed on 25 March 2019).
21. https://www.un.org/development/desa/dspd/wp-content/uploads/sites/22/2018/05/Concept-Note-for-the-workshop-on-revisiting-socio-economic-policies-to-address-poverty-in-all-its-dimensions-in-MIC.pdf (accessed on 25 March 2019).
22. http://wcr.unhabitat.org/wp-content/uploads/2017/03/Chapter4-WCR-2016.pdf (accessed on 7 October 2019).
23. https://academic.oup.com/oep/article-abstract/20/2/250/2360432/?redirectedFrom=PDF (accessed on 7 October 2019).
24. https://www.downtoearth.org.in/news/economy/it-is-official-unemployment-rate-in-rural-urban-india-highest-in-47-years-64902 (accessed on 7 October 2019).
25. The above definition of ILO is given in Economics Revision, for details see http://economicsrevision.co.uk/measurign-unemployment (accessed on 21 March 2014).
26. https://www.investopedia.com/ask/answers/032515/why-does-unemployment-tend-rise-during-recession.asp (accessed on 8 October 2019).
27. https://www.urban.org/urban-wire/long-term-unemployment-and-poverty-produce-vicious-cycle (accessed on 7 October 2019).
28. http://jedsnet.com/journals/jeds/Vol_3_No_2_June_2015/8.pdf (accessed on 25 March 2019).
29. https://siteresources.worldbank.org/EXTNWDR2013/Resources/8258024-1320950747192/8260293-1322665883147/WDR_2013_Report.pdf (accessed on 25 March 2019).
30. https://www.dailymaverick.co.za/article/2017-09-10-cdes-opportunities-first-the-key-to-urban-growth-is-creating-cities-of-hope-for-the-poor/ (accessed on 25 March 2019).

References

ADB. (2014). *Urban poverty in Asia*. Asian Development Bank.

Adebayo, A. (1999). Youth unemployment and national directorate of employment and self-employment programmes. *Nigerian Journal of Economics and Social Studies, 41*(1), 81–102.

Ajufo, B. I. (2012). Challenges of youth unemployment in Nigeria: Effective career guidance as a Panacea. *An International Multidisciplinary Journal, Ethiopia, 7*(1), 307–321.

Ali, S. (2000). Urban poverty in India: An introduction. *Social Change, 30*(1 & 2).

Americana Corporation. (1995). *The Encyclopedia Americana International* (Vol. 27, p. 316). Americana Corporation.

Attia, S. M. (2009, January 27). *The informal economy as an engine for poverty reduction and development in Egypt* (MPRA Paper No. 13034). https://mpra.ub.uni-muenchen.de/13034/1/Microsoft_Word-Informal_Economy_as_an_engine_of_Development_in_Egypt.pdf (accessed on 29 May 2019).

Baker, J. L., & Schuler, N. (2004). *Analyzing urban poverty: A summary of methods and approaches* (Vol. 3399). World Bank Publications, The World Bank. https://pdfs.semanticscholar.org/90c2/c833b876770c2b6a4d745b0d2140a5b2266a.pdf (accessed on 3 October 2019).

Bayarjargal, A. E. (1996). *Income, social and political inequality*. ANU College of Asia and Specific, Royal Economic Society. http://www.ecineq.org/ecineq_nyc17/FILESx2017/CR2/p179.pdf (accessed on 4 June 2019).

Bennel, P. (2000). *Improving youth livelihood*. SSA Report to the International Development Center.

Birdsall, N. (2005). *The world is not flat: Inequality and injustice in our global economy.* WIDER Annual Lecture 9. UNU-World Institute for Development Economics Research (UNU-WIDER).

Broussard, N. H., & Tekleselassie, G. (2012). *Youth unemployment: Ethiopia country study* (Working Paper). International Growth Centre, The Ohio State University. https://www.theigc.org/wp-content/uploads/2014/09/Broussar-Tekleselassie-2012-Working-Paper1.pdf (accessed on 25 March 2019).

Bukhari, M., & Munir, K. (2016). *Impact of globalization on income inequality in selected Asian countries* (MPRA Paper No. 74248) https://mpra.ub.uni-muenchen.de/74248/1/MPRA_paper_74248.pdf (accessed on 7 October 2019).

Chaudhuri, S. (2015). Urban poor, economic opportunities and sustainable development through traditional knowledge and practices. *Global Bioethics, 26*(2), 86–93.

Chigunta, F. (2002). The socio-economic situation of youths in Africa: Problems, prospects and options [Paper presentation]. Youth Employment Summit, Alexandria, Egypt. 1–13.

D'Souza, V. S. (1979). Socio-cultural marginality: A theory of urban slums and poverty in India. *Sociological Bulletin, 8*(1/2), 9–24.

Dandekar, V. M., & N. Rath. (1971). *Poverty in India*. Indian School of Political Economy. Also see https://www.jstor.org/stable/pdf/29793621.pdf (accessed on 24 December 2018).

DFID. (2001). *Meeting the challenges of poverty in urban areas.* Department of International Development.

DFID. (2005). *Reducing poverty by tackling social exclusion*. A DFID Policy Paper, International Division, DFID, London.

Eite, J. H., & Ashipala, J. M. (2010). Determinants of unemployment in Namibia. *International Journal of Business and Management, 5*(10), 92–104.

Ejike, E. C. C. (2016). Malnutrition affects the urban-poor disproportionately: A study of Nigerian urban children of different socio-economic statuses. https://www.ncbi.nlm.nih.gov/pmc/articles/PMC5184792/ (accessed on 27 May 2019).

Englama, A. (2001). Unemployment: Concepts and issues. *Bullion Publication of the Central Bank of Nigeria, 25*(4), 1–6.

Ezeani, E. O., & Otaki, O. A. (2003). Youth unemployment in Nigeria: Some implication for the third millennium. *Global Journal of Social Sciences, 2*(1), 21–26.

Frank, C. R. (1968). Urban unemployment and economic growth in Africa. *Oxford Economic Papers,20*(2), 250–274.

Fukuchi, T. (1998). The simulation analysis of the urban informal sector. *The Developing Economies, XXXVI*(3), 225–256.

Ghani, Z. A. (2017). A comparative study of urban crime between Malaysia and Nigeria. *Journal of Urban Management, 6*(1), 19–29.

Gibb, A. A., & George, M. (1990). The design of extension and related support services for small scale enterprise development. *International Small Business Development Journal, 8*(3), 10–12.

Glaeser, E. L., Resseger, M., & Tobio, K. (2009). *Urban inequality* (Policy Brief). Harvard Kennedy School, Taubman Centre for State and Local Government. https://www.hks.harvard.edu/sites/default/files/centers/taubman/files/urban_inequality_final.pdf (accessed on 25 March 2019).

Goldstein, M., & Holister, R. (1994). *Reforming labour markets in the near East.* International Center for Economic Growth. Also see https://pdfs.semanticscholar.org/19ee/5a198585a0a0f3d66a23e822f2bfc8fd0419.pdf (accessed on 24 December 2018).

Grant, U. (2010). *Spatial inequality and urban poverty* (ODI Working Paper, No. 326). ODI.

Gupta, S., & Abed, G. (2002). Does corruption affect income inequality and poverty. *IMF eLibrary.* https://asean.elibrary.imf.org/abstract/IMF071/02861-9781589061163/02861-9781589061163/ch17.xml?redirect=true (accessed on 6 June 2019).

Haddad, L., Ruel, M. T., & Garrett, J. L. (1999). *Are urban poverty and under-nutrition growing? Some newly assembled evidence.* Food Consumption and Nutrition Division, International Food Policy Research Institute.

Haughton, J., & Khandker, S. R. (2009). *Handbook on poverty and inequality.* World Bank.

Hamnett, C. (2010). Urban inequality and polarization. In F. Wu, & C. Webster (Eds.), *Marginalization in urban China (international political economy series)* (pp. 17–28). Palgrave Macmillan.

IIEP. (2006). Building skills for poverty reduction. *Newsletter, XXIV*(3, July–September). Also see http://www.iiep.unesco.org/sites/default/files/nl_2006–3_en.pdf (accessed on 29 May 2019).

ILO. (2011). *A skilled workforce for strong, sustainable and balanced growth.* International Labour Office.

Jolly, R. (2005). *Global inequality in historical perspective.* https://www.wider.unu.edu/publication/global-inequality-historical-perspective (accessed on 15 April 2020).

Kim, W. B. (1987). Urban unemployment and labor force participation in Korea. *The Annals of Regional Science, 21*(1), 44–55.

Kuznets, S. (1955). Economic growth and income inequality. *American Economic Review, 45,* 1–28.

Litwin, B. S. (2015). Determining the effect of the minimum wage on income inequality. *Student Publications, 300*(Spring). https://cupola.gettysburg.edu/cgi/viewcontent.cgi?article=1388&context=student_scholarship (accessed on 6 June 2019).

Malenbaum, W. (2011). Urban unemployment in India. *Pacific Affairs, 30*(2), pp. 138–150.

McKay, A. (2002). *Defining and measuring inequality* (Briefing Paper No. 1 (1 of 3)). Inequality Briefing, ODI. Also see https://www.odi.org/sites/odi.org.uk/files/odi-assets/publications-opinion-files/3804.pdf (accessed on 21 December 2018).

McCullouch. (1977). *The effect of minimum wage legislation on income equality: A theoretical analysis* (NBER Working Paper No. 171). National Bureau of Economic Research. Also see https://www.nber.org/papers/w0171 (accessed on 7 October 2019).

McDonald, J. F., & McMillen, D. P. (2008). *Urban economics and real estate.* Blackwell Publishing.

Mitlin, D. (2003). *The economic and social processes influencing the level and nature of chronic poverty in urban areas* (Working Paper 29). Chronic Poverty Research Centre, University of Manchester.

Mitra, A. (1992). Urban poverty: A rural spill-over? *Indian Economic Review, New Series, 27,* 403–419.

Moser, C. O. (1998). The asset vulnerability framework: Reassessing urban poverty reduction strategies. *World Development, 26*(1), 1–19.

Musgrove, P. (1980). Household size and composition, employment, and poverty in urban Latin America. *Economic Development and Cultural Change, 28*(2), 249–266.

Odonwodo, C. U., & Abdullahi, G. (2009). The imperative of information and communication technology in reducing unemployment among Nigerian graduates. *International Journal of Creativity and Technical Development, 1*(1–3), 54–65.

Okafor, E. E. (2011). Youth unemployment and implications for stability of democracy in Nigeria. *Journal of Sustainable Development in Africa, 13*(1). http://www.arcnjournals.org/images/arc-ijbse-11-2-5.pdf (accessed on 15 April 2020).

Onah, F. O. (2001). Urban unemployment situation in Nigeria. In E. O. Ezeani and N. N. Elekwa (Eds.), *Issues in urbanization and urban administration in Nigeria* (pp. 154–167). Jamo Enterprises.

Pigou, A. C. (1933). *Theory of unemployment.* Macmillan & Co.

Planning Commission of India. (2002). *National human development report 2001.* National Planning Commission, Government of India.

Ravallion, M. (2004). *Pro-poor growth: A primer* (Policy Research Working Paper Series 3242). World Bank.

Ravallion, M. (2007, September). Urban poverty. *Finance and Development, 44*(3). Also see https://www.imf.org/external/pubs/ft/fandd/2007/09/ravalli.htm (accessed on 19 December 2018).

Satterthwaite, D. (2001). Reducing urban poverty: Constraints on the effectiveness of aid agencies and development banks and some suggestions for change. *Environment & Urbanization, 13*(1, April).

Simelane, H. S. (1995). Labour migration and rural transformation in post colonial Swaziland. *Journal of Contemporary African Studies, 13*(2), 206–207.

Singh, D. P. (2009). Poverty and migration: Does moving help? In *India Urban Poverty Report 2009*. Ministry of Housing and Urban Poverty Alleviation.

Stephenes, C. (2012). Urban inequalities; urban rights: A conceptual analysis and review of impacts of children and policies to address them. *Journal of Urban Health, 89*(3), 464–485.

Streeten, P. (1979). From growth to basic needs. *Finance and Development, 16*(3), 28–31.

Thampi, A., & Anand, I. (2017, November 23–25). *Income Inequality and Polarization in India: The Role of Caste* [Paper presentation]. IARIW-ICIER Conference on Experiences and Challenges in Measuring Income, Inequality, and Poverty in South Asia, New Delhi, India. http://www.iariw.org/India/thampi.pdf (accessed on 27 September 2019).

Todaro, M. (1992). *Economics for a developing world* (2nd ed.). Longman Group.

Traeger, B. (2011). Poverty and fertility in India: Some factors contributing to a positive correlation. *Global Majority E-Journal, 2*(2), 87–98.

UN-Habitat. (2007). Slum dwellers to double by 2030: Millennium development goal could fall short. Twenty First Session of the Governing Council Nairobi, Kenya. https://www.preventionweb.net/files/1713_463146759GC202120Slum20dwellers20to20double.pdf (accessed on 29 May 2019).

UN-Habitat. (2014). The widening urban divide. UN-Habitat. Also see http://wcr.unhabitat.org/wp-content/uploads/2016/05/Chapter-4-WCR-2016.pdf (accessed on 7 October 2019).

UNCHS. (1996). *Global report on human settlements.* Oxford University Press for the United Nations Centre for Human Settlements.

UNDP. (2005). *Human development report 2005.* New York, NY: UNDP.

UNDP. (2016). *Samoa hardship and poverty report analysis of the 2013/14 household income and expenditure survey.* Samoa Bureau of Statistics and UNDP Pacific Centre, Government of Samoa.

United Nations. (2002). *World urbanization prospects; the 2001 Revision: Data tables and highlights.* United Nations Population Division, Department of Economic and Social Affairs. Cited by Child, R. E. (2002). Friendly cities: good governance in the best interests of the child. *Environ Urban,14*(2): 45–58.

United Nations. (1993, 30 June). *Secretary-General says basic objective of social development is to redress economic, social, cultural and ecological deprivation.* Press Release, SG/SM/1457, ECOSOC/1409, Geneva.

Unni. (2009). The unorganized sector and urban poverty: Issues of livelihood. In *India Urban Poverty Report 2009.* Ministry of Housing and Urban Poverty Alleviation.

WCED. (1987). *Our common future.* Oxford University Press.

William, C. C. (2014). *The informal economy and poverty: Evidence and policy review.* Joseph Rowntree Foundation. https://www.sheffield.ac.uk/polopoly_fs/1.358671!/file/JRF-informal-economy-and-poverty.pdf (accessed on 27 May 2019).

World Bank. (2000). *World development report 2000/2001: Attacking poverty.* Oxford University Press.

World Bank. (2012). *World Development Report 2012, Gender Equality and Development.* World Bank.

World Health Organization. (2008). *Closing the gap in a generation: Health equity through action on the social determinants of health, final report of the commission on social determinants of health.* World Health Organization.

Yao, S. (2004). Unemployment and urban poverty in China: A case study of Guangzhou and Tianjin. *Journal of International Development, 16*, 171–188.

Yunus, M. (2006, 5 May). *We can put poverty into museum*. Speech delivered on the occasion of receiving the honorary degree from the University of Venda, Thohoyandou, South Africa.

Zenou, Y. (1999). *Urban unemployment and city formation: Theory and policy implications* (Seminar Paper No. 662). Institute for International Economic Studies, Stockholm University. Also see https://www.diva-portal.org/smash/get/diva2:328248/FULLTEXT01.pdf (accessed on 24 December 2018).

Zhuang, J., & Kanubur, R. (2013). *Urbanization and inequality in Asia* (working Paper). Charles H. Dyson School of Applied Economics and Management, Cornell University.

9 Urban Education and Healthcare

Social performance in education, health and social security has to be made sufficient and sustainable over the long term in order for countries to prepare their citizens for today and for the future.

—Carlson (1998)

Education must be viewed as an important intermediary for capitalizing on the physical, intellectual and social capital available in cities.

—Joshi (2017a)

Urban areas provide great opportunities for individuals and families to prosper and can provide a healthy living environment through enhanced access to services, culture and recreation. However, city dwellers continue to face health hazards and new health challenges have emerged.

—WHO (2010)

Introduction

Effective, efficient and equitable social performance of governments and societies is a necessary public policy ingredient for making a fundamental transition in the structure of society (Carlson, 1998). The social backwardness is one of the important responsible factors of poverty, inequality and unemployment in the developing countries. Mukherjee and Banerjee (2009) were of the view that education and health are considered to be two vital sectors that can play a crucial role in determining the level of social development. Economic development and growth of a nation depend on its educated and skilled manpower ensured through high-quality education and healthcare services with the help of efficient education and healthcare system. One of the reasons for migration of rural people to urban areas is to have access to quality education and healthcare facilities. Health and education are the two important attractions of urban areas to the cities. Cities are known for their higher educational and healthcare institutions. Not only the government but also the corporate sector invests a lot of money in the health and education sector in the cities. This chapter deals with urban education and healthcare.

LEARNING OBJECTIVES

After reading this chapter, you should be able to:

- Explain the role of education and healthcare in urban development
- Describe the features of urban education and healthcare
- Discuss the various issues and challenges of urban education and healthcare
- Explain various measures to be taken for the improvement of urban education and healthcare

I
EDUCATION AND URBAN DEVELOPMENT

In the knowledge age, nothing counts more for economic success than the educational qualifications of the workforce.......... a country with a high percentage of tertiary education graduates is generally credited with greater innovative potential and a higher ability to move into high value added sectors of the economy, than a country featuring a lower share of graduates.

—The Schleicher (2006)

The distribution of educational opportunity within cities must be monitored to ensure that education plays a role in reducing and not exacerbating urban inequalities.

—Joshi (2017)

Education is the seed of socioeconomic development of a nation state. The role of education in development has been recognized ever since the days of Plato, who considered that education is indispensable to the economic health of good society. Adam Smith in his illustrious book *The Wealth of Nations* identified human capital as skills, dexterity (physical, intellectual and psychological) and judgement essential for economic growth and development. It is believed that it is the human resources that ultimately determine the character and pace of economic and social development of a nation. Alfred Marshall (1961) affirmed that the most valuable of all capital is investment in human beings. The role of education in the development of the rural as well as urban areas has been veritably recognized by both developed and developing countries. According to Krueger and Lindahl (2001), each additional year of schooling appears to raise earnings by about 10 per cent in the USA, although that rate of return to education varies overtime as well as across countries. Estimates done by Chen and Feng (2000) show that the stock of higher educated population has had a statistically significant, positive and robust relationship with economic growth across provinces of China in the 1980s and 1990s. Urban education is an effective input for sustainable urbanization. There needs to be more appreciation of education's role in transformative urban development (Joshi, 2017).

The Role of Education in Urban Development

It is not a flight of fancy, but it is true that the contribution of urban areas to the economic growth rate of both developed and developing nations is higher than the rural areas. This is one of the leading reasons which is why the developing nations are nowadays urbanizing in a faster pace than the developed nations. Among all the social factors of urban development, education is one of the key factors which help in the acceleration of urban areas contribution to economic growth.

Some of the roles played by education in urban development are as follows:

1. *Helps to raise contribution of urban areas to GDP:* Education is an instrument that both directly and indirectly contributes to raise productivity and output of the industrial and service sectors and thus can contribute greatly towards urban economic growth rate. Lim (1996) noted that education contributes to economic growth in the following six ways: (a) it improves generally the quality of the labour force by imparting skills and work knowledge; (b) it increases labour mobility and therefore promotes the division of labour; (c) it enables new information to be absorbed faster and unfamiliar inputs and new processes applied more effectively; (d) it improves management skills which leads to a more efficient allocation of resources; (e) it removes many of the social and institutional barriers to economic growth; and (f) it encourages entrepreneurship by promoting individual responsibility, organizational ability, risk-taking in moderation and planning over the long term.
2. *Inclusive urban development:* Education is a great social and economic equalizer. It helps to empower people irrespective of caste, class, ethnicity and gender. For urban development, in general, and inclusive urban development, in particular, education is of paramount importance. It enhances capability of the socially weaker sections and enables them to contribute towards economic growth rate. The UNDP (2016) has defined human resources development as empowering people by fostering the contributory capacities that they can bring to the improvement of their own quality of life and that of their families, communities, enterprises and societies. B. R. Ambedkar (1997), the architect of the Indian Constitution and one of the prominent Dalit leader, said:

   > coming as I do from the lowest order of the Hindu society. I know what the value of education is. The problem of raising the lower order is deemed to be economic. This is a great mistake. The problem of raising the lower order is not to feed them, and to make them serve the higher order, as is the ancient ideal of this country. The problem of lower order is to remove from them that inferiority complex, which has stunted their growth and made them slaves to others, to create in them the consciousness of the significance of their lives for themselves and for the country, of which they have been cruelly robbed by the existing social order. Nothing can achieve this except the spread of higher education. This in my opinion is the panacea of our social trouble.

3. *Sustainable urban development:* The development of various education facilities contributes substantially to the development of an urban area. Education, in general, and higher and skill education, in particular, are critical to sustainable development. It is a fact

that quality educational institutions exist in the cities of both developed and developing countries. Educational facilities available in the urban areas not only help to develop urban areas but also the skilled manpower produced in the urban areas help in the country's rural development.

4. *Help to reduce urban inequality:* Education is a great equalizer. It enhances the capability of an individual irrespective of caste, class, ethnicity and gender and enables him or her to earn more. It entices individuals to earn respect in the society. In the urban society, education is very essential for survival in the social and economic sphere. Urban areas are more competitive as compared to the rural areas. Therefore, education, in general, and higher and skill education, in particular, are essential for fighting with the social and economic evil of inequality in the era of rapid urbanization. The early modernization theorists argued that education weakens traditional, ascriptive attachments based on characteristics such as gender, hereditary positive, ethnicity and religion in favour of achievement and merit (Levy, 1966).
5. *Urban education can reduce urban conflict:* Education is a great instrument to be helpful to reduce urban conflict. According to the UNESCO 2011 report, an increased primary school enrolment, from 77 per cent to universal provision, reduced the likelihood to civil war by nearly 50 per cent. Thyne (2006) found that an increased male enrolment from 30 per cent to 81 per cent in secondary schools seemed to reduce the probability of civil war by 67 per cent. Evidence shows that educational inequalities significantly heightened the risk of conflict (Fasih, 2008).
6. *Education provides solace to urban crime:* The urban crime seems to be committed by the people largely less educated and uneducated living in the unorganized colonies and slums. Enhancement of higher education among these deprived sections of urban population would be helpful to reduce urban crime. In the United States, if 5 per cent more men graduated from high school it would add US$20 billion to the economy via reduced crime and higher earnings (UNESCO, 2016).
7. *Education builds knowledge society:* Knowledge society can be built only with the help of educated and knowledgeable persons. For which educational infrastructure and expansion of educational facilities are essential in urban areas. Knowledge society is a fundamental requisite for development, as innovation and development have always been based on the creative and imaginative capacity of the human mind. Knowledge contributes to development in several ways: as a productive resource; as an essential input for education, scientific research and industrial technology; as a catalyst for social change and economic development; and as a basis for civilization and capture values that promote social integrity and harmony, which is an essential foundation of all development. Without adequate knowledge all the other essential inputs—land, infrastructure, factories, capital, technology, administrative and social organization—cannot yield full result (Jacobs & Asokan, 2003).
8. *Enhance employment opportunity:* The education, in general, and skill education, in particular, will enhance the employment opportunities for the youth in urban areas irrespective of their social background. The importance of skill education has immensely enhanced in the cities of both developed and developing countries after globalization. The unskilled youth in urban areas are found to be working in the informal sector with lower wage rate and put up in unorganized settlements devoid of minimum basic amenities. Education, skilled workforce and urban development go hand in hand.

Features of Urban Education

The features of urban education are as follows:

1. The literacy rate and gross enrolment ratio (GER) of urban areas is higher as compared to the rural areas.
2. The educational status of population living in the urban slums and unorganized colonies is higher as compared to the city population.
3. The education and educational infrastructure and institutions in the urban areas are more heterogeneous as compared to rural areas. It is envisaged that schools in urban settings are larger, tend to benefit from better educational resources and often enjoy greater autonomy in how they can allocate those resources.[1]
4. The private sector plays an equally important role in the secondary and tertiary educational system in the urban areas.
5. Urban education system in many developing countries is a tri-track system. First, schools governed by the respective states; second set of schools being opened and managed by the private sector and the third category of schools being managed by the municipal corporations and councils.
6. The education in the urban areas is more commercialized as compared to the rural areas. The commercialization process of the schools and tertiary education system in the developing countries and more particularly in its urban areas have been escalated after the globalization.
7. Quality educational institutions both general and technical are found to be present largely in the metropolitan cities among the urban areas. The economic costs of education in these institutions are also higher as compared to those present in the smaller cities.
8. The student community belonging to urban education system comparatively belongs to educated and economically sound families. The OECD has remarked that urban schools are usually larger, have a more socioeconomically advantaged student body, enjoy greater responsibility for resource allocation, are less likely to experience staff shortages, are more likely to have a higher proportion of qualified teachers and have higher student–teacher ratios than schools in rural areas and towns, especially in partner countries and economies.[2]

Determinants of Urban Education Status

It is pertinent to discuss various determinants of urban education status, as it enables the urban administration to take appropriate steps for development of urban education. Some of these important determinants are narrated as follows:

1. *Literacy rate and GER:* It is one of the conventionally recognized determinants of education status of any nation, both rural and urban. According to UNESCO (2002), a person is functionally literate, if he or she is able to engage in all those activities in which literacy is required for his/her effective functioning to continue to use reading, writing and calculation for both his/her and the community's development. Nowadays literacy is not considered enough for the nation states to enable their citizens to effectively participate in the nation-building process. GER is being considered as the other important determinant of the

Table 9.1 Gross Enrolment Ratio of a Few Countries, 2017

Countries	Tertiary
China	51.0
Brazil	50.5
Finland	87.0
India	27.5
Pakistan	10.1
United Kingdom	59.4
USA	88.8

Source: World Development Indicators, World Bank 2019.

Table 9.2 Government Expenditure on Education as a Percentage of GDP, 2017

Countries	% of GDP
Bhutan	7.1
Brazil	6.2
Finland	7.1
Nepal	5.1
Japan	3.5
United Kingdom	5.5
SriLanka	2.8

Source: World Bank, World Development Indicators, 2019. http://wdi.worldbank.org/tables (accessed on 27 September 2019).

educational development status of the population. The GER of a few countries is given in Table 9.1.

2. *Expenditure on education:* Any expenditure on education by the family, society and the nation states needs to be considered as an investment. Investment on educational infrastructure, manpower and capacity building is critical to the manpower development. The skilled and trained manpower effectively contribute towards the growth and development of the nation states. It is viewed that education as an investment secures returns in the form of skilled manpower that geared to the needs of development, both for accelerating economic development and for improving the quality of the society (Yogish, 2006). The expenditure on education as a percentage of GDP is given in Table 9.2.
3. *Ranking of the educational institutions:* Nowadays ranking of the educational institutions is considered as one of the yardsticks of the educational development of the nation states. In the present times, world ranking of the universities and educational institutions belonging

Table 9.3 World University Ranking, 2018

Countries	Rank
University of Oxford	1
University of Cambridge	2
California Institute of Technology	3
Stanford University	3
Massachusetts Institution of Technology	5
Harvard University	6
Princeton University	7
Imperial College of London	8
University of Chicago	9
ETH Zurich-Swiss Federal Institute of Technology Zurich	10
University of Pennsylvania	10

Source: https://www.timeshighereducation.com/world-university-rankings/2018/world-ranking#!/page/0/length/25/sort_by/rank/sort_order/asc/cols/stats (accessed on 23 April 2018).

to the USA and the United Kingdom occupy copious places. Yeravdekar and Tiwari (2014) were of the opinion that the present global higher educational milieu is typified by its preoccupation with rankings. As the higher educational institutions of nation states are established in its cities, therefore, both national and international rankings of the institutions are a vital indicator of the city educational development. The ranking of various universities is given in Table 9.3.

4. *Educational policy and educational regulators:* The other important determinants of educational development of the nation states are formulation of effective educational policies and establishment of educational regulators. Different countries in the world have formulated different education policies and established educational regulators for enlisting the vision and mission and implementing them through regulators. The education policy needs to give specific direction about the urban education, its thrust areas and mechanism to promote quality skill education institutions in urban areas.
5. *Use of technology in education:* Use of technology in education is considered as one of the vital indicators of educational status in the globalized era. The smart classrooms with computer facility and Internet connectivity are considered as vital inputs to promote smart learning and impart smart education. ICT is a powerful tool that upgrades quality and efficiency of education. It promotes virtual learning and there is no need to be physically present in the classroom. Some of the important features of ICT are that it promotes distance education, flexibility in teaching and learning, virtual interaction, active learning and motivation.
6. *Skill and vocational education:* Skill education in general, and in urban areas in particular, is vital to raise the living condition of a city's population and reduce income disparities in urban areas. The World Bank envisages that one-third of the working age population in low- and middle-income countries lacks the basic skills required to get quality jobs, leaving them

Table 9.4 Classification of Skill Levels

Skill Levels	Definition	Examples
Level 1	Skills involving simple and routine physical or manual work	Hawker, street vendor, gardener, cook, household servant, construction worker, mason and so on
Level 2	Skills involving operation of machinery and electronic equipment	Plumber, electrician, artisan, barber, mechanic, tailor and so on
Level 3	Skills involving written records of work, simple calculations, good persona communication skills in specialized fields	Clerical, supervisory level and so on
Level 4	Skills involving decision-making and creativity based on theoretical and factual knowledge	Doctor, lawyer, chartered accountant, engineer, architect, scientist, actor, author and so on

Source: https://www.financialexpress.com/opinion/skill-india-why-there-is-a-gap-between-current-status-and-goals-explained/1520633/ (accessed on 6 February 2020).

unable to achieve their full productive potential and limiting economic investment and growth. According to the latest India Skill Report (2019), only 45.6 per cent of the youth graduating from educational institutions are employable. Imparting more and more skill education to the youth for employment across the sector is vital for raising economic growth and development of the nation.[3] The shortage of skilled manpower across the sector is a vital issue in developing countries. To cite the example of India, the proportion of formally skilled workers in India is extremely low, at 4.69 per cent of total workforce, compared to 24 per cent in China, 52 per cent in the USA, 68 per cent in the UK, 75 per cent in Germany, 80 per cent in Japan and 96 per cent in South Korea. According to the World Bank, low skills perpetuate poverty and inequality, and the skills development and education can reduce unemployment, raise incomes and improve standards of living. The World Bank has noted three types of skills such as (a) cognitive skills, (b) socioemotional skills and (c) technical skills. The National Skill Development Mission in India has categorized skills at different levels given in Table 9.4.

Issues and Challenges of Urban Education

'Urban' education is fraught with impositions, deficit approaches and even racist mindsets in dealing with teaching and learning tied particularly to ethnicity, race, gender, ability and choice.[4] The urban education in many urban areas of the developed as well as developing countries and more particularly in the developing countries faces a lot of issues and challenges.

1. *Educational disparities:* One of the biggest challenges which the urban education system is facing is the vertical and horizontal disparity in education and educational system in

urban areas. The education being offered by the private schools in urban areas is being offered with better pedagogy and by highly qualified teachers as compared to the education students receive from the educational institutions present in the urban slums and other unorganized colonies. Moreover, schools situated in cities have better infrastructural facilities, good-quality teachers, having better educational aids and the students' performance is far better as compared to the ones in the suburban areas and in the unorganized colonies and slums. Logan and Burdick-Will from their research on school segregation and racial/ethnic disparities in America have found continuing segregation in metropolitan schools, inequalities between urban and suburban schools, and disparities between relatively advantaged white and Asian students in comparison to black and Hispanic students.[5]

2. *Commercialization of education:* After globalization, education, in general, and tertiary education, in particular, in the cities of both the developed and developing countries have become highly commercialized. They have gone beyond the affordability capability of the common men. City schools and particularly the private schools are largely meant for the rich and high middle-class people. The government schools are largely found to be having students from the middle- and lower-middle-class families. The craze for private schools has pauperized many impoverished families in the urban areas. It is one of the biggest challenges of the urban education system.
3. *Two-track system:* The urban education system is largely a two-track system; one being offered by the government schools belonging to the traditional state-centric education system and the other one being offered by the private educational institutions, largely English medium. The former is largely opted by the families having lower and moderate income and the latter by the higher income group of people. The cost of education of the private English-medium schools is higher as compared to the state language medium schools.
4. *Structural challenges:* The urban education system suffers from structural challenges, which deprive the underprivileged from their right to education. It is remarked that the urban school systems tend to have specific structural challenges that impede their ability to effectively educate the most vulnerable students and while these structural challenges may be evidenced across all types of educational contexts, they are perhaps most potent in urban settings.[6] They include the following: (a) persistently low student achievement, (b) a lack of instructional coherence, (c) inexperienced teaching staff, (d) poorly functioning business operations and (e) low expectations of students (Kincheloe, 2010).
5. *Cultural challenges:* It is one of vital challenges of the urban education system. Migrant students from different cultural backgrounds sometimes fail to cope with the urban culture and environment. This affects their educational achievements. The principles of culturally responsive pedagogy recognize that culture is central to learning and pivotal not only in communicating and receiving information but also in shaping the thinking process of groups and individuals (Ladson-Billings, 1994). A pedagogy that acknowledges, responds to and celebrates knowledge, information and processes as culturally bound offers fuller and more equitable access to education for culturally and linguistically diverse student groups (Gay, 2000). Steele's (2010) research indicates that African Americans and other racial/ethnic minority groups for whom there is a societal perception of intellectual inferiority display greater psychological vulnerability to failure and other identity-threatening, social-environmental cues.
6. *Politics of reform:* The frequent reforms in educational system by various governments in power have created a lot of confusion in the minds of the teachers, pupils and parents. The education systems of the urban areas are being the first target of educational politics of

reform. For example, the introduction of four-year graduation during the time of the UPA government and choice-based credit system in the NDA period in India has created a lot of confusion and also apprehensions in the mind of the teachers, students as well as parents. The urban education is the immediate target of politics of educational reform.

Measures to Improve Urban Education

Education is a very vital sector to promote urban development. Many youths migrate from rural to urban areas in order to pursue quality higher education in the cities. Customarily, cities are the hub of quality higher educational institutions. Therefore, the governments of the nation states have to take appropriate measures for the development of urban education. Some of the measures to be taken for strengthening urban education for urban development are as follows:

1. *Building partnership with the parents and stakeholders:* One of the important tasks of the urban education system is to build trust and relationships between students and various stakeholders involved in the process of urban education system. Moreover, careful coordination of services with community partners to meet specific nutrition, healthcare and counselling needs is vital to raise enrolment and student attendance and reduce dropout. It will be also helpful to build infrastructure with community support. Effective urban schools should seek to build relationships with NGOs and other CBOs. It is remarked that the urban schools should see these other agencies as not having outside interests but, rather, being equal stakeholders in the long-term goals of the school.[7]
2. *Not frequent but need-based reform:* The education system need not to be the victim of politics of reform. However, reforms are required, therefore they should be need-based and serve the need of the urban community and make the students socially and culturally considerate and economically useful to the nation. The educational curriculum must be need based and continuously revised keeping in mind the need of the market and society.
3. *Building relationship between students and teachers to mend behaviour and achievement:* The teaching–learning system and the teaching pedagogy need to be both teacher and students friendly. It is said that good teaching in urban schools is often a function of leveraging trust and relationships to challenge students to meet the high expectations for learning. In this way, extracurricular activities can be utilized as tools to engage students, and these activities should be designed to develop skill sets beyond athletics that create opportunities for youth leadership and civic engagement.[8]
4. *Building quality educational infrastructure:* There is a wide gap between the infrastructural facilities available in the public and private schools in urban areas. As education is a public good, the municipal government needs to improve the educational infrastructure which will motivate the students to enrol and pursue the cost-effective education in government schools.
5. *Educational governance:* Improvement in educational governance is the key to urban education system. The educational administrators and teachers need to be accountable to the student's achievement. The transparency in recruitment of teachers will go a long way to improve the standard of teaching–learning in the schools of urban areas which cater to the need of the urban middle- and lower-income groups of population. The government needs to focus on teacher absenteeism, student enrolment and attendance, classroom teaching, student satisfaction and so on. Governing body of the educational institutions

must be carefully formulated with educational experts who can provide constructive suggestions to educational institution.

6. *Urban educational management:* Management of urban education, in general, and school education, in particular, is critical to quality assurance of urban education. The management of the both urban primary, secondary and tertiary schools and higher educational institutions plays a critical role in effective delivery of education to the pupils. Several studies have found that the educational management is a key factor for students' achievement and schools' performance. Management holistically refers to finance and fee, manpower, logistic management, educational management information system and so on.
7. *Teacher education system:* The teacher education system is one of the important components of education system. It helps the teachers to be knowledgeable about the educational pedagogy, changes in curriculum, technological advancement and other educational reforms being taken up from time to time by the government. The teacher education system is very weak in many developing countries which do not equip the teacher with skill and knowledge and attitudinal changes and how to deal with diversified student groups in an urban situation. A strong teacher education system is required in order to improve the quality of urban education system. It is remarked that developing educators for rapidly transitioning schools requires a re-examination of the current models of teacher and leadership preparation because 'continuing with business as usual will mean failure or mediocrity' (Howard, 2007).
8. *Education of the disadvantaged:* The urban education system has to give special attention to the education of the disadvantaged sections of society and the people living in the urban slums. The literacy and GER of the slum dwellers have to be improved in order to enable them to stand at par with their counterparts.

Education plays a crucial role in urban development. Education, in general, and skill education, in particular, in urban areas help the cities to contribute more effectively and efficiently to economic growth of the nation states. Therefore, the urban administration has to give adequate importance to establishing quality educational institutions in the cities. Moreover, educating the urban disadvantaged sections of population who are staying in the slums and informal settlements will promote inclusive and sustainable development of the cities. Moreover, use of technology in the educational institutions of the cities will make city classrooms smart. Smart education is a key ingredient in smart city development. Smart cities need education facilities and educational system which provide smart classrooms and enable students to acquire the 21st-century skills, including digital literacy, creative thinking, innovations, effective communication, teamwork and the ability to create high-quality projects.

II
HEALTH AND URBAN DEVELOPMENT

Improving the state of health contributes to the realization of other developmental objectives such as economic development, labour productivity growth, responsiveness to innovation and future orientedness.

—Szirmai (2006)

WHO considers better health central to human happiness and well being and makes an important contribution to economic progress, as healthy populations live longer, are more productive and save more.

—CWS (2010)

Healthy urbanization is a course of action towards the attainment of optimum and equal population health and development.

—WHO (2011)

According to WHO, urban areas provide great opportunities for individuals and families to prosper and can provide a healthy living environment through enhanced access to services, culture and recreation.[9] Health and development whether rural or urban are intertwined. A country with high percentage of morbid and unhealthy population cannot escalate its economic growth rate. Most of the African countries where there is high prevalence of HIV/AIDS are less developed as compared to their counterparts. In a historical research, it was claimed that about one-third of economic growth in England in the past 200 years is due to improvements in nutrition and health. Investments in healthcare make substantial positive contribution to economic growth and development. Therefore, any expenditure on healthcare must be considered as an investment as a healthy population is an asset of a nation and contributes towards its economic growth and development.

Urban Health: Need and Importance

Following are a few important factors for which there is a need for improvement in urban healthcare status.

1. *Raise economic growth rate:* In order to raise the contribution of urban areas to the overall growth rate of a nation, the improvement in the health status of the urban population is very essential. Basta et al. (1979) found that in Indonesia, men with anaemia were 20 per cent less productive than men without anaemia.
2. *Control Health Hazards:* Growth of population and rise in the population of vehicles and other gadgets have raised the level of pollution in almost all the advanced cities in both developed and developing countries. WHO has rightly remarked that the cities concentrate risks and hazards for health, and they magnify some long-standing threats to health and introduce others.[10] Therefore, improving the health status of the urban population is of utmost importance in the drive for urban development.
3. *Unhealthy lifestyle of city population:* The healthcare of urban population is sine qua non as in most of the cities and particularly in the metropolitan and large cities people follow an unhealthy lifestyle. This causes a lot of damage to their health. WHO has rightly remarked that cities tend to promote unhealthy lifestyles, such as 'convenient' diets that depend on processed foods, sedentary behaviour, smoking and the harmful use of alcohol and other substances. These lifestyle choices are directly linked to obesity and the rise of conditions such as heart disease, stroke, some cancers and diabetes.[11]
4. *Slum population:* Most of the cities have a sizeable number of slum populations. In the developing countries, the health and hygienic conditions in these slums are very poor. This causes a lot of morbidities and mortalities in these colonies. Provisioning of healthcare and

raising the health status of these marginalized sections of urban population are vital for the nation. WHO has remarked that today, around one-third of urban dwellers, amounting to nearly one billion people, live in urban slums, informal settings or sidewalk tents. They are the people who over-consume healthcare and people who forego the most basic and essential care for financial and other reasons.[12]

5. *Rapid urbanization:* One of the vital reasons to look after the health of the urban population is the rapid unplanned urbanization in the developing countries. The migration of impoverished rural population to urban areas has put tremendous pressure on the government to ensure healthcare infrastructure, personnel and medicines to them. The budget of the municipalities on healthcare is being enhanced from year to year. To narrate it for the first time in history, more people are now living in urban settings than in rural areas. By the year 2030, it is estimated that six out of every ten people will be living in towns or cities, with the most explosive growth expected in Asia and Africa.
6. *Urban health matters:* WHO in its urban health matters has envisaged that in urban areas health matters in critical ways, for more and more people, and WHO will be doing more, today and well into the future, to support these efforts by:
   a. Promote urban planning for healthy behaviours and safety;
   b. Improve urban living conditions;
   c. Ensure participatory urban governance;
   d. Build inclusive cities that are accessible and age friendly; and
   e. Make urban areas resilient to emergencies and disasters.[13]

Features of Urban Health

One of the documents of WHO has envisaged that cities are confronted by the triple threat of infectious diseases exacerbated by poor living conditions; non-communicable diseases and conditions fuelled by tobacco use, unhealthy diets, physical inactivity and the abuse of alcohol; and injuries, road accidents, violence and crime.[14] Some of the important features of urban healthcare are narrated as follows:

1. *Health disparities:* There is a wider disparity in the access to healthcare services in urban areas. The people belonging to marginalized sections of society are largely accessing government healthcare services, while the rich sections of the community and those who have healthcare security have access to quality emergency care services in the specialized private hospitals. In urban areas, access to quality healthcare institutions and healthcare specialists depends on the affordability abilities of the healthcare seekers.
2. *Differences in healthcare indicators:* The healthcare indicators such as mortality, morbidity, fertility, death rates and birth rates vary from one group to that of the other. Although the healthcare status such as infant and maternal mortality and morbidity is higher in rural areas as compared to urban areas, these are higher among the people living in urban slums and pathways. It is higher among the migrated population from rural to urban areas. The nutritional status, reproductive health indicators such as teenage pregnancy, total fertility rate, maternal mortality, infant mortality, child mortality, communicable and non-communicable diseases are all worse among the urban poor than the urban non-poor.

3. *Rising cost of healthcare services:* The cost of healthcare services is rising day by day in urban areas because of shortage of the tertiary healthcare institutions in urban areas. The growing urbanization is one of the vital reasons. This has led to growing foothold of private healthcare institutions in urban areas which are charging exorbitant fees for healthcare and other associated services. For the poor to have access to quality healthcare services is becoming dearer day by day.
4. *Air pollution and urban health:* One of the critical features of urban health is health related problems associated with urban pollution. The rising pollution in the cities because of various reasons such as rise in the number of vehicles, growing construction activities, sanitation-related pollution, industrial pollution and heat generation are causing a lot of cardiovascular problems among all age groups. According to WHO, urban air pollution kills around 1.2 million people each year around the world, mainly due to cardiovascular and respiratory diseases.[15]
5. *Incidence of communicable diseases:* There is a good number of incidences of communicable diseases like TB in the cities. The unhygienic food, living conditions, consumption of unhygienic foods from small food caterers and so on are some of the factors among many. According to WHO, TB incidence is much higher in big cities. In New York City, TB incidence is four times the national average. In the Democratic Republic of the Congo, 83 per cent of people with TB live in cities.[16] The incidences of HIV/AIDS are found to be higher in the urban areas as compared to the rural areas.
6. *Unhealthy urban environment:* Urban environments tend to discourage physical activity and promote unhealthy food consumption. Participation in physical activity is made difficult by a variety of urban factors including overcrowding, high-volume traffic, heavy use of motorized transportation, poor air quality and lack of safe public spaces and recreation/sports facilities.[17]
7. *Rising incidence of lifestyle diseases:* In the urban areas there has been growing incidences of lifestyle diseases such as high/low blood pressure and diabetes. While under nutrition has given rise to vitamin deficiencies, anaemia and stunted growth, over nutrition is the reason behind the rise of non-communicable diseases such as cardiovascular diseases, cancer, hypertension and diabetes mellitus, among urban population.[18]
8. *Mental and occupational health problems:* Because of work pressure, unemployment, lower wage rate, family problems and so on many of the urban population are suffering from mental and occupational health problems. The work cultures such as night shifts, over work burden have added to woos. The range of disorders and deviancies associated with urbanization is enormous. Some of the disorders are severe mental disorders, depression, substance abuse, alcoholism, crime, family disintegration and alienation (Srivastava, 2009).

Determinants of Urban Health Status

Identification of health indicators for the determination of health status of the urban population is vital to finding solution to the urban health problems. Urban health indicator tools provide evidence about the health impacts of the physical urban environment which can be used in making environment policy and decision-making.[19] Several indictors are being used by various researchers and government policymakers in the determination of health status. A few of them are discussed as follows.

1. *Housing:* At the outset, healthy housing is an important determinant of urban health. Healthy house keeps the household members happy and healthy. A WHO document has rightly envisaged,

   > The quality of housing has major implications for people's health. Housing in cities is of particular concern, with the world's urban population predicted to double by 2050 and, with it, the demand for housing. Raising housing standards is therefore a key pathway for providing healthy housing conditions and improving health and well-being for all.[20]

   A healthy house in minimum needs to have following facilities: (a) adequate rooms while taking into consideration the number of household members; (b) proper ventilation; (c) separate bathroom and toilet facility; (d) separate kitchen for cooking with safe energy for cooking; (e) electricity connection and energy for lighting; (f) sewerage system for the passage of waste water and safe garbage disposal tank for waste disposal; and (g) safe drinking water facility. It is observed that the people living in the urban slum and on the pavements are largely devoid of all these minimum facilities.
2. *Population and demography:* The population and the demographic dynamics, that is, birth rate, death rate and fertility rate are important indicators of health status. Migration of impoverished population from the rural to urban areas has put tremendous pressure on the heathcare infrastructure and service delivery in the cities. Thus, checking population migration from rural areas to urban areas would improve the healthcare status of the urban population. Moreover, the migrant impoverished population has larger family size than the original urban population. A large percentage of them live in the informal settlements and are incapable to pay for expensive quality healthcare services thus impacting their health status. The research based on medical and epidemical records in China has found that the migrants had worse health than the urban residents (Zhang et al., 2015).
3. *Water and sanitation:* Safe drinking water and sanitation are two important determinants of the health. The WHO figure shows that about 80 per cent of urban dwellers have access to piped drinking water and 96 per cent have access to improved drinking water sources. It has also mentioned that often the bacteriological quality of this water remains poor; more than 50 per cent of urban residents in developing countries are still affected at one time or another by diseases related to insufficient access to safe drinking water and improved sanitation.[21] The sanitation conditions of the people staying in the urban slums and beside the railway tracks are quite sordid. They are also devoid of safe drinking water. Moreover, solid waste disposal and open defecation are also problems in many cities of the developing countries. Recent estimates also suggest that cities generate 1.3 billion tonnes of solid waste per year, a figure expected to rise to 2.2 billion tonnes by 2025. Failure to adequately collect and dispose of solid waste can increase the proliferation of disease-carrying vectors, such as rodents and insects.[22] The sanitation and drinking-water-related health problems occurring in most of the developing countries are malaria, cholera, dengue, diarrhoea and so on. Provision of healthcare services without adequate provision of safe drinking water and sanitation facilities would not be helpful to improve the health and health-related quality of life in urban areas.
4. *Mortality and morbidity:* Mortality, such as infant and maternal mortality rates are two important worldwide indicators of health development. Although the infant and maternal

mortality occurring in the urban areas of the developing countries is lower as compared to their rural areas, yet as compared to the urban areas of the developed countries these are very high. It is remarked that the scale and speed of urbanization in Sub-Saharan Africa and parts of Asia has outpaced the ability of cities to absorb new arrivals and provide basic services. In Latin America, an estimated 55 per cent of under-five deaths occur in urban areas. In Africa and Asia, cities account for approximately 30 per cent of under-five deaths and the expectation is that the number will increase.[23] The infant and maternal mortality rates in the urban slum areas of the developing countries are quite high and sometimes even equal to the figures in rural areas. Vaid et al. (2007) have found that neonatal mortality, which is preventable by better antenatal and perinatal care, continues to be high in urban slums in South India. Similarly, in the post-neonatal period of infancy, infectious disease mortality is high, although healthcare is accessible.

5. *Food and nutrition:* Food and nutrition are two important determinants of health status in urban areas. The nutritional anaemia among the children and women in the urban areas of the developing countries is high and in the urban slums it is higher. Moreover, the nutritional anaemia is also prevalent in adolescent girls living in urban areas of the developing countries, which causes problem in their future maternity. The nutritional status of slum children is worst among all urban groups and is even poorer than the rural average. Under nutrition and malnutrition impair physical, mental and behavioural development of millions of children. Srinivas and Mankeshwar (2015) from his study on anaemia in urban adolescent has remarked that the high prevalence of anaemia among adolescent girls indicates need for additional nutritional support, iron folic acid supplementation including prevention and control of worm infestation in urban communities.
6. *Pollution and air quality:* Pollution and air quality are major issues which determine the health condition of the people in the cities. It has been constantly reported that the air quality of Delhi is poor because of pollution. According to WHO's most recent survey of 4,300+ cities worldwide, only 20 per cent of the urban population surveyed live in areas that comply with WHO air quality guideline levels for PM2.5. About 80 per cent of those deaths are due to heart disease and stroke, while another 20 per cent are from respiratory illnesses and cancers related to exposure to fine particulate matter (PM2.5), the most harmful air pollutant.[24] Besides air pollution, sound pollution is also a cause of concern in metropolitan cities, which causes many health problems, especially among the aging population. WHO highlights in recent reports that environmental noise can be considered as a pollutant that has a significant impact on public health. This is due to the existence of evidence that links environmental noise and specific health effects, including cardiovascular disease, cognitive impairment, sleep disturbance and tinnitus.[25]
7. *Healthcare expenditure:* Healthcare expenditure done by the government of a country for the urban area population is also one of the important determinants of health status. The per population availability of trained health personnel is also low in the developing countries as compared to the developed countries. The per capita expenditure in the developed countries is higher than the developing countries. Because of the lack of adequate provision and non-availability of experts on critical healthcare services in the government hospitals, even in the cities of the developing countries, people incur a lot of healthcare expenditure out of their pocket. The healthcare status of various developed and developing countries is given in Table 9.5.

Table 9.5 Health Expenditure in Selected Developed and Developing Countries, 2017

Country	Out of Pocket Health Expenditure (%)	% of GDP	Public % Current Expenditure
US	11.1	17.1	81.8
UK	15.1	9.8	80.2
Japan	13.5	10.9	83.6
China	35.9	5.0	58.0
India	64.6	3.7	25.4
Sri Lanka	50.1	3.9	43.1
Nigeria	75.2	3.6	13.0
Zambia	12.1	4.5	38.3

Source: World Development Indicators, World Bank, http://wdi.worldbank.org/tables (accessed on 27 September 2019).

8. *Health infrastructure and manpower:* Availability of healthcare infrastructure and trained health manpower are also critical factors influencing the health status of population in a city. It is observed that all the specialized healthcare facilities are available in the metropolitan and larger cities of the nation states and the smaller municipalities are devoid of the same. This is a prominent feature of the developing countries. One of the WHO documents has envisaged that urban public health services suffer from inadequate manpower, infrastructure and supplies, weak referral systems and sub-optimal allocation of resources.[26]
9. *Lifestyle diseases:* Lifestyle diseases such as high/low blood pressure, diabetes and obesity in the globalized era, nowadays, are being considered as important indicator of health status of the population in both developed and developing countries. It is not a flight of fancy, but truly the percentage of urban population suffering from lifestyle diseases in urban areas is higher than those who are in rural areas. Rapid urbanization and industrialization are leading to increased lifestyle risk factors and thus lifestyle diseases. Lifestyle diseases have caused more deaths and disability worldwide in recent years. Kumar and others (2018) have commented that the current lifestyle(s) of an average city dweller includes fast-paced life with sedentary jobs, a stressful environment and unhealthy food habits predisposing him/her to non-communicable diseases such as obesity, diabetes and hypertension.

Issues and Challenges of Urban Healthcare System

The urban healthcare system is facing a lot of issues and challenges particularly in developing countries. Some of them are as follows.

1. *Migration and health problems:* It is not a flight of fancy, but delicately the demand for healthcare services in the developing countries has been constantly rising in their urban

areas because of migration of rural population to the urban areas. It can be said that the flow of population from rural to urban areas is increasing in a geometric proportion, while the supply of services is increasing in an arithmetical proportion. The big issue before these nations is how to check the migration of population from rural to urban area.

2. *Scanty allocation of resources for healthcare:* The allocation of resources for provisioning of healthcare services in urban areas is not adequate as compared to the requirement of healthcare services. In most of the developing countries, the allocation of resources for health is less than 5 per cent. It has been viewed that we not only want to allocate resources proportionate to the greater morbidity among the poor but also want to reduce the social inequalities in health; we have to look more closely at the vertical aspects of equity, that is, the unequal treatment of unequal. In other words, deprived groups should receive preferential allocation of healthcare resources to achieve more rapid improvements in their health, thereby reducing inequalities in their health vis-à-vis richer groups.[27]
3. *Urban physical environment:* The urban physical environment includes the built environment: the air city dwellers breathe, the water they drink, the indoor and outdoor noise they hear, the park land inside and surrounding the city and the geological and climate conditions of the site where the city is located.[28] The physical environment determines the physical and mental health conditions. Lack of clean air, playgrounds, parks and recreation centres lead to health problems such as asthma and other respiratory problems, obesity and psychological distress. Because of lack of space in the big cities, the physical environment is more congested and vulnerable to noises and other disturbances. Physical environment has a strong correlation with human health.
4. *Urban infrastructure, water and sanitation:* Urban infrastructure, particularly water and sanitation, are big issues in the cities which challenge the health of the city population. The urban infrastructure is a critical part of the physical environment. It determines how a city provides water, disposes of garbage and provides energy. In long-standing urban areas, the decline of an aging infrastructure, coupled with frequently declining municipal resources, may challenge cities' ability to continue to provide safe water and sanitation for urban residents. Breakdown of these water and sanitation infrastructures may increase health problems related to water, sewage or disposal of solid waste. In rapidly urbanizing areas, frequently in less wealthy countries, cities often face the challenge of maintaining an adequate fresh water supply to growing numbers of urban residents and transport accumulating sewage and other waste.[29]
5. *Health governance:* The poor governance of healthcare services is a big issue in urban areas. The public sector healthcare institutions are devoid of adequate health manpower. Moreover, the number of healthcare institutions is also not adequate compared to the pace of urbanization. The healthcare personnel have a lacklustre attitude towards the health problem and are not adequately motivated to serve in slums and other unorganized pockets. The issues such as accountability, punctuality and responsiveness towards the patients have been complained by many beneficiaries. There is also a lack of proper monitoring mechanism of healthcare institutions and personnel.
6. *Health planning and management:* The nation states do not have comprehensive health policy, which needs to clearly spell out the planning and management of urban healthcare system. The poor urban health planning and management has led to poor performance of health sector in the urban areas. As the health needs of the urban area population are different from those of the rural areas, separate planning for urban areas is required.

Moreover, as three parallel healthcare delivery systems run in urban areas—one by the municipal government, one by the concerned state and the other by the central government—proper planning and management are required to do away with overlapping. On World Health Day, 7 April 2010, WHO launched a campaign to highlight urban planning as a crucial link to building a healthy 21st century. It highlighted the following five actions which will significantly increase the chances of people enjoying better urban living conditions:

a) Promote urban planning for healthy behaviours and safety
b) Improve urban living conditions
c) Ensure participatory governance
d) Build inclusive cities that are accessible and age friendly
e) Make cities resilient to disasters and emergencies[30]

7. *Healthcare of the disadvantaged and urban slum population:* Last but not least, promoting healthcare of the disadvantaged sections, largely staying in urban slums, is a big challenge in the cities. It is remarked that the increase in proportion of urban poor and vulnerable groups including slum populations, their financial instability and predisposition to slip BPL on account of medical expenditures is well known. Living and working in the harsh and hazardous urban environment, often as 'illegal' occupants of the urban space, the urban poor are in fact more vulnerable than their rural counterparts.[31] Several innovative attempts by the government, NGOs and private sector are being made by opening mohalla clinic and mobile health clinic in order to provide healthcare and medical services to these disadvantaged sections of urban population. However, despite these endeavours with rapid urbanization and migration of rural poor to urban areas, it will always remain a challenge for the government.

Measures to Promote Urban Health

With rapid urbanization, majority of the world's population is now living in urban areas and this proportion is expected to grow. This is largely due to uninterrupted migration of poor and impoverished population from rural areas to urban areas. This is putting pressure on limited resources in cities, especially in underdeveloped countries to spend on social services such as health and education. Urban health should become a major focus of global public health policy. Healthcare of the urban poor is critical to the healthcare of all urban population. Healthy urban population is sine qua non for the economic growth and development of the nation. According to WHO (2011), 'healthy urbanization' is defined as the process of 'enabling people to gain greater control over their health and their determinants through good urban governance that creates equal social opportunities for health for all'.

Some of the measures required to be taken for the improvement of the urban health status are as follows.

1. *Check unplanned urbanization:* The unplanned urbanization process particularly in the developing countries needs to be checked. The migration of rural population to the urban areas needs to be checked. The measure for the development of rural areas through comprehensive planning of PURA is needed. The Kerala model of rural–urban continuum will be helpful to defuse rural to urban migration.

2. *Strengthening primary healthcare services:* There is a need to strengthen the provision of primary healthcare services in the disadvantaged colonies of the urban areas. The urban areas not only need to largely focus on the tertiary healthcare but also on the primary healthcare in the urban slums. The mohalla clinic introduced in Delhi is one of such experiments aimed at fulfilling the primary and secondary healthcare needs of the people living in the slums and unorganized colonies.

Mohalla Clinic in Delhi

- *The idea:* To provide free healthcare services through a health facility within a walking distance (around 2–3 km radius or 10–15 min walking), open for at least 4–6 hours of every working day, assured availability of identified basic health services, medicines and diagnostic tests. Estimated 80–90 per cent of health problems are likely to get treated at this level reducing the number of patients in need of referral.
- *Population targeted:* Underserved, migrants, *jhuggi jhopri* colony; each clinic aims to serve approximately 10,000–15,000 population.
- *Services provision:* An assured package of health services includes outpatient consultations, basic first aid services, maternal and child health services including immunization, antenatal and postnatal services, family planning, counselling and referral to next level of facilities for specialized treatment. These clinics aim to implement national health programmes as well.
- *Specialist and referral services and continuum of care:* Specialists proposed to be available on weekly basis (paediatrician, gynaecologist and ophthalmologist). A system of referral through a tiered approach to health facilities has been proposed (though yet to be made fully functional).
- *Medicines and diagnostics:* Sufficient supplies of medicines and diagnostics, free of cost to the people availing these facilities, form an approved list of 108 medicines and provision of >200 diagnostic tests.
- *Location:* Migrant and poor population live in demarcated areas called slums and *jhuggi jhopri* colonies. First such clinic was established in North-West Delhi in *jhuggi jhopri* colony and was situated around 400 m walking distance from the main road, in the centre of *jhuggi jhopri* settlement. The locations are decided with inputs from local community/RWA/survey by planning branch/verification of sites by a team of health personnel.
- *Physical infrastructure and accessibility:* Proposed to be housed in two or three rooms. The rooms could be either made of prefabricated material (called portacabin) or in private houses with similar amenities. Of the rooms, one to be assigned to a doctor and for medical examination, sufficient enough to maintain privacy. The other or second room is used for laboratory functions, dispensing medicines and the waiting seat for next patient to be seen by doctor. If there is a third room available, it could be used as waiting room; else, the open space covered through a roof should be used as waiting area. The provision of drinking water dispenser and a washroom attached to these facilities. There has to be provision of air conditioning and television with cable connection as part of the design. These clinics to be located in areas easily accessible to beneficiaries, with an all-weather road, accessible by an ambulance and an open area.

3. *BCC:* BCC is critical to improve the health status of urban population. The change in food habits and lifestyle of the urban area people, particularly the adults and adolescents, will be helpful to control lifestyle-related diseases in the urban areas which are on the rise. Community-based maternal and new-born programmes should revise BCC interventions to strengthen inter personal communication using rigorously tested print materials as aids

and stand-alone media. Messages about birth preparedness, recognition of danger signs and immediate self-referral to biomedical health services should be carefully aligned and effectively delivered to women, men and older members of the community.[32]

4. *PPP:* Public sector alone cannot meet the health needs and health challenges of the cities and particularly the metropolitan cities. The private sector needs to be encouraged to play a role in provisioning healthcare services in urban areas. However, it is seen that these private hospitals in urban areas are charging exorbitant consultation fees and other services which have become beyond the reach of common men. A regulation mechanism needs to be developed for the operation of private sector in health sector by controlling their fees and other charges. It is recommended that PPP is more preferred in the urban areas of the developing countries in health sector rather than exclusive private sector with clearly defined role and responsibility. ADB has rightly remarked that in the absence of a strong regulatory environment, relying on the private sector raises issues of quality, accountability and reliability.[33]
5. *NGOs and CVOs:* The role of NGOs and CVOs is day by day increasing in urban areas particularly in education and health sector. NGOs instead of looking for fund from the government for implementing government-directed programmes, need to work based on needs of the urban areas. They should work towards raising awareness, improvement of health, drinking water and sanitation in urban slums. They also need to operate mobile clinics on maternal and child healthcare in urban slums. Researchers have commented that the role of NGOs as advocates for the urban poor also has diminished, as many were drawn into becoming implementers of government programmes. In effect, this increase in participation can be seen as a new form of centralization, strengthening the position of senior bureaucrats and bypassing the elected politicians.[34]
6. *Role of local self-government institutions:* In the decentralization process in both high-income and developing countries, the local self-government institutions in the urban areas have been assigned the duties and responsibilities of looking after the health. The proactive role of the municipalities and the Ward Sabha will improve community participation in sanitation, drinking water and availability of health services. The capacity building of the functionaries and elected representatives of the local self-government institutions on health and its related issues will improve the health status of urban population.
7. *Inter-sectoral coordination and convergence of action:* Inter-sectoral action for health refers to 'actions undertaken by sectors outside the health sector, possibly, but not necessarily, in collaboration with the health sector, on health or health equity outcomes or on the determinants of health or health equity' (PHAC & WHO, 2008). The health sector does not need to work in silos rather take the help of other related sectors such as education, public health, local self-government institutions and women and child development for the effective delivery of health services in the urban areas. It is rightly pointed out that another factor aggravating the poor health scenario of the urban slum population is lack of intra-sectoral and inter-sectoral coordination. Although there are a number of projects on water and sanitation, nutrition and maternal and child health that involve various stakeholders, including the government, NGOs and corporate and private sector organizations, they operate without any coordination and convergence.[35]
8. *Community participation:* The community participation is considered important in primary healthcare development and it results in positive health outcomes (Preston et al., 2010). According to WHO (2002),

> [C]ommunity participation is a process by which people are enabled to become actively and generally involved in defining the issues of concern to them, in making decisions about factors that affect their lives, in formulating and implementing policies, in planning, developing and delivery services and in taking action to achieve change. A participatory health development process involves relevant partners for health at all levels i.e. home, school, and worksite, local community and country—and that promotes joint decision-making, implementation and accountability.

The government health functionaries working in the primary health sector in the urban areas have to take the help of the community-level organization such as *mahila mandals*, youth club members, cooperative society members and any other community-level organizations for the effective implementation of healthcare services in the urban slum areas.

9. *Focus on unserved urban population:* The primary focus of the urban healthcare delivery system is to reach the unreachable and the people who are deprived of expert healthcare facilities. Therefore, the national health policy prioritizes addressing the primary healthcare needs of the urban population with special focus on poor populations living in listed and unlisted slums, other vulnerable populations such as homeless, rag pickers, street children, rickshaw pullers, construction workers, sex workers and temporary migrants.[36]

Summing Up

Education and healthcare are the two important social development indicators for both urban and rural areas. The development of education depends on the educational infrastructure and quality and trained teachers and good educational regulatory mechanism. GER and percentage of technical education to the total education are nowadays being considered as two important indicators of educational development. Customarily, cities are the hop of higher education in both developed and developing countries. Like education, healthcare is also another important indicator of social development of the nation states. Quality tertiary healthcare institutions and specialized healthcare institutions are found to be located in the cities. However, there is a saying that there exists darkness beneath the lamp. Likewise, in the cities of the developing countries the education and health status of the people staying in the urban slums are astoundingly low as compared to other city dwellers. The welfare state has to take adequate public measures to improve the education and health status of slum dwellers and other migrants staying on the pathways and temporary sheds in the cities. WHO calls on a wide range of groups—from municipal authorities and the private sector to concerned citizens, NGOs and advocates for healthy living—to take a close look at health inequities in cities and take action.[37] It is also noted that promoting health and confronting disease challenges require action across a range of activities in the health system. This includes improvements in the policymaking and stewardship role of governments, better access to human resources, drugs, medical equipment and consumables, and a greater engagement of both public and private providers of services.[38]

Keywords

Inclusive Education, Educational Deprivation, Two-track Education, Primary Healthcare, Community Participation, Inter-sectoral Coordination, Behavioural Change Communication

REVIEW QUESTIONS

1. Briefly explain the role of education in urban development.
2. Explain various issues and challenges of urban education.
3. Describe various features of urban education. How it differs from rural education?
4. Narrate various measures to be taken for the educational development of the cities.
5. Why urban healthcare is important for urban development? Explain.
6. What are the various determinants of urban health status?
7. Explain various issues and challenges of urban healthcare.
8. Suggest measures for how to improve the health status of urban population.

Notes

1. https://www.oecd.org/pisa/pisaproducts/pisainfocus/pisa%20in%20focus%20n28%20%28eng%29--FINAL.pdf (accessed on 2 January 2019).
2. https://www.oecd.org/pisa/pisaproducts/pisainfocus/pisa%20in%20focus%20n28%20%28eng%29--FINAL.pdf (accessed on 2 January 2019).
3. https://www.financialexpress.com/opinion/skill-india-why-there-is-a-gap-between-current-status-and-goals-explained/1520633/ (accessed on 16 June 2020).
4. http://www.uh.edu/education/research/jsshe/9-16-issue/white-urban-ed.pdf (accessed on 1 January 2019).
5. https://www.ncbi.nlm.nih.gov/pmc/articles/PMC5804745/ (accessed on 2 January 2019).
6. http://www.rtinetwork.org/learn/diversity/urban-school-challenges (accessed on 3 January 2019).
7. http://www.rtinetwork.org/learn/diversity/urban-school-challenges (accessed on 3 January 2019).
8. http://www.rtinetwork.org/learn/diversity/urban-school-challenges (accessed on 3 January 2019).
9. https://www.who.int/world-health-day/2010/media/whd2010background.pdf (accessed on 3 January 2019).
10. https://www.who.int/world-health-day/2010/media/whd2010background.pdf (accessed on 3 January 2019).
11. https://www.who.int/world-health-day/2010/media/whd2010background.pdf (accessed on 3 January 2019).
12. https://www.who.int/world-health-day/2010/media/whd2010background.pdf (accessed on 3 January 2019).
13. https://www.who.int/world-health-day/2010/media/whd2010background.pdf (accessed on 3 January 2019).
14. http://apps.searo.who.int/PDS_DOCS/B4682.pdf (accessed on 6 January 2019).
15. https://www.who.int/bulletin/volumes/88/4/10-010410/en/ (accessed on 3 January 2019).
16. https://www.who.int/bulletin/volumes/88/4/10-010410/en/ (accessed on 3 January 2019).
17. https://www.who.int/bulletin/volumes/88/4/10-010410/en/ (accessed on 3 January 2019).
18. https://www.downtoearth.org.in/news/lifestyle/lifestyle-diseases-change-in-nutrition-consumption-pattern-make-urban-india-unhealthy-58814 (accessed on 4 January 2019).
19. https://link.springer.com/article/10.1007/s11524-018-0228-8 (accessed on 4 January 2019).
20. https://www.who.int/hia/housing/en/ (accessed on 4 January 2018).
21. https://www.who.int/sustainable-development/cities/health-risks/water-sanitation/en/ (accessed on 5 January 2019).

22. https://www.who.int/sustainable-development/cities/health-risks/water-sanitation/en/ (accessed on 5 January 2019).
23. https://www.mhtf.org/2017/02/15/the-urban-disadvantage-rethinking-maternal-and-newborn-health-priorities/ (accessed on 5 January 2019).
24. https://www.who.int/sustainable-development/cities/health-risks/air-pollution/en/ (6 January 2019).
25. https://www.mdpi.com/2504-3900/2/20/1311/pdf (accessed on 25 November 2019).
26. http://apps.searo.who.int/PDS_DOCS/B4682.pdf (accessed on 6 January 2019).
27. http://siteresources.worldbank.org/HEALTHNUTRITIONANDPOPULATION/Resources/281627-1095698140167/Chap8DiderichsenRAforHlthEqtyFinal.pdf (accessed on 25 November 2019).
28. https://pdfs.semanticscholar.org/7390/1041848737dff423a2b89cacb6a2144db2b8.pdf (accessed on 6 January 2019).
29. https://pdfs.semanticscholar.org/7390/1041848737dff423a2b89cacb6a2144db2b8.pdf (accessed on 6 January 2019).
30. https://www.who.int/mediacentre/news/releases/2010/urban_health_20100407/en/ (accessed on 7 January 2019).
31. https://www.researchgate.net/publication/306267583_Urban_Health_in_India_Policies_Practices_and_Current_Challenges (accessed on 7 January 2019).
32. https://www.ncbi.nlm.nih.gov/pmc/articles/PMC4987986/ (accessed on 7 January 2019).
33. https://www.adb.org/sites/default/files/linked-documents/47354-003-ssa.pdf (accessed on 25 November 2019).
34. https://journals.sagepub.com/doi/full/10.1177/0956247811416433 (accessed on 7 January 2019).
35. http://www.ijcm.org.in/article.asp?issn=0970-0218;year=2011;volume=36;issue=1;spage=3;epage=7;aulast=Yadav (accessed on 25 November 2019).
36. http://nrhmchd.gov.in/sites/default/files/nuhm.pdf (accessed on 17 April 2020).
37. https://www.who.int/world-health-day/2010/media/whd2010background.pdf?ua=1 (accessed on 12 January 2019).
38. http://siteresources.worldbank.org/HEALTHNUTRITIONANDPOPULATION/Resources/281627-1095698140167/Chap8DiderichsenRAforHlthEqtyFinal.pdf (accessed on 25 November 2019).

References

Basta, S. S., Karyadi, D. & Scrimshaw, N. S. (1979). Iron deficiency anaemia and the productivity of adult males in Indonesia. *American Journal of Clinical Nutrition, 32*(4), 916–925.

Carlson, B. (1998). *Education at a glance: OECD indicator 1998 (Latin America).* ECLAC. https://repositorio.cepal.org/bitstream/handle/11362/19824/S9812929_en.pdf?sequence=1 (accessed on 16 April 2020).

Chen, B., & Feng, Y. (2000). Determinants of economic growth in China: Private enterprise, education and openness. *China Economic Review, 11*, 1–15.

Fasih, T. (2008). *Linking education policy to labor market outcomes.* The International Bank for Reconstruction and Development/The World Bank.

Gay, G. (2000). *Culturally responsive teaching: Theory, research, and practice.* Teachers College Press.

Howard, G. R. (2007). As diversity grows, so must we. *Educational Leadership, 64*(6), 16–22.

Jacobs, G., & Asokan, N. (2003). *Towards a knowledge society: final draft for the vision 2020 Committee.* https://www.mssresearch.org/?q=Towards_a_Knowledge_Society (accessed on 16 April 2020).

Joshi, P. (2017a). Education for people, prosperity and planet: Can we meet the sustainability challenges? *European Journal of Education, Research, Development and Policy, 52*(5), 399–403.

Joshi, P. (2017b). A perspective on education's importance for urban development. *European Journal of Education Research, Development and Policy, 52*(4), 399–562.

Kincheloe, J. L. (2010). Why a book on urban education? In S. Steinberg (Ed.), *19 urban questions: Teaching in the city* (2nd ed., pp. 1–28). Peter Lang Publishing.

Krueger, A., & Lindahl, M. (2001). Education and growth: why and for whom? *Journal of Economic Literature, 39*(4), 1101–1136. https://link.springer.com/article/10.1186/s40172-017-0061-4 (accessed on 16 April 2020).

Kumar, S., Kumar, S., & Gupta, B. (2018). Urban health: Needs urgent attention", *Indian Journal of Public Health, 62*(3), 214–217.

Ladson-Billings, G. (1994). *The dream-keepers: Successful teachers of African American children.* Jossey-Bass.

Levy, M. (1966). *Modernization and the structure of society.* Princeton University Press.

Marshall, A. (1961). *The principles of political economy.* Macmillan.

Mukherjee, J., & Banerjee, S. (2009). Education and health: Strategic sequencing in social development contemporary issues and ideas in social sciences. www.worldwewant2015.org/file/300184/download/325641 (accessed on 28 September 2013).

Preston, R., Waugh, H., Larkins, S., & Taylor, J. (2010). Community participation in rural primary health care: Interventions or approach? *Australian Journal of Primary Health, 16*(1), 4–16.

Public Health Agency of Canada, & World Health Organization. (2008). *Equity through intersectoral action: An analysis of 18 country case studies.* World Health Organization.

Schleicher, A. (2006). *The economics of knowledge: Why education is key for Europe's success.* Lisbon Council Policy Brief.

Srinivas, V., & Mankeshwar, R. (2015). Prevalence and determinants of nutritional anemia in an urban area among unmarried adolescents girls: A country-based cross-sectional study. *International Journal of Medicine and Public Health, 4*(5), 283–288.

Srivastava, K. (2009). Urbanization and mental health. *Industrial Psychiatry Journal, 18*(2, July–December), 75–76.

Steele, C. (2010). *Whistling Vivaldi: And other clues to how stereotypes affect us.* Norton.

Szirmai, A. (2006). *The dynamics of socio-economic development: An introduction.* Cambridge University Press.

Thyne, C. L. (2006). ABC's, 123's, and the golden rule: The pacifying effect of education on civil war 1980–1999. *International Studies Quarterly, 50*(4), 733–754.

UNESCO. (2002). *The 2002 global education for all monitoring report: Is the world on track?* UNESCO.

UNESCO. (2016). *Education for people and planet: Creating sustainable future for all, global education monitoring report 2016.* UNESCO.

UNDP. (2016). *Human development report 2016: Human development for Everyone.* UNDP.

Vaid, A., Mammen, A., Primrose, B., & Kang, G. (2007). Infant mortality in an urban slum. *Indian Journal of Pediatric, 74*(5), 449–453.

WHO. (2002). *Community participation in local health and sustainable development approaches and technique.* WHO.

WHO. (2010). *Why urban health matters.* World Health Organization. https://www.who.int/world-health-day/2010/media/whd2010background.pdf (accessed on 17 April 2020).

WHO. (2011). *Healthy regional framework for scaling up and expanding healthy cities in the Western Pacific 2011–2015.* World Health Organization. Also see http://www.wpro.who.int/health_promotion/healthy_urbanization_regional_framework_2011_2015.pdf (accessed on 4 January 2019).

World Bank. (2019). *World development indicators.* World Bank.

Yeravdekar, V. R., & Tiwari, G. (2014, November 27). Global rankings of higher education institutions and India's effective non-presence: Why have world-class universities eluded the Indian higher education system? And, how worthwhile is the Indian government's captivation to launch world universities? *Procedia-Social and Behvioural Sciences, 157*, 63–83.

Yogish, S. N. (2006). Education and economic development. *Indian Journal of Social Development, 6*(2), 255–270.

Zhang, L., Liu, S., Zhang, G., & Wu, S. (2015). Internal migration and health of the returned population: A nationally representative study of China. *BMC Public Health, 15*(1). https://www.ncbi.nlm.nih.gov/pmc/articles/PMC4517553/ (accessed on 16 April 2020).

10 Urban Heritage

Nowadays the role of cultural heritage is becoming unquestioned.

—CIVVIH (2012)

The principle of sustainable development provides for the preservation of existing resources, the active protection of urban heritage and its sustainable management is a condition sine qua non of development.

—UNESCO (2011b)

Increasingly, there is a general acknowledgement that cultural heritage plays a crucial role in the creation of a sustainable city as a vital non-renewable resource of cities, a catalyst for social cohesion, as an identity and creativity element, as an economic attractor for tourism revenues and as a mitigation factor for climate change.

—UNESCO (2014)

Culture will be key in the success of sustainable development policies, as driver and enabler of development and people-centered societies. A holistic and integrated approach to development needs to take creativity, heritage, knowledge and diversity into account. Poverty is not just a question of material conditions and income, but also of lack of capabilities and opportunities, including in cultural terms.[1]

Introduction

Urban heritage is one of the important dimensions of city development. Urban heritage plays an important role in depicting the role of history and culture of the city. It also tries to exhibit the importance of history and culture in the sustainable development of the city. Urban heritage is an important source of livelihood for millions of people since long in many countries of the world and more particularly in India. Preservation of urban heritage in the city not only attracts tourists from both within and outside the nation states but also significantly contributes towards the economic growth and development of the nation state. It promotes social connectivity and cultural integration. It strengthens beliefs and values of the people towards their cultural past, faith in history and religion. In a historic sense, urban areas play a fundamental role in the formation of local identity as place of memory, tradition, social values and as magnets for economic and creative activities (Bandarin & Van Oers, 2012). Urban conservation in a new way and with renewed tools appears clearly in order to 'better integrate and frame urban heritage conservation strategies within the larger goals of overall sustainable development' (UNESCO, 2011). It is one of the important means of national integration and international attraction. This chapter deals with urban heritage.

LEARNING OBJECTIVES

After reading this chapter, you should be able to:

- ❒ Define heritage and various types of heritage
- ❒ Describe the importance of heritage to the development of the nation
- ❒ Explain various issues and challenges related to the conservation and management of heritage
- ❒ Suggest measures for the effective conservation and management of urban heritage

Urban Heritage: Meaning and Types Heritage

Heritage is a historical monument or imprint which has significance even today from the social, cultural and human and development perspectives. The *Cambridge Dictionary* defines heritage as features belonging to the culture of a particular society, such as traditions, languages or buildings, that were created in the past and still have historical importance.[2] *Larousse Dictionary* defines heritage as the common goods of a collectivity (community or social group), while *Oxford Dictionary* perceives it as works of art and cultural achievements that have been passed on from earlier generations.[3] Another definition goes like this, 'By the term "heritage" we mean all kinds of natural and cultural goods, tangible or intangible which have a historic, symbolic or aesthetic meaning'.[4] Susan Tonkin from the standpoint of Australia has noted that[5]:

> Heritage and culture are at the heart of community identity. They define how we as a people view ourselves and our place in the world and how we define and respect each other. The engagement with heritage places, stories and cultural activities enables Australians to feel confident about their national and local identity, better understand the different cultures, races and ethnicities that have shaped communities, and face a changing future with hope and optimism.

Etymologically, urban 'heritage' means what a city has inherited from the past or history, which it can be proud of and can showcase to the nation and to the world for which it is famous. The Habitat III Issue Papers have envisaged that the urban heritage represents a social, cultural and economic asset and resource reflecting the dynamic historical layering of values that have been developed, interpreted and transmitted by successive generations and an accumulation of traditions and experiences recognized as such in their diversity. Urban heritage comprises urban elements (urban morphology and built form, open and green spaces, urban infrastructure), architectural elements (monuments, buildings) and intangible elements.[6] There are several cities in India which are known for its heritage such as Agra in Uttar Pradesh for the Taj Mahal, Amritsar in Punjab for the Golden Temple and many palaces in Jaipur, Rajasthan. Some of the important heritage sites recognized by UNESCO are:

1. City of Angkor, Cambodia
2. Acropolis of Athens, Greece
3. Machu Picchu, Peru
4. Mount Kilimanjaro, Tanzania
5. Sigiriya, Sri Lanka
6. Cinque Terre, Italy
7. Kinkaku-ji Temple, Japan

It is very difficult to precisely identify and classify the types and scope of heritage. However, many charters, principles, recommendations and other agreements have tried carefully to define the scope of heritage and its types. The scope has broadened considerably from mere concern for individual buildings and sites to include groups of buildings, historical areas, towns, environments, social factors and, lately, intangible heritage. Broadly, both UNESCO and the International Council on Monuments and Sites agreed in principle that the scope of heritage should cover both cultural and natural heritage. Australia refers to its heritage as 'place, cultural significance and fabric', Canada refers to 'material culture, geographic environments and human environments', New Zealand to 'place' and China to 'immovable physical remains' to name a few.[7] According to Steinberg (1996), when we want to define 'urban heritage', what comes to the mind of most urban planners and managers are usually 'monuments', that is, churches, temples, all sorts of religious buildings, palaces, castles, fortresses, historic city walls and gates and other types of institutional buildings (e.g., of education, science, administration or other social purposes). Various countries have tried to define and determine the scope of heritage in their own way. However, some common international standard and parameters are being used by the international agencies to classify heritage.

From the above discussions it is amply clear that there are four types of heritage sites: cultural, natural, built and mixed.

1. *Cultural heritage:* Cultural heritage sites include hundreds of historic buildings and town sites, important archaeological sites and works of monumental sculpture or painting. Cultural heritage was defined by UNESCO in 1972 as follows.
   a. *Monuments:* Architectural works, works of monumental sculpture and painting, elements or structures of an archaeological nature, inscriptions, cave dwellings and combinations of features, which are of outstanding universal value from the point of view of history, art or science.
   b. *Groups of buildings:* Groups of separate or connected buildings which, because of their architecture, their homogeneity or their place in the landscape, are of outstanding universal value from the point of view of history, art or science.
   c. *Sites:* Works of man or the combined works of nature and of man, and areas including archaeological sites, which are of outstanding universal value from the historical, aesthetic, ethnological or anthropological points of view.[8]

   The cultural heritage can be further expanded as: (a) archaeological heritage, (b) art galleries, (c) theatres, (d) museums and (e) memorials.
2. *Natural heritage:* Heritage refers to those valuable places and sights that have come to us from yesterday, we have to maintain it today and pass it on to the future generation,

who can pride themselves on their past. The natural heritage refers to important natural resources having natural values such as forests, waterfalls, bio-diversity parks, lakes and lagoons, wetlands, water bodies and so on. The natural heritage is vital from the perspectives of environment and ecology. Natural heritage sites are restricted to those natural areas that (a) furnish outstanding examples of Earth's record of life or its geologic processes, (b) provide excellent examples of ongoing ecological and biological evolutionary processes, (c) contain natural phenomena that are rare, unique, superlative or of outstanding beauty or (d) furnish habitats for rare or endangered animals or plants or are sites of exceptional biodiversity.[9] Healthy natural heritage is critical for preserving and building local environmental resilience and helps to adapt to climate change.

The natural heritage can be further classified into the following categories: (a) geological heritage, (b) botanical heritage, (c) biological heritage and (d) zoological heritage.

3. *Built heritage:* The built heritage consists of historical homes, institutions, monuments, gardens and industrial sites and other historical buildings. This can be further categorized as institutional heritage and industrial heritage.
4. *Mixed heritage:* Mixed heritage sites contain elements of both natural, cultural and built heritage.

Some of the widely recognized urban heritage are as follows:

1. Palaces and buildings having historical and cultural importance
2. Places of religious importance: temples, churches, mosques, gurudwaras and so on
3. Monuments
4. Caves
5. Statues
6. National parks
7. Lakes and water bodies
8. Waterfalls
9. Wildlife sanctuaries
10. Ancient historical cities
11. Forests
12. Ancient complexes
13. Archaeological sites
14. Rock-art sites
15. Art galleries
16. Classical gardens
17. Historical forts
18. Cultural landscapes
19. Memorials
20. Old city walls
21. Heritage in the event of armed conflict

These are some broad categories; however, the heritage sites vary from one country to the other depending on their place of historical and cultural importance. The number of world heritage sites by region is given in Table 10.1 while ten important heritage sites in India are given in Table 10.2.

Table 10.1 Number of World Heritage Sites by Region

Regions	Cultural	Natural	Mixed
Africa	53	38	5
Arab States	78	5	3
Asia and the Pacific	189	67	12
Europe and North America	453	65	11
Latin America and the Caribbean	96	38	8
Total	869	213	39

Source: https://whc.unesco.org/en/list/stat/ (accessed on 26 March 2020).

Table 10.2 Ten Important Heritage Sites in India

Name of the Sites	State
Taj Mahal	Uttar Pradesh
Qutab Minar	Delhi
Sun Temple	Odisha
Khajuraho	Madhya Pradesh
Mahabodhi Temple	Bihar
Kaziranga national Park	Assam
Chola Temple	Tamil Nadu
Ajanta Caves	Maharastra
Fatehpur Sikri	Uttar Pradesh
Mahabalipuram	Tamil Nadu

Role and Importance of Heritage in Urban Development

Urban heritage contributes towards the economic, social, cultural and human development of the cities. Many of the cities of the West have encashed the rich dividend of the urban heritage. The developing nation states have to invest for the rejuvenation of heritage places of their cities. It is remarked that urban conservation in its broader term is preserving the traditional, social and cultural aspects, as well as the physical improvement of historic buildings is often witnessed as an approach towards higher levels of sustainability (Elnokaly & Elseragy, 2013). According to Throsby (2002), a heritage has the following values.

1. *Historical value:* A connection with the past.
2. *Symbolic value:* Objects as repositories or conveyors of meaning.
3. *Aesthetic value:* Connection with others or a sense of identity.
4. *Spiritual value:* Understanding, enlightenment or insight.
5. *Social value:* Connections with others or a sense of identity.

Some of the important roles of heritage towards the economic growth and development of the cities are narrated as follows.

1. *Contributes towards economic growth:* A heritage site enables the city to contribute to the income of the state as well as that of the nation. It is said that cultural heritage assets represent an essential resource for sustainable human development, economic growth and job creation and their protection is not only a moral call but also a necessary financial investment to progress towards the creation of inclusive and sustainable cities (Angrisano et al., 2016; Girard, 2013). The UN-Habitat II document has envisaged that the volume of world trade of creative goods and services has doubled between 2002 and 2011, reaching $624 billion. Exports of creative goods in developing countries grew 12.1 per cent annually on average over this period. Cultural industries account for a growing portion of urban jobs, representing 16 per cent of all jobs in Mumbai or 12 per cent in London.[10]
2. *Promotes tourism:* Tourism is considered a cultural phenomenon since tourists seek to know the characteristics of the area of destination from historical, cultural and environmental perspectives. Customarily, tourists are largely interested to see heritage places. Tourist flow to the heritage places creates infrastructure such as roads, hospitals and hotels and opens employment opportunities for the local people. Many countries have cherished and revived parts of the archaeological sites, museums, old cities, traditional handicrafts and cultural events in order to boost cultural tourism (Dweik, 2014).
3. *Promote social development:* Urban heritage in the real sense is the social capital of a city. It promotes national and international networking among the people of nation states and also with other countries. People not just see and enjoy the heritage and culture but also if motivated, practise and propagate. Many foreign tourists visiting various religious places in India are found to be engaged in social networking and developing contacts, which promotes brotherhood among the nations. Heritage promotes social networking and understanding. UN-Habitat III believes that the cultural infrastructures such as museums can offer civic spaces for intercultural dialogue and knowledge sharing and contribute to social cohesion and mutual understanding.[11]
4. *Heritage helps to promote human development:* Culture is integral to human development. Culture is the fabric for the dynamic construction of individual and collective identities. The active participation of people in local cultural activities (such as poetry, dance, sculpture, theatre and music) improves their quality of life and well-being and enhances life opportunities and options. Local cultures encompass the traditional, long-standing and evolving cultures of a territory as well as the cultures of new arrivals to the area—and the evolutionary and hybrid transformations that evolve from creating and living within culturally diverse contexts. Local cultural vitality and its dynamic transmission and growth are desirable ends in themselves.
5. *Promotes nationalism and national unity:* To this extent, conservation of both tangible and intangible heritage is a peace-building process (UNESCO, 2017). Heritage sites are the places which integrate people of the nation states. They get to know each other and their culture such as language, dress code, food habits and festivals. It is one of the cheapest sources to promote non-violent national integration and promote nationalism in an easy way. It is being remarked that the national museum in Europe has the capacity to create and reinforce concepts such as social cohesion, unity, mutual understanding and tolerance among nations and cultures of Europe.[12]
6. *Promotes inclusive development:* Heritage in rural as well as urban areas and particularly in urban areas promotes inclusive development. The people irrespective of caste, class,

religion and ethnicity visit the heritage sites. It is a place for cultural convergence and inclusive development. Nobody is excluded or denied a visit to heritage sites and everybody takes keen interest in seeing those places. The World Bank, Cities Alliance, at the request of GoI in 2011, is implementing a phased Inclusive Heritage Based City Development Programme in India. This is to contribute towards filling the knowledge and application gaps for integrating cultural heritage management with city development.[13] The World Heritage Convention intends that the states parties should commit to and implement policies, interventions and practices of conservation and management in and around world heritage properties that achieve the following for all stakeholders, and in particular, for local communities: (a) improve the ability, opportunities and dignity of all, irrespective of age, sex, disability, ethnicity, origin, religion or economic or other status and (b) promote equity, reduce social and economic inequalities and reduce exclusion of all, irrespective of age, sex, disability, ethnicity, origin, religion or economic or other status.[14]

7. *Promotes sustainable development:* Heritage promotes sustainable development. It integrates three components of sustainable development such as environment, society and economy for the national development. The World Heritage Convention has rightly envisaged that: (a) it intends to promote environmental sustainability, by valuing and conserving places of outstanding natural heritage value, containing exceptional biodiversity, geo-diversity or other exceptional natural features, which are essential for human well-being; (b) it intends to promote respect and equity of all stakeholders, including local and concerned communities and indigenous peoples, together with a commitment to gender equality, as a fundamental premise for inclusive social development; and (c) as far as economy is concerned, it intends to promote sustainable forms of inclusive and equitable economic development, productive and decent employment and income-generating activities for all. It intends to offer great potential to alleviate poverty and enhance sustainable livelihoods of local communities, including those of marginalized populations.[15]
8. *Heritage propagates national identity:* Heritage projects the image of a nation in the world portal. Heritage is the mirror through which a nation sees its face. It is rightly mentioned that the construction of a national heritage is an important part of nation-building, and historic buildings and monuments can be powerful symbols of nation's aspirations and identity (Light & Dumbraveanu-Andone, 2007). A. O. Altwaijri in his work 'Heritage and Identity' has envisaged,

   > It should first be noted that there is a strong correlation between heritage and identity. They cannot exist in isolation from one another, both being constituent elements of the self and integral parts of individuals and communities. Every nation has its own heritage and distinctive cultural identity of which they are either mindful or oblivious.[16]

Issues and Challenges of Preservation and Conservation of Urban Heritage

Historically and today, heritage sites and landscapes in the city have faced neglect, or worse, demolition in the absence of local mechanisms that can identify, designate, preserve and protect them.[17]

1. *Financial crunch:* Availability of limited financial resources to local government agencies is being identified as a key problem in the preservation and maintenance of urban heritage. All

the forms of government, be it local self-government, state or central government, they give little priority and allocate scanty finance to the urban heritage preservation and maintenance.

2. *Lack of political will:* Political interference in the work of implementation agencies is also a problem in many developing countries. Moreover, there is a fight between the local self-government, state government and the central government over the jurisdiction of the preservation and maintenance of the urban heritage. Local governments also lack authority to enforce rules and carry out conservation projects.
3. *Disaster risks to urban heritage:* Historic urban areas are becoming increasingly vulnerable to natural as well as man-made hazards such as earthquakes, floods, fires, cyclones and vandalism. In the absence of any comprehensive legal framework for protection, historic urban areas are vulnerable not only to impending disasters but also during emergency and post-disaster recovery phases (Jigyansu, 2016). The agencies both internal and external involved in disaster management took little interest in the preservation and maintenance of disaster risks during various phases of disaster, such as the pre-disaster, during disaster and post-disaster stages.
4. *Rapid urbanization:* Rapid urbanization and migration of rural people to urban areas pose challenge to urban heritage. It is remarked that the heritage legacies are facing intensive pressures rising mainly due to rapid urbanization; a notion resulted from population growth and rural migrant's influx.[18] The government of the developing countries assign more importance to meet the basic needs and other infrastructural provisioning, while giving least importance to the preservation and maintenance of heritage. Patrizia Riganti has remarked that the current upwardly urbanization trends cause an excessive pressure on Indian cities' fragile cultural heritage, which is prone to irreversible damage and ultimate loss.[19]
5. *Environment and climate change:* In recent years, the built-in heritage and natural heritage are vulnerable to environmental risks and climate change. It is remarked that as a consequence of the ever-changing environmental and economic climate, heritage sites may currently be exposed to a greater risk from various threats than ever before in history (Croft, 2013). It is also commented that the climate change severely impacts cultural heritage leading to irreversible damage and losses because of its age and fragility.[20]
6. *War and armed conflict:* Many past histories have recorded that how the external invasion and armed conflict have affected the heritage. It outlined that the protection of world heritage and culture from human-induced threats, like armed conflict, should be a priority at both national and international levels, and further underlined that these sites require safeguarding and treating with the utmost respect.[21]
7. *Globalization and uninterrupted tourism:* Globalization and uninterrupted tourism are also a big issue and challenge for the conservation and management of urban heritage. The authority hardly finds space to carry out maintenance activities of the built heritage which leads to their further deterioration. It is remarked that often coming alongside tourism, development is another threat to historic sites.[22]
8. *Modernity:* The process of modernization has diminished the significance of heritage. There is a general lack of interest towards heritage and its values. Citing the case of Nepal, Mateo (2014) has remarked that cultural heritage is threatened by the fast urbanization and modernization happening in recent decades.
9. *Deficiency in community participation:* Community participation plays an important role in the conservation and preservation of heritage in their local areas. Cooperation of the

community-level organizations such as youth club, *mahila mandals* and opinion leaders are crucial for generation of moral and financial support for the preservation of heritage sites. Wong (2018) was of the view that there is an increasing social demand that local communities should be included in the decision-making process in heritage management.

10. *Poor PPP:* PPP is very vital for the sustainable preservation and conservation of urban heritage. However, it is seen that in most of the countries there is lack of PPP with regards to the preservation and conservation of urban heritage. The corporate sector under CSR needs to invest in the conservation and preservation of urban heritage, however, it is not seen. Cheong and Macdonald (2014) were of the view that the conservation of cultural heritage requires the involvement of multiple actors from across the public, private and non-government sectors, not only to initiate and carry out conservation but also to sustain the heritage place after the intervention.

Measures for the Conservation and Management of Urban Heritage

Heritage conservation is important for identifying, recording, analysing and protecting heritage and cultural resources. Conservation of heritage buildings is an important tool in city development, which can be seen in some cities in the world. It plays an important role to define the landmark within the heritage area as well as to generate economic returns and to support the tourism industry.[23] Elias considers that conservation is a set of procedures, which guarantees the protection of the architectural and historical characteristics of the important old areas and buildings, such as repairing, removing erosion and sedimentation signs, and securing acceptable standards for the protection of open spaces and squares.[24] Preserving the world's cultural heritage for the enrichment and education of present and future generations is one of the responsible tasks of the nation states. Heritages are the placards that glorify the identity of nation states. It is rightly remarked that urban heritage preservation and development activities must become part of a larger urban rehabilitation process that tackle not only the historic preservation problem posed by the heritage sites and buildings but also the larger issue of turning the urban area that contains the heritage into a fully functional and developed portion of the city (Rojas, 2007).

Some of the measures that the countries have to take for the conservation and management of heritage are given as follows:

1. The government of various nations and its states have to do a sincere exercise on heritage mapping. Heritage mapping is a set of activities and processes for exploring, discovering, documenting, examining, analysing, interpreting, presenting and sharing information related to various heritage existing in various places of the states. Moreover, it has also to map the people, communities, societies and material products and practices associated with the management of heritages in various places. Heritage mapping will make the endeavour easy for the government to plan, execute various heritage management strategies and promotion of heritage tourism in a systematic manner.
2. At the outset, the role of various levels of government have to be clearly defined while assigning them the task of preservation and management of heritages. Moreover, the role of various departments has to be also demarcated while assigning duties and responsibility to them. It is rightly suggested that the key to success is a strong, centralized governance

framework, with skilled heritage professionals as well as other urban experts who understand the role of heritage conservation and an informed, engaged citizenry (UNESCO, 2011).

3. The nation state has to formulate appropriate legislation for the preservation and conservation of heritage. For example, the Jammu and Kashmir Heritage Conservation and Preservation Act, 2010 aims to provide for conservation and preservation of heritage both tangible and intangible, including buildings, structures, monuments, precincts, areas/sites, artefacts, sculptures, paintings, handicrafts, manuscripts, music, dance, drama, performing arts and poetry, living traditions such as crafts and cuisine, traditional knowledge systems, folklores, spiritual traditions, respectively, of historic or cultural or religious or aesthetic or architectural or environmental significance and for matters connected therewith or incidental thereto.[25]
4. Involvement of local community and local-level organizations such as youth club, *mahila mandals*, cooperative societies, municipalities and village Panchayati Raj institutions in the preservation and management of heritage will be more effective rather than outside agencies. The government should promote community participation for the conservation and management of heritage. UNESCO (2011a) has rightly envisaged that 'the involvement of inhabitants and local people is indispensable and can endure through political cycles. Successful conservation is a result of simultaneous top-down and bottom-up support. Building long-term support for heritage and its conservation is critical'.
5. Involvement of private and corporate sectors in the conservation and maintenance of the heritage is being encouraged by a few countries. The role of government and the privates sector has to be clearly demarcated while doing so. Susan Macdonald viewed that the conservation of cultural heritage requires an interdisciplinary approach with the involvement of multiple players across the public, private and non-government sectors, not only to initiate and carry out conservation but also to sustain the place.[26] According to Rojas (2007), the success of urban heritage conservation efforts through PPP depends on the efficient allocation of costs, benefits and risks among the participants who are best suited to assume them or have the greatest interest in taking them given the potential returns: profits in the case of real estate investors, better relations with the community in the case of private philanthropies and votes in the case of elected officials.
6. The role of NGOs and PVOs has to be promoted in the conservation and maintenance of heritage. The NGOs can better involve the community in the process of raising awareness about the need and importance of the conservation of heritages.
7. The attitudes of the politician, bureaucrats, planners and policymakers have to be changed towards the role and importance of heritage in the economic growth and development of the nation states. They have to allocate necessary funds for the preservation and maintenance of urban heritage.
8. The nation state has to take adequate steps to check unbridled urbanization particularly in the heritage cities. The country should formulate its 'national heritage policy' which should clearly delineate the vision, mission and actions on the heritage conservation and management.
9. The urban development plan and policy document of the nation state need to have a separate section on national heritage, which may find a place in the service sector chapter of the document. Unless and until the role and importance of urban heritage find a place in the plan and policy documents, its conservation and management programmes will not be taken seriously and would not be adequately promoted.
10. For the effective propagation of a heritage city, the government has to promote information education and communication programme. A national guidebook on national heritage has

to be published and be placed in the social media so that everybody can access and get knowledge about the heritage sites.

11. Appropriate monitoring and management strategies have to be developed for the sustainable management of urban heritage. The built heritages have to be monitored by a group of experts consisting of multi-disciplinary backgrounds, that is, architectures, engineers, social scientists and so on. Corrective measures must be taken from time to time so that these heritages do not deteriorate.
12. In the preservation and promotion of the religious heritage cities, the government can take the help of religious organizations. These organizations are well trained and for centuries have been involved in the management and monitoring of various activities. One of the illustrious examples is the Shiromani Gurudwara Prabandhak Committee (SGPC). The Sikh Gurdwara Act, 1925, enables the SGPC to control all the historical gurdwaras as well as gurdwaras under Section 87 of this Act. The type and dynamics of involvement can vary from one state to the other.
13. The country needs to promote research in heritage and its management. The National Research Institute on Heritage has to be created in order to promote research, education and training in heritage. The interdisciplinary research will take into account the historical, cultural, built-in, architectural, planning aspects of heritage.
14. Last but not the least, a group of well-trained engineers and builders and masons should be identified for the maintenance of built heritages. As far as non-tangible heritage is concerned, time-to-time fairs, seminars, workshops for their protection and preservation have to be conducted. An interdisciplinary approach consisting of social scientists, scientists, engineers, architectures is needed for the preservation and conservation of heritage.

System Approach to Development of Sustainable and Smart Heritage Cities

Various steps of the system approach to development of sustainable and smart heritage city are as follows:

Step I: At the outset, there is a need to understand the value and importance of preserving and conserving local heritage.
Step II: The second step is to identify these heritage assets and classify them as cultural, natural, historical, religious and other heritage assets.
Step III: Defining the role and purpose of heritage conservation concerning the type of heritage. Then addressing the issues related to the governance, finance, infrastructure, technology, IEC, community participation and other related aspects relating to the sustainable conservation of the heritage. Feilden (1982) identified seven degrees of intervention arguing that the minimum the intervention the better is the conservation. These terms are prevention of decay, preservation, consolidation, restoration, rehabilitation, reproduction and reconstruction.
Step IV: Identification of risks, challenges or barriers facing heritage conservation.
Step V: Identifying and defining the role and responsibility of various stakeholders, that is, multilateral and bilateral agencies, government, private, corporate, NGOs, community and so on, and any other in terms of contributing in cash, kind and manpower in heritage conservation.
Step VI: Initiating actions in various areas of heritage conservation, that is, infrastructure development, renovation, beautification, need-based business activities, hotels and restaurant and rest houses, communication network, publicity, tourism promotion and so on.

Step VII: Monitoring and evaluation of conservation activities and taking remedial measures.
Step VIII: The final product is to develop a smart heritage city taking into consideration various features of smart city.

Aspects Related to Urban Heritage Rehabilitation and Management

A few important aspects for which conservation and preservation of urban heritage are vital are discussed as follows.

1. *Political aspects:* For undertaking rehabilitation and conservation of urban heritages, there is a need for political support. Formulation of appropriate policy by the parliament and assemblies on conservation and rehabilitation and allocation of resources for its implementation requires political support and will power. The lack of adequate consistency of political support and resources strongly affects the interpretation of heritage policies and the allocation of resources for heritage management.[27]
2. *Administrative aspects:* The administrative machinery situated at various levels need to actively support the rehabilitation process. Without active support of the executives, heritage conservation and rehabilitation cannot take place effectively and efficiently. Adelino Goncalves was of the view that the central argument in the safeguard of urban scale heritage is mainly a question of urban management and urban planning, which necessarily implies a framework that results from conciliation among the culture and the land-use administrations.[28]
3. *Cultural aspects:* The heritage is a cultural pride of the nation states. The historic buildings, houses, monuments and so on situated in the nation states strengthen their cultural supremacy and their tradition and indigenous culture outside. Therefore, cultural consideration occupies an important place in heritage conservation. UNESCO has noted that culture has the power to make cities more prosperous, safer and sustainable and protection and promotion of culture and heritage can benefit cities.[29]
4. Social aspects: The community feels proud of its cultural heritage and monuments. They actively participate in the conservation and rehabilitation process. The social issues are critical to rehabilitation and conservation of urban heritage. It is recognized that a heritage resource contributes to enhancing contemporary social interaction in a community (Feilden & Jokilehto, 1998). However, a clear understanding of the social factors which contribute to successful heritage conservation in urban renewal is still lacking (Yung et al., 2017).
5. *Economic aspects:* The economic aspect customarily covers the financing of urban heritage rehabilitation and management; PPP with modalities of cooperation and collaboration; and anticipated revenue and income from the heritage tourism after the rehabilitation. The cost-benefit analysis and social and cultural impact assessment would be helpful for project funding for the rehabilitation of the heritage from the national as well as international agencies. A book on economic evaluation of urban heritage has rightly mentioned that today, development actors see urban heritage as a resource for their territory, which is why they need to define its economic value. This evaluation is a delicate exercise as such patrimony is generally a complex reality, consisting of four interdependent dimensions, that is, economic, cultural, social and environmental.[30] Further, T. Baycan and L. F. Girard in their article 'Heritage in Socioeconomic Development: Direct and Indirect Impact' have envisaged

that cultural heritage constitutes an essential engine for economic development. The possibility to generate income from cultural assets creates employment, reduces poverty, stimulates enterprise development, fosters private investment and generates resources for environmental and cultural conservation.[31]

6. *Tourism aspects:* Heritage tourism is one of the vital aspects that substantiates the need for conservation and preservation of heritage both in urban and rural areas. Tourism in heritage places not only promotes the feeling of brotherhood but also generates income and employment opportunities for the local people. Heritage is one of the vital sources of livelihood for many people both in developed and developing countries. Graham Brooks was of the view that the enormous potential for the world's heritage resources combined with well-managed 'tourism' to be a major driver for the intellectual, emotional, moral and spiritual 'development' of the communities that sustain that heritage.[32]
7. *Environmental aspects:* The urban heritage needs to take into consideration the environmental aspects. The impact of rehabilitation of the cultural and built-in heritage on the city environment needs to be assessed. In other words, impact of rehabilitation of heritage on human beings, fauna and flora; on the soil, water, air, climate and the landscape; and atmospheric pollution. The European Commission has rightly remarked that in a world where the climate is changing, our heritage will be faced with a range of new pressures that are quite different to those experienced in the past.[33]
8. *Entrepreneurial aspects:* There is need to promote heritage entrepreneurship for the conservation and effective utilization of heritage building into tourist spots and commercial purposes keeping its cultural heritage value intact. Some of the important requirements of effective entrepreneurship are access to finance, technology and research and development, entrepreneurial capability, market conditions, regulatory framework and heritage entrepreneurial attitude and culture. The government of the nation state needs to encourage students of architecture and urban planning to take up start-up programmes on heritage rehabilitation. Moreover, internship on urban heritage will also motivate the students to pursue heritage rehabilitation as an entrepreneurial carrier. The heritage entrepreneurship of Ahmedabad city is given in Box 10.1.

Box 10.1 Heritage Entrepreneur: A Case Study, Ahmedabad

Rajiv Patel, a member of a renowned family of realtors, has been diversifying his enterprise from modern economy to heritage economy and has developed some of these edifices into heritage hotels, stay-homes and art galleries. One of these havelis, Diwanji ni Haveli, today serves as the office of the City Conservation Project with provision for holding classes, displaying art and holding audio-visual shows. The centre organizes a 'Heritage Walk' into the old city, which begins with a sumptuous Gujarati breakfast. The programmes now yield enough for the heritage structures to be economically viable projects, which justify the expenditure incurred on their restoration, conservation and maintenance.

Similarly, the haveli of Seth Mangaldas Giridhardas, a textile baron, was restored and converted into a heritage hotel named 'House of MG' in 2008. The haveli built in 1924 had iconic moments in history and had hosted even Mahatma Gandhi for a couple of days. Following the success of the two ventures, many such properties are being coveted by heritage entrepreneurs.

Source: https://www.thehindu.com/life-and-style/homes-and-gardens/preserving-urban-heritage/article23457105.ece (accessed on 1 October 2019).

Smart and Sustainable Heritage City

The 'smart city' concept dates from the 1990s when academics and scientific experts initiated an effort to merge ICT, cognitive maps, global cities and the network society (Castells, 1996; Sassen, 2001). The six major factors identified by Giffinger et al. (2007) for the 'smartness' of city are as follows: mobility, economy, governance, environment, living and people. Many cities in different countries of the world have immense potential of heritage, which can be developed and a few of them can be developed into smart heritage cities. It will not only attract both internal and external tourists to the cities but also provide livelihood, income and employment opportunities to the local people. As cultural development is one of the important components of the holistic development, therefore, the significance of the heritage cities to the economic growth and development of a nation state cannot be underestimated. However, a study has revealed that cultural heritage is not systematically exploited and formally incorporated in smart city initiatives, despite the fact that it offers an array of opportunities for smart city development, while significant technological advancements have taken place in the cultural heritage domain in recent years as well (Angelidous et al., 2017).

Some of the essential requirements of the smart heritage cities are as follows:

1. *Smart infrastructure:* A smart heritage city needs to have smart infrastructure such as roads, sanitation, electricity, water supply, shopping complexes, parks, recreation centres, hotels and smart airports.
2. *Smart governance:* A smart city needs to have smart governance and there is law and order, and smart safety and security systems. The administrative system in the heritage city follows smart governance principles and provides prompt and hassle-free services to the visitors and tourists. Moreover, there is a need for appropriate participatory approaches to the governance of cultural heritage, involving public, private and civil society stakeholders and, whenever possible, enabling everyone in a community to be engaged in relevant decisions.[34]
3. *Smart e-governance:* A smart heritage city must have smart ICT facilities. It needs to have smart city website and Internet connectivity. Online booking of hotels, taxi services and attractive places must be available in the website.
4. *Smart environment:* A smart heritage city needs to have smart environment. It needs to take appropriate measures to check environmental pollution.
5. *Smart mobility:* Smart mobility is one of the key features of a smart heritage city. Smart mobility means smart traffic management, smart surface communication system, smart taxi and metro rail services, smart air communication system and so on. The world heritage city surveillance system using smart CCTV is a system that detects the movement around the monitoring area and then counts the number of tourists who enter and exit the word heritage city.[35]
6. *Smart PPP:* Smart PPP will be an add-on advantage to provide quality services in the heritage city. The opening of malls, hotels, hospitals, recreation centres and management of public spaces with PPP are essential requirements of a smart heritage city.
7. *Smart people and smart community participation:* People living in the heritage city need to be cooperative with the visitors and tourists and be courteous and should be honest and amiable. People and community-level organizations are responsible to keep the city clean and smart.
8. *Smart ULBs:* The urban municipality must be active, the functionaries and elected representatives of the municipality must be well trained in the management of city affairs.

9. *Smart entrepreneurship and businesses:* The entrepreneurs managing the businesses, guest houses, hotels, motels, resorts must be smart and show entrepreneurial quality. More number of women entrepreneurs must be trained in the management of home guesthouses.
10. *Inclusive and gender sensitive:* Last but not least, the heritage city needs to be inclusive and gender sensitive. Women must feel secured and must be well trained to run the city affair. There should not be any discrimination in the heritage city on the basis of caste, class, ethnicity, gender, religion and so on.

Summing Up

'Heritage is our legacy from the past, what we live with today, and what we pass on to future generations. Our cultural and natural heritages are both irreplaceable sources of life and inspiration'. UNESCO defines a world heritage site as 'a place of outstanding universal value and belonging to all the peoples of the world, irrespective of the territory on which they are located'.[36] Heritage is not limited in time. In fact, the historical works of intellectuals, scientists, scholars, philosophers, poets, historians and authors in various fields of knowledge are intellectual, cultural and scientific heritage. Thus, heritage lives in our minds, hearts and souls and is part of our collective memory. It is not only the past but also the present and the future alike.[37] Heritage projects the image and identity of a nation state within and outside the nation. It attracts tourists and promotes cultural goods and services and helps to contribute towards the economic growth and development of the nation.

Keywords

Cultural Heritage, Natural Heritage, Mixed Heritage, Rehabilitation of Heritage, Heritage Entrepreneur

REVIEW QUESTIONS

1. What is urban heritage? Describe different types of urban heritage.
2. Explain the need and importance of urban heritage.
3. Describe various issues and challenges of urban heritage in urban development.
4. What factors are responsible for deterioration of urban heritage? Describe measures to be taken for the conservation and preservation of urban heritage.
5. Discuss the system approach to conservation and preservation of urban heritage.
6. Describe various aspects related to preservation and conservation of urban heritage.
7. Write short notes on the following:
   a. Smart and sustainable heritage
   b. Heritage entrepreneurship
   c. Cultural heritage
   d. Natural heritage
   e. Mixed heritage

Notes

1. http://www.agenda21culture.net/sites/default/files/files/documents/en/culture_sd_cities_web.pdf (accessed on 13 January 2019).
2. https://dictionary.cambridge.org/dictionary/english/heritage (accessed on 13 January 2019).
3. http://www.isocarp.net/Data/case_studies/2221.pdf (accessed on 13 January 2019).
4. http://www.isocarp.net/Data/case_studies/2221.pdf (accessed on 13 January 2019).
5. https://www.environment.gov.au/system/files/pages/f4d5ba7d-e4eb-4ced-9c0e-104471634fbb/files/essay-whatisheritage-tonkin.pdf (accessed on 13 January 2014).
6. https://webdosya.csb.gov.tr/csb/dokumanlar/mpgm0006.pdf (accessed on 13 January 2019).
7. https://www.tandfonline.com/doi/full/10.1080/13527250600604639?src=recsys (accessed on 14 January 2019).
8. https://www.tandfonline.com/doi/full/10.1080/13527250600604639?src=recsys (accessed on 14 January 2019).
9. https://www.britannica.com/topic/World-Heritage-site (accessed on 14 January 2019).
10. https://webdosya.csb.gov.tr/csb/dokumanlar/mpgm0006.pdf (accessed on 13 January 2019).
11. https://webdosya.csb.gov.tr/csb/dokumanlar/mpgm0006.pdf (accessed on 13 January 2019).
12. http://www.ep.liu.se/ecp/083/006/ecp12083006.pdf (accessed on 14 January 2019).
13. http://www.citiesalliance.org/sites/citiesalliance.org/files/AdP-n%C2%B0107-GB%205.pdf (accessed on 14 January 2019).
14. https://whc.unesco.org/archive/2015/whc15-39com-5D-en.pdf (accessed on 25 November 2019).
15. https://whc.unesco.org/en/compendium/?id_faq_themes=1334,1332,1330,1322,1314,1312,1310,1304,1302,1300,892&action=list&index=41&maxrows=20 (accessed on 25 November 2019).
16. https://www.isesco.org.ma/wp-content/uploads/2015/11/heritage-identity.pdf (accessed on 14 January 2019).
17. https://architexturez.net/doc/krishna2014urban (accessed on 15 January 2019).
18. http://eprints.lincoln.ac.uk/32830/1/HERITAGE2018_Elseragy_Elnokaly_AbuELa_2018_Final.pdf (accessed on 15 January 2019).
19. http://irep.ntu.ac.uk/id/eprint/32811/1/10165_Riganti.pdf (accessed on 15 January 2019).
20. https://era.gv.at/object/document/475/attach/ProposalJPI_CulturalHeritage_final_4_11_09.pdf (accessed on 15 January 2019).
21. https://dspace.lboro.ac.uk/dspace-jspui/bitstream/2134/21734/1/Chmutina%20et%20al_CIB_cultural%20heritage.pdf (accessed on 15 January 2019).
22. https://hyperallergic.com/87139/five-issues-threatening-the-destruction-of-cultural-heritage-sites/ (accessed on 15 January 2019).
23. https://www.ukessays.com/essays/environmental-sciences/heritage-conservation-is-important-for-identifying-environmental-sciences-essay.php (accessed on 15 January 2019).
24. https://www.intechopen.com/books/urban-and-architectural-heritage-conservation-within-sustainability/introductory-chapter-heritage-conservation-rehabilitation-of-architectural-and-urban-heritage (accessed on 9 November 2019).
25. See https://indiacode.nic.in/bitstream/123456789/5516/1/heritahe_conservation_and_preservation_act%2C_2010.pdf (accessed on 5 November 2019).
26. http://openarchive.icomos.org/1303/1/IV-3-Article2_Macdonald.pdf (accessed on 16 January 2019).
27. https://www.encatc.org/media/2688-encatc_journal_vol3_issue_1_20132432.pdf (accessed on 9 November 2019).
28. http://www.ceci-br.org/novo/revista/docs2008/CT-2008-108.pdf (accessed on 9 November 2019).
29. https://whc.unesco.org/en/news/1572 (accessed on 9 November 2019).
30. https://issuu.com/objectif-developpement/docs/economic-valuation-urban-heritage (accessed on 9 November 2019).
31. http://openarchive.icomos.org/1299/1/IV-2-Article9_Baycan_Girard.pdf (accessed on 9 November 2019).

32. http://openarchive.icomos.org/1207/1/III-1-Article1_Brooks.pdf (accessed on 9 November 2019).
33. https://www.coe.int/t/dg4/majorhazards/activites/2009/Ravello15-16may09/Ravello_APCAT2008_44_Sabbioni-Jan09_EN.pdf (accessed on 9 November 2019).
34. http://www.agenda21culture.net/sites/default/files/files/documents/en/report_7_-_cultural_heritage_sustainable_development_-_eng.pdf (accessed on 10 November 2019).
35. https://www.sciencedirect.com/science/article/pii/S1877705811000749 (accessed on 10 November 2019).
36. https://www.isturin.it/uploaded/Website_uploads/TOMUNRisingProbWorldHeritage.pdf (accessed on 16 January 2019).
37. https://www.isesco.org.ma/wp-content/uploads/2015/11/heritage-identity.pdf (14 January 2019).

References

Angelisous, M., Karachaliou, E., Angelidous, T., & Stylianidis, E. (2017, August 28–September 1). Cultural heritage in smart city environments. The International Archives of the Photogrammetry, Remote Sensing and Spatial Information Sciences (Vol. XLII–2/W5). 26th International CIPA Symposium 2017, Ottawa, Canada.

Angrisano, M., Biancamano, P. F., Bosone, M., Carone, P., Daldanise, G., De Rosa, F., Franciosa, A., Gravagnuolo, A., Iodice, S., Nocca, F., Onesti, A., Panaro, S., Ragozino, S., Sannicandro, V., & Fusco Girard, L. (2016, December). Towards operationalizing UNESCO recommendations on 'historic urban landscape'. Aestimum n. 69, 165–210. Also see http://irep.ntu.ac.uk/id/eprint/32811/1/10165_Riganti.pdf (accessed on 13 January 2019).

Bandarin, F., & Van Oers, R. (2012). *The historic urban landscape: Managing heritage in an urban century*. John Wiley & Sons.

Castells, M. (1996). *Rise of the network society: The information age.* Cambridge, Blackwell.

Cheong, C., & Macdonald, S. (2014). The role of public-private partnerships and the third sector in conserving heritage buildings, sites, and historic urban areas. The Getty Conservation Institute. https://www.getty.edu/conservation/publications_resources/pdf_publications/pdf/public_private.pdf (accessed on 9 November 2019).

CIVVIH. 2012. *Resolutions of Naples' international symposium on the role of integrated conservation of cultural heritage for a creative, resilient and sustainable city*. CIVVIH. Also see http://iopscience.iop.org/article/10.1088/1757-899X/245/6/062002/pdf (accessed on 13 January 2019).

Croft, A. (2013). *Assessment of heritage at risk from environmental threat: Key messages.* Report in Partnership with English Heritage. https://dspace.lboro.ac.uk/dspace-jspui/bitstream/2134/21734/1/Chmutina%20et%20al_CIB_cultural%20heritage.pdf (accessed on 15 January 2019).

Dweik, G. J. (2014). Urban heritage and its role in the development of the tourism sector: A model of two cities—Hebron and Bethlehem, Palestine. *The Sustainable City IX, 1*, 247–257.

Elnokaly, A, & Elseragy, A. (2013). Sustainable heritage development: Learning from urban conservation of heritage projects in non Western contexts. *European Journal of Sustainable Development, 2*, 31–54.

Feilden, B. M. (1982). *Conservation of historic buildings.* Butterworth Scientific.

Feilden, B. M., & Jokilehto, J. (1998). Evaluation for conservation. Chap management guidelines for world heritage sites. ICCROM. https://www.iccrom.org/sites/default/files/2018-02/1998_feilden_management_guidelines_eng_70071_light_0.pdf (accessed on 17 April 2020). Giffinger, R., Fertner, C., Kramar, H., Kalasek, R., Pichler-Milanović, N., & Meijers, E. (2007). *Smart cities: Ranking of European medium-sized cities.* Vienna University of Technology.

Girard, L. F. (2013). Toward a smart sustainable development of port cities/areas: The role of the 'historic urban landscape' approach. *Sustainability,* 5(10), 4329–4348.

Jigyansu, R. (2016). Reducing disaster risks to unban cultural heritage: Global challenges and opportunities. *Journal of Heritage Management, 1*(1), 1–11.

Light, D., & Dumbraveanu-Andone, D. (2007). Heritage and national identity: Exploring the relationship in Romania. *International Journal of Heritage Studies, 3*(1), 28–43.

Mateo, B. V. (2014). *Community based development and urban conservation in Kathmandu valley of Nepal: Learning from conservation and development program in Madhyapur Thimi* (Master's thesis, Technische Universität Berlin). https://www.urbanmanagement.tu-berlin.de/fileadmin/f6_urbanmanagement/Study_Course/student_work/2014_Blanca_Villar.pdf (accessed on 6 November 2019).

Rojas, E. (2007). The conservation and development of the urban heritage: A task for all social actors. *City & Time, 3*(14), 41–47.

Sassen, S. (2001). *The global city*. Princeton University Press.

Steinberg, F. (1996). Conservation and rehabilitation of urban heritage in developing countries. *Habitat International, 20*(3), 463–475.

Throsby, D. (2002). Cultural capital and sustainability concepts in the economics of cultural heritage. In M. de la Torre (Ed.), *Assessing the values of cultural heritage: research report* (pp. 101–117). Also see http://www.ceci-br.org/novo/revista/docs2007/CT-2007-73.pdf (accessed on 10 April 2019).

UNESCO. (2011a). *Recommendation on the historic urban landscape*. https://www.isturin.it/uploaded/Website_uploads/TOMUNRisingProbWorldHeritage.pdf (accessed on 15 January 2019).

UNESCO. (2011b). Preamble. *Recommendation on the historic urban landscape*. http://iopscience.iop.org/article/10.1088/1757-899X/245/6/062002/pdf (accessed on 13 January 2019).

UNESCO. (2014). Culture for sustainable development: Sustainable cities. http://iopscience.iop.org/article/10.1088/1757-899X/245/6/062002/pdf (accessed on 13 January 2019).

UNESCO. (2017). *Unite4Heritage Partnership*. UNESCO.

Wong, W. H. (2018). Community participation in heritage management: A case study of Hong Kong conservation approaches. https://www.academia.edu/37594809/Community_Participation_in_Heritage_Management_A_Case_Study_of_Hong_Kongs_Conservation_Approaches (accessed on 7 November 2019).

Yung, E. H. K., Zhang, Q., & Chan, E. H. W. (2017). Underlying social factors for evaluating heritage conservation in urban renewal districts. *Habitat Intentional, 66*, 135–148.

11 Urban Water Bodies

Water bodies have played an important role in the development of our towns and cities. In addition to maintaining the ecosystem and providing a source of freshwater, these water bodies have provided recreational spaces to the city dwellers.[1]

Water bodies constitute the most productive ecosystems with vast ecological services to the mankind. These ecosystems serve as life support systems and as habitat for a variety of organisms including migratory birds for food and shelter. Water bodies aid in bio-remediation and therefore regarded as the 'kidneys of the landscape'. Water bodies also constitute as vital components of the regional hydrological cycle.[2]

Introduction

Water bodies are critical elements in the ecological health of the cities. Water bodies are the water wealth of the nation states. The size, shape and connectivity of water bodies (lakes, ponds and wetlands) can have important effects on ecological communities and ecosystem processes. In the cities, water bodies not only strengthen ecological health but are also sources of recreation and tourism. Effective development and utilization of water bodies can earn revenue for the municipal bodies. It was suggested that intensive alteration of water bodies during urban development, including construction, burial, drainage and reshaping, may select for certain morphometric characteristics and influence the types of water bodies present in cities.[3] The water bodies are great sources to meet the water crisis in the cities as the water preserved in the water bodies is used for various purposes in the cities such as drinking, cleaning and watering plants. Water systems play an important role in urban areas, providing vital services such as drinking water, irrigation, flood control, transportation, recreation and wildlife habitat (Postel & Carpenter, 1997). It is also remarked that the water bodies, the aquatic systems on land, are one of the important storehouses for a variety of wildlife as well as nesting and breeding sites for different kinds of avifauna (Prasad et al., 2009). This chapter deals with urban water bodies and wetlands.

LEARNING OBJECTIVES

After reading this chapter, you should be able to:

- ❒ Define water bodies and explain various types of water bodies
- ❒ Describe need and importance of water bodies and wetlands
- ❒ Explain impact of urbanization on water bodies and wetlands
- ❒ Discuss various measures to be taken for the restoration of water bodies

Water Bodies: Meaning and Types

Historically, towns and cities have flourished on the banks of water bodies. These water bodies have played an important role in their growth and development. India's water bodies are extraordinarily diverse—ranging from lakes and ponds to marshes, mangroves, backwaters and lagoons (Bindu & Mohamed, 2016). A 'water body' is a structure where water from ice melt, streams, springs, rain or drainage of water from residential areas is accumulated or water is stored by diversion from a stream, *nala* or river.[4] To Laloo and Ranjan (2017), a lake or pond is the water body which holds a certain volume of water generally in all seasons of the year and is an intrinsic part of the ecosystem. The 'Manual for Data Collection in Census of Water Bodies', Government of India, has defined water bodies as all natural or man-made units bounded on all sides with some or no masonry work used for storing water for irrigation or other purposes (e.g., industrial, pisciculture, domestic/drinking, recreation, religious, ground water recharge and so on). These are usually of various types known by different names such as tanks, reservoirs, ponds and *bundhis*. Different types of water bodies are given in Exhibit 11.1.

Three types of water bodies largely found in the urban areas are as follows:

1. *Ponds:* A pond is a body of standing water. The ponds are created either through natural water or artificially by putting water into the dogged ponds. Ponds are smaller as compared to lakes and are used for limited purpose. Ponds may arise naturally in floodplains as part of a river system, or they may be somewhat isolated depressions (examples include vernal pools and prairie potholes).[5] They might contain shallow water with marsh and aquatic plants and animals (Clegg, 1986). The type of life in a pond is generally determined by a combination of factors including water-level regime (particularly, depth and duration of flooding) and nutrient levels, but other factors may also be important, including the presence or absence of shading by trees, presence or absence of streams, effects of grazing animals and salinity (Paul, 2010).
2. *Lake:* A lake is an area filled with water and surrounded by land. Lakes lie on land and are not part of the ocean, and therefore, are distinct from lagoons, and are also larger and deeper than ponds, though there are no official or scientific definitions.[6] In India, the National Lake Conservation Plan under the Ministry of Environment and Forests (2010) defines lakes as 'standing water bodies which have a minimum water depth of three metres, generally cover a water spread of more than ten hectares and have no or very little aquatic vegetation'. Most lakes are fed and drained by rivers and streams and many

Exhibit 11.1 Different Types of Water Bodies in India

Bawri	Small, usually shallow pond, sometimes man-made
Beel	Oxbow lakes in Assam
Bheel	Oxbow lakes in Bengal
Bheri	Estuarine/brackish water impoundments
Chaur	Oxbow lakes in Bihar
Jheel	Usually large and deep lakes
Johad	Natural or man-made shallow water bodies in Rajasthan, small or large
Kayal	Backwater lakes in Kerala
Kere	Tanks in Karnataka
Kund	Small, relatively deep water bodies, often associated with temples
Maun	Oxbow lakes in Uttar Pradesh & Bihar
Pat	Shallow natural floodplain lakes in Manipur
Pokhar	Small pond (in Nepali, it refers to even large shallow lakes)
Sagar	Very large and deep man-made lakes
Samand	Very large and deep man-made lakes (Rajasthan dialect for *samudra*)
Sar	Sanskrit word for lakes
Sarassu	Telugu word for lakes
Sarovar	Sanskrit word for relatively shallow lakes
Tal	Large spread of water, generally an oxbow, but also natural lakes
Talao	Usually a small pond, natural or man-made
Talaiya	Shallow small pond
Tso	Tibetan word for lakes

Source: http://www.moef.nic.in/sites/default/files/nlcp/Lake_Conserv-Manage_India.pdf (accessed on 20 May 2019).

even depend on rainwater. There are different types of lakes. The common types of lakes are as follows:

a. *Ephemeral lake:* It is a short-lived lake or pond (Gangstad, 1979). If it fills with water and dries up (disappears) seasonally it is known as an 'intermittent lake' (Poehls & Smith, 2009).
b. *Dry lake:* It is a popular name for an ephemeral lake that contains water only intermediately at irregular and infrequent intervals (Last & Smol, 2001).
c. *Perennial lake:* It is a lake that has water in its basin throughout the year and is not subject to extreme fluctuations in level (Neuendorf et al., 2005).
d. *Playa lake:* It is typically a shallow, intermittent lake that covers or occupies a playa either in wet seasons or in wet years but subsequently dries up in an arid or semi-arid region (Neuendorf et al., 2005).[7]

3. *Wetlands:* Wetlands are popular forms of water bodies in the cities situated near to the riverines and seashores. The National Academics of Sciences, Engineering and Medicine has envisaged that the wetlands are those land and water areas subject to regular inundation by tidal, riverine or lacustrine flowage. Generally included are inland and coastal shallows, marshes, mudflats, estuaries, swamps and similar areas in coastal and inland navigable waters. Many such areas serve important purposes relating to fish and wildlife, recreation

and other elements of the general public interest.[8] The Ramsar Convention on Wetlands defines wetlands as: 'areas of marsh, fen, peat land or water, whether natural or artificial, permanent or temporary, with water that is static or flowing, fresh, brackish or salt, including areas of marine water the depth of which at low tide does not exceed six metres.[9] The concept 'wetland' is still known differently in different places. For example, the US Congress granted to Louisiana in 1849 certain wetlands, which were described as 'those swamp and overflowed lands, which may be or are found unfit for cultivation....'[10]

The Ramsar Convention on Wetlands has mentioned the five different types of wetlands that are generally recognized are:

a. Marine (coastal wetlands including coastal lagoons, rocky shores and coral reefs)
b. Estuarine (including deltas, tidal marshes and mangrove swamps)
c. Lacustrine (wetlands associated with lakes)
d. Riverine (wetlands along rivers and streams)
e. Palustrine (meaning 'marshy'–marshes, swamps and bogs)[11]

Some of the famous lakes and the country to which they belong in the world are given in Table 11.1. The distribution of wetlands in India is given in Table 11.2. The ecosystem services provided by or derived from wetlands is given in Table 11.3.

Table 11.1 Famous Lakes in the World

Name of the Lake	Country
Lake Baikal	Russia
Lake Eyre	Australia
Lake Van	Turkey
Great Salt Lake	USA
Lake Titicaca	Bolivia
Lake Onakal	Uganda
Lake Aswan	Egypt
Chilka Lake	India

Source: https://www.onlinegk.com/geography/famous-lakes-and-rivers-in-india-and-world (accessed on 17 April 2020).

Table 11.2 Distribution of Wetlands in India

Sl. No	State	Natural Nos.	Area (ha)	Nos	Artificial Area (ha)
1	Andhra Pradesh	219	100,457	19,020	425,892
2	Arunachal Pradesh	2	20,200	NA	NA
3	Assam	1394	86,355	NA	NA
4	Bihar	62	224,788	33	48,607

(Table 11.2 Continued)

(Table 11.2 Continued)

Sl. No	State	Natural Nos.	Area (ha)	Nos	Artificial Area (ha)
5	Goa	3	12,360	NA	NA
6	Gujarat	22	394,627	57	129,660
7	Haryana	14	2,691	4	1,079
8	Himation Pradesh	5	702	3	19,165
9	Jammu and Kashmir	18	7,227	NA	21,880
10	Karnataka	10	3,320	22,758	539,195
11	Kerala	32	24,329	2,121	210,579
12	Madhya Pradesh	8	324	53	187,818
13	Maharashtra	49	21,675	1,004	279,025
14	Manipur	5	26,600	NA	NA
15	Meghalaya	2	NA	NA	NA
16	Mizoram	3	36	1	1
17	Nagaland	2	210	NA	NA
18	Orissa	20	137,022	36	148,454
19	Punjab	33	17,085	6	5,391
20	Rajasthan	9	14,027	85	100,217
21	Sikkim	42	1,107	2	3
22	Tamil Nadu	31	58,068	20,030	201,132
23	Tripura	3	575	1	4,833
24	Uttar Pradesh	125	12,832	28	212,470
25	West Bengal	54	291,963	9	52,564
	TOTAL	2167	1,458,580	65,251	2,587,965

Source: http://ces.iisc.ernet.in/energy/TR86/intro.html (accessed on 5 December 2019).

Table 11.3 Ecosystem Services Provided by or Derived from Wetlands

Services	Comments and Examples
Provisions	
Food	Production of fish, wild game, fruits and grains
Fresh water	Storage and retention of water for domestic, industrial and agricultural use
Fiber and fuel	Production of logs, fuelwood, peat, fodder
Bichemical	Extraction of medicines and other materials from biota
Genetic materials	Genes for resistance to plant pathogens ornamental species and so on

(Table 11.3 Continued)

(Table 11.3 Continued)

Services	Comments and Examples
Regulations	
Climate regulation	Sources of and sink for greenhouse gases, influence local and regional temperature, precipitation and other climatic processes
Water regulation (hydrological flows)	Ground water recharge/discharge
Water purification and Waste treatment	Retention, recovery, removal of excess nutrients and other pollutants
Erosion regulation	Retention of soils and sediments
Natural hazard regulation	Flood control, storm protection
Pollination	Habitat for pollinators
Cultural	
Spiritual and inspirational	Sources of inspiration; many religions attach spiritual and religious values to aspects of wetland ecosystem
Recreational	Opportunities for recreational activities
Aesthetic	Many find beauty or aesthetic value in aspects of wetland ecosystem
Educational	Opportunities for formal and information education and training
Supporting	
Soil formation	Sediment retention and accumulation of organic matter
Nutrient cycling	Storage, recycling, processing and accusation of nutrients

Source: http://iced.cag.gov.in/wp-content/uploads/C-22/PresentationCAG_Wetlands.pdf (accessed on 5 December 2019).

Importance of Water Bodies and Wetland to Urban Development

The water bodies in urban areas provide a diversity of values and uses ranging from ecological goods and services to direct production values. The stored water may be used for consumptive purpose as well as non-consumptive use such as irrigation, fishing and ecotourism. These are also sites of artistic, religious and spiritual pursuits.[12] The presence of water bodies gives added social, psychological and environmental value. It includes (a) enhancing the aesthetic quality and place quality, thereby contributing to the image of the city or town; and (b) enhancing the social and recreational value and thus increasing the liveability of the residents and land value manifold (Bindu & Mohamed, 2016). Some of the benefits of the water bodies and wetlands are as follows. The value of water bodies is given in Figure 11.1.

1. *Economic value:* The water bodies have a lot of economic value. It helps in maintenance of livestock and urban vegetation. Near to the cities it also provides irrigation facilities to the agricultural land with wetlands and water bodies. The tourism activities in the water bodies generate employment opportunities and revenue for the ULBs. For example, in Kerala, the backwater boating attracts a lot of tourists to the state and the state government earns a lot of revenue from it and also many people earn livelihoods. The places such as Srinagar and

Figure 11.1 Values of Water Bodies

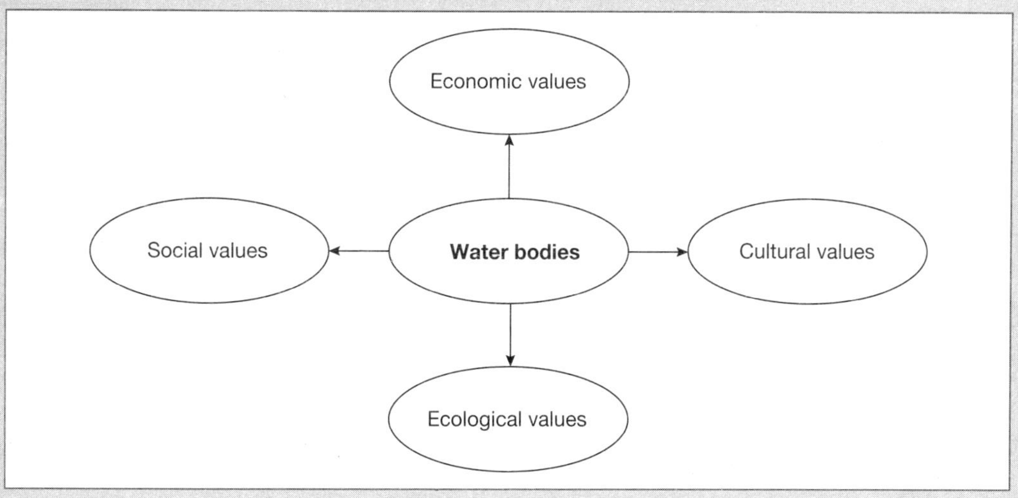

Nainital in Jammu and Kashmir and Uttarakhand also earn a lot of revenue from tourist activities from their lakes. Wetlands in Kerala are important rice cultivation land.

2. *Biodiversity:* Lakes and wetlands are among the world's most productive environments, which promote biodiversity. They are the cradles of biological diversity. Countless species of plants and animals depend for survival on them. Many migratory birds travel from far-flung places to the wetlands and lakes of different countries and are dependent for their livelihoods on the lakes and wetlands. It is rightly remarked that they support high concentrations of birds, mammals, reptiles, amphibians, fish and invertebrate species. Wetlands are also important storehouses of plant genetic material.[13]
3. *Cultural value:* The wetlands have special attributes as part of the cultural heritage of humanity; they are related to religious and cosmological beliefs, constitute a source of aesthetic inspiration, provide wildlife sanctuaries and form the basis of important local traditions.[14] Shootings of many films, songs and dances take place in the water bodies, especially in the lakes and lagoons. For example, many Hindi film shootings have taken place in the Dal Lake of Kashmir.
4. *Social development:* Well-developed water bodies in a city in many countries has promoted service sector activities such as tourism, hotel industries, transport system, educational institutions and health institutions. Near the popular water bodies, the service sector activities such as hospitals, hotels, banks, schools and colleges have opened and gradually many of them have become mini cities and municipal bodies. Water bodies attract tourists to the nation states, and therefore, promote networking among the people of different states and their social and cultural systems.
5. *Industrial development:* The water bodies in many places generate energy and promote small and medium industries in the nearby areas. However, on the other hand, excessive growth of industrial activities has affected the sanctity and biodiversity of the water bodies. The Centre for Science and Environment has opined that lakes are an easily available source of water for the needs of many sectors of economy such as agricultural, domestic and industrial.[15]

6. *Basic needs:* Water is one of the basic needs of human beings. Safe drinking water is an essential requirement for the health of human beings and even livestock. It is rightly remarked that although 70 per cent of the Earth is covered by water, only water bodies such as lakes, ponds, rivers, reservoirs and streams provide us with fresh water, so keeping them clean is an issue of survival not only for humans but for all other forms of life.[16] Thus, water bodies are essential for human consumption and livestock, and these are far more important in the hilly and desert areas.
7. *National integration:* Water bodies promote national integration. The water bodies in different states attract tourists and thus promote communal harmony and national integration. Bathing in a holy river is considered to be symbolic cleansing of both mind and body. Prayers are recited while bathing, invoking the names of all holy rivers such as Ganga, Narmada, Godavari and Kaveri. The four Kumbh Melas at Nashik, Ujjain, Prayag and Haridwar are being held for thousands of years and are even popular today. The holy dips during the time of Kumbh Mela integrate people across the various states and even across the globe.
8. *Ecological values:* One of the greatest advantages of water bodies to the cities is their favourable impact on the environment. Water bodies enable flora to grow and attract fauna to the cities. As environmental and human health is interrelated, in the same vein, water bodies and ecosystem of the cities are interrelated. It is said that the presence of water in various forms in its natural setting plays an important role in enhancing the quality of the physical and socioeconomic environment (Bindu & Mohamed, 2016).
9. *Control urban flooding:* It is not a flight of fancy, but delicately and primarily water bodies act as sponge and soak up the rainwater. However, increasing population in the cities of the developing countries has led to increased waste and the cities' water bodies have turned into dumping grounds for MSWs. The recent flood and urban disasters in Chennai and Srinagar are illustrious examples of shrinking urban spaces, in general, and water bodies, in particular, in these cities.
10. *Generates income and livelihood opportunities:* Urban water bodies generate income for the city municipalities. Srinagar is an illustrious example where the Dal Lake and other lakes not only generate income for the municipalities but also provide livelihood to many boat owners and boat drivers. In many water bodies the impoverished people perform pisciculture (fishing activities) activities and earn their livelihood. The important wetlands in selected few cities are given in Table 11.4.

Table 11.4 Important Wetlands in the Cities of the World

Wetland	City, Country
Camargue	France
Wasur Naitonal Park	Indonesia
Mekong Delta	Vietnam
Kerala Backwater	India
Everglades	Florida, USA
Sundarbans	Inida/Bangladesh
Pantanal	Bolivia/Paraguay

Source: https://www.touropia.com/important-wetlands-in-the-world/ (accessed on 17 April 2020).

Impact of Urbanization on Water Bodies and Water-related Problems

It is a universal observation that all the urban expansions have engulfed almost all the water bodies in their territories and in the peripheral regions (Beura, 2017). Water bodies are missing due to the construction of various urban infrastructures. However, the depletion of water bodies has adversely affected the water supply, groundwater development and local climate. It has also affected the urban environment and biodiversity. Some of the adverse impacts of urbanization on water bodies are narrated as follows.

1. *Water scarcity:* The immediate and most prominent adverse impact of urbanization on the water bodies is that the number of water bodies is diminishing day by day. One of the reasons of scarcity of water for drinking and for other essential uses is landfilling of water bodies. The increasing urban sprawl in proportion to population growth has posed severe pressure on urban and rural lakes by making them non-potable, impairing their absorption capacity, deteriorating water quality, disturbing aquatic biodiversity and finally resulting in vanishing of the water body.[17]
2. *Livelihood and livestock:* The decrease in a number of water bodies has also proportionately affected the number of livestock, plants and species of birds in the cities. The cities have become monotonous with only population, buildings and vehicles with decreasing number of flora and fauna. The livelihood of many poor people depending on fisheries and animals has vanished. The cities have become dry. Water bodies, the aquatic systems on land, such as lakes, reservoirs, tanks, ponds, act as storehouses for a variety of wildlife, especially for avifauna, serving as breeding and nesting sites.[18]
3. *Flood control:* The water bodies play an important role in disaster management, especially flood control. The decrease in number of water bodies in Kashmir has resulted in a lot of devastation in the recent floods. The rapid urbanization and decrease in water bodies have made the cities more prone to natural calamities like flood. The decrease in the number of water bodies and wetlands affects the water balance in the city. Zheng et al (2016) were of the view that urban flooding has become more and more severe and pervasive in China due to (a) loss of natural water bodies, (b) urban land use and imperviousness and (c) fragmentation of natural water systems.
4. *Groundwater recharge:* The water bodies are vital for the urban groundwater recharge. Most of the water supply in the urban areas is through groundwater boring. The urbanization and decrease in the water bodies have pushed the water level in the urban areas down. In many metropolitan cities, the scope of boring water is decreasing day by day. The rapid growth of urban areas has two basic effects on groundwater resources: effects on natural recharge of aquifers due to sealing of ground with concrete and pollution of groundwater due to leakage from drainage, industrial wastage and effluents (Baier et al., 2014).
5. *Water quality:* The unbridled urbanization and decrease in urban water bodies have affected the water quality. It is said that healthy streams are essential for protecting the water quality. They also add to the quality of life in our area, providing recreational opportunities such as fishing and swimming, and an attractive element of green in the parched desert.[19]
6. *Flora and fauna:* The decrease in the water bodies due to urbanization has affected the flora and fauna. For example, excessive urbanization in the hill state of Himachal Pradesh

has affected the flora and fauna of many of the cities, especially Shimla. Shimla, the summer capital, has started looking dry, and water scarcity is a common problem in the city. The varieties of birds and other species are decreasing. The selected water bodies in India is given in Table 11.5 and the role of water bodies in city development is given in Figure 11.2.

Table 11.5 Selected Water Bodies in India

Name of the Water Bodies	Place and State
Naini Lake	Nainital, Uttarakhand
Dal Lake	Srinagar, Jammu and Kashmir
Powai Lake	Mumbai, Maharashtra
Hussain Sagar Lake	Hyderabad, Telangana
Deepor Beel	Gawahati, Assam
Surajkund Lake	Faridabad, Haryana
Sukhna Lake	Chandigarh
Okhla Barrage	New Delhi
East Kolkata Wet Land	Kolkata, West Bengal
Swaroop Sagar	Udaipur, Rajasthan

Figure 11.2 Role of Water Bodies in City Development

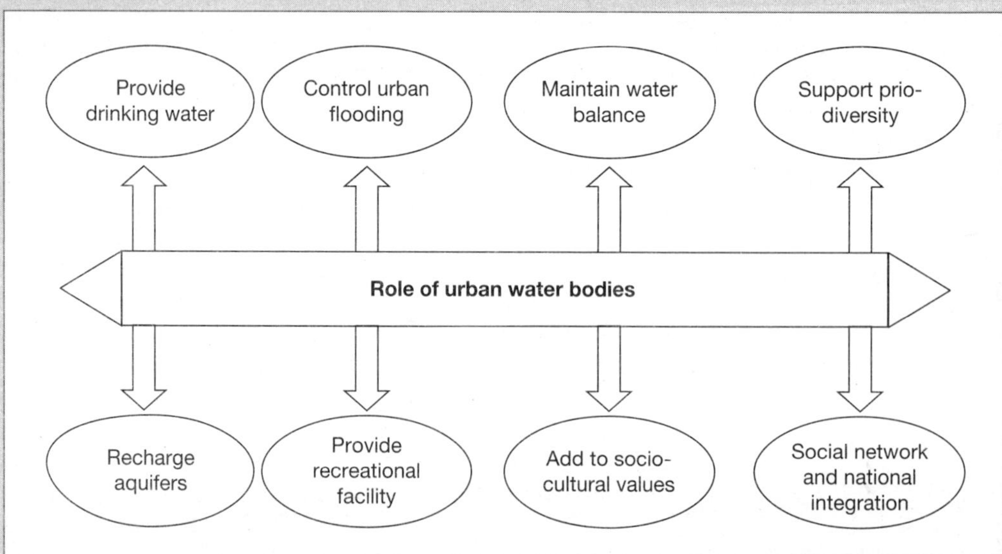

Issues and Challenges for the Loss of Water Bodies

The urban water bodies are facing many challenges and many of these bodies have died, while others are in dying conditions. The GoI has even recognized that in the last half of the 20th century, the lakes underwent unprecedented environmental degradation on account of (a) population explosion, (b) large-scale industrialization, (c) chemical-intensive agriculture and (d) water-intensive lifestyles (MoUD, 2013). Kerala has submitted that the total number of water bodies has declined in the state due to (a) increase in population and density of population per square kilometre, (b) change in land-use pattern, (c) shift from paddy-based agriculture to cash crop cultivation, (d) depletion of groundwater, (e) rapid urbanization, (f) unplanned urbanization and development activities, and (f) boom in construction activity.[20] Some of the issues and challenges that the water bodies in the cities are facing are narrated as follows.

1. *Urbanization:* Urbanization and uninterrupted growth of population in urban areas are one of the major issues which have affected the water bodies leading to the loss of water bodies. It is said that urbanization is one of the main driving forces for large-scale changes and homogenized land-use practices over large areas (Prasad et al., 2009).
2. *Dynamics of land use and faulty land-use planning:* The land-use pattern and pressing demand for land for the residential and official purposes in urban areas have resulted in landfilling of water bodies for these purposes. The land-use planning in most of the cities neglects the planning of water bodies.
3. *City infrastructure development:* The infrastructure development of the cities such as the construction of roads, waterworks, commercial centres and offices has demanded additional land. The most preferred solution that has been seen in the developing countries is filling of open spaces, in general, and water bodies and wetlands, in particular.
4. *Lack of emphasis on sustainable urbanization:* The presence of water bodies is essential for sustainable urbanization. The water bodies preserve the environment and improve the health of human beings as well as other natural resources of the cities. Because of lack of emphasis on sustainable urbanization, the numbers of water bodies in most of the cities of the developing nation states are declining. It is one of the major issues.
5. *Pollution and waste management:* The water bodies in the cities have become the soft target of waste management strategies. The governments as well as municipalities at the first site prefer to choose water bodies and wetlands as landfilling sites. This is a major issue. Besides, the pollution in the cities is also affecting the water bodies, their water quality and victimizing these bodies by converting into landfill sites.
6. *Lack of availability of data on water bodies:* There is no clear-cut data available with the nation states on the number of water bodies. In other words, there is no census of information regarding water bodies. For example, in 2001, by the order of the high court, a joint survey committee assessed the number of natural water bodies in Delhi and came up with a list of 508 water bodies, which differed from a count of 794 submitted by TAPAS (a Delhi-based NGO). The court asked for another survey and DDA came up with a new count of 580 water bodies in Delhi in 2004.[21] Without clear-cut information, it will be difficult to take appropriate measures for the restoration of water bodies.
7. *Ambiguity in the definition of water bodies:* The ambiguity in definition sometimes helps the private player to take advantage of converting the water bodies into housing projects, shop complexes, industries and so on. The Centre for Science and Environment has commented that in the case of Somepeta thermal power plant in Andhra Pradesh and Nirma plant in

Bhavnagar, attempts have been made to convert these water bodies for commercial use. Fortunately, the quick action of the central government saved these wetlands.[22]

8. *Corruption:* The corruption is also one of the important reasons for the decline in the water bodies in the cities. It is only through the political and bureaucratic decision-making the water bodies in the cities are converted into other purposes like construction of official and residential buildings and selling them to the private parties. Mohit Ray, in the context of Kolkata's mission of water bodies, has remarked that urbanization, the negligent attitude of city planners to look after the water requirement of common citizens, the partition of the state and corruption in administration, all helped in the disappearance of hundreds of water bodies in the city.[23]

Protection, Restoration and Revitalization of Urban Water Bodies

The major factor that contributes to the sustainable development of an area is its water bodies. Moreover, the presence of water bodies gives added social, psychological and environmental value. It includes (a) enhancing the aesthetic quality and place quality, thereby contributing to the image of the city or town; (b) enhancing the social and recreational value and thus increasing the liveability of the residents and land value manifold (Bindu & Mohamed, 2016). These water bodies are to be protected and used properly for sustainable growth of the city. A water body is an important infrastructure of urban landscape. Water bodies such as tanks and ponds are constructed to harvest rainwater for local use. Such water bodies serve many environmental functions including flood and soil erosion control and are useful for irrigation, drinking water supply and groundwater recharge. Therefore, urban lakes and other water bodies have to be in the focus of urban planning and decision-making processes as these surface water sources, if protected and managed properly, will create tremendous potential to augment the water supply, if not immediately for drinking, but for other non-potable water requirements of ever-increasing urban population.

A few important measures required to be taken for the protection, conservation and revitalization of water bodies are as follows.

1. *Restriction on dumping in water bodies:* The city government and municipality need to enact strict regulations that restrict dumping of wastes in the water bodies. Most of the water bodies are becoming dead because of dumping of waste in them. The National Green Tribunal and the Central Pollution Control Board of India have suggested a few measures to improve the health of water bodies which include steps such as levying a fine on those found dumping waste into water bodies and creation of a green belt around the water resources.[24]
2. *Check unplanned urbanization:* Urbanization, in general, and unplanned urbanization, in particular, are the root cause of the decline of water bodies and wetlands in the cities. The construction of housing projects by filling of water bodies and wetlands is seen in many cities. Therefore, check on unbridled migration of people from rural to urban areas will also control the declining of water bodies. It is remarked that urbanization in most cases results in downgrading the integrity of water bodies and watershed in urban and urbanizing areas.[25]
3. *Forestation activities:* The planting of trees around the catchment areas of the water bodies will check degradation of water bodies. Like in the rural areas, in urban areas also trees need to be planted in the catchment areas of the ponds, lake and rivers. Many water bodies are customarily sites for migratory birds; the trees planted by the side of the water body and water channels provide suitable environment for egg-laying birds and propagation of bird

species. The Bharatpur Bird Sanctuary is one of the illustrious examples where planting of high-growing trees with more branches provide a healthy environment for migratory birds and large varieties of birds come to the sanctuary.

4. *Desilting and rainwater harvesting in water bodies:* The desilting of water bodies must be done regularly. It will check the decay of water bodies. If it is done every year, then fresh water is injected into them. Besides, rainwater harvesting in the water bodies will also maintain them for a longer period.
5. *Checking the growth of industrial activities in the cities:* The passing and dumping of industrial waste in the water bodies have degraded water bodies and wetlands nearer to the cities. This needs to be stopped.
6. *Stopping cleaning and washing activities:* Customarily, washing of vehicles, clothes and animals in water bodies deteriorates the quality of water in the water bodies. And when human beings bathe in these water bodies, they become prone to many types of skin diseases. The cleaning of animals and clothes in the water bodies and wetlands needs to be banned. Water bodies need to be recognized as municipal assets.
7. *PPP:* PPP in the conservation, restoration and revitalization of water bodies needs to be promoted. The corporate sectors functioning in the cities may be requested by the government for the conservation of water bodies. The private sector may be allowed to promote hotels and boating and other activities which will raise revenue for the conservation of water bodies. One of the examples of the PPP model is given in Box 11.1.
8. *Monitoring of water balance:* The government and municipality from time to time continuously monitor the water balance in the water bodies. If required, water may be injected and the inflow of water to various water bodies may be allowed. Water resource assessment and water audit in the water bodies of the cities will go a long way to improve the ecological health of the water bodies.

Box 11.1 Mansagar Lake: An Alternate Institutional Arrangement

In recent years, new institutional arrangements are also being implemented, particularly the public–private partnerships (PPP). However, these forms of arrangements often face strong resistance from civil society. The restoration of Mansagar Lake in Jaipur is an example of such an arrangement where the government decided to imply the PPP approach to restore the lake. Until a few years back, Mansagar Lake, an artificial lake of 300 ha. in Rajasthan was suffering from serious problems of siltation and contamination, inflow of wastewater, eutrofication and loss of water due to the outflow for downstream irrigation during summer. During the past years, several attempts were made by the government of Rajasthan to restore the lake but none of these attempts yielded any positive result particularly because of the lack of funds. In 2002, the government decided to created a PPP of the state government and a private player called Jal Mahal Resorts Pvt. Ltd. (JMRPL). Under the agreed restoration plan, the lakebed was dredged to enhance its holding capacity. The authorities implemented a scheme to discharge treated sewage in the lake to ensure that the water balance was maintained in spite of high evaporation losses. Three wetlands of total 40,000 sqm were constructed in the vicinity of the lake to facilitate filling up of the Mansagar Lake with clean water. The sewage water is diverted into these wetlands before releasing into the lake. The lakefront was leased out to a hospitality group and the lake's health was tied to revenues from tourism to generate money for further investments on the restoration of the lake. The water quality of the lake has immensely improved over the past five years.

Source: http://www.saconenvis.nic.in/publication/Lake%20Protection%20and%20Management%20of%20Urban%20Lakes%20in%20India.pdf (accessed on 5 December 2019).

9. *Capacity building of local self-government institutions:* Government should conduct training on water bodies conservation, restoration and management for the local self-government institutions, functionaries and elected representatives. Moreover, integrated training programmes for the parallel bodies and opinion leaders along with the local self-government institution functionaries may be considered.
10. *Stormwater management plan:* The central, state and the local self-government need to have a proper plan for stormwater management. One of the objectives of it is to restore and conserve water bodies. The stormwater management can mitigate intense rainfall events and enhance local water sources. The appropriated policy for stormwater management during the rainy season in the water bodies would improve the health of the water bodies and in another way would be able to control flood and rainwater related disasters.
11. *Creating multiple amenities:* Creating multiple recreational facilities in and around the water bodies in order to attract the attention of the local people as well as the tourists. It will not only raise the importance of water bodies in the national scenario but also generate revenue for the municipality. For example, the Sukhna Lake in Chandigarh attracts attention of the tourists and also the locals spend their summer evening there for recreation purpose. The lake offers the following amenities to the visitors: (a) boating, (b) wide pathway for walking and benches for sitting, (c) amusement park for children, (d) evening concert by opera groups and performance by well-recognized singers and folk dancers, (e) Rock Garden at a walking distance and (f) a small zoo nearby.
12. *Citizens' responsibility and public awareness:* It is the duty of every responsible citizen to protect its water bodies for the ecological and human health. The Indian Constitution has also envisaged the same. It has a separate chapter, Part IV-A, on the 'Fundamental Duties of a Citizen'. Clause (g) of Article 51-A of the Constitution states, 'It shall be the duty of every citizen of India to protect and improve the natural environment including forests, lakes, rivers and wild life and to have compassion for living creatures'.
13. *Monitoring of water bodies:* Time-to-time monitoring of the water bodies by the state government and initiating restoration activities would protect the water bodies from extinction. Neelakantan and Ramakrishnan (2017) in their study on 'Protection of Urban Water Body Infrastructure—Policy Requirements' have envisaged that to monitor and prioritize conservation works of six water bodies in and around Chennai city, a Water Bodies Protection Index was developed. To formulate the index, five factors, namely (a) quality of water, (b) biodiversity, (c) encroachment of water body, (d) involvement of local community in the management and preservation of water body and (e) role of government agencies in protecting water bodies were considered.
14. *Heritage water bodies:* The government of the provinces needs to declare some of the old water bodies having historical and ancient linkages as heritage water bodies. The

Box 11.2 **Reality Check: Delhi's Five Lakes at Deep End**

At a time when the Delhi government is planning to spend hundreds of crores to revive more than 200 water bodies, the city's existing lakes—some as large as the Nainital Lake—are dying a slow death. Naini Lake, Bhalswa Lake, Purana Qila Lake, Sanjay Lake and Hauz Khas Lake are all in a sorry state.

Source: Times City (2019).

Mansarovar is one of the illustrious examples of heritage water bodies. It will earn revenue for the government from tourist activities and will also boost service sector activities around the heritage water bodies. There are many such water bodies in different states having religious importance and those may be promoted as heritage water bodies. The sorry state of affair of a few water bodies in Delhi is given in the Box 11.2.

15. *Allocation of resources:* Government and the Ministry of Culture need to allocate resources for the maintenance and restoration of water bodies in the states. The municipalities also need to allocate budget for the restoration of water bodies. One of the reports of the GoI has envisaged during the Twelfth Five-year Plan that the planned outlay of the scheme is ₹10,000 crore and is envisaged to provide central assistance for restoration of about 10,000 water bodies (9,000 water bodies in rural areas and 1,000 water bodies in urban areas) with an earmarked central outlay of ₹6,235 crore and respective state share of ₹3,765 crore for the scheme with likely restoration of 6.235 lakh hectare.[26]
16. *Women empowerment:* Women are the main actors of conserving water for the family and society. The women groups and self-help groups for women need to be given charge for the restoration, preservation and management of water bodies.

Summing Up

Water bodies are vital for humans as well as for the flora and fauna of the urban areas. It not only enhances the beauty of the cities but also attracts tourists from distant places and enable the municipalities to earn revenue. However, in many cities, the municipalities are not taking adequate steps to improve the condition of water bodies. As a result, many water bodies are dying day by day. Traditional water bodies were built to harvest the rainwater and prevent any flooding into the city core and use this water for various purposes; even to tide over the situation of drought.[27] It is well remarked that the size, shape and connectivity of water bodies (lakes, ponds and wetlands) can have important effects on ecological communities and ecosystem processes (Steele & Heffernan, 2014). Efforts must be made to preserve these water bodies, reduce/control the anthropogenic impacts and enhance their ecological benefit for achieving a balance between the urbanization and environmental conditions (Prasad et al., 2009).

Keywords

Water Bodies, Wetlands, Ponds, Perennial Lake, Ephemeral Lake, Biodiversity, Groundwater Recharge

REVIEW QUESTIONS

1. Define water bodies. Explain various types of water bodies.
2. Why water bodies are important for urban development? Explain.
3. Describe in detail the impact of urbanization on water bodies.
4. What are various issues and challenges associated with water bodies and how can they be overcome?

5. Explain various measures to be taken for the protection, restoration and revitalization of urban water bodies.
6. Write short notes on the following:
   a. Ponds
   b. Wetlands
   c. Biodiversity
   d. Groundwater recharge
   e. Lake

Notes

1. http://ficci.in/spdocument/20206/Safeguarding-Urban-FreshWater-Bodies.pdf (accessed on 16 January 2019).
2. http://shodhganga.inflibnet.ac.in/bitstream/10603/203913/13/13_chapter%205.pdf (accessed on 16 January 2019).
3. https://www.ncbi.nlm.nih.gov/pubmed/25154097 (accessed on 16 January 2019).
4. http://164.100.47.193/lsscommittee/Water%20Resources/16_Water_Resources_10.pdf (accessed on 16 January 2019).
5. https://en.wikipedia.org/wiki/Pond (accessed on 17 January 2019).
6. https://en.wikipedia.org/wiki/Lake (accessed on 17 January 2019).
7. https://en.wikipedia.org/wiki/Lake (accessed on 17 January 2019).
8. https://www.nap.edu/read/4766/chapter/5 (accessed on 17 January 2019).
9. http://mohua.gov.in/upload/uploadfiles/files/Advisory%20on%20Urban%20Water%20Bodies.pdf (accessed on 16 January 2019).
10. See as mentioned in Chapter 87, An Act to aid the State of Louisiana in draining the Swamp Lands therein, 9 Stat. 352, 1849. Also see https://www.nap.edu/read/4766/chapter/5#44 (accessed on 17 January 2019).
11. https://www.ramsar.org/sites/default/files/documents/library/info2007-01-e.pdf (accessed on 17 January 2019).
12. https://www.informea.org/sites/default/files/imported-documents/info2007-01-e.pdf (accessed on 18 January 2019).
13. https://www.informea.org/sites/default/files/imported-documents/info2007-01-e.pdf (accessed on 18 January 2019).
14. https://helpsavenature.com/industrial-water-pollution (accessed on 18 January 2019).
15. http://www.saconenvis.nic.in/publication/Lake%20Protection%20and%20Management%20of%20Urban%20Lakes%20in%20India.pdf (accessed on 5 December 2019).
16. http://www.soulhyd.org/articles/MS_JSS_waterbodies.pdf (accessed on 18 January 2019).
17. http://www.soulhyd.org/articles/MS_JSS_waterbodies.pdf (accessed on 18 January 2019).
18. https://www.unce.unr.edu/publications/files/ho/2005/av0514.pdf (accessed on 18 January 2019).
19. http://www.tucson.ars.ag.gov/icrw/Proceedings/Novotny.pdf (accessed on 20 January 2019).
20. http://164.100.47.193/lsscommittee/Water%20Resources/16_Water_Resources_10.pdf (accessed on 6 December 2019).
21. http://www.saconenvis.nic.in/publication/Lake%20Protection%20and%20Management%20of%20Urban%20Lakes%20in%20India.pdf (accessed on 5 December 2019).
22. http://www.saconenvis.nic.in/publication/Lake%20Protection%20and%20Management%20of%20Urban%20Lakes%20in%20India.pdf (accessed on 5 December 2019).
23. https://www.indiawaterportal.org/articles/curious-case-kolkatas-missing-water-bodies (accessed on 6 December 2019).

24. https://m.dailyhunt.in/news/india/english/the+logical+indian-epaper-tlogin/fine+those+dumping+waste+into+water+bodies+says+pollution+watchdog-newsid-122421480 (accessed on 6 December 2019).
25. https://www.dailyo.in/politics/smart-cities-water-bodies-rural-india-flood-prevention/story/1/16467.html (accessed on 1 April 2019).
26. http://164.100.47.193/lsscommittee/Water%20Resources/16_Water_Resources_10.pdf (accessed on 6 December 2019).
27. https://www.dailyo.in/politics/smart-cities-water-bodies-rural-india-flood-prevention/story/1/16467.html (accessed on 1 April 2019).

References

Baier, K., Schmitz, K. S., Azzam, A. & Strohschon, A. (2014). Management tools for sustainable ground water protection in mega urban areas—small scale land use and ground water vulnerability analyses in Guangzhou, China. *International Journal of Environmental Research, 8*, 249–262.

Beura, D. (2017). Depletion of water bodies due to urbanization and its management. *International Education and Research Journal, 3*(6), 204–205.

Bindu, C. A., & Mohamed, A. R. (2016). Water bodies as a catalyst to growth and development—a case of Kodungallur town, Kerala. *Procedia Technology, 24*, 1790–1800.

Clegg, J. (1986). The new observer's book of pond life (p. 460). Frederick Warne.

Gangstad, E. O. (1979). *Glossary of biolimnological terms* (p. 22). United States Army Corps of Engineers.

Keddy, Paul A. (2010). Wetland ecology: Principles and conservation. Cambridge University Press.

Laloo, S. W. L., & Ranjan, A. (2017). Urban development impacts on water bodies: A review in India. International Journal on Emerging Technologies, 8(1), 363–370.

Last, W. M., & Smol, J. P. (2001). *Tracking environmental change using lake sediments. Vol. 1. Basin analysis, coring, and chronological techniques*. Springer Science & Business Media.

Ministry of Environment and Forests. (2010). *Conservation and management of lakes: An Indian perspective.* Ministry of Environment and Forests.

MoUD. (2013). *Advisory on Conservation and Restoration of Water Bodies in Urban Areas*. Central Public Health and Environmental Engineering Organization (CPHEEO), Ministry of Urban Development. http://mohua.gov.in/upload/uploadfiles/files/Advisory%20on%20Urban%20Water%20Bodies.pdf (accessed on 17 April 2020).

Neelakantan, T. R., & Ramakrishnan, K. (2017). Protection of urban water body infrastructure—policy requirements. *IOP Conference Series: Earth and Environmental Science, 80*. https://iopscience.iop.org/article/10.1088/1755-1315/80/1/012068/pdf (accessed on 27 March 2020).

Neuendorf, K. K. E., Mehl Jr., J. P., & Jackson, J. A. (2005). *Glossary of geology* (5th revised and Enlarged ed.). Springer.

Poehls, D. J., & Smith, G. J. (Eds.). (2009). *Encyclopedic dictionary of hydrogeology* (p. 517). Academic Press.

Postel, S., & Carpenter, S., (1997). Freshwater ecosystem services. In G. C. Daily (Ed.), *Nature's services: Societal dependence on natural ecosystems* (pp. 195–214). Island Press.

Prasad, P. R. C., Raja, K. S., Bhole, V., & Dutt, C. B. S. (2009). Is rapid urbanization leading to loss of water bodies? *Journal of Spatial Science, II* (2), 43–52.

Steele, M. K., & Heffernan, J. B. (2014). Morphological characteristics of urban water bodies: Mechanisms of change and implications for ecosystem function. *Ecological Applications, 24*(5), 1070–1084.

Times City. (2019, May 23). Reality check: Delhi's five lakes at deep end. *Times City*.

Zheng, Z., Gao, J., Ma, Z., Wang, Z., Yang, X., Luo, X., Jacquet, T., & Fu, G. (2016). Urban flooding in China: Main causes and policy recommendations. *Hydrological Processes, 30,* 1149–1152.

12 Urban Open Spaces

Urban open spaces have increasing importance in city developments due to the urban expansion characteristic of the last decade.[1]

Open spaces are valued by theorists who relate them to the social, political, and physical health of urban residents and communities.

—Stanley et al. (2012)

Introduction

Open spaces play an important role in the lifestyle of the urban dwellers. It is not a flight of fancy, but delicately the cities having high green-coverage rate have better ecological and environmental importance than their counterparts. The green spaces help to improve the urban climate and enhance the quality of life of the city dwellers. These act as an ecological balancer and reduce environmental damages. Open spaces can help the residents to enjoy a healthy lifestyle through not only their environmental importance but also their social importance. By their aesthetic importance, open spaces determine the characteristics of the urban settlements. It is estimated that well-designed public open areas increase the value of the surrounding properties and attract new investors. City residents, when offered easily accessible high-quality green open areas, they tend to spend more time in outdoors, which could have a positive impact on their life expectancy, health, happiness and general well-being. It also adds to their efficiency and enhances productivity of individuals and the whole society. Open spaces are required for the well-being of all the sections of the urban society. Children use these for activities, youth for sports and recreation, women for chatting and the old in utilizing these for their leisure. According to WHO (2017), green spaces and other nature-based solutions offer innovative approaches to increase the quality of urban settings, enhance local resilience and promote sustainable lifestyles, improving both health and well-being of urban residents. This chapter is on urban open space.

LEARNING OBJECTIVES

After reading this chapter, you should be able to:

- Describe the meaning and need for open space
- Explain the importance of open space to urban development
- Discuss factors responsible for the deterioration of urban open space
- Note down measures for the renewal and revitalization of urban open space

Urban Open Space: Concept and Meaning

A simple definition of urban open space is—open areas for public use that are situated within the urban fabric of a city. The term, urban open space, is also often used interchangeably with terms such as public space, green space or urban parkland; although, these all can have slightly different meanings.[2] In a broader sense, however, open space can also be considered as something wider and more all-encompassing, namely, the continuous matrix of all un-built land in urban areas—public parks as well as private gardens, urban streets as well as city squares.[3] Open space is any open piece of land that is undeveloped (has no building or other built structures) and is accessible to the public. Box and Harrison (1993) were of the view that for instance 'opens space', 'natural space' and 'natural open space' have been used interchangeably by the planners, landscape designers and other professionals. Public spaces such as streets, school yards, outdoor sport complexes, cemeteries and public squares are important open spaces (Hall, 1998). Open space can include the following.

1. *Green space (land that is partly or completely covered with grass, trees, shrubs or other vegetation):* Green space includes parks, community gardens and cemeteries.
2. *Schoolyard:* It is the region within the boundaries of the school that is used for extracurricular, sports and other physical activities.
3. *Playground:* It is the area which is specifically designed for the children and youth to play various outdoor games such as football, hockey and cricket. Grounds are specially built in the cities. Salt Lake Stadium in Kolkata is such an example that is especially meant for football.
4. *Public seating area:* The public seating area is such places where chairs and benches in either wood or cement are built for seating in open public places.
5. *Public plaza:* An unused open public place in the city square.
6. *Vacant lot:* A vacant lot is the neglected parcel of property in the city that has no building on it.
7. *City forest area:* In some cities, particularly situated in hilly and forest areas, forest land is being treated as an open space. Dehradun is an illustrious example of this.

Stanley et al. (2012) have defined open space as any urban ground space, regardless of public accessibility, that is not roofed by any architectural structure. From all these definitions, it can be said that urban open spaces are the urban public land that remain vacant for public use for various recreational and sociocultural and political activities. These may be parks, playgrounds, open grounds for public activities such as conducting electioneering campaigning, book fairs and trade fairs, cultural functions, religious functions, yoga and other physical activities and so on. Carr et al. (1992) define public space as 'open, publicly accessible places' that facilitate the popular activities necessary for community building. The report of Rogers and Urban Task Force (1999) says:

To achieve urban integration means thinking of urban open space not as an isolated unit—be it a street, park or square—but as a vital part of urban landscape with its own specific set of functions. Public space should be conceived of as an outdoor room within a neighbourhood, somewhere to relax, and enjoy the urban experience, a venue for a range of different activities, from outdoor eating to street entertainment; from sport and play areas to a venue for civic or political functions; and most importantly of all a place for walking or sitting-out. Public spaces work best when they establish a direct relationship between the space and the people who live and work around it.

Some of the benefits and needs for open spaces are as follows:

1. Deal with climatic change and modification
2. Check noise pollution
3. Give space for wildlife habitat
4. Use for recreation
5. Improve quality of life
6. Enhance community and personal interaction
7. Promote social networking
8. Protect water quality
9. Recharge water
10. Retain flood water
11. Increase property value
12. Enhance income from tourism
13. To build a sustainable city
14. To build a smart city
15. Help in land-use planning

It is noted that rapid urbanization, the rise of income level, change of lifestyle and concerns on healthy living have increased the demand for urban open space recreational facilities (Berg et al., 2015). Further, the change of lifestyle also requires more public open spaces in the cities to fulfil different socio, economic and environmental needs of the city population (Wolch et al., 2014). Therefore, many studies have emphasized the importance of accessing the monetary value of intangible and non-market benefits of open urban green spaces (Jim & Chen, 2006). Some of the open spaces in a few important cities of the world are given in Table 12.1.

Table 12.1 Open Spaces in a Few Important Cities of the World

Open Spaces	City, Country
Forsyth Park	Savannah, Georgia
Asramam Maidan	Kollam, Kerala, India
Washington park	Tory, New York, USA
Sad Janka Krala Park	Bratislava, Slovenia
Ariel Slaron Park	Tel Aviv, Israel
Cheoiggyecheo Strcam Park	Seoul, South Korea
Ram Lila Maidan	New Delhi, India

Importance of Open Space to Urban Areas

Urban open spaces are an inevitable necessity for the physical and mental health of the urbanites. It is necessary for the economic, social, political and cultural reasons also. Urban green space exists in and surrounds urban areas. The idea of urban green space is understood by referring to all publicly owned and publicly accessible open spaces with a high degree of cover by vegetation, such as parks, woodlands, nature areas and other green spaces in urban areas (Schipperijn et al., 2010). Such space plays a critical role in supporting urban ecological and social systems and providing important services in urban areas (Levent & Nijkamp, 2004). One vital role that urban open space plays is providing space for the expression of diversity, both personal and cultural; this raises issues of democratic provision for accessing public open space.[4] Open spaces are often planned and controlled by states and lower-level governance institutions or influenced by voluntary associations. They also provide critical venues for populations with limited means and little private space to perform many social, economic and cultural activities (Stanley et al., 2012). The need for open space cannot be ignored in the cities. It is not only required for performance of entertainment activities and recreations, but also for the health of ecology and environment of the cities. According to WHO (2017), parks, playgrounds or vegetation in public and private places are central components of open space, and these can help to ensure the following:

1. Urban residents have adequate opportunities for exposure to nature.
2. Urban biodiversity is maintained and protected.
3. Environmental hazards such as air pollution or noise are reduced.
4. The impacts of extreme weather events (heat waves, extreme rainfall or flooding) are mitigated.
5. The quality of urban living is enhanced.
6. The health and well-being of residents is improved.

It is well remarked that a well-designed open space that encourages outdoor activity and social communication is a community asset that could potentially contribute to the health of local residents and social harmony of the community (Chen et al., 2016). The six important values of open spaces are described further (Figure 12.1).

Figure 12.1 Values of Open Space

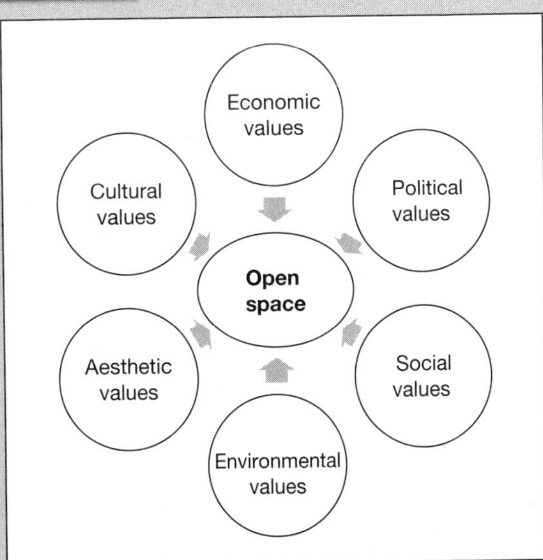

1. *Environmental values:* Open space is one of the pivotal assets of environment and is considered an essential environmental capital of the cities. It provides support to the city environment and maintains and improves it. Through natural conservation, it increases biodiversity of flora and fauna. It

produces a positive effect on urban climate, and thus helps in the reduction of air temperature and urban heat. It improves air quality and decreases air pollution. WHO has rightly envisaged that through improved air and water quality, buffering of noise pollution and mitigation of impacts from extreme events, urban green spaces can reduce environmental health risks associated with urban living.[5] Some of the noted environmental benefits of open space are as follows: (a) adaptation to climate change; (b) air quality improvement; (c) biodiversity support; (d) temperature regulation; (e) sound and pollution regulation; (f) soil protection; (g) water table and water quality regulation and (h) carbon storage and healthy breathing. The diversities of Yamuna Biodiversity Park as given by Patwal are given in Box 12.1.

2. *Economic values:* Open spaces are being rented out by the municipalities for performing many activities such as organizing concert, marriages and political campaigning. The municipalities get an income out of it. It also noted that open spaces such as parks and recreation areas, can have a positive effect on nearby residential property values, and can lead to proportionately higher property tax revenues for local governments.[6] Hamilton and Quayle (1999) at the University of British Columbia from their study indicated that proximity to greenways has a positive property value effect of around 15 per cent. Numerous reports quote the cost of treatment of the diseases where lack of physical activity is a risk factor and imply that green space provision for the activity has some economic justification.[7] Some of the noted economic benefits of the open space are as follows: (a) it enhances property prices; (b) it increases the property tax income of the municipality; (c) it earns rental income to the municipality; and (d) it indirectly enhances productivity and capability of the workforce.

Box 12.1 Yamuna Biodiversity Park

For the better preservation of nature and to retain the ecological, aesthetical and cultural qualities of Biodiversity sites in the National Capital Territory of Delhi, the DDA has set up a biodiversity park. The Yamuna Biodiversity Park is one among them. Some of the features of the biodiversity park are given as follows:

1. The Yamuna Biodiversity Park has been able to grow a wide variety of plants, shrubs, trees, herbs and so on. About 350 species of the most well-known herbal plants are maintained in the conservatory. The most noteworthy among them are Brahmi, *Safed Musali, Dama-bel,* six varieties of *Tulsi,* four varieties of lemon grass, three species of Phyllanthus, *Isabgol* and several species are used to cure multiple ailments.
2. About 850 plant species are ecologically assembled into 30 different forest communities. These communities include riparian, tropical dry deciduous, tropical thorn, shrub forest communities and salt bush land.
3. It has seven varieties of citrus fruit, eight varieties of *anar* (pomegranate), six varieties of *sapota* and six varieties of guava.
4. It has 75 species of butterfly; some of the notable among them are Common Castor, Peacock Pansy, Lime Butterfly and Common Silverline.
5. It has 196 spices of resident and migratory birds, and the most easily and frequently sighted ones are parakeets, 43 bulbuls, peafowls, prinias, munias and shikra.
6. It has biologically rich communities of animals such as civet, mongoose, hares, nilgai, jungle cat, wild pig and many herpetofauna and diverse food webs with three tropic levels. It has also breeding population of the Indian Cobra.
7. The other special areas of Yamuna Biodiversity Park are nurseries, amphitheatres, poly houses, orchards of Acacia and grasslands.

Source: Patwal (2019).

3. *Social values:* Public spaces are open to all, regardless of ethnic origin, age or gender, and as such, they represent a democratic forum for citizens and society. When properly designed and cared for, they bring communities together, provide meeting places and foster social ties of a kind that have been disappearing in many urban areas.[8] Urban open green spaces have been viewed not only as a setting for recreation and leisure but also as a significant part of the community and urban development, which can be used to eliminate social distinction. (Coley et al., 1997). They contribute to social justice by creating opportunities for all the people to participate in close interaction between social layers of diverse ethnic and racial backgrounds (Fainstein, 2005). Urban open green spaces contribute to human and social well-being and are essential for liveable and sustainable cities.[9] People irrespective of sex, caste, class and ethnicity have access to open space and this promotes inclusive social development. Some of the noted social benefits of the open space in general and the green open space, in particular, are as follows: (a) improve citizens' quality of life; (b) promote social inclusion; (c) strengthen personal relationship among people; (d) improve social networking; and (e) reduce crime and anti-social activities. Rogers and Urban Task Force (1999) had rightly proposed that we '... create beautiful places (in our towns and cities) that are socially cohesive, avoiding disparity of opportunity and promoting equity and social solidarity'.
4. *Cultural values:* Open space has significant cultural value. One vital role that urban parks play is providing space for the expression of diversity, both personal and cultural; this raises issues of democratic provision for accessing public open space (Thompson, 2002). The municipalities rent out open places for holding various cultural programmes, such as melodies, marriages, festivals, operas, circus and so on. Besides the government, the open places belonging to private individuals and corporates are rented out to the general public for the aforementioned programmes. Open space, recreation, public art and cultural amenities enhance the quality of life attributes in 'urban living' by (a) providing events and activities that project a creative, energetic 'vibe' that is attractive to business, visitors and residents alike; (b) ensuring that as the community grows, amenities are in place such as public art and art centres, museums, library, walking and biking network, neighbourhood, community and regional parks and recreational facilities; (c) promoting healthy community living with diverse choice in recreation and (d) supporting active lifestyles, strengthening public arts and culture offerings and activities.[10] One of UNESCO's documents has rightly envisaged that 'Public Spaces serve as the basic framework for urban landscape and reflect the history and cultural diversity of urban societies while allowing for a greater level of social diversity. They also have an economic dimension and promote development in communities and societies'.[11]
5. *Aesthetic values:* The open space in general and green space, in particular, is helpful in relaxation and stress reduction. Well-maintained green space in the cities with flora and fauna provides peace of mind. Individuals enjoy the serenity of nature along with their families and relax from their busy, stressful life by spending some quiet time with nature. Studies have also observed that people use green spaces for rest and restoration and also as means to de-stress.[12] Green spaces perceived to be 'serene', 'social' and 'natural' were said to have greater restorative effects. One meta-analysis reported that exercise undertaken in all green environments improved both self-esteem and mood (Lee et al., 2015). Regular physical activity in the green open space has shown to increase health and reduce the risk of a wide range of diseases, including heart disease, hypertension and diabetes. Physical

activity also relieves symptoms of depression and anxiety, improves mood and enhances psychological well-being. Numerous studies have also demonstrated that access to adequate open space for activities as well as passive recreational pursuits contributes to an individual's mental and physical well-being.[13] It is not a flight of fancy, but in reality, well-maintained green open spaces give aesthetic sense and values to the city. It gives a 'feel good' feeling to the individual.

6. *Political values:* This public ideal is closely intertwined with controversial arguments emphasizing the 'contact hypothesis', that socio-spatial contact between different ethnic and class groups generate the healthy psychological, social and political development of urban citizens (Hajer & Reijndorp, 2001; Sennett, 1971). Streets, parks, squares and other shared spaces of a city have been seen as symbols of collective well-being and possibility, expressions of achievement and aspiration by urban leaders and visionaries, sites of public encounter and formation of civic culture, and significant spaces of political deliberation and agonistic struggle.[14] The political parties both in power in national, state and municipal government try to maintain and upkeep the open spaces for organizing electioneering campaigns for their respective political parties. The Ramlila Maidan (ground) of Delhi and Gandhi Maidan (ground) in Patna, Bihar are illustrious examples of open spaces being used for political rallies and other rallies of farmers, labourers, social activists and religious rallies.

Open Space for Sustainability

Open spaces play an important role in generating and sustaining 'urban sustainability'. One of the vital indicators of urban sustainable development is the availability and accessibility of green spaces in the cities. In other words, urban sustainability depends on the quality and quantity of green spaces available in the cities. Greening of the city or green urbanism is supposed to be an important design concept for sustainable urbanization. There is a growing realization that urban green spaces are required for creating sustainable urban forms. Rapid urbanization leads to a decline in open spaces available across the cities. It affects the biodiversity and urban ecosystem which is essential for sustainable urbanization. A recent study estimated the total environmental economic value of Beijing's urban forest to be around 19,339 million CN¥. Out of this estimate, timber and fuelwood accounted for only 15.66 per cent and rest was composed of new value sources such as carbon sequestration, oxygen emission, rainfall interception, dust retention, biodiversity conservation and so on.[15] The three important aspects of green space in urban form which have bearing on sustainable development are as follows.

1. *Quantity of urban space:* This is the percentage of the urban area covered with green space.
2. *Quality of urban space:* This is the capability of the available green space to improve biodiversity and provide better ecosystem services in the urban area.
3. *Connectivity:* This means inter-connectedness between the green spaces with the biodiversity and the ecosystem on the one hand and city dwellers on the other hand.
4. *Accessibility:* This is the percentage of city population having access to green space. Global standards typically recommend at least a 33 per cent green cover for the urban areas.

It is rightly remarked that urban open spaces are the key ingredients in the cities' sustainability.

Factors Responsible for Deterioration of Open Spaces

Some of the factors responsible for the deterioration of the open spaces are as follows.

1. *Urbanization:* Over the past two decades, studies have shown that urban green spaces are disappearing fast. In many cities, these green open spaces are being seen to be destructed at an alarming rate. Urbanization remains the single most important factor that has been predominantly linked to causing such destructions. Honu et al. (2009) found out that rapid urbanization has resulted in the conversion of several urban lands into built-up structures and excessive destruction of the natural ecosystem including green spaces.
2. *Globalization:* The globalization is also another vital reason for the destruction of urban green open space. The government is doing construction activities in its vacant green spaces. Because of the rise in land value, private individuals are also selling out their green patches in the urban areas for making a profit. Gradually, the open spaces in the urban areas and most particularly in the million-plus cities are decreasing day by day.
3. *Poor attitude of the general public:* The ultimate beneficiaries of the green space are the general public. However, the uncooperative attitudes of the general public have resulted in the destruction of many public parks, playgrounds and green patches in many cities. Inadequate involvement of the general public in the management of green spaces is a probable cause for this problem. The general public many a time leave the stray animals in the open spaces. They have found to have destroyed many lawns, shrubs and other green environments. People think that preservation of green spaces is the work of the government and municipality. Instead of helping municipalities to preserve the green spaces, they are unconcerned and found to have destroyed many aspects of green spaces.
4. *Lack of care from the government and municipalities:* There is a lack of concern about urban open space on the side of the government and municipality. Many municipalities do not consider them as municipal assets. Rather, they think that if they construct some shops and shopping complexes, they will get some revenue out of it. They lack understanding about the aesthetic value of the open space to the city dweller.
5. *Conflict of ownership:* Sometimes, conflict of ownership over the open space leads to selling out of the open space. Sometimes, the state and municipal government also fight with each other over the ownership of the open space, and if the dispute continues for a longer period then the open space starts deteriorating.
6. *Poor maintenance:* Because of lack of finance, the municipal government gives cursory attention to the maintenance of the green open space. This leads to deterioration in the standard of the open space. It is seen that in many parks, the trees and plants start dying and the pathways are destroyed over a period of time because of poor maintenance.
7. *Landfilling:* Management of solid waste has become a super headache for the municipal administration in many cities. It is observed that many open spaces which could have been developed into parks and space for other recreational activities are being converted into landfill sites. The increased demand for landfilling sites for the disposition of urban solid waste is one of the reasons for the deterioration and reduction of open spaces in the highly urbanizing cities of the developing countries.
8. *Growth of urban slum:* Growth of slums in the cities and particularly in the populous cities has led to a decrease in quantity and quality of urban open space. It is largely being observed that the migrant and impoverished people mostly occupy the open spaces near the cities

and many of these areas have also come within the city after the expansion of the cities. The acquisition of open spaces by the slum population has led to deterioration of the quantity as well as the quality of the urban open space.

Renewal and Revitalization of Urban Open Space

Open space is a critical urban infrastructure which improves physical, social and mental health of urbanites. It strengthens urban communities and makes cities an attractive place to live and work. The renewal and revitalization of urban open space would be helpful to the city dweller in many ways that are to (a) enhance economic activities in the city; (b) increase daily physical activities; (c) reconnect children and elderly with nature; and (d) reduce crime by providing safe, healthy, alternatives for at-risk youth. The report of Rogers and Urban Task Force (1999) states:

> To achieve urban integration means thinking of urban open space not as an isolated unit—be it a street, park or square—but as a vital part of urban landscape with its own specific set of functions. Public space should be conceived of as an outdoor room within a neighborhood, somewhere to relax, and enjoy the urban experience, a venue for a range of different activities, from outdoor eating to street entertainment; from sport and play areas to a venue for civic or political functions; and most importantly of all a place for walking or sitting-out. Public spaces work best when they establish a direct relationship between the space and the people who live and work around it.

Some of the measures to be taken for the renewal and revitalization of urban open space are given as follows.

1. *Financial support:* The state and local self-government need to allocate finance for the renewal and revitalization of the open space. The political and bureaucratic willpower is essential for this purpose. Without additional financial support, planning and maintenance of open spaces are impossible.
2. *PPP:* The state government and the municipalities can involve the private and corporate sectors in the renewal and revitalization of open space. The involvement of the private sector in the provision of open spaces of the city has enormous potential. Involvement of the private sector is a form of participation of the urban community through the planning and design process. The implementation of design and even financing is done through the provision of CSR funds.[16]
3. *Role of NGOs and CSOs:* The government needs to promote the role of the NGOs and CSOs in the rejuvenation and management of open spaces and more particularly parks. It is noted that the initiative collaborated with various non-profits to help provide resources, in some cases offering financial assistance, maintenance and management of each park to help offset expenses.[17]
4. *Change in public attitude:* Public attitude towards the value and importance of open space needs to be changed. Government and municipalities need to conduct an awareness campaign on the need and importance of open space for the physical and psychological development of the residents. The public should consider it as their community asset and try to protect the health of open space for their well-being.
5. *Checking growth of slum:* The cities need to decide the optimum population it should have. The growth of slum and temporary sheds of the poor migrant rural population in the open

spaces of the urban areas also reduce the number and size of open space in the cities. Therefore, the cities need to impose a restriction on the proliferation of the slums.

6. *Open space planning and management policy:* Government needs to formulate a policy on open space planning and management. The implementation of these policies is done at the municipality level. Without an effective open space policy, open space creation, renewal and revitalization would not be possible in a systematic way.
7. *Create a shared vision:* The open spaces are meant not only for the beautification of the cities but also for the physical and psychological development of the urbanites. The renewal and revitalization of the open space need to be a shared vision of all the stakeholders such as the government—both centre and state, the urban local bodies, the private sector, NGOs and the city population at large. The participatory approach needs to be followed for the growth, renewal and revitalization of the open space in the cities.

Aspects for Revitalization of Open Space

Urban open space is important to urban development and well-being of the urban dwellers. Open space adds value to the name and fame of the city. For example, Chandigarh is known for its rose garden and rock garden. The art of open space is treated as an effective tool of energizing city life, and therefore, its revitalization is essential. Revitalization of open space has many aspects. The most common typology refers to dominating aspects: spatial (including technical, architectonic, urban and aesthetic), economic, social, cultural and environmental (Sas-Bojarska, 2018). A few important aspects of urban open space are as follows.

1. *Political aspects:* Keeping public space in the city landscape depends on political decision-making and political power. The growing slums in the open spaces of various cities and political parties supporting it and regularizing slums in the open spaces of the city for vote bank politics gradually synchronize public spaces in many cities. Grabbing of the public land by the political leaders and their musclemen is being reported. Thus, the political aspect of open space is one of the critical aspects to sustain, maintain and keep the sanctity of open space in the cities.
2. *Bureaucratic aspects:* Besides political willpower, bureaucracy is also equally important for the revitalization and sustenance of urban open space. For example, in Bangalore city in India, planning authorities converted several tanks into bus depots, residential layouts and sports stadiums; thus, irreversibly changing the ecological, social and cultural functions of the pre-colonial water bodies (Srinivas, 2004). A report on open spaces in Bangalore revealed a decline in the growth rate of the city's parks, playgrounds and recreational spaces between 1960 and 2003 (Ravindran, 2007).
3. *Economic aspects:* Urban green space constitutes a vital element of all the cities. It affects the overall physical space and built environment of the city. It makes cities attractive. Availability of open space enhances the land values and helps the urban administration to earn more revenue. In other words, availability of open space is an economic gain to the city. Besides keeping the open space green, cleaning and its beautification require investment. Erica Gies has rightly noted that the parks and preserved lands boost land values and property taxes, attract residents and businesses, encourage economic development, boost the economy of surrounding areas, save money over some types of

development, preserve ecosystem services and reduce healthcare costs. Thus, the economic aspect is crucial to open space.[18]

4. *Ecological aspects:* Urban green open spaces are indispensable elements of ecological, aesthetic and recreational value. The flora and fauna grow and develop in the open space and improve the environmental health of the city. It improves the health and quality of living of the city dwellers. Environmental consideration is one of the important considerations for the growth and development of the city. Urban ecology and ecosystem depend on urban green open space.
5. *Social and cultural aspects:* The last but not the least aspect of open space is the social and cultural aspect. The open space gives opportunity and provides space for social networking among all age group of the population in the city. It enables to build a healthy neighbourhood in the city. Moreover, within the open space, the cultural heritage and historical values are manifested. It provides space for cultural activities to take place. Fairs and festivals are organized and the social and cultural values are glorified.

Summing Up

Open space creation, renewal and revitalization can no longer be dismissed as a frill. The open spaces are essential for the economic, social, cultural and political well-being of the urbanites. These places bring significant and diverse values to society. It promotes social networking and the well-being of the urban community. It promotes aesthetic sense and gives happiness. Open space protection is an important component behind successful community development projects, and a major contributor to the character of a place that forms the foundation of its economy. The preservation of green spaces is the work of only the city authorities but also all the stakeholders such the municipalities, private sectors, NGOs and city dwellers at large. According to WHO, the living conditions in the urban environment are the key to the health and well-being of its inhabitants. Evidence from the literature indicates that there is an association between the availability of green open space and the health and well-being, and the levels of physical activity. City parks and open spaces improve our physical and psychological health, strengthen our communities and make our cities and neighbourhoods more attractive places to live and work.[19] It is remarked that the lack and poor quality of open/green space in urban neighbourhoods can be a serious restriction for the well-being of the inhabitants as it does not support developing healthy lifestyles, including spending time outdoors, walking, playing and so on (Mitchell & Popham, 2008). Modern urban lifestyle is associated with chronic stress, insufficient physical activity and exposure to anthropogenic environmental hazards. Urban green space, such as parks, playgrounds and residential greenery, can promote mental and physical health and reduce morbidity and mortality in urban residents by providing psychological relaxation and stress alleviation, stimulating social cohesion, supporting physical activity and reducing exposure to air pollutants, noise and excessive heat.[20]

Keywords

Open Space, Environmental Value of Open Space, Economic Value of Open Space, Cultural Value of Open Space, Aesthetic Value of Open Space, Public–Private Partnership.

REVIEW QUESTIONS

1. Discuss the meaning and importance of open space for urban development.
2. What is open space? What are its values to the cities?
3. Explain various factors responsible for deterioration of urban open space.
4. Why open space is required? Describe the steps to be taken for the renewal and restoration of open space in urban areas.
5. Write short notes on the following:
   a. Open space
   b. Economic values of open space
   c. Environmental values of open space
   d. Cultural values of open space
   e. Role of stakeholders in the renewal and revitalization of open space

Notes

1. http://www.acta.sapientia.ro/acta-agrenv/Supl2011/11_Balogh.pdf (accessed on 20 January 2019).
2. https://cdr.lib.unc.edu/indexablecontent/uuid:39297d97-89cb-4c2f-881a-3b69fb9c3271 (accessed on 20 January 2019).
3. http://ln-institute.org/urban-spaces/urban-spaces.php?encyclopedia_id=255 (accessed on 20 April 2019).
4. https://www.sciencedirect.com/science/article/pii/S0169204602000592 (accessed on 20 January 2019).
5. https://www.researchgate.net/publication/322775387_THE_ENVIRONMENTAL_BENEFITS_OF_URBAN_OPEN_GREEN_SPACES (accessed on 20 January 2019).
6. https://activelivingresearch.org/sites/activelivingresearch.org/files/Synthesis_Shoup-Ewing_March2010_0.pdf (accessed on 20 January 2019).
7. http://www.hphpcentral.com/wp-content/uploads/2010/09/Economic-Benefits.pdf (accessed on 20 January 2019).
8. https://www.designcouncil.org.uk/sites/default/files/asset/document/the-value-of-public-space1.pdf (accessed on 21 January 2019).
9. http://www.euro.who.int/__data/assets/pdf_file/0010/342289/Urban-Green-Spaces_EN_WHO_web.pdf (accessed on 20 January 2019).
10. https://www.tempe.gov/Home/ShowDocument?id=18995 (accessed on 20 January 2019).
11. https://en.unesco.org/news/culture-public-spaces-key-shaping-new-urban-agenda (accessed on 20 January 2019).
12. https://www.ncbi.nlm.nih.gov/pmc/articles/PMC4556255/ (accessed on 20 January 2019).
13. https://www.burlingtonvt.gov/sites/default/files/PZ/OpenSpaceProtectionPlan/2.Value%20of%20Urban%20Open%20Space.pdf (accessed on 20 January 2019).
14. http://publicspace.org/en/text-library/eng/b003-collective-culture-and-urban-public-space (accessed on 20 January 2019).
15. http://sustainabilityoutlook.in/content/open-spaces-urban-sustainability (accessed on 31 September 2019).
16. https://www.researchgate.net/publication/328291271_The_Role_of_CSR_in_the_Revitalization_of_Urban_Open_Space_for_Better_Sustainable_Urban_Development/download (accessed on 21 January 2019).
17. https://www.ourla2040.org/open-space (accessed on 20 January 2019).

18. https://conservationtools.org/library_items/topic/132-Economic-Benefits-of-Open-Space (accessed on 2 October 2019).
19. https://conservationtools-production.s3.amazonaws.com/library_item_files/48/40/parks_for_people_Jan2004.pdf?AWSAccessKeyId=AKIAIQFJLILYGVDR4AMQ&Expires=1554811005&Signature=RbCkL3ru%2F67EoUqTC7KzPyIlef4%3D (accessed on 9 April 2019).
20. https://link.springer.com/chapter/10.1007/978-3-319-56091-5_11 (accessed on 26 April 2019).

References

Berg, M. V. D., Wendel-Vos, W., Proppel, M., Kemper, H., Mechelen, W. V., & Maas, J. (2015). Health benefits of green spaces in the living environment: A systematic review of epidemiological studies. *Urban Forestry & Urban Greening, 14*(4), 806–816. file:///C:/Users/new%20world/Downloads/30-61-1-PB.pdf (accessed on 23 January 2019).

Box, J., & Harrison, C. (1993). Natural spaces in urban places. *Town and Country Planning, 62*(9), 231–235. https://rsa.tandfonline.com/doi/pdf/10.1080/713691902 (accessed on 9 April 2019).

Carr, S., Francis, M., Rivlin, L. G., & Stone, A. M. (1992). *Public space.* Cambridge: Cambridge University Press.

Chen, T., Liu, T., Xie, X., & Marusic, B. G. (2016). What attracts people to visit community open spaces? A case study of the overseas Chinese town community in Shenzhen, China. *International Journal of Environmental Research and Public Health, 13*(7), 2–17.

Coley, R. L., Sullivan, W. C., & Kuo, F. E. (1997). Where does community grow? The social context created by nature in urban public housing. *Environment and Behavior, 29*(4), 468–494.

Fainstein, S. S. (2005). Cities and diversity: Should we want it? Can we plan for it? *Urban Affairs Review, 41*(1), 3–19.

Hajer, M., & Reijndorp, A. (2001). *In search of new public domain.* Rotterdam: NAi Uitgevers.

Hall, P. (1998). *Sociable cities: The legacy of Ebenezer Howard.* Chichester: Wiley.

Hamilton, S., & Quayle, M. (1999). *Corridors of green and gold: Impact of Riparian Suburban Greenways on property values.* Vancouver: Fraser River Action Plan, Department of Fisheries and Oceans. http://citeseerx.ist.psu.edu/viewdoc/download?doi=10.1.1.605.4950&rep=rep1&type=pdf (accessed on 21 January 2019).

Honu, Y. A. K., Chandy, S., & Gibson, D. J. (2009). Occurrence of non-native species deep in natural areas of the Shawnee Natural Forest, Southern Illinois, USA. *Natural Areas Journal, 29*(2), 177–187.

Jim, C. Y., & Chen, W. Y. (2006). Recreation–amenity use and contingent valuation of urban greenspaces in Guangzhou, China. *Landscape and Urban Planning, 75*, 81–96.

Lee, A. C. K., Jordan, H. C., & Horsley, J. (2015). Urban green spaces in promoting healthy living and well-being: Prospects for planning. *Risk Management Healthy Policy, 8*, 131–137.

Levent, T. B, & Nijkamp, P. (2004). Urban green space policies: Performance and success conditions in European cities, in preliminary vision. 44th European Congress of the European Regional Science Association, Regions and Fiscal Federalism, Portugal. https://pdfs.semanticscholar.org/15b8/3caaf9f8bf6b105f9ee60a47cfd5f793940d.pdf?_ga=2.182972262.1128365025.1588849480-1385769566.1559037232 (accessed on 8 May 2020).

Mitchell, R., & Popham, F. (2008). Effect of exposure to natural environment on health inequalities: An observational population study. *Lancet, 372*, 1655–1660.

Patwal, J. (2019). *A comparative study of Yamuna Biodiversity Park and Aravalli Biodiversity Park* [Dissertation Report]. New Delhi: PGDUPDL, IGNOU.

Ravindran, D. S. (2007). *Wither open spaces? A politico-economic analysis of open spaces provisioning in Bangalore, India* [PGPPM Dissertation]. Indian Institute of Management, Bangalore.

Rogers, R., & Urban Task Force. (1999). *Towards an urban renaissance: Final report of the Urban Task Force* (Chaired by Lord Rogers of Riverside). London: Department of the Environment, Transport and the Regions. http://citeseerx.ist.psu.edu/viewdoc/download?doi=10.1.1.463.2355&rep=rep1&type=pdf (accessed on 1 March 2019).

Sas-Bojarska, A. (2018). Linear revitalization: Problem and challenges. *Urban Development Issues, 53*(1). https://content.sciendo.com/view/journals/udi/53/1/article-p5.xml (accessed on 17 April 2020).

Schipperijn, U. K., Stigsdotter, T. B., & Troelsen, J. (2010). Influences on the use of urban green space—A case study in Odense, Denmark. *Urban Forestry & Urban Greening, 9*, 25–32.

Sennett, R. (1971). *The uses of disorder*. New York: Vintage.

Srinivas, S. (2004). *Landscapes of urban memory: The sacred and the civic in India's high-tech city*. Hyderabad: Orient BlackSwan.

Stanley, B. W., Stark, L. B., Johnston, K. L., & Smith, M. E. (2012). Urban open spaces in historical perspective: A trans-disciplinary typology and analysis. *Urban Geography, 33*(8), 1089–1117.

Thompson, C. W. (2002). Urban open space in the 21st century. *Land Scape and Urban Planning, 60*(2), 59–72.

WHO. (2017). *Urban Green Spaces: A brief for action*. Copenhagen: Regional Office of Europe, World Health Organization. http://www.euro.who.int/__data/assets/pdf_file/0010/342289/Urban-Green-Spaces_EN_WHO_web3.pdf?ua=1 (accessed on 9 April 2019).

Wolch, J. R., Byme, J., & Newell, J. P. (2014). Urban green space, public health, and environmental justice: The challenge of making cities 'just green enough'. *Landscape and Urban Planning, 125*, 234–244.

13 Urban Slum, Informal Settlements and Urban Informal Sector

Slums are a manifestation of the two main challenges facing human settlements development at the beginning of the new millennium: rapid urbanization and the urbanization of poverty. Slums areas have the highest concentrations of poor people and the worst shelter and physical environmental conditions.

—UN-Habitat (2003)

As the world continues to urbanize and globalize at the most rapid pace in modern history, the global population of slum dwellers also continues to grow tremendously. Urban slums are the world's fastest-growing human habitat.[1]

Informal Settlements and urban informality is a serious and common problem in Third World countries. The Informal Settlements emerged in and around big cities since the sixties of the twentieth century, due to natural growth and the flux of rural-urban migration.

—Nassar and Elsayed (2018)

Introduction

Urbanization is taking place at a rapid pace in the developing countries. It is estimated that more than half of the world's population lives in urban areas, and it is projected that by 2030 over half of the residents in low- and middle-income countries will reside in cities (Montgomery, 2008). The UN-Habitat has rightly termed that the world is rapidly moving towards 'maximum urbanization', which has already largely been completed in Europe and North and South America. The unplanned growth of population in the cities has laid to the growth of slums in most of the cities of the developing countries. It is estimated that more than 40 per cent of the population in the million-plus cities in India are living in slums. The impoverished people, who are staying in a slum, constitute a gigantic element of vote bank politics in the developing countries. The political parties allure these impoverished people with the hope of providing them basic amenities, such as houses, free electricity and water and other benefits for votes. It is sometimes thought that political parties sincerely do not want to abolish or demolish slums and informal settlements in the cities for their vested political interests. Informal settlements are seen near construction sites, adjacent to railway lines, close to sewerage lines, which are largely rejected and filthy places devoid of basic amenities. To Zarate

(2016), 'informal settlements' do not indicate the relevance of the places in their cities that they occupy or the spatial segregation they usually suffer from; the lack of access to affordable and public transportation, places of employment, schools, hospitals and other basic facilities; the lack or limited access to financial resources such as credits, subsidies and so on. According to UN-Habitat in our world, one in eight people lives in slums. In total, around a billion people live in slums today.[2] Worldwide, at least 860 million people are now living in slums, and the number of slum dwellers grew by six million each year from 2000 to 2010 (UN-Habitat, 2012). Therefore, any deliberations on urban development without taking into consideration urban slum would be incomprehensive.

LEARNING OBJECTIVES

This chapter deals with urban slums and informal settlements and the urban informal sector. After reading this chapter, you should be able to:

- ❒ Define urban slum and informal sector
- ❒ Describe various characteristics of urban slums and informal settlements
- ❒ Narrate factors responsible for the growth of urban slums and informal settlements
- ❒ Discuss the issues and challenges pertaining to urban slums and informal settlements
- ❒ Define the informal sector and describe the characteristics of the urban informal sector
- ❒ Describe the need and importance of the urban informal sector
- ❒ Narrate the issues and challenges pertaining to the urban informal sector
- ❒ Discuss the measures to be taken for the improvement of life of the people working in the urban informal sector

I
URBAN SLUMS AND INFORMAL SETTLEMENTS

Urban Slums and Informal Settlements: Definition and Characteristics

The word 'slum' was first used in London at the beginning of the 19th century to describe a 'room of low repute' or 'low, unfrequented parts of the town'.[3] A slum is defined by the United Nations Program on Human Settlements (UN-Habitat, 2002) as 'a contiguous settlement where the inhabitants are characterized as having inadequate housing and basic services. A slum is often not recognized and addressed by the public authorities as an integral or equal part of the city'. According to a document by UNESCO, 'a slum is a building, a group of buildings or an area characterized by overcrowding, deterioration, unsanitary conditions or absence of facilities or amenities, which because of these conditions or any of them endanger the health, safety or morals of its inhabitants or the community'.[4] As far as informal settlement is concerned, the Habitat-III (2015) has defined informal settlements as the residential areas where (a) inhabitants have no security of tenure vis-à-vis the land or dwellings they inhabit, with modalities ranging from squatting to informal rental housing; (b) the neighbourhoods usually lack, or are cut off from, basic services and city infrastructure; and (c) the housing may not comply with the current planning and building regulations, and is often situated in geographically and environmentally hazardous areas. The words 'informal settlements' and 'slums' are interchangeably used in the developing countries to characterize the dilapidated living condition of the impoverished in the cities. The United Nations operationally defines a slum as 'one or a group of individuals living under the same roof in an urban area, lacking in one or more of the following five amenities':

1. Durable housing (a permanent structure providing protection from extreme climatic conditions).
2. Sufficient living area (no more than three people sharing a room).
3. Access to improved water (water that is sufficient, affordable and can be obtained without extreme effort).
4. Access to improved sanitation facilities (a private toilet or a public one shared with a reasonable number of people).
5. Secure tenure (*de facto* or *de jure* secure tenure status and protection against forced eviction; UN-Habitat, 2006).

The country-specific definition of slum also more or less is analogous to the one given by the United Nations. Uganda, for example, in a document outlining a slum upgrading strategy and an action plan from 2008, defines slums as combining the UN definition with more localized characteristics reflecting the 'Ugandan situation': (a) attracting a high density of low-income earners and/or unemployed persons with low levels of literacy; (b) an area with high rates/levels of noise, crime, drug abuse, immorality (pornography and prostitution) and alcoholism, and high HIV/AIDS prevalence; or (c) an area where houses are on environmentally fragile lands, for example, wetlands. (The Republic of Uganda, 2008). In the Indian context, a slum is defined in Chapter II Section 3 of the Slum Areas Act, 1956 as 'those houses which require repair, stability, natural light and air, a system of dump, water supply drainage and sanitary conveniences, facilities for storage, preparation or cooking of food and disposal of wastewater, the building deemed to be unfit if it is so for defective in one or more of the same matter and not found reasonably suitable for occupation in that condition'. For the survey in 1993 and 2002, the National Sample Survey Organization adopted the definition of slums as 'a slum is a compact settlement with a collection of poorly built tenements, mostly of temporary nature, crowded together usually with inadequate sanitary and drinking water facilities in unhygienic conditions. Such an area, for the purpose of this survey was considered as "non-notified slum" if at least 20 households lived in that area. Areas notified as slums by the respective municipalities, corporations, local bodies or development authorities are treated as "notified slums". Census 2011 explained slums as residential areas where dwellings are unfit for human habitation by reasons of dilapidation, overcrowding, faulty arrangements and design of such buildings, narrowness or faulty arrangement of street, lack of ventilation, light, or sanitation facilities or any combination of these factors which is detrimental to the safety and health.[5] Various indicators and threshold of defining slums are given in Table 13.1.

From all these definitions, it can be concluded that the urban slums and informal settlements are those places in urban areas, which are predominated with low-income migrant workers whose housing conditions are very poor and many of these houses are kutcha houses deprived of basic amenities like safe drinking water, kitchen, toilet and bathroom facilities and also lack of other

Table 13.1 Indicators and Threshold of Defining Slums

Characteristic	Indicator	Definition
Access to water	Inadequate drinking water supply	A settlement has inadequate drinking water supply if less than 50% of HHs have improved water supply: • HH connection • Access to public stand pipe • Rainwater collection with at least 20 lpcd within an acceptable collection distance
Access to sanitation	Inadequate sanitation	A settlement has inadequate sanitation if less than 50% HHs have improved sanitation: • Public sewer • Septic tank • Pour flush latrine • Ventilated improved pit latrine The excreta disposal system is considered adequate if it is private or shared by a maximum of two HHs
Structural quality of housing	Location	Proportion of HH residing on or near hazardous site. The following locations should be considered: • Housing in geologically hazardous zones (landslides/earthquakes and floodareas) • Houses on or under garbage mountains • Housing around high industrial pollution areas • Housing around other unprotected high risk zones (railroads, airports, energy transmission lines)
	Permanency of structures	Proportion of HHs living in temporary and/or dilapidated structures. Following factors could be considered when placing a housing unit in these conditions: • Quality of construction (eg material used for wall, floor and roof) • Compliance with local building codes, standards and byelaws
Overcrowding	Overcrowding	Proportion of HH with more than two persons per room. The alternative is to set a minimum standard for floor area per person (5sq. metres).
Security of tenure	Security of tenure	• Proportion of HHs with formal title deeds to both land and residence • Proportion of HHs with formal title deeds to either one of land and residence • Proportion of HHs with enforceable agreements or any document as a proof of a tenure arrangement

Source: https://www.researchgate.net/publication/319988165_Slums_and_Urban_Environmental_Challenges_in_India_An_Appraisal_of_Planning_and_Policy_Issues (accessed on 24 January 2019).

basic household amenities. There is a poor provision of education and health facilities in the slum areas. In South Asia, slums are known by various names: *chawls/chalis* (Ahmedabad, Mumbai), *ahatas* (Kanpur), *katras* (Delhi), *bustee* (Kolkata), *jhopadpattis* (Maharashtra), *cheris* (Chennai), *katchi abadis* (Karachi), *watta, pelpath, udukku* or *pelli gewal* (Colombo). In the USA, the slums are called 'hood' and 'ghettos' (UN-Habitat, 2003).

Characteristics of Slums and Informal Settlements

Some of the characteristics of urban slums and informal settlements are as follows.

1. *Illegal and temporary settlements:* The slums in most parts of the world are illegal settlements. The slum dwellers do not have the ownership right of the land in which they reside. UN-Habitat has envisaged that a number of definitions consider the lack of security of tenure as a central characteristic of slums, and regard lack of any formal document entitling the occupant to occupy the land or structure as prima facie evidence of illegality and slum occupation.
2. *Substandard housing:* The housing structure in the slums is largely substandard and is just for eking out a living for the sake of living. They are made of low-quality materials and most of them are kutcha houses made of low-quality bricks, mud, tarpaulin shades and so on. To UN-Habitat, the slum areas are associated with a high number of substandard housing structures, often built with non-permanent materials unsuitable for housing in given local conditions of climate and location.
3. *Lack of basic amenities:* The slum dwellers lack basic amenities such as notorious food, proper clothing, safe drinking water, sanitation, electricity and cooking gas facilities. Except a very few, most of them do not have these facilities. Moreover, their children are also found to be deprived of basic education and healthcare. According to UN-Habitat, the slums' lack of access to improved sanitation facilities and improved water sources are the most important features, sometimes supplemented by the absence of waste collection systems, electricity supply, surfaced roads and footpaths, street lighting and rainwater drainage.
4. *Overcrowding:* The slum areas are generally seen to be overcrowded. Most of the houses are single rooms which house all the family members. The parents, children and even the fellow relatives if visit also share the same room. According to UN-Habitat, overcrowding is associated with a low space per person, high occupancy rates, cohabitation by different families and a high number of single-room units.
5. *Predominated with impoverished and low income population:* The slums are largely populated by low-income and poverty-stricken population. The male members are employed in menial casual and low-income activities and are petty shopkeepers, rickshaw pullers, street vendors, ragpickers, bicycle mechanics and so on, while women work as casual labour, housemaids and so on. In a few families, even children support the family for eking livelihood.
6. *Migrant population:* The slum dwellers are largely the migrant population from the poorer regions and states and from the rural areas. Some are even found to be seasonal migrant labours.
7. *Social exclusion:* The slum people, because of their characteristics and locations, are largely excluded from the rest of the urban population. It is commented that the slum areas are the residences of criminal elements. The UN-Habitat has rightly remarked that the slums are the areas of social exclusion that are often perceived to have high levels of crimes and other measures of social dislocation. In some definitions, such areas are associated with certain vulnerable groups of population, such as recent immigrants, internally displaced persons or ethnic minorities.
8. *Hazardous location:* Last but not the least, the slums are largely found in unhealthy locations such as near the railway stations, by the side of the sewerage canal, near the waste disposal sites of the factories. Therefore, most of the slum population is found to be suffering from

Table 13.2 Population Living in the Slums (% of Urban Population), 2014

Countries	% of Urban Population Living in Slums
Afghanistan	63
Bangladesh	55
China	25
Ethiopia	74
India	24
Iraq	47
Kenya	56
Nepal	54
Nigeria	50
Pakistan	46
Thailand	25

Source: https://data.worldbank.org/indicator/EN.POP.SLUM.UR.ZS?view=chart (accessed on 23 January 2019).

various types of diseases. The UN-Habitat has envisaged that the slums houses might be built on hazardous locations or land unsuitable for settlement, such as floodplains, in proximity to industrial plants with toxic emissions or waste disposal sites and on the areas subjected to landslip. The percentages of urban population living in the slums of a few selected countries of the world are given in Table 13.2. The status of five largest slums of the world is given in Box 13.1.

Box 13.1 Five Largest Slums in the World

1. *Khayeltisha, Cape Town, South Africa:* Khayeltisha's population is projected to be around 400,000, with a striking 40 per cent of its residents under 19 years of age.
2. *Kibera, Nairobi, Kenya:* The largest urban slum in Africa, Kibera is estimated to be housing anywhere from 200,000 to 1 million people.
3. *Dharavi, Mumbai, India:* Also famous among journalists and development organizations, Dharavi is home to somewhere between 600,000 and 1 million people. Dharavi is located squarely in the heart of Mumbai.
4. *Orangi Town, Karachi, Pakistan:* Orangi has crept up in notoriety as the largest slum in Asia, compared to its long-time predecessor, Dharavi. With a population of over 1 million, Orangi was once the centre of ethnic conflict between the Pathans and Bihari gangs.
5. *Neza-Chalco-Itza, Mexico City, Mexico:* With around 4 million residents, Neza-Chalco-Itza barrio has been considered as the largest slum area in the world. Unique to this area is its diversity in housing arrangements. Most residents live illegally on authorized land.

Source: https://borgenproject.org/5-largest-slums-world/ (accessed on 21 January 2019).

Box 13.2 Features of India's Urban Slum

1. Urban slum contributes to 7 per cent of the country's GDP.
2. In million-plus cities, nearly 40 per cent of the households live in slums.
3. Five metro cities, namely, Mumbai, Delhi, Chennai, Hyderabad and Kolkata account for more than 50 per cent of the total slum households in the country.
4. A total of 36 per cent of the slum households do not have three basic facilities: electricity, tap water and sanitation within the house premises.

Source: https://economictimes.indiatimes.com/news/economy/indicators/people-in-urban-slums-contribute-over-7-of-gdp-study/articleshow/24199742.cms (accessed on 25 June 2020).

Nassar and Elsayed (2018), in the context of Egypt in their article on 'From Informal Settlements to Sustainable Communities', have noted that in 2008, the Informal Settlement Development Facility redefined 'Slums' or 'Informal Settlements' to 'Unsafe Areas' and 'Unplanned areas', where unsafe areas are characterized by being subjected to life threat, or having inappropriate housing, or exposed to health threat or tenure risks. Whereas, the unplanned areas are principally characterized by their noncompliance to planning and building laws and regulations. Thus, the features of slums and informal settlements are characterized by many negative aspects of human living conditions: unsafe, unplanned, overcrowded, illegal and so on. People eke out their living in the slums and informal settlements in urban areas out of compulsion and inability to afford to live in formal settlements. The features of India's urban slum are given in Box 13.2.

Factors Responsible for the Formation and Growth of Urban Slums and Informal Settlements

With the unbridled urbanization in the developing countries, the number of slums and also the number of populations living in the city slums is increasing. It is more visible in the developing countries of Africa and South Asia. Many factors are responsible for the growth of slums in the cities. According to UN-Habitat in general, slums are the products of failed policies, bad governance, corruption, inappropriate regulation, dysfunctional land markets, unresponsive financial systems and a fundamental lack of political will.[6]

Let us describe some of the important factors responsible for the growth of slums in the developing countries.

1. *Urbanization:* At the outset, urbanization in general, and unplanned urbanization in particular, is one of the important causes of slums in the cities. The cities are incapable of providing gainful employment and infrastructure for the growing number of people in the cities. As a result, the impoverished, those who are illiterate and are casual labourers, are sheltering in the slums by making temporary housing.
2. *Globalization:* Globalization is also one of the factors for urbanization and growth of slums in the cities. The developing countries in general are not able to cope with the globalization process and are largely incapable of providing the required infrastructure for the globalization process. This has resulted in the growth of urban slums. The Global Report on

Human Settlements 2001 was concerned largely with the globalization and its effect on urban settlements.

3. *Urban pull and rural push:* It is also one of the important factors of the increasing number of slums in the cities. The urban relatives staying in the slums pull their friends and kith and kins from the village to the cities. A high percentage of slum population belongs to the rural areas of the poorer states. Thus, rural-to-urban migration is one of the important reasons for the rising population in the slums.
4. *Informal sector:* The urban informal sector is also responsible for the growth of slums. The people who migrate from the rural to urban areas get employed in the urban informal sector, where the income is very low and there is no job security. With low wage rate and income, these people are forced to live in slums and in slum-like areas where they do not have to pay any house rent and low rent. The UN-Habitat has rightly remarked that the urban poor are trapped in an informal and 'illegal' world—in slums that are not reflected on maps, where waste is not collected, where taxes are not paid and where public services are not provided (UN-Habitat, 2003).
5. *Urban governance:* The poor urban governance in the developing countries also fails to check the growth of slums in the cities of the developing countries. There is no proper urban planning and the urban administration does not take any proactive step to check the growth of slums. UN-Habitat has rightly remarked that the slums must be seen as the result of failure of housing policies, laws and delivery systems, as well as of national and urban policies (UN-Habitat, 2003).
6. *Market forces:* One of the factors for the growth of slums in the cities in general, and metro cities in particular, is the foul play of the market forces. The draw of lots system by the government and foul play of private land-market player forces the impoverished people to resort to urban slums, the illegal land. For the poor working in the fragile informal sector, buying a land from the government and also from the private is a herculean task. This has promoted growth of slums in the cities. The neo-liberal urban economists regarded slums as the natural response of the market in providing housing for poor people: the housing that they can afford.[7]
7. *Politics of slum:* In the developing countries, there is a strong politics of slums. The political parties are not keen to eradicate slums from the cities and rather use them as a vote bank by giving them menial benefits and subsidies. No political party wants to touch a slum because of fear to be voted out of power. One of the former Chief Ministers of Delhi has admitted that slums have growth in the city because they are a potential vote bank for the political parties.[8]
8. *Poor land-use planning:* The land-use planning of most of the developing countries and the municipalities is extremely poor. Moreover, lack of finance for infrastructure development activities keeps many open spaces vacant for a long period of time. This gives an opportunity to the migrant people to make temporary makeshift houses, and gradually with the growth of population the area develops into a slum. In Brazil, the slums grow up in the invaded lands. These invaded areas are generally located close to the city centres, but mostly unsuitable for human occupation due to geographical and ecological factors.[9]
9. *Poverty and unemployment:* Last but not the least, two important causes for the growth of slums in the cities are poverty and unemployment. A large percentage of people living in the slums belong to the BPL families and are employed casual and petty self-employment activities. The wage rate and earnings are very low. The government and the municipalities

have also failed to eradicate urban poverty and unemployment mostly in the developing countries.

10. *Peoples' attitude and family compulsion:* Last but not the least, the cause for the growth of slums is the attitude of the people. Large family size, responsibility to send money to families and parents staying at home in the village and saving to buy land in the native place are some of the compulsions which compel many slum dwellers to stick to slums even after they become well-up to affording a better accommodation.

Issues and Challenges of Slums and Informal Settlements

Issues and challenges of slums and informal settlements are as follows:

1. *Poverty:* The most vital and pressing issue of the urban slum is poverty. People living in slums are predominantly impoverished migrant population from rural areas of economically weaker states and provinces of the nation. UN-Habitat document has envisaged that slums have, however, also come to include the vast informal settlements that are quickly becoming the most visible expression of urban poverty in the cities of developing countries, including squatter settlements and illegal subdivisions (UN-Habitat, 2003). The greatest challenge before the government is to eradicate poverty from the urban slums.
2. *Inequality:* The slum people are victims of economic, social and political inequality. Their income is astoundingly low as compared to other sections of the urban population. Income inequality is a necked feature of urban paradox amidst slums. The other economic inequality is with regard to the quality of employment, a large percentage of slum people work in the urban informal sector and many of them are menial casual workers. Besides economic inequality, the slum dwellers are subjected to social inequality as their social networking with other urban sections of the population is very low. Their social status in terms of education, health and women empowerment is also low.
3. *Quality of life:* The standard of living of slum dwellers is very low. They live in low-quality houses and many of them lack access to safe drinking water, sanitation, nutrition and other basic amenities of life. The UN-Habitat report has envisaged that the quality of dwellings in such settlements varies from the simplest shack to permanent structures, while access to water, electricity, sanitation and other basic services and infrastructure is usually limited. Such settlements are referred to by a wide range of names and include a variety of tenure arrangements (UN-Habitat, 2003). Many families in the slums do not have even a ration card and BPL card which deprive them of having access to basic food grains at subsidized prices.
4. *Infrastructure:* One of the biggest issues in the slum is low-quality infrastructure. There is lack of proper road, sewerage system, electricity connections and piped drinking water infrastructure. One of the documents of the Asian Development Bank has rightly commented that the settlements labelled as slums are characterized by inadequate basic facilities, and limited accessibility to the city's basic infrastructure, including clean water resources, sanitation, roads, drainage, electricity and other public facilities.[10]
5. *Education:* The literacy and education status of slum population are very low. The slums lack proper educational infrastructure. Many of the slums do not even have a primary school. As far as education is concerned, many of the slums are under the apathy of the NGOs and even if there are government schools, they are not properly functioning. Because

of lack of residential proof, many of the slum children are not permitted to take admission in formal education system. The quality of educational infrastructure such as teaching aid, bench and desk, quality of teachers, playgrounds and so on are lacking in slums, which demotivate slum children to attend school. One of the surveys conducted in Delhi slums found that many children did not attend school, due to constraint of space within slums. Schools within slums are either run in small houses or smaller buildings than schools outside the slums.[11]

6. *Health:* One of the critical issues and important challenges of urban slum is the health problems of the slum population. Their location and unhygienic living conditions are responsible factors for poor health status. The slum populations do not have adequate access to safe drinking water and sanitation. The water-borne and sanitation-related diseases are rampant in slums. Several studies have recorded that the immunization status of the children and the antenatal mothers is low as compared to other urban population. The infant mortality rate, maternal mortality rate and morbidity rate of the population are high in slum. The slum populations are more prone to problems like sexually transmitted diseases (STDs) and HIV/AIDS.
7. *Environmental pollution:* Environmental pollution because of slum is one of the pertinent issues in urban areas. It is remarked that slum indicates a form of pollution which broadly covers all the environmental aspects of degradation, namely, poor water quality, unwanted noise from areas close to railway lines and people themselves, poor air quality and unorganized solid wastes and sewage lines lead to pollution of all sorts.[12]
8. *Urban crime:* Because of poverty and low income, the youth of the urban slum families are found to be involved in many crimes. Many of the youth regard the income earned from the various criminal activities as a part of their livelihood. Some of the common criminal activities observed in the slums are theft and hijacking, drug addiction, smuggling, trafficking, prostitution and so on. Crime against women and girl children are also rampant in the slums. Poverty and crime and slums and crime are interrelated in the urban slums. One of the studies has reflected that unemployment is a driving force of youth criminality in slum areas. The slum areas serve as hideouts for criminals since accessibility to these areas is difficult.[13]
9. *Deprivation and identity crisis:* The people who live in slums lack in wealth, power and social connections; probably under-counted in national surveys; and under-served by both government and non-government organizations, whose focus has traditionally been on rural development.[14] Poor urban children are devoid of basic rights of survival, development and protection and are marginalized in challenging conditions in overcrowded settlements.[15] In the case of some states like Rajasthan, Gujarat and Bihar, the entire slum population of several lakhs remains unrecognized by the state governments.[16]
10. *Status of women:* One of the vital challenges in the slums is how to improve the socioeconomic status of women living in the slums. The women are not only illiterate, but also economically and mentally exploited. They suffer from various types of diseases and are mentally and sexually harassed. The reproductive health status of women in slums is very low and many women and even adult girls suffer from STDs for unhygienic conditions and practices. Most of them work as maids and do other menial jobs with low-wage rate. They are also a subject of domestic and external violence. Gender poverty and lack of decision-making power of women are other gender issues and challenges in urban slums. The Census data shows that more than two out of five women workers living in the slums are marginal workers, who do not have employment throughout the year.[17]

Benefits of Slum

Box

Urban slums should not be considered as a burden and waste for the city, rather these should be rehabilitated so that the slum population can have a better quality of life. Why do slums need to be upgraded and organized? Though it is acknowledged that slum communities are the homes of desperation, research has also shown that the slum dwellers contribute meaningfully to the urban economy and that they make tremendous efforts to fend for themselves (Grigorovich, 2008; Simone, 2001). Slums play many roles in city life; they are the bastions of low-cost labour that keeps various parts of the city working in many different ways (UN-Habitat, 2003).

Following are some of the benefits of slums to the urban areas.

1. *Contribute to urban GDP:* The slum contributes to the economic development of the nation. The slum population effectively contributes to the GDP of the city. They are found to be working in the service sector and also in the urban industrial sector as industrial labour. By some account, 8 per cent of GDP of Dhaka City is contributed by its slums.[18] Urban slums contribute to 7 per cent of India's GDP.[19]
2. *Slum supplies domestic workers to the city households:* Most of the domestic workers in the city reside in the slums. They are low-paid workers. In case of households, where both husband and wife are working, the cost benefit of the slum domestic worker is higher.
3. *Contribute to clean and smart city:* It is an irony that the slum people themselves live in unhealthy and insanitary locations, but they significantly contribute towards the sanitation of the city. Most of the sanitary workers reside in slums.
4. *Produce low-cost domestic use material:* It is observed that many NGOs and voluntary organizations have helped the slum people in income-generating activities through capacity building. These people produce many low-cost materials such as toys for children, clay pots, brooms and so on, which are being used by the urban lower-middle class.
5. *Urban infrastructure building:* All high-rise buildings, city roads, big malls, hospitals, schools and other infrastructure have been largely built with the hard labour of labourers who stay in slums and in slum-like conditions. The entire infrastructure could not have been possible without their physical labour contribution. It is rightly remarked that slums may be a 'necessary' phase in the evolution of a city as they perform the function of housing for a section of the society that has not been 'integrated in the city life' yet (Stokes, 1962).

It is righty remarked that 'slums are not a necessary evil. They are just necessary. They are necessary for the growth and functioning of the city; for the city to act as the path out of poverty; and for the transformation of India.'[20] The slum people should not be considered as a liability to the city; they are a rather useful asset that have contributed a lot to the growth and development of the cities. In their happiness lies the well-being of urbanites. Therefore, rehabilitation of slums is sine qua non for the development of the city.

Measures for Rehabilitation and Upgradation of Slums

The slums are an indispensable part of the urban areas and cities of the third world countries. The solution is not to uproot them but to upgrade them so that the slum dwellers have a better quality of life. This includes: provision of basic infrastructure (water, sewerage, drainage, street lighting,

Box 13.3 Odisha Accorded Land and Property Rights to Slum Dwellers

The state government today decided to accord land and property rights to slum dwellers; a move that will have a bearing on urban polls scheduled for next year. The decision is expected to benefit slum dwellers, which constitute a majority of the state's urban poor. Announcing the decision, the chief minister said, 'They (the urban poor) are the silent ones who keep our homes secure and comfortable. It is because of their sacrifice and hard work that the kitchens run, the gardens bloom, the city breathes and we feel secure. The fear of eviction coupled with harassment is always on their mind.'

The state government has promulgated two ordinances—the Odisha Municipal Corporation (Amendment) Ordinance, 2017 for providing property rights to slum dwellers and Odisha Land Rights to Slum Dwellers Ordinance, 2017 to amend the existing law and facilitate its decision. Odisha became the first state to confer land rights to the urban poor. The beneficiaries will have the rights for residential use and can mortgage the land. The property, however, cannot be transferred to anyone else.

Source: https://www.telegraphindia.com/india/right-of-land-for-slums/cid/1502152 (accessed on 28 January 2019).

street paving, parks and sport areas, reforestation); social services (childcare centres; social service referral centres; income and work-generating activities); community organization and development; and land titling (Jaitman & Brakarz, 2013).

1. *Land tenure:* The basic problem of slum dwellers for which they are being evicted is the lack of land ownership. The government needs to issue land tenure to the slum dwellers and rehabilitate them in a place with proper land ownership rights. An example of measures taken by Odisha to ensure land and property fights to slum dwellers is given in Box 13.3.
2. *Citizenship identity:* The slum dwellers need to be issued Aadhar Card (citizenship identity) and Voter Identity Card so that they can cast their votes in the election. Many slum dwellers complained that without an identity card, the police torture them. They are worthy citizens and contribute towards the infrastructure development of the city. They must be issued BPL and ration cards so that they can get all the benefits given by the government for eradication of poverty.
3. *Provision of basic infrastructure:* Slums are deficient of basic infrastructure facilities which affect their quality of life. The basic infrastructure facilities like road, electricity, sewerage system, tapped drinking water, gas connection, houses and so on needs to be provided to the slum dwellers. They are the worthy urban poor and their standard of living needs to be upgraded.
4. *Employment and poverty eradication programme:* The urban employment and poverty eradication programmes need to be provisioned to the slum dwellers. The banking facilities and opening of bank accounts of the slum dwellers will ensure for them hassle-free and transparent transactions of financial benefits.
5. *Social capital:* Slum dwellers are devoid of social capital institutions such as medical institutions and educational institutions. Besides, they do not have other social institutions such as *mahila mandals*, youth clubs, self-help groups and cooperative societies which can raise their social issues at the highest level. The social networking among the slum dwellers is very less. Education, healthcare and social networking need to be promoted in the slum areas.

Box 13.4 The Slum Networking Programme Called Parivartan

The Slum Networking Programme is a slum improvement programme with the participation of beneficiaries and has been implemented in some of the cities of Gujarat and Madhya Pradesh. This partnership-based slum development programme has community at its core, partnering with the social institutions, industry organization (private sector), local government (the implementing agency) and the NGO acting as a facilitator for providing physical and social infrastructure and extending education and health facilities like non-formal education programmes, maternal and child health in the slums.

Source: https://cept.ac.in/UserFiles/File/CUE/Working%20Papers/Revised%20New/27CUEWP%2027_Slum%20Rehabilitation%20Schemes%20(SRS)%20across%20Ahmedabad%20-%20Role%20of%20an%20External%20Agency.compressed.pdf (accessed on 28 January 2019).

6. *Role of private sector:* The private sector under the CSR can play a vital role in slum upgradation. They can provide education, health, water supply, sanitation and other infrastructure facilities in the slum. The private sector needs to adopt slums under their corporate social responsibilities. The private sector can engage with (a) local government; (b) community organizations; (c) rich consumers and (d) directly with the poor. In other words, private sector through public–private partnership and participatory approach can play an important role in slum rehabilitation. The slum networking programme called Parivartan is given in Box 13.4.
7. *Role of NGOs and international agencies:* The NGOs, PVOs and other civil society organizations can play an important role in the slum rehabilitation programmes. Many NGOs are playing an important role in the education and health improvement in the slum areas. Even the international organizations such as WHO, UNICEF and UNDP are giving funds to the government and NGOs for the implementation of various slum upgradation programmes and provisioning of basic infrastructure facilities and services in the slums. An example of NGO endeavour in slum rehabilitation is given in Box 13.5.
8. *Community development and participation:* Community participation is an important strategy for slum development. Any slum upgradation programme conducted either by the government or by the private sector has to involve the slum community in order to hasten the process. The slum dwellers have to be encouraged to in-kind contribution for ensuring basic infrastructure in their locality. There are many examples where NGOs have encouraged community participation and participation of slum dwellers for the effective implementation of slum development projects. Hamada and Ragab from the findings of their study have suggested that an effective mechanism is needed to activate the role of community participation not only in identifying problems and priorities, but also participating in

Box 13.5 Slum Rehabilitation Society—An NGO in Mumbai

Slum Rehabilitation Society works to improve the quality of life of the urban poor across Mumbai. Its primary focus is to enable slum dwellers to transition to legal and permanent housing; and implement various social welfare programs, including vocational training, legal awareness, micro-credit, female empowerment, medical clinics and early childhood learning in the slum.

Source: https://www.unitedwaymumbai.org/ngo-467 (accessed on 28 January 2019).

Box 13.6 The Urban Community Development Programme

The Urban Community Development programme, launched in 1966 as a centrally sponsored scheme, got transferred to the state sector in 1969. This programme aimed to involve the community in the improvement of slums (included provision of facilities such as sewer lines, public standposts, roads, street lights, etc.), provision of health facilities and the construction of dwelling units (included as a part of the project), thereby reducing the cost of the project and for the post-project maintenance. It was successfully implemented in Hyderabad in three major stages, namely, granting *pattas* (tenure regularization), finalizing the layout plan of the colony and actual construction of the dwelling units. The project has delivered nearly 20,000 *pattas* and upgraded 12,000 houses.

Source: https://cept.ac.in/UserFiles/File/CUE/Working%20Papers/Revised%20New/27CUEWP%2027_Slum%20Rehabilitation%20Schemes%20(SRS)%20across%20Ahmedabad%20-%20Role%20of%20an%20External%20Agency.compressed.pdf (accessed on 28 January 2019).

proposing solutions, development plans, implementation and dissemination of awareness among the citizens in the slum.[21] An example of community development programme in slum development is given in Box 13.6.

9. *Capacity building of local government:* The urban local bodies have an important role to play in the management of slums within their municipalities. The capacity building of urban local bodies on slum development and rehabilitation and dealing with various issues and challenges which the slums are facing will go a long way to improve the lifestyle of the slum dwellers. One of the World Bank documents has envisaged that measures to facilitate and strengthen the organizational capacities of citizen groups and local governments will increase access to information, and guidance on solutions to slum communities.[22]
10. *Women empowerment and women involvement:* The empowerment of slum women and their involvement in various upgradation programmes of slums will make these programmes more effective and beneficiary friendly. Women empowerment can be promoted through SHGs, *mahila mandals* and other need-based women groups formulated from time to time in the slum by the government. NGOs and other private actors are involved in the slum upgradation programme. The skill development programme will socially and economically empower women in the slums. A study conducted by the Institute for Study of International Development has noted that to achieve the New Urban Agenda goals of the UN-Habitat (2017), slum upgradation processes need to be aided by interventions that empower both men and women slum residents. Furthermore, women-focused policy making and gender mainstreaming are essential to ensure an equitable economic development process for both male and female slum residents as urbanization and growth continue.[23]
11. *Slum safety and security programme:* There is an urgent need to strengthen the safety and security programme in the slums. The slum people are victims of insecurity. The life of women and adult girls are in risk and report of molestation and rapes are being reported in the slums. The police post needs to be established in the slum to protect them from exploitation and theft. It will also check illegal activities in the slums. The slum dwellers are also subjected to disasters like flood, cyclone and fire outbreaks in the slum. These calamities cause a lot of damage to their paltry household assets and further add to their difficulties. Slums dwellers are needed to be effectively protected against various crimes. It is remarked that there exists a significant relationship between slum characteristics and

crime rates, and therefore better accessibility, lighting and better infrastructure facilities in the slums are required.[24]

12. *Stopping force eviction:* One of the heinous human right violations committed against slum dwellers is forced eviction. According to UN-Habitat (2007), the main causes of large-scale forced evictions are public infrastructure development, international mega events (including global conferences and international sporting events, such as the Olympic Games) and urban beautification projects. Often, such evictions are undertaken with bulldozers, supported by heavy police presence, and the targets of such forced evictions are nearly always the residents of poor informal settlements or slums (UN-Habitat, 2007). The government should not conduct any forced eviction in the slum. It should be done with the consent of the community and after giving proper notice and making alternative rehabilitation arrangements.
13. *Slum free city plan:* The government needs to prepare strategic master plan for slum development in the cities. The strategic plan would take into account slum prevention, rehabilitation and upgradation. The resource allocations along with the actors to be involved in the slum rehabilitation and upgradation programmes have to be clearly delineated. In order to make Chandigarh a slum-free city, the Chandigarh administration has proposed to make it 'mandatory for all private houses and industrial plots of 1 kanal and above, who engage servants or labour to make available suitable accommodation for them within their premises.'[25]
14. *Good urban governance:* The upgradation of slum necessitates good and inclusive urban governance. Here, slums need to be taken as an important and inclusive part of urban governance and administration. UN-Habitat has envisaged that a good urban governance is characterized by the principles of sustainability, subsidiary, equity, efficiency, transparency and accountability, civic engagement and citizenship, and security. These principles must be interdependent and mutually reinforcing (UN-Habitat, 2003).

One of the documents of the World Bank and United Nations Centre for Human Settlements (Habitat) has nicely concluded the slum upgrading actions. Slum upgrading consists of physical, social, economic, organizational and environmental improvements undertaken cooperatively and locally among citizens, community groups, businesses and local authorities. Actions typically include:

1. Installing or improving basic infrastructure, for example, water reticulation, sanitation/ waste collection, rehabilitation of circulation, storm drainage and flood prevention, electricity, security lighting, and public telephones;
2. Removal or mitigation of environmental hazards;
3. Providing incentives for community management and maintenance;
4. Constructing or rehabilitating community facilities such as nurseries, health posts, community open space;
5. Regularizing security of tenure;
6. Home improvement;
7. Relocation/compensation for small number of residents dislocated by the improvements;
8. Improving access to healthcare and education as well as social support programs to address issues of security, violence, substance abuse and so on;
9. Enhancement of income-earning opportunities through training and micro-credit; and
10. Building social capital and the institutional framework to sustain improvements.[26]

The Cities Alliance notes of slum upgrading consists of a whole range of physical, social, economic, organizational and environmental improvements undertaken cooperatively and locally among citizens, community groups, private-sector actors and local authorities. It has identified the following essential ingredients for any successful national slum upgradation programme.

1. *Demonstrate political will:* Both national and local governments must provide the vision, commitment and leadership required to sustain nationwide upgradation.
2. *Set national and city targets:* Set clear targets and ensure public-sector accountability by engaging stakeholders in planning and monitoring results.
3. *Put it in the budget:* Support slum upgrading as a part of core business, nationally and locally.
4. *Implement policy reforms:* Ensure necessary reforms dealing with land, finance and institutional frameworks.
5. *Ensure open and transparent land markets:* Reform closed and opaque land markets that encourage corruption, patronage and exploitation of the urban poor as well as constrain capital markets.
6. *Mobilize non-public-sector resources:* Engage slum dwellers themselves who have both the ability and the interest in promoting upgradation, and the private sector, which should be engaged as a risk-sharing partner rather than a mere contractor to the public sector.
7. *Prevent the growth of new slums:* Facilitate access to land and services by planning realistically for future growth (Cities Alliance, 2003).

II
URBAN INFORMAL SECTOR

The urban informal sector of developing countries is often described as low productivity back water 'sponage', observing those who cannot find productive employment in formal urban activities.

—Ranis and Stewart (1999)

The informal economies in both the third world and the developed world are characterized as being survival mechanisms for those people who have no choice.

—Henry (1982)

The informal sector is the key of the economic system in most of the underdeveloped and developing economies of the world. It is the unregulated sector which provides livelihood to millions in the developing countries. Its root is so strong in the developing countries that it is very difficult to do away with them soon from the landscape of the developing economies. Arvin-Rad et al. (2010) said that often described alternatively as the 'unorganized sector', 'unorganized economy', 'third economy', 'parallel economy' and the 'shadow economy', amongst others, the urban informal sector has become an integral part of the economic landscape across the developing economies of Africa, Asia and Latin America. Becker (2004) defined the informal sector as the unregulated non-formal portion of the market economy that produces goods and services for sale or for other form of remuneration. Portes et al. (1989) have said that the informal sector is 'a process of income generation characterized by one central feature: it is unregulated by the institutions of society in the legal and social environment in which similar activities are regulated.' Informal sector activities are those activities which are not subjected to the rules and regulation of the government and are free from taxes and duties and are being too individualistic in nature and character, and its main objective is to sustain the livelihood of its owner and employees through informal employment. The informal sector is sometimes referred to as hidden, grey, shadow, informal, clandestine, illegal, unobserved, unreported, unrecorded, second, parallel and black (Feige, 1990). It is considered as 'economy of the poor' or 'backyard economy' (Hemmer & Mannel, 1989).

To ILO, the informal sector is broadly characterized as consisting of units engaged in the production of goods or services with the primary objective of generating employment and incomes for the persons concerned.[27] Sinha and Kanbur (2012) were of the view that the informal economy is generally understood to include economic activities that fall largely outside the purview of official regulation because the regulations do not apply due to some combination of weak enforcement and evasion. To Seshamani (1990), the informal sector is comprised of all those activities which generate incomes that are unrecorded in the formal accounts of the national economy. USAID (2013) viewed that enterprises that do not or cannot register, for whatever reason, as official entities are called informal and they generally operate outside government oversight. According to legalistic definition, a worker is declared informal if he/she does not possess a written labour contract or does not have access to social security (mostly the pension system) or health insurance (ILO, 2010).

The First National Commission of Labour constituted in India defined the unorganized sector as that part of the workforce that has not been able to organize in pursuit of a common objective because of constraints such as (a) casual nature of employment; (b) ignorance and illiteracy; (c) the small size of employments with low capital investment per person employed; (d) scattered nature of establishments; and (e) superior strength of employer operating singly or in combination. The unorganized workforce are (a) contract labour including construction workers; (b) casual labour; (c) labour employed in small scale industries; (d) handloom/power-loom workers; (e) *beedi*/ cigarette workers; (f) workers in tanneries; (f) tribal labour; and (g) other unprotected labour.[28] In the context of developing countries, particularly having a dualistic structure the informal economy in the urban sector could be called as '*bazaar* economy' and its counterpart in the rural sector would be known as '*haat* or *mandi* economy' and both the forms of informal economies co-exist in the informal form.

According to ILO,[29] one of the important criteria which an informal sector enterprise has is that it is an unincorporated enterprise, which means that (a) it is not constituted as a legal entity separate from its owners; (b) it is owned and controlled by one or more members or more households; and (c) it is not a quasi-corporation (it does not have a complete set of accounts, including balance sheets).

Informal Sector in Urban Areas

The urban informal economy includes a wide array of activities, from street vending to domestic services, from home-based enterprises to the informal employees of formal enterprises, and from waste picking to urban agriculture (Brown & McGranahan, 2016). In urban areas, people found to be engaged in informal activities are those who are poor, illiterate, less skilled and have migrated from rural and semi-urban areas in order to eke out a livelihood in urban areas. ILO (2002a) therefore has rightly remarked that informal economic activities should not be confused with the illegal goods and services. It is remarked that in countries with high rates of population growth or urbanization, the informal economy tends to absorb most of the growing labour force in the urban areas when the manufacturing industry and off-farm activities, in general, do not grow at the same pace (Becker, 2004).

There are three main schools of thought regarding the relationship between the formal and informal economies.

1. *The dualists:* The dualist believes that the informal economy is a separate marginal economy. It is not directly linked to the formal economy. It provides income or a safety net for the poor.
2. *The structuralists:* They consider that the informal economy is a structural issue. The structuralists are of the opinion that informal economy is subordinated to the formal economy. The main intention is to reduce costs. It acts as feeder and is subordinate to the capitalists.
3. *The legalists:* The legalists believe that the individual entrepreneurs and micro-enterprises prefer to operate in the informal sector in order to avoid the cumbersome registration and taxation process as required by the state. It is viewed that the informal work arrangements are a rational response by micro-entrepreneurs to over-regulation by government bureaucracies (De Soto, 2000).

Some of the features of urban informal economy are as follows:

1. Informal economy or informal sector in the urban areas is not temporary in nature, rather a continuous phenomenon.
2. The size of informal economy in the urban areas of the developed as well as developing countries and more particularly in the developing countries is on the rise.
3. In the informal sector in urban areas, there is an ease of entry, more dependence on indigenous technology and resources, family ownership of enterprises or activity operated by the owner with few or no employees.
4. These operate on a small scale by using labour incentive and adaptive technology.
5. It provides job and income-earning opportunities to illiterate and low literate, unskilled and semi-skilled and poor migrants in urban areas.
6. Anyone can enter the informal sector with only minimum of capital and without sector-specific professional skills (Fukuchi, 1998).
7. The informal workers in the urban areas are of different categories such as wage-earning labourers, petty businessmen, household maids, ragpickers, rickshaw pullers, auto-rickshaw drivers, taxi drivers, street vendors, hawkers, shoe-shiners, barbers and so on.
8. The percentage of women engaged in the informal sector in urban areas is higher than those engaged in the formal sector. The women's share of informal economy employment worldwide has remained between 60 and 80 per cent and women in the informal economy most probably are much more in number than reflected in available statistics (Becker, 2004).
9. In the urban sector, informal workers are also found to be prevalent in the government sector and they are largely daily wagers, contractual workers and part-time workers customarily hired by the government from the private agencies.
10. The workers in the informal sectors are dispersed and unorganized, and therefore do not form any union to fight for their rights.

Table 13.3 Traditional and Modern Perspectives of Informal Sector

Traditional Perspective of Informal Sector	Modern Perspective of Informal Sector
Informal sector will vanish with the advent of the modern and industrial sector.	Informal sector has expanded with the advent of the modern and industrial sector.
The informal sector is mutually exclusive to the formal sector.	The informal sector is linked to the formal sector.
Most of the activities in the informal sector are illegal and informal enterprises are unregistered.	The informal sector activities are very much recognized by the government. It comprises enterprises and self-employed persons producing legal goods and services.
The informal sector hardly provides any sustainable employment, income and livelihood.	The informal sector is the main source of employment and income in many developing countries. Many enterprises and self-employment activities are providing sustainable livelihood to unskilled and illiterate people in both urban and rural areas.
The informal sector activities are present in rural economy.	The informal sector is present both in rural and urban economy.
It does not contribute to economic growth.	It contributes substantially to economic growth. It contributes to nearly fifty per cent to India's GDP.

11. Many of the workers in the informal sector stay in slums and informal settlements and are found without having identity or ration card to avail government subsidy facilities.
12. The informal workers face difficulty in getting their children admitted to schools and also open their bank accounts because they fail to produce residential proof.
13. Many of the people working in the informal sector and staying in the informal settlements and slums are reported to be involved in anti-social activities.
14. The people working in the informal sector in urban areas have low income and have lower standards of living compared to their counterparts working in the urban formal sector.
15. Last but not the least, a lot of changes have happened in recent years and with the endeavour of the public, private and NGO sector activities, the standard of living of people working in the informal sector has improved. They have been given land rights; better infrastructure facilities are available in the unorganized colonies, where these informal workers reside, and health and social security measures have been implemented for the well-being of the informal sector workers. The informal sector has become more vibrant and there has been real-time difference between the old informal sector and new informal sector (Table 13.3).

Need and Importance of the Urban Informal Sector

The informal sector occupies a pivotal place in the economic, social and political structure of the urban areas. It is not exclusive rather an integral part of urban economy. The need and importance of the urban informal sector are as follows.

1. *Employment and income:* The informal sector and its activities constitute an important source of employment and income in urban areas. Mijere (1989) was of the view that the informal sector usually emerges due to the inability of the formal sector to create job opportunities for the urban as well as the rural labour force in the third world countries. In most of the developing countries of South Asia and Latin America, informal sector occupies a lot of labour force in both their rural as well as urban areas. A gigantic percentage of the labour force earns its livelihood and income from the informal sector activities.
2. *Poverty alleviation:* In developing countries, the urban informal sector plays an important role in the alleviation of poverty. It is largely observed that the impoverished people from rural areas migrate to urban areas with a hope to earn more income and overcome the curse of poverty and hunger. Customarily, the income of the wage earners in urban areas is higher and job opportunities available in the urban areas are more as compared to the rural areas. In other words, the urban informal sector provides 'opportunities' to the poor to fight against poverty. Based on Nepal's experiences, Agarwal and Dhakal (2010) viewed that the informal sector is a good source of livelihood for poor and marginalized groups. They were of the opinion that earnings from the informal sector have been making a strong impact on the households' livelihood and poverty.
3. *Provides job and livelihood opportunities to the marginalized:* The urban informal sector provides livelihood opportunities to the women. The percentage and number of women employed in the informal sector in urban areas are on the rise. It also provides employment and livelihood opportunities to the low-skilled and unskilled workers. The female participation in the informal sector is highest (80.1%) among the South Asian countries (ILO, 2014). In India, almost 94 per cent of the total women workers are engaged in the informal sector and nearly 50 per cent of these women workers are sole supporters of their families (Sansiya, 2013).
4. *Urban infrastructure building:* The informal sector workers in urban areas are the key actors in the building of urban infrastructure such as housing, market complexes, road, parks, hospitals, schools and so on. They provide valuable support to the formal economy and help it to contribute towards economic growth and development. They protect properties of the rich in the night and the maids in urban areas extend a helping hand to the urban women. The urban formal sector is dependent on the informal sector. In other words, the informal sector supplements and complements the urban formal sector in enhancing its efficiency.
5. *Urban trade and commerce:* The informal workers are found to be employed in many key businesses and industries having export potentials such as handloom, jewellery, wood carving, embroidery, ordinary garments, meat products and so on that are feeders to the exporters. Carr and Chen (2001) viewed that a large share of the workforce in key export industries, including garments, textiles, sport shoes and electronics, work in export processing zones, sweatshops or from their homes under informal employment arrangements.
6. *Contributes towards economic growth and development:* The contribution of the informal sector to the economic growth in urban as well as rural areas in the developing countries is proportionately higher than the formal sector. The informal sector absorbs about 80 per cent of the total labour force, contributing about 55 per cent of Sub-Saharan Africa's GDP (AfBD, 2013). As far as India is concerned, the informal sector comprises of 86 per cent of workforce

and contribute 50 per cent of GDP of the Indian economy in the year 2004–2005 (NCEUS, 2008). It can be rightly said that the informal sector is quite essential for the economic growth and development of the developing countries.

7. *It is one of the important segments of the labour market:* The informal sector economy comprises immigrant entrepreneurship keen to introduce innovation, competitiveness and a positive output in terms of total factor productivity into a market in order to earn profit. The informal sector absorbs most of the migrant and unskilled and semi-skilled labours migrated from the rural to the urban areas. It has a vast labour market in urban areas as compared to the formal sector labour market.
8. *Interconnectedness of informal economy:* The most valuable importance of informal economy is its interconnected nature. It acts as a supply chain to the formal sector economy. Therefore, it is rightly remarked that the informal sector economy acts as an important and strategic distribution channel for the formal sector economy. Many a time, the formal sector buys the unfinished and preliminary material produced by the informal sector in order to produce the final product. The informal sector economy opens up the market for the formal sector economy by distributing products and services produced in the formal sector economy into grassroots markets previously inaccessible to the formal sector economy. It is many a time argued that the informal sector economy is fundamentally connected to the formal sector economy. A considerable amount of enterprises in the informal sector economy either have production or distribution relationships with the formal sector economy enterprises in terms of supply, whether it is through products (finished goods) or services (transactions or subcontracting) (Bashe, 2012).

Causes of the Growth of Urban Informal Sector

Some of the reasons for the growth of the informal sector in the urban areas and cities are as follows:

1. The rural push and urban pull have been recognized as one of the leading factors for the migration of the rural population to urban areas and the growth of the informal sector in the urban areas of the developing countries. People migrate to the urban areas with the hope of getting a formal sector job and when they do not find it preferable to be engaged in the informal sector.
2. The stagnation of the agriculture and lack of job opportunities in the rural areas are also the leading causes of growth of the urban informal sector. The low-skilled and people with lower level of education are being absorbed into the informal sector of urban areas.
3. The rise in population in general, and in the youth population in particular in the developing countries, is also one of the factors for the growth of the urban informal sector. The wrong assessment of considering youth as 'demographic deveined' by the developing countries, failing to promote skill among them leads to a rise in the informal sector activities among the youth.
4. The increase in the rate of urban unemployment and poverty leads to raise the informal sector activities in the urban areas. The people working in the informal sectors are largely the poor, less skilled and are with low levels of education.
5. The low rate of industrialization both in public and the private sectors and less skill-oriented education among the youth compel them to be absorbed in the informal sector activities.

6. The starting of informal activities is very easy and requires low capital, therefore, the impoverished people prefer to go for it. There is also less or no taxation burden.
7. Illegal migration from the neighbouring countries to the targeted countries are also one of the factors for the growth of informal sector activities in many countries having porous border.
8. Lack of political will is also one of the reasons for the prevalence and continuation of the gigantic informal economy in the developing countries. The vote bank politics is a factor for urban population growth and rising informal activities in the developing countries.
9. With the restructuring and rationalization of the public sector and the deregulation of the labour market in the private sector, the informal sector phenomena has also assumed significant proportions in many developed economies (ILO, 2000). The urban labour market in most of the cities in the developing countries is informal and the area is dependent on the informal labour force.
10. As the governments of most of the countries and particularly in the developing countries are unable to provide employment to its population in the formal sector, they also do not restrict people to start informal sector activities. There is no burden on the government's part to pay any incentives and benefits to the people engaged in the informal sector.

Issues and Challenges of the Informal Sector

Some of the issues and challenges of the informal sector are as follows:

1. *Urban informal sector and labour market discrimination:* Labour market discrimination, although visible among the informal workers in both formal and informal sectors, it is more prominent in the informal sector. As most of the informal activities are owned by individual entrepreneurs, the wage rate paid to the informal workers depends on the whims and profit of the individual entrepreneurs. It also varies from one informal worker to another depending on their education, skill and other soft skills. For the same type of work different wages are being paid to different workers. In urban areas, the labour market varies widely for the informal workers working in the formal sector and informal sector.
2. *Financial risk and vulnerability:* The entrepreneurs and businessmen in the urban informal sectors face financial risk and are vulnerable to market shocks. The firm and business in the informal sector is largely based on personal funding, loan from the money lenders, small loan from the government banks and so on. USAID (2013) remarked that the informal enterprises have notoriously poor access to credit, with their borrowing options generally restricted to the 'Three Fs'—'friends, family and fools'—or to more ominous sources, such as loan sharks or disreputable middlemen. In case of any failure, they are vulnerable to be closed and even at financial risk of selling their property, gold and other assets to vanquish the loss.
3. *Working and living conditions:* The majority of urban informal workers live in poor areas, lack basic health and welfare services and social protection and work in an unhealthy and unsafe working environment.[30] The working conditions of the informal workers are very sordid and is found to be largely characterized by long hours of work, low wages, no facility for food and recreation, no maternity benefit to the pregnant and lactating mothers, no drinking water and sanitation facilities and so on, which affect their health and well-being astoundingly in many cases. According to some ad-hoc surveys carried out by the ILO in the

Philippines, Nigeria, Senegal and Tanzania, hazards vary according to occupation. Some of the most prevalent problems were poor lighting, lack of ventilation, excessive heat, poor housekeeping, inadequate workspace and working tools, lack of protective equipment, exposure to hazardous chemicals and dusts and long hours of work.[31]

4. *Vulnerability of women:* Women are most vulnerable among all the workforces working in the urban informal sector. The women in the urban informal sector are largely seen to be working as daily wagers in lower posts, casual labour in the urban construction sector and domestic workers. There is income gap between the urban informal male and female workers. Neog and Sahoo (2016) from their study have found that the gender wage gaps are significantly higher in the informal economy—a major part of which is attributable to discrimination effect.[32] Women informal workers are mute spectators and silent bearers of discrimination. In many cases, they are being paid less than the signed amount by their contractors. They fear to be thrown out of the job if they raise their voice and some of them are also victims of sexual exploitation at the workplaces.
5. *Skill and competencies deficiencies:* Most of the workers working in the urban informal sector lack adequate skills. The lack of skill is also one of the factors for not getting adequate income and wage rate to eke out a decent lifestyle in urban areas. Some of the examples of unskilled labour force found to be working and earning their livelihood in the urban informal sector are street vendors, petty shop owners, ragpickers, household businesses, domestic servants, casual labour and so on. However, it is believed that if effective skill-oriented training is given to this workforce, it will enhance the earning of the urban informal workforce. Catherine and Jacob (2014) were of the view that the development of the relevant skills is an important instrument for improving productivity and working conditions and also for the promotion of decent work in the informal economy.
6. *Undefined boundaries of informal sector:* The informal sector has undefined boundaries as it is presented in various sub-sectors of the urban sector. It's elasticity in terms of types and form is vast in the urban areas of the developing countries. It is very difficult to draw a boundary and activity mapping of the informal sector activities. ILO has rightly remarked that due to the informal sector's heterogeneity and vastness, the concept of the informal sector is difficult to operationalize, and its magnitude is not easy to quantify.[33]
7. *Entrepreneurship and innovation:* Most of the activities operational in the informal sector of the urban areas are individual in character and casual in nature. There is a lack of innovations by the entrepreneur in this sector. However, a large number of successful entrepreneurs had their humble beginning in the informal sector (Patric, 2004). For example, many important large enterprises in Japan were stated as subcontractors and later evolved into independent manufacturers (Watabane, 1978). Britain kept a special interest with small firms during the 1980s because of the fact that a number of entrepreneurs who started up small firms grew up and perhaps became millionaires in the process (Paul & Dewhurst, 1996). In India, the Reliance Company which is one of the largest multinational companies had a humble beginning by Dhirubhai Ambani from a very small business. Taking clues from these examples, there is a challenge before the government to promote entrepreneurship and innovation in the informal sector entrepreneurs to bring them into the fold of the formal sector in future.
8. *Culture of excellence and progression:* Promoting healthy working culture in the informal sector for the development of individual excellence is one of the biggest challenges of the informal sector reform. A large percentage of entrepreneurs engaged in informal business and entrepreneurship in the informal sector find stagnation in their progression because of lack of innovation. This not only kills the individual but also the organization in the long run.

Most of the entrepreneurs functioning in the informal sector believe in avoiding registration of their business and paying tax to the government. In other words, they believe in the culture of avoidance. It is commented that the informal entrepreneurs are viewed as 'rational-economic actors' who will evade tax as long as the pay-off is greater than the expected cost of getting caught and punished (Allingham & Sandomo, 1972). Therefore, international organizations like the ILO and OECD emphasized on developing a culture of excellence and progression in the informal sector.

Measures to Improve Livelihood Conditions of People in the Urban Informal Sector

Some of the measures to be taken to improve the livelihood of the people in the informal sector are as follows:

1. *Dealing with informal workers with a humane face:* The informal sector workers such as vendors, housemaids, ragpickers, labourers and so on are needed to be treated with a humane face. Urban vending is not only a source of employment but also provides 'affordable' services to the majority of the urban population. Their support and contribution to city dwellers is immense. It is rightly remarked that the role played by the hawkers in the economy and also in society needs to be given due credit but they are considered as unlawful entities and are subjected to continuous harassment by the police and civic authorities (Government of India, 2004).
2. *Provision of security for the workers in informal sector:* The workers working in the informal sector are needed to be provided with health and social security. The healthcare insurance for the major diseases and pensions coverage during old age will enhance their quality of living. D. Batangan and T. D. U. Batangan (2007) said that in realizing decent work, it is essential to extend social security coverage to the working population in the informal economy, including the rural areas and urban informal sector, as social security benefits are considered key instruments in the fight against poverty; hence, it plays an important role in achieving the Millennium Development Goals on poverty reduction and healthcare. The seven essential categories of security denied to informal workers as noted by the ILO (2002b) are as follows.
   a. *Labour market security:* Adequate employment opportunities through high levels of employment are ensured by macroeconomic policies.
   b. *Employment security:* Protection against arbitrary dismissal, regulation on hiring and firing, employment stability compatible with economic dynamism.
   c. *Job security:* A niche designated as an occupation or 'career', the opportunity to develop a sense of occupation through enhancing competencies.
   d. *Work security:* Protection against accidents and illness at work, through safety and health regulations, limits on working time and so on.
   e. *Skill reproduction security:* Widespread opportunities to gain and retain skills through innovative means for decent work and the informal economy as well as apprenticeships and employment training.
   f. *Income security:* Provision of adequate incomes and representation security (protection of collective voice in the labour market through independent trade unions and employers' organizations and social dialogue institutions).
3. *Infrastructure facilities in the informal workers settlements:* There is a need to provide infrastructure facilities such as good quality roads, sanitation, drinking water, electricity

and so on in the unorganized colonies where the workers of the informal sector dwell. Lack of infrastructure facilities affects their quality of living and makes them susceptible to many kinds of diseases and ills.

4. *Promoting role of private and NGO sectors in the development activities of the informal sector:* The role of private and NGO sector needs to be encouraged by the government and international agencies for the improvement of the living conditions of informal sector workers. The private sector under the corporate social responsibility can invest in the well-being of the people staying in the unorganized colonies by building houses, sanitation facilities, safe drinking water and so on. As they are closer to the people, they can implement development activities in a better way, aiming at the well-being of workers working in the informal sector and staying in informal settlements.
5. *Formalization for informal sector:* The formalization of the informal sector by ensuring them job security and social security will be one of the important steps to strengthen the informal sector. The developed countries are doing this, however, the developing countries are lagging behind. The entrepreneurs operating in the informal sector need to be registered and adhered to the labour laws of the government. However, to support the formalization process, the government should provide tax concessions, relax import duties and access to formal credit from the public sector banks. Capacity building of the entrepreneurs operating in the urban informal sector will go a long way to motivate them to formalize their business and entrepreneurship.
6. *Simplification of laws and policies for the informal sector:* The government needs to simplify the registration system and taxation system for the entrepreneurs working in the informal sector. It is a fact that the informal sector entrepreneurs do not try to formalize their business and expand their activities because of fear of stringent law and policies of the government. The informal sector has tremendous entrepreneurial quality and scope to expand the labour and productivity market in both developed as well as developing countries particularly in the cities.
7. *Skill development in the urban informal sector:* Last, but not the least, the skill development in the urban informal sector will go a long way to improve productivity and raise the income of the informal workers. It is rightly remarked that a strategy to improve productivity and income in small businesses and household enterprises of the informal sector needs to be considered as factors behind the sector's shortfall in skills (Adams et.al, 2013).

Summing Up

Cities are often viewed as drivers of economic growth and innovation. It is one of the suggested measures for the structural changes of development of the developing countries. Urban areas contribute a larger share of GDP of the states of the nation. However, rapid urban growth can cause significant environmental and societal problems and challenges. It can lead to growth of slums in the cities, which will make the cities uglier and environmentally poor. The negative effects of rapid, unplanned urbanization include lack of proper housing and growth of slums, inadequate and out-dated infrastructure, escalating poverty and unemployment, safety and crime problems, pollution and health issues, as well as poorly managed natural or man-made disasters and other catastrophes.

According to UN-Habitat (2003), some 923,986,000 people, or 32 per cent of the world's total urban population live in slums; some 43 per cent of the urban population of all the upper-middle income regions combined lives in slums; some 78 per cent of the urban population in the countries with least high incomes lives in slums; some 6 per cent of the urban population in developed regions lives in slum-like conditions. For the first time, the census data on slums in India has identified slum dwellers as the people living in compact areas with a population of at least 300, in unhygienic environment with inadequate infrastructure and lacking proper sanitation and drinking water facilities. Slum dwellers are not only a burden on the city, but they also contribute a lot to the city's development and making the city dweller's life comfortable. It is largely felt that the growth of the city cannot do away with the slum and the only solution is to upgrade the slum and provide better quality of lifestyle to the slum dwellers. Instead of treating them as a burden on the city, they should be considered as necessary assets and, in their well-being, lies the happiness of the urbanites. The slums and their problems need special attention for improving the quality of life of the people living in the slums. It is therefore rightly remarked that 'If cities do not deal with the problems of the slums in constructive way, they will deal with the cities in a destructive way' says Robert McNamara, former president of World Bank.[34]

Keywords

Slums, Hazardous Location, Informal Settlements, Unorganized Slums, Citizenship Identity, Slum Networking, Slum Upgradation, Slum Rehabilitation

REVIEW QUESTIONS

1. Define slum. Discuss the main characteristics of a slum.
2. Give a few definitions of slum. Describe the factors responsible for the growth of slums in the cities.
3. Explain the various issues and challenges of slums.
4. What is urban informal sector? Explain the importance of the informal sector in the urban economy of developing countries.
5. Define informal sector. Describe the causes of growth of the informal sector in the urban economy of the developing countries.
6. What are the various issues and challenges confronting the urban informal sector? Describe the various steps to be taken for strengthening the urban informal sector.
7. What are the positive and negative effects of slums on the city?
8. Explain the various measures to be taken for slum upgradation in the city.
9. Write short notes on the following:
   a. Organized and unorganized slums
   b. Politics of slum
   c. Role of private organizations and NGOs in slum upgradation
   d. Women empowerment and slum upgradation
   e. Quality of life in slums
   f. Key problems in the slum
   g. Slum-free city planning
   h. Community participation in slum rehabilitation

Notes

1. https://borgenproject.org/tag/urban-slums/ (accessed on 16 January 2019).
2. https://www.jstor.org/stable/pdf/24639396.pdf (accessed on 16 January 2019).
3. https://unhabitat.org/slum-almanac-2015-2016/ (accessed on 21 January 2019).
4. http://shodhganga.inflibnet.ac.in/bitstream/10603/84847/16/16_chapter-viii.pdf (accessed on 24 January 2019).
5. http://www.censusindia.gov.in/2011-Documents/Slum-26-09-13.pdf (accessed on 25 November 2019).
6. https://unhabitat.org/wp-content/uploads/2003/07/GRHS.2003.0.pdf (accessed on 23 January 2019).
7. https://www.un.org/ruleoflaw/files/Challenge%20of%20Slums.pdf (accessed on 24 January 2019).
8. https://timesofindia.indiatimes.com/city/delhi/Politicians-let-slums-grow-as-vote-banks-Sheila-Dikshit/articleshow/20824009.cms (accessed on 24 January 2019).
9. http://siteresources.worldbank.org/INTKNOWLEDGEFORCHANGE/Resources/491519-1193429621722/brazil_slum_formation_072406.pdf (accessed on 24 January 2019).
10. https://www.adb.org/sites/default/files/linked-documents/46094-001-ssa.pdf (accessed on 24 January 2019).
11. https://pdfs.semanticscholar.org/1efe/28ed3908c00bbdf6e7336a852ce77d7e3551.pdf (accessed on 24 January 2019).
12. http://shodhganga.inflibnet.ac.in/bitstream/10603/84847/16/16_chapter-viii.pdf (accessed on 24 January 2019).
13. https://www.ajol.info/index.php/ahds/article/view/154574 (accessed on 24 January 2019).
14. http://www.create-rpc.org/pdf_documents/PTA45.pdf (accessed on 24 January 2019).
15. https://www.ncbi.nlm.nih.gov/pmc/articles/PMC3702140/ (accessed on 24 January 2019).
16. https://economictimes.indiatimes.com/33-of-slum-population-live-without-basic-facilities/articleshow/23440441.cms (accessed on 26 January 2019).
17. https://economictimes.indiatimes.com/33-of-slum-population-live-without-basic-facilities/articleshow/23440441.cms (accessed on 26 January 2019).
18. http://bbs.portal.gov.bd/sites/default/files/files/bbs.portal.gov.bd/page/303f0460_e79c_40d2_8157_acfcf64845a8/Economics_Slums.pdf (accessed on 26 January 2019).
19. https://economictimes.indiatimes.com/news/economy/indicators/people-in-urban-slums-contribute-over-7-of-gdp-study/articleshow/24199742.cms (accessed on 26 January 2019).
20. https://www.indiatoday.in/magazine/special-report/story/20130128-partha-mukhopadhyay-why-we-cannot-live-without-slums-761475-1999-11-30 (accessed on 26 January 2019).
21. https://www.researchgate.net/publication/234162784_Activating_the_role_of_community_participation_in_slums_upgrading_projects_A_case_study_of_El-sahaby_area_in_Aswan_Egypt (accessed on 27 January 2019).
22. http://web.mit.edu/urbanupgrading/sponsor/ActionPlan.pdf (accessed on 28 January 2019).
23. http://grow.research.mcgill.ca/publications/working-papers/gwp-2018-17.pdf (accessed on 28 January 2019).
24. http://inpressco.com/wp-content/uploads/2013/12/Paper2134-145.pdf (accessed on 28 January 2019).
25. https://indianexpress.com/article/cities/chandigarh/master-plan-aims-to-make-chandigarh-slumfree/ (accessed on 29 January 2019).
26. http://web.mit.edu/urbanupgrading/sponsor/ActionPlan.pdf (accessed on 28 January 2019).
27. http://mospi.nic.in/sites/default/files/publication_reports/wcms_182300.pdf (accessed on 27 October 2017).
28. Quoted in IInd Labour Commission Report, Report of the National Commission of Labour, Shri Ravindra Verma (Vol.I Part I) Akalank Publication New Delhi, 2002.
29. http://mospi.nic.in/sites/default/files/publication_reports/wcms_182300.pdf (accessed on 27 October 2017).

30. Quoted by Simo Manila in his paper 'Informal employment and vulnerability in less developed markets. file:///C:/Users/hcl/Downloads/9789401797979-c2%20(1).pdf (accessed on 17 October 2017).
31. http://www.ilo.int/wcmsp5/groups/public/---ed_protect/---protrav/---safework/documents/publication/wcms_110306.pdf (accessed on 17 October 2017).
32. http://www.ilo.int/wcmsp5/groups/public/---ed_protect/---protrav/---safework/documents/publication/wcms_110306.pdf (accessed on 17 October 2017).
33. http://www.ilo.org/wcmsp5/groups/public/@ed_emp/@ifp_skills/documents/publication/wcms_104010.pdf (accessed on 17 October 2017).
34. http://iigeo.org/wp-content/uploads/2015/02/3-Quality_of_Life_in_Slums_of_Varanasi_Comparative_Study-IIG-Vol.36-No.2.pdf (accessed on 31 January 2019).

References

Adams, A. V., de Silva, S. J., & Razmara, S. (2013). *Improving skills development in the informal sector strategies for Sub Saharan Africa*. Washington, DC: World Bank. http://documents.worldbank.org/curated/en/736731468194635805/pdf/Improving-skills-development-in-the-informal-sector-strategies-for-Sub-Saharan-Africa.pdf (accessed on 21 September 2019).

AfBD. (2013). *African economic outlook: Structural transformation and natural resources*. Tunis: African Development Bank.

Agarwal, M. K., & Dhakal, R. C. (2010). *Impact of informal sector on poverty and employment in Nepal—Micro-level study of Chitwan District*. Paper presented at the International conference, 'The informal sector and informal employment: Statistical measurements, economic implications and public policies', Hanoi, Vietnam.

Alligham, M., & Sandomo, A. (1972). Income tax evasion. In M. Pickhardt, & A. Prinz (Eds.), *Tax evasion and the shadow economy* (pp. 13–32). Edward Elgar.

Arvin-Rad, H., Basu, A. K., & Willumsen, M. (2010). *Economic reform, informal–formal sector linkages and intervention in the informal sector in developing countries: A paradox*. Discussion Paper Series, IZA D P No. 5229. Bonn: Institute for the Study of Labour.

Bashe, A. (2012). *The formalization of the informal sector economy: Panacea or chimera*? https://pdfs.semanticscholar.org/ad75/5f16b25582450233d9c82036eeaf5695f797.pdf (accessed on 21 September 2019).

Batangan, D., & Batangan, T. D. U. (2007). *Social security needs assessment survey for the informal economy in the Philippines*. Final Report on the ILO-SRO Manila Survey Results. https://pdfs.semanticscholar.org/c761/47321a14cdfc5d1eb5161e831f86dbcf682b.pdf (accessed on 20 September 2019).

Becker, F. K. (2004). *The informal economy*. Department for Infrastructure and Economic Cooperation, SIDA.

Brown, D., & McGranahan, G. (2016). The urban informal economy, local inclusion and achieving a global green transformation. *Habitat International, 33*, 97–105.

Carr, M., & Chen, M. A. (2001). *Globalization and the informal economy: How global trade and investment impact on the working poor*. WIEGO http://natlex.ilo.ch/wcmsp5/groups/public/---ed_emp/documents/publication/wcms_122053.pdf (accessed on 8 October 2017).

Catherine, K., & Jacob, M. (2014). Vocational skills development for youths in the informal sector of the economy in Africa. *IOSR Journal of Business and Management (IOSR-JBM), 15*(6), 81–87.

Cities Alliance. (2003). *Annual report*. Washington, DC: World Bank.

De Soto, H. (2000). *The mystery of capital: Why capitalism triumphs in the West and fails everywhere else*. New York: Basic Books.

Feige, E. L. (1990). Defining and estimating underground and informal economies: The new institutional economics approach. *World Development, 18*(7), 989–1002.

Fukuchi, T. (1998). A simulation analysis of the urban informal sector. *The Developing Economics, 36*(3), 225–256.

Government of India. (2004). *National policy for urban street vendors.* New Delhi: Ministry of Urban Employment and Poverty Alleviation. file:///C:/Users/ignou/Downloads/innovative_policies_for_the_urban_informal_economy_-_unhabitat_2006.pdf (accessed on 20 September 2019).

Grigorovich, J. (2008). Informality and autonomy in the slums of the developing world. *Undercurrent Journal: The Canadian Undergraduate Journal of Development Studies, 5*(3), 20. file:///C:/Users/Administrator/Downloads/154657-404262-1-SM.pdf (accessed on 27 January 2019).

Habitat-III. (2015). *Habitat-III Issue Papers, 22-Informal Settlements.* New York: UN-Habitat. file:///C:/Users/new%20world/Downloads/Habitat-III-Issue-Paper-22_Informal-Settlements-2.0%20(2).pdf (accessed on 2 April 2019).

Hemmer, H. R., & Mannel, C. (1989). On the economic analysis of the unban informal sector. *World Development, 17*(10), 1543–1552.

Henry, S. (I982). The working unemployed: Perspectives on the informal economy and unemployment. *Sociological Review, 30,* 460–477.

ILO. (2000). *Employment and social protection in the informal sector. ILO activities concerning the urban informal sector: Thematic evaluation.* ILO. https://www.ilo.org/public/english/standards/relm/gb/docs/gb277/pdf/esp-1-1.pdf (accessed on 17 April 2020).

ILO. (2002a). *Decent work and the informal economy.* Geneva: Sixth item on the agenda, Report VI, International Labour Office. http://www.gdrc.org/informal/ilo-decentwork.pdf (accessed on 21 September 2019).

ILO. (2002b). *Women and men in the informal economy: A statistical picture.* International Labour Organization.

ILO. (2010). *World Social Security Report 2010/11, Providing coverage in times of crisis and beyond.* Geneva: ILO.

ILO. (2014). *Transition from the informal to the formal economy* (2nd Ed.). Geneva: International Labour Organization.

Jaitman, L., & Brakarz, J. (2013). *Evaluation of slum upgrading programs: Literature review and methodological approaches.* InterAmerican Development Bank.

Mijere, N. J. (1989). Youth and development of self-reliance. In K. Osei-Hwedie, & M. Ndulo (Eds.), *Studies in youth and development.* Multimedia Publications. http://www.academicjournals.org/app/webroot/article/article1383742132_Tshuma%20and%20Jari.pdf (accessed on 17 April 2020).

Montgomery, M. R. (2008). The urban transformation of the developing world. *Science,* 319, 761–764.

Nassar, D. M., & Elsayed, H. G. (2018). From informal settlements to sustainable communities. *Alexandria Engineering Journal, 57*(4), 2367–2376.

NCEUS. (2008). Contribution of the unorganized sector to GDP report of the sub-committee of the NCEUS Task Force (Working Paper No. 2). New Delhi: National Commission for Enterprises in the Unorganized Sector.

Neog, B. J., & Sahoo, B. (2016). Discrimination in India's formal and informal labour market. *SSRN Electronic Journal.* https://www.researchgate.net/publication/314476400_Discrimination_in_India's_Formal_and_Informal_Labour_Markets (accessed on 17 April 2020).

Patric, M. (2004). *Informal sector: Seedbed of industrial entrepreneurship* (Discussion Paper No. 79). Kerala Research Programme on Local Level Development. Thiruvananthapuram: Centre for Development Studies. http://www.cds.ac.in/krpcds/publication/downloads/79.pdf (accessed on 17 April 2020).

Paul, B., & Dewhurst, J. (1996). *Small business and entrepreneurship.* Macmillan Business.

Portes, A., Castells, C., & Benton, L. A. (Eds). (1989). *The informal economy—Studies in advanced and less developed countries.* Baltimore; London: Johns Hopkins University Press.

Ranis, G., & Stewart, F. (1999). V-goods and the role of the urban informal Sector in development. *Economic Development and Cultural Change, 47*(2), 259–88.

Sansiya, P. (2013). Women in informal sector (A sociological inquiry). *International Journal of Research in Social Sciences and Humanities, 2*(4).

Seshamani, V. (1990). *The informal sector in Zambia: An overview of issues, problems and prospects*. Lusaka: University of Zambia.

Simone, A. M. (2001). Between ghetto and globe: Remaking urban life in Africa. In M. Vaa, I. Tvedten, & A. Tostensen (Eds.), *Associational life in African cities: Popular responses to the urban crisis* (pp. 46–62). Uppsala: Nordic Africa Institute. file:///C:/Users/Administrator/Downloads/154657-404262-1-SM.pdf (accessed on 27 January 2019).

Sinha, A., & Kanbur, R. (2012). Introduction: Informality-concepts, facts and models margin. *The Journal of Applied Economic Research*, *6*, 91–102.

Stokes, C. J. (1962). A theory of slums. *Land Economics*, *38*, 187–197.

The Republic of Uganda. (2008). *National slum upgrading strategy and action*. Kampala: Ministry of Lands, Housing and Urban Development. https://www.jstor.org/stable/pdf/24639396.pdf (accessed on 17 January 2019).

UN-Habitat. (2002). *Expert group meeting on urban indicator, secure tenure, slums and global sample cities, Monday 28 to Wednesday 30th October 2000*. United Nations Human Settlements Programme (UN-HABITAT).

UN-Habitat. (2003). *The challenges of slums global report on human settlements, 2003*. Nairobi: UNDP.

UN-Habitat. (2006). *State of the world's cities 2006/2007*. Nairobi: UNDP.

UN-Habitat. (2007). *Enhancing urban safety and security global report on human settlements, 2007*. Nairobi: UNHSP.

UN-Habitat. (2012). *State of the world's cities 2006/2007*. Nairobi: UNDP.

UN-Habitat. (2017). *New urban agenda (A/RES/71/256)*. New York, NY: United Nations.

USAID. (2013). *Feed the future, Informal Economy Regional Agricultural Trade Environment (RATE) Summary*. Bangkok: USAID Regional Development Mission for Asia. https://www.usaid.gov/sites/default/files/documents/1861/Informal_Economy.pdf (accessed on 8 October 2017).

Watabane, S. (1978). *Technical linkages between formal and informal manufacturing industries* (WEP Working Paper, No. 34). International Labour Organization.

Zarate, L. (2016). *They are not 'informal settlements'—They are habitats made by people*. https://www.thenatureofcities.com/2016/04/26/they-are-not-informal-settlements-they-are-habitats-made-by-people/ (accessed on 15 April 2019).

14 Urban Safety and Security

Crime and violence are fundamental threats to human security and safety from crime, and violence—including the resulting fear and insecurity—is increasingly being acknowledged internationally as a public good, as well as a basic human right.

—UN-Habitat (2007)

Enhancing Urban Safety and Security addresses three major threats to the safety and security of cities: crime and violence; insecurity of tenure and forced evictions; and natural and human-made disasters.

—UN-Habitat (2007)

Even where there is a downward trend in homicide rates, urban crime and violence still bring dramatic and unacceptable direct and indirect costs to communities and individuals. The United States is estimated to lose 3.5% of its GDP to criminal activity (Waller 2016); the regional estimate for Central America is 8% (World Bank 2011).[1]

Over the past decade the world has witnessed growing threats to the safety and security of cities and towns. Some have come in the form of catastrophic events, while others have been manifestations of poverty and inequality or of rapid and chaotic urbanization processes.

—The UN Secretary-General, Ban Ki-moon[2]

Introduction

We are living in a primarily urban world with approximately 3.5 billion people living in cities today (UN, 2015). This trend is projected to continue in the next few decades, with 95 per cent of urban expansion happening in cities to occur in the developing world (UN, 2015). By 2050, the urban population will be bigger than the world population today.[3] Urban areas are becoming increasingly larger day by day. This increase in population in urban areas without any proper urban planning, urban safety and security, and law and order measures, has resulted in the rise of urban crime. This brings with it not only the direct effects of displacement, injury and death, but also cumulative and long-term impacts on essential services with consequences for people's health, education, livelihoods and dignity (ICRC, 2016). Terrorism and radicalization of young people are also increasingly urban-cantered today. Most of the cities and mostly the metropolitan cities are becoming highly unsafe for the women and elderly. Many of those who commit terrorist acts are being radicalized in their local urban communities. There is a need for the government to engage more systematically and effectively for urban safety with particular attention to the systems of urban planning, legislation and governance. According to UN-Habitat, 60 per cent of all urban residents in developing countries have been victims of crime at least once over the past five years—70 per cent of these residents live in Latin America and Africa.[4] This chapter deals with urban safety and security.

LEARNING OBJECTIVES

After reading this chapter, you should be able to:

- Explain the key components of urban safety and security
- Describe meaning, importance, issues and challenges of urban crime and violence
- Discuss the urban insecurity of tenure and forced eviction
- Analyse urban disaster and its impact on urban development

Urban Safety and Security: Meaning and Importance

Before dealing in detail about urban safety and security, it is essential to define urban safety. It has been argued that today's definition of urban safety is complementary to crime prevention, as it considers how to enhance a person's individual rights and well-being, in terms of their physical (Kelly, 2015), social and psychological integrity, in addition to addressing the prevention of crime and violence (Habitat III, 2015a). To Roberts (2018), urban safety refers to the extent to which a city's inhabitants are able to live, work and participate in urban life without fear of bodily harm or intimidation. It should be viewed as a complex set of ever-changing and interconnected problems related to the following:

1. Physical built environment
2. Socioeconomic practices
3. Systems (governmental, service provision, environmental)

The urban areas having heterogeneous groups of population are more subjected to insecurity. Urban safety and security are largely related to various aspects such as safety of life and property and to live and move in the city without fear. The city administration needs to control and effectively deal with the antisocial elements indulging in eve teasing, chain snatching, burglary, and similar activities for which people largely feel unsafe to move and live in the city. Urban safety and security are critical to urban governance and development. Some of the important reasons because of which urban safety and security are important are narrated below.

1. *Sustainable development:* One of the edifices of the SDGs is sustainable cities and communities. It cannot be possible if the city dwellers live in fear and their life and properties are insecure.

Urban safety development is necessary to ensure a sustainable development of urban environment. Urban safety is a built environment which ensures safe life to the population in the city. A safe city is good for the present and also for the future generation. It promotes sustainable growth and development by enhancing the contribution of individuals. P. Cozens was of the view that sustainability will not achieve its full potential unless it explicitly includes measures to address the ubiquitous problems of crime and the fear of crime within the community.[5]

2. *Economic growth:* Crime and violence affect the psycho-social well-being and physical safety of citizens and have a negative impact on productivity.[6] People contribute more to the development if they feel that their life and property are secure. Safety and security are required for urban prosperity. Moreover, land security also helps in enhancing employment, productivity and income opportunities in urban areas. Evidence on tenure options shows that individual land titles and freehold home ownership are not the only means of providing security and may only be available to those in full-time, stable employment with reasonable incomes.[7]
3. *Human well-being and happiness:* Safety and security promote well-being and happiness among the city dwellers. If the city dwellers remain in fear of their life and property, then it is not a good sign of prosperity and happiness. When people feel unsafe, this feeling can easily overwhelm their world view so that they can feel a drastic reduction of well-being in a similar way to an unemployed or an individual who is feeling pain.[8]
4. *Land price:* Land price and the price of property such as housing and business depend on the safety and security status in the city. The land price in the disaster prone and crime-ridden cities are low as compared to their counterparts where there is peace and security. Land grabbing, forced eviction, forged selling and so on are some of the land security concerns in the cities. Besides, constant occurrences of communal conflicts, terrorism and extremist activities, which affect the safety and security of life and property in the city will influence the land price in the cities. In many settings, enjoying tenure security is far more important to dwellers than home-ownership or being provided with a title to a land plot (UN-Habitat, 2007).
5. *Quality of life:* The safety and security in the cities improve the quality of life of the people. If the land tenure is secure, people are enticed to build healthy houses with all amenities and facilities which add to their quality of life. The safety and security in slums would enhance the quality of life of the slum dwellers. Several types of security such as land security, health security, income and employment security and security against crime and violence of the slum dwellers would improve their quality of life.
6. *Women empowerment:* Women frequently do not feel safe in cities. Their insecurity limits their ability to work and have careers, let alone reach their potential as game changers for economic growth (UN Women, 2015). Safety and security in the workplace and on city roads and secure communication systems improve women's mobility in urban areas. Many women are not adequately motivated to work in a place where they feel insecure. The parents also do not prefer to send their girl children to school if travel in the school bus and other communication facilities are insecure. It is found that women are reluctant to participate in activities outside their homes for fear of sexual harassment and other forms of sexual violence.[9] Women empowerment in urban areas calls for safety and security in the cities.

7. *Security and poverty reduction:* Evidence on tenure options shows that individual land titles are helpful in providing employment opportunity to the urban poor with reasonable income and thus can reduce urban poverty. One of the documents of the United States Agency for International Development envisaged that when tenure rights of insecure people reduce the incentives to invest in and upgrade land and housing, they may be forced to leave a family member home to guard property rather than go to work or school; and, they may often lack access to services to devote significant portions of their time and income to acquire these.[10]

Figure 14.1 Dimensions of Urban Safety and Security

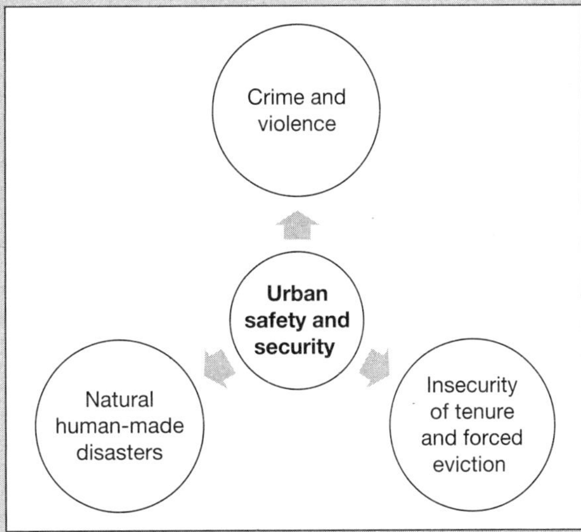

Dimensions of Urban Safety and Security

According to the UN-Habitat, documents enhancing urban safety and security address three major threats to the safety and security of cities: crime and violence; insecurity of tenure and forced evictions; and natural and human-made disasters. The three critical dimensions of urban safety and security are given in Figure 14.1.

I
CRIME AND VIOLENCE

The crime and violence occurring in the urban areas is a cause of concern and a central preoccupation of policymakers, planners, and development practitioners.

—UN-Habitat (2007)

Crime and violence occur at regular intervals in cities of the developed as well as developing countries and more particularly in developing countries. It is remarked that many of the fastest growing metropolises are also witnessing a sharp escalation in the incidence and severity of various forms of urban violence, particularly in Latin America and the Caribbean and Sub-Saharan Africa (Muggah, 2012). Crimes and violence are pernicious, continuing threats to human security, generally, and especially for the poor, who are disproportionately victimized as individuals and whose communities are strongly affected (UN-Habitat, 2007). Several types of crime and violence occur in the society. However, of course the types of crime and violence differ from one society to the other and from one country to the other. A few types of crime occurring in the developed as well as developing countries are noted below.

1. Assault
2. Murder
3. Robbery
4. Homicide
5. Property-related crime
6. Domestic abuse
7. Arson
8. Fraud
9. Residential burglary
10. Non-residential burglary
11. Kidnapping
12. Sexual harassment
13. Revenge porn
14. Auto theft
15. Snatching
16. Criminal homicide
17. Forcible rape
18. Trafficking in prostitutes
19. Terrorism and naxalism and cross-border terrorism
20. Child abuse
21. Pickpocketing
22. Illicit drug trafficking
23. Arms trafficking
24. Mob lynching
25. Intimate partner violence

Robbery is a frequently-occurring crime in the urban areas of the developing countries. Customarily, it can be defined as the taking of property through the use of force, fear and threat of violence. Robbers create terror in the society; as a result, people are frightened and even forced to leave the areas of the city where such incidents frequently occur. Violence starts at home and homicides frequently occur in globalized cities because of rising aspirations and lack of understanding among family members. It is envisaged by the UN-Habitat (2007) that the homicide rates for cities are extremely variable with Asian cities demonstrating generally low rates compared to cities in Africa, Latin America and the Caribbean, Eastern Europe and North America. Interpersonal violence is widespread with women and children being the main victims. Burglary is another popular form of crime that takes place in most of the cities. It is generally defined as the unlawful entry into someone else's property by using force with the intention to commit a crime. Commercial and residential properties are frequent targets for burglaries, and data shows that, on an average, one out of five urban residents worldwide is reported for being victimized within a five-year period. The UN-Habitat report (2007) has envisaged that intimate partner violence has global, national and local significance as a type of contact crime that may culminate in homicide, assaults and property damage or public order offences. Close intimate partners, particularly women in the younger age groups, are at a higher risk of this kind of crime. In most countries, the illegal trade of drugs, use of drug and drug trafficking are vital risk factors underlying crime and violence at global, national and local levels. Drug trafficking, simply defined as buying and selling illegal drugs, is a huge worldwide industry that is often the province of organized crime (UN-Habitat, 2007). Possession of illegal weapon with the intentions to carry out criminal activities is also a driving factor for urban crime and violence, and it is mostly found among the youth. Like drug trafficking, arms trafficking is also one form of organized crime. In recent years, many countries having common borders are victims of urban terrorism in general and cross-border terrorism in particular in some parts of their territory. India is a victim of cross-border terrorism. Besides child abuse, child trafficking, human trafficking, urban terrorism is one type of violence that has serious consequences for cities in both developed and developing countries. Women and girls are especially vulnerable to human trafficking. It is estimated that people between 700,000 and 1 million are trafficked around the world each year (UN-Habitat, 2007). The other form of urban crimes recently seen are stone pelting and mob lynching. Crime and violence commonly reported in the print and electronic media in the cities are chain snatching, sexual harassments, kidnapping, auto-theft, women lifting and rape in vehicles, revenge-prone, arson, murder, assault and so on.

Impact of Crime and Violence on Urban Development

Crime and violence adversely affect the growth and development of the city and contribute to the state and national GDP. It also produces adverse impact on human and social development. Some of the impacts of crime and violence on urban development are narrated below.

1. *GDP and Economic development:* Violence can have strong, negative impacts on economic development by drastically reducing the growth. It will produce long-lasting detrimental social impacts. At the national level, the cost of violence can add up to a substantial portion of the GDP and can harm economic growth.[11] In 2005, in Guatemala, the direct costs of violence, concentrated primarily in the capital city, were estimated at $2.4 billion or 7.3 per cent of GDP (World Bank, 2011). The WHO has estimated that 90 per cent of violence-related deaths in the year 2000 occurred in low- and middle-income countries, with violent deaths at 32.1 per 100,000 people, compared to 14.4 per 100,000 in developed countries. In Brazil, more than 100 people are killed by guns every day, and the gun-related death rate in Rio de Janeiro is more than double the national average.[12]
2. *Land and property price:* The cities experiencing frequent crimes of various types will gradually erode its creditability. The land and property value will go down. In other words, an increase in crime rate will decrease the property value and vice versa. The people believing in peace and tranquillity will leave the city by selling their property, and as a result the number of people with criminal mindsets would rise in the city. A 2012 report by the Federal Reserve Bank of New York, 'Crime, House Prices, and Inequality,' looks at how the issue plays out in Latin America. The authors found that a decrease of crime generated by heightened policing in Rio de Janeiro contributed to a fall in crime and a rise in property values: Homicides dropped to 10 per cent from 25 per cent and robberies to 10 per cent

from 20 per cent, while the selling price of the properties increased between 5 per cent and 10 per cent—and was proportionally higher in low-income neighbourhoods.[13]

3. *Growth of business and industries:* Urban crime and violence will affect the growth of business and small and medium industrial activities in the cities. This will also hamper the ease of doing business in the city. One of the documents of the World Bank on Jamaica has highlighted that crime and violence leads to (a) higher cost of doing business, because of the need to employ different forms of security, and diverts investment away from business expansion and productivity improvement, and may lead to a less than optimal operating strategy; (b) business losses arise from looting, arson, theft, extortion and fraud; and (c) can also cause a permanent shutdown of firms or relocation to less crime-prone countries.[14]
4. *Diversion of resources from productive use*: The occurrences of crime and violence in the cities will require more police force, and judicial and criminal judges, which will divert the allocated resource from other social and essential spending, such as education, health, women and child welfare, housing, safe drinking water and sanitation. Between 1988 and 1989, and 2001 and 2002, Jamaica's budgetary expenditure for health, in nominal terms, grew by 23 per cent annually, whereas the budget for national security and justice grew by 62 per cent due to the impact of crime.[15]
5. *Children, youth and women*: The crime and violence will produce long-lasting social impact particularly on children and youth. If the crime and violence frequently occur in the cities, the children and youth of those areas will remain in fear, and gradually it will change their attitude and they may follow the path of crime and violence. One of the studies conducted in the violence-prone areas of Jammu and Kashmir have mentioned that the children who have experienced nothing but hatred, fear, bloodshed and violence in their surroundings have grown up with traits of overwhelming aggression, instability, obstinacy, irresponsibility and an obsession with vengeance (Sanyal, 1999).

   The crime and violence would have adverse impact on women empowerment. The crime against women such as molestation, rape, snatching, sexual abuse in workplace and so on would not adequately motivate women to participate in the urban workforce. It will hamper the economic empowerment of women and also directly impact household income and poverty.
6. *Physical and Mental Health:* Crime and violence will affect the physical and mental health of the people living in the crime- and violence-like situations in the areas of the cities. A report from Jammu and Kashmir has envisaged that terrorism has affected the physical and mental health of the elderly in the following ways: (a) a large proportion of the patients treated in hospitals exhibit symptoms of fear psychosis; and (b) heath ailments are becoming increasingly common (Ahmed, 1996). It is also remarked that crime, and especially the fear of crime, affects the mental and physical well-being of victims, causing behavioural alterations with serious consequences for the whole community.[16]

Factors Responsible for Urban Crime

It is important to study the factors responsible for the growth of crime and violence in the cities. UN-Habitat has rightly quoted that urban safety thus 'starts from the observation that inadequate urban development and local governance and social and territorial exclusion patterns encourage crime and violence. In this perspective, urban safety adopts a citywide and participatory process to address the risk factors, and above all, protection factors of insecurity in cities, creating the conditions of more sustainable, inclusive, cohesive and just cities' (UN-Habitat III, 2015b). Some of the important reasons for the increased rate of crimes and violence in the cities are discussed below.

1. *Urbanization:* Unbridled urbanization is one of the vital causes of crime and violence in the cities of the developing countries. The unplanned urbanization in the developing countries is in full swing, which is attracting people from rural to urban areas. Because of lack of employment opportunities and other avocations, the youth from rural areas are resorting to crime to eke out a livelihood in the cities. The pickpocket or, chain snatchers, drug abusers, molesters and so on are largely migrant youth residing in the unauthorized localities and in slums and slum-like situations. Malik (2016) was of the view that increasing urbanization causes less integration among people, and as a consequence generates less informal social control. Less integration and less informal control explain higher levels of crime, disorder, victimization and fear of crime.
2. *Ethnic non-homogeneity:* Cities are a place of national integration. People from different caste, class, religion and ethnicity come to cities for varieties of purposes such as business, study, employment and so on. There is a lack of homogeneity which sometimes creates mistrust and leads to group and individual crimes. Lack of sociocultural homogeneity is also one of the factors for rising crimes in urban areas. Charis E. Kubrin was of the view that racial heterogeneity is a strong predictor of neighbourhood violent crime independent of other socioeconomic and demographic factors.[17]
3. *Sociocultural values:* Many a time, some communities and some cities are socioculturally tagged as cities with higher criminal records. The UN-Habitat report has envisaged that globally, informal forces embedded in social and cultural values are arguably the most powerful factors acting to encourage or discourage crime and violence. In some societies, crime and violence are common components of daily life and are accepted on social and cultural norms, or (in the case of 'structural violence') are built into, or encouraged by, law (UN-Habitat, 2007). For example, in Kabul, Karachi and Managua, violence is so interwoven into the fabric of daily life that it has become 'routinized', or normalized, as 'terror as usual' for many slum dwellers (UN-Habitat, 2007).
4. *Poverty:* Poverty is also an important influencing factor of crime and violence. UN-Habitat (2007) report has also mentioned that poverty has long been recognized as an important factor associated with increased crime and violence. The poverty-stricken households use crime as survival tactics. Many researchers have observed that the uppermost crime rates are within the poorest urban slums (Patterson, 1991) and foremost criminologists trust that the poverty–crime connection is direct and clear (Hipp, 2007). In Kenya, crime is often perceived as a problem in areas with high poverty levels. However, many other factors such as unemployment, population density, minority population, age distribution and locality are correlated with crime and affect poverty.[18]
5. *Inequality:* Socioeconomic inequality is considered as one of the factors promoting crime in urban areas. The gap between the rich and poor and income gap between the people living in the organized urban areas and unorganized urban areas, entices people belonging to the latter area to resort to crime as a method to enhance their income. The UN-Habitat (2007) has mentioned that inequality may be an important underlying factor in the perpetration of crime and violence than poverty. The research has shown that the racial inequality in

urban areas—black and white residential segregation and economic inequality—is associated with increased levels of homicide offending.[19] Alexander Cotte Poveda's research finding shows that factors such as inequality, poverty, education and the labour market influence urban violence.[20]

6. *Labour market and unemployment:* UN-Habitat (2007) report has envisaged that the proportion and growth of youthful populations have long been connected with increased crime and violence rates. Unemployment is a fundamental risk factor related to crime and violence. Mainstream economists generally believe that unemployment is associated with crime because reduced expected utility from legitimate work decreases the opportunity costs of illegitimate work (Becker, 1968; Ehrlich, 1973). The employment in the informal sector is largely casual which is insufficient for the urban youth to eke out a reasonable standard of living, and many of them—particularly the illiterate and low literate youth living in slums and slum-like conditions—resort to crime and violence to justify it as a cause of unemployment. The reservation for the other backward caste communities done by the Mandal Commission of India and its implementation has resulted in a lot of violence particularly by the unemployed youths.
7. *Political transitions:* In many countries, particularly in the African and Latin American countries, the political transition from the autocratic system to the democratic system has led to violence, more particularly in urban areas. The transition towards democratization often brings social and economic disruption that may be associated with increased crime and violence, at least in the short term. Findings suggest that some nations undergoing transition from autocratic governance to democracy have had significant increases in homicide rates. These include countries in Eastern Europe and in the Latin American and Caribbean region (UN-Habitat, 2007).
8. *Urban planning and governance:* There is increasing evidence that poor planning, design and management of the urban environment puts citizens at risk of death, injury and loss of property (UN-Habitat, 2007). Faulty urban planning is also one of the key reasons of crime and violence. The root of crime and violence is formed in the informal and unplanned settlements of the cities. Most of the criminals take asylum in these unorganized areas which act as safe haven for them in the cities. Busy marketplace, congested roads, lack of proper streetlight, ghettos within the cities, scanty police posts, are some out of many faults in urban planning that provide support to crime and violence in the cities. UN-Habitat (2007) has rightly mentioned that land-use juxtapositions, street layouts, building and site design, transportation system planning, infrastructure improvements—especially lighting and facility and landscape maintenance, as well as activity and space scheduling—have been shown to have variable impacts on crime opportunity and on the subsequent incidence and fear of the crime. It is therefore remarked that crime needs to be taken into account during the planning process, as valuable components can be provided that can offer effective approaches to crime prevention and the improvement of community safety.[21]

Indeed, studies of crime distribution patterns within cities have shown that the absence of natural surveillance functions as a variable that influence the incidence of certain kinds of crimes in places where motivation and opportunities are plentiful (Harries, 2000). Lack of orientation of the local self-government institutions regarding crime and violence is also many a time a responsible factor for occurrences of crime and violence in the municipal areas.

Measures for Crime and Violence Prevention and Control

There is also an urgent need for strategies to combat crime, promote security in communities and contribute to their sustainable development (UN, 2005b). Crime, and especially the fear of crime, affects the mental and physical well-being of victims, causing behavioural alterations, with serious consequences for the whole community. It is also the main contributor to the decline of quality of life in urban areas.[22] Inclusive prevention of violence not only can improve safety in towns, cities and urban areas but also will open up opportunities for the local population to access, influence and participate in urban life.

Table 14.1 shows that the crime problem is more serious in the African countries as compared to other regions of the world.

Some of the measures to be taken for the control and prevention of crime and violence are as follows:

1. *Active policing:* The quantity and quality of policing matter in the control and prevention of crime and violence in the cities. Police force is needed to be trained in the prevention and control of various types of crimes and violence occurring in the cities. However, police effectiveness requires cooperation by the public. Night patrolling in all areas with special focus on the security risk areas is sine qua non for prevention and control of crime.
2. *Private sector intervention:* The private sector also has a direct role in crime control—as many private security guards are being deployed by the housing societies and also by the public and corporate sector hired from security agencies. Proper orientation to these security guards by the government police department would enable them to effectively control crime in the cities.
3. *City planning and infrastructure development:* Widening of city roads, street light during night hours and proper housing in the cities would be helpful to control crimes. Most of the

Table 14.1 Crime Index of Selected Countries, 2019

Country	Crime Index Value	Rank
Venezuela	83.23	1
Afghanistan	76.63	5
Brazil	70.24	7
Bangladesh	65.82	11
Nigeria	62.55	17
United States	47.13	45
Pakistan	46.73	48
China	45.46	54
India	42.72	63
Singapore	21.47	110
Japan	17.73	117
Qatar	13.26	118

Source: https://www.numbeo.com/crime/rankings_by_country.jsp (accessed on 4 January 2019).

crimes occur in the unorganized colonies and are also conducted by people living in the unorganized colonies.

4. *Public education:* The police and law and order department must conduct public education on crime and its prevention in the cities. The CSOs like youth clubs, *mahila mandals* and residential welfare association need to be a part of it.
5. *Community policing:* In order to reduce the cost of policing by the government, the system of community policing may be encouraged. It will not only empower the community to take care of themselves, but also reduce the cost on security. Many successful examples of community policing are being reported. It is also remarked that communities should be involved in all stages of crime prevention planning and implementation. Community driven approaches are most effective.[23]
6. *Capacity building of local self-government institutions:* Capacity building of the municipal-elected representatives and the functionaries on crime prevention and control will be helpful to control crime and violence at the *mohalla* and ward level of the municipalities. As they belong to the community, they can be better able to identify the areas vulnerable to crime and take appropriate action for their prevention and control. It is remarked that at a local level, the municipalities are a key factor in crime prevention work.[24]
7. *Bad crime control policy:* Bad crime control policy is but one of the ways that public policy is implicated in the crime problem. Excessive punishment and illegal crime-control methods may affirm already existing views of the unjust nature of the criminal justice system and justify non-cooperation with it as well as self-help alternatives to it.[25]
8. *Good governance:* Last but not the least, good governance is the safest answer to crime prevention and control. The legislative, executive and judicial system need to act in tandem to control crime in the cities. The criminals need not to be protected by the executive, legislative and judicial system. Strong rule of law and their adherence will be able to effectively control crime.

The UN-Habitat report has envisaged that the policy initiatives at the local level to address issues of urban crime and violence have been grouped into six broad categories (UN-Habitat, 2007).

1. Enhancing urban safety and security through effective urban planning, design and governance;
2. Community-based approaches to enhancing urban safety and security;
3. Strengthening formal criminal justice systems and policing;
4. Reducing risk factors;
5. Non-violent resolution of conflicts; and
6. Strengthening social capital.

The majority of cities today are marred by inequalities and lack social cohesion. The divides and dualities that are manifested in the form of urban inequalities are important root causes of crime. For example, as cities expand, so does the establishment of gated communities and informal settlements. In both cases, the availability of urban services including safety services and the police are often lacking. On the one hand, public police service facilities are being replaced by private services. In many cases, these are either absent or inadequate. It is in informal settlements, areas characterized by poverty, lack of access to quality basic services, unplanned settlements and high rates of insecurity and crime that we find some of the greatest challenges to urban safety.

II
INSECURITY OF TENURE AND FORCED EVICTION

There's too many land disputes, too many rich people, greedy companies. Property is really the key to prosperity and freedom and once people are not secure in what they own, everything else falls apart.

—UN-Habitat (2007)

Secure tenure is a major contribution to the alleviation of poverty, to advancing sustainable livelihoods, to improving choices and opportunities for men and women; for accessing services; and for the recognition of the citizenship of the urban poor and the rights that go with such citizenship.

—UN-Habitat (2007)

The second vital aspect of urban safety and security is the insecurity of tenure and forced eviction. The colonies developed outside the legal purview of the urban administration and slums most of the time face harsh forced evictions. The tenureship of land is a big issue and urban challenge. In simple terms, tenure systems determine who can use what resources, for how long, and under what conditions.[26] There are many forms of tenure arrangements, ranging from full ownership and formal rental agreements to emergency housing and occupation of land in informal settlements (Wyckoff, 2016). Customarily, people living in informal settlements, who are often internally displaced, may not possess a 'legal' right to occupy the land but do still possess the right to adequate housing and the protection against forced eviction from their home (UN Committee on Economic Social and Cultural Rights, 1997).

Security of tenure is a certainty that a person's rights to housing, land and property will be protected. It guarantees legal protection against forced eviction, harassment and other threats and enables one to live in one's home in security, peace and dignity (NRC, 2011). Therefore, all persons should possess a degree of security of tenure that guarantees legal protection against forced eviction, harassment and other threats.[27]

Tenure formed in urban areas largely but not exhaustive are given as follows:

- Tenant with contract
- Tenant without formal contract
- Tenant in informal settlement
- Owner in informal settlement
- Owner of unauthorised construction
- Freeholder
- Cooperative housing dweller[28]

It is rightly remarked that notwithstanding the type of tenure, all persons should possess a degree of security of tenure which guarantees legal protection against forced eviction, harassment and other threats (UN Committee on Economic Social and Cultural Rights, 1997).

On the other hand, forced eviction is using force to vacate the acquired land. It is defined as 'the permanent or temporary removal against the will of individuals, families and/or communities from the homes and/or land which they occupy, without the provision of, and access to, appropriate forms of legal or other protection' (UN Committee on Economic Social and Cultural Rights, 1997).

Importance of Security of Tenure to Urban Development

1. *Economic development:* There is a correlation between security of tenure and economic development. If too many urban dwellers do not have security of tenure, then the city is not getting the economic (tax and business), social and cultural benefits that come from having a secure place to live; these become prime risks for political and social turmoil.[29]
2. *Quality of life:* Security of tenure will enable people with the weakest tenures to have a more secure framework. This would ultimately enable them to improve their homes and livelihood situations. Positive urbanization occurs when people feel secure.
3. *Empowerment of the marginalized:* Security of tenure will empower the marginalized community that are staying in the informal settlement of the cities. It will enable them to contribute effectively towards the development of the city.
4. *Reduce conflict and violence:* It is remarked that ensuring the security of land tenure through de facto protection against evictions or de jure formalization of land tenure can have obvious benefits in terms of enhanced investment incentives, improvements in equity, and reduction of the potential for conflicts. Land and right to property are the main bone of contention between the urban dwellers and the urban landowners and government. Secure of tenure will enable the nation state to build sustainable human settlements in the urban areas.
5. *Women empowerment:* It is recognized that the secure of tenure will empower women. The women-headed households in the urban areas are largely found in the informal settlements. If they get security of tenancy, it will enable them to contribute more to the city's development.

Effects of Forced Eviction on Urban Development

Development projects, which include many urban development schemes, displace 10 million people a year in the countries with less high income. Such forced eviction makes more people homeless than armed conflict, but this issue mostly goes unnoticed.[30] According to the Special Rapporteur on adequate housing, 'forced evictions intensify inequality, social conflict, segregation and "ghettoization", and invariably affect the poorest, most socially and economically vulnerable and marginalized sectors of society, especially women, children, minorities and indigenous peoples.'

1. *Economic effect:* Forced eviction would affect the economic development and growth rate of the economy. In the developing countries in particular, most of the labour force stay in illegal settlements and their forceful eviction would not only affect their lives and livelihood but also the economic growth rate of the city. The slum dwellers are the backbone of the urban economy in many developing countries of Asia and Africa. It also enhances the unemployment rate in the developing countries.
2. *Poverty effect:* Forced evictions enforce poverty and impoverishment on the people who are being forced to evict. Forced evictions result in severe trauma and in serious declines in the standard of living of those that are already marginalized or vulnerable within their respective societies, often leaving them homeless, landless, and living in extreme poverty and destitution.[31]
3. *Income Inequality:* Forced eviction increases economic inequality between the evicted and non-evicted people in the cities. Eviction affects the physical and psychological health of the evicted and reduces their productivity capacity which ultimately affects their income. It is

remarked that evictions cause significant socioeconomic hardship to individuals, affecting cities and whole nations.[32]

4. *Health effect:* Forced eviction produces negative effect on the physical and psychological health of the evicted families. Its effect on the health of the pregnant women and infant and also people suffering from the cardiovascular diseases is significant. A study in Mumbai shows that repeated eviction has had a profound effect on the health of this already impoverished population; there is evidence of widespread infection such as diarrhoea, respiratory infections including pneumonia, and skin infections.[33]
5. *Effect on education:* The frequent forced eviction affects the education of the children of the impoverished people staying in informal settlements. It affects the physical and mental health of their children, which ultimately influences their attitude towards education; some of them become dropout and others lose interest, which even affect the pass-out rate of their children because of lack of space for study. The parents too are not motivated to send their children to school.
6. *Effect on women and children:* Women and children are the worst suffers during the eviction and post-eviction period. They are more traumatized and tensed than any other persons in the evicted households. One of the researchers found that eviction often results in multiple and multidimensional negative consequences for urban mothers. Mothers who were evicted the previous year experienced about 20 per cent higher levels of material hardship and parenting stress.[34] Women and girls are particularly vulnerable to violence, including sexual violence, before, during and after an eviction (UN-Habitat, 2014).
7. *Effect on elderly and disabled:* Forced eviction would affect negatively the physical and psychological health of the elderly. These two groups of population are more vulnerable to forced eviction in the informal settlements. Like the women and children, their mental and physical health are utterly disturbed during eviction and also after the eviction.
8. *Human rights:* Forced evictions are among the most widespread forms of human rights violation, and they affect people in both developed and developing countries. Such evictions violate not only the right to housing, but also the rights to information, participation, and remedy.[35] During forced evictions, people are frequently harassed or beaten and occasionally subjected to inhumane treatment or killed (UN-Habitat, 2014).
9. *Political rights:* Forced evictions may also result in indirect violations of political rights, such as the right to vote, if persons are rendered homeless (UN-Habitat, 2014).

Eviction is detrimental to the development of the human being as well as the urban economy. Research results of a study conducted in Sweden indicates that imminent eviction is significantly associated with subsequent depression, even accounting for a range of social, economic, geographic and behavioural characteristics.[36]

Measure for Security of Tenure

The UN Committee on economic, social and cultural rights recognize legal security of tenure as a key component of the right to adequate housing. It urged that 'notwithstanding the type of tenure, all persons should possess a degree of security of tenure which guarantees legal protection against forced eviction, harassment and other threats. States parties should consequently take immediate measures aimed at conferring legal security of tenure upon those persons and households currently lacking such protection, in genuine consultation with affected persons and groups.'[37]

Developed by a Special Rapporteur on adequate housing to assist the states and others in addressing the current tenure insecurity crisis faced by the urban poor in an increasingly urbanized world, the 'Guiding principles on security of tenure for the urban poor' cover the 10 areas given as follows:

1. Strengthening diverse tenure forms;
2. Improving security of tenure;
3. Prioritizing in situ solutions;
4. Promoting the social function of property;
5. Combating discrimination on the basis of tenure;
6. Promoting women's security of tenure;
7. Respecting security of tenure in business activities;
8. Strengthening security of tenure in development cooperation;
9. Empowering the urban poor and holding states accountable; and
10. Ensuring access to justice (UN-Habitat, 2014).

III
URBAN DISASTER

Despite their destructive powers, disasters in urban areas are yet to receive the attention they merit within the field of urban development planning. Indeed, disasters are neither pure natural events nor acts of God, but, rather, products of inappropriate and failed development.

—UN-Habitat (2007)

Successive disasters can reduce the resilience of people or households to subsequent shocks and stresses. Small disasters can pave the way for large events by eroding people's assets and the integrity of critical infrastructure, progressively lowering society's thresholds of resilience.

—Kasperson et al. (1996)

In the new urban millennium, natural and human-made disasters are likely to have their greatest impact in cities where half of humanity is expected to reside (UN-Habitat, 2007). The growing numbers of the urban poor, especially the 1 billion slum dwellers worldwide, who reside in hazardous locations within cities such as industrial waste sites, floodplains, riverbanks and steep slopes, are perhaps most vulnerable to the impacts of disasters. Disaster refers to an emergency caused by natural hazards or human-induced actions that results in a significant change in circumstances over a relatively short time period. Typical examples are death, displacement, disease and loss of crops. Others may include damage to physical infrastructure, depletion of natural and social capitals, institutional weakening and a general disruption of economic and social activity.[38]

The UNISDR (2009) defines disaster as 'a serious disruption of the functioning of a community or a society causing widespread human, material, economic or environmental losses which exceed the ability of the affected community or society to cope using its own resources.' Broadly, disaster can be classified into two categories, that is, natural disaster and man-made disaster. If disasters occur because of natural forces, they are called natural disasters. Over the natural disaster, man has hardly any control. Some of the common examples of natural disasters are earthquakes, landslides floods, droughts, cyclones and so on. Tsunamis, volcanic eruptions and wildfires are also included under natural disasters. On the other hand, when disasters occur due to the fault of the human being and wrongdoing of the human being these are called man-made disasters. Some prominent examples of man-made disasters are city floods, collapse of the dam and bridges, train accidents, aeroplane crashes, collapse of buildings, bridges, mines, tunnels and so on. J. M. Albala-Bertrand had remarked that an urban hazard is a risk that threatens a city, its population, and related socioeconomic activities. If a risk threatens a capital or large city, the risk may resonate beyond the area of impact.[39] Some examples of urban natural disaster that occurred in India at different point of time are given in Box 14.1, Box 14.2 and Box 14.3.

Box 14.1 Bhopal: A Deadly Human-made Disaster

The accident at Union Carbide's pesticide plant in Bhopal, Madhya Pradesh (India), in 1984, exposed 500,000 people, the majority living in low-income settlements close to the plant, to toxic gas. To date, assessments of the death toll vary from 4000 to 20,000. The majority of deaths have been in the years since the disaster, as its chronic health effects unfold. Even by conservative estimates, it remains the worst industrial disaster on record, and the victims are still dying.

Source: https://www.un.org/ruleoflaw/files/urbansafetyandsecurity.pdf (accessed on 6 February 2019).

Box 14.2 Tsunami of December 2004: The Most Devastating Natural Disaster

Tsunami of December 2004, caused by a 9.0 magnitude earthquake, is the most infamous tsunami of modern times with disastrous consequences in many areas:

Humanitarian toll: It affected more than 18 countries from Southeast Asia to Southern Africa, killing more than 250,000 people in a single day and leaving more than 1 million homeless.
Economic toll: It left several millions of dollars of economic loss affecting fishing and tourist industries.
Environmental and medical threats: It includes water pollution and flooding and endemic diseases.

Source: https://www.hindawi.com/journals/emi/2011/920813/ (accessed on 6 February 2019).

Box 14.3 Severe Cyclone 'Fani' Odisha, 4 May 2019

The severe cyclone Fani, windstorm gusted up to 240 kmph which had blown away thatched houses in the urban and rural areas. It uprooted lakhs of trees, electric poles, and mobile towers. The electricity and water supply to the cities of Puri and Bhubaneswar remain disrupted for several days. People severely suffered and many of them even flew from urban areas to the rural areas. The districts affected were Puri, Cuttack, Kendrapada, Jagatsinghpur, Balasore, Mayurbhanj, Keonjhar, Dhenkanal. Several crores worth of properties were damaged. An estimation of 1 crore people in 10,000 villages and 52 urban agglomerations in around 14 districts were affected by Cyclone Fani.

Source: https://www.indiatoday.in/india/story/cyclone-fani-odisha-government-mounts-massive-restoration-work-1517293-2019-05-04 (accessed on 13 May 2019).

Effect of Disaster on Urban Development

Disaster, both natural as well as man-made, produces adverse impact on the social, economic and human development of the cities. It is remarked that a disaster impact is normally the result of a physically or socially uncompensated tension that leads to fatalities, damage, destruction and the disarticulation of societal frameworks.[40] The effects of disasters on such human and economic sectors as employment, balance of trade, indebtedness from reconstruction and loss of capital continued to be felt for many years after disaster events (CERD, 2000; Mcentire, 2001). Developing nations in particular, experience pervasive risk of devastation, human and property loss resulting from human and natural disasters (Gbadegesin et al., 2010).

1. *Economic effects:* The natural disasters cause a serious damage to the economy of the nation state. It not only destroys productive assets of the economy but also requires lot of monetary investments on reconstruction. It will make impoverished people indebted and thus can add to household impoverishment. To Kreimer (2001), natural disasters can cause sharp increase in poverty and impose financial cost of physical damage. It is commented that natural disasters such as earthquakes, floods, typhoons and hurricanes inflict serious damage and so seem to be bad for the economy. For firms, natural disasters destroy tangible assets such as buildings and equipment—as well as human capital—and thereby deteriorate their production capacity.[41] It is not a flight of fancy, but truly, disasters will affect the economic growth and the contribution of disaster-affected cities will affect the GDP of the nation states. A study conducted by Haddad and Teixeira (2013) in the city of Sao Paulo, Brazil estimates that floods contributed to reducing city growth and residents welfare, as well as to hamper local competitiveness in both domestic and international markets.
2. *Effect on urban land market:* The disaster affects the land price of the disaster-prone areas. The cities, which are in the disaster-prone areas, the value of land is lower as compared to the cities which are not in the disaster-prone zone. It is remarked that if in the disaster-prone areas, the land tenure rights are not secure and people face a real risk of either the government preventing them from rebuilding in the same place, or of being the victims of land-grabbing.[42]
3. *Human effect:* Disaster, both natural as well as man-made, posits loss of human capital. Any disaster occurring due to collapse of building and fire in the factories and the death of skilled labour force is a loss to the nation and also to their families. Numerous studies have shown that natural disasters could pose a great challenge to human development in particular to the developing countries. In the aftermath of a disaster, the poor could be losing access to some basic services, with reversals in the accumulation of physical and human capital and these could result in an increase in child labour and criminal activities.[43]
4. *Social and cultural effect:* Natural hazards, such as earthquake, tsunami, cyclone and so on can destroy centres of social and cultural activities. In such cases, a devastating natural disaster can disturb the social and cultural aspects of communities. By destroying the individual buildings, critical facilities, or economic of cultural centres, natural hazard disturbs or destroys the existing inter-relationship and interaction between or among the different groups and activities of the society or a nation. Such relationships and inter-dependence are established in any society on the long term. These are dynamic, and it is the responsibility of social organizations to guide the dynamics of such relationships in a progressive direction. This is especially important in developing countries.[44]

The Great Tangshan Earthquake of 26 July killed 250,000 people and another 250,000 went missing. This shows the vulnerability of society. China had to mobilize all possible resources for rescue and relief operations. This earthquake was the reason why the Cultural Revolution came to a halt in China (Shah, 2001).

By social impacts we mean the consequences to human populations of any public or private actions that alter the ways in which people live, work, play, relate to one another, organize to meet their needs and generally cope as members of society. The term also includes cultural impacts involving changes to the norms, values, and beliefs that guide and rationalize their cognition of themselves and their society. (Inter-organizational Committee on Principles and Guidelines for Social Impact Assessment, 2003)

Source: https://www.academia.edu/17367903/Principles_and_guidelines_for_social_impact_assessment_in_the_USA_The_Interorganizational_Committee_on_Principles_and_Guidelines_for_Social_Impact_Assessment (accessed on 17 April 2020).

5. *Political effect:* Natural disaster has political effects too. The natural disaster management capability of the government and political party in power and the local political leader's capability to deal with the disaster and its effective management create image on the minds of the public. It influences the voter's attitude. For example, during the devastating flood in Germany in 2002, the government offered immediate monetary help and cleverly staged a visit of the chancellor, wearing rubber boots, to flooded villages, which the media took up as a symbol of the chancellor's credibility as a crisis manager (Boin et al., 2009). After the floods and at least partly due to what was perceived as successful disaster management, the government gained support among the public and won the federal elections several months later (Bechtel & Hainmueller, 2011; Bytzek, 2008). To give another example, posting of Narendra Modi as the Chief Minister of Gujarat and the way he managed the devastating earthquake disaster of Bhuj remain imprinted in the minds of the people of Gujarat and this is sighted as one of the strong reasons for which he won consecutive elections in Gujarat for three terms.
6. *Effect on disadvantaged:* Women suffer more in disaster situations. Economic dependence on men makes them highly vulnerable in developing countries. During disasters, they are the victims of the disaster as well as the victims of the male-dominated social order. Besides women, the other disadvantaged sections of the population affected by the disasters are the disabled and aged population. Their situation becomes precarious during disasters and they also suffer during post-disaster management.
7. *Business and trading effect:* Trade and businesses are the foundation of local, regional and national economies. Disasters affect trade and business, and produces both direct and indirect effects on business. It not only leads to direct business losses due to disruptions, but also indirect losses and economic ripple effects. Destruction of and damage to businesses, along with disaster-related closures, result in the loss of jobs, negatively affecting incomes and creating even greater challenges for households, neighbourhoods and communities as they attempt to recover from disasters. After disasters, business owners face a host of challenges, including how to finance business recovery, and often how to cope simultaneously with damage to both business and residential property. Disasters can produce both psychological distress and additional debt burdens for business owners.[45]

8. *Environmental effect:* Natural disasters are caused by hydro-meteorological, climatological, geophysical and biological phenomena which adversely impact the natural and built environment of affected regions.[46] Tornadoes, hurricanes and typhoons can cause loss of life, terrain and habitat destruction and severe erosion. Volcanoes spew gigatons of CO_2 and more noxious gases into the atmosphere, destroy local terrain and any life that it comes in contact with. Floods also cause widespread destruction of terrain and habitat.[47]

Urban Disaster Management: Strategies and Challenges

Urban areas are the largest contributors to the national GDP of any nation. The urban disaster risk and vulnerability of the cities to disaster could reduce the contribution of the cities to the nation states economic growth and development. Therefore, disaster risk reduction and management are a vital concern of the city administration and local self-government. Disaster management is generally understood as a planned way of dealing with the impacts of disasters, defined widely according to the needs of particular agencies. To take the definition of one of the most globally prominent agencies, the International Federation of Red Cross and Red Crescent Societies 'Disaster Management can be defined as the organization and management of resources and responsibilities for dealing with all humanitarian aspects of emergencies, in particular preparedness, response and recovery in order to lessen the impact of disasters'. It is remarked that the ultimate aim of Urban Disaster Risk Management is to manage and enhance the capacity of the cities to reduce disaster risk in an atmosphere of sustainable development, while enhancing the quality of life of urban populations.[48]

Disaster Management Strategies

The urban disaster management follows a disaster management cycle for the effective management of urban disaster. The four components of the cycle as envisaged by the UNDP are:

1. *Preparedness:* It comprises activities in anticipation of and prior to the impact of likely or immediate hazards. These actions include the disaster plans, the training of responders, the maintenance of human, material and financial resources and the establishment of public education and information system (National Research Council, 2006).
2. *Response:* It comprises activities and provision of emergency services during and immediately after a disaster. Emergency response covers the indispensable services and activities that are undertaken during the initial impact or in the aftermath of a disaster including those to save lives and to prevent further damage to property (Bhatti, 2003).
3. *Recovery:* It comprises activities relating to restoration and improvement of facilities, livelihoods and living conditions after a disaster. Recovery is the action or process of getting back something that has been lost (Hornby, 2000). Recovery, in disaster management, refers to the activities that are taken after the initial impact to develop socioeconomic and environmental conditions that are destroyed by the disaster aimed at achieving return to normality (Kapucu, 2008) that is, disaster recovery activities are related to the re-establishment of pre-disaster social and economic routine provision of financial and other services to the victims, as well as repairment of destroyed properties (National Research Council, 2006).

Figure 14.2 Phases of Disaster Management

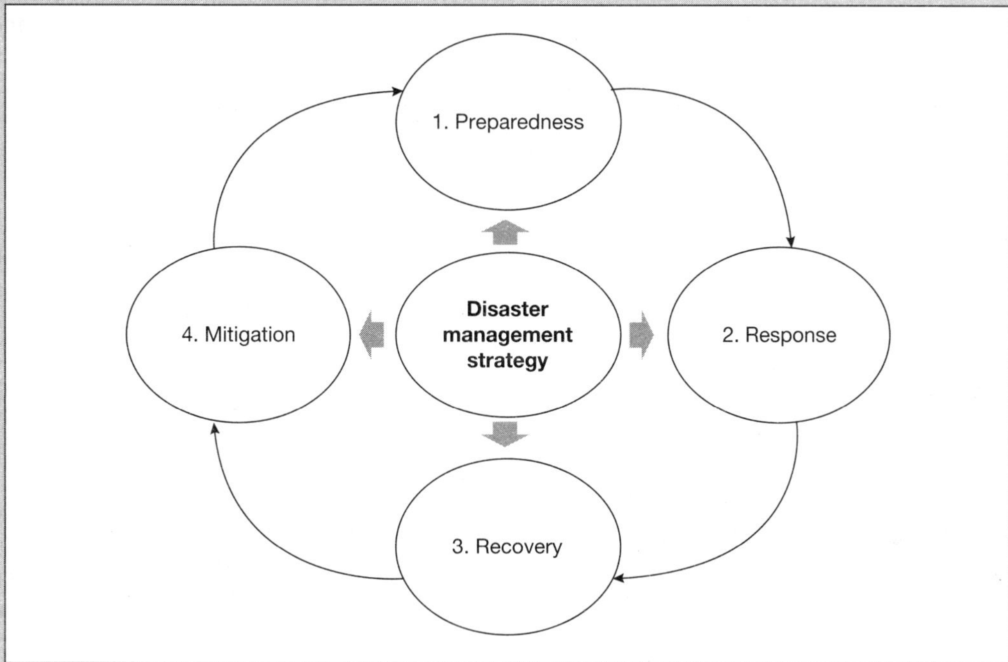

4. *Mitigation:* It comprises activities to lessen or limit the adverse effects of disaster. Mitigation involves the measures that can be adopted to minimize the destructive effects of hazards and to lessen the magnitude of the disaster. These activities can occur before, during and in the aftermath of the disaster and overlapping of all the phases of disaster management (Fernando, 2001).

The effective disaster management can broadly cover four phases (Figure 14.2).

Phase 1: Disaster Preparedness (Before a Disaster)

These exercises are being done before the disaster occurs. These activities aim to reduce the impact of an earthquake before it strikes. These activities largely cover:

- Public awareness activities;
- Implementing seismic building codes;
- Strengthening existing structures;
- Planning and training for emergency response activities;
- Earthquake research;
- Training volunteers and local leaders;

- Making ready following essential items such as medicine, clothes, food, utensils, cooking gas, cash, etc.; and
- Making ready National Disaster Rapid Action Force team comprising forces, doctors, nurses, veterinarians, counsellors and so on.

Phase 2: Disaster Response (During and Immediately After the Disaster)

Actions shortly after an earthquake which address the emergency needs of the community are as follows:

- Search and rescue of buried victims
- Emergency medical care
- Fire suppression
- Shelter for homeless victims
- Distribution of food, water and supplies

Phase 3: Disaster Recovery (Long Term After a Disaster)

The long-term processes of rebuilding all the aspects of a community following an earthquake are as follows:

- Rebuilding houses and buildings
- Financing for rebuilding
- Repair of roads, bridges, water system and so on
- Psychological counselling

Phase 4: Disaster Mitigation (Before Disaster, During Disaster and After Disaster)

The disaster mitigation activities include cross-cutting activities of all these above-said three phases. These broadly include the following:

- Creating public awareness about the possible disaster
- Public participation
- Rapid action by the volunteers and local leaders
- Making available essential items such as medicine, clothes, food, utensils, cooking gas, cash and so on
- Repair of roads, bridges, water system and so on
- Search and rescue operation
- Emergency medical care
- Shifting of victims to disaster shelter homes

In the 2005 World Conference on Disaster Reduction, the current framework for disaster risk management was developed in the Hyogo Framework for Action 2005–2015: Building the Resilience of Nations and Communities to Disasters and was summoned as follows:

1. Ensure that disaster risk reduction is a national and a local priority with a strong institutional basis for implementation.
2. Identify, assess and monitor disaster risks and early warning.
3. Use knowledge, innovation and education to build a culture of safety and resilience at all the levels.
4. Reduce the underlying risk factors.
5. Strengthen disaster preparedness for effective response at all levels (UN, 2005a).

Issues and Challenges of Urban Disaster Management

Some of the issues and challenges of urban disaster management are as follows:

1. *Disaster risk assessment:* One of the important issues of disaster management is the disaster risk assessment. The two terms are vital to the assessment of disaster risk, that is, hazard and vulnerability. A hazard can be defined as a potentially damaging physical event, phenomenon or human activity, which may cause the loss or life or injury, property damage, social and economic disruption or environmental degradation. Each hazard is characterized by its location, intensity and probability.[49] On the other hand, vulnerabilities are a set of prevailing or consequential conditions resulting from physical, social, economic and environmental factors, which increase the sustainability of a community to the impact of hazards (ISDR, 2002). It can comprise physical, socioeconomic, environmental and/or political factors that adversely affect the ability of communities to respond to events (Jegillos, 1999). Risk is usually associated with the inability of people to manage hazard events that may eventually lead to negative consequences like destruction of the environment, socioeconomic activities, properties and losses of lives.[50] According to ISDR (2002), disaster risk is thc product of thc combination of three elements—vulnerability, coping capacity and hazard. The formula given by the ISDR for the calculation of disaster risk is as follows:

$$\text{Disaster Risk}(R) = \frac{\text{Vulnerability}(V) \times \text{Hazard}(H)}{\text{Capability}(C)}$$

2. *Social impact assessment:* The sole goal of disaster management and mitigation endeavour is how it has ultimately benefited the disaster-affected people. In other words, the assessment of the social impact of the disaster-management endeavour is either inadequate or has not been undertaken religiously. According to the Inter-organizational Committee of the US Department of Commerce, National Oceanic and Atmospheric Administration, and National Marine Fisheries Service 'social impacts' refers to the consequences to human populations of any public or private actions that alter, or are capable of altering, the ways in which people live, work, play, relate to one another, organize to meet their needs and generally cope as members of the society. The term also includes cultural impacts involving changes to the norms, values and beliefs that guide and rationalize their cognition of themselves and their society. Social Impact Assessment (SIA) is the process of analysing,

monitoring and managing the social consequences of policies, programmes and projects.[51] The SIA could broadly cover the following: (a) impact of the disaster management programme on the people to their access to basic needs such as house, clothing, food, safe drinking water, sanitation, healthcare and education facilities, communication and poverty; (b) its impact on the status of the women, children, elderly and disabled and (c) its social impact on the disadvantaged sections of the society.

3. *Community participation:* Participation of the people in the management of disaster is one of the vital strategies adopted by the government of various countries in the process of disaster management. Whether a disaster is major or minor, or happens in the rural or urban areas or is at the local and national proportion; it is the people at the community or village level or ward level in the rural and urban areas who suffer from its adverse effects. They use coping and survival strategies to face and respond to the situation long before outside help arrives from the NGOs or the government. They try to protect themselves from damage and harm. The community-based disaster management (CBDM) philosophy involves local-level people, leaders and community to provide necessary services and logistics to their victims during and after disaster has been encouraged both in the developed and developing countries and launched the generation of CBDM strategy.[52] Some of the steps to be followed for the effective community participation for disaster management are as follows: (a) selection of the community level organizations such as youth club, *mahila mandals*, cooperative societies, farmers association and so on and community level members; (b) rapport building and enhancing community support; (c) participatory disaster risk assessment along with the community members; (d) participatory disaster risk management planning; (e) capacity building and community awareness campaign; (f) implementation of disaster planning at all stages of disaster management; (g) participatory monitoring; (h) participatory impact assessment of disaster mitigation programmes; and (i) final action on gap finding. Participation of the community in the disaster risk assessment, SIA, resource identification, coping mechanism, capacities identification and vulnerability assessment will go a long way in the effective management of disaster.
4. *Role of CVOs and NGOs:* The government alone cannot effectively manage disasters and therefore, the role of CVOs and NGOs is vital to disaster management. The international as well as national NGOs and CVOs play an important role during and after the disaster. They provide financial, material and human support in the disaster-prone areas. The NGOs can play an important role before disaster, during disaster and after the disaster. The role of NGOs during disaster includes awareness generation, education, training and formation of task force and also the conduction of mock drills. During disaster, they can keep themselves alert and help people to shift to safer places, look after the critical clients like pregnant women, children and elderly; distribute food items and so on. The NGOs can play a key role in the immediate aftermath of disasters by extending assistance in rescue and first aid, sanitation and hygiene, damage assessment and distribution of relief materials and so on. During the post-disaster phase, the NGOs can take a lead by providing building infrastructure, restoration of means of livelihood and assist the government in the social need assessment, monitoring and impact assessment of implementation for various reconstruction and recovery programmes. Yukie Osa has remarked that East Asia has been the most disaster-prone region in the world. In order to meet the urgent humanitarian needs that arise out of these disasters, CSOs, especially NGOs, have begun playing a major role in the region in providing disaster relief.[53]

5. *Role of local self-government in disaster management:* Nowadays, much attention is paid to local governments in managing disasters (Kusumasari et al., 2010). Customarily, local governments such as municipalities play a vital role in disaster management at the local level. As they are closer to the people, they can better and effectively attend to their needs before, during and after the disaster and can aptly deal with the situation. They can better assess who will be the most affected during the disaster and how to effectively manage the disaster. It is remarked that local governments can also play the most active role in emergency operations because the local governments are more familiar with local conditions, communities and culture (Herman, 1982; Stewart et al., 2009). Solway (2004) notes that the task of local governments is to facilitate local situations and as such, the local government is not usually involved in disaster mitigation programmes at the national level. Cheong (2011) was of the view that the central government and local governments should work together in order to develop a comprehensive disaster management framework and reduce vulnerability towards disasters. A strong partnership among all the levels of the government helps ensure that all the levels are integrated and involved in resilience building and disaster planning (Helsloot & Ruitenberg, 2004).
6. *Role of PPP:* The private sector under their corporate social responsibility are playing important roles in various stages of disaster management. They are extending support to the government in the better delivery of services to the disaster-affected areas and people along with the government. Tomasini and Van Wassenhose (2009) point out that disasters have forced private organizations to re-examine their role and consider humanitarian activities in terms of strategy and social responsibility. By becoming better corporate citizens, these companies believe that they can be of benefit to both their business and society, despite the risks involved.[54] It is remarked that the public and private sectors, the civil society organizations and the academies should work more closely together and create opportunities for collaboration, and integrate disaster risks into business management practices (UNISDR, 2015).

Summing Up

According to the United Nations (2019), more people live in urban areas than in rural areas globally, with 55 per cent of the world's population residing in urban areas in 2018. In our world, one in eight people lives in slums. In total, around a billion people live in slum conditions today. In its document Slum Almanac 2015–2016, UN-Habitat has noted that in spite of great progress in improving slums and preventing their formation—represented by a decrease from 39 per cent to 30 per cent of urban population living in slums in developing countries between 2000 and 2014—absolute numbers continue to grow and the slum challenge remains a critical factor for the persistence of poverty in the world (UN-Habitat, 2015).

The unplanned urbanization particularly in the developing countries has given rise to crimes and violence in the cities of these countries. The urban safely and security is a major concern in the cities of the developing countries. The three important components of urban safety and security are as follows: (a) crime and violence; (b) insecurity of tenure and forced evictions; and (c) natural and human-made disasters. The crime and violence, forced eviction in the informal and unorganized colonies and the natural and man-made disasters are regular features in the overpopulated cities of the developing countries. The governments of these countries have to take adequate steps to deal with these urban adversaries in order to ensure a sustainable quality of life of the people living in the cities.

Keywords

Urban Safety and Security, Urban Crime and Violence, Urban Disasters, Disaster Risks Assessment, Disaster Preparedness, Disaster Response, Disaster Recovery, Disaster Mitigation, Security of Tenure, Community Policing

REVIEW QUESTIONS

1. Define the concepts of urban safety and security. Explain why safety and security are vital to urban development.
2. What is security of tenure? What are the various challenges of security of tenure and why security of tenure is important for urban development?
3. What are key components of urban safety and security? Briefly explain each of them.
4. What is urban crime? Describe the various factors responsible for urban crime.
5. What different crimes take place in urban areas? Explain the various steps to be taken for the prevention and control of crimes in urban areas.
6. Explain various types of urban disasters. Describe the various measures to be taken for the control of urban disaster.
7. Describe in detail various strategies of urban disaster management. What are the various challenges of urban disaster management?
8. What is urban disaster? Explain the effect of disaster on urban development.
9. What is forced eviction? Describe the effects of forced eviction on urban development.
10. Write short notes on the followings:
    a. Disaster risk assessment
    b. Social impact assessment of disaster
    c. Community participation in disaster management
    d. Types of urban violence and crimes
    e. Security of tenure and its challenges
    f. Disaster management strategies
    g. Forced eviction

Notes

1. https://www.gpplatform.ch/sites/default/files/PP%2022%20-%20Urban%20safety%20and%20security_0.pdf (accessed on 29 January 2019).
2. http://www.citiesalliance.org/node/724 (accessed on 29 January 2019).
3. http://www.crime-prevention-intl.org/fileadmin/user_upload/Publications/International_Report/CIPC_5th-IR_EN_Chapter-2.pdf (accessed on 29 January 2019).
4. https://www.saferspaces.org.za/understand/entry/urban-safety-in-south-africa (accessed on 29 January 2019).
5. https://www.witpress.com/Secure/elibrary/papers/SDP07/SDP07018FU1.pdf (accessed on 31 January 2019).
6. https://www.saferspaces.org.za/understand/entry/urban-safety-in-south-africa (accessed on 29 January 2019).
7. https://www.land-links.org/wp-content/uploads/2016/09/USAID_Land_Tenure_Urban_Brief_061214-1.pdf (accessed on 31 January 2019).

8. https://www.researchgate.net/publication/290446281_Feeling_Safe_and_Subjective_Well-being (accessed on 25 November 2019).
9. https://www.saferspaces.org.za/understand/entry/urban-safety-in-south-africa (accessed on 29 January 2019).
10. https://www.land-links.org/wp-content/uploads/2016/09/USAID_Land_Tenure_Urban_Brief_061214-1.pdf (accessed on 31 January 2019).
11. https://www.unicef.org/protection/Violence_in_the_City.pdf (accessed on 31 January 2019).
12. https://www.un.org/ruleoflaw/files/urbansafetyandsecurity.pdf (accessed on 31 January 2019).
13. https://journalistsresource.org/studies/economics/real-estate/the-impact-of-crime-on-property-values-research-roundup/ (accessed on 1 February 2019).
14. http://siteresources.worldbank.org/INTLAWJUSTINST/Resources/JamaicaPaper.pdf (accessed on 1 February 2019).
15. http://siteresources.worldbank.org/INTLAWJUSTINST/Resources/JamaicaPaper.pdf (accessed on 1 February 2019).
16. https://www.ukessays.com/essays/geography/impact-urbanization-crime-rates-2643.php (accessed on 1 February 2019).
17. https://www.researchgate.net/publication/255699204_Racial_Heterogeneity_and_Crime_Measuring_Static_and_Dynamic_Effects (accessed on 1 February 2019).
18. https://www.the-star.co.ke/news/2017/08/18/poverty-increases-crime-rate-in-urban-areas_c1618167 (accessed on 3 January 2019).
19. https://journals.sagepub.com/doi/abs/10.1177/0011128708328442 (accessed on 3 January 2019).
20. https://www.tandfonline.com/doi/abs/10.1080/13600818.2011.620085?src=recsys&journalCode=cods20 (accessed on 3 January 2019).
21. http://www.uc.pt/fluc/gigs/GeoHealthS/doc_apoio/crime_ambienteurbano_santana.pdf (accessed on 3 January 2019).
22. http://www.uc.pt/fluc/gigs/GeoHealthS/doc_apoio/crime_ambienteurbano_santana.pdf (accessed on 3 January 2019).
23. http://www.csvr.org.za/docs/urbansafety/socialcrimeprevention.pdf (accessed on 4 January 2019).
24. https://www.government.se/49d966/contentassets/f2054a68786949d9a321dbc4b50cd02b/combating-crime-together.pdf (accessed on 4 January 2019).
25. https://www.government.se/49d966/contentassets/f2054a68786949d9a321dbc4b50cd02b/combating-crime-together.pdf (accessed on 4 January 2019).
26. http://pubs.iied.org/pdfs/10827IIED.pdf (accessed on 4 January 2019).
27. http://pubs.iied.org/pdfs/10827IIED.pdf (accessed on 4 January 2019).
28. http://pubs.iied.org/pdfs/10827IIED.pdf (accessed on 4 January 2019).
29. http://www.mypsup.org/content/libraryfiles/155.pdf (accessed on 4 January 2019).
30. http://www.mumbaidp24seven.in/reference/health_effects_of_orced_evictions_in_mumbai.pdf (accessed on 4 January 2019).
31. https://unhabitat.org/books/assessing-the-impact-of-eviction-handbook/ (accessed on 4 January 2019).
32. https://www.researchgate.net/publication/229771364_Forced_Evictions_in_Kenyan_Cities (accessed on 4 January 2019).
33. http://www.mumbaidp24seven.in/reference/health_effects_of_orced_evictions_in_mumbai.pdf (accessed on 4 January 2019).
34. http://news.rice.edu/2015/03/09/eviction-can-result-in-depression-poorer-health-and-higher-stress-according-to-new-rice-and-harvard-study-2/ (accessed on 4 January 2019).
35. https://www.amnesty.org.uk/files/forced_evictions_briefing_2010.pdf (accessed on 4 January 2019).
36. http://su.diva-portal.org/smash/get/diva2:940068/FULLTEXT02.pdf (accessed on 4 January 2019).
37. https://www.amnesty.org.uk/files/forced_evictions_briefing_2010.pdf (accessed on 4 January 2019).
38. https://www.intechopen.com/books/environmental-change-and-sustainability/disaster-risk-management-and-social-impact-assessment-understanding-preparedness-response-and-recove (accessed on 7 January 2019).

39. http://citeseerx.ist.psu.edu/viewdoc/download?doi=10.1.1.838.7175&rep=rep1&type=pdf (accessed on 6 January 2019).
40. http://citeseerx.ist.psu.edu/viewdoc/download?doi=10.1.1.838.7175&rep=rep1&type=pdf (accessed on 6 January 2019).
41. https://www.weforum.org/agenda/2015/02/how-do-natural-disasters-affect-the-economy/ (accessed on 6 January 2019).
42. https://www.researchgate.net/publication/279764940_Land_valuation_a_key_tool_for_disaster_risk_management/link/559cb3e208ae0035df249066/download (accessed on 25 November 2019).
43. https://www.tandfonline.com/doi/full/10.1080/1331677X.2018.1504689 (accessed on 6 February 2019).
44. http://www.adpc.net/casita/Course%20Modules/Earthquake%20vulnerability%20reduction%20for%20cities/EVRC0302A_Social_cultural_and_economic_Vulnerability.pdf (accessed on 7 February 2019).
45. https://link.springer.com/chapter/10.1007/978-0-387-32353-4_16 (accessed on 8 February 2019).
46. http://www.scielo.br/scielo.php?pid=S1414-753X2013000300004&script=sci_arttext&tlng=en (accessed on 8 February 2019).
47. https://socratic.org/questions/how-can-natural-disasters-impact-the-environment (accessed on 8 February 2019).
48. http://www.adpc.net/udrm/udrm.html (accessed on 10 February 2019).
49. http://dx.doi.org/10.5772/55736 (accessed on 12 February 2019).
50. https://www.idpublications.org/wp-content/uploads/2016/03/Full-Paper-COMMUNITY-BASED-DISASTER-MANAGEMENT-STRATEGY-IN-BANGLADESH.pdf (accessed on 13 February 2019).
51. http://dx.doi.org/10.5772/55736 (accessed on 12 February 2019).
52. https://www.idpublications.org/wp-content/uploads/2016/03/Full-Paper-COMMUNITY-BASED-DISASTER-MANAGEMENT-STRATEGY-IN-BANGLADESH.pdf (accessed on 13 February 2019)
53. http://www.jcie.org/researchpdfs/growingforce/5_Osa.pdf (accessed on 14 January 2019).
54. https://jamba.org.za/index.php/jamba/article/view/277/556 (accessed on 14 February 2019).

References

Ahmed, R. (1996, August 11–16). *Focus*. India Today.

Bechtel, M. M., & Hainmueller, J. (2011). How lasting is voter gratitude? An analysis of the short- and long-term electoral returns to beneficial policy. *American Journal of Political Science*, *55*(4), 852–868.

Becker, G. S. (1968). Crime and punishment: An economic approach. *Journal of Political Economy*, *76*(2), 169–217.

Bhatti, A. (2003). Disaster risk reduction through livelihood concerns and disaster policy in South Asia. In P. Sahni, & M. M. Ariyabandu (Eds.), *Disaster Risk Reduction in South Asia*. New Delhi: Prentice-Hall of India. http://www.antrocom.net/upload/sub/antrocom/090113/16-Antrocom.pdf (accessed on 13 February 2019).

Boin, A., Hart, P., & McConnell, A. (2009). Crisis exploitation: political and policy impacts of framing contests. *Journal of European Public Policy*, *16*(1), 81–106.

Bytzek, E. (2008). Flood response and political survival: Gerhard Schröder and the 2002 Elbe flood in Germany. In A. Boin, A. McConnell, & P. 't Hart (Eds.), *Governing after Crisis. The Politics of Investigation, Accountability, and Learning*. Cambridge: Cambridge University Press, 85–113.

CERD. (2000). *EM-DAT: The OFDA/CRED International Disaster Database.* https://www.intechopen.com/books/environmental-change-and-sustainability/disaster-risk-management-and-social-impact-assessment-understanding-preparedness-response-and-recove (accessed on 18 April 2020).

CESCR. (1997). *General Comment No. 7: The right to adequate housing (Art. 11.1): Forced evictions.* UN Doc. E/1998/22.www.refworld.org/docid/47a70799d.html; also see http://pubs.iied.org/pdfs/10827IIED.pdf (accessed on 4 January 2019).

Cheong, S. M. (2011). The role of government in disaster management: The case of the Hebei Spirit oil spill compensation. *Environment and Planning C: Government & Policy, 29*, 1073–1086.

Ehrlich, I. (1973). Participation in illegitimate activities: A theoretical and empirical investigation. *Journal of Political Economy, 81*(3), 521–565.

Fernando, W. B. J. (2001). Disaster mitigation. In: P. Sahni, A. Dhameja, & U. Medury (Eds.). *Disaster Mitigation: Experiences and Reflections*. New Delhi: Prentice Hall of India Private Limited.

Gbadegesin, A. S, Olorunfemi, F. B., & Raheem, U. A. (2010). Urban vulnerability to climate change and natural hazards in Nigeria. In H. G. Brauch, U. O. Spring, C. Mesjasz, J. Grin, P. Kameri-Mbote, B. Chourou, P. Dunay, J. Birkmann (Eds.), *Coping with Global Environmental Change, Disasters and Security-Threats, Challenges, Vulnerabilities and Risks*. Hexagon Book Series, Berlin-Heidelberg- New York- Hong Kong-London- Milan- Paris- Tokyo: Springer-Verlag, 5.

Habitat-III (2015a). *3 - Safer Cities* (Issue Paper No. 3). http://www.crime-prevention-intl.org/fileadmin/user_upload/Publications/International_Report/CIPC_5th-IR_EN_Chapter-2.pdf (accessed on 29 January 2019).

Habitat-III. (2015b). *21 - Smart Cities* (Issue Paper No. 21). http://www.crime-prevention-intl.org/fileadmin/user_upload/Publications/International_Report/CIPC_5th-IR_EN_Chapter-2.pdf (accessed on 29 January 2019).

Haddad, E. A., & Teixeira, E. (2013). *Economic impacts of natural disasters in megacities: The case of floods in Sao Paulo, Brazil*. http://www.usp.br/nereus/wp-content/uploads/TD_Nereus_04_2013b.pdf (accessed on 6 February 2019).

Harries, K. (2000). Filters, fears, and photos: Speculations and explorations in the geography of crime. *Analysing Crime Patterns: Frontiers of Practice*. Thousand Oaks: Sage Publications. http://www.uc.pt/fluc/gigs/GeoHealthS/doc_apoio/crime_ambienteurbano_santana.pdf (accessed on 3 January 2019).

Helsloot, I., & Ruitenberg, A. (2004). Citizen response to disasters: a survey of literature and some practical implications. *Journal of Contingencies and Crisis Management, 12*, 98–111.

Herman, R. E. (1982). *Disaster planning for local government*. New York: Universe Books.

Hipp, J. R. (2007). Income inequality, race, and place: Does the distribution of race and class within neighborhoods affect crime rates? *Criminology, 45*, 665–697.

Hornby, A. S. (2000). *Oxford Advanced Learner's Dictionary of Current English* (6th Edition). S. Wehmeier (Ed.). Oxford: Oxford University Press.

ICPG. (2003). Principles and guidelines for social impact assessment in the USA. *Impact Assessment & Project Appraisal, 21*(3), 231–250.

ICRC. (2016). *Armed violence and the new urban agenda the ICRC's recommendations for habitat III*. International Committee of the Red Cross.

ISDR. (2002). *Living with risk: A global reviews of disaster reduction initiatives* preliminary version. Geneva: ISDR Secretariat.

ISDR. (2009). *UNISDR terminology on disaster risk reduction*. UN/ISDR.

Jegillos, S. (1999). Fundamentals of disaster risk management: How are South East Asian countries addressing this? In A. Holloway (Ed.) *Risk, Sustainable development and Disasters, Southern Perspective*. Cape Town: Periperi Publications.

Kapucu, N. (2008). Collaborative emergency management: better community organizing, better public preparedness and response. *Disasters, 32*. 239–262.

Kasperson, J. X., Kasperson, R. E., & Turner, B. L. (1996). *Regions at risk: Comparisons of threatened environments*. Washington: United Nations University Press.

Kelly, B. (2015). *Why "Smart Cities" improve safety and sustainability*. http://www.crime-prevention-intl.org/fileadmin/user_upload/Publications/International_Report/CIPC_5th-IR_EN_Chapter-2.pdf (accessed on 29 January 2019).

Kreimer, A. (2001). Social and economic impacts of natural disaster. *International Geology Review, 43*, 401–405.

Kusumasari, B., Alam, Q., & Siddiqui, K. (2010). Resource capability for local government in managing disaster. *Disaster Prevention and Management, 19*, 438–451.

Malik, A. A. (2016). Urbanization and crime: A relational analysis. *IOSR Journal of Humanities and Social Science, 21*(1-IV), 68–74.

Mcentire, D. A. (2001). Triggering agents, vulnerabilities and disaster reduction: Towards a holistic paradigm. *Disaster Prevention and Management: An International Journal, 10*(3), 189–196.

Muggah, R. (2012). *Researching the urban dilemma: Urbanization, poverty and violence.* DFID.

National Research Council. (2006). *Facing hazards and disasters: Understanding human dimensions.* Washington: The National Academies Press.

NRC. (2011). *Housing, land and property training manual.* www.nrc.no/what-we-do/speaking-up-for-rights/training-manual-on-housing-land-and-property; http://pubs.iied.org/pdfs/10827IIED.pdf (accessed on 4 January 2019).

Patterson, E. B. (1991). Poverty, income inequality, and community crime rates. *Criminology, 29*, 755–776.

Roberts, J. (2018). *Urban safety projects: Urban safety and security in Myanmar.* The Asia Foundation. https://asiafoundation.org/wp-content/uploads/2018/07/Urban-Safety-Brief-Series-No-1_Urban-Safety-and-Security-in-Myanamr_Eng-EN.pdf (accessed on 29 January 2019).

Sanyal, S. (1999).One man's terrorist law enforcers: Attitude towards terrorism (Vol. 3). *Faultlines.*

Shah, H. (2001, September 5). *The Coming Killer Quake.* The Times of India.

Solway, L. (2004). Reducing the effect of natural hazards on urban areas. In: R. Casale, C. Margottini (Eds.). *Natural Disasters and Sustainable Development. Environmental Science.* Berlin: Springer. https://ac.els-cdn.com/S2212567114010065/1-s2.0-S2212567114010065-main.pdf?_tid=93779237-91f3-4f07-83c1-69318ea04f7d&acdnat=1550119577_37669da5ce0991587d388fcdab5d37bb (accessed on 14 February 2019).

Stewart, G. T., Kolluru, R., & Smith, M. (2009). Leveraging public-private partnerships to improve community resilience in times of disaster. *International Journal of Physical Distribution & Logistics Management, 39*, 343–364.

Tomasini, R., & Van Wassenhove, L. (2009). *Humanitarian logistics.* Insead Business Press. https://jamba.org.za/index.php/jamba/article/view/277/556 (accessed on 14 February 2019).

UN-Habitat. (2007). *Global report on human settlements 2007: Enhancing urban safety and security.* United Nations Human Settlement Programme.

UN-Habitat. (2014). *Forced Evictions Human Rights* (Fact Sheet No. 25/Reve.1). New York: United Nations.

UN-Habitat. (2015). *Slum almanac 2015–16, tracking improvement in the lives of slum dwellers.* UN-Habitat. https://unhabitat.org/sites/default/files/download-manager-files/Slum%20Almanac%202015-2016_PSUP.pdf (accessed on 17April 2020).

UN Women. (2015). *Progress of the world's women 2015-2016.* New York, NY: UN Women.

UN. (2015). *Cities – United Nations Sustainable Development Action 2015.* http://www.crime-prevention-intl.org/fileadmin/user_upload/Publications/International_Report/CIPC_5th-IR_EN_Chapter-2.pdf (accessed on 29 January 2019).

UNISDR. (2015). *Sendai framework for disaster risk reduction 2015 – 2030 A/CONF.224/CRP.1 gives Third World Conference.* https://jamba.org.za/index.php/jamba/article/view/277/556 (accessed on 14 February 2019).

United Nations. (2005b, April 18–25). *Strategies and best practices for crime prevention, in particular in relation to urban áreas and youth at risk.* Bangkok: Eleventh United Nations Congress on Crime Prevention and Criminal Justice,.

United Nations. (2019). *World urbanization prospects: The 2018 revision.* Department of Economic and Social Affairs Population Division, United Nations.

United Nations (UN) Millennium Project. (2005). *A home in the city. Task force on improving the lives of slum dwellers.* Earthscan.

World Bank. (2011). *Violence in the city understanding and supporting community responses to urban violence.* Washington DC: The World Bank Social Development Department, The World Bank.

Wyckoff, M. E. (2016). *Securing Tenure in Shelter Operations: Guidance for Humanitarian Response.* NRC. www.sheltercluster.org/sites/default/files/docs/nrc_shelter_tenure_guidance_external.pdf; http://pubs.iied.org/pdfs/10827IIED.pdf (accessed on 4 January 2019).

15 Sustainable Urbanization and Smart City

Cities are the primary engines of global economic activity, accounting for 70 percent of world's GDP. As their populations continue to grow, so too can cities' potential for job creation, trade, business opportunity, and investment.[1]

Sustainable urbanism is a widely used phrase, often with ecological and green connotations, constituting a rather complete framework for the interdisciplinary planning and urban design of contemporary cities, neighbourhoods and residential places.

—Metzger (2013)

A smart sustainable city is an innovative city that uses information and communication technologies (ICTs) and other means to improve quality of life, efficiency of urban operation and services, and competitiveness, while ensuring that it meets the needs of present and future generations with respect to economic, social and environmental aspects.

—ITU (2015)

Introduction

Urban areas are now occupied by more than one half of the world population, and the number and percentage of population living in urban areas is on the rise. In recent years, cities are becoming the hub of economic, social, cultural and political progress both in developed as well as developing countries. Urbanization is the order of the day and almost every country of the world is becoming increasingly urbanized. The urbanization is influencing the landscape scenario and determining significantly the living conditions, environment and development of the various regions of the world. Urban areas are significantly contributing towards the economic growth and national income of the various countries of the globe. In other words, global development is being determined by the urban development. Urbanization is thus, providing the setting, base and momentum for global change. It is rightly remarked that cities are no longer functioning as areas for settlement, production and services, instead they now profoundly shape and influence social and political relations at every level; determining advances and setbacks in modes of production and providing new content to the norms and culture.[2] However, unbridled and unplanned urbanization is detrimental to sustainable urban development.

The urbanization in hill and forest areas is also significantly influencing the environment and climate change of the nation states. Sustainable urbanization is an inevitable pre-requisite for the development and formulation of smart cities. Sustainable urbanization and smart city go hand in hand, and both are supplementary and complementary to one another. This chapter deals with sustainable urbanization and the smart city.

LEARNING OBJECTIVES

After reading this chapter, you should be able to:

- ❒ Define sustainable urbanization
- ❒ Explain the meaning and importance of sustainable urbanization
- ❒ Describe measures to promote sustainable urbanization
- ❒ Narrate the issues and challenges of sustainable urbanization
- ❒ Explain the meaning of smart city
- ❒ Describe need and importance of smart city
- ❒ Explain the dynamics and characteristics of smart city
- ❒ Dovetail the strategies for development of smart city
- ❒ Explain issues and challenges of smart city development

I
SUSTAINABLE URBANIZATION

Ensuring that urbanization in the developing world happens sustainably is an urgent priority as cities' populations and areas are growing faster than the ability of national and local governments to plan for, build, and manage these changes. Poorly managed and chaotic urban development can undermine economic growth and business opportunities and threaten security through increased crime, violence, and extremism.[3]

Cities will play a key role in halting climate change and meeting the SDGs.[4]

Cities do not enjoy good reputations for development or for ecological sustainability.[5]

Urban areas have been recognized as the key elements for the future of global societies, and the locus of major social and environmental transformations. Urbanization affects the physical shape of a region as well as the social experience of those who live there. Physical urban growth alters the natural and built landscape while population growth reshapes politics and culture. Socially, urbanization may increase the richness and diversity of a region's population on the one hand and on the other may cause tension and conflict between the competing groups. Physically, urbanization may produce new urban spaces and liveable neighbourhoods, and at the same time may cause damage to critical environmental features and important cultural resources.

Sustainable Urbanization: Concepts and Dimensions

Sustainable urbanization occurs when the urbanization and city development process harmonize with principles of sustainable development. The sustainable urbanization presupposes that the urban development activities being conducted at present should be done keeping the future in consideration, and it should not create problems and put the life of the future generation in inconvenience. The three important components of sustainable development are people, environment and economy need to function in harmony. The harm to the environment caused by the excessive desire of the economy to achieve a higher growth rate and of the huge population to fulfill their greed needs to be avoided.

The World Bank (2013) has identified four key concepts for urban sustainability that are

1. *Green growth:* Green growth refers to making growth processes more resource efficient, cleaner and more resilient, without necessarily slowing them (Hallegatte et al. 2011). Green growth necessarily intends to use green inputs in the production and consumption process. In other words, green growth desires to use more green and renewable sources of energy in the production and consumption process of the urban economy. Green growth is otherwise called healthy growth. It will lead to Green Urban Economy.
2. *Green city:* Green city is otherwise called an environment-friendly city. It has adequate flora and fauna and has open spaces for enjoyment and recreation. Urban green spaces can contribute to climate change mitigation. The Intergovernmental Panel on Climate Change 2014 report has emphasized on: (a) energy efficiency and conservation; (b) low-carbon electricity; and (c) switching to lower carbon fuels.
3. *Smart cities:* The cities have to adopt technical and information platforms to better manage the use of their resources, improve management, monitor developments, develop new business models, and help citizens to make informed decisions about the use of resources (World Bank, 2013). In other words, cities can be and must become places of innovation and drivers of economic growth, where wealth and jobs are created and resources are used efficiently (World Bank, 2018). The smart cities are known as ICT-driven cities. The other features of smart cities are smart people, smart location, smart energy, smart governance, smart local self-government and so on.
4. *Resilient cities:* Resilient cities need to have the ability to respond to natural disasters and system shocks. It can provide reliable services under a wide set of unpredictable circumstances. It is adequately prepared to face the challenges of natural disasters and has the ability to overcome the shocks within a short period. It makes the life and property of people safe and secure. These are the cities that have built-in systems, such as diverse transport and land use that can adapt to changes (Newman et al., 2009).

Four dimensions of sustainable development identified in building a more sustainable city are as follows:

1. *Environmental dimension:* It is related to the objectives of the conservation and preservation of the environment. This includes aspects such as atmosphere, soil, water, oceans and seas, biodiversity, and sanitation. The sustainable development is intricately linked to sustainable environment.

2. *Social dimension:* The sustainable development is for the people, by the people and of the people. People are the creators and destructors of sustainability. It is rightly said that sustainable development is related to the objective that involves the satisfaction of human needs. They include population, employment and income, health, education, housing and security, which aim to reflect the level of education, income distribution and living conditions.
3. *Economic dimension:* It is concerned with the efficiency of production processes and changes in consumption patterns.
4. *Institutional dimension:* It includes the ability and effort spent by governments and societies to implement changes required for an effective implementation of sustainable development.[6]

The sustainable city must keep better coordination among the urban economy, urban society and urban environment with the help of effective institutions. It is remarked that cities of the future should be a socially diverse environment where economic and social activities overlap and where communities are focused around neighbourhoods.[7] Sustainable urbanization is that process which effectively integrates its possible future impact on the economy, society and environment. In other words, it has to take into consideration all the three components of sustainable development that are society, economy and environment while implementing various urban development projects and programmes.

The key themes that lie at the core of Sustainable Smart City operations are given as follows:

1. Society—the city is for its inhabitants (the citizens).
2. Economy—the city must be able to thrive—in terms of jobs, growth and finance.
3. Environment—the city must be sustainable in its functioning for future generations.
4. Governance—the city must be robust in its ability to administer policies and put together the different elements (ITU, 2015).

Need and Importance of Sustainable Urbanization

It is not a flight of fancy, but truly, cities with constantly increasing urban population will turn to a more resource, land, food, energy and employment demanding consumers. Therefore, this growing mass of population should be productive to be genuinely sustainable. Unproductive and consumption-driven urban areas are likely to face with poverty, inequality of individuals, pollution, illnesses and other external economic dependency. According to UN-Habitat, the dynamism of cities represents a major sustainable development opportunity. By getting urban development right, cities can create jobs and offer better livelihoods; increase economic growth; improve social inclusion; promote the decoupling of living standards and economic growth from environmental resource use; protect local and regional ecosystems; reduce both urban and rural poverty; and drastically reduce pollution. Sound urban development will accelerate progress towards achieving SDGs, including the end of extreme poverty.[8] According to the USAID, sustainable urbanization is essential for (a) strengthening resilience to respond and adapt to disasters, economic shocks and extreme weather; (b) improving global health and reducing the spread of infectious diseases; (c) improving domestic resource mobilization, fiscal self-reliance and government accountability; (d) increasing women's economic empowerment and access to services and reducing gender-based violence; and (e) improving agricultural development and food security by strengthening rural-urban linkages.[9]

Some of the important reasons for which sustainable urbanization is needed are as follows:

1. *Sustainable economic growth:* The contribution of urban areas to the economic growth in both developed and developing countries is on the rise. However, unplanned and irresponsible urbanization may not lead to sustainable contribution of urban areas to the economic growth rate of the nation states. Sustainable urbanization focuses on the impact of urbanization in present as well as future contribution to growth rate of the nation states. The urbanizations which promotes better integration of the economy, society and environment, would lead to steady and sustained growth rate. Turok and Granahan (2013), from their research, have suggested that governments should seek ways of enabling forms of urbanization that contribute to growth, poverty reduction and environmental sustainability, rather than encouraging (or discouraging) urbanization per se.
2. *Quality of life:* Sustainable urbanization, which focuses on reduction of poverty, inequality and ensuring basic needs such as healthcare, sanitation, drinking water and housing, would raise the quality of life of the people. One of the UN documents has rightly envisaged that without appropriate planning, design and investment in the development of sustainable cities, a growing number of people will continue to face unprecedented negative impacts, not only of climate change but also of reduced economic growth, low quality of life and increased social instability.[10]
3. *Minimize risks and disasters:* Cities and towns in general, and those that are situated at the bank of a seashore in particular, are bearing the brunt of natural disasters such as flooding and tropical storms. As many of the world's largest cities and towns are located along coastlines, rivers and floodplains, these are mostly vulnerable to natural disasters. One of the objectives of the sustainable city is to effectively deal with the disaster and ensure a risk-free living. Ana Cristina Thorlund has rightly viewed that reducing the risks posed by natural and man-made hazards will be critical to keep cities around the globe on a sustainable development track, according to the delegates preparing the way for the UN's Habitat III conference on urbanization.[11] In the same vein, the Asian Development Bank has envisaged that enhanced integration of disaster risk concerns into development policies, plans and individual initiatives would both strengthen disaster resilience and contribute to sustainable development.[12]
4. *Deal with climate change:* Cites are more vulnerable to climate change. Sustainable urbanization is important to deal with the climate change-related effects in the cities. Rapid urbanization is making people more vulnerable to the impacts of climate change. The cities ranked most 'at risk' today (as measured by annual average losses due to floods) span high-income and developing countries: Guangzhou, Miami, New York, New Orleans, Mumbai, Nagoya, Tampa-St. Petersburg, Boston, Shenzhen, Osaka-Kobe and Vancouver.[13] As a measure, many nation states are taking diverse initiatives that are bolstering the resilience of cities, towns and villages under their sustainable development endeavour. One of the documents have mentioned that the 100 Resilient Cities programme was launched by the Rockefeller Foundation in 2013 as a way to select 100 cities to be provided with necessary resources in developing road maps to resilience. Support that has been provided ranges from financial and logistical guidance, expertise in strategy development, access to solutions and service providers, as well as membership to a global network of cities.[14]
5. *Infrastructure and energy:* It is estimated that as urban populations grow, trillions of dollars will be spent on expanding and renewing urban infrastructure. Meeting increasing demands

will require more than doubling annual physical capital investment to over US$20 trillion by 2025, mostly in emerging economies.[15] One of the goals of the sustainable development initiatives is to provide quality infrastructure to the city population. The energy saving initiative which is also an important objective of the sustainable urbanization provides more renewable sources of energy by reducing fossil energy. It will check pollution and improve the health status of urban population.

6. *Technology and innovation:* Sustainable development is important from the standpoint of technology and innovation. The introduction of technology and continuous innovation will sustain the urban economy in an effective and efficient way. Investments in sustainable industries, as well as in scientific research and innovation are important ways to facilitate sustainable development. Chai-Lee said that with urban areas containing the increasing majority of the population, it is very important to focus on how technological innovation can help deliver a sustainable future. A sustainable city must strive to create a sustainable living environment through the use of technology and innovations. The urban areas are the hope of innovations both in developed as well as developing countries. Urban economy is only capable of investing in modern technology and innovations which are essential for sustainable urbanization. USAID in its holistic approach to sustainable urban development emphasizes on (a) creating knowledge through scientific research and geospatial analysis to identify and disseminate emerging trends, evidence and best practice and (b) providing technical assistance to address complex challenges that threaten stability or security and pose barriers to equitable economic growth.[16]
7. *Sustainable Urban Village:* Many cities comprise a lot of urban villages. For example, Delhi has more than 300 urban villages. Imagining a smart and sustainable city bereft of smart and sustainable urban villages is inconclusive. The sustainable and smart cities need to have smart and sustainable urban villages existing within it. The villages need to have smart boundary, smart energy and drinking water supply, smart municipal ward, smart e-connectivity and so on. The municipal government needs to take adequate steps to eradicate poverty and unemployment from the village and provide smart healthcare and education facilities in these villages in order to make them sustainable.

Mass urbanization can lead to social instability, undermining the capacity of cities to be environmentally sustainable and economically successful. A new model of sustainability is needed, including greater incentives to save energy, reduce consumption and protect the environment while also increasing levels of citizen wellbeing.[17] One of the World Bank documents has envisaged the following:

1. The sustainable cities are critical to sustainable development given their position as engines of economic growth, centres of population growth and resource consumption, and crucibles of culture and innovation.
2. Cities must adopt sustainable development policies as soon as possible because today's infrastructure investments will be locked in for hundreds of years. This is all the more urgent in developing countries that are rapidly urbanizing.
3. Sustainable cities should be defined broadly, integrating environmental, economic and social objectives, and should be supported with a comprehensive and customizable how-to menu.
4. Making cities sustainable requires addressing knowledge gaps, broadening participation across stakeholders, and incentivizing behavioural change at the individual, corporate and local government levels.[18]

Measures to Promote Sustainable Urbanization

Various areas to be covered in the sustainable urban development in tandem with the SDGs declared by the UNDP are discussed below. These are the strategic areas where countries have to take appropriate actions in fulfilling various goals of sustainable cities.

1. *Access to basic services:* One of the vital components of SDG is to provide basic services to all population. The basic needs customarily include food, clothing, shelter, sanitation, safe drinking water, basic education and basic healthcare. The Asian Development Bank desires sustainable urbanization to provide basic services to an increasing number of urban residents. It is rightly remarked that many cities are already struggling with the lack of basic services, such as water supply, sanitation and waste management.[19]
2. *Zero poverty:* Sustainable urbanization desires to remove poverty from the cities. Urban poverty poses great challenge to urban sustainability because most of the urban poor suffer from social exclusion, unemployment, homelessness, lack of paid income and vulnerability to environmental risks and poor health. This has resulted in the growth of slums, squatters' settlements, shacks, dirty run-down housing. These are found in most of the cities of the developing countries especially belonging to South Asia and Africa. The sustainable urbanization emphasizes on raising the living standard and quality of life of the urban poor through the removal of urban poverty.
3. *Zero hunger and absence of malnutrition:* Hunger and malnutrition are still prevailing among the urban people living in the slums and squatters that are working in the low-paid unorganized sector. The children of the families living in the slums are devoid of proper nutrition. As a result, many of them are found to be stunted and wasted, which is affecting their mental growth. Sustainable urban development emphasizes not only on improving food security, but also on more healthy diets and enhancing sustainable and resilient food and nutrition systems for the urban residents. The end of hunger, achieved food security and improved nutrition aim to identify options, opportunities and strategies for improving nutrition and strengthening sustainable global and local food systems by developing science-based solutions, creating partnerships and delivering change.[20]
4. *Reduction of inequalities:* One of the goals of sustainable urban development is to reduce inequality. It is remarked that the right to equitable urban development is the right for all the citizens to share equally the benefits and burdens of urban development. City planning, regulation and management should be designed to equitably distribute services and resources among inhabitants, promote social cohesion, and ensure that the social function of the city and property is being fulfilled.[21] The sustainable urbanization believes in inclusive urbanization where all the city dwellers must contribute and equally share the benefits of urban development. Emphasis is on three levels of inclusive urbanization: eliminating discriminatory exclusion; giving the disadvantaged a bigger voice in existing institutions; and guaranteeing human rights.
5. *Good health and well-being:* The rapid urbanization process taking place both in developed as well as developing countries in order to be sustainable needs to look after the health and well-being of the city dwellers. Because of increasing pollution and other human-laid activities, the health and well-being of the city dwellers have been greatly disturbed. UNEP (2012) has remarked that while urban areas occupy just 3 per cent of the land surface, they are responsible for perhaps three-quarters of carbon emissions and natural resource utilization. Urban people are suffering from many communicable and non-communicable

diseases, such as diabetes, blood pressure, tuberculosis, cancer, dengue, chikungunya and so on. The human health and well-being have to be promoted for sustainable urban development.

6. *Inclusive and quality education:* Education is an important instrument of sustainable development. Inclusive and quality education at all levels starting from the primary up to higher education are required for sustainable development. Education must be strengthened in the backward provinces and also among the marginalized sections of the population. The UN-Habitat believes that universities, colleges, research and training institutions and students alike play a critical role in finding and implementing strategies to realize the potential of urbanization for sustainable development. It helps them in dealing with issues of air quality, climate change mitigation and adaptation, and contributing to the creation of more sustainable cities from various angles. The role of education in its broader sense, including training and capacity building, communication, creating public awareness and enabling knowledge exchange, is thus critical for the transformation of human and institutional capacities, as well as enabling local communities to strengthen their resilience and planning for inclusive, safe and sustainable cities.[22]
7. *Clean water and sanitation:* Sustainable urbanization ensures clean drinking water and better sanitation to the city dwellers in order to promote their health and well-being. Clean drinking water and sanitation are the two vital basic needs of human beings. Both are critical for the future well-being of the city dwellers. Besides this, better urban sanitation unquestionably contributes to environmental protection through a reduction in pollution of soils, waterways and groundwater. It also helps to mitigate the adverse impacts of flooding exacerbated by climate change.[23]
8. *Women empowerment and gender equality:* Contribution of women to development needs to be increased for attainment of sustainable urbanization. Women empowerment and sustainable development go hand in hand. Gender equality and sustainability reinforce each other and create alternative pathways of development, which is more inclusive and sustainable. It is said that women's knowledge, agency and collective actions are often central in managing local landscapes, adapting to climate change, producing and accessing food, or securing sustainable water, sanitation and energy services.[24] It is remarked that the effects of unsustainable patterns of development often intensify gender inequalities, as women and girls are disproportionately affected by economic, social and environmental shocks and stresses.[25]
9. *Affordable and clean energy:* Sustainable urbanization requires affordable and clean energy. Cities contribute to global climate change and environmental disturbances by emitting anthropogenic greenhouse gases. Besides the use of innumerable vehicles, other electrical and electronic gadgets produce heat and pollution. It is estimated that urban electricity used in and cooling together contribute 37 per cent of global energy-related emissions, buildings contribute 25 per cent and urban transportation contributes 22 per cent (WRI, 2009).Therefore, it is critical to create cities that produce low carbon and are resilient and liveable. The use of renewable sources of energy by the household and institutions in the urban areas will further strengthen the sustainability dimensions of urban development.
10. *Innovation and urban infrastructure:* Urban infrastructure in many developing countries and particularly in the least developed countries of Asia, Africa and Latin America is inadequate and insufficient to meet the needs of rapidly growing populations and conduction of various economic development activities. The urban infrastructure such as road, electricity, energy, housing, safe drinking water, sanitation, transport, safety and security infrastructure are inadequate and utterly lacking as compared to the growing

population in the cities. Besides this, rapid urbanization leads to the expansion of the cities to its vicinities known as peri-urban areas, which also demands infrastructure facilities. Urban infrastructure is central to building sustainable cities. Moreover, scientific and technological innovation in various sectors will further strengthen sustainable urbanization endeavour. The UNDP envisages that the concentration of resources, ideas and energy in urban areas is useful for creativity and technological innovation.[26] The UN has rightly remarked that science, technology and innovation can help achieve sustainable urban development by taking into account the economic, environmental and social dimensions of urbanization.[27]

11. *Addressing environmental issues and climate change:* The urbanization of the global population has fundamental ramifications for the economy, society and the environment. Cities cover a small part of the nation states landscape, but their physical and ecological footprints are much larger. City environments are vulnerable to climate change and extreme events. Climate change posits challenges to the city dwellers especially on the impoverished population. In a similar vein, the UNDP feels that its impact is expected to hit those living in poverty the hardest. The UNDP has noted that the human dimensions of climate change, especially its impacts on the daily challenges of the urban poor in terms of employment, livelihoods, safety, health, housing and access to basic services are critical for successful policies to create inclusive and resilient cities.[28] The control of pollution, heat and green house effects in the cities are viable strategies for building sustainable cities.
12. *Urban safety and security:* Safety and security is a big issue in the cities and particularly in the metropolitan and big cities of the developing countries. The two main challenges of urban safety and security are to prevent urban crime and violence, to reduce the risk and impact of urban disasters. To UN-Habitat, crime and violence occur within a physical setting, whether a public open space, a park, a street, a market, or a transportation hub. Urban physical planning, design and management can contribute to the prevention of crime and violence within the cities through integrated approaches that incorporate strategic and systematic upgrading of public spaces, and apply security-conscious design and management principles, revision of city by-laws and regulations, mixed zoning and planning for diversity, integrated management of public space, conflict resolution and rapid maintenance responses.[29] Besides effective prevention, reduction and management of both man-made and natural disasters are vital requisites of sustainable urbanization. UNISDR has rightly said that reducing the risks posed by natural and man-made hazards will be critical to keep cities around the globe on a sustainable development track.[30]
13. *Accountable and inclusive institutions:* The local self-government institutions need to be accountable for the effective implementation of the various parameters of sustainable urbanizations. Political leadership at the sub-government level is vital for building accountable and inclusive institutions. It is said that without leadership by cities and territories, it is impossible to decrease poverty, reduce inequality or achieve effective, accountable and inclusive institutions.[31] Besides this, the nation state has to establish strong institutions and parastatal bodies to formulate and execute policies and programmes for sustainable cities. In India, the Housing and Urban Development Corporation (HUDCO) plays an important role in the housing sector in urban areas. The parastatals working at the state levels are needed to be oriented and energized on various aspects of sustainable urbanization.
14. *Decent work, employment and economic growth:* The decent work phenomenon emphasizes on combating inappropriate working conditions, improving social protection and respecting labour standards in human settlements. Its objective is to pay sustainable wage rate to the workers, particularly those who are working in the informal sector in the cities in order to

enable them to have a decent lifestyle. It will enable them to further contribute towards the economic growth rate. The inclusive growth cannot be possible if the workers in cities have decent work and working conditions. It is remarked that the societies are resilient when decent jobs are available and can be created in the future in a context of inclusive and environmentally sustainable economic growth. More resource-efficient production generates room for productivity increases that can have positive effects on value added and therefore on workers' remuneration.[32]

15. *Global partnership:* For building sustainable cities, the national and provincial government have to build partnership with the international and national NGOs and the corporate sectors. They also need to have government-to-government collaboration and need to adopt the best available practices in various countries. The role of multilateral and bilateral agencies such as the World Bank, ADB, JICA, CIDA and so on will go a long way to strength the sustainable urbanization initiatives in the developing countries. Goal 17 recognizes that the implementation of the SDGs is a challenge for governments and therefore seeks to strengthen the global partnership by calling upon all the stakeholders to take part in implementing the SDGs.[33] The World Bank (2013) has rightly said that a sustainable urbanization process needs to enable cooperative networks towards a common sustainable future. The prosperity of a city is measured through the amenities it has ensured to its population. Some of the dimensions of City Prosperity Index are given in Box 15.1.

Box 15.1 City Prosperity Index

In 2012, UN-Habitat created the City Prosperity Index as a tool to measure the sustainability of the cities. It has six critical dimensions:

- *Productivity:* A prosperous city contributes to economic growth and development, generating income, employment and equal opportunities that further provide adequate living standards for the entire population.
- *Infrastructure development:* A prosperous city deploys the infrastructure, physical assets and amenities—adequate water, sanitation, power supply, road network, information and communications technology and so on—required to sustain both the population and the economy, and provide a better quality of life.
- *Quality of life:* Prosperous cities provide amenities such as social services, education, health, recreation, safety and security required for improved living standards, enabling the population to maximize individual potential and to lead fulfilling lives.
- *Equity and inclusion:* A city is only prosperous to the extent that poverty and inequalities are minimal. No city can claim to be prosperous when large segments of the population live in abject poverty and deprivation. This involves reducing the incidence of slums and new forms of poverty and marginalization.
- *Environmental sustainability:* The growth of cities and their economic development do not destroy or degrade the environment; instead, the city's natural assets are preserved for the sake of sustainable urbanization.
- *Governance and legislation:* Cities are best able to combine sustainability and shared prosperity through effective urban governance and transformational leadership, deploying appropriate and effective policies, laws and regulations, and creating adequate institutional frameworks with strong local institutions and sound institutional arrangements.

Source: https://unhabitat.org/wp-content/uploads/2019/02/CPI-METADATA.2016.pdf (accessed on 1 March 2019).

Issues and Challenges of Sustainable Urbanization

Some issues and challenges of sustainable urbanization are as follows:

1. *Socioeconomic equity and inclusiveness:* One of the outstanding issues and challenges in the process of sustainable urbanization is how to energize the socioeconomic equity and inclusiveness in the cities. Cities are not only places of great opportunity, but also places of disparities. The sustainable urbanization will become sustainable and endure only when each and every section of the urban society contributes towards urban growth and development.
2. *Land-use planning:* Sustainable urbanization calls for integrated land-use planning. Land-use planning must be done after careful assessment and planning of available land space for the city within and in its periphery so that the community needs such as housing, environmental protection, healthcare, education and other infrastructure needs of the present and projected future population are meaningfully incorporated. Customarily, land-use zoning was the dominant approach to urban planning. Zoning means creation of defined areas within a city that were being assigned for different activities such as residential, commerce, industry, social services, recreation, open space and so on.
3. *Green initiatives:* The faster pace of globalization and use of non-renewable fossil fuel energies have made the green city initiative more challenging. It has been noted that the cities are now the main sources of global greenhouse gas emissions, responsible for 80 per cent of global CO_2 according to UN-Habitat, while cities are the ones most vulnerable to climate change. The rapid urbanization will bring more carbon emissions to cities and expose urban dwellers to increased climate risks.[34] It calls for great will power among the various actors of green city initiatives and sustainable city missions such as government, local self-government institutions, multilateral and bilateral organizations, corporate sector and so on to take lead in implementing green city and climate actions.
4. *Demographic challenge:* One of the critical challenges for sustainable urbanization is to handle the issue of urban population pressure and rural-to-urban migration. It is not a flight of fancy, but truly 'Human beings are at the centre of concern for sustainable development.' Any discussion on sustainable development must take into consideration the population issue and recognize its impacts on the environment, and their vulnerabilities to risk broadly depend on their age, gender, location and other socioeconomic characteristics in urban areas. The urban population growth also presents challenges for urban planning and good governance: challenges that are especially acute in environmentally fragile locations. The principal demographic factors that increase vulnerability are poverty, poor health, low levels of education, gender inequality, declining family support for the elderly and unfavourable geographic location especially for those who are living in the slums and other disadvantaged location of the cities. Populations with these characteristics also often lack a political voice, putting them at even greater risk.[35] The challenge is how to check egregious migration and control unplanned urbanization for sustainable urban development particularly in the developing countries.
5. *Urban resilience:* One of the most critical features of the challenges of sustainable urbanization is urban resilience. The cities have to tackle the internal and external shocks such as violence and disasters in order to provide a sustainable living culture to the city dwellers. The resilience cities also have to effectively deal with the environment and climate-related changes and adversaries. The sustainable cities are therefore otherwise known as resilience cities. The UN-Habitat has rightly remarked that urban resilience is the

measurable ability of any urban system, with its inhabitants, to maintain continuity through all shocks and stresses, while positively adapting and transforming toward sustainability. A resilient city assesses, plans and acts to prepare and respond to hazards—natural and human-made, sudden and slow-onset, expected and unexpected—in order to protect and enhance people's lives, secure development gains, foster an environment for investment, and drive positive change.[36]

6. *Decentralized urban governance and participation:* Strengthening decentralized governance and promoting peoples' participation in municipal activities is one of the vital challenges for fulfilling the goal of sustainable cities. Greater devolution of funds, functionaries and functions with full freedom to do need-based activities to the local self-government institutions at various levels will enable them to effectively indulge in development activities. Their capacity building and empowerment is vital to sustainable urbanization. However, it is seen that in most of the countries they are not effectively empowered to discharge their constitutionally assigned duties and responsibilities. The elected representatives of the local self-government institutions can only effectively promote peoples' participation for sustainable urbanization. The UN-Habitat has righty envisaged that urban governance is inextricably linked to the welfare of the citizens. Good urban governance must enable women and men to access the benefits of urban citizenship. Good urban governance, based on the principle of urban citizenship, affirms that no man, woman or child can be denied access to the necessities of urban life, including adequate shelter, security of tenure, safe water, sanitation, a clean environment, health, education and nutrition, employment and public safety and mobility. Through good urban governance, citizens are provided with the platform which will allow them to use their talents to the full to improve their social and economic conditions.[37]
7. *Public–private partnership:* Government in silos cannot handle various issues and challenges of sustainable urbanization. They need the cooperation and partnership of the private and corporate sectors to handle various issues and challenges of sustainable urbanization. Some of the positive aspects of PPP are quality of work, timely completion of the projects, better maintenance of the projects and so on. According to the European Investment Bank, PPP is a general name defining all relations between the private sector and public organizations, aiming at the application of private resources or experience to support the public sector in providing assets and services.[38] The challenge before the urban government is to promote effective PPP through choosing the appropriate areas and modalities of PPP in various areas of SDGs in the cities. An example of sustainable PPP model is given in Box 15.2.

Box 15.2 PPP—A Felt Need Model for Sustainable Development

'Jalanidhi' is a model of PPP which is a community demand-driven project that changed the role of the government from direct service delivery to that of the facilitator. The implementation of the project was ensured through a partnership between Kerala Rural Water supply and Sanitation Agency, district project management units, gram panchayats, beneficiary committee, beneficiary groups, support organizations, mostly NGOs, which are recruited through a public process. The study has also revealed that the participation of community in the programme helps reducing the corruption and the service becomes more effective.

Source: https://www.cppr.in/wp-content/uploads/2012/10/intensivepublicprivatepartnershipforsustainableurabizationofcochi.pdf (accessed on 25 November 2019).

8. *Fiscal sustainability:* Last but not the least, finance is the kingpin to carry out all the activities aimed at sustainable urbanization. However, the available sources of finance and its quantity always fall short of the rapid urbanization. Effective tax collection, devolution of fund from the central and provincial governments to the local government and peoples' participation in partially financing the developmental projects in their areas would go a long way to achieve the goal of sustainable urbanization. It is said that national governments should consider strategies to strengthen local capacities and diversify local sources of finance for sustainable urbanization.[39] Besides this, UNDP has suggested the various alternative sources of financing such as crowed funding, social impact bonds, youth employment bonds for meeting the sustainable financing challenges for the cities of the developing countries.[40]

II
SMART CITY

The Smart City is and will definitely be one of the most important challenges over the next few decades. Although the smart city is a trend for some and a necessity for others, it is obvious that, with the demographic explosion of our cities, we have to rethink our way of life and how we use our resources, consume and move about.[41]

The idea of Smart Cities is rooted in the creation and connection of human capital, social capital and Information and Communication Technology (ICT) infrastructure in order to generate greater and more sustainable economic development and a better quality of life.

–European Parliament[42]

The phenomenon of the so called "Smart Cities" is spreading worldwide as a synonym of an innovative and improved model of sustainable city.

–European Investment Bank Institute[43]

It is estimated that by 2050, more than 6 billion people will be living in urban environments. It is nearer to the 75 per cent of the world's population. No doubt, the cities are the places of many opportunities. Cities are becoming the hub of human and economic activity. However, at the same time, urbanization carries with it a sundry of urban-management problems, that is, pollution, poverty, unemployment and under-employment, housing, slums, sanitation, drinking water, cost of living, mobility and so on. Moreover, cities are also the places where inequalities are stronger. Therefore, city development initiatives call for sustainable and smart cities which can ensure a good quality of life to the city dwellers.

Smart City: Concept and Meaning

The smart city is a new and vibrant concept. With the acceleration of the pace of urbanization, the issues of sustainable urbanization and smart city have emerged in order to enhance the facilities to the growing population and raise the quality of life of the city dwellers. The alternative names used for the smart cities are Hi-tech City, Resilience City, Knowledge City, Sustainable City, Green City, Eco-City and so on.

A few definitions of Smart City are narrated below:
Mark and Husam (2011) list four factors that contribute to the definition of a smart city.

1. The application of a wide range of electronic and digital technologies to communities and cities.
2. The use of ICT to transform life and working environments within a region.
3. The embedding of such ICTs in government systems.
4. The territorialization of practices that brings ICTs and people together to enhance the innovation and knowledge that they offer.

According to Caragliu and Nijkamp (2009), 'a city can be defined as 'smart' when investments in human and social capital and traditional (transport) and modern (ICT) communication infrastructure fuel sustainable economic development and a high quality of life, with a wise management of natural resources, through participatory action and engagement.'

The Institute of Electrical and Electronics Engineers Smart Cities defined that 'a smart city brings together technology, government and society to enable the following characteristics: smart cities, a smart economy, smart mobility, a smart environment, smart people, smart living, smart governance.'[44]

To a Business Dictionary, a smart city is 'a developed urban area that creates sustainable economic development and high quality of life by excelling in multiple key areas; economy, mobility, environment, people, living, and government. Excelling in these key areas can be done so through strong human capital, social capital, and/or ICT infrastructure.'[45]

The British Standards Institute defines the term smart city as 'the effective integration of physical, digital and human systems in the built environment to deliver sustainable, prosperous and inclusive future for its citizens'.[46]

The UK Department for Business, Innovation and Skills considers smart cities a process rather than a static outcome, in which increased citizen engagement, hard infrastructure, social capital and digital technologies make cities more liveable, resilient and better able to respond to challenges.[47]

Kumar (2017) has mentioned a few salient features of a smart city given as (a) Digital ICT appears to form the core of a smart city project; (b) Role of the private sector in central government is only an enabler in the smart city project; (c) To become a smart city, a city must be competitive, efficient and productive; (d) To become competitive, a city should house a large number of creative and innovative people. Human capital is critical to the smart city mission; and (e) Integration of the various elements of a smart city through technology is another central aspect of a smart city.

From all these definitions, it can be deduced that smart city's aims and objectives are to:

1. achieve a sustainable and inclusive urban growth rate;
2. ensure smart environment and effectively attain climate change effects;
3. promote the use of technology and information systems;
4. promote smart social, human and cultural capital;
5. ensure smart infrastructure and mobility;
6. ensure smart energy;
7. smart resilience to disaster;
8. ensure smart governance and smart institutions;
9. promote smart participation in city development; and
10. smart good quality of living.

Need and Importance of Smart City

The need for smart cities is being called for due to followings:

1. *Effective management of city population:* The migration of rural population to the urban areas for various reasons have led to population pressure in the city. If the migration of population to the cities is not effectively managed, it may lead to various problems such as housing, sanitation, employment, safety and security and so on. One of the objectives of the smart city is smart population. The smart city is necessary in order to provide various basic amenities to the city dwellers such as housing, healthcare, sanitation, education, employment and so on and raise their quality of life. Another perspective of city population management is the decision-making process of city development. People are to be encouraged to contribute in cash and kind for the development of various socio-welfare activities. It is argued that The Smart People concept merges with the governance through the participative role of citizens in the urban milieu within a smart but transparent decision-making process.[48]
2. *Enhance contribution of city to national growth rate:* The smart cities are vital to enhance the contribution of the city to national economic growth. The use of technology with the help of smart population could bolster and make the city's economy smarter and enhance its potential and productivity. Smart city projects contribute to economic growth by establishing an economy of scales. The use of Information Technology in the production of goods and services, in particular, has a strong influence on the productivity and economic growth.[49]
3. *Infrastructure and technological development:* One of the objectives of the smart cities is to ensure smart, sustainable and secured infrastructure to city population. These includes better housing, water works, sanitation projects, city road, transport and traffic system, school, hospitals and so on. It saves time and enables the city population to contribute towards the economic growth. Information Technology has been 'a powerful catalyst' in addressing economic challenges for cities, and it has simply become the 'foundation of every sector of every economy.'[50] According to the World Economic Forum's 2015 Global Information Technology Report, several studies have shown a significant and positive impact on GDP from Information Technology (WEF, 2015). Smart technologies have changed cities in many ways, such as infrastructure, communications, education and social interaction (Aribilosho & Usoro, 2016). The United Kingdom Government Department for Business, Innovation, and Skills noted that 'A smart city uses digital technologies to enhance performance and wellbeing, to reduce costs and resource consumption, also to engage more effectively and actively with its citizens.'[51]
4. *Enhancement of resilience capabilities:* The smart cities are important from the point of view of resilience. The smart cities are being promoted on the ground of effectively managing the natural and man-made disasters and dealing with urban crimes and violence. Smart cities open the door to public safety. Gun detectors and GIS are being used to reduce crimes by geographically spotting areas with high crime rates, identifying specific crime patterns. Besides using the upgraded surveillance system, it can easily identify the culprits and punish them. The Detotto and Otranto (2010) study concluded that higher crime rates discourage domestic and foreign direct investments and reallocates resources, creating uncertainty and inefficiency. The study also concluded that crimes play a role in determining a country's economic progress and negatively impact the economic performance. Moreover, the smart cities equip the administration and governance system to effectively deal with the disasters.

5. *Inclusive urbanization:* The smart city is vital from the point of view of inclusive urbanization. One of the characteristics of the smart city is that it is an inclusive city. During the process of formulation and implementation of smart city projects and programmes, adequate care is being taken for the well-being of the marginalized sections of the city dwellers. It is pertinent to mention here that they contribute significantly towards the city's development, however, they do not enjoy the fruits of the development. Therefore, the smart cities are being called as inclusive cities, where rejuvenation of slums is being carried out for raising the quality of life of the slum dwellers. These smart cities should have the capacity to absorb, adapt and provide opportunities for both the poor rural migrants as well as the educated professionals.
6. *Sustainable urbanization:* Traditional cities are going through serious urban challenges, nowadays, ranging from environmental (i.e., climate change, energy and pollution), economic (i.e., globalization), to social (i.e., urbanization). These challenges make cities more of consumers than preservers of the environmental resources, which threaten the sustainability of the cities for years to come. To achieve sustainability, cities need to implement smart solutions enabled by smart technology. These smart technology solutions require 'smart city initiatives' from the society (Albino et al., 2015). Smart city initiatives have to involve citizens, government, businesses and non-government institutions in collaboration and partnership efforts (Mosterman & Zander, 2013; Vanolo, 2014). This social involvement has to focus on organizing a team with a dedicated manager, diagnosing the current situation with regard to urban challenges specific to the city and current ICT infrastructure, identifying smart technological solutions, setting action plan (i.e., goals, schedules, costs and performance indicators), financing the smart city action plan, implementing the smart city project and evaluating it. The smart cities are have the objective to effectively deal with the various SDGs with prime focus on sustainable environment and resilience to deal with the impact of climate change.
7. *Ease of doing business:* Smart cities are important for ease of doing business. The cities have better infrastructure facilities and IT resources attract FDIs. The smart cities can promote ease of doing business through unlocking efficiency by harnessing business expertise, technology and data, deploying private-sector investment, and developing well-executed PPPs. Smart cities can create a smart business community through a transparent system of ease of doing business. Ease of doing business can be effectively promoted in the smart cities as smart cities are skilled and innovative, high-tech and technology driven, green and sustainable and resilient to natural hazards. The corporate sector from within and outside the nation would love to invest in smart cities.

Dynamics and Characteristics of Smart Cities

The widely cited indicators for the 'smartness' of a city are mapped to six characteristics: smart economy, smart people, smart governance, smart mobility, smart environment and smart living (Giffinger et al., 2007). SMART City is defined with elaboration of the word SMART as:

S—Sustainable
M—Measurable
A—Accessible
R—Replicable
T—Technical

Hence the definition of SMART is accepted in a similar way by the National Planning Commission and Department of Urban Development and Building Construction.[52]

The letters used in SMART can be elaborated as:

S—Sustainable: The development projects and programmes to be carried out in the smart city or under the smart city mission at present must take into consideration its impact on the future. The cities need to be smart enough to provide sustainable, environment-friendly urban infrastructure to its citizens.

M—Measurable: The impact of the development projects and programmes carried in the smart city or under the smart city mission are measurable both in quantitative as well as qualitative terms.

A—Accessible: The benefits of the development projects and programmes in the smart city should be inclusive in nature so that it is accessible to all. The inclusive principle emphasizes that the development benefits must be more directed towards the marginalized sections that are staying in urban slums and other impoverished sections.

R—Replicable: The paradigm of development adopted in the smart city or under the smart city mission is needed to be such that it could be replicable both within the country by various cities and also by other countries in their cities. In other words, to be replicable it must be exemplary. We should make our cities globally competitive so that they emerge as engines of inclusive growth.

T—Technical: The use of technology in the smart city. In a border sense, smart cities use ICTs to be more intelligent and efficient in the use of resources, resulting in cost-saving and improved service delivery.

The characteristic features of the smart cities vary from one city to another, and there is no universally acceptable characteristics framework for the smart cities. It is designed and developed by conducting need assessment by fulfilling the gaps required to meet the exigencies of smartness of the city. It is one of the most dynamic concepts and cannot be defined and its features cannot be stipulated for universal satisfaction. In other words, smart cities cannot be framed, rather it is an out-of-box phenomenon. Some of the characteristics features of a smart city are follows:

1. *Smart people:* The smart cities are otherwise known as 'intelligent city' or 'knowledge city'. The smart city uses digital technologies to enhance performance and promote the well-being of city dwellers. Therefore, a smart city necessitates smart people who can use ICTs for faster delivery of services to the common men. There should be quality technology-driven educational institutions in the smart cities which can provide smart education and training to the city dwellers. The smart people must be tolerant, creative and versatile in nature and respect ethnicity and pluralistic culture of the city.
2. *Smart environment:* One of the important features of smart city is smart environment. The smart city must use an environment-friendly energy system that reduces pollution and greenhouse effects. The smart city promotes smart environment through climate action, waste management, use of renewable sources of energy and air quality monitoring. Smart environment would improve health status by controlling environmental degradation-related health problems and ensure a good quality of living to the city dwellers. The smart environment enhances the efficiency and productivity capacity of the people as people in a smart environment do not feel fatigue.

3. *Smart technology:* Smart city uses smart technology to enhance efficiencies, improve sustainability, create economic development and enhance the quality of life of the people living and working in the cities. Smart cities are cities, where everything is connected to each other and this is highly dependent on technologies. The smart phone, internet connectivity are illustrious examples of smart technology which has promoted connectivity not only in the cities but has also connected city with the countryside. Smart cities use technologies to find solution to the modern problem.
4. *Smart economy:* Smart economy is crucial to smart city. The smart economy raises productivity and growth rate by using technology. The on-line transactions, virtual supermarket, near field communication or payment through smart phone are a few among many features of smart economy. The smart economy has smart market, smart entrepreneurs, smart investors, smart consumers, smart producers, smart banking and insurance system and so on. Besides these, smart digital transaction, digital transfer of social benefits to the poor, e-banking and so on are being popularized in the smart economy. The other name of smart economy is digital economy.
5. *Smart governance:* Smart governance plays an important role in a smart city. The smart government prefers developing smart governance through the application of emergent ICT for governing. Smart governance prefers the intelligent use of ICT to improve decision-making through better collaboration and coordination among various stakeholders of development, including the government, the corporate sector, bilateral and multilateral agencies, NGOs and citizens at large. The smart city uses smart governance in order to address the challenges of the digital society, collaborative governance, information sharing, citizen engagement, transparency and accountability.
6. *Smart land-use planning:* Smart city requires smart land-use planning. The smart planning uses various planning models and GIS techniques for the urban land-space planning. Smart cities and smart land-use planning are intimately connected. It is remarked that the way we use and plan the development of the space in which our communities exist is crucial to the creation of sustainable infrastructure and vibrant healthy communities. The sustainable infrastructure demands planning that is efficient, helps support or creates closer knit neighbourhoods and the sense of community with them, and preserves natural systems that existed on the land prior to human development.[53]
7. *Smart infrastructure:* Smart infrastructure is eco-friendly and sustainable infrastructure, which is cost-effective and durable for a longer period. Smart infrastructure provides the foundation for all the key themes related to a smart city, including smart people, smart mobility, smart economy, smart living, smart governance and smart environment.[54] Various components of smart infrastructure are smart buildings, smart roads, smart malls and shopping complexes and so on.
8. *Smart mobility:* Smart mobility is best described as an approach that reduces congestion and foster faster, greener and cheaper transportation options. Smart mobility systems include mass transit systems as well as individual mobility systems that feature bicycle sharing, ride sharing (or carpooling), vehicle sharing and, more recently, on-demand transportation. Smart mobility uses network of sensors, global positioning system-tracked public transportation, dynamic traffic lights, passenger information panels, automatic vehicle registration plate readers, closed-circuit television systems, navigation facilities, signalling systems and so on.[55]
9. *Smart energy:* A smart city uses smart energy systems. Smart energy management systems use sensors, advanced meters, renewable energy sources, digital controls and analytic

tools to automate, monitor and optimize energy distribution and usage. Such systems optimize grid operation and usage by balancing the needs of the different stakeholders involved (consumers, producers and providers).[56] Smart energy is otherwise being called smart grid.

10. *Smart territory:* One of the important features of a smart city is smart territory. The territory of the city must be unique and should not have any dispute between the states and provinces. For example, the beautiful city of Chandigarh in India belongs to Haryana and Punjab, which sometimes leads to political battle between the two states. It needs to have a wider periphery. Smart territories are also described as geographical areas in which knowledge-intensive activities are undertaken and are environment and technology friendly. Some of the territorial divisions commonly seen in recent years are IT zones, business zones, residential complexes and so on.
11. *Smart participation:* In the open market economy, where the corporate and privates sectors are playing important roles in the development process, smart participation in the development of the smart city is also equally vital. The various actors of development such as government, private sector, NGOs, CSOs and people at large could play an important role in smart city management. The PPP in the smart city mission of India is an illustrious example. Smart interaction and collaboration with various stakeholders would lead to smart decision-making.
12. *Smart institutions:* Smart institutions are important requisites of smart cities. At the outset, smart cities need to have smart local self-government institutions, which are equipped with technology and have trained elected representatives and functionaries to smartly carry out their duties and responsibilities. Moreover, smart urban parastatal bodies are also sine qua non for implementing the goals and objectives of the smart city mission. Names of few parastatal bodies are: HUDCO, DDA and so on. Moreover, for smart cities, smart urban education, training and research organizations are also needed for carrying out further innovations.
13. *Smart safety and security:* A smart city needs to have smart safety and security system. The three important dimensions of safety and security are prevention of urban crime, control and prevention of violence and smart urban disaster management system in place. It is the duty of the urban governance to protect the life and property of city dwellers. It needs to have a strong surveillance system and effective law and order enforcement system. In the IT-driven smart cities, prevention of cybercrime and ensuring cyber security is essential to smart cities. It is impossible to have a smart city when your citizens do not feel safe. Mr Dixon was of the view that 'As cities concentrate a growing share of the national economy, it is imperative that they have systems to manage natural hazards and prevent them from becoming human and economic disasters'.[57]
14. *Smart social, human and cultural capital:* A smart city enriches its social, human and cultural capital. It makes optimum use of sustainable urbanization. Smart cities need to have good social-networking systems and social institutions, particularly health and educational institutions, for the enrichment of its human and cultural capital. The cultural capital includes preservation of cultural heritage, cultural practices such as song, dance, drama, theatre, languages, cultural foods and dress and so on. Smart city needs to realize the role of culture in sustainable urbanization.
15. *Smart identity:* A smart city has smart identities. It is based on its main economic activity, such as local cuisine, health, education, arts and craft, culture, sports goods, furniture,

hosiery, textile, dairy and so on. Some of the popular words used in classifying the cities based on their importance are: 'religious city', 'heritage city', 'wood carving city', 'brass work city', 'pink city' and so on. The smart city mission in India aims at upgrading religious and heritage cities into smart cities.

16. *Smart open space:* In smart cities, smart open spaces have strong urban effect. They are places for relaxation, recreation and social networking, and promotion of healthy living. The features of the smart open spaces like parks, stadiums, water bodies and so on are that they should be clean, well-maintained and have toilet facilities. It is said that urban green spaces in contemporary culture are no longer seen as an aesthetic element only, but also a factor in combating pollution, industrialization and anthropization. Maintaining green areas is a delicate balance between environmental and economic sustainability.[58]
17. *Smart living:* Last, but not the least, is smart living in smart cities. The smart cities need to ensure smart living and smart quality of life to the city dwellers. Smart living comprises smart schools, smart hospitals, smart traffic management, smart parking, smart water management, smart waste management, smart metering, smart grid, smart crime control management, smart disaster management, smart integration and several other smart things, which require the effective involvement of smart people or smart citizens.[59] It is also further remarked that the quality of life is much better in smart cities as a smart city offers better safety and security, inclusiveness, entertainment, ease of seeking and obtaining public services, cost efficient healthcare, quality education, and opportunity for participation in governance.[60]
18. *Smart slums:* It is not a flight of fancy, but truly slums are the part and parcel of the city life particularly in the cities of the developing countries. However, the governments of these countries have to make these slums smart by providing proper housing, sanitation, drinking water, electricity, ration cards, schools, health centres and so on. The government and the municipalities need to have smart slum development policies in the smart cities.

Strategies for Development of Smart City

The four strategies customarily being used for the development of smart cities in India are as follows: (a) city improvement (retrofitting); (b) city renewal (redevelopment); (c) city extension (green field development); and (d) pan city development (Table 15.1).

1. *Retrofitting:* The retrofitting or redevelopment is done in an existing built-up area to make it smart under the smart city mission in order to achieve the smart city objective. It is needless to mention that in the retrofitting, the existing structure largely remains intact. The improvement is done depending on the need of the existing built-up area. Here, usually a large number of smart applications are inflicted into retrofitted smart cities. Retrofitting is done in an area of 500 acres under the Smart City Mission. Some of the demerits associated with the retrofitting are (a) Expensive and inconvenient; (b) Internal spaces may be reduced during the time of application and installation; and (c) Might cause negative impact to heritage and archaeological assets.
2. *Redevelopment:* Redevelopment is the replacement of the existing built-up environment. It is done with the objective of embarking a co-creation of a new layout with enhanced infrastructure by using mixed land-use and increased density. Redevelopment is being done

Table 15.1 Strategies for Development of Smart City

Area-based Development	Options
Retrofitting	Identify an area of more than 500 acres and prepare a plan to make it more efficient and livable with citizen's participation (Connaught Place in Delhi, Bhendi Bazar in Mumbai).
Redevelopment	Replace existing built-up area (50 acres) and prepare a new layout plan with enhanced infrastructure by way of mixed land use (Kidwai Nagar in Delhi).
Greenfield	Introduce solutions in an area of 250 acres by using innovative planning (land pooling/land reconstitution in Outer Delhi, GIFT city in Gujarat).
Pan-city development	Use technology, information and data to make existing city-wide infrastructure and services better. For example, initiating waste water recycling and smart metering which can make substantial contribution to better water management in the city.

Source: Smart City Guideline, MoUD.
Also see: https://www.downtoearth.org.in/news/urbanisation/what-s-the-progress-of-smart-cities-mission--58147 (accessed on 7 March 2019).

Figure 15.1 Strategy of Smart City Development in India

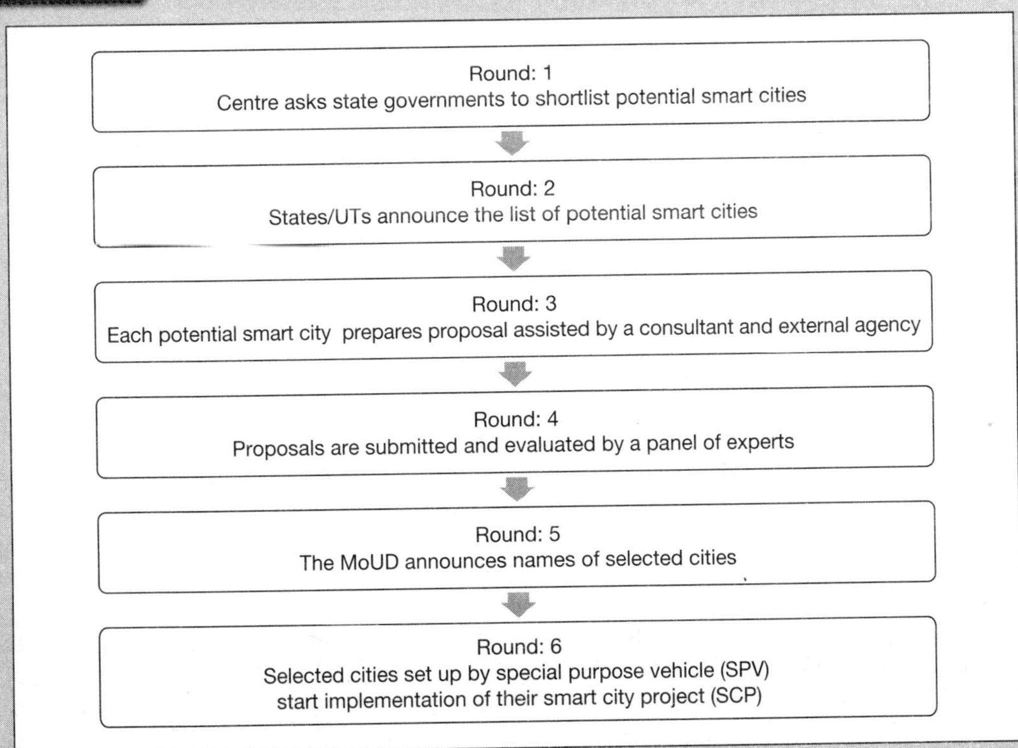

in an area of more than 50 acres. It is done in consultation with the urban local bodies and citizens.

3. *Greenfield Development:* Greenfield land is green open fields which lie between cities and towns or in suburban areas. As and when the cities and towns grow and the city population increases, more and more greenfield land is being used for development. Under the smart city mission, greenfield development introduces smart city solutions in a vacant area of usually more than 250 acres. It is done by using innovative planning, plan financing, and through plan implementation strategies. Greenfield development is being done with the objective to accommodate the expanding population with the provision of affordable housing especially for the poor in the city.
4. *Pan city development:* The pan-city development strategy envisages application of selected smart solutions to the existing city-wide infrastructure. It uses technology, information and data in order to make existing city-wide infrastructure and services better. In other words, pan-city solution is that solution where almost everything is automated, a city which is so well-connected that things happen seamlessly. Under the pan-city development strategies, a number of initiatives are being considered such as improving urban transport and electricity, water supply and drainage as well as development of tourism infrastructure, smart waste management and traffic decongestion through smart traffic management.

Modalities of Smart City Development in India

There is no watertight or particular prescribed model suggested by the government for the development of smart city. In other words, the approach is not 'one-size-fits-all'. Each city has to formulate its own concept, vision, mission and plan (proposal) for a smart city that is appropriate for its local context, levels of ambition and taking into consideration available resources.

Cities prepare Smart City Proposals (SCPs) using the principles of strategic planning process and the proposals containing area-based development plans and pan-city initiatives. Preparing SCPs is a collaborative effort because the objectives and funds of all government departments, parastatals and private agencies are being taken into consideration. The citizens participate during the process of preparing the SCPs. As the task of preparing the SCPs is quite challenging, the states/ULBs seek technical assistance by either hiring consulting firms or engaging with handholding agencies.[61]

The implementation of the smart city scheme is done by a Special Purpose Vehicle (SPV) created for the purpose. The SPV plans, appraises, approves, releases fund, implements, manages, monitors and evaluate the smart city projects. Each smart city has a SPV headed by a full-time CEO and has nominees of the central government, the state government and ULBs on its Board.

The SCM is operated as a Centrally Sponsored Scheme and the Central Government proposes to give ₹48,000 crores over five years, with an average ₹100 crore per city per year. The states/ULBs are also required to contribute a matching amount. The total amount likely to be allocated for smart cities development will be about ₹1 lakh crore.

The project cost of each SCP varies depending upon the level of ambition, model and capacity to execute and repay. The funds from the centre and the matching contribution by the states/ULB will meet only a part of the project cost. Balance funds are expected to be mobilized from the private sector through PPPs.[62]

Challenges of Smart City Development

Some of the key challenges of smart city development are discussed below.

1. *Demographic challenge:* One of the vital challenges the smart city will be facing is the population and its related problems such as poverty, unemployment and underemployment, basic needs issues such as house, sanitation, drinking water, education, healthcare and other amenities of life. The smart cities, therefore, need to make adequate planning to accommodate the migrated population to the cities and its related issues and challenges. Dispersion of population from the mega cities to the small cities with the sifting of public sector offices and private investment would be helpful in the promotion of the smart city mission. However, it is a big challenge.
2. *Financing smart city development:* Financing smart city missions is a big challenge. The state or the provincial government having poor financial resources would not be able to provide matching grants as desired by the central government for the smart city mission. However, attracting private investment for smart city development is also a challenge. It is rightly remarked that smart city projects often require multiple investors. Attracting appropriate sources of capital (debt or equity) for a given project requires effort, innovation and a sophisticated understanding of the project's fundamental components.[63]
3. *Smart technology and skilled manpower:* Smart cities necessitate smart technology and to operate them requires skilled manpower. However, both of these exigencies are lacking in developing countries. Creating skilled labour and capacity building requires a lot a financial investment, which is a Herculean task before both the central and state governments. Moreover, such projects also involve training, research and a hefty database for execution.
4. *Land acquisition and land-use planning:* Another vital challenge for the development of smart cities is land acquisition and land-use planning. Land acquisition is the most arduous task before the government, which faces a lot of resistance from the people. Clearly stating the purpose of land acquisition has also sometimes put the government in a fix such as (a) the purpose for which land is to be acquired; (b) the amount of compensation to be paid; (c) the process of acquisition; (d) use of the land acquired; and (e) dispute settlement mechanisms. After the use of GIS, land-use planning is a challenge also before the urban administration.
5. *Partnership:* Getting the support of the private sector and the people at large is also a challenge before the smart city mission. As cities look to upgrade their infrastructure with smart technologies, paying for those projects presents a significant challenge of introducing smart technologies on a wide-scale basis. Constrained by tight budgets, cities need to identify business models that can help to attract private financing in order to make the introduction viable and financeable.[64] Therefore, PPPs have been at the forefront of infrastructure development and management of infrastructure in the smart cities. However, developing a smart PPP model is sine qua non. The existing models of PPP need to be significantly restructured, to be able to provide an adequate response to the smart infrastructure challenges.[65]
6. *Smart security:* Smart security is a big challenge before the smart city. The increased use of technology has enhanced the risk of e-crime. Cybercrime and hacking is mostly being reported. Moreover, the security of people against violence, theft, snatching and physical crime against women requires lot of police and traffic infrastructure. The prevention of accidents and disaster is also another aspect of smart security posing challenges before the formation of smart cities.

7. *Inclusive city:* One of the objectives of smart city is that it is being promoted as an inclusive city. It is vital that smart city planning involves the consideration of all groups of people, and not just the affluent and technologically advanced. Technology should always be working to bring people together, rather than dividing them further based on income or education levels.[66] The development of slum and squatters and entailment of property right and other basic amenities to these marginalized sections of the urban dwellers who work hard in toiling from dawn to dusk in the development of infrastructure for the city deserve adequate attention. In most of the cities, development of an inclusive city is an arduous challenge.

   The UN-Habitat in its Global Campaign on Good Urban Governance, Concept Paper 2000 has asked several questions on inclusive city that are narrated below.

   a. How Inclusive is your city?
   b. How informed are citizens about the municipal budget?
   c. Do people in your city have equal access to clean water, clean neighbourhood and other services?
   d. How attractive is your city to investors?
   e. How safe is your city to live and work in?
   f. How often do the elected representatives meet their constituencies?
   g. Are all ethnic groups given equal opportunities?
   h. How much are women involved in citywide decision-making?
   i. How participatory is the decision-making process?
   j. Are the poor given proper consideration?[67]

8. *Smart governance:* The development of smart cities involves multi-stakeholders at various levels. Therefore, it calls for multi-level governance. However, governance of smart cities affairs is a big challenge. It is rightly remarked that smart governance deals with all the complexity related to supporting a city, region or a nation governance towards a smart city, region or nation, with suitable technologies, information systems, human and financial resources, policies, laws, regulations, norms and best practices.[68] To set right all these dimensions of governance is a challenging affair.

9. *Smart government:* Last but not the least, the development of smart city requires smart government, smart political party in power, smart bureaucracy and smart local self-governing institutions. All the power of decision-making regarding the selection of smart city, and allocation of resources for the smart city development depends on the government in power and its interest in urban development. The government directs the executive to carry forward the vision and mission of smart city. It is said that if a horse is not thirsty, any amount of dragging it to the water will not make it drink. Likewise, if the government in power at the central and provincial levels is not interested in developing a smart city, any amount of academic emphasis on smart city will not be successful.

Summing Up

Asia is host to half of the world's urban population, and that population continues to grow. This rapid urbanization has caught some governments by surprise, both at the local and national levels. Cities across the region face increasing poverty; lack of basic amenities and services such as water supply, electricity, sanitation, housing, education and healthcare; worsening pollution and depletion of natural resources; crippling traffic congestion; declining safety and security, and increased dissatisfaction by urban residents. These problems are exacerbated by the challenges brought on by the adverse impacts of climate change. Many Asian cities lack the mandate, resources and capability to deal with these multiple issues. It is rightly remarked that 'A smart sustainable city is an innovative city that uses information and communication technologies (ICTs) and other means to improve quality of life, efficiency of urban operation and services and competitiveness, while ensuring that it meets the needs of present and future generations with respect to economic, social, environmental, as well as cultural, aspects.'[69]

Keywords

Green City, Green Growth, Resilient City, Inclusive City, Green Initiatives, Fiscal Sustainability, Smart Solutions

REVIEW QUESTIONS

1. What do you mean by sustainable urbanization? Why is there a need for sustainable urbanization?
2. Enumerate a few key features of sustainable urbanization. Describe various measures to be taken for the promotion of sustainable urbanization.
3. Explain in detail various issues and challenges of sustainable urbanization.
4. What do you mean by smart city? Describe the need and importance of smart city.
5. Explain in detail various components and features of a smart city.
6. Describe various strategies for the development of smart city laid down by India.
7. Discuss various challenges for the development of smart cities. What measures have to be taken for the development of smart cities?
8. Write short notes on the followings
   a. Green city
   b. Green economy
   c. Green growth
   d. Smart governance
   e. Smart participation for smart city
   f. Resilient city and smart security
   g. Inclusive city
   h. Sustainable city

Notes

1. https://www.usaid.gov/urban (accessed on 22 February 2019).
2. https://www.essarp.org.ar/wp-content/uploads/2018/05/ECOSOC-Promoting-sustainable-urbanization.pdf (22 February 2019).
3. https://www.usaid.gov/urban (accessed on 17 February 2019).
4. https://www.wbcsd.org/Programs/Cities-and-Mobility/Sustainable-Cities/News/Sustainable-urbanization-is-key-to-your-business (accessed on 22 February 2019).
5. https://www.bu.edu/pardee/files/2010/04/UNsdkp004fsingle.pdf (accessed on 22 February 2019).

6. https://www.econstor.eu/bitstream/10419/176488/1/10.1186_s40887-017-0014-9.pdf (accessed on 24 February 2019).
7. https://futurecitiesandenvironment.com/articles/10.1186/s40984-016-0014-2/ (accessed on 24 February 2019).
8. https://sustainabledevelopment.un.org/content/documents/2569130918-SDSN-Why-the-World-Needs-an-Urban-SDG.pdf (accessed on 22 February 2019).
9. https://www.usaid.gov/urban (accessed on 28 January 2019).
10. https://unchronicle.un.org/article/addressing-sustainable-urbanization-challenge (accessed on 20 February 2019).
11. https://www.unisdr.org/archive/49761 (accessed on 20 February 2019).
12. https://www.adb.org/sites/default/files/publication/182652/sdwp-041.pdf (accessed on 20 February 2019).
13. https://www.oecd.org/env/cc/Cities-and-climate-change-2014-Policy-Perspectives-Final-web.pdf (accessed on 20 February2019).
14. https://unfccc.int/news/rapid-urbanization-increases-climate-risk-for-billions-of-people (accessed on 20 February 2019).
15. See https://unfccc.int/news/rapid-urbanization-increases-climate-risk-for-billions-of-people (accessed on 20 February 2019).
16. https://www.usaid.gov/urban (accessed on 24 February 2019).
17. https://futurecitiesandenvironment.com/articles/10.1186/s40984-016-0014-2/ (accessed on 24 February 2019).
18. http://documents.worldbank.org/curated/en/622651468320375543/pdf/801060REVISED00170Partnership0Paper.pdf (accessed on 28 February 2019).
19. https://www.unenvironment.org/regions/asia-and-pacific/regional-initiatives/supporting-resource-efficiency/sustainable-cities (accessed on 25 February 2019).
20. https://www.wur.nl/upload_mm/e/a/9/6d101598-1ecf-40c2-be76-29633c84c21b_8412102763_RvB_SDG_boekje_LR.pdf (accessed on 24 February 2019).
21. http://www.tadamun.co/2013/12/07/right-of-equitable-and-sustainable-urban-development/?lang=en#.XHS8sC8zbIU (accessed on 26 February 2019).
22. https://unhabitat.org/wp-content/uploads/2016/03/2016Mar18_Prague_SE_Agenda_v07.pdf (accessed on 26 February 2019).
23. https://www.iddri.org/en/publications-and-events/blog-post/sanitation-developing-cities-imperative-sustainable-urban (accessed on 26 February 2019).
24. https://steps-centre.org/blog/gender-equality-sustainable-development-melissa-leach/ (accessed on 26 February 2019).
25. https://steps-centre.org/blog/gender-equality-sustainable-development-melissa-leach/ (accessed on 26 February 2019).
26. http://www.undp.org/content/dam/undp/library/Sustainable%20Development/Urbanization/UNDP_Urban-Strategy.pdf (accessed on 26 February 2019).
27. https://unctad.org/meetings/en/SessionalDocuments/ecn162013d2_en.pdf (accessed on 27 February 2019).
28. http://www.undp.org/content/dam/rbap/docs/Research%20&%20Publications/poverty/RBAP-PR-2013-Urbanization-Climate-Change-Issue-Brief-01.pdf (accessed on 27 February 2019).
29. https://www.un.org/ruleoflaw/files/urbansafetyandsecurity.pdf (accessed on 25 November 2019).
30. https://www.unisdr.org/archive/49761 (accessed on 28 February 2019).
31. https://www.undp.org/content/undp/en/home/blog/2016/10/12/Ciudades-sostenibles-si-no-es-ahora-cu-ndo-.html (accessed on 1 March 2019).
32. https://sustainabledevelopment.un.org/content/documents/18233HLPF_Decent_Work_for_Sustainable_Development_2018.pdf (accessed on 1 March 2019).
33. http://www.internationaldisabilityalliance.org/content/global-partnership-sustainable-development (accessed on 1 March 2019).

34. https://www.unido.org/sites/default/files/2016-10/sustainable_cities_brochure_0.pdf (accessed on 1 March 2019).
35. http://www.iiasa.ac.at/web/home/research/researchPrograms/WorldPopulation/Research/Options%20LaxDec.pdf (accessed on 2 February 2019).
36. http://urbanresiliencehub.org/wp-content/uploads/2018/08/WCD-Concept-Note2.pdf (accessed on 2 February 2019).
37. http://www.isocarp.net/Data/case_studies/1664.pdf (accessed on 4 March 2019).
38. https://core.ac.uk/download/pdf/82500220.pdf (accessed on 4 March 2019).
39. https://www.uclg.org/en/media/news/challenge-financing-sustainable-urbanization-not-only-unresolved-largely-ignored (accessed on 4 March 2019).
40. https://www.undp.org/content/undp/en/home/blog/2018/Meeting-the-urban-finance-challenge.html (accessed on 4 March 2019).
41. https://www.effigis.com/en/smart-city-importance-of-the-where/ (accessed on 5 March2019).
42. https://institute.eib.org/wp-content/uploads/2017/02/2017_0131-ASCIMER-DELIVERABLE-1A-CONCEPT-CHALLENGES.pdf (accessed on 45 March 2019).
43. https://institute.eib.org/wp-content/uploads/2017/02/2017_0131-ASCIMER-DELIVERABLE-1A-CONCEPT-CHALLENGES.pdf (accessed on 5 March 2019).
44. https://en.wikipedia.org/wiki/Smart_city (accessed on 5 March 2019).
45. https://en.wikipedia.org/wiki/Smart_city (accessed on 5 March 2019).
46. https://www.centreforcities.org/reader/smart-cities/what-is-a-smart-city/1-smart-cities-definitions/ (accessed on 7 March 2019).
47. https://www.centreforcities.org/reader/smart-cities/what-is-a-smart-city/1-smart-cities-definitions/ (accessed on 7 March 2019).
48. https://www.mdpi.com/2624-6511/1/1/2/htm (accessed on 5 March 2019).
49. https://scholars.fhsu.edu/cgi/viewcontent.cgi?article=1500&context=theses (accessed on 5 March 2019).
50. https://scholars.fhsu.edu/cgi/viewcontent.cgi?article=1500&context=theses (accessed on 5 March 2019).
51. https://scholars.fhsu.edu/cgi/viewcontent.cgi?article=1500&context=theses (accessed on 5 March 2019).
52. See https://pusprajbhatt.wordpress.com/2018/05/27/smart-city-context-of-nepal-2/ (accessed on 5/3/2019)
53. https://www.crcresearch.org/sustainable-infrastructure/land-use-planning (accessed on 6 March 2019).
54. https://unctad.org/meetings/en/SessionalDocuments/ecn162016d2_en.pdf (accessed on 6 March 2019).
55. https://unctad.org/meetings/en/SessionalDocuments/ecn162016d2_en.pdf (accessed on 6 March 2019).
56. ibid
57. http://www.worldbank.org/en/news/press-release/2011/11/21/investing-smarter-cities-smart-economics-help-malaysia-achieve-high-income-country-status-says-world-bank-malaysia-economic-monitor (accessed on 6 March 2019).
58. https://www.mondomacchina.it/en/smart-cities-maintenance-and-management-of-public-green-spaces-c1703 (accessed on 6 March 2019).
59. https://www.semaphore-software.com/blog/smart-cities-in-india/ (accessed on 6 March 2019).
60. https://timesofindia.indiatimes.com/city/nagpur/Smart-cities-can-provide-a-much-better-quality-of-life-to-citizens/articleshow/48688825.cms (accessed on 6 March 2019).
61. https://www.downtoearth.org.in/news/urbanisation/what-s-the-progress-of-smart-cities-mission--58147 (accessed on 8 March 2019).
62. https://www.downtoearth.org.in/news/urbanisation/what-s-the-progress-of-smart-cities-mission--58147 (accessed on 8 March 2019).
63. https://www2.deloitte.com/content/dam/Deloitte/us/Documents/public-sector/us-ps-the-challenge-of-paying-for-smart-cities-projects.pdf (accessed on 11 February 2019).
64. https://www2.deloitte.com/content/dam/Deloitte/us/Documents/public-sector/us-ps-the-challenge-of-paying-for-smart-cities-projects.pdf (accessed on 11 February 2019).
65. https://journals.sagepub.com/doi/full/10.1177/1783591717734794 (accessed on 11 February 2019).
66. https://ubidots.com/blog/the-key-challenges-for-smart-cities/ (accessed on 11 February 2019).

67. https://unhabitat.org/books/a-guide-for-municipalities-inclusive-and-sustainable-urban-development-planning-volume-1/ (accessed on 19 March 2019).
68. https://ieeexplore.ieee.org/document/8372349 (accessed on 11 February 2019).
69. https://www.unece.org/fileadmin/DAM/hlm/documents/Publications/U4SSC_Deliverable-Connecting-Cities-and-Communities.pdf (accessed on 23 September 2019).

References

Albino, V., Berardi, U., & Dangelico, R. M. (2015). Smart cities: Definitions, dimensions, performance, and initiatives. *Journal of Urban Technology*, *22*(1), 3–21.

Aribilosho, M., & Usoro, A. (2016). *A review on smart cities: Impact of technology and social factors. Computing and Information Systems*, 1, 21. https://scholars.fhsu.edu/cgi/viewcontent.cgi?article=1500&context=theses (accessed on 5 March 2019).

Caragliu, A, Del Bo, C., & Nijkamp, P. (2009). Smart cities in Europe. *Serie Research Memoranda 0048*. https://en.wikipedia.org/wiki/Smart_city (accessed on 5 March 2019).

Chai-Lee, G (2017). The impact of technological innovation on building a sustainable city. *International Journal of Quality Innovation*, *3*(6), 1–13.

Detotto, C., & Otranto, E. (2010). Does crime affect economic growth? *Kyklos*, *63*(3), 330–345. https://scholars.fhsu.edu/cgi/viewcontent.cgi?article=1500&context=theses (accessed on 5 March 2019).

Giffinger, R., Fertner, C., Kramar, H., Kalasek, R., Milanović, N. P., & Meijers, E. (2007). *Smart cities: Ranking of European medium-sized cities*. http://www.smart-cities.eu/download/smart_cities_final_report.pdf (accessed on 5 March 2019).

Hallegatte, S., Heal, G., Fay, M., & Treguer, D. (2011). *From growth to green growth: A framework* (Policy Research Working Paper 5872). Washington, DC: World Bank.

ITU. (2015). *Setting the state for stakeholders 'engagement in smart sustainable cities* (Focus Group Technical Report). Geneva: International Telecommunication Union.

Kumar, K. (2017). Can the smart city allure meet the challenges of Indian urbanization. In: P. Sharma, & S. Rajput (eds.). *Sustainable Cities*, Chapter 2. New Delhi: Springer International Publishing, 17–39.

Mark, D., & Al Wear, H. (2011). From intelligent to smart cities. *Journal of Intelligent Buildings International: From Intelligent Cities to Smart Cities*, *3*(3), 140–152. https://en.wikipedia.org/wiki/Smart_city (accessed on 5 March 2019).

Metzger, J., & Olsson, A. R. (2013). *Sustainable Stockholm, exploring urban sustainability in Europe's, Greenest City, New York*. London: Routledge.

Mosterman, P. J., & Zander, J. (2013). *Computation for Humanity: Information Technology to Advance Society*. Florida: CRC Press.

Newman, P., Beatley, T., & Boyer, H. (2009). Resilient Cities: Responding to Peak Oil and Climate Change. Washington: Island Press.

Turok, I., & Granahan, G. (2013). Urbanization and economic growth: The arguments and evidence for the Africa and Asia. *Environment and Urbanization*. https://journals.sagepub.com/doi/full/10.1177/0956247813490908 (accessed on 20 February 2019).

UNEP. (2012). *Sustainable, resource-efficient cities: making it happen*. Paris: United Nations Environment Programme.

Vanolo, A. (2014). Smartmentality: The smart city as disciplinary strategy. *Urban Studies*, *51*(5), 883–898.

WEF. (2015). *The Global Information Technology Report 2015*. https://scholars.fhsu.edu/cgi/viewcontent.cgi?article=1500&context=theses (accessed on 5 March 2019).

World Bank. (2013). *Building sustainability in an urbanizing world: A partnership report*. Washington, DC: The World Bank.

World Bank. (2018). *Urban sustainability framework*. Washington, DC: The World Bank.

WRI. (2009). *World Greenhouse Gas Emissions in 2005*. Washington, DC: World Resources Institute.

Index